THE TWELVE PROPHETS

BERIT OLAM
Studies in Hebrew Narrative & Poetry

The Twelve Prophets

VOLUME TWO

Micah
Nahum
Habakkuk
Zephaniah
Haggai
Zechariah
Malachi

Marvin A. Sweeney

David W. Cotter, O.S.B.
Editor

Jerome T. Walsh
Chris Franke
Associate Editors

A Michael Glazier Book
THE LITURGICAL PRESS
Collegeville, Minnesota

A Michael Glazier Book published by The Liturgical Press.

Cover design by Ann Blattner.

Volume Two: ISBN 0-8146-5091-0

1   2   3   4   5   6   7   8   9

Library of Congress Cataloging-in-Publication Data

Sweeney, Marvin A. (Marvin Alan), 1953–
    The twelve prophets / Marvin A. Sweeney ; David W. Cotter, editor ;
Jerome T. Walsh, Chris Franke, associate editors.
      p.   cm. — (Berit olam)
    Includes bibliographical references and index.
    ISBN 0-8146-5095-3 (alk. paper) (volume one)
    1. Bible. O.T. Minor Prophets—Commentaries.   I. Cotter, David W.
II. Walsh, Jerome T., 1942–   III. Franke, Chris.   IV. Title.   V. Series.
    BS1560.S94   2000
    224'.907—dc21   00-035651

For
Terry and Candy

Georgia, Walter Issac, Jake, Lakie,
and Mary

CONTENTS

ABBREVIATIONS

ASOR	*Annual of the American Schools of Oriental Research*
ABD	*The Anchor Bible Dictionary*, ed. D. N. Freedman et al. 6 volumes. New York: Doubleday, 1992.
ABS	*Archeology and Biblical Studies*
AnBib	*Analecta Biblica*
ANEP	*The Ancient Near East in Pictures Relating to the Old Testament*, ed. J. Pritchard. Princeton: Princeton University Press, 1969.
ANET	*Ancient Near Eastern Texts Relating to the Old Testament*, ed. J. Pritchard. Princeton: Princeton University Press, 1969.
AOAT	Alter Orient und Altes Testament
ARAB	*Ancient Records of Assyria and Babylonia*, ed. D. D. Luckenbill. London: Histories and Mysteries of Man, 1989.
AT	Altes Testament
ATSAT	*Arbeiten zu Text und Sprache im Alten Testament*
BA	*Biblical Archaeologist*
BASOR	*Bulletin of the American School of Oriental Research*
BBET	*Beiträge zur biblischen Exegese und Theologie*
B.C.E.	Before Common Era
BDB	Brown, Driver, Briggs: *Hebrew and English Lexicon of the Old Testament*, ed. F. Brown, S. R. Driver, and C. A. Briggs. Oxford: Clarendon, 1972.
BEATAJ	*Beiträge zur Erforschung des Alten Testaments und des Antike Judentums*
BibSem	*Biblical Seminar*
BJS	Brown Judaic Studies
BLS	Bible and Literature Series
BN	*Biblische Notizen*
BO	*Biblica et Orientalia*
BTS	*Biblisch-Theologische Studien*
BZAW	Beihefte zur Zeitschrift für die Alttestamentliche Wissenschaft
CAH	*The Cambridge Ancient History*. Cambridge: Cambridge University Press.

CBQ	*The Catholic Biblical Quarterly*
C.E.	Common Era
ConBibOT	*Coniectanea Biblica, Old Testament Series*
CR:BS	*Currents in Research: Biblical Studies*
CRINT	Compendia Rerum Iudaicarum ad Novum Testamentum
DDD²	*Dictionary of Deities and Demons in the Bible,* ed. K. van der Toorn, B. Becking, and P. van der Horst. 2nd edition; Leiden: E. J. Brill; Grand Rapids: Eerdmans, 1999.
DJD	*Discoveries in the Judaean Desert*
EB	*Études bibliques*
EvT	*Evangelisches Theologie*
Fest.	Festschrift
FOTL	Forms of the Old Testament Literature Commentary Series
FRLANT	Forschungen zur Religion des Alten und Neuen Testaments
GCT	Gender, Culture, and Theory Monograph Series
HBD	*HarperCollins Bible Dictionary,* ed. P. Achtemeier et al. 2nd edition; San Francisco: HarperSanFrancisco, 1996.
HKAT	Handkommentar zum Alten Testament
HSM	Harvard Semitic Monographs
HUCA	*Hebrew Union College Annual*
ICC	*International Critical Commentary*
IDB	*Interpreter's Dictionary of the Bible,* ed. G. Buttrick. 4 volumes. Nashville: Abingdon, 1962.
IDB[S]	*Interpreter's Dictionary of the Bible. Supplementary Volume,* ed. K. Crim. Nashville: Abingdon, 1976.
IEJ	*Israel Exploration Journal*
JAOS	*Journal of the American Oriental Society*
JBL	*Journal of Biblical Literature*
JCS	*Journal of Cuneiform Studies*
JNES	*Journal of Near Eastern Studies*
JR	*Journal of Religion*
JSOT	*Journal for the Study of the Old Testament*
JSOTSup	Journal for the Study of the Old Testament, Supplement Series
JSS	*Journal of Semitic Studies*
JTS	*Journal of Theological Studies*
KAT	Kommentar zum Alten Testament
KHAT	Kurzer Hand-Commentar zum Alten Testament
LXX	Septuagint
MT	Masoretic Text
NEAEHL	*New Encyclopedia of Archaeological Excavations in the Holy Land,* ed. E. Stern et al. 4 volumes. Jerusalem: Carta and the Israel Exploration Society.
NICOT	New International Commentary on the Old Testament
NRSV	New Revised Standard Version
OBO	Orbis biblicus et orientalis
OT Guides	Old Testament Guides
OTL	Old Testament Library Commentary Series

OTS	*Oudtestamentische Studiën*
RB	*Revue biblique*
RBL	*Review of Biblical Literature*
SBLDS	Society of Biblical Literature Dissertation Series
SBLMS	Society of Biblical Literature Monograph Series
SBLResBS	Society of Biblical Literature Resources for Biblical Study Monograph Series
SBS	Stuttgarter Bibelstudien
SBT	Studies in Biblical Theology
SJOT	*Scandinavian Journal of the Old Testament*
TA	*Tel Aviv*
TB	Theologische Bücherei
TDOT	*Theological Dictionary of the Old Testament*, ed. H. Ringgren et al. Grand Rapids: Eerdmans, 1977ff.
VT	*Vetus Testamentum*
VTSup	Vetus Testamentum Supplements
WMANT	Wissenscaftliche Monographien zum Alten und Neuen Testaments
ZAW	*Zeitschrift für die Alttestamentliche Wissenschaft*
ZDPV	*Zeitschrift des deutschen Palästina Vereins*

MICAH

MICAH

Overview

Micah is the sixth book in the Masoretic version of the Book of the Twelve and the third book in the Septuagint version. Because of its emphasis on northern Israel's punishment at the hands of the Assyrian empire as a model for the experience of Jerusalem and Judah (Micah 1–3) and because it anticipates the Babylonian exile and the ultimate restoration of Zion at the center of the nations (Micah 4–5), it plays a key role in the overall conceptualization of both versions. It follows Obadiah and Jonah in the MT which deal respectively with the themes of YHWH's judgment and mercy in relation to the nations, and it precedes Nahum, Habakkuk, and Zephaniah, which respectively take up the fall of Nineveh, the threat of the Babylonians, and the renewed call to adhere to YHWH in the aftermath of punishment. Micah thereby aids in giving direction to the book by pointing to the punishment suffered by Israel and Judah at the hands of the nations, first Assyria and later Babylonia, as a key element in realizing the future idealized role of Zion at the center of creation. It follows Hosea and Amos in the LXX, which take up the punishment of the northern kingdom of Israel, and it precedes Joel, Obadiah, and Jonah, which respectively deal with G–d's protection of Zion from the threats of the nation, G–d's punishment of Edom as representative of the nations, and G–d's mercy toward Assyria again as representative of the nations. The LXX version of Micah thereby emphasizes the paradigmatic role of the punishment of northern Israel for Jerusalem and Judah, and extends this perspective as a model for the experience of the nations as well. Again, the ideal vision of a world at peace with Zion set in the midst of the nations defines an overall goal of divine process in the LXX version of the Book of the Twelve.

Relatively little is known about the prophet Micah.[1] According to the superscription of the book, he was active during the reigns of the Judean kings, Jotham (742–735 B.C.E.), Ahaz (735–715 B.C.E.), and Hezekiah (715 B.C.E.), which would make him a contemporary of the prophet Isaiah ben Amoz. He is a Moreshtite, which indicates that he likely lived in a town or village called Moreshet. The term simply means, "possession" or "property." Scholars have argued that Micah's home must be Moreshet Gath, which is identified as Tell Judeidah, a site located in the Judean Shephelah about twenty-one miles southwest of Jerusalem, nine miles east of the Philistine city of Gath, and one mile north of Beth Guvrin.[2] Moreshet Gath would have been one of the forty-six cities and numerous villages that the Assyrian king Sennacherib claims to have conquered during his invasion of Judah in 701 B.C.E.[3] Wolff identifies him as an elder of the village, based upon his identification as a Moreshtite rather than in relation to his patronymic, his references to the "heads" of the people, his use of the term "my people" to designate Israel/Judah, his concerns for social justice, and his presence in Jerusalem for the festival of Sukkoth.[4] Micah may well have been an elder of Moreshet Gath, but his presence in Jerusalem is very likely the result of his having been forced to flee for safety before the advancing Assyrian army. His frequent references to social abuse and the desperation to obtain the means for survival (Mic 2:1-2; 3:1-12), the terror of the towns and villages of Philistia and the Shephelah (Mic 2:8-9), and the exile of the people and destruction of Jerusalem (Mic 2:12-13; 3:12), all point to a man who knows first-hand the terrors of war and the brutality of life in an ancient city under siege.

Indeed, the prophet's message appears to be based on this experience. As a resident of the Shephelah, he knows first-hand of the movements of the Assyrian army against both Israel and Judah from the time of the Syro-Ephraimitic War until Hezekiah's revolt. When the Assyrians attacked Israel in 734–732 to relieve Judah from the Syro-Ephraimitic coalition, they stripped northern Israel of its territories in the Trans-Jordan, Galilee, and along the coastal plain. When the Assyrians invaded

---

[1] For an overview of critical study concerning both the prophet and book Micah, see R. Mason, *Micah, Nahum, Obadiah,* OT Guides (Sheffield: JSOT Press, 1991) 9–53.

[2] See Karl Elliger, "Die Heimat des Propheten Micah," *ZDPV* 57 (1934) 81–152, reprinted in *Kleine Schriften zum Alten Testament,* Theologische Bücherei, vol. 32 (Munich: Chr. Kaiser, 1966) 9–71.

[3] For Sennacherib's account of his 701 B.C.E. invasion of Judah and siege of Jerusalem, see Pritchard, *ANET* 287-8.

[4] Wolff, *Micah* 6–9; idem, *Micah the Prophet,* trans. R. D. Gehrke (Philadelphia: Fortress, 1981) 17–25.

and destroyed Israel in 724–722/1 B.C.E., they made sure in 720 B.C.E. to secure control of the coastal plain by moving against Philistia to cut off Egyptian assistance.[5] Sennacherib employed this strategy once again in 701 B.C.E., and then continued to ravage the bordering Judean Shephelah as a means to deprive Jerusalem of its buffer territory, agricultural produce, and man power, prior to moving against the city itself. From his location in Moreshet Gath, Micah would have witnessed each of these moves, and would easily have drawn the conclusion that Judah would suffer the same fate as Israel if it dared to challenge Assyria. His constant criticism of Israel's and Judah's leadership indicates the perspective of a man who lives in an outlying village that suffers as a result of the decisions made in Samaria and especially in Jerusalem. Although many consider Micah to have been entirely a prophet of doom, the materials in Micah 6–7 call upon the people to do justice, return to YHWH, and await the time when Israel's/Judah's punishment will come to an end.[6] Many scholars consider these chapters to be late, but there is little evidence that this is the case. Such a perspective is absolutely essential for Micah's reputation as the prophet who convinced King Hezekiah to change his course of action and thereby saved Jerusalem from the destruction that he had previously announced. Micah's announcement of Jerusalem's destruction in Mic 3:12 is reportedly quoted in Jeremiah's defense at the trial of the latter for sedition about a century later (Jer 26:18). Although Isaiah is given the credit for this accomplishment in Isaiah 36–37 and 2 Kings 18–19, it was Micah who was remembered in Jeremiah.

Indeed, there appears to be some debate or differences of perspective between the traditions that represent the two prophets. Although both books share the vision of world peace centered on Zion in which the nations will beat their swords into plowshares (Mic 4:1-5; Isa 2:2-4), the overall punishment of the land and creation of a remnant of Israel/Jacob (Micah 1–3; 4:6–5:9; Isa 2:6–4:6), and the emergence of a new Davidic monarch who will subdue nations and bring justice and peace (Mic 5:9-14 [NRSV: 5:10-15]; Isa 9:1-6; 11:1-16), each tradition construes these elements along somewhat different lines. Whereas the book of

[5] For Sargon II's accounts of his campaigns at this time against Hanno of Gaza and the Egyptians, see Pritchard, *ANET* 285.

[6] For discussion on the interrelationship between doom and hope in Micah, see Lamontte M. Luker, "Beyond Form-Criticism: The Relation of Doom and Hope Oracles in Micah 2–6," *Hebrew Annual Review* 11 (1987) 285-301; Jan Aart Wagenaar, *Oordeel en Heil. Een Onderzoek naar Samenhang Tussen de Heils-en Onheilsprofetieën in Micha 2–5/Judgement and Salvation. A Study into the Relationship between the Oracles of Hope and the Oracles of Doom in Micah 2–5* (Ph.D. diss., University of Utrecht, 1995).

Isaiah envisions Jacob joining the nations at Zion (Isa 2:5) as part of the process by which YHWH will establish sovereignty and peace over all creation, the book of Micah points especially to the differences in the worship practices of Israel and the nations (Mic 4:5) and looks to a time when the remnant of Jacob will establish its dominance over the nations (Mic 4:11-13; 5:1-8 [NRSV: 5:2-9]). Insofar as Mic 4:1-5 and 5:9-14 [NRSV: 5:10-15] appear to draw upon and rework Isa 2:2-4 and 2:6-21 extensively, it appears that the present book of Micah is designed in part to provide a counterpoint to the present form of Isaiah.

Overall, the book of Micah is designed to address the future of Jerusalem or Israel in the aftermath of the Babylonian exile.[7] Although Micah lived and spoke during the Assyrian period of the late-eighth century B.C.E., the reference to Babylonian exile in Mic 4:10 and the debate with and use of the Isaiah tradition as mentioned above indicate that this is the case. In this respect, Micah 4–5 appear to be reworked versions of some of the prophet's own statements. Unlike Isaiah, Micah the prophet was probably not heavily focused on the Jerusalem/Davidic tradition, but he does rely on the traditions of YHWH's promises to the ancestors, Abraham and Jacob (Mic 7:20), the traditions of the Exodus, the Wilderness Wandering, and the entry into the promised land (Mic 6:3-5), and the role of Bethlehem/Ephrata in the births of Israel's kings (Mic 5:1-5 [NRSV: 5:2-6]).[8] The book of Micah indicates strong support for the Jerusalem/Davidic tradition, however, as Zion and the Davidic monarch will play the key roles in YHWH's and Zion's role in world dominion. In this respect, Micah 4–5 apparently result from extensive reworking of some of Micah's earlier material. The present form of the book thereby begins in typical fashion with the superscription of Mic 1:1, but then Mic 1:2–7:20 is formulated as a prophetic announcement concerning YHWH's plans for the anticipated exaltation of Zion at the center of the nations. Although many scholars allow their views concerning the compositional history of the book to determine their understanding of its literary structure, a synchronic reading of the book points to a four part structure.[9] Micah 1:2-16 announces that YHWH's punishment of Samaria

---

[7] For a redaction-critical analysis of the book of Micah, see the relevant sections of my *King Josiah of Judah: The Lost Messiah of Israel* (Oxford and New York: Oxford University Press, 2000).

[8] See Walter Beyerlin, *Die Kulttraditionen Israels in der Verkündigung des Propheten Micah*, FRLANT, vol. 72 (Göttingen: Vandenhoeck & Ruprecht, 1959), for discussion of Micah's use of tradition.

[9] For discussion of the structure of Micah, see esp. John T. Willis, "The Structure of the Book of Micah," *Svensk Exegetisk Årsbok* 34 (1969) 5–42; David Gerald Hagstrom, *The Coherence of the Book of Micah: A Literary Analysis*, SBL Dissertation Series, vol. 89 (Atlanta: Scholars Press, 1988).

and Israel will stand as a paradigm for the punishment of Jerusalem and Judah. Micah 2:1–5:14 [NRSV: 2:1–5:15] provides a detailed overview of the process of punishment and restoration in which Zion and the Davidic monarch will emerge as the central figures in YHWH's plans to establish sovereignty over the nations of the world at Zion. Micah 6:1-16 then appeals to the people of Israel/Judah to return to YHWH and YHWH's expectations of justice as a prelude to this process. Finally Mic 7:1-20 expresses the prophet's trust that YHWH will carry out this process in the form of a prophetic liturgy or psalm of confidence that YHWH will act on behalf of Israel once the punishment is complete.

The Superscription: 1:1

The superscription for the book of Micah appears in Mic 1:1. In keeping with the typical characteristics of superscriptions in the Hebrew Bible, Mic 1:1 is formulated as a third person archival or reporting statement that is addressed to the audience that will read or hear the following material in the book.[10] It thereby introduces, identifies and characterizes the following material in Mic 1:2–7:20 as "the word of YHWH that was unto Micah the Moreshtite . . ." This statement represents a relatively common form of superscription for a prophetic book that appears elsewhere in Hos 1:1; Joel 1:1; Zeph 1:1; and LXX Jer 1:1. Variants of the form appear in Jer 1:2; Ezek 1:3; Jon 1:1; Hag 1:1; Zech 1:1; and Mal 1:1. This particular formulation appears to be derived from the formula, "and the word of YHWH was unto X," which frequently introduces prophetic oracles. Micah 1:1 further states that the historical context of this material is "in the days of Yotham, Ahaz, Hezekiah, kings of Judah," and it qualifies it as a prophetic vision "which he saw concerning Samaria and Jerusalem." Because of its typical formulation and its function to introduce and identify the following material in the book, Mic 1:1 is structurally and generically distinct from the material in Mic 1:2–7:20. It is not the work of Micah himself, but of an anonymous editor who sought to identify the contents of the book for its reading or listening audience.

The prophet Micah the Moreshtite is known primarily from the contents of the book of Micah. He is also mentioned in Jer 26:18, which re-

---

[10] See Gene M. Tucker, "Prophetic Superscriptions and the Growth of a Canon," *Canon and Authority*, ed. G. W. Coats and B. O. Long (Philadelphia: Fortress, 1977) 56–70.

lates the prophet Jeremiah's trial for sedition against the state in the time of King Jehoiakim ben Josiah. Jeremiah had been accused of attempting to undermine the Judean state on the basis of his Temple sermon (Jeremiah 7) which announced destruction for Judah and the Jerusalem Temple if the people did not observe YHWH's commands. During the course of his trial, Jeremiah's defenders cited the precedent established by Micah who prophesied concerning the destruction of Jerusalem (cf. Mic 3:12) and thereby prompted King Hezekiah and the people of Judah to turn to YHWH so that the city was in fact saved. The name Micah is relatively common in the Hebrew Bible where it appears as the name of the man from Ephraim who established the sanctuary at Dan (Judges 17–18), a descendant of Reuben (1 Chr 5:5), the son of Merib-aal/Mephibosheth and grandson of Jonathan ben Saul (1 Chr 8:34-35; 24:24-25; cf. 2 Sam 9:12), a Levite in the time of David (1 Chr 23:20; 24:24-25), and the father of Abdon in the time of Josiah (2 Chr 34:20; cf. 2 Kgs 22:12, where he is identified as Michiah). It appears in a number of variant forms, including Michael, Michiah, Michayahu, Michayehu, and the woman's name Michal. The name Micah appears to be derived from Michayahu, which means, "Who is like YHWH?" (cf. Michael, "who is like G–d/El?"). The names *mi-kà-yà* and *mi-kà-il* are also attested in the Sumero-Akkadian tablets found at Tell Mardikh, the late-third/early-second millennium city of Ebla in north Syria.

Micah is identified by the gentilic name, "the Moreshtite," which indicates that he is probably from the city of Moreshet Gath (see Mic 1:14). Moreshet Gath is identified with Tell Judeideh (Tell Godéd), located in the Shephelah about 2 kilometers or 1 mile north of Beth Guvrin, 15 kilometers or 9 miles east of the Philistine city of Gath, and 35 kilometers or 21 miles southwest of Jerusalem. The site is in the vicinity of Mareshah and Lachish (cf. Mic 1:14).[11] It may have been among the cities fortified by King Rehoboam ben Solomon (cf. 2 Chr 11:8, which lists Gath and Mareshah, but many think that Gath should read Moreshet Gath). Moreshet Gath would have been situated directly in the path of Sennacherib's invasion of Judah in 701 B.C.E. which focused on the city of Lachish. It was undoubtedly one of the forty-six Judean cities taken by his soldiers.[12] Most scholars maintain that Micah's presence in Jerusalem was the result of his flight from Moreshet Gath to escape the Assyrian invasion.

The placement of Micah's prophetic career in the days of Yotham (742–735 B.C.E.), Ahaz (735–715 B.C.E.), and Hezekiah (715–687/6 B.C.E.)

---

[11] See Lamontte M. Luker, "Moresheth," *ABD* IV:904-5.

[12] See Sennacherib's account of his campaign against Judah in 701 B.C.E. in *ANET* 287–8.

provides quite a long period for his activities, which corresponds to the initial period of Assyrian intervention in the region of Israel and Judah from the time of the Syro-Ephraimitic War (734–732 B.C.E.) through the time of Sennacherib's invasion of 701 B.C.E. During this period, Tiglath-Pileser III attacked Israel and stripped it of its territories in the Trans-Jordan and Galilee (734–732 B.C.E.); Shalmanezer V and Sargon II destroyed the northern kingdom of Israel (722/1 B.C.E.); and Sennacherib devastated Judah at the time of Hezekiah's revolt (701 B.C.E.). Micah had ample opportunity to witness the dismemberment and destruction of Israel as well as the devastation of Judah.

These experiences appear to provide the basis for his prophetic speeches. Overall, Mic 1:1 characterizes his message as one "concerning Samaria and Jerusalem," the respective capitals of northern Israel and southern Judah. As a resident of Moreshet Gath, a border city situated at the southwestern edge of Judah close to Philistia, Micah would have felt the full impact of the Assyrian invasions during this period. His life and those of his family and neighbors in Moreshet Gath were destroyed as a result of decisions made by the kings of Israel and Judah in Samaria and Jerusalem. The book of Micah therefore presents him as arguing throughout his oracles that Israel and Judah have been judged by YHWH as a result of the sins of Samaria and Jerusalem, and that following the punishment YHWH will see to the restoration of Jerusalem and Israel under proper Davidic leadership.

Prophetic Anticipation of YHWH Plans for Zion's Exaltation: 1:2–7:20

Micah 1:2–7:20 constitutes the second major structural component of the book of Micah following the superscription in Mic 1:1, but this observation has not generally been recognized in the overall assessments of the book's literary form. Most scholars allow a combination of thematic and redaction-critical considerations to guide their decisions concerning the structure of the book. Thus, there is almost universal agreement that Micah 1–3 represent the authentic oracles of the prophet Micah concerning judgment against Israel and Judah, and chapters 4–5 and 6–7 represent later expansions of the text that focus on the themes of Jerusalem's and Israel's restoration at the center of the nations. By and large, this view of the compositional history of the book underlies the four major structural proposals for the book that have been put forward in recent years: 1) Micah 1–3; 4–5; 6–7; 2) Micah 1–3; 4–5; 6:1-7(7);

7:7(8)–20; 3) Micah 1–5; 6–7; and 4) Micah 1–2; 3–5; 6–7.[13] But these proposals frequently overlook significant generic, linguistic, and syntactic
indicators that point to a different assessment of Micah's structure.
First, of course, is the above-mentioned distinction between the superscription for the book in Mic 1:1 and the material that it introduces in
Mic 1:2–7:20. Although many scholars group chapters 1–3 or 1–2 together as a major structural component, there is no syntactic connector
that would link chapters 1 and 2 as Mic 2:1 begins with the exclama-
tion, "Woe *(hôy)* for those who devise wickedness . . ." Chapter 3,
however, does begin with the *waw-consecutive* statement, "and I said"
(wāʾōmar), which establishes a syntactical link between chapters 2 and
3. Likewise, chapter 4 begins with the *waw-consecutive* statement, "and
it shall come to pass *(wĕhāyâ)* in days to come . . .," which again establishes a syntactical relationship between chapters 3 and 4. Chapter 5
[NRSV: 4:13] begins with conjunctive formulations, "and you *(wĕʾattâ)*,
Beth Lehem, Ephrathah . . .," which links chapter 5 to chapter 4. Chapter 6 lacks any syntactical link to chapter 5 in that it begins with the imperative call to attention, "Hear now *(šimʿû-nā)* what YHWH says . . .,"
which indicates that chapter 6 forms the beginning of a new structural
component. Likewise, chapter 7 lacks a syntactical connection to chapter 6 in that it begins with the interjection, "woe is me *(ʾalĕlay lî)*," which
marks the beginning of another new structural component.

When these syntactical features are considered in relation to the
generic characteristics and contents of the book of Micah, a very different view of the book's structure emerges. The superscription in Mic 1:1,
of course constitutes the first major component of the book, and the
material in Mic 1:2–7:20, which anticipates YHWH's plans for Zion's
exaltation following a period of punishment, constitutes the second.
Micah 1:2–7:20 breaks down into four sub-units of its own. Micah 1:2-16
constitutes a prophetic announcement of punishment against Samaria/
Israel as a basis or paradigm for the punishment of Jerusalem/Judah.
Micah 2:1–5:14 [NRSV: 2:1–5:15] then provides a detailed overview of
the process of punishment and restoration, including a woe speech that
points to Israel's exile in Mic 2:1-13 and the prophet's announcement of
YHWH's plans to exalt Jerusalem in Mic 3:1–5:14 [NRSV: 3:1–5:15]. The
third major sub-unit is Mic 6:1-16, in which the prophet appeals to the
people to return to YHWH. Finally, Mic 7:1-20 constitutes the last major
sub-unit of the body of the book which presents the prophet's song of
confidence in YHWH's faithfulness to Israel and the view that the exal-

---

[13] For an overview of these proposals, see David Gerald Hagstrom, *The Coherence
of the Book of Micah: A Literary Analysis*, SBLDS, vol. 89 (Atlanta: Scholars Press, 1988)
11–22.

tation of Zion will indeed result from the punishment that is coming upon the people.

Prophetic Announcement of Punishment against Samaria/Israel as Paradigm for the Punishment against Jerusalem/Judah: 1:2-16

Micah 1:2-16 constitutes the prophet's announcement of punishment against Samaria and Israel, which stands as a paradigm for the judgment that will also come upon Jerusalem and Judah. Such a correlation between the two kingdoms presupposes their past relationship as allies for much of the eighth century, particularly during the reigns of Jeroboam ben Joash of Israel (786–746 B.C.E.) and Uzziah ben Amaziah of Judah (783–742 B.C.E.) when Judah served as a vassal to Israel. The superscription of Mic 1:1 clearly places the prophet's oracles in the period following the reigns of these two kings when the relationship began to unravel as a result of Israel's decision to break its longstanding alliance with the Assyrian empire that had stood since the early years of the Jehu dynasty. A series of royal assassinations rocked the northern kingdom during the years after the death of Jeroboam ben Joash as various proponents of confrontation with Assyria vied for power against those who sought to continue the alliance. Thus, Shallum assassinated Jeroboam's son Zechariah in 746, but Shallum in turn was assassinated a month later by Menahem who continued the alliance with Assyria during his reign (745–738 B.C.E.). Menahem's son Pekahiah was assassinated in 737 by Pekah (737–732 B.C.E.), who allied with Aram in an attempt to oppose the Assyrians. When Pekah and Rezin of Aram attempted to force Jotham (742–735 B.C.E.) and subsequently Ahaz (735–715 B.C.E.) of Judah to join the anti-Assyrian coalition, the Syro-Ephraimitic War (734–732 B.C.E.) broke out in which Ahaz finally called upon the Assyrians to protect his throne against the Syro-Ephraimitic threat. The result was a disaster for Aram, Israel, and Judah. Aram was destroyed and Rezin killed as the Assyrians first attacked their western neighbor. During the course of the Assyrian invasion of Israel, Pekah was assassinated by Hoshea (732–724 B.C.E.), who promptly surrendered to Tiglath Pileser III, but the Assyrians stripped Israel of its outlying territories in the Trans-Jordan, Galilee, and coastal plain, incorporating them as provinces of the Assyrian empire, and left Israel with only the central hill country of Ephraim. Judah was forced to become a vassal of Assyria and was obligated to pay a heavy tribute to the Assyrians in return for the protection provided to the small kingdom. Later years saw the destruction of northern Israel following its revolt in 724–722/1 B.C.E., Assyrian intimidation of Judah by Sargon II in 720 B.C.E., and the invasion of Judah in 701 B.C.E. by Sennacherib as a result of Hezekiah's (715–687/6 B.C.E.) revolt against the Assyrians.

Micah's statements concerning YHWH's judgment of Israel and Judah clearly presuppose the Assyrian actions against both Israel and Judah during this period, which he understands and portrays as acts of punishment by YHWH against the two kingdoms for their sins. As a resident of the Shephelah, the border territory of Judah with the Philistines, Micah was far removed from the centers of power in both Israel and Judah, but his life was heavily impacted by the decisions of the kings in Israel and Judah as the Assyrians generally chose an invasion route that took their armies down the coastal plain. Such a strategy ensured that the Shephelah would be one of the major areas hit by the Assyrian army as they attempted to surround and isolate Israel and Judah from potential Egyptian assistance. As he is presented in the book of Micah, the prophet seems to have cared little for the political differences in Samaria and Jerusalem that led to Israel's shift of alliance from Assyria to Aram or Judah's opposition to such a move. His oracles demonstrate no overt sentiments either for or against alliance with Assyria throughout the book. From his perspective, the catastrophe that was overtaking both Israel and Judah was evidence enough that the kings of both nations had acted irresponsibly. Israel was clearly the leader in provoking YHWH's punishment according to Micah, but Judah too would suffer as it followed in Israel's course by attempting to play such hardball politics in a world for which it was evidently ill-prepared.

Micah 1:2-16 appears to reflect the prophet's theological evaluation of the events that were overtaking both Israel and Judah during the late eighth century B.C.E. Based upon form and content, the passage comprises two major components. Verses 2-7 present the prophet's condemnation of Israel and Judah in the form of a prophetic announcement of judgment against the two kingdoms, and verses 8-16 express the prophet's anguish over the punishment that his home territory in the Shephelah will suffer as a result of the decisions made by the kings of Israel and Judah. Altogether, Israel's experience provides a paradigm for that of Judah regardless of the politics involved; i.e., just as Israel erred grievously and suffered destruction as a result, so Judah was committing similar errors and would suffer punishment like that of Israel.

Many scholars maintain that the prophetic announcement of judgment in verses 2-7 is based in the covenant lawsuit pattern because of the characteristic call to attention formula in verse 2 and the forensic reference to YHWH as a "witness" (*ʿēd*) to the nations and earth concerning Israel's and Judah's transgressions. The concept of a covenant lawsuit pattern has begun to break down in recent years, and the passage lacks any overt reference to a covenant between G–d and Israel to begin with.[14] Nevertheless, the passage does appear to reflect the pattern of a prophetic announcement of judgment in which both the punishment and the basis for punishment are laid out;[15] it is formulated to portray the destruction of northern Israel or Samaria as an act of punishment by G–d. Such a portrayal serves a rhetorical strategy of attempting to convince a presumably Judean audience that Jerusalem will suffer a similar fate for similar reasons.

The syntactical break at the beginning of verse 5 indicates that verses 2-7 contain two major sub-units. Verses 2-4 employ theophanic language and images of destruction in the natural world to portray YHWH's judgment that is applied specifically to Samaria and potentially to Jerusalem in verses 5-7.

Verses 2-4 begin with an example of the typical call to attention formula in verse 2a (cf. Judg 5:3; Prov 7:24; 2 Kgs 18:28-29; Amos 3:1; Hos 4:1; Mic 6:1) that is designed to engage the attention of the audience to the remarks that will follow.[16] In this case, the call is directed to both the "peoples" or the nations of the earth and the "earth" itself "and all that is in it" (literally, "its fullness") as the nations and the earth apparently must be convinced that YHWH's actions are justified. Of course, the true audience for this discourse is neither the nations nor the earth, but the prophet's own Judean listeners and readers. But by formulating the call in relation to the nations and the earth, the prophet portrays the destruction of Samaria and potentially Jerusalem as acts of universal or cosmic significance, and thereby asserts both YHWH's cosmic or worldwide role and the Assyrian actions against Samaria and perhaps Jerusalem as acts of YHWH. This perspective is evident in verse 2b, which provides the rationale for the nations and the world to pay attention to what is taking place. Verse 2b states that YHWH is serving as a "witness to you" from YHWH's "holy Temple." The reference to YHWH's role as a "witness to you *(bākem lĕʿēd)*" indicates that the statement is a direct address to the nations and the earth in keeping with the imperative address formulation of verse 2a, "Hear, you nations, all of you; listen, O earth and of its fullness." The designation of YHWH as "witness" apparently draws upon the imagery and roles of a courtroom or legal setting in which a witness is required to testify concerning the wrongdoing of the accused or the legality of an action (cf. Num 5:13; Josh 24:22; 1 Sam 12:5), although two witnesses are normally required in cases of capital

---

[14] For discussion, see Renaud, *Formation* 38-41; Ben Zvi, ad loc.

[15] Sweeney, *Isaiah 1–39* 530–1.

[16] Ibid., 544.

offenses (Deut 17:6). The designation of YHWH as a witness thereby lends credibility to the prophet's portrayal and understanding of Samaria's destruction as an act of YHWH. The reference to YHWH's "holy Temple" likewise adds credibility to the prophet's case by asserting the role of the Temple, presumably in Jerusalem, as the site from which YHWH carries out these acts of judgment. In this manner, the prophet identifies his message with the Temple and thereby attempts to draw institutional support and legitimacy for his message.

Verses 3-4 then employ theophanic imagery of YHWH's actions in nature as a basis for his contention that YHWH is acting against Samaria and potentially against Jerusalem. The use of such imagery is particularly important in relation to the preceding reference to the Temple in verse 2 in that the Temple serves as the holy center of both the natural world of creation and the human world.[17] The introductory *kî hinnēh*, "for behold!" indicates that verses 3-4 are designed to provide evidence for the prophet's initial contention in verse 2. Verse 3 states that "YHWH is coming out of his place," i.e., that YHWH proceeds from the Temple, and that YHWH "will come down and tread upon the high places of the earth." The reference to YHWH's treading upon the "high places" indicates an element of cultic apostasy on the part of Israel among the prophet's charges. The high places refer to illegitimate worship sites that challenged the assertion of Jerusalem as the only legitimate worship site in the land. The prophet thereby suggests that Israel and Judah have abandoned YHWH, which further substantiates his claim that YHWH is acting to punish the people. Verse 4 then employs imagery from the natural world that metaphorically portrays the destruction of the land. The first image is that of mountains which "dissolve." This does not mean that the mountains will literally disappear, but it refers to the natural phenomenon of flooding during the rainy season in Israel in which the rains will wash down the sides of the mountains and potentially destroy or carry away anything that stands in their path. The imagery of hillside disintegration is, of course, well known to the residents of Malibu along the Pacific coast as the winter rains claim hillsides and houses every year. The imagery of valleys that will "burst open," literally "be split/divided," refers to the cleavages created in the low-lying areas as the flooding waters rage through and cut channels along the floors of the valleys, again washing away everything in their path. The second half of the verse shifts to the imagery of wax melting before a fire, which suggests the flames of war. Such an image is particularly pertinent in the ancient near-eastern world as Mesopotamian accounts of the flood also make reference to the torches and

---

[17] See Jon D. Levenson, "The Temple and the World," *JR* 64 (1984) 275–98.

fires that consume the land along with the raging waters. Finally, the imagery returns to water once again with a description of waters cascading down a slope.

Verses 5-7 then refer specifically to Samaria/Israel and Jerusalem/ Judah to make the prophet's points concerning the fate of both nations clear. Verse 5a constitutes the basic thesis of the prophet's discourse, "all this is for the transgressions of Jacob and for the sins of the house of Jacob," i.e., the prophet charges that Israel's suffering is the result of its sins. The Hebrew term *peš^ca*, "transgression," frequently refers to political revolt of one nation against another (e.g., Amos 1:3, 6; cf. the use of the verb *pš^c* in 1 Kgs 12:19; 2 Kgs 1:1; 3:5, 7; 8:22) as well as to acts of revolt against G–d (e.g., Isa 58:1; 59:12; Amos 5:12). The use of the term *ḥaṭṭ'ōt*, "sins," is much more general. The reference to Jacob, of course, employs the name of Israel's eponymous ancestor, the patriarch Jacob (Genesis 25–35), in parallel with the designation "house of Israel." The initial assertion of 5a is reinforced by two rhetorical questions in verse 5b that point specifically to the capital city of Samaria as the cause for Israel's problems and then to the capital city of Jerusalem as the cause for Judah's potential problems. In this manner, the prophet points to the decisions made by the kings of Israel who ruled in Samaria as the cause of Israel's transgression. He then establishes the analogy between Israel and Judah by pointing to Jerusalem, and thus the Judean kings, as the cause for Judah's wrongdoing. The prophet employs the metaphor of "high places" in reference to Judah to highlight the motif of Judah's rejection of YHWH by calling to mind the image of illegitimate worship places that were forbidden in the Jerusalem cult tradition. Ironically, northern Israel's sin against YHWH in the Deuteronomistic History is the establishment of alternative and illegitimate places of worship that demonstrated the northern kingdom's rejection of the Jerusalem Temple (see 1 Kings 12–13; 2 Kings 17). In this respect, Judah is likened to Israel so that the prophet can assert that Judah will suffer the same consequences.

Verses 6-7 then build upon the assertions of Israel's and Judah's sins in verse 5 by pointing to YHWH's acts of punishment against them. This segment is syntactically joined to verse 5 by the *waw-consecutive* verbal structure of verse 6 and the conjunctive *waw's* of verse 7. Verse 6 is formulated as a first person speech by YHWH in which the Deity graphically describes the destruction of Samaria by a conqueror. As a resident of the Shephelah, it is doubtful that Micah actually witnessed Samaria's demise, but the imagery is common enough for the destruction of cities. YHWH states the intention to make Samaria into a "ruin" or a "heap" in the field that is fit only for planting vineyards rather than as the site of a settled city. Its stones will be cast down the side of the hill or tell on which cities are commonly built in the ancient world into the valley below. The use of the *hiphil* verb *ngr*, "to pour down," of course calls to mind the use of the same verb in the portrayal of the waters washing down the slope in verse 4. The uncovering of foundation stones enables a conqueror to undermine the defensive walls of a city and thereby destroy its defenses. Excavations at Samaria demonstrate the strong and well-crafted walls that defended eighth-century Samaria, thereby confirming its reputation as an extremely well protected fortress.[18] Verse 7 then shifts from the imagery of destruction to that of moral evaluation. It begins with a description of the city's images or idols that will be beaten to pieces as the city is destroyed by the enemy soldiers, and then describes how its "wages" shall be burned with fire. The term *ʾetnan*, "wage," is generally taken as a reference to a harlot's wage (Deut 23:19 [NRSV: 23:18]; Ezek 16:34, 41; Hos 9:1), although it might actually designate offerings to a deity or to an idol or goods acquired in trade (see Isa 23:17, 18). In any case, the use of the term here is clearly polemical as the prophet clearly uses the term as a reference to a harlot's wage in the second part of the verse. The concluding charge of verse 7b, "for as the wages of a prostitute she gathers them, and as the wages of a prostitute they shall again be used (literally, "unto the wages of a prostitute they shall return")," indicates the prophet's view that the destruction of the city results from sin on the part of Israel. In this case, the shift in alliance from Assyria to Aram and the exchange of goods, tribute, or gifts that would take place as part of the establishment of such an alliance would provide a basis for the prophet's focus on the motif of prostitution, i.e., Israel metaphorically "changed lovers" when shifting from Assyria to Aram (cf. Hosea 1–3), and suffered the consequences when the new relationship went sour. The statement, "unto the wages of a prostitute they will return," likely refers to the fact that the conquering Assyrians would have dedicated part or all of the spoil of the city to their own gods.

Verses 8-16 then present the prophet's lament over the fate of Judah and Jerusalem. Insofar as the prophet mentions, in addition to Jerusalem, some eleven cities and villages in Judah, all of which may be located in the Shephelah or nearby, it would seem that the lament presupposes Sennacherib's invasion of Judah by way of the coast plain in 701 B.C.E. According to his accounts of the action, Sennacherib concentrated his assault against the city of Lachish, the second capital of Judah which served as the Davidic administrative center for Judean territory in the Shephelah. The reason for Sennacherib's attack in this region is that the coastal plain would enable his army to move quickly

---

[18] Nahman Avigad, "Samaria (City)," *NEAEHL* 4:1300-10, esp. 1303.

against Judah and to block any assistance that might come from Egypt to the southwest or the sea to the west. Furthermore, the Shephelah is a rich agricultural area which would allow his troops plenty of food and water. The conquest of this region would open the soft underbelly of Judah, and give his troops a good base of support for a push up into the Judean hill country toward Jerusalem. It would seem that Sennacherib's invasion of Judah forced Micah to flee his home city of Moreshet Gath for refuge in Jerusalem, and prompted his prophecy against Jerusalem and Israel.

The introductory particle *ʿal-zōʾt*, "for this," in verse 8 establishes a syntactical link between the lamentation material in verses 8-16 and the prophetic announcement of judgment in verses 2-7. It therefore indicates that the prophet's lament is for the anticipated punishment of Jerusalem and Judah that was announced in the preceding pericope. The specific references to the cities and villages of the Shephelah suggests that the Assyrian invasion is already under way and that the prophet can draw upon his own experience of the terror of the Assyrian assault as he formulates his lament. In this case, the suffering of the Shephelah is the direct result of the transgressions of both Israel and Judah that he condemns in verses 2-7.

The prophet is clearly the speaker as indicated by the first person formulation of verses 8-9. He employs the characteristic vocabulary for mourning and lamentation as he cries out, "for this I lament and wail; I will go barefoot (literally, "despoiled") and naked." Normally, a person in mourning would put on sackcloth rather than go about naked (cf. Gen 37:34; 1 Kgs 21:27; Joel 1:8), but the nakedness symbolizes the status of prisoners of war who are marched off naked and barefoot, sometimes with their hair shaved off, by their captors (cf. Isa 7:20; 20:1-6).[19] The prophet metaphorically compares his lamentation to the howling of jackals and the screeching of ostriches in verse 8b. The introductory *kî*, "because," of verse 9 indicates the cause of the prophet's mourning as he states that "her wound (literally, "wounds") is incurable" because it has reached Judah, the gate of my people, and Jerusalem (cf. Jer 15:18; Isa 1:5-6). The antecedent to "her" is not entirely certain, although it likely anticipates the reference to "the daughter of Zion" in verse 13. The sequence, "Judah," "gate of my people," and "Jerusalem," suggest Assyrian movement from the Shephelah and into the Judean hills toward Jerusalem.

---

[19] See also the portrayal of the prisoners on the Megiddo ivory (*ANEP* 332), Shalmanezer III's palace reliefs (*ANEP* 358), and the impaled captives in Sennacherib's relief of the conquest of Lachish (*ANEP* 373).

Verses 10-16 then present a sequence of the prophet's cries of lamentation and warning which enumerate the cities and towns of the
Shephelah and the ultimate threat to Jerusalem. Not all of the sites are
known. It is interesting however that, apart from Gath in verse 10,
those that are known appear in verses 13-16 in association with Jerusalem whereas those that are not known appear in verses 10-12 in association with Gath. Sennacherib's account of the campaign indicates
that Hezekiah had forced the Philistines onto his side in the revolt, and
that he had imprisoned Padi, King of Ekron, in Jerusalem in order to
make sure that Ekron supported him during the revolt.[20] It is possible,
therefore, that the cities mentioned in verses 10-12 are Philistine sites
associated with Gath that would have been located in the coastal plain
at the base of the Shephelah whereas those listed in verses 13-15 are in
fact Judean cities located in the Shephelah itself. This would explain
why the cities in verses 10-12 seem to have been already taken whereas
those in verses 13-16 are still being warned. Sennacherib's forces would
have taken the Philistine lowlands first before proceeding up the ascent
of the Shephelah into the heartland of Judah. Indeed, the statement in
verse 12b, "for ($k\hat{\imath}$; NRSV reads, "yet") disaster has come down from
YHWH to the gate of Jerusalem," reprises the statement in verse 9, and
suggests the closure of a sub-unit of verses 10-16 that returns to the initial theme of the threat to Jerusalem in verses 8-9. A similar observation
may be made about verse 16, which employs feminine singular address
forms for an unspecified addressee. Just as the feminine singular reference in verse 9 ("for her wound is incurable") refers to Jerusalem, so
the references in verse 16 also refer to Jerusalem. Both verse 12b and
verse 16 would conclude the two sub-units of verses 10-16 by returning
to the initial concern with Jerusalem in verses 8-9. Verses 10-12 take up
Philistine cities that have been incorporated into Judah by Hezekiah as
part of his preparations for revolt, and verses 13-16 take up cities that
were always a part of Judah. Both sections together point to the impending threat against the Judean capital in Jerusalem.

Scholars have had a great deal of difficulty in identifying the sites of
the cities or towns listed in verses 10-12, but each of the city or town
names provide the basis for a pun in the prophet's lamentation. Thus,
Gath, one of the five principle cities of the Philistines, was initially
identified as Tel Erani just north of modern Kiryat Gath in the Shephelah, but the site was not occupied in the Iron Age.[21] Most scholars
now identify Gath with Tel Zafit/Safi, about ten miles southeast of Tel
Miqne/Ekron, although full confirmation of this hypothesis awaits fur-

---

[20] See *ANET* 287–8.
[21] See Joe D. Seger, "Gath," *ABD* II:908-9.

ther excavation at the site. The pun on the name Gath lies in the formation of the verb formation, "tell it not *(ʾal-tagîdû),*" in that the verb relates
assonantally to the name Gath *(gat).* The town name Beth Leaphrah is
otherwise unknown in the Hebrew Bible, and the site has not been
identified.[22] The pun is based upon the command, "roll yourselves *(hitpallāšî)* in the dust *(ʿāpār),*" which relates assonantally to the name Beth
Leaphrah *(bêt lᵉʿaprâ).* In addition, the *Ketiv* form of the verb *hitpallāšî,*
i.e., *htplšty,* employs the consonants of the Hebrew term for Philistine
(plšty), which suggests a Philistine association for the town. The town
Shapir is not mentioned elsewhere in the Hebrew Bible, and the site is
unknown.[23] The name Shaphir means, "beautiful, fair," and contrasts
with the depiction of the city in Micah's lament, "pass by on your way
inhabitants of Shaphir in nakedness and shame." Zaanan is probably to
be identified with Zenan in Josh 15:37, but the site is unknown.[24]
Micah's lament, "the inhabitants of Zaanan do not come forth," plays
upon the assonance of the name Zaanan *(ṣaʾănān)* and verb "do not
come forth *(lōʾyāṣᵉʾâ)."* Beth Ezel is otherwise not mentioned in the Hebrew Bible, and the site is unknown.[25] The prophet's statement, "he
(i.e., the enemy; contra NRSV) shall remove/take his support from you,"
relates to the meaning of the name Beth Ezel, which employs the verb
root *ʾṣl,* "to remove, withdraw, withhold." Maroth is not mentioned
elsewhere in the Hebrew Bible and the site is unknown.[26] The name
means "bitter" or "evil," and relates ironically to the prophet's statement, "for the inhabitants of Maroth wait anxiously for good, yet disaster has come down from YHWH to the gate of Jerusalem."

Verses 13-16 refer to sites that are well known in the Judean Sheph-
helah, and likewise employ puns based upon the name of the city or
town. Lachish, present-day Tel Lakhish/ed-Duweir in the western
Shephelah, was the Judean royal administrative center for the Sheph-
helah.[27] Sennacherib's conquest of the city in 701 B.C.E., depicted as a

---

[22] See Lamontte M. Luker, "Beth-Le-aphrah," *ABD* I:689. Karl Elliger, "Die
Heimat des Propheten Micha," *Kleine Schriften zum Alten Testament,* TB, vol. 32 (Munich: Chr. Kaiser, 1966) 9–71, esp. 47–8, identifies Beth Leaphrah with Tell et-Taiyibeh
based upon the association of the latter with a demon figure known to the local
Arabs as Aphrit, but this is only conjectural.

[23] See Lamontte M. Luker, "Shaphir," *ABD* V:1160.

[24] See Lamontte M. Luker, "Zaanan," *ABD* VI:1029. Luker notes that some scholars identify the city with ʿAraq el-Kharba west of Lachish on the basis of the meaning of the Hebrew and Arabic place names, but there is no consensus.

[25] See Lamontte M. Luker, "Beth Ezel," *ABD* I:686.

[26] See Lamontte M. Luker, "Maroth," *ABD* IV:559.

[27] See David Ussishkin, "Lachish," *NEAEHL* 3:897-911.

major triumph in his palace reliefs,[28] secured his control over western Judah and opened the way to Jerusalem. The name Lachish *(lākîš)* relates assonantally to the term *rekeš*, "the steeds," in Micah's statement, "Harness the steeds to the chariots, inhabitants of Lachish." From the prophet's perspective, the city has not yet been conquered. The introductory "therefore" *(lākēn)* in verse 14 indicates that the reference to Lachish in verse 13 introduces the following statements concerning the cities of Judah. Indeed the prophet's reference to the transgressions of Israel in Bath Zion ("daughter Zion") apparently indicates Jerusalem's role revolting against Assyria analogous to that of Samaria in relation to the northern kingdom of Israel some twenty years before (cf. Mic 1:5). As the second capital of Judah (cf. 2 Kgs 14:19/2 Chr 25:27), Lachish would have played a central role in preparing the Shephelah for revolt against Assyria. It was known as one of Solomon's chariot cities (1 Kgs 9:19; 10:26; cf. 2 Chr 11:9). The prophet's references to "parting gifts" for Moresheth Gath employs the term *šilûḥîm*, a term that refers to the payment that a husband makes when sending away his wife (e.g., Exod 18:2, when Moses sends Zipporah away) or that a father makes when he sends away his daughter to be married (e.g., 1 Kgs 9:16). Here, the term indicates the loss of Moresheth Gath, Micah's hometown, which would have been located in the vicinity of Gath (Tel Judeidah, cf. Mic 1:1). The term Moreshet, "possession, settlement," relates assonantally to the verb root *ʾrš*, "to be betrothed." Likewise, the name Gath (Hebrew, *gat*) relates assonantally to the Rabbinic Hebrew term *get*, which refers to a divorce. The town Achzib is identified with Tell Beida, northeast of Lachish (see Josh 15:44).[29] The name provides a pun for the prophet's statement, "the houses of Achzib *(ʾakzîb)* shall be a deception *(ʾakzāb)* to the kings of Israel," i.e., Achzib will be lost. Mareshah is modern Tell Maresha, about four miles/6.5 km northeast of Lachish (cf. Josh 15:44; 2 Chr 11:5-12; 15:9-15).[30] The name Mareshah, Hebrew *mārēšâ*, forms a pun with the prophet's reference to the "conqueror" (Hebrew, *yōrēš*) that YHWH will bring against the city. Adullam is identified with Tell Adullam/Madkur, about five miles south of Beth Shemesh (cf. 2 Chr 11:7).[31] The prophet's reference to the "glory of Israel" that shall come to Adullam plays satirically upon the name, which means "refuge," and the tradition in 1 Sam 22:1; cf. 2 Sam 23:13 concerning David's hiding in a cave at Adullam while fleeing from Saul. The prophet clearly indicates that the "glory of Israel" will be

---

[28] See *ANEP* 372-3.

[29] See Eilat Mazar and Moshe W. Prausnitz, "Achzib, *NEAEHL* 1:32-6.

[30] See Michael Avi-Yonah, "Mareshah (Marisa)," *NEAEHL* 3:948-51.

[31] See Jeffries M. Hamilton, "Adullam," *ABD* 1:81.

forced to flee for safety. Finally, the prophet calls upon an unidentified feminine singular addressee, undoubtedly Jerusalem (cf. verses 9, 12), to shave her hair in mourning over the loss of her "pampered" (literally, "children of delight") children. Shaving the head was a common sign of mourning, loss, or sense of threat (Deut 14:1; Isa 3:24; 15:2; 22:12; Jer 47:5; Ezek 7:18; Amos 8:10). The prophet employs the metaphor of the eagle to portray such baldness in mourning for the people who will be lost. Likewise, just as the eagle soars away, so the people of these cities and towns will be exiled or removed (n.b., the verb root *glh* means "to exile, remove") away from their homes.

Prophetic Announcement Concerning the Punishment and Restoration of Jerusalem and Judah: 2:1–5:14 [NRSV: 2:1–5:15]

The second major component of the body of the book of Micah in Mic 1:2–7:16 is the prophetic announcement concerning the punishment and restoration of Jerusalem and Judah in Mic 2:1–5:14 [NRSV: 2:1–5:15]. As noted above, this textual block is held together by syntactical joins at three major points, i.e., the *waw-consecutive* statement, "and I said" *(wā'ōmar),*" in Mic 3:1; the *waw-consecutive* temporal formula in Mic 4:1, "and it shall come to pass in later days *(wĕhāyâ bĕ'aḥărît hayyāmîm),*" in Mic 4:1; and the *waw-conjunctive* address, "and you, O Beth Lehem, Ephratah *(wĕ'attâ bêt-lehem 'eprātâ)* in Mic 5:1 [NRSV: 5:2]. In addition, it is held together conceptually by an overall perspective that presents the exile of the northern kingdom of Israel as the impetus for the process by which YHWH will exalt the remnant of Israel/Jacob in Jerusalem/Zion at the center of the nations and all creation. Thus, Mic 2:1-13 presents the prophet's extended "woe" speech against the northern kingdom of Israel, which culminates in Mic 2:12-13 with a much-debated portrayal of Israel's exile led by its king and YHWH. Although the scenario of Micah 2 is one of judgment against Israel, the prophet responds to and elaborates upon this scenario in Mic 3:1–5:14 [NRSV: 3:1–5:15] with an extended speech that lays out the means by which YHWH will form a remnant of Israel from the exiles that will then be established in Jerusalem/Zion. The prophet's speech is signaled by the introductory speech formula in Mic 3:1aα^1, "and I said," and it appears in Mic 3:1aα^2–5:14 [NRSV: 3:1aα^2–5:15]. Within this speech, the prophet focuses first in Mic 3:1aα^2-8 on Israel's leaders as the parties responsible for the failures of the nation that led to punishment. The prophet then turns to the core of the unit, the general announcement concerning the punishment and restoration of Jerusalem and Zion in Mic 3:9–5:14

[NRSV: 3:9–5:15]. Micah 3:9–5:14 [NRSV: 3:9–5:15], of course, constitutes the rhetorical goal of the entire unit in Micah 2–5 in that it points to a glorious future for Israel at Jerusalem that stems from the initial situation of defeat and humiliation.

THE PROPHET'S WOE SPEECH AGAINST ISRAEL: 2:1-13

Micah 2–5 begins with a presentation of the prophet's "woe" speech against the northern kingdom of Israel in Mic 2:1-13.[32] The passage begins with the prophet's syntactically independent "woe" address in verse 1, provides an overview of the reasons for Israel's punishment throughout, and culminates in a portrayal of the nation's exile in verses 12-13. The speech formula in Mic 3:1aα[1] marks the beginning of an entirely new, but related, sub-unit of Micah 2–5. Micah 2:1-13 contains three basic sub-units: the basic "woe" speech of the prophet in verses 1-5, formulated as a prophetic judgment speech against Israel; a disputation speech in verses 6-11, in which the prophet attempts to counter the claims of his opponents who contend that YHWH will act to protect the nation; and a concluding announcement by the prophet in verses 12-13 of Israel's impending exile. Altogether, Mic 2:1-13 is designed to convince its listening or reading audience that the exile of northern Israel is an act of YHWH that is intended to punish the nation for enabling its more powerful elements to seize the property of small landowners and householders.

The presentation of the prophet's "woe" speech against northern Israel in Mic 2:1-5 employs the basic pattern of the prophetic judgment speech.[33] Verses 1-2 lay out the causes for the punishment, and verses 3-5, introduced by the particle lākēn, "therefore," takes up the consequences that the guilty parties are to suffer. Although the passage initially employs third person references in verses 1-3a to speak *about* the guilty parties, second person masculine plural or singular address forms appear throughout verses 3b-5 to indicate that the prophet's speech shifts to a direct address to those whom the prophet holds to be responsible for Israel's current situation.

The initial interjection hôy, "alas!" or "woe!" that typically introduces prophetic "woe" oracles that are concerned with announcing punishment against a guilty party or warning a party of the potential consequences of its actions (e.g., Amos 5:18-20; Isa 1:4; 3:11; Nah 3:1). It

---

[32] For discussion of the prophetic "woe" speech, see Sweeney, *Isaiah 1–39* 543.

[33] For discussion of the prophetic judgment speech, see Sweeney, *Isaiah 1–39* 533–4.

is generally followed by a participial formation that describes the actions of those who are to be condemned or warned by the prophet. In the present case, the objects of the prophet's address are described as "those who devise wickedness *(hōšĕbê ʾāwen)* and those who work evil (deeds) upon their beds *(ûpōʿălê rāʿ ʿal-miškĕbôtām)*." This statement is followed immediately in verse 1b by one formulated with finite verbs indicating that the guilty parties carry out their plans at the first opportunity in the morning because they have the power to do so. The statement certainly suggests the eagerness with which these persons act as they are awake at night devising their plans, and act at first light in the morning. The statement, "because it is in their power" reads literally, "because their hand is (for) god," which suggests that the prophet intends to portray the guilty parties as persons who would see themselves as exercising absolute power or the power of G–d. The prophet's portrayal of the guilty certainly is designed to turn the audience against them.

Whereas verse 1 expresses the actions of the guilty in very general terms, verse 2 becomes much more specific by pointing to crimes of economic abuse against home- and landowners. The statements are self-explanatory, "they covet fields, and seize them, and take them away." It is essential to keep in mind the role that land ownership plays in ancient Israelite and Judean society, i.e., land is the fundamental form of wealth or property in the ancient world, and a family's right to own land is protected throughout ancient Israelite law by provisions that disallow the transfer of land outside of the family or the normal line of family succession or inheritance. Although an Israelite man or woman could certainly go into debt and become a slave (Exod 21:1-11; Deut 15:12-18), the sabbatical and Jubilee laws protected ownership of property within the family by stipulating that any land transfer or loan to pay a debt could continue only for a term of six years; at the end of six years in the sabbatical seventh year or at the end of forty-nine years in the Jubilee fiftieth year, debts were canceled, land would revert to its original owner, and the term of service as a slave would conclude (in addition to the above-cited slave laws, see Leviticus 25; Deut 15:1-11). The inheritance rights of the firstborn son were paramount and protected (Deut 21:15-17); the charging of interest on a loan was forbidden and the collection of pledges strictly regulated (Exod 22:25-27; Lev 25:35-38; Deut 23:19-20; 24:10-15); Levirate marriage was instituted to protect the lines of inheritance of a man who died without an heir (Deut 25:5-10; cf. Ruth 4); and the inheritance of land by daughters or other family members was instituted and regulated to ensure that land would remain within the family and the larger tribal group (Num 27:1-11; 36:1-12; cf. Jer 32:1-15). Nevertheless, the problems posed by those who would attempt to take land or other property from its owners appears frequently (e.g., 1 Kings 21; Isa 5:8-24; Amos 2:6-8; 8:4-6). The prophet's condemnation of those who would take away family property or inheritance is evident in verse 2b, "they oppress householder and house, people and their inheritance."

The prophet's presentation of the consequences for such actions appears in verses 3-5. As noted above, this segment begins with the particle, *lākēn*, "therefore," which typically introduces the announcement of consequences in a prophetic judgment speech. The particle is followed by an example of the messenger formula, "thus says YHWH," which indicates that the prophet's oracle is intended to represent YHWH's own statement concerning the matter. This perspective is reinforced by the first person formulation of the actual statement in verse 3aβ-b so that YHWH is indicated as the speaker. YHWH presents the announcement in terms that are designed to relate to the prophet's initial statements in verses 1-2 concerning the actions of those to be condemned. Thus, the statement reads, "Behold (NRSV, "now"), I am devising against this family an evil from which you cannot remove your necks; and you shall not walk haughtily, for it is (NRSV, "will be") an evil time." The initial verb, "I am devising," employs a participial form of the verb *ḥšb*, which also appears in the prophet's initial "woe" statement concerning "those who devise wickedness" in verse 1. Some hold the reference to YHWH's judgment "against this family *(mišpāḥâ)*" to be a later addition because of the unusual syntax and the uncertainty concerning the reference to Israel as a family,[34] but the syntax merely emphasizes "this family" as the indirect object of the verb.[35] The reference to a nation as "family" is not unknown as the term is used in this fashion in Gen 12:4 ("all the families of the earth shall be blessed") and Jer 8:3 ("all the remnant that remains of this evil family [i.e., Judah]"). In the present context, however, it highlights the issue of property ownership in that the seizure of property referred to in verse 2 runs contrary to the above-mentioned property laws that are designed to protect family property holdings. On the surface, the feminine noun "evil" *(rāʿâ)* reprises the masculine noun *rāʿ*, "evil (deeds)," of verse 1, but it also plays upon the meaning of the verb root *rʿh*, which means "to pasture, tend, graze." The noun *rōʿeh*, "shepherd, herdsman," is derived from this root, and it is oftentimes used as a reference to a ruler (e.g., Jer 17:16; Zech 10:2; 11:16; 13:7; Ezek 34:2; Nah 3:18). The metaphor is particularly apt when considered in relation to the following image of those judged who will not be able to remove their necks from the "evil/

---

[34] See the discussion in Renaud, *Formation* 73–4.
[35] Hillers, *Micah* 31.

herdsman," i.e., like an ox placed in a yoke, they will not be able to lift their necks. It also provides a basis for the imagery in verses 12-13 of Israel being led like sheep from a pen into exile with their king at their head. Verse 3 concludes with a reference to the shame of the guilty parties in this evil time because they will no longer walk haughtily (cf. Isa 3:16).

The prophet follows up his quotation of YHWH with his own reference to a taunt song in verses 4-5 in order to drive home the point concerning the humiliation of those condemned. The segment begins with the future temporal formula, *bayyôm hahû᾿*, "in that day," which simply indicates that the song will be sung in the future when the punishment takes place. The term for "taunt song," *māšāl*, denotes any kind of proverb (Prov 1:1; 10:1), parable (Ezek 17:2; 24:3), common saying or by-word (1 Sam 10:12; Ezek 18:2; Deut 28:37), or the type of artistic composition frequently ascribed to prophets (Num 23:7; Isa 14:4; Hab 2:6). In this case, the "taunt song" is qualified by the reference to the wailing with bitter lamentation so that the so-called "taunt song" actually functions as a sort of lament. The song itself employs a great deal of assonance with the letter *shin* and word play in its initial two couplets: "We are utterly ruined *(šādôd nĕšaddunû)*; He changes the inheritance of my people *(ḥēleq ῾ammî yāmîr)*; How he removes it from me/ what is mine *(᾿êk yāmîš lî)*; To the one who restores/burns(?) our fields, he apportions *(lĕšôbēb šādênû yĕḥallēq).*" Although the NRSV understands YHWH to be the primary protagonist who acts against the people and thus the subject of the verbs, it seems more likely that the subject "he" should refer to the "shepherd" or conqueror indicated in verse 3 who will carry out the punishment. Certainly the imagery of land confiscation and reassignment would play into such an interpretation. The NRSV translation, "how he removes it from me," is not well supported by the Hebrew *᾿êk yāmîš lî* which is more properly rendered as "how he removes what is mine (literally, 'what is to me')." The term *lĕšôbēb* is very problematic as many suppose it to be corrupt,[36] but the term means literally, "to one who returns/restores," although the Hebrew noun *šābîb*, "flame," (Job 18:5) suggests the existence of a root *šbb*, "to blaze, burn" (cf. Assyrian, *šabābu*, "to blaze"). There is no Hebrew attestation for such a verb, however, and the meaning, "to one who returns/ restores," may refer to the conqueror whose conquest would restore misappropriated land to its rightful owners by taking away from those who misappropriated it in the first place. In this manner, those who abused their positions of power by misappropriating the land of the

---

[36] BHS notes; but see the comments by Rudolph, *Micha–Nahum–Habakuk–Zephanja* 52–3 and Wolff, *Micah* 70.

people, suffer a similar fate as the conqueror in turn takes away the land from them. Verse 5 begins with *lākēn*, "therefore," and thereby states the consequence of this loss, "therefore you will have no one to cast the line by lot." The casting of lots in order to make major tribal or national decisions (cf. Prov 18:18), such as the selection of the first king of Israel (see 1 Sam 10:17-27, which does not use the term "lot"), was apparently a privilege of land ownership in ancient Israel. The casting of lots was also employed to apportion land (see Josh 15:1; 18:6; Num 26:55; 36:2). At the time of punishment, those who had misappropriated land would be cut out altogether. Although many note that the reference to "the assembly of Yʜwʜ" must denote the religious community,[37] there is little basis for such a view; it simply refers to the people of Israel assembled publicly regardless of whether the occasion is religious or not.

Micah 2:6-11 constitutes the prophet's disputation speech concerning Yʜwʜ's ability or willingness to protect the people of Judah.[38] The identity of the prophet's opponents is unclear—van der Woude maintains that they are other prophets,[39] and this is certainly possible given the prophet's reference to those of who would preach to the people of wine and strong drink in verse 11. Whatever their institutional identity might be—prophets, village elders, or just common persons—the prophet's opponents apparently hold to the opinion that Yʜwʜ will act to protect the people. This is clear from verse 7 in which the prophet quotes those who challenge his contention that Yʜwʜ has lost patience with the people and that the threat against the people actually comes from Yʜwʜ. In defending himself, he points throughout the passage to the suffering of the people who are apparently fleeing from the advancing Assyrian army (cf. verse 8), and argues that his words concerning Yʜwʜ's judgment against the people are designed to benefit them by pointing to the reality that Yʜwʜ is the cause of their suffering. In the end, however, he recognizes that the people are desperate, and that they will listen to anyone who will give them some comfort even if they speak of delusions such as wine and strong drink.

The prophet begins his disputation by quoting the words of his opponents in verses 6-7a. Apparently, they call upon Micah to cease his preaching, i.e., "'Do not preach!' they preach," but the prophet quickly points out that his opponents are unwilling to preach about the catastrophe that is overtaking the people. The NRSV translates the following statement as, "disgrace will not overtake us," but this is clearly mis-

[37] E.g., Mays, *Micah* 66.
[38] For discussion of the disputation genre, see Sweeney, *Isaiah 1–39* 519.
[39] A. S. van der Woude, "Micah and the Pseudo-Prophets," *VT* 19 (1969) 244–60.

taken as the Hebrew term *kĕlimmôt* is a feminine plural noun that means "disgraces" or "humiliations," but *yissag* is a third person masculine singular *niphal* imperfect form of the verb *sûg*, which means "to turn back" or "to turn aside." The feminine plural *kĕlimmôt* cannot possibly serve as the subject for the masculine singular *yissag*. In keeping with the suggestion of the BHS textual apparatus, NRSV emends the verb to *yassigēnû* which is based on the root *śgg*, "to overtake," but this presupposes a rendition of the verb root with *sgg* and it does not address the lack of correspondence in gender and number. Interpreters have failed to note, however, that YHWH is in fact the implicit subject of the verb, and that the statement represents Micah's contention, "(YHWH) will not turn aside humiliations," i.e., YHWH will not defend the people in their time of distress. In verse 7, the prophet quotes the contention of his opponents among the people, "Is it said, O house of Jacob, 'Is YHWH's patience exhausted? Are these his (YHWH's) doings?' " The paired rhetorical questions represent the challenge that is posed to the prophet's contention that YHWH will not protect the people, i.e., the rhetorical questions must be answered, "No!" and thereby assert that YHWH's patience is not exhausted and that the calamity that is overtaking the people is not YHWH's work. The people are in trouble and they do not want to hear that YHWH will not come to their rescue.

The prophet presents his response to this challenge in verses 7b-10, beginning with his own rhetorical question, "Do not my words do good to one who walks uprightly?" The rhetorical response to such a question is "Of course they do!" Although it would be difficult for the prophet's audience to imagine how his message of YHWH's hostility might be of benefit, the prophet is basically attempting to convince the people to accept the reality of their situation, i.e., YHWH is not going to come to their rescue and they had better flee if they hope to save their lives (cf. verse 10). The reader is not told what catastrophe the people face, but the following verses portray scenes of men, women, and children, stripped of their dignity, homes, and even clothing, in the face of someone who has arisen as an enemy. It seems likely, given that Micah's home in Moreshet Gath was located in the Shephelah which was taken by Sennacherib's army in 701 B.C.E., that the prophet addresses a situation in which people are fleeing in terror before the advancing Assyrian troops as they overrun the entire land. At a time like this, they are desperate for a message of hope that YHWH will intervene and deliver them; Micah indeed tells them that YHWH has come, but he also tells them that YHWH is the cause of their suffering. This is evident in verse 8a, which the NRSV translates in the notes as "but yesterday my people arose as an enemy." The main translation, "But you rise up against my people as an enemy," actually captures some of the meaning of the statement, although it clearly deviates from the Hebrew text. Indeed, YHWH is again the implicit subject of the verb *yĕqômēm*, which in the *polel* form always refers to the (re)establishment of something, such as the (re)building of a ruined city (cf. Isa 44:26; 58:12). In this case, the verb means, "he shall establish," so that the entire statement reads, "and yesterday, he (YHWH) would establish my people as an enemy." He then goes on to list the various indignities suffered by the people at the time of the Assyrian invasion, which is particularly ironic in the present context because these same indignities were visited upon them by those who would seize their land and homes in Mic 2:1-5. The first, "from before/the front of a garment, you strip off glory/a cloak." The meaning of the Hebrew term *ʾeder* is somewhat enigmatic in that it can mean either "glory" or "cloak." In this case, it seems to refer to an outer cloak or mantle that is worn over a *śimlâ*, the basic "garment" worn by people in ancient Israel, and indicates that people are being stripped of their garments as they flee. The party referred to by "you" is uncertain, but successive occurrences of this address form seem to be directed to the prophet's audience who apparently take advantage of the fugitives as they pass by. This would be suggested by the continuation of the statement in verse 8b, "from those passing by for safety, returning from war," i.e., the cloaks are stripped off from those who are fleeing the scene of war for safety as the enemy advances. Such actions would be characteristic of the treatment of the poor addressed in Mic 2:1-5 as well. The reader must keep in mind that garments were frequently taken in pledge for a loan, and strict guidelines had to be devised in order to prevent the abuse of such a practice (Exod 22:25-27; Deut 24:10-13, 17). In verse 9, the prophet charges that his audience drives out "the women of my people" from their homes and that they take away "my glory" from "her young children." The latter reference is uncertain, although it may mean that children are taken or separated from their parents as they are driven from their homes. Such realities would also have been experienced by those forced out of their homes and land (cf. Mic 2:1-5). In verse 10, the prophet calls upon the audience to "arise and go," i.e., they must flee themselves like the refugees who are streaming past because even "this is no resting place." Presumably, the prophet refers to his own hometown of Moreshet Gath, which is situated inland in the Shephelah, so that refugees from the lower portion of the Shephelah would stream through Moreshet Gath as they fled from the Assyrian army to the higher ground of Jerusalem and what they hoped would be safety (cf. verse 8). In verse 10b, the prophet maintains that even "this (place)" has become unclean. Verse 10bβ, translated in the NRSV as, "that destroys with a grievous destruction," is clearly a difficult text as indicated by the NRSV note. It seems to read literally, "it is ravaged and a violent district/portion of land," thereby indicating that the region of this place, Moreshet Gath, is no longer safe and that the people must flee. The Hebrew term *ḥebel*, "district" or "portion of land," recalls the use of the term in reference in verse 5 to the casting of lots in the assembly of YHWH, i.e., "to cast the line *(ḥebel)* by lot in the assembly of YHWH." The basic meaning of the term *ḥebel* is "line," and refers both to the use of a line or cord in the casting of lots and to the measuring line that is used to apportion land. Just as Mic 2:1-5 indicates that those who oppress people will lose their right to make decisions when the enemy takes their land, so Mic 2:6-11 indicates that the time of reckoning has come. Indeed, those addressed in Mic 2:1-5 will experience the same suffering that they have inflicted upon others.

At the close of the disputation speech in verse 11, the prophet expresses his exasperation at his audience which is not prepared to hear his message of warning in a time of crisis. He simply states that if someone were to go about lying to the people and claiming to preach to them about wine and strong drink, the people would listen. The reference to wine and strong drink clearly serves as a metaphor for the delusory nature of the lying message from such a person. In this case, the delusion or the lie is the initial contention of the prophet's opponents that YHWH will protect the people. That such a person would be considered a preacher to the people certainly indicates their desperation for something to hold on to and to hope for as their world disintegrates around them.

Finally, the prophet's announcement concerning Israel's impending exile appears in Mic 2:12-13, which portrays the remnant of Israel as sheep that break out of their pen and proceed out into the open with their king and YHWH at their head. Based upon their similarities with Mic 4:6-7, which speak of YHWH's intention to gather and restore the remnant of Israel, these verses are generally construed as an oracle of salvation that portrays YHWH's deliverance of Israel from captivity.[40] The initial verbal statements, "I will surely gather *(ʾāsōp ʾeʾĕsōp)* all of you, O Jacob, I will gather *(qabbēṣ ʾăqabbēṣ)* the survivors of Israel," play a role in this construction as well as the general scholarly understanding of the imagery of YHWH's gathering the remnant of Israel as a reference to salvation and restoration (cf. Isa 27:12-13; 48:20-21; 49:8-12; Jer 23:1-4; Ezekiel 34). The portrayal of YHWH at the head of the people, of course, reinforces this understanding.

The construction of Mic 2:12-13 as an oracle of salvation has prompted a great deal of discussion as scholars have sought to explain why such an oracle appears in the context of material that deals largely with pun-

---

[40] For a full discussion of this issue, see Renaud, *Formation* 104–14.

ishment. Most argue that it is a later addition to the text, but the discussion fails to account adequately for the threatening elements of the scenario presented in this text. The statement, "I will surely gather (*ʾāsōp ʾeʾĕsōp*)," elsewhere indicates not a situation of restoration, but a situation of threat in which people are swept away (Zeph 1:2) or "gathered" and cut down like the grapes of a harvest (Jer 8:13). Likewise, the statement, "it will resound with the people," misrepresents the meaning of the Hebrew *tĕhîmenâ mēʾādām*, "they/you shall be discomfited/confused by people," which suggests that the people are not at all content about what is taking place. Furthermore in the context of a pastoral and agricultural society, the image of sheep led out of their pens into the wilderness hardly conveys an image of security. Rather, it points to the potential loss of sheep as they scatter into the wilderness. This sense of threat is also conveyed by the references to "the one who breaks out (*happōrēṣ*)" and goes up before them and to the actions of the sheep who "break through (*pārĕṣû*) and pass the gate." The verb *prṣ* generally describes a destructive act, such as breaking down a wall (2 Kgs 14:13/2 Chr 25:23; Neh 3:35 [NRSV: 4:3]) or a fence (Isa 5:5; Pss 80:13 [NRSV: 80:12]; 89:41 [NRSV: 89:40]) or the breaking out of violence (2 Sam 5:20/1 Chr 14:11; Hos 4:2). Although some take these statements as references to an escape from captivity, they represent the loss of security. When the image is applied to the people of Israel, it conveys an image of people who are led out from the protective walls of their cities into the open where they are subject to danger. The image appears to pertain to captives who are led off by a conqueror, an image that is well known from Assyrian reliefs and inscriptions that relate the victories of the Assyrian kings.[41] After all, the Assyrians were the ones who broke down or overcame the defensive walls of the Judean cities during their campaign in 701. After placing the surviving Judeans into holding areas, many were exiled by the Assyrian king Sennacherib who claims to have driven out 200,150 people from Judah's cities during his campaign as well as cattle, sheep, etc.[42]

The imagery presented by Mic 2:12-13 conveys the exile of the Shephelah at the hands of Sennacherib in 701 B.C.E. In such a scenario, the portrayal of the king and YHWH at the head of the people must also be considered. The king here does not serve as a leader who rescues his people; rather, he is led away with them as the chief captive. YHWH's place at the head of the people must be understood from the context of Mic 2:1-13 as a whole, i.e., YHWH is the cause of the exile and leads them

---

[41] See esp. *ANEP* figs. 350–73; Sennacherib's account of his 701 campaign against Judah appears in *ANET* 287–8.

[42] *ANET* 288.

into their punishment. Such a view is consistent with the prophet's condemnation of the abusive leadership of the nation in Mic 2:1-5 which deprived the people of land, including the prophet's oblique reference to a "shepherd" or "evil" that YHWH plans for them in verse 3. It is also consistent with the prophet's contention in Mic 2:6-11 that YHWH will not protect the people, but is rather the source of the threat against them. In this case, the prophet identifies YHWH with the Assyrian conqueror who leads the people away into exile. Micah 2:12-13 speaks of the exile of "the remnant of Jacob," and thereby recalls Micah 1 in which the punishment of northern Israel would serve as the paradigm for that of southern Judah. By employing the term "Jacob" that normally designates the northern kingdom, the prophet defines Judah as the remnant of Israel, and thereby sets the stage for the scenario of restoration in Micah 3; 4; and 5 in which Israel is punished and reduced to a remnant and then restored at the center of the nations in Jerusalem/Zion.

THE PROPHET'S RESPONSE TO THE EXILE OF ISRAEL:
PROPHETIC ANNOUNCEMENT CONCERNING THE PUNISHMENT AND
EXALTATION OF THE REMNANT OF ISRAEL/JACOB IN ZION: 3:1–5:14
[NRSV: 3:1–5:15]

Micah 3:1–5:14 [NRSV: 3:1–5:15] presents the prophet's response to the preceding announcement of Israel's exile in Mic 2:1-13. These chapters are introduced by the introductory speech formula, "And I said (wā'ōmar)," which identifies the following material as the prophet's discourse.[43] The conjunctive *waw* of the *waw-imperfect* formation ties these chapters syntactically to Mic 2:1-13. As noted above, the syntactical joins at Mic 4:1 and 5:1 [NRSV: 5:2] bind the material in Mic 3:1–5:14 [NRSV: 3:1–5:15] together. The call to attention in Mic 6:1 marks the beginning of an entirely new unit within the book of Micah. Overall, Mic 3:1–5:14 [NRSV: 3:1–5:15] presents a scenario in which "the remnant of Jacob" (Mic 5:6, 7 [NRSV: 5:7, 8]; cf. Mic 4:2; 5:2 [NRSV: 5:3]) will provide the basis for the restoration of Jerusalem and Judah in the aftermath of the downfall of both the Assyrian (Mic 5:4-5 [NRSV: 5:5-6]) and the Babylonian empires (Mic 4:10). In this respect, Mic 3:1–5:14 [NRSV: 3:1–5:15] builds upon the statements in Mic 2:12-13 that YHWH will

---

[43] For a full discussion of the function of this term and its role in establishing the literary history of this unit, see J. T. Willis, "A Note on ואמר in Micah 3:1," *ZAW* 80 (1968) 50–4.

gather the remnant of the remnant of Israel, but it points ultimately to the restoration of the remnant of Israel at Zion. Micah 3:1–5:14 [NRSV: 3:1–5:15] thereby asserts that the exile of Israel is part of a much larger process in which the restoration of the remnant of Israel at Zion signals YHWH's sovereignty over the cosmos and the nations at large. The emergence of a new monarch in Israel from Bethlehem signals the restoration of (presumably) Davidic kingship and an era of peace and security for Israel.

The superstructure of Mic 3:1–5:14 [NRSV: 3:1–5:15] is determined at the outset by the appearance of the above-mentioned speech formula, "and I said," in Mic 3:1aα¹, which identifies the balance of the unit in Mic 3:1aα²–5:14 [NRSV: 3:1aα²–5:15] as the presentation of the actual speech by the prophet. Although several examples of the messenger speech or oracular formulas which indicate speech by YHWH appear throughout the unit (Mic 3:5; 4:6; 5:9 [NRSV: 5:10]), they are included within the presentation of the prophet's speech as indicators that he is quoting YHWH. Within the prophet's speech, the formulaic examples of the call to attention in Mic 3:1aα²-β and 3:9a mark the two major components of the prophet's speech in Micah 3:1aα²-8 and 3:9–5:14 [NRSV: 3:9–5:15]. Micah 3:1aα²-8 specifically blames Israel's failures on its leaders, and Mic 3:9–5:14 [NRSV: 3:9–5:15] lays out the process by which Zion will be punished and then exalted.

Concerning the Failure of Israel's Leadership: 3:1aα²-8

The first major component of the prophet's speech appears in Mic 3:1aα²-8 which points to the misconduct of Israel's leadership as the cause for the nation's punishment. The passage is introduced by the call to attention formula in verse 1aα²β which is directed to the "heads of Jacob" and the "rulers of the house of Israel," and it concludes in verse 8 with reference to the transgressions of Jacob and the sins of Israel.[44] The passage includes two basic components. Verses 1aα²-4 address the mistreatment of the people in general by Israel's leaders. Verses 5-8, which are introduced by the prophetic messenger formula, focus specifically on the actions of the prophets and diviners whom the prophet charges with having led the people astray.

The introductory call to attention in verse 1aα²β employs a relatively common imperative to address the leadership of the nations, "Listen *(šimʿû-nā)*, you heads of Jacob and rulers of the house of Israel."

---

[44] For discussion of the call to attention, see Sweeney, *Isaiah 1–39* 544.

The titles for the leadership of Israel, i.e., "head" (rō'š) and "ruler" (qāṣîn), appear at first sight to be rather general designations, but the use of qāṣîn elsewhere points to a specifically military function (see Josh 10:24; Dan 11:18), especially in Judg 11:6, 11 where rō'š and qāṣîn together are applied to Jephthah when the elders of Gilead ask him to serve as their commander in war against the Ammonites. The use of such terminology in this context suggests that Micah speaks to Israel's military commanders in a time of war. Although no specific setting is identified in this passage, the following imagery of the stripping of skin and flesh from people, the boiling of meat in a pot, and the presentation of food to prophets suggests a desperate situation of threat, such as Sennacherib's invasion of Judah and the siege of Jerusalem in 701 B.C.E. Others have indicated that the setting might relate to earlier Assyrian campaigns against the northern kingdom of Israel,[45] but there is no indication that Micah was in a position to witness the conditions of a siege during these earlier incursions.

Having addressed the commanders of the people in verse 1aα²β, the prophet then turns to a detailed account of the commanders' abuse of the people in verses 1b-4a. The prophet begins with a rhetorical question addressed to the commanders in a 2nd person masculine address form, "Should you not know justice?" The rhetorical answer is, "of course you should," so that the prophet's question actually functions as an assertion that the leadership of the people does not know justice. Verse 2a then employs participles, which may or may not directly address the leaders, to charge Israel's commanders with a warped sense of values, i.e., "you who hate the good and love the evil (literally, 'haters of good and lovers of evil')." Verses 2b-4a then turn to a much more specific portrayal of what the prophet has in mind. A literal reading of this passage points to cannibalism; certainly the text describes the stripping off and eating of human flesh, but these statements employ the metaphor of cannibalism to charge the leadership with abuse of the people. Certainly, the imagery of the meat cooking in pots and the following imagery of the presentation of food to prophets and diviners suggests that the prophet describes a scene of sacrifice which would accompany the request for a prophet's or diviner's oracle (cf. Numbers 22–24). The absence of any reference to the eating of human flesh by the prophets and diviners suggests that the imagery is metaphorical.[46] Overall, the stripping of skin and flesh from bones, the breaking of bones and the chopping of meat for the kettle, and the crying out to YHWH does express the desperation of cannibalism, although it

---

[45] Renaud, *Michée* 57; Hillers, *Micah* 42–3; Wolff, *Micah* 97.

[46] E.g., Mays, *Micah* 79; Allen, *Micah* 307–8; Simundson, "Micah," 557.

could suggest the possibility of human sacrifice (cf. 2 Kgs 3:27 in which the Moabite king sacrifices his firstborn son in a situation of military desperation). Nevertheless, there is no indication that such human sacrifices were eaten by human beings (but see 2 Kgs 6:28-29, which relates the eating of human flesh during a siege), nor do verses 5-8 suggest that the prophets and diviners ate human flesh. As in earlier oracles, Micah charges the leadership of Israel with abuse of the people; in this instance he chooses the imagery of cannibalism rather than the taking of houses and property to make his point.

The prophet relates the results of the leaders' efforts in verse 4b. YHWH chooses not to answer their pleas, but instead "hides" the divine face from them on account of their wrongdoing. There is an extensive tradition in Judaism concerning the "hidden face" of G–d (hestēr pānîm), in which G–d deliberately withdraws the divine presence as an act of punishment or as a means to test worthiness (cf. Isa 8:17; 54:8; 64:4 [NRSV: 64:5]; Deut 31:17, 18; 32:20; Jer 33:5; Ezek 39:23, 24, 29; Pss 13:2 [NRSV: 13:1]; 22:25 [NRSV: 22:24]; 27:9; 30:8 [NRSV: 30:7]; 69:18 [NRSV: 69:17]; 88:15 [NRSV: 88:14]; 102:3 [NRSV: 102:2]; 143:7; Job 13:24; 34:29).[47] This, of course, raises questions concerning the righteousness of G–d, particularly in the aftermath of the modern experience of the Shoah or Holocaust. Here, the prophet attempts to assert the righteousness of G–d by maintaining that the leadership of the nation had sinned and thereby brought the nation to punishment.

The prophet then presents an oracle from YHWH in Mic 3:5-8 that condemns the prophets and diviners for delivering oracles based upon the offerings that they receive from the people. The oracle begins with a somewhat unusual form of the messenger formula in verse 5 that blends into a series of accusations against the prophets and diviners, "thus says YHWH concerning the prophets who lead my people astray . . ." Normally, the messenger formula introduces a self-contained speech by YHWH, but in this case the prophet's use of the formula together with a syntactically dependent accusation suggests that the prophet does not quote YHWH directly. Instead, the prophet appears to summarize YHWH's statement or to represent it in his own words. The accusations begin with the general charge that the prophets "lead my people astray"; the syntax of the statement indicate that the referent for "my people" appears to be the prophet. It continues with the imagery of prophets who deliver oracles in return for something to eat. Many

---

[47] See Eliezer Berkovitz, *Faith After the Holocaust* (New York: KTAV, 1971); Martin Buber, *Eclipse of G–d: Studies in the Relation between Religion and Philosophy* (New York: Harper, 1952); Samuel Balentine, *The Hidden G–d: The Hidden Face of G–d in the Old Testament* (Oxford and New York: Oxford University Press, 1983).

contemporary readers seem to feel that such an action is unwarranted and that the prophets represented in this oracle must be false prophets,[48] but it must be kept in mind that prophecy and oracular divination were professions in the ancient world for which people were extensively trained and paid for their services.[49] Micah's indignation in these verses is not directed against such payment per se, but against those who cry "peace!" only when they are fed and declare war against those who do not feed them (n.b., verse 5bβγ reads literally, "and whomever does not give upon their mouth [i.e., feed them], they sanctify [i.e., declare] against him war"). In any case, it must be kept in mind that Micah's statements constitute charges of corruption against other prophets and diviners. The book of Micah hardly provides an objective or even sympathetic account of the words of the other prophets; its presentation is polemical. We therefore cannot know to what extent Micah's charges are true;[50] we only know that he accuses other prophets of professional misconduct.[51] The book of Isaiah may be quite instructive, however, as Isaiah condemns Hezekiah's policy of revolt against Assyria, but declares that there will be peace if Hezekiah refrains from military action (see e.g., Isaiah 28–31; cf. Isaiah 2; 36–37). Furthermore, unlike Micah, Isaiah never states that Jerusalem will be destroyed (cf. Mic 3:12; Jer 26:18). It is entirely possible that Micah's charges are directed against the prophet Isaiah among others. Isaiah would hardly be considered a false prophet, but other legitimate prophets would have opposed his message. Jeremiah 27–28 contains an example of Jeremiah's opposition to the prophet Hananiah, whose message mirrored Isaiah's proclamation that Jerusalem would be freed from threat (cf. Isa 7:1–9:6) a century later.[52]

Verses 6-7 present Micah's statements concerning the consequences for those prophets whom he charges with professional misconduct. In keeping with the form of the prophetic judgment speech, this section begins with the particle *lākēn*, "therefore." Micah's statements begin in verse 6 by employing the imagery of darkness to express his contention that such prophets will no longer experience the visions that are necessary for prophetic practice in the ancient world. His statements are ironic in that such visions are often perceived to be dreams or visions of

---

[48] E.g., Allen, *Micah* 310–5.

[49] Frederick H. Cryer, *Divination in Ancient Israel and its Near Eastern Environment: A Socio-Historical Investigation*, JSOTSup, vol. 142 (Sheffield: JSOT Press, 1994).

[50] Cf. Mays, *Micah* 80–6.

[51] Cf. Smith, *Micah* 32–4.

[52] For a detailed study of Micah's conflict with other prophets, see van der Woude, "Micah in Dispute."

the night in which the prophet sleeps (cf. 1 Samuel 3; Genesis 15) or otherwise goes into a trance-like state to receive prophetic revelation (cf. 1 Sam 10:5-6, 9-13; 19:19-24). The irony of Micah's statements is well expressed by his statement, "The sun shall set upon the prophets, and the day shall darken upon them." Interestingly, Isaiah likewise employs the imagery of darkness to express the inability of diviners to discern the instruction of YHWH (Isa 8:16–9:6).

Micah then turns to the motif of shame in verse 7 in that the prophets will be ashamed and the diviners will "be put to shame (literally, 'turn red')." His statement that "they shall all cover their lips" is particularly ironic because speech is the prophet's primary tool for conveying divine oracles to the people. It is doubly ironic, however, in that one of the few portrayals of a prophet or oracle diviner in action indicates that the prophet's face is covered, i.e., Moses must wear a veil as a result of his encounter with YHWH (Exod 34:29-35). Many have speculated that Moses' veil reflects ancient shamanistic practice in Israel, but the absence of other examples leaves the question open.[53] Leviticus 13:45 employs the same terminology to indicate that a leper must cover his upper lip and cry out "unclean, unclean." Such a comparison suggests that Micah intends that the prophets are to be shunned much like a leper.

Finally, the prophet concludes this oracle in verse 8 with a statement that he is filled with power, or the spirit of YHWH, justice, and might to declare Jacob's sin and Israel's transgression. Indeed, the reference to the spirit of YHWH appears to be an appositional definition of the term "power" (*kōaḥ*) that ascribes prophetic power to Micah. Interestingly, the book of Micah nowhere refers to Micah as a prophet, and some speculate that this expression is a gloss to indicate that he is indeed a prophet of YHWH.[54] The NRSV translates the introductory particle, *wĕʾûlām*, "but as for (me)." The particle means literally, "but" or "however," and indicates that Micah saw himself in opposition to the prophets that he charges with misconduct. This should come as no surprise to the readers of verses 5-8, but it might also suggest that he does not see himself as a prophet. Much like Amos, he is not a trained professional but simply a person who sees himself as speaking on behalf of G–d (cf. Amos 7:10-17). From his perspective, that means that he must condemn Israel and declare that Jerusalem will be destroyed. Anyone who disagrees with him is wrong.

---

[53] For discussion, see Brevard S. Childs, *The Book of Exodus: A Critical, Theological Commentary*, OTL (Philadelphia: Westminster, 1974) 609–10, 617–9.

[54] Rudolph, *Micha* 68; Wolff, *Micah* 91–2; but contra Renaud, *Formation* 132–3.

Concerning the Punishment and Exaltation of Jerusalem and Judah: 3:9–5:14 [NRSV: 3:9–5:15]

Following the condemnation of Israel's leaders, Mic 3:9–5:14 [NRSV: 3:9–5:15] turns to the prophet's scenario of the punishment and exaltation of Jerusalem and Judah in which the remnant of Israel is established at the center of the nations and the cosmos. This unit is demarcated by the introductory call to attention directed to the heads of Jacob and the chiefs of the house of Israel in Mic 3:9a, and it continues until Mic 6:1a where another example of the call to attention introduces the following unit. Micah 3:9–5:14 [NRSV: 3:9–5:15] begins in Mic 3:9-12 with the announcement of punishment against Jerusalem/Zion that blames the leadership of Israel for Jerusalem's impending destruction. Although Mic 3:9-12 very likely constituted the prophet's original conclusion to the condemnations of Israel's leadership in Mic 3:1-8, in the present form of the text, the material in Mic 4:1–5:14 [NRSV: 3:9–5:15] is syntactically linked to Mic 3:9-12 so that the oracle now serves as the introduction to Mic 3:9–5:14 [NRSV: 3:9–5:15] as a whole. The formula, "and it shall come to pass in later days (NRSV, 'In days to come')," marks the transition in the unit from the condemnation of Jerusalem to the presentation of Jerusalem's and Judah's exaltation. Jerusalem's/Zion's exaltation is basically stated in Mic 4:1-5, and Mic 4:6–5:14 [NRSV: 4:6– 5:15], introduced by the formula *bayyôm hahû'*, "in that day," then elaborates by laying out the details as to how that exaltation will be manifested.

CONCERNING THE PUNISHMENT OF ZION: 3:9-12

Although Mic 3:9-12 likely constituted the concluding sub-unit of the prophet's condemnation of Israel's leadership in Mic 3:1-8, the syntactical and conceptual relation with the material in Mic 4:1–5:14 [NRSV: 4:1–5:15] requires that the oracle be read as the introduction to Micah's presentation of Jerusalem's restoration.[55] Although many see Mic 4:1–5:14 [NRSV: 4:1–5:15] as a much later addition to the original words of Micah,[56] a synchronic reading of the text cannot be guided by a model of the text's compositional history. In the present case, the condemnation of Israel's leaders in Mic 3:1-8 facilitates a transition to the presentation as to how the destruction of Jerusalem (Mic 3:9-12) will lead ultimately to its exaltation at the center of the cosmos.

[55] A number of scholars see Micah 3:1-2 as a kerygmatic unity, e.g., Wolff, *Micah* 92–5; Rudolph, *Micha* 68; Renaud, *Michée* 56–7, interestingly sees the prophet Micah as the redactor of this chapter. See also the discussion by Hagstrom, *The Coherence of the Book of Micah* 29–43.

[56] See the discussion in Mason, *Micah, Nahum, Obadiah* 27–42.

The passage begins with an example of the formulaic call to attention in verse 9a that very clearly relates to the prior example in Mic 3:1aα²β, "Hear this you rulers of the house of Jacob and chiefs of the house of Israel *(šimˁû-nāˀ zōˀt rōˀšê bêt yaˁăqōb ûqṣînê bêt yiśrāˀēl)*." The repetition of the verb and the addressee from Mic 3:1aα²β indicates a relationship between the two texts, and the variations in the formula indicate an attempt to emphasize the following message of judgment against Jerusalem ("this") and the simple vagaries of oral speech ("house of Jacob"). Another series of accusations directed against the leadership of the nation follows in verses 9b-11, which rehearse the basic concerns of Mic 3:1-8, but lead instead to the prophet's announcement that the city of Jerusalem will be destroyed. The sequence begins in verse 9b with a general statement concerning the propensity of Israel's leaders to "abhor justice" and to "pervert all equity." The term *mišpāṭ* is the common Hebrew term for "law" or "justice," and *yĕšārâ* generally refers to what is "straight" or "upright." Together, the use of these terms indicates that Micah charges Israel's leadership with corruption and gross incompetence, which is hardly surprising if the setting of these statements is during Sennacherib's siege of Jerusalem in 701 B.C.E. After all, it was the decision of the leadership of the nation to revolt against Assyria, and the results were very clear to a man like Micah. This perspective informs the next charges in the sequence, i.e., that Zion is built with "blood" and Jerusalem with "wrong." Zion is the poetic name for Jerusalem, and likely designates the site of the Temple. The prophet's reference to building Zion with blood would naturally call to mind the images of animal sacrifice that were normally made at the Temple, and which likely increased as the nation implored YHWH for blessing as it prepared for war against Assyria (cf. Isa 1:10-17[57]). It would also call to mind the many thousands who died as the Assyrians overran the nation (cf. Isa 1:4-9[58]). The reference to "wrong" employs the Hebrew word *ˁawlâ*, "injustice," and likely conveys the prophet's resentment of the leadership of his country whose decisions cost him his home and the lives of many of his neighbors. The prophet then points specifically to the various classes of leaders or authority figures in Judean society whom he hold responsible for the present state of the nation. He charges in verse 11aα¹⁻³ that the "rulers" or "heads" of the people "give judgment" for a bribe. The verb *špṭ*, translated here as "give judgment," may be used for judicial decisions but more generally means "to rule, govern" i.e., "to make decisions." In this manner, the prophet condemns those who made the decision to oppose Assyria in the first place and suggests that the decision was influenced by the expectation of

---

[57] For discussion of Isa 1:10-17, see Sweeney, *Isaiah 1–39* 78–81.

[58] For discussion of Isa 1:4-9, see Sweeney, *Isaiah 1–39* 75–8.

reward. He then follows up in verse 11aα[4-6] that the priests teach or give instruction for a price. Insofar as the priests are responsible for instructing the people in proper understanding of G–d's requirements (cf. Hos 4:5-6, 7-10; Hag 2:10-19), the prophet charges the priesthood with failing to instruct the people that the decision to revolt ran contrary to G–d's will (at least in his view, which was supported by the results). He then turns to a condemnation of the prophets in verse 11aα, whom he charges with divining oracles for money. As noted above, this is not unusual for the professional prophecy, but it feeds into his charges in Mic 3:5-8 that the prophets give oracles according to what they receive from their clients. In this case, the prophets are responsible for informing the king and people whether or not their actions conform to YHWH's will (cf. 1 Kings 22; Jeremiah 27–28). Micah's condemnation charges them with not doing their job. Finally, the prophet summarizes what each of these classes of leaders, all of whom depend upon YHWH for support, apparently have said to the people, i.e., "Surely YHWH is with us! No harm shall come upon us." Hezekiah and his advisors had made a decision to revolt against Assyria, and apparently had concluded that YHWH would protect the nation. As the results of Sennacherib's invasion of Judah demonstrate, Hezekiah and his advisors were wrong; Judah was devastated.

This oracle concludes with the prophet's announcement of punishment, introduced by the particle *lākēn*, "therefore," which typically expresses the statement of the consequences in the prophetic judgment speech. He declares that "because of you," i.e., the leaders of the nation who had failed in their responsibility, Jerusalem would be destroyed. The imagery is graphic: Zion would be plowed as a field; Jerusalem would become a ruin; and the mountain of the house would become a wooded height. The last statement is particularly significant because "the house" refers to the Temple of YHWH in Jerusalem. Likewise, the statement that it would become "a wooded height" employs the term *bāmôt*, "high places," which throughout the Bible typically refers to the high places that were used for illegitimate worship of YHWH or foreign gods. The reference to "wooded" must be understood in relation to wooded areas in Israel, i.e., the Temple mount would be covered with scrub brush and other wild growth. Ironically, Micah's prediction of Jerusalem's destruction did not come true, at least in his own lifetime, as Hezekiah and Sennacherib were able to come to terms before Jerusalem could be taken.[59] As noted above, Micah's statement that Jerusalem

---

[59] For discussion of this issue, see Sweeney, *Isaiah 1–39* 478–9; Bustenay Oded, "Judah and the Exile," *Israelite and Judaean History*, ed. J. H. Hayes and J. M. Miller, OTL (Philadelphia: Westminster, 1977) 446–51.

would be destroyed is quoted in the narrative concerning Jeremiah's sedition trial as a defense for the prophet (Jer 26:18). According to the Jeremiah narrative, Micah's words convinced Hezekiah to turn to YHWH so that the destruction of the city was averted.

Concerning the Exaltation of Zion:
4:1–5:14 [NRSV: 4:1–5:15]

Most scholars maintain that Mic 4:1–5:14 [NRSV: 4:1–5:15] is a later exilic or post-exilic redactional composition that has been added to the original words of the prophet in Micah 1–3.[60] Although the reference to the Babylonian exile in Mic 4:10 and the Zion-centered theological perspective among other factors indicate that this is undoubtedly the case, a synchronic reading of the present form of Micah cannot be guided by diachronic models concerning the book's literary history. Rather, analysis must be guided by the literary signals in the present form of the text. In the present case, syntactical and thematic factors play an especially large role in that Micah 4–5 is joined to Mic 3:9-12 by the syntactically conjunctive formula, *wĕhāyâ bĕ'aḥărît hayyāmîm*, "and it shall come to pass in later/future days," and by the concern to demonstrate that the previously announced punishment of Jerusalem will lead ultimately to its restoration and exaltation in the midst of the nations as the process of Jerusalem's punishment and purification together with the manifestation of YHWH's sovereignty over the nations takes place.

Micah 4:1–5:14 [NRSV: 4:1–5:15] is defined throughout by its consistent focus on the future restoration and exaltation of Jerusalem/Zion, including the rise of a new, presumably Davidic, monarch from Bethlehem who will see to the security of the people of Israel and Judah and guide them into the projected era of peace. The passage draws heavily on other biblical traditions,[61] particularly the book of Isaiah and the Jacob traditions of Genesis, in an effort to present a distinctive understanding of Jerusalem's punishment and restoration that points especially to the submission to YHWH at Zion of the nations that had

[60] For brief overviews of the history of scholarship, see J.M.P. Smith, with W. H. Ward and J. A. Bewer, *A Critical and Exegetical Commentary on Micah, Zephaniah, Nahum, Habakkuk, Obadiah and Joel*, ICC (Edinburgh: T. & T. Clark, 1985) 9–12; Mays, *Micah* 95; Smith, *Micah* 37.

[61] For a full discussion of the use of earlier biblical tradition in Micah 4–5, see B. Renaud, *Structure et Attaches Littéraires de Michée IV–V*, Cahiers de la Revue Biblique, vol. 2 (Paris: Gabalda, 1964) 37–74.

previously oppressed Israel and Judah. This concern is signalled initially by Mic 4:1-5, which presents a future scenario of world-wide peace in which the nations will stream to Zion in order to receive instruction from YHWH concerning YHWH's Torah and ways. The introductory formula, *bayyôm hahû²*, "in that day," indicates that Mic 4:6–5:14 [NRSV: 4:6–5:15] elaborates extensively on this presentation of future peace at Zion by providing a detailed portrayal of the process by which the remnant of Jacob will be redeemed by YHWH so that the idyllic scenario will be achieved.

CONCERNING THE EXALTATION OF ZION AT THE
CENTER OF THE NATIONS: 4:1-5

Micah 4:1-5 is perhaps one of the best-known oracles of the entire prophetic corpus in the Hebrew Bible. The oracle also appears in Isa 2:2-4 in a somewhat different form and context. There has been extensive discussion of these two passages, particularly in relation to their origins. Most maintain that the passage represents an exilic-period liturgical composition that has been taken up and adapted to the respective contexts of the books of Micah and Isaiah,[62] although some argue that Isaiah is the original author of the passage[63] and even fewer argue that Micah is the original author.[64] Although the passage appears to have been composed in relation to the rebuilding of the Jerusalem Temple in the late-sixth century, the literary features of the Mican text indicate that it was adopted and modified from the Isaian version for its present literary context (cf. Mic 5:9-14 [NRSV: 5:10-15], which draws upon Isa 2:6-21).[65] The Isaian version points specifically to an interest in inviting Israel/Jacob to join the nations in recognizing YHWH's sovereignty at Zion (see esp. Isa 2:5, "O House of Jacob, come, let us walk in the light of YHWH") following a process in which the land is punished by YHWH for arrogance (see esp. Isa 2:6-22) and Jerusalem and Judah

[62] See Sweeney, *Isaiah 1–39* 97–100.

[63] E.g., Hans Wildberger, *Isaiah 1–12*, Continental Commentaries (Minneapolis: Fortress, 1991) 81–96.

[64] E. Cannawurf, "The Authenticity of Micah IV 1-4," *VT* 13 (1963) 26–33.

[65] Sweeney, *Isaiah 1–39* 97–100; cf. Renaud, *Formation* 160–81, who dates the passage to the late fifth century. See also A. S. van der Woude, "Micah IV 1–5: An Instance of the Pseudo-Prophets Quoting Isaiah," *Symbolae biblicae et mesopotamicae Francisco Mario Theodoro de Liagre Böhl dedicate*, ed. M. A. Beek et al. (Leiden: Brill, 1973) 396–402; idem, "Micah in Dispute," who sees in Micah 4:1-5 the prophet's attempts to refute those who would quote Isa 2:2-4 in their attempts to challenge Micah's statements.

are punished and purified by YHWH from their sins (see esp. Isa 3:1–4:6). The Mican version, on the other hand, accentuates the differences between Israel and the nations by emphasizing that the nations adhere to their own gods (Mic 4:5), by pointing to the role of the Davidic king in punishing the nations that have oppressed Israel (Mic 5:1-8 [NRSV: 5:2-9]), and by describing YHWH's destruction of the weapons and idols of the nations (Mic 5:9-14 [NRSV: 5:10-15]).

Micah 4:1-5 comprises two major portions in verses 1-2 and 3-5, each of which describes a sequence of events together with one or two motivating clauses introduced by the particle *kî*, "because," that provides the rationale for the previously described actions. Together, these components present the overall scenario of the nations streaming to Zion to receive YHWH's instruction and the resulting situation of world peace.

Verses 1-2 describe the future scenario of the nations pilgrimage to Zion. It begins with the formula in verse 1aα¹⁻³, *wĕhāyâ bĕʾaḥărît hayyāmîm*, "and it shall come to pass in later/future days." Under the influence of the Septuagint's rendition of the verse, *kai ʾestai ʾepʾ ʾeschatōn tōn ʿemerōn*, "and it shall come to pass at the end of days," the passage is frequently understood as a reference to the eschatological end of time. Semantic study of the Hebrew expression, particularly in relation to the cognate Akkadian expression, *ina aḥrat umi*, "in future days," indicates however that it merely refers to the future and not to the end of time.[66] A sequence of five statements, i.e., two paired statements followed by a fifth, then follows to describe the exaltation of Zion and the nations' actions. The first pair in verse 1aα⁴⁻¹⁰β relates Zion's exalted status, and especially emphasizes that Zion is the location of YHWH's Temple, "the mountain of the House of YHWH shall be established *(nākôn)* as the highest of the mountains, and it *(hûʾ)* shall be raised above the hills." The order and wording of the Mican verse differs slightly from the Isaian verse, "established *(nākôn)* shall be the mountain of the House of YHWH as the highest of the mountains, and shall be raised above the hills." Anyone familiar with the topography of Jerusalem and environs would dispute this assertion as the Temple Mount is hardly the highest hill in the vicinity, but it must be understood as a statement concerning the status and importance of Zion and the Jerusalem Temple as the center of the cosmos. The second pair of statements in verses 1b-2aα¹⁻³ then present the nations' approach to Zion, "Peoples *(ʿammîm)* shall stream to it, and many nations *(gôyim rabbîm)* shall come." Again, the Isaian

---

[66] See Simon J. De Vries, *Yesterday, Today, and Tomorrow* (Grand Rapids: Eerdmans, 1975) 50; idem, *From Old Revelation to New* (Grand Rapids: Eerdmans, 1995) 88.

version differs slightly in that it reverses the references to "peoples" (*ʿammîm*) and "nations" (*gōyim*), "Nations (*gōyim*) shall stream to it, and many peoples (*ʿammîm rabbîm*) shall come." Nevertheless, the statement (in both Micah and Isaiah) expresses the common motif of the Zion tradition concerning the pilgrimage of the nations to Zion to acknowledge YHWH's sovereignty at the Temple (cf. Isaiah 60–62; Haggai 2; Zechariah 8), although many of the Psalms portray YHWH's defeat of the nations as a basic premise of the traditions (Psalms 46; 47; 48). The fifth statement in verse 2aα⁴⁻¹²-b presents the nations' statement of their willingness to receive YHWH's instruction, "and they shall say, 'come, let us go up to the mountain YHWH, to the house of the G–d of Jacob; that he may teach us his ways and that we may walk in his paths.'" Apart from orthographic differences, this statement is the same as that of Isaiah. The reference to Jacob is particularly pertinent in the present context, however, in that Micah portrays northern Israel's punishment as a paradigm for that of Judah. By the same token, Judah or Jerusalem forms the remnant of Jacob, i.e., the remnant of all Israel, that will be restored in Zion (cf. Mic 4:6-7; 5:6 [NRSV: 5:7]). Likewise, the submission of the nations to YHWH's instruction represents the fulfillment of creation as presented in the Pentateuch in that Israel and the wilderness tabernacle/Temple provide the means by which YHWH's Torah is revealed in the world at large to complete creation. The goals of revealing YHWH's Torah/instruction and word is clear in the concluding statement of this pericope in verse 2b, "for out of Zion shall go forth instruction (*tôrâ*) and the word of YHWH from Jerusalem." In the Isaian text, the absence of a motivating clause at the end of the passage indicates that this statement introduces the entire scenario of peace that follows and thereby presents peace as the rationale for Zion's exaltation. In Micah, however, the following scenario of peace has its own rationale in YHWH's command (see verse 4), so that the reference to YHWH's Torah only serves as the conclusion to the portrayal of the nations' approach to Zion. It thereby presents YHWH's Torah as the rationale for Zion's exaltation and the nations' approach, whereas YHWH's word or command in verse 4 enforces the peace among the nations. Although the nations are motivated to come by the prospect of YHWH's Torah, the Mican text gives greater emphasis to YHWH's role in exercising authority and sovereignty and thereby seeing to peace among the nations.

Verses 3-5 then presents YHWH's judgment of the nations and the arbitration of their disputes which makes the peace possible. The pericope is organized into a series of three paired statements followed by a concluding statement that includes two motivating clauses. The first pair relates YHWH's judgment of the nations, "He shall judge between many peoples (*ʿammîm rabbîm*) and shall arbitrate between strong nations

far away *(gôyim ʿǎṣumîm ʿad-rāḥōq)*." The Mican statement differs from
its counterpart in Isaiah by emphasizing "many peoples *(ʿammîm
rabbîm)*" as opposed to simply "the nations *(haggôyim)*" and "strong nations far away *(gôyim ʿǎṣumîm ʿad-rāḥōq)*" as opposed to "many peoples
(ʿammîm rabbîm)." In comparison to the reference in Isaiah, the Mican
passage emphasizes the number, power, and distance of the nations involved and thereby emphasizes the threat posed by the nations and the
difficulty in compelling them to submit. The next pair of statements in
verse 3bα emphasizes the disarmament of the nations as they prepare
for peaceful agricultural pursuits, "they shall beat their swords into
plowshares and their spears into pruning hooks." Likewise, verse 4bβ
emphasizes the resulting cessation of war as a result of YHWH's appli-
cation of judgment and arbitration, "nation shall not lift up sword
against nation, neither shall they learn war any more." Finally, the concluding statement in verses 4-5 emphasizes the tranquility and content-
ment to be realized by everyone in the world once war is put to an end,
"but they each shall sit under their own vines and under their own fig
trees, and no one shall make them afraid; for the mouth of YHWH of
hosts has spoken."

Verses 4-5 are particularly important, not only because they define
the rhetorical goal of the pericope in their portrayal of peace, but also
because of their dependence upon other texts and the means by which
they shape the meaning of the Mican form of this passage. The reference to each nation or man sitting under his own vine and fig tree
draws upon formulaic language that appears elsewhere in 1 Kgs 5:5
[NRSV: 4:25]; 2 Kgs 18:31/Isa 36:16; Zech 3:10. It is not original to the
passage as the Isaian version would have included it as well, although
the reference to 2 Kgs 18:31/Isa 36:16 suggests that it might have been
drawn from Isaiah. The formulaic statement, "and no one shall make
them afraid *(wĕʾên maḥrîd)*," appears Isa 17:2 in reference to the safety
of flocks that lie down at the ruins of Damascus. Otherwise, it appears
frequently in the blessing and cursing traditions of Leviticus (Lev 26:6)
and Deuteronomy (Deut 28:26) and in the prophetic traditions (Jer 7:33;
30:10; 46:27; Ezek 34:28; 39:26; Nah 2:12 [NRSV: 2:11]; Zeph 3:13), and
serves here as a means to emphasize the tranquility and security of the
world. As noted above, the motivating statement in verse 4b, "for the
mouth of YHWH of hosts has spoken," emphasizes YHWH's active role in
rendering judgment between the nations and settling their disputes as
the necessary prelude to an idyllic scenario of peace. In this respect, the
Mican passage emphasizes YHWH's exercise of sovereignty in dealing
with the nations, and not simply the nations' willingness to submit as
in Isaiah, as the cause of world peace. Verse 5 also begins with *kî*, "because," which indicates its explanatory role. By stating that all of the

peoples walk in the name of their own respective gods and that "we" (Israel) walk in the name of YHWH our G–d, the verse emphasizes the fundamental difference in perspective between Israel and the nations. It points to the continuing tensions among the nations that required YHWH's judgment as well as between the nations and Israel and between the nations and YHWH as articulated in the following material. It thereby provides some explanation for the abuses committed by the nations against Israel and for Israel's actions against the oppressing nations in Mic 4:6–5:14 [NRSV: 4:6–5:15].

The Exaltation of Zion Defined:
4:6–5:14 [NRSV: 4:6–5:15]

Micah 4:6–5:14 [NRSV 4:6–5:15] provides a much more detailed presentation concerning the process by which Jerusalem/Zion will be restored in the aftermath of its punishment to serve as the center of the cosmos to which the nations will come to receive YHWH's instruction. This section begins in Mic 4:6-7 with an initial statement concerning the intention to form the lame and the outcast into a remnant and strong nation over which YHWH will rule. Micah 4:8–5:14 [NRSV: 4:8–5:15] then constitutes paired addresses to Zion and Bethlehem Ephrata concerning their respective roles in YHWH's plans. The address to Zion in Mic 4:8-14 stresses Zion's present situation of distress, indicated by the three occurrences of *ʿattâ/wĕʿattâ*, "now/and now," in verses 9, 11, and 14, and the coming redemption and dominance over its former enemies and oppressors that will result from its present destitute state. The address to Bethlehem Ephrata in Mic 5:1-14 [NRSV: 5:2-15] stresses the future emergence of a King from Bethlehem and the resulting situation of peace for Jacob/Israel at the center of the nations, indicated by the three occurrences of *wĕhāyâ*, "and it shall come to pass," in verses 4, 6, and 9 [NRSV: 5, 7 and 10].

THE INITIAL STATEMENT OF YHWH'S PLANS:
YHWH/THE SHEPHERD WILL GATHER THE LAME AND OUTCAST
TO FORM A STRONG NATION AT ZION: 4:6-7

The syntactically independent introductory formula *bayyôm hahûʾ*, "in that day,"[67] marks the beginning of this unit, and indicates that it

---

[67] De Vries, *From Old Revelation to New* 38–55.

follows upon the previous scenario that will take place "in the later/future days." Micah 4:6-7 states the central premise or thesis of the entire unit concerning Zion's exaltation in chapters 4–5, i.e., that YHWH will gather the lame and the outcast of Jacob in the aftermath of Israel's and Judah's punishment, and form them into a "strong nation" over which YHWH will rule at Zion. The use of the verbs *ʾōsĕpâ*, "I will assemble," and *ʾăqabbēṣâ*, "I will gather," as well as the metaphorical portrayal of YHWH as shepherd reaches back to Mic 2:12-13 in which YHWH is portrayed as shepherd who "assembles" and "gathers" the sheep in order to lead them into exile. Micah 4:6-7 points to the ultimate goals of YHWH's actions in Mic 2:12-13 as well as the projected destruction of Jerusalem in Mic 3:9-12.

The use of the images of the "lame" (*haṣṣōlēʿâ*) and the "outcast" (*hannidāḥâ*) is hardly accidental. Both images portray the desperate and wounded state of those who have suffered the punishment of Jerusalem, Judah, and Israel outlined throughout the book of Micah, but they also hold significance beyond the immediate scenario of punishment. Other biblical traditions indicate that Jerusalem was a stronghold where even the blind and the lame (*pisseaḥ*) could defend themselves against attack (2 Sam 5:6, 8), and the place where the exiled blind and lame would eventually return (Isa 35:6; Jer 31:8; cf. Zeph 3:19, which employs the same terminology at Mic 4:6). Indeed, the return of the blind and lame remnant of Jacob to Jerusalem (Jer 31:8) points to the lame (*ṣōlēʿa*) figure of Jacob in Gen 32:32. Jacob's exile from the land of Israel to Aram in order to find a bride and to escape the wrath of his brother Esau and his eventual return (Genesis 25–35) forms the basis for prophetic conceptualizations of the exile of Israel and its return to the land (e.g., Jeremiah 30–31; Isaiah 40–55), although the traditions tend to portray the exiled and returning Israel as a woman who has lost or regained her children, i.e., Rachel (Jer 31:15; cf. 31:4, 8) or Lady Zion (Isa 50:1-3; 51:17-52:12; 54:1-17). Apparently, the image of the dying Rachel from the Jacob tradition (Genesis 35) and the images of Israel as bride of YHWH (Hosea 1–3; Jeremiah 2) play a role in this construction of Israel's exile to the wilderness. This would explain the feminine formulation of the terms for "lame" and "outcast" in Mic 4:6, i.e., the "lame" and "outcast" represent YHWH's cast-off bride who was exiled to the wilderness like Jacob and Rachel and who will now be restored as YHWH reestablishes the "remnant" of Israel as a "strong nation" (*gôy ʿāṣûm*, cf. the reference to "the strong nations" in verse 3) in Zion. Given the following scenario of the defeat of the nations that oppress Israel, the establishment of Israel as a "strong nation" alongside "the strong nations" that will flock to Zion essentially designates Israel for its role at the center of the nations (see Mic 5:6 [NRSV: 5:7]; 4:13).

The Addresses to Zion and Bethlehem Ephrata
concerning YHWH's Plans: 4:8–5:14 [NRSV: 4:8–5:15]

As noted above, the addresses to Zion and Bethlehem are paired so that they will portray Zion's present state of desolation from which it will emerge as the center of the nations (Mic 4:8-14) and the future emergence of the Davidic king from Bethlehem who will defeat Israel's enemies and bring about this era of peace. Each address is indicated by an introductory *wĕ'attâ*, "and you," followed by the proper names of the cities addressed. The combination of the names Migdal Eder ("Tower of the Flock") and "Daughter Zion" in Mic 4:8 and Bethlehem and Ephrata in Mic 5:1 [NRSV: 5:2] meld together the place names of the royal Davidic tradition and the Jacob traditions concerning the death of Rachel. Daughter Zion refers to Jerusalem where David ruled (2 Samuel 6–7) and Bethlehem refers to David's home (1 Samuel 16). Migdal Eder ("Tower of the Flock") refers to the place where Jacob camped immediately following the death of Rachel (Gen 35:21) in the vicinity of Ephrata (Gen 35:16). The traditions are tied together here because Ephrata is near to Bethlehem, and because Rachel died giving birth to Benjamin, the ancestor of Saul, Israel's first king (cf. Gen 35:18; cf. Gen 35:11). Just as Rachel gave birth to Benjamin and future kings at her entry to the land from wilderness, so the remnant of Jacob will see the birth of future kings as its exile comes to an end. Stylistically, the three occurrences of *'attâ/wĕ'attâ*, "now/and now," in Mic 4:9, 11, 14 contrast Jerusalem's present desolation with its future exaltation as indicated by the three occurrences of *wĕhāyâ*, "and it shall come to pass," in Mic 5:4, 6, 9 [NRSV: 5:5, 7, 10].[68]

THE ADDRESS TO ZION/MIGDAL EDER: 4:8-14

The address to Zion/Migdal Eder in Mic 4:8-14 begins with the statement, "and you, Migdal Eder ("Tower of the Flock"); hill *('ōpel)* of daughter Zion." The "hill *('ōpel)*" designates the site of the royal Davidic palace in Jerusalem (2 Chr 27:3; 33:14; cf. Neh 3:26; 11:21), and it may have been associated with a watchtower (Isa 32:14). As noted above, this statement combines references to the royal Davidic tradition and to the death of Rachel and birth of Benjamin so that the themes of royal authority and death and restoration in the wilderness are brought together to express Israel's restoration. Although the location

[68] Cf. Eduard Nielsen, *Oral Tradition*, SBT, vol. 11 (London: SCM, 1954) 79–93 and Renaud, *Structure et Attaches* 11–26, who argue that the structure of Micah 4–5 is constituted by paired segments in chapters 4 and 5 at large.

of Migdal Eder is unknown, Gen 35:16-22 places it in the vicinity of
Ephrata and Bethlehem, apparently on the way south to Hebron, the
home and burial place of Abraham (Genesis 23; 25) and the burial place
of Jacob (Gen 50:13). The name Migdal Eder, "Tower of the Flock," of
course plays on the motif of Y<small>HWH</small> as the shepherd who will gather the
sheep for exile in Mic 2:12-13 and for restoration in the present context
(cf. Mic 4:6-7). The combination of the Davidic and Jacob/Rachel traditions clearly draws upon the promises of rule to the house of David
(e.g., 2 Samuel 7) and to possession of the land of Israel by Jacob (e.g.,
Gen 28:35). This concern appears in the second half of verse 8 which
promises the return of Zion's "former dominion" and "sovereignty."
By this means, the verse looks back at the tradition of Davidic rule over
the nations (e.g., 2 Samuel 8) and forward to Zion's domination of the
nations in Mic 4:13; 5:1-14 [N<small>RSV</small>: 5:2-15].

Verses 9-10 constitute the first of three segments that begin with
ʿattâ/wĕʿattâ, "now/and now," which focuses the reader's or the listener's attention on the present state of Jerusalem.[69] These verses employ second person feminine singular address forms directed to "the
daughter Jerusalem" or "the daughter Zion" mentioned in verse 8. The
prophet begins by asking Zion why she cries aloud, and then explains
the question with two rhetorical questions that speak to Jerusalem's
current desolate state. The first, "is there no king in you?" of course asserts that there is not. This calls to mind the fact that Jerusalem's king
would have been removed as a result of the nation's defeat and exile; it
also calls to mind the death of Rachel in childbirth as Benjamin, the ancestor of the first king of Israel, was born. The rhetorical impact of such
a question would suggest that Jerusalem's situation is not as desperate
as that of Rachel; Rachel died, but Jerusalem will not. The second question follows from the first, "has your counselor perished?" to assert
that counselors or advisors to the king are gone now that Jerusalem is
defeated. The kî ("because") clause, "that pangs have seized you like a
woman in labor," ensures that the reader's or listener's attention will
be drawn to the image of Rachel dying in childbirth. It also relates to the
various references to childbirth and labor in the book of Isaiah that point
to the rebirth of Israel in the aftermath of the exile (Isa 13:8; 21:3; 26:17;
33:11; 51:2; 66:7, 9, 13) and the restoration of Davidic and divine kingship in Zion. The prophet calls upon Jerusalem in verse 10 to "writhe"
and "groan" like a woman giving birth. The verb "writhe" (ḥûlî) is a
standard term employed in relation to labor pains, but "groan" (gōḥî)
actually means "burst forth" or "bring forth." The term indicates that
the time of birth is at hand, even as Jerusalem is exiled into the wilder-

[69] See De Vries, *From Old Revelation to New* 23–33.

ness. The root *gyḥ*, "burst forth," also serves as the basis for the name of the Gihon spring in Jerusalem (2 Chr 32:30; 33:14) where Solomon was anointed as king (1 Kgs 1:33, 38, 45). The second half of the verse points to Jerusalem's exile in the wilderness (cf. Jacob and Rachel). It states that she will come to Babylon, indicating the Babylonian exile, and that this is the place where Jerusalem will be redeemed. In essence, the Babylonian exile serves as a means both to punish Jerusalem and to prepare it for its role at the center of the nations.

The second textual sub-unit introduced by "and now" appears in verses 11-13. It continues the second person feminine singular address forms to Jerusalem, and shifts to the image of the nations that are gathered against the city. The verb "assembled," *neʾespû* also means "gathered," and is often employed in reference to the gathering of a harvest (Exod 23:10, 16; Lev 23:39; 25:3, 20; Deut 11:14; 16:13). It plays upon the previous uses of the same verb in references to "gathering" the people for exile (Mic 2:12-13) and for restoration (Mic 4:6-7), and it introduces the motif of gathering the harvest in verse 13. The term "many nations," *gôyyim rabbîm*, also appears in the portrayal of the nations streaming to Zion (Mic 4:2). Its use here emphasizes that the nations constitute a threat to Jerusalem/Zion. This is particularly evident in the imagery of verse 11b, which suggests a scene of rape and degradation for Jerusalem as she is "profaned" before the eyes of the nations. Verse 12 provides a key statement in the author's reasoning concerning the means by which YHWH will use Jerusalem's exile and defeat as the basis for its future exaltation in the midst of the nations. By stating that the nations do not know YHWH's thoughts or understand YHWH's plan, the verse indicates that the nations do not realize that their actions against Zion at her time of humiliation will become the basis for their own punishment at the hands of YHWH and the Davidic king who will rule in Jerusalem once the restoration takes its course (cf. Mic 5:1-14 [NRSV: 5:2-15]). The references to YHWH's "thoughts" *(maḥšĕbôt)* and "his plan" (literally, "his counsel"; *ʿăṣātô)* recall similar references to YHWH's thoughts and plans in Isa 55:8, 9; Jer 51:29; Pss 40:6 [NRSV: 40:5]; 92:6 [NRSV: 92:5] *(maḥšĕbôt)* and Isa 5:19; 14:26; 19:17; 25:1; 46:10, 11; Jer 32:19; 49:20; 50:45; Pss 73:24; 106:13; 107:11 *(ʿēṣâ).* The reference to YHWH's plan or counsel likewise ironically contrasts with the statement in verse 9 that Jerusalem's "counselor has perished." Because the nations do not know YHWH's plans, they will indeed be "gathered" (*ʾsp*, cf. verse 11), but verse 12b indicates that they will be "gathered" *(qbṣ)* "as sheaves to the threshing floor." The reader must bear in mind that ancient temples, including the Jerusalem Temple, were the sites of threshing floors that were used to process or prepare the grain that was brought to the temple as offerings to the Deity at the major festivals and other occasions (Exod

23:14-19; 34:21-26; Deut 16:1-17; cf. 2 Sam 24:9-25/1 Chronicles 21–22, which identify the threshing floor of Araunah/Ornan the Jebusite as the site for the future Temple). In this manner, verse 12b introduces the motif of Zion's domination over the nations. Verse 13 then builds upon this motif by calling upon "daughter Zion" to "thresh" the nations that have been gathered for Zion's harvest. The metaphorical portrayal of Zion's iron horns and bronze hoofs draws upon the image of an ox that pulls a threshing sledge over raw grain in order to crush it and separate the wheat and the chaff (Deut 25:4; cf. Judg 16:21 where the Philistines use Samson for this purpose). The reference to beating in pieces "many peoples" (*ʿammîm rabbîm*) recalls the "many peoples" (*ʿammîm rabbîm*) who will be judged by Yʜwʜ in Mic 4:3. Verse 13b indicates that "their gain" (*biṣʿām; beṣʿa* frequently refers to "ill-gotten gain, plunder" e.g., Judg 5:19; 1 Sam 8:3; Ps 119:36; Prov 28:16) will be "devoted" to Yʜwʜ. The verb *ḥrm*, "to devote," is employed to indicate spoil or offerings that are dedicated to Yʜwʜ (e.g., Lev 27:28; Ezra 10:8), although it is also frequently employed to refer to the destruction of Israel's enemies who are devoted "to Yʜwʜ" (e.g., Deut 7:2; Josh 10:28; 11:11; 1 Sam 15:3). Yʜwʜ's sovereignty over the nations is indicated by the designation, "L–rd of all the earth."

The third sub-unit introduced with *ʿattâ*, "now," is verse 14. The second person feminine address form is again directed to Jerusalem/Zion. The section begins with a somewhat enigmatic pun that is not well understood in the NRSV, "now you are walled around with a wall." The Hebrew reads *ʿattâ titgōdĕdeî bat-gĕdûd*, "now, assemble/cut yourself, daughter of troops/cuttings." The verb root *gdd* on which both *titgōdĕdeî*, "gather/cut yourself," and *gĕdûd*, "troops/cuttings," are based basically means "to penetrate, to cut." The derivative root *gûd* is employed in reference to the invasion of troops (Gen 49:19; Hab 3:16; Ps 94:21), but the root *gdd* is frequently employed in reference to the self-inflicted incisions that were a part of the Canaanite mourning rituals for Baal during the time the time that he was in the netherworld (cf. 1 Kgs 18:28; Deut 14:1) or for the mourning in relation to Yʜwʜ (Jer 41:5). Jeremiah 5:7 indicates that the verb is used in reference to gathering at a harlot's house. The noun *gĕdûd* appears to presuppose either root as it refers to bands or troops that attack or make incursions into a territory (cf. 1 Sam 30:8; 1 Kgs 11:24; 2 Kgs 5:2; 6:23, etc.). The expression here builds upon the motif of "gathering" or "assembling" in that Jerusalem must be prepared to gather itself before the enemy invader, but it also builds upon the motif of cutting oneself in mourning, particularly as the ruler of the nation is about to be struck on the cheek by the invader. Zion is called Bat Gedud, "daughter of troops/cutting," to signify its defeated and humiliated status before an enemy who lays siege. The reference to the striking of Israel's ruler on the cheek with a "rod" *(šebeṭ)* recalls the image of the Assyrian monarch who strikes Judah with a rod in Isa 10:5, 24. The term *šōpēṭ*, "ruler," normally means "judge," but can be applied more generally as a designation for a "ruler" or "leader" as it is used throughout the book of Judges.

The Address to Bethlehem Ephrata concerning the New King: 5:1-14 [NRSV: 5:2-15]

The address to Bethlehem Ephrata concerning the new king in Mic 5:1-14 [NRSV: 5:2-15] draws heavily upon the traditions of eternal Davidic kingship in Israel in order to point to a time when Israel will enjoy peace and security from its enemies. The appearance of the introductory verb *wĕhāyâ*, "and it shall come to pass," in verses 4, 6/7, and 9 [NRSV: 5, 7, 10] indicates the structure of the passage. It begins in verses 1-3 [NRSV: 2-4] with an announcement that a shepherd or ruler will emerge to restore the security of Israel, and it continues with announcements concerning the peace that will come when Assyria is stricken (verses 4-5 [NRSV: 5-6]), Israel's role in the midst of the nations (verses 6-7 [NRSV: 7-8]), and a summation that relates how Israel's punishment will lead to the punishment of the nations and Israel's restoration (verses 9-14 [NRSV: 10-15]).

The initial announcement concerning the emergence of the shepherd or ruler of Israel signals its interest in looking forward to the rise of a new Davidic monarch who will inaugurate an age of security for Israel. It thereby builds upon Mic 4:9-10, which states that there is no king in Zion. In addition, it builds upon the imagery of childbirth in Mic 4:9-10 by pointing to the "birth" of the new king. Micah 5:1-3 [NRSV: 5:2-4] begins with a direct address to Bethlehem Ephrata in verse 1aα [NRSV: 2aα], "and you, O Bethlehem Ephrata, the youngest among the clans of Judah." Bethlehem, of course, is the city where David was born and in which he was anointed by Samuel as Israel's next king after Saul (1 Sam 16:1-13), and Ephratha is oftentimes identified with Bethlehem (see Ps 132:6; Gen 35:16, 18; 48:7; 1 Sam 16:1, 18; 17:12; Ruth 4:11). The NRSV renders this address as, "but you, O Bethlehem of Ephrata, who are one of the little clans of Judah," in an attempt to address the problem of the identities of Bethlehem and Ephrata. The two names are sometimes distinguished, particularly since 1 Chr 4:4 names Ephratah as the father of Bethlehem and Ruth 1:2 identifies Elimelech, Naomi, and their two sons as Ephrathites from Bethlehem in Judah. The issue is complicated, however, by various traditions that identify Ephratah and Bethlehem, i.e., both Gen 35:16, 18 and 48:7 explicitly identify

Ephratha as Bethlehem, and 1 Sam 16:1, 18 and 17:12 respectively identify Jesse, the father of David, as a Bethlehemite and as an Ephrathite.
Given that both Ephratha (Ps 132:6) and Bethlehem are identified as
place names in their own right, and that Ephrathites might live in the
city of Bethlehem, it seems reasonable to conclude that Ephratha is a
clan name that might designate a territory in which the clan lives, and
that the town of Bethlehem is located within that territory. The NRSV
translation, "who are one of the little *(ṣāʿîr)* clans of Judah," misses the
force of the Hebrew word *ṣāʿîr*, "young." The term plays upon the common Israelite tradition that the younger overcomes the older or that the
less powerful overcomes the more powerful.[70] This motif is expressed
especially in relation to Jacob's supplanting of his older brother Esau
(Genesis 25–27; 32–35), Joseph's supplanting his older brothers (Genesis 37–50), the selection of the small tribe of Benjamin as the royal tribe
of Israel (1 Sam 10:17-27), and the selection of David as king over his
older brothers (1 Sam 16:1-13). This motif expresses the notion that
those selected by G–d will possess the qualities for success, but it also
expresses some sense of Israel's self-identity as a late-comer which sup-
planted older Canaanite peoples in the land of Israel. The address to
Bethlehem Ephratha continues in verse 1aβ-b [NRSV: 2aβ-b] with statements that a ruler in Israel will emerge "from you," and that origins of
this ruler are "from of old *(miqqedem)*, from ancient days *(mimê ʿôlām;*
lit., 'from days of old/eternity')." Elsewhere, the Davidic traditions
emphasize the antiquity of David's covenant as "an eternal/ancient
covenant" *(běrît ʿôlām;* 2 Sam 23:5) that ensures that his descendants
will rule "forever" *(lěʿôlām,* Pss 89:29, 37; cf. Ps 110:4; *ʿad ʿôlām,* Ps 89:5
[NRSV: 89:4]; 2 Sam 7:13, 16; Isa 9:6 [NRSV: 9:7]). Fundamentally, the address to Bethlehem Ephrata points to the birthplace of David in order
to anticipate the emergence of a new Davidic king who will bring peace
to Israel from its enemies.

Verse 2 [NRSV: 3] follows upon the initial address to Bethlehem
Ephrata with the enigmatic statement, "therefore he shall give them up
until the time when she who is in labor has brought forth." The one
who shall give them up must be identified as the David ruler who will
emerge from Bethlehem Ephrata, and those who are given up must be
identified as the clans of Judah. Apparently, this statement points to a
period of waiting in which Israel is subjected to the oppression of enemies before the projected monarch is able to act. The oracle employs
the metaphor of a woman giving birth to express the necessary interval

---

[70] See Frederick E. Greenspahn, *When Brothers Dwell Together: The Preeminence of
Younger Siblings in the Hebrew Bible* (New York and Oxford: Oxford University Press,
1994).

until the rest of his kindred, i.e., the people of Judah or Israel are sufficiently restored so that they might bring about the new era of peace for
Israel. Indeed, the Mican oracle may draw upon the tradition in Isa 7:14
concerning the birth of Immanuel as a sign to the house of David (cf.
Isa 13:8; 26:18 for other uses of the childbirth motif in Isaiah). Verse 3
[NRSV: 4] employs the metaphor of a shepherd who stands over the
flock to express the rule of this monarch who acts in the strength of
YHWH. This metaphor draws upon the common portrayals of kings as
shepherds in the ancient world (cf. Ezekiel 34), and it especially draws
upon the portrayal of the young David as a shepherd who protects his
flock against powerful attacking lions and bears (see 1 Sam 16:11; 17:31-
37; 2 Sam 7:8). The image of the shepherd protecting the flock from
lions or bears is particularly apt in the Assyrian period, as the Assyrian
monarchs frequently liked to depict themselves as hunters of lions and
other dangerous game.[71] The imagery is also particularly apt in the
present context in which Israel is portrayed as a flock of sheep led by
YHWH and its king (Mic 2:12-13) and in which Zion is portrayed as the
"tower of the flock" (Mic 4:8). Once the new monarch is in place and
the people are restored, verse 3b [NRSV: 4b] indicates that Israel will
dwell securely as the monarch shall be recognized (literally, "become
great") "until the ends of the earth." In this manner, the presentation of
the new monarch draws upon the traditions that YHWH's (and David's)
kingship in Zion will be recognized by all the nations of the earth (cf.
Psalms 2; 46; 47; 48; 89; cf. 2 Sam 7:1; Ps 132:18; Isa 9:1-6; 11:1-16).

Micah 5:4-5 [NRSV: 5:5-6] is the first of the sequence of pericopes introduced by *wĕhāyâ*, "and it came to pass," that elaborates upon the
announcement of the new monarch in verses 1-3 [NRSV: 2-4]. The initial
statement of this pericope in verse 4a, [NRSV: 5a] "and this shall be
peace" *(wĕhāyâ zeh šālôm)*, has prompted a great deal of comment as interpreters from ancient times until the present have struggled to understand "this" *(zeh)*. For example, LXX renders "this" in relation to the
woman who shall give birth in verse 2, reading, "and she shall have
peace when Assur shall come . . .," whereas Targum Jonathan renders
"this" in relation to Israel, "and there shall be peace for us when the
Assyrian comes into our land." The statement must be taken literally,
however, not as a reference to the woman giving birth, the people of
Israel, or the new king, but simply as an introduction that identifies the
following portrayal of the process by which peace will come about in
verses 4b-5 [NRSV: 5b-6], i.e., "and this will be peace: when comes into
our land . . . and we raise against him seven shepherds . . . and they
shepherd/afflict the land of Assyria with the sword . . . and he delivers

[71] See *ANEP* 184–7.

us from Assyria." Verses 4b-5 [NRSV: 5b-6] clearly relate four basic steps
to the process. The first appears in verse 4bα [NRSV: 5bα], which points to
the entry of Assyria into the land of Israel and its treading down of Israel's palaces (n.b., NRSV incorrectly emends "our palaces" [*ʾarmĕnōtênû*]
to "our land" [*ʾadmātēnû*] in accordance with the LXX reading of the passage). This statement relates the initial oppression of Israel by Assyria.
The second appears in verse 4bβ [NRSV: 4bβ] in which the people states
that they will raise seven shepherds and indeed eight rulers against the
Assyrian invaders. The numbers seven and eight have prompted some
discussion as interpreters have struggled to understand them in relation to the one monarch of verse 1 [NRSV: 2], but they are simply an example of the common graduate numerical sequence that appears in
biblical and ancient Near Eastern literature to express a multiplicity of
examples, e.g., "for three transgressions of Damascus and for four, I
will not revoke the punishment" (Amos 1:3) or "three things are too
wonderful for me; four I do not understand" (Prov 30:18). The statement
again employs the metaphor of shepherds for rulers, and qualifies the
metaphor as such by the explicit reference to those "installed (literally,
'ordained') as rulers." In the present case, Mic 5:4bβ [NRSV: 5:5bβ]
merely expresses the expectation that the Assyrians will have their
hands full as they will be unable to contain the revolts of the people of
Israel that break out against them. The third statement in verse 5a
[NRSV: 6a] indicates that these "rulers" will overcome Assyria, and take
the battle back into the Assyrian homeland. It begins with a pun in that
the verb *wĕrāʿû*, "and they shall shepherd," based upon the root *rʿh*, "to
pasture, tend, graze," which can also be read as a form of the root, *rʿʿ*,
an Aramaic loanword, that means "to break," i.e., "and they shall break
the land of Assyria with the sword." The reference to "the land of Nim-
rod" in the second part of the statement recalls the ancient Mesopotamian king and culture hero who established the Assyrian cities of
Nineveh and Calah as well as the cities of Babylon, Erech, and Accad
(Gen 10:8-12; cf. 1 Chr 1:10). The NRSV emends "in its entrances/gates/
doors" to "with the drawn sword," but this eradicates the intent of the
passage to indicate that Assyria will suffer in its own land just as Israel
did as a result of Assyria's oppression. Finally, verse 5a [NRSV: 6a] indicates that the people of Israel will be delivered from Assyria. This statement reiterates the initial premise of the sequence, i.e., "when (Assyria)
comes into our land, and when (Assyria) treads upon our borders" (cf.
verse [NRSV: 5aβ]). It may well react against the statement in Mic 4:10b
that Zion must go to Babylon in order to be redeemed.

Micah 5:6 [NRSV: 5:7] and Mic 5:7-8 [NRSV: 5:8-9] are the second and
third passages in the sequence of oracles that are introduced by *wĕhāyâ*.
Although they are formally distinct, they appear to form a pair. Both

begin with reference to "the remnant of Jacob . . . in the midst of many
peoples" and provide contrasting images of that motif by portraying
Jacob first as life-giving dew or rain (verse 6 [NRSV: 7]) and then as a
lion that threatens its prey (verses 7-8 [NRSV: 8-9]). In this manner, they
present the options that are available to the nations in their relationship
with Zion, i.e., either a peaceful and beneficial relationship or a con-
flicted and threatening one. Together, these pericopes build upon Mic
4:11-13 which portrays Zion surrounded by many nations that are
ready to humiliate her and then calls upon her to "thresh" or take action against her enemies.

The terminology of Mic 5:6 [NRSV: 5:7] relates to previous pericopes
in this context. The reference to "the remnant of Jacob" *(šĕʾarît yaʿăqōb)*
recalls Mic 4:6-7 in which YHWH announces the intention to gather the
lame and outcast and to constitute them as the "remnant" *(šĕʾarît)* and a
"strong nation." Likewise, the reference to the remnant's placement "in
the midst of many peoples" *(bĕqereb ʿammîm rabbîm;* cf. NRSV, 'surrounded
by many peoples') takes up the language of Mic 4:3 which states that
YHWH "will judge between many peoples *(ʿammîm rabbîm;* cf. Mic 4:1-2)."
Micah 5:6 [NRSV: 5:7] (and 5:7-8 [NRSV: 5:8-9]) thereby portray a scenario
by which that judgment will be carried out in relation to the remnant of
Jacob, either for the benefit of the nations or their punishment. Micah
5:6 [NRSV: 5:7] clearly portrays the potential benefits for the nations by
portraying the remnant of Jacob metaphorically as "dew from YHWH"
and "showers on the grass." Such images take up YHWH's role as creator of the natural world, and indicate the continuing fertility and blessing in nature that the nations will enjoy as a result of the remnant of
Jacob's presence in their midst. The statements that the dew and rain
"do not depend upon people" or "wait for any mortal" merely indicate
that such dew and showers are not controlled by human means, but
only by YHWH who bestows such blessings in the created world order.

Micah 5:7-8 [NRSV: 5:8-9] the follows, beginning with a variant of the
same formula that appears in verse 6 [NRSV: 7], "and the remnant of
Jacob shall be among the nations in the midst of many peoples." The
introduction of *baggôyim,* "among the nations," takes up language from
Mic 4:2, "many nations *(gôyim rabbîm),"* and 4:3, "strong nations *(gôyim
ʿaṣumîm),"* and thereby relates the following images of threat to earlier
image of Zion's ascendancy among the nations. The balance of the passage in Mic 5:7aβ-8 [NRSV: 5:8aβ-9] focuses on the image of the remnant
of Jacob as "a lion among the animals of the forest" or as "a young lion
among the flocks of sheep." This image builds upon the earlier references to Israel as sheep that are led into exile by YHWH (Mic 2:12-13), the
reference to Zion as "the tower of the flock" (Mic 4:8), and the portrayal
of the new Davidic monarch as a shepherd (Mic 5:1-3 [NRSV: 5:2-4]).

Nevertheless, Jacob now becomes the predator rather than the prey, so that this image builds upon the above-mentioned pun on the verb *wĕrāʿû* in Mic 5:5 [NRSV: 5:6] in which the new monarch (or the seven or eight shepherds) will either "shepherd" or "afflict" Assyria in its own land. The statement at the end of verse 7 [NRSV: 8] that there will be "no one to deliver" *(wĕʾên maṣṣîl)* the (enemy) nations contrasts with the statement concerning the time of peace in Mic 4:5 that there will be "no one (to) make them afraid" *(wĕʾên maḥrîd)*. In order to achieve that peace, the judgment against the oppressors mentioned in Mic 4:3 must be carried out. Verse 8 addresses the remnant of Jacob directly with second person masculine singular address language by calling upon Jacob to raise its hand against its adversaries and to cut off its enemies. As presented in Mic 5:7-8 [NRSV: 5:8-9] (cf. Mic 5:1-3, 4-5 [NRSV: 5:2-4, 5-6]), the remnant of Jacob will be the agent by which YHWH carries out the judgment against the oppressing nations so that peace may be achieved.

The fourth pericope introduced by *wĕhāyâ* appears in Mic 5:9-14 [NRSV: 5:10-15], which presents an overview of Jacob's punishment or cleansing and the subsequent punishment of the nations.[72] Overall, this passage indicates YHWH's actions to remove military strength and idolatrous installations and practices from Jacob as a prelude to the punishment of the nations that do not listen to YHWH. In this respect, it corresponds to Mic 4:14, which expresses Zion's conquest and humiliation. The passage draws heavily on Isa 2:6-21, which presents an overview of YHWH's actions against the land on the Day of YHWH following the invitation to Jacob (Isa 2:5) to join the nations streaming to YHWH at Zion (Isa 2:2-4).[73] Whereas the Isaian text appears to be directed from the outset against all the earth, including both Jacob/Israel and the nations, the Mican text differentiates between Jacob in verses 9-13 [NRSV: 10-14] and the nations in verse 14 [NRSV: 15].

The structure of the passage is constituted by a simple sequence of *waw-consecutive* imperfect verbs. It begins with the prophet's statement in verse 9aα [NRSV: 10aα] that identifies the following material as an oracle by YHWH, "and it shall come to pass on that day, oracle/utterance of YHWH." The balance of the passage is formulated as a first person speech by YHWH. The second person masculine singular address forms indicate that the addressee is Jacob/Israel. The first four statements

---

[72] See John T. Willis, "The Structure of Micah 3–5 and the Function of Micah 5, 9–14 in the Book," *ZAW* 81 (1969) 191–214; idem, "The Authenticity and Meaning of Micah 5, 9–14," *ZAW* 81 (1969) 353–68, who sees Mic 5:9-14 [NRSV: 5:10-15] as a composition of the eighth-century prophet. Contra Renaud, *Formation* 262–71, who argues that the passage is an exilic composition.

[73] Renaud, *Formation* 267.

begin with the verb *wĕhikratî*, "and I shall cut off." Verse 9β-b [NRSV: 10β-b] begins YHWH's address to Jacob with a statement that the Deity promises to cut off and destroy "your horses from among you" and "your chariots." This statement obviously speaks to YHWH's intention to destroy Israel's military forces, and it draws upon the language of Isa 2:7 which portrays the land as full of horses and chariots. Verse 10 [NRSV: 11] then states YHWH's intention to cut off and throw down Jacob's cities and strongholds. Again, this indicates the intention to destroy Israel's defenses, and it draws upon the images of Isa 2:15 which speaks of YHWH's intentions to destroy high towers and fortified walls. Verse 11 [NRSV: 12] then turns to the issue of forbidden religious practices by stating YHWH's intentions to cut off sorceries (cf. Exod 22:17) and soothsayers. This draws upon Isa 2:6 which charges that the land is full of soothsayers and foreigners. Verse 12 [NRSV: 13] states that YHWH will cut off images and pillars. Images refers to idols, and pillars (*maṣṣēbôt*) may also serve as divine representations,[74] perhaps of the sacred trees that symbolize Asherah (but see Gen 28:22, where Jacob sets up a stone as a *maṣṣēbâ* at Beth El). Verse 12 [NRSV: 13] stipulates that Jacob will no longer worship "the work of your hands," which takes up language from Isa 2:8 concerning the worship of idols and the work of human hands (cf. Isa 2:20). Verse 13 [NRSV: 14] then breaks the sequence of *wĕhikratî* statements with the climactic use of the verbs *wĕnātaštî*, "and I will uproot," and *wĕhišmadtî*, "and I will destroy," in reference to Jacob's Asherim and cities. The statement appears to be a climactic summation of the prior statements to Jacob in that Asherim takes up the issue of idolatry in verses 11-12 [NRSV: 12-13] and cities takes up the concern with Israel's military forces and defenses in verses 9aβ-10 [NRSV: 10aβ-11]. It must be considered as a penultimate statement, however, as verse 14 [NRSV: 15] then turns to the general issue of YHWH's anger and vengeance upon "the nations that did not obey." This final shift in the passage reinforces previous statements throughout Micah 4–5 that Israel's punishment would eventually lead to YHWH's punishment of the nations at the time of Zion's restoration.

Prophetic Appeal to People to Return to YHWH: 6:1-16

The third major component of the body of the book of Micah is the prophet's appeal to the people of Israel/Judah to return to YHWH in Mic 6:1-16. The passage begins with a syntactically independent version

---

[74] For a convenient survey of the function of such pillars, see Dale W. Manor, "Massebah," *ABD* IV:602.

of the call to attention formula, "Hear what YHWH says," which introduces the following material.[75] Although Mic 6:1-16 is frequently re-
garded as a collection of two (Mic 6:1-8. 9-16)[76] or three (Mic 6:1-5, 6-8,
9-16)[77] independent oracular units, the entire chapter is held together
by the overriding interest in defining what YHWH requires from the
people and in pointing to their present situation of distress as the basis
for the prophet's appeal to them to do what YHWH wants. Although
Micah 6 contains quotes by YHWH, the prophet is the speaker throughout the entire chapter. Micah 6:1-5 constitutes the prophet's presentation
of YHWH's "lawsuit" against the people in which the Deity rehearses
prior actions on behalf of the people. Micah 6:6-8 then presents a set of
rhetorical questions by the prophet concerning what the people shall
give to YHWH in order to assert YHWH's desire for justice. These verses
thereby function rhetorically as an appeal for justice from the people.
Finally, Mic 6:9-14 asserts that the lack of justice among the people is
the cause for their current suffering. The formula, "Woe is me!" in Mic
7:1 marks the beginning of an entirely new component of the book of
Micah. When read synchronically in relation to the preceding material
in Micah 2–5, Micah 6 functions as the prophet's call to the people to
take the appropriate self-corrective action so that the ideal scenario of
Micah 2–5 might be realized.

Many scholars view this chapter as a very late addition to the book
of Micah that reflects upon the destruction of Jerusalem and the Babylonian exile.[78] This conclusion is based primarily on the presence of
priestly concerns and liturgical language in the chapter as well as the
references to Moses, Aaron, Miriam, and Balaam in verses 4-5 and to
Ahab in verse 16. Nevertheless, such a conclusion ignores the role that
the Temple would play in the life of the people of monarchic Judah,
particularly when the people would be making their own liturgical
appeals and sacrifices to YHWH for deliverance from the Assyrian army
at the time of Sennacherib's invasion (cf. Hezekiah's appeal to YHWH
for deliverance in Isaiah 36–37). Furthermore, Moses, Aaron, Miriam,
and Balaam all appear in the early J traditions of the Pentateuch so that
they could be well known in the eighth century B.C.E.[79] Ahab preceded

[75] For discussion of the call to attention formula, see Sweeney, *Isaiah 1–39* 544.

[76] E.g., Wolff, *Micah* 163–99; Renaud, *Michée* 119–38; Ben Zvi, *Micah* ad loc.

[77] Mays, *Micah* 127–49.

[78] For surveys of the relevant literature, see esp. Renaud, *Formation* 318–26, 340–2.

[79] See the standard treatments of Pentateuchal sources in Martin Noth, *A History of Pentateuchal Traditions*, trans. B. W. Anderson (Englewood Cliffs: Prentice-Hall, 1972); Antony F. Campbell and Mark O'Brien, *Sources of the Pentateuch: Texts, Introductions, Annotations* (Minneapolis: Fortress, 1993).

Micah by at least a century, and there is some evidence of a Hezekian edition of the DtrH that would have presented a very critical assessment of this Omride monarch.[80] It would appear instead that the chapter reflects upon the crisis prompted by Sennacherib's 701 B.C.E. invasion of Judah and siege of Jerusalem. Micah, after all, is a refugee from the Shephelah who apparently was forced to seek shelter in Jerusalem from the Assyrian invaders. This chapter appears to reflect his perspectives on the causes of the disaster and the attempts by the people to appeal to YHWH for help.

THE PROPHET'S PRESENTATION OF YHWH'S "LAWSUIT" AGAINST THE PEOPLE: 6:1-5

Micah 6:1-5 constitutes the prophet's presentation of YHWH's lawsuit or contentions against the people of Israel/Judah. The unit is frequently identified as an example of the so-called "covenant lawsuit" or "trial" genre because of the forensic term *rîb*, "controversy, contention," in verse 2, the appeal to natural features of the earth as witnesses in 1 and 2, and the accusatory questions that are directed by YHWH to the people in verses 3-5.[81] The passage presupposes an attempt by an injured party, in this case YHWH, to obtain redress from a court or other legal authority for the wrongs done by the offending party. In the present instances, the wrongs done by the people of Israel/Judah are only identified in verses 6-8 and 9-14 as the lack of justice and honesty after the pattern of the northern Israelite Omride dynasty. Micah 6:1-5 must therefore be read together with Mic 6:6-8 and 6:9-16.

The unit begins with the prophet's rendition of the call to attention formula in verses 1-2 in which he introduces the following speech by YHWH. The initial statement in verse 1a, "Hear what YHWH says," *šimĕ'û-nā' 'ēt 'ăšer-yhwh 'ōmēr*, would seem to introduce a direct quote of YHWH by the prophet, but the third person references to YHWH throughout verses 1b-2 indicate that these, too, continue the prophet's introductory statements. The following appeal to "arise, plead your case before the mountains, and let the hills hear your voice," appears to be directed by the prophet to YHWH, so that the prophet essentially invites

---

[80] Baruch Halpern and David Vanderhooft, "The Editions of Kings in the 7th–6th Centuries B.C.E.," *HUCA* 62 (1991) 179–244; Marvin A. Sweeney, *King Josiah of Judah: The Lost Messiah of Israel* (New York and Oxford: Oxford University Press, 2000).

[81] For discussion of the "covenant lawsuit" or "trial genres," see Sweeney, *Isaiah 1–39* 541–2 and the literature cited there.

YHWH to begin the legal proceedings against the people. It has long
been recognized in discussion of the trial genres that the natural features of creation, i.e., the mountains, hills, streams, etc., must function
as witnesses to the legal testimony of YHWH against Israel/Judah. Because they have stood since the beginning of creation and because
there are no other neutral parties in a controversy between G–d and
human beings, creation thereby stands as the only realistic witnesses to
the proceeding. The prophet then calls upon the "mountains" and the
"eternal streams, the foundations of the earth" in verse 2a to hear
YHWH's "controversy." The term *rîb*, "controversy," is a technical term
for a legal dispute that might arise between two parties (e.g., Exod 23:2,
3, 6; Deut 21:5; 25:1). The noun is derived from the verb *rîb* which
means, "to strive, contend," and likewise portrays a situation of conflict between two parties, such as Jacob's challenge to Laban for accus-
ing him of theft (Gen 31:36) or the potential charges of the fathers
whose daughters will be taken (not given) for marriage by the men of
Benjamin (Judg 21:22). The expression *wĕhā'ētānîm mōsĕdê 'āreṣ*, translated by the NRSV as "and you enduring foundations of the earth," has
proved to be very problematic. The term *'ētān* means both "perpetual,
permanent," and "everflowing stream"; apparently the notion of an
ever-flowing underground stream (Deut 21:4; Ps 74:15; cf. Exod 14:27)
became the basis for the abstract expression of permanence (e.g., Gen
49:24; Jer 5:15; Job 33:19). The image is particularly pertinent in that the
ancient conception of the universe posited that the earth was placed between the waters in the heavens above and those that flowed beneath
(see Gen 1:6-10; 6:11; cf. Ps 74:13-15). Insofar as water flows below the
earth as well as above, such perpetual streams would constitute the
foundations on which the earth rests. Water thereby flows from below
the Temple in Jerusalem, which serves as the center of the earth in ancient Israelite thought (cf. Ezek 47:1; Joel 3:18; Zech 13:1; 14:8; cf. Gen
2:10-14; Ps 46:4). Finally, verse 2b employs a *kî* ("because, for") clause to
state the reason why the mountains and streams must listen, i.e., YHWH
has a case against YHWH's own people. The verb *yitwakāḥ*, "he will content, arbitrate," is a common technical term for legal arbitration (Gen
31:37; Job 9:33; 16:21; Isa 2:2; Mic 4:3).

The first person speaker and the second person addressee of verses
3-5 identify this section as the quotation of YHWH's speech to the
people. The Deity begins with a pair of rhetorical questions directed to
the people followed by a demand for a response, "O my people, what
have I done to you? In what have I wearied you? Answer me!" The
questions presuppose the setting of legal dispute in which the parties
are assembled before a court or judge to make their respective claims.
In this case, YHWH's questions to Israel/Judah presuppose that the

people have taken some action against YHWH, or that they have failed to fulfill some obligation to the Deity. Essentially, YHWH's questions demand some explanation from the people so that a decision can be made concerning the issue. The verb *'nh* generally means simply, "to answer," but it also frequently serves as a technical term for legal testimony (Deut 31:21; Ruth 1:21; Num 35:30; Deut 19:6; Exod 20:16). The lack of an answer from Israel/Judah represents a deliberate rhetorical strategy to indicate that, of course, there is no answer and that the people are guilty as charged. Nevertheless, the reader of this text never has the opportunity to hear from the people. Undoubtedly, they might have a few things to say to a Deity who had failed to protect them from Sennacherib's armies!

YHWH then turns in verses 4-5 to a rehearsal of the various actions of deliverance and protection performed on behalf of Israel/Judah. The purpose of this rehearsal in the context of a legal dispute is to establish YHWH's credibility as protector or defender of the people, which would be essential in a context in which Assyrian troops were swarming all over the land and laying siege to the city of Jerusalem, the site of YHWH's own Temple. This segment draws upon traditions concerning the foundation of the nation Israel at the time of the Exodus from Egypt and the wilderness wanderings, which were apparently well known among the people in both the northern kingdom of Israel and the southern kingdom of Judah (cf. Hosea 11; 12; 13). YHWH begins in verse 4a by reminding the people of the Exodus from Egypt and the redemption from Egyptian bondage, and follows up in verse 4b with a reference to the sending of Moses, Aaron, and Miriam to serve as leaders for the people during this period. Commentators are fond of pointing out that the three figures appear together only in Numbers 12 (see also Num 26:59; 1 Chr 5:29 [NRSV: 1 Chr 6:3]), in which Miriam challenges Moses' leadership because of his marriage to a Cushite or Ethiopian woman (presumably Zipporah, as the Midianites are equated with Cushites in Hab 3:7). Some seem to feel that this has some bearing on the date of this text since early covenant traditions in Joshua 24; 1 Samuel 12; and Psalm 105 mention only Moses and Aaron.[82] This has little bearing on the date or the interpretation of this passage, however, as all three figures appear throughout the J versions of the Pentateuchal narrative from the tenth-ninth centuries B.C.E. (n.b., Numbers 12 is a J text), which indicates that they were well known by the late-eighth century B.C.E. YHWH then calls upon the people in verse 5 to remember how Balak, the king of Moab, attempted to engage the Mesopotamian diviner/prophet Balaam ben Beor to curse Israel as they passed through

---

[82] E.g., Wolff, *Micah* 171–2.

the land of Moab on their journey to the land of Israel. This, of course, refers to the traditions in Numbers 22–24 in which Balaam was unable to curse Israel because he was able to speak only what YHWH willed for him to say. The result was that Balaam provided Israel with a great blessing on the eve of their entry into the promised land. The reference to Shittim indicates the site in the plains of Moab where the Israelites were encamped at the time that Balaam delivered his oracles of blessing (Num 25:1; cf. Num 22:1) and Gilgal indicates the site where Israel encamped under the leadership of Joshua once they had crossed the Jordan River into the land of Israel (Joshua 3–5). The final phrase of the passage, "that you may know the saving acts of YHWH," indicates the purpose of YHWH's recitation, i.e., that YHWH has acted to save Israel in the past and is capable of doing so again. The statement thereby is a rhetorical attempt to convince the people to undertake action that will motivate YHWH to act on their behalf. It is noteworthy that the expression, ṣidqôt yhwh, does not mean literally, "saving acts of YHWH," but "righteous acts of YHWH." The expression thereby reinforces the attempt to establish YHWH's credibility to the people.

THE PROPHET'S APPEAL FOR JUSTICE FROM THE PEOPLE: 6:6-8

Micah 6:6-8 draws upon the language of cultic instruction in order to define what YHWH requires from the people (cf. Hag 2:10-14).[83] Scholars frequently understand this passage to be an example of the generic form of the Temple entrance liturgy (cf. Psalms 15; 24; Isa 33:14-16) because of its initial questions concerning the proper offering to bring to YHWH, presumably at the Temple, and its interest in defining the fundamental observance of justice, loyalty (NRSV, "kindness"), and walking humbly with G–d.[84] Indeed, the various examples of the Temple entrance liturgy noted above posit similar characteristics for those who are considered to be sufficiently pure to enter the Temple. By defining such characteristics as that which YHWH desires, the oracle calls upon the people to emulate such practice. It thereby points indirectly to the causes for YHWH's "lawsuit" in verses 1-5, and prepares the reader for the explicit charges of misconduct in verses 9-16.

The prophet begins with a series of four rhetorical questions that propose a sequence of sacrificial offerings that he or the people might

[83] For a full discussion of this passage, see Theodor Lescow, *Micha 6, 6-8. Studien zu Sprache, Form und Auslegung*, Arbeiten zur Theologie, vol. I/25 (Stuttgart: Calwer, 1966).

[84] See Lescow, *Micha 6, 6-8* 9–22; Wolff, *Micah* 167–8.

present to YHWH. The proposed offerings presuppose a situation such that the people make offerings to YHWH as a means to ask for deliverance in the face of crisis (Judg 20:26; 21:4; 1 Sam 7:9; 2 Sam 24:10-25; 1 Kings 18; Jer 14:1-22, esp. 11-12; cf. Psalms 44; 60; 79; 80; Isaiah 37). To a certain extent, it is already clear that YHWH does not want sacrifices as they would have been performed already as part of the preparations for revolt against the Assyrians (cf. 1 Sam 13:9). The questions also presuppose a situation of want. During Sennacherib's siege of Jerusalem, food supplies would have been very scarce and the proposal to sacrifice animals and oil would have placed some strain on the supplies that were at hand (cf. 2 Kgs 18:27; Isa 36:12). Micah's questions already represent the state of the besieged people; they don't have much to offer anyway.

The prophet's questions begin with a general question concerning sacrifice in such a situation, and move progressively to the more specific and desperate. The first set of questions in verse 6a simply raises the question of sacrifice by asking, "With what shall I come before YHWH, and bow myself before G–d on high?" Israelite/Judean tradition makes it clear that the people are to present an offering to YHWH on the major festivals (Exod 23:14-15; 34:18-20; Deut 16:16-17). Offerings are considered to be normative when one approaches YHWH. The second set of questions then specifies the presentation of "whole burnt offerings" and "calves a year old." The "whole burnt offering" (*ʿōlâ*) is the standard daily offering at the Temple that is designed to maintain the relationship between the people and YHWH and to ensure the stability of the created world (Leviticus 2). The whole burnt offering could be cattle, sheep, goats, turtledoves, or pigeons. The specification of a year-old calf reflects the requirement that the burnt offering (Lev 12:6; 23:12; Num 6:14), the daily offering (Exod 29:38; Ezek 46:13), the guilt offering (Num 6:12), the festival offerings (Exod 12:5; Lev 23:18, 19; Numbers 28–29), the sin offering (Lev 9:3), the offerings for the dedication of the altar (Num 7:17, etc.) be year-old lambs or cattle. The prophet's third set of questions in verse 7a specifies the presentation of "thousands of rams" and "rivers of oil." The question employs the technical term *rṣh*, "to want, desire, be pleased," which indicates YHWH's acceptance of sacrifice (cf. Deut 33:11; Mal 1:10, 13; Ps 51:18 [NRSV: 51:17]; 119:108; Amos 5:22). Rams are generally included among the animals that are presented at the new moon and the festivals (see Num 28:11–29:39), and oil is always included with the animal and grain offerings (Numbers 28–29). The specification of "thousands of rams" and "ten thousands of rivers of oil" is an example of hyperbole that is intended to indicate that no quantity of these sacrifices would be acceptable to YHWH in these circumstances. Finally, the prophet asks if he should offer his firstborn. Again, this proposal is an example of hyperbole as human sacrifice is forbidden in ancient Israel and Judah (see Lev 18:21; 20:2-5; Deut 12:31; 18:10), although it was known to be practiced in times of crisis or desperation (see 2 Kgs 3:27 [Moab]) or in relation to illicit forms of worship (2 Kgs 16:3; 21:6; Jer 7:31; 19:5; 32:35; Ezek 16:20-21; 20:26, 31).

The prophet's rhetorical strategy reaches its climax in verse 8, which defines what Yʜᴡʜ requires instead of the various sacrifices enumerated in verses 6-7: justice, kindness, and walking humbly with G–d. The term "justice," *mišpāṭ,* is the technical term for "law" (e.g., 1 Sam 8:9, 10:25; Lev 5:10; Exod 15:25; Num 27:11; 35:29; Jer 8:7, etc.), and refers to doing what is "right" or "just." The term "kindness," *ḥesed* is more properly translated as "loyalty" or "fidelity," and conveys a sense of social and moral obligation and responsibility.[85] The term to walk "humbly" with G–d employs the verb *ṣnʿ,* "to be modest, humble," which appears only here as an infinitive absolute construction that serves as an adverb and as an adjectival form in Prov 11:2. In Prov 11:2, "the humble" *(ṣĕnûʿîm)* are labeled as "wise," and contrasted with those who exhibit "pride" or "arrogance" *(zādôn)* and will therefore suffer disgrace. As noted above, these characteristics correspond to those sought in the Temple entrance liturgies, which call for "walking blamelessly, doing what is right, speaking truth, (Ps 15:2), and who have "clean hands, pure hearts," etc. (Ps 24:4).

Tʜᴇ Pʀᴏᴘʜᴇᴛ's Assᴇʀᴛɪᴏɴs ᴏғ Isʀᴀᴇʟ's Lᴀᴄᴋ ᴏғ Jᴜsᴛɪᴄᴇ ᴀs ᴛʜᴇ Cᴀᴜsᴇ ᴏғ Pᴜɴɪsʜᴍᴇɴᴛ: 6:9-16

Micah 6:9-16 then turns to the prophet's charges that the actions of the people are the cause of their present calamity. Essentially, he maintains that the people have not acted in accordance with the principles of justice, loyalty, and humbleness that Yʜᴡʜ requires, but that they have acted deceitfully, particularly in economic matters and marketplace transactions. This would be particularly pertinent to a refugee such as Micah, who flees to Jerusalem before the advancing Assyrian army and then finds that he is charged exorbitant rates for food and other necessities of life. This is not surprising in a situation of siege when such items become increasingly scarce, but it offends Micah's sense of social justice. Interestingly, the Temple entrance liturgies cite economic abuse (Ps 15:5; Isa 33:15) and deceit *(mirmâ;* Ps 24:4; cf. Mic

---

[85] See Nelson Glueck, *Ḥesed in the Bible,* trans. A. Gottschalk (Cincinnati: Hebrew Union College, 1967).

6:11, "dishonest weights," *ʾabnê mirmâ*) as the characteristics of those who are not fit to enter the Temple premises and appear before YHWH. Likewise, the above-cited Proverbs 11 begins with similar economic concerns in defining the actions of the arrogant over against those of the humble and wise. By charging the people with such actions, Micah provides the basis for his appeal that they should change and thereby put an end to their current national crisis.

The pericope begins in verse 9aα with the prophet's announcement that the voice of YHWH cries out to the city. It thereby stands as the introduction to the speech by YHWH in verses 10-16. The statement in verse 9aβ, "it is sound wisdom to fear your name," is very problematic. Although the statement reads literally, "and success/wisdom your name will see," the word order is somewhat awkward *(wĕtûšîyâ yirʾeh šĕmekā)*. Many repoint *yirʾeh*, "he/it will see," as a form of *yrʾ* in keeping with the Vulgate and LXX (see NRSV),[86] but these merely represent ancient attempts to render a difficult text so that it will make sense in the immediate context. The second person address to YHWH, however, indicates that this statement is a marginal gloss that has found its way into the text. It was probably written by someone who wished to affirm the sentiments that are expressed in verses 9-16. The term *tûšîyâ*, "success, wisdom," elsewhere refers to sound wisdom that comes from YHWH (Isa 28:29; Prov 3:21; 8:14).

YHWH's speech then follows in verses 9b-16. The deity's speech begins with a general call to attention in verse 9bα, "hear, O tribe," which directs the audience's attention to the following speech. The prophet follows up with a rhetorical question in verse 9bβ, "and who has appointed it?" in order to call the audience's attention to the fact that YHWH has directed that the Assyrian invasion take place. This question is frequently emended because of its awkward formulation *(ûmî yĕʿādāh)*, which begins with a conjunction and lacks an antecedent for the third person feminine object of the verb.[87] The issue is also tied up with text critical problems in verse 10 as the initial *ʿôd*, "yet, again, still," is often mistakenly read with this question (see NRSV note, "and who has appointed it yet?").[88] Nevertheless, the question by the prophet makes perfect sense in the present context in which the prophet wishes to argue that YHWH has brought the Assyrian army as a means to punish the people. As evidence for this contention, the prophet quotes the Deity's own speech in verses 10-16.

[86] See Rudolph, *Micha* 114–5.
[87] Wolff, *Micah* 186.
[88] Rudolph, *Micha* 115–6.

YHWH's speech is styled according to the general rubrics of a judgment speech in which the charges are leveled against the people in verses 10-12, and the announcement of punishment follows in verses 13-16. YHWH begins the charges with a series of rhetorical questions that are designed to assert wrongdoing on the part of the people. The first in verse 10 has been particularly problematic because of the difficulties posed by the expression ʿôd hᵃʾiš. The particle ʿôd means simply, "yet, still." The particle hᵃʾiš has been frequently emended,[89] but it is simply a combination of the interrogative particle hă and the particle ʾiš. The particle ʾiš is a variant of the usual Hebrew particle yēš, "there is/are," which appears elsewhere in 2 Sam 14:19 ("one cannot [ʾim-ʾiš, literally, 'if there is'] turn right or left from anything that my lord the king has said").[90] The particle ʿiš may be a variant form of the Aramaic ʾitay/ʾîtay, "there is/are." When these factors are taken into consideration, the verse reads, "Are there still a wicked house, wicked storehouses, and an accursed lean ephah?" The Deity's initial question points to the continued exorbitant charging for food or grain within the besieged city. The references to a "wicked house" and "wicked storehouses" point to those who have grain to sell, and do so by cheating on the measures and prices that are offered. This may refer directly to the royal house or to the Temple, particularly since the Temple was the place where ancient Judean brought their grain offerings for presentation to the priests (cf. Deut 26:1-15). It was built with storehouses for silver and gold (1 Kgs 7:51; 15:18; 2 Kgs 12:19 [NRSV: 12:18]), although no mention is made of grain storage. Nevertheless, the quantity of grain brought to the Temple would require some sort of storage facility. The use of royal or Temple stores of grain in a time of crisis is analogous to that of Joseph in Egypt (Genesis 41), who stored grain during times of plenty and then sold it to the people during times of famine. This would account for the phrase wĕʾêpat rāzôn zĕʿûmâ, "and an accursed lean ephah." The ephah was the standard measure for grain in ancient Israel and Judah, equivalent to 20.878 quarts or 0.652 bushels. The designation of the ephah as "lean" indicates that someone has been cheating in the measurement of grain for sale. In this regard, it is particularly interesting that the Hebrew term rāzôn, "lean" (derived from the root rzh) may also mean "ruler" or "potentate" when it is derived from the root rzn, "to be weighty, judicious, commanding" (cf. Prov 14:28 where rāzôn is parallel with melek, "king"). The use of the term rāzôn by the prophet might constitute a pun that indicates his views concerning the source of the dishonesty in pricing grain. Finally, the

[89] Ibid.
[90] Hillers, *Micah* 80–1.

use of the adjective *zĕ'ûmâ*, "accursed, detested," indicates the prophet's and the people's evaluation of such a practice. Prices for food inevitably go up in a situation of want, but refugees such as Micah will rightfully resent this situation. YHWH continues with a second rhetorical question in verse 11, "Can I tolerate wicked scales and a bag of dishonest weights?" The answer, of course, is "no," but the question once again asserts the charges that people are being cheated when purchasing food and other goods that must be priced by measure. The verb *zkh* normally means, "to be clean, bright, pure," but in the present context it takes on an abstract meaning, "to be justified" (cf. the use of the verb in parallel to *ẓdq*, "to be righteous," in Ps 51:6 [NRSV: 51:4]). YHWH's charges in verse 12 that the wealthy inhabitants of the city are "full of violence," "speak lies," and are deceitful again reflect the general concerns of the Temple entrance liturgies.

Verses 13-16 then turn to a delineation of Israel's/Judah's punishment in which YHWH claims to be the source of Israel's and Judah's suffering. The rendition of verse 13 in the NRSV reflects the problems of interpretation that this verse prompts, "Therefore I have begun to strike you down, making you desolate because of your sins." The verse reads literally, "And I also have grievously smitten you, making (you) desolate because of your sins." The primary problem lies with the interpretation of the verb *heḥĕlêtî*, "I have made sick." The *hiphil* form of *ḥlh* is not elsewhere followed by the infinitive *hakkōlekā*, "smiting you"; (but cf. Nah 3:19; Jer 10:19; 30:12, "your wound is grievous," *naḥlâ makātekā*) many scholars follow LXX and Vulgate in rendering the verb as *haḥillôtî*, "I have begun" (cf. Deut 2:31, *haḥillôtî tēt*, "I have begun to give").[91] This creates problems, however, because it requires a somewhat different consonantal reading, i.e., *hḥlwty* as opposed to the MT *hḥlyty*, although it is not impossible for a *waw* and a *yod* to be interchanged. At this point, the oracle expressly states that YHWH is responsible for smiting the people. The rendition of the verse in the MT may reflect an attempt by later scribes to wrestle with the moral problems posed by divine punishment.

Verses 14-15 employ a series of five statements that outline the failure of human efforts to provide food and sustenance. The form of each statement employs the particle *wĕlō*, "but not," and reflects the typical formulation of cursing statements from ancient Near Eastern treaty texts.[92] Because such (blessings and) curses conclude some of the major law collections of the Hebrew Bible (see Leviticus 26; Deuteronomy 28),

---

[91] Rudolph, *Micha* 116.

[92] Hillers, *Micah* 82; idem, *Treaty Curses and the Old Testament Prophets*, BO, vol. 16 (Rome: Pontifical Biblical Institute, 1964).

it would appear that Micah draws upon this tradition as the basis for his claim that YHWH is now punishing the people for violating the terms of their covenant. Such a claim would be in keeping with the initial use of the trial genre form in verses 1-5 as YHWH would seek redress from the courts for such a breach of contract. Such a conceptualization might well reflect the Assyrian rationalization for their own invasion of Judah, i.e., Hezekiah was a vassal or ally of Assyria and his revolt constituted grounds for invoking the punishments called for in the treaty that defined the relationship between Assyria and Judah. The first statement in verse 14a, "you shall eat, but not be satisfied, and there shall be a gnawing hunger within you," reflects the similar statement in Lev 26:26b, "and though you eat, you shall not be satisfied." The next statement in verse 14b, "you shall put away, but not save, and what you save, I will hand over to the sword," indicates that the people will not be able to store sufficient food for future needs. Whatever is saved will be taken by enemies (cf. Deut 28:47-57, which describes the effects of enemy invasion that YHWH will bring if the people do not keep the terms of the covenant). The third statement in verse 15a, "you shall sow, but not reap," reflects similar sentiments in Lev 26:16 and Deut 28:38 which indicate that enemies or locusts will consume seed that is planted in the field. The fourth statement in verse 15bα, "you shall tread olives, but not anoint yourselves with oil (literally, 'pour out oil')," corresponds to Deut 28:40, which also speaks of the failure to reap the olive harvest. The NRSV translation presupposes the use of oil as a cleansing agent, but oil is more frequently used for cooking in both the ancient and modern worlds. Finally, the fifth statement in verse 15bβ, "(and you shall tread) grapes, but not drink wine," actually draws the initial verb from the preceding statement concerning oil. It corresponds to Deut 28:30b, 39, which indicate that the people will plant vineyards but not drink the wine.

The concluding statements in verse 16 charge the people with keeping "the statutes of Omri" and walking in the counsels of "all the works of the house of Ahab." This is a clear reference to the northern Israelite king Ahab ben Omri (869–850 B.C.E.), who was condemned by Elijah for idolatry and murder in that he followed the gods of his Phoenician wife Jezebel (1 Kgs 16:31-34; 18) and murdered Naboth in order to claim his land in the Jezreel Valley (1 Kings 21). After Jeroboam ben Nebat, Ahab is judged to be the most wicked of the northern Israelite kings because of his erection of an Asherah in Samaria (1 Kgs 16:33; cf. 2 Kgs 17:16; and 21:3, which compares Manasseh's actions to those of Ahab). The choice of Ahab is particularly interesting. The Omride dynasty was overthrown by Jehu in 842 B.C.E. (see 2 Kings 9–10), and there is plenty of condemnation of the Jehide kings in the Deuteronomistic

History (2 Kings 11–15). Nevertheless, the Jehide kings maintained a policy of alliance with Assyria throughout much of their history following the reign of Jehu, and it was this policy that enabled Israel to emerge as the dominant power in the Syro-Israelite region throughout much of the mid-eighth century B.C.E. It was only when the Jehides were overthrown that Israel began its attempts to revolt against Assyria, which brought about the Assyrian invasions of the late-eighth century, the destruction of the northern kingdom of Israel, and subservience of Judah. Ahab and the house of Omri, on the other hand, were once allied with Aram to oppose the attempted invasion of the Assyrian monarch Shalmaneser III in 853 B.C.E., but later abandoned its alliance as it went to war with Aram over the trans-Jordanian territories in Gilead region (cf. 1 Kings 22). Because Israel abandoned its alliance with Aram, Ahab was killed in battle with the Arameans, the Omride dynasty was overthrown, Aram took control of Israel, and the situation was not rectified until the later Jehide kings, Jehoahaz, Jehoash, and Jeroboam, reestablished the Israelite alliance with Assyria (see 1 Kings 22–2 Kings 14). Like Ahab and the Omrides, Hezekiah had proved to be an unreliable ally, and the country suffered invasion as a result. Micah knew fully well the costs of such maneuvering; it cost him his home and probably the lives of most of his family and neighbors. The final statements concerning the desolation of the people and the hissing and scorn that they will endure reflect similar statements concerning the humiliation of the people in Deut 28:25, 37 (cf. Jer 18:16; 19:8; 25:9, 18; 29:18).

*Prophet's Expression of Confidence in Y*HWH*'s Faithfulness to Israel: 7:1-20*

Micah 7:1-20 constitutes the fourth section of the body of the book of Micah. As the conclusion of the "Prophet's Anticipation of YHWH's Plans for Zion" in Mic 1:2–7:20, Micah 7 expresses the prophet's confidence that YHWH will indeed act to realize the plans outlined throughout the book for Israel's and Judah's punishment as well as Zion's restoration at the center of the nations. The chapter is demarcated by the introductory ʾalĕlay lî, "Woe is me!" which is syntactically independent from the preceding appeal for the people's return to YHWH and expresses the prophet's concern over his perception of the degenerate state of the people. The chapter is generally considered to be two originally independent units, based upon the generic identification of verses 1-6 as a lament and verses 7-20 as a liturgical psalm or prophetic liturgy.[93] Nevertheless, they are clearly interrelated as the two major structural components of the present form of the chapter by the over-arching concern with YHWH's willingness to intervene on behalf of the people despite the problems outlined in verses 1-6.

Many scholars see this chapter as a late post-exilic addition to the book of Micah.[94] The basic reasons are the liturgical forms of the lament and the psalm of confidence, which would have their settings in the Jerusalem Temple, and the references to Abraham and Jacob, which ap-pear to presuppose the Pentateuchal narrative. Such views overlook the role of the Temple in pre-monarchic Judah, not only as a site for worship and sacrifice but as a site at which public figures can address the people as a whole on issues of importance (cf. Jeremiah 7). They also overlook the fact that major Pentateuchal figures were known among the people in pre-monarchic times (cf. Hosea 12, in which the prophet cites the Jacob tradition as part of his efforts to argue against continued alliance with Assyria) even if the Pentateuch had not yet achieved its present form. Overall, the chapter reflects the desperate circumstances of a city under siege, such as the 701 siege of Jerusalem by Sennacherib, in which food and other necessities are so scarce that no one can be trusted. It also represents the attempt of the prophet, himself a refugee in Jerusalem at the time of Sennacherib's siege, to ex-press his confidence that YHWH will indeed deliver the people from this situation of extreme threat. As subsequent tradition indicates, Micah was credited with convincing Hezekiah to take the appropriate action that would see to the deliverance of Jerusalem from the Assyrian threat (Jeremiah 26).

THE PROPHET'S LAMENT OVER THE CURRENT STATE OF THE PEOPLE: 7:1-6

Micah 7:1-6 constitutes the prophet's lament over the current state of the people. The passage begins in verse $1a\alpha^{1-2}$ with the formula, *'alĕlay lî*, "Woe is me!" which is syntactically independent from the pre-ceding appeal for Israel's return to YHWH and marks the beginning of an entirely new section that focuses on the degenerate state of the people. Verse 7 is tied to verses 1-6 syntactically by a conjunctive *waw*, "and," which prompts many scholars to argue that verse 7 must be considered together with verses 1-6.[95] Nevertheless, the first person

---

[93] See Renaud, *Formation* 345–6, for an overview of the scholarly discussion.

[94] For discussion of the date and compositional unity of the material in this chap-ter, see Renaud, *Formation* 352–7, 372–82.

[95] See Wolff, *Micah* 203, for discussion.

perspective of the verse and its expression of the prophet's confidence in YHWH marks it as the introduction to the psalm of confidence that follows in verses 8-20. Thus, the first person perspectives of both verses 1aα$^{1-2}$ and 7 indicate the two major components of the chapter in verses 1-6 and 7-20, and the conjunctive *waw* in verse 7 ties them together.

The introductory formula, *ʾalĕlay lî*, "Woe is me!" is rare in that it appears elsewhere only in Job 10:15. Nevertheless, it provides an appropriate introduction to the overall lamentation character of the passage in that it appears to be derived from the root *ʾll*, "to be weak, worthless," which is sometimes associated with *ʾlh*, "to wail." Verses 1α$^{3-6}$-4a then lay out the reasons for the prophet's lament beginning with the *kî*, "because, for," statement of verse 1α$^{3-6}$β, "for I have become like those gathering the summer fruit, like the gleanings of the vintage" (cf. NRSV, "for I have become like one who, after the summer fruit has been gathered, after the vintage has been gleaned"). The summer fruit and the vintage are among the last crops that are brought in at the end of the harvest season in the late summer or early fall, just prior to the festival of Sukkoth (Tabernacles) which marks the conclusion of the fruit harvest and the beginning of the rainy season. The following image concerning the lack of grape clusters and first-ripe figs calls to mind the practice of allowing the poor to glean the fields and vineyards for food (Deut 23:24-25; cf. Lev 19:9-10; see also Deut 25:4), particularly every seventh year when the fields lie fallow (Exod 23:11; cf. Leviticus 25). The biblical commands are designed to support the poor during times of hardship, but the situation that Micah describes is so desperate that these means are no longer available. Many interpreters charge the people described in this passage with greed or evil intent,[96] but the statements of the Assyrian officials in 2 Kgs 18:27/Isa 36:12 indicate the desperate circumstances of the siege, i.e., there simply is little or no food to be had. The prophet goes on in verse 2 to describe the disappearance of "the faithful" and "the upright" from the land; rather, he finds those who lie in wait for blood and hunt each other. Again, a siege with its attendant starvation tends to bring out the worst in people as they struggle, even against each other, to survive. A refugee such as Micah would likely find himself on the streets of the city scrounging for food and fighting off those with whom he was forced to compete. In verses 3-4a, he recounts the collapse of social order and hierarchy as even the officials and judges demand payment for their services—and perhaps for special consideration—and the powerful say whatever they like to achieve their interests. Siege and starvation have a way of making equals of everyone. The NRSV renders the final statement of verse 3,

---

[96] E.g., Allen, *Micah* 383–90.

"thus they pervert justice," in an attempt to render the meaning of the verb, *wayĕʿabbĕtûhā*, "and they weave it." This verb is meant to be read with the following similes in verse 4a that compare goodness and righteousness with briers and thorn bushes, i.e., goodness and righteousness are so interwoven or tangled up with evil (see verse 3) that they have become like thorn bushes which are impossible to untangle. In this sense, justice and social order have completely collapsed.

The second portion of the prophet's lament begins in verse 4b, in which he announces to the people that punishment has come upon them, i.e., in contrast to his remarks concerning his own situation and the reasons for it in verses 1-4a, verses 4b-6 point to what the people may expect. The experience of the refugee in time of siege will now become the experience of the entire city. The indications of the siege appear in the prophet's statements in verse 4b that "a day of watching you/your punishment has come; now their confusion is at hand." The reference "your punishment" (*pĕquddātĕkā*) apparently stands as an appositional specification of "watching you/your watchers" (*mĕṣappeykā*). According to Sennacherib's own accounts of his actions against Jerusalem in 701, he did not bring up his entire army, but only posted sufficient forces to molest those who attempted to pass and thereby restricted passage into and out of the city.[97] In verses 5-6, the prophet announces to the people that will not be able to trust even those closest to them in this time of extreme trial. At a time of starvation, verse 5 indicates that they will not be able to trust even their friends, their closest family members, or even their spouses. The reasons are outlined in verse 6 with a description of complete social breakdown in which the son despises the father, the daughter rises against the mother, the bride (rises) against the groom, and the people who live in one's own household become one's enemies. In such a situation, the prophet maintains that absolutely no one can be trusted.

THE PROPHET'S PSALM OF CONFIDENCE IN YHWH'S FIDELITY: 7:7-20

The prophet then turns to a presentation of the prophetic liturgy or psalm of confidence in YHWH's fidelity to Israel/Judah in Mic 7:7-20.[98]

[97] For Sennacherib's account, see Pritchard, *ANET* 288.
[98] For the definition of Mic 7:7-20 as a psalm, see Bernhard Stade, "Streiflichter auf die Entstehung der jetzigen Gestalt der alttestamenlichen Prophetenschriften," *ZAW* 23 (1903) 153–71. For the definition of this text as a prophetic liturgy, see Hermann Gunkel, "The Close of Micah: A Prophetical Liturgy. A Study in Literary History," *What Remains of the Old Testament and Other Essays*, trans. by A. K. Dallas

The introduction to the psalm in verse 7 is linked syntactically to the preceding material in verses 1-6 by the introductory conjunctive *waw* and the first person presentation of the speaker that corresponds to verse 1. Furthermore, the reference to the prophet's "watching" for YHWH (NRSV, "I will look to YHWH") employs the *piel* imperfect form of the verb *ʾăṣappeh*, "I will watch," which contrasts the prophet's actions with those of Jerusalem's besiegers, who are described as *mĕṣappeykā*, "your watchers/watching you,"in verse 4, i.e., while the Assyrians "watch" Jerusalem, Micah will "watch" for YHWH. Overall, verse 7 sets the basic theme of the prophet's psalm, YHWH hear the prophet and bring deliverance in this time of distress (cf. Hab 2:1, in which the prophet employs *ʾăṣappeh* to describe his standing watch to await YHWH's response to his complaints in Hab 1:2-4 and 1:12-17). The social setting for such standing watch is uncertain, although it may refer to a sort of vigil before the ark or the Temple to await divine oracular response to a petition by the prophet or psalmist (cf. Isaiah 37/2 Kings 19, in which Hezekiah enters the Temple to petition YHWH and receives a divine response through the prophet Isaiah, and Ezek 3:16-27, in which the prophet functions as a "sentinel for the house of Israel" [verse 17] or oracle diviner before the people; see also Exod 34:29-35, which describes Moses in a similar role).

Following the introduction in verse 7, the psalm proceeds according to four basic stanzas. Verses 8-10 relate the prophet's address to an unnamed enemy in which he expresses his confidence that YHWH will act to deliver him. Verses 11-13 relate the prophet's address to Jerusalem, advising it to prepare for the influx of people from abroad. Verses 14-17 relate the prophet's address to YHWH to show divine power on behalf of Israel. Finally, verses 18-20 relate the prophet's praise of YHWH for incomparability and fidelity in acting on behalf of Israel.

The prophet's expression of confidence in verses 8-10 begins with an address in verse 8aα to an unnamed enemy that calls upon it not to rejoice. The term for "my enemy" is feminine, *ʾōyabtî*, and appears in the Bible only here and in verse 10. There is no clear reference to the identity of the enemy, although it is not unusual for enemies to be personified as women in prophetic oracles (e.g., Philistia in Isa 14:29 or Edom in Lam 4:21; but note the masculine reference to Edom or Esau in Obad 12). In such a case, Jerusalem must be conceived as "the daughter of Jerusalem" in the present context (see verse 11). The psalmist's initial statement to the enemy not to rejoice is followed in verse 8aβb with two *kî* ("because, for") that provide reasons for the prohibition. The first

---

(London: George Allen and Unwin, 1928) 115–49. For a full overview of discussion, see J. T. Willis, "A Reapplied Prophetic Hope Oracle," *VTSup* 26 (1974) 64–76.

indicates that although the psalmist has fallen, the psalmist will rise once again having not been defeated. The second expresses the psalmist's confidence that YHWH will provide light even though the psalmist currently sits in darkness. The second cluster of statements in verse 9abα presupposes that YHWH has brought the enemy as a punishment for some perceived sin of the psalmist, i.e., the psalmist bears YHWH's wrath on account of having sinned against YHWH. But the verse also expresses the psalmist's confidence that once YHWH hears the facts of the case, justice will be done. The language here is forensic. The statement, "until he takes my side," employs verbal and noun forms of the root *ryb*, "to contend," which is used in reference to legal dispute or contention (e.g., Gen 31:36; Isa 3:13 [verb]; Exod 23:2, 3, 6; 2 Sam 15:2, 4 [noun]). Here it indicates that YHWH must first hear the psalmist's contention or case, after which YHWH will conclude that the psalmist deserves no further punishment. At that point, YHWH will "execute judgment (for me)," *ʿāśâ mišpāṭî*, i.e., act to redress the psalmist's situation. The results are expressed metaphorically once again with the imagery of light in verses 9bβ-10aα, in which YHWH will bring the psalmist out to the light to look upon YHWH's righteousness and the enemy will be covered in shame. The section concludes with the psalmist's repetition of the enemy's mocking question, "Where is YHWH your G–d?" which expresses the helplessness of the psalmist in a time of distress. The answer then follows in the assertion that her eyes will look upon the enemy as she is trampled in the mud of the streets.

Micah 7:11-13 then shifts to an address that is presumably directed to Jerusalem. At first glance, it is not entirely clear that this is the case because the initial second person feminine singular address form, "your walls" (*gĕdērāyik*), appears to continue the address to the feminine singular enemy of verses 8-10. Nevertheless, the identification of Assyria and Egypt as the lands from which people will come indicates that Jerusalem must be the addressee in this pericope. At this point, the psalmist employs the motif of enemy nations that will advance against Jerusalem, but the language is ambiguous enough to allow for a shift in perspective in which the threat posed by the enemy will become the basis for Israel's or Zion's redemption in verses 14-17 and 18-20. This, of course, is in keeping with the initial theme of the psalm that the psalmist has fallen, but will rise again after vindication from YHWH. The passage begins with three statements introduced by the formulaic expression, "a day" (*yôm*, verse 11a) or "(in) that day" (*yôm hahûʾ*, verse 11b; *yôm hahûʾ*, verse 12a), which appear to be a variation of the standard formula, *bayyôm hahûʾ*, "in that day." Verse 11a calls upon Jerusalem to rebuild its walls, presumably for defense against potential invaders. Verse 11b follows with a call to extend "the boundary." The meaning of the Hebrew expression *ḥōq* is rendered as "boundary" in keeping with the use of the term in Isa 5:14 and Jer 5:22, but it more properly means "statute, decree, authority." The statement apparently refers to extension of royal authority over outlying areas or even over peoples' houses within a city during a time of military emergency (cf. Isa 22:8-11, which describes the measures taken to strengthen the fortifications of Jerusalem, including the demolition of houses so that their stones could be used to fortify the walls of the city).

Verse 12 then states that "and unto you he/it will come" *(wĕ'ādeykā yābô²)*. There are problems in this statement, however, in that the second person addressee is now masculine singular, and there is no clear identification of that which will come. Most suggest that the masculine singular addressee should be read as the feminine singular addressee of verse 11a,[99] and that the coming threat must be understood as the people of the following nations that will come up against Jerusalem. Verse 12aβ-b specifies that this threat will come "from Assyria and the cities of Egypt and from Egypt to the River, from sea to sea and from mountain to mountain." The rendering of "Egypt" as *māṣōr* rather than the usual *miṣrayim* is sometimes questioned as the term *māṣōr* also means "fortress" or "siege,"[100] but this functions, whether deliberately or not, as a means to enhance the ambiguity of the language. The term *māṣōr* is used elsewhere in reference to Egypt (Isa 19:6; 2 Kgs 19:24/Isa 37:25), but the meaning of the term as "fortress" or "siege" aids in conveying the threat that is posed against the city (see the use of this term in Mic 4:14). The reference to "the River" indicates the Euphrates River of Mesopotamia (see Gen 15:18; Deut 1:7; Josh 1:4; 2 Sam 8:3; 1 Chr 18:3), and thereby plays upon the traditional ideal boundaries of Israel, which extends from the Euphrates River to Egypt (Gen 15:18; Numbers 34; 2 Samuel 8; Ezek 47:13-20). It is at this point that the meaning of the verse becomes somewhat ambiguous, i.e., do the nations come to threaten Jerusalem or to witness its restoration as indicated in verses 14-17? In keeping with the general tenor of the psalm, this ambiguity is probably deliberate. The last statement of this pericope that "the land/ earth will be desolate because of its inhabitants" reinforces the ambiguity. The Hebrew word *hā²āreṣ* can refer either to "the land" of Israel in particular (e.g., Gen 12:1) or to the world or "earth" at large (e.g., Gen 1:2). The verse refers either to the devastation of Israel or to the devastation of the world at large from which the nations come, and the deeds that caused this devastation can be attributed either to Israel or to the nations. Although these statements will be read in relation to Israel

---

[99] See BHS note; Rudolph, *Micha* 129; Wolff, *Micah* 213.
[100] Cf. Wolff, *Micah* 224–5.

from the beginning of the psalm, they will be understood in relation to the earth and the nations as the reader approaches its end.

Micah 7:14-17 then shifts to an address directed to Yhwh as indicated by the second person masculine address forms and the role of the addressee as the One who delivers the people of Israel from the threat of the nations. The initial imperative statement, "shepherd your people with your staff . . ." builds upon the earlier metaphor of Israel as sheep that are to be led first into exile (Mic 2:12-13) and then into restoration (Mic 4:6-10; 5:3 [NRSV: 5:4]) under the leadership of Yhwh or the anointed king. The NRSV translation of verse 14aα⁴⁻⁵, "the flock that belongs to you," masks the term *naḥălātekā*, "your inheritance," which signifies Israel's status as Yhwh's special possession (e.g., Deut 4:20; 9:26, 29; 1 Kgs 8:51, 53; 2 Kgs 21:14). The tranquil scene of Yhwh's sheep settling or residing alone in the "forest" or "the garden land (*karmel*, generally understood to be vineyard country, especially in the hills overlooking the Mediterranean just south of Haifa) envisions a people that is not molested by invaders (cf. Mic 5:3 [NRSV: 5:4]; cf. Isa 11:6-9) and prepares the reader for the following statements concerning Yhwh's deliverance of the people from the threat of the nations. The shift from metaphor to national reality begins in verse 14b, which calls for "the flock" to graze "in Bashan and Gilead as in days of old." The Bashan refers to the plains of southwest Syria that overlook the Sea of Galilee, roughly equivalent to the modern Golan heights. The territory has always been good grazing land (cf. Ps 22:12; Amos 4:1; Ezek 27:6). The Gilead refers to the Israelite region of the Trans-Jordan south of the Sea of Galilee and north of the Dead Sea, and it is likewise well suited for grazing (Num 32:1; Cant 6:5). The Gilead was assigned to the tribes of Manasseh, Reuben, and Gad (see Joshua 13). Both the Bashan and the Gilead were lost first to Aram in the ninth century (1 Kgs 22:3; Amos 1:3) and later to Assyria in the eighth century (2 Kgs 15:29). Micah 7:14b apparently envisions the return of these territories to Israelite control. Verse 15 then defines "the days of old" in verse 14 in reference to the Exodus from Egypt. This shift provides a means to establish the basis for the claim that Yhwh will act with "miracles" or "marvelous things" (*niplāʾôt*, cf. Exod 3:20; Ps 78:11) to redeem Israel from the threat of the nations in the present just as Yhwh did in the past. Verse 16 focuses on the shame, astonishment, and amazement of the nations that threaten the people of Israel when they see Yhwh's miraculous acts of deliverance. The witness of the nations is also an important element of the Exodus traditions in which Egypt and the rest of the nations tremble in dismay and fear as Yhwh defeats the Egyptians and leads the people to Yhwh's sanctuary (Exod 15:1-19, esp. 11-18). Having been left speechless and deaf by Yhwh's deliverance of Israel, the enemy nations are only able to "lick" the dust like snakes or other crawling creatures. Verse 17b concludes with a depiction of their trembling in their own fortresses (literally, "enclosures") as they stand in dread and fear of YHWH.

Finally, Mic 7:18-20 concludes the psalm (and the book of Micah) with the psalmist's/prophet's praise of YHWH's incomparability for divine forgiveness, fidelity, and mercy on behalf of the people of Israel. In this regard, these verses express the rhetorical goal of the book in that the punishment that the people currently suffer will turn to forgiveness and restoration in the future. The psalmist continues to draw upon the Exodus tradition with the opening rhetorical question addressed to YHWH, "Who is a G–d like you . . . ?" which corresponds to the question posed in Exod 15:11, "Who is like you among the gods, O YHWH?" (cf. Jer 10:7; Ps 89:9 [NRSV: 89:8]). But whereas the Exodus tradition focuses on YHWH's holiness, power, and miraculous actions on behalf of Israel, Mic 7:18-20 focuses upon YHWH's pardoning the sins of the people, and thereby returns to the initial theme of the prophetic liturgy in verse 9. The references to YHWH's "pardoning iniquity *(nōśēʾ ʿāwôn),*" "passing over transgression *(ʿōbēr ʿal pešʿa),*" "not retaining anger *(lōʾ heḥĕzîq lāʿad ʾappô),*" and "delights in showing clemency *(ḥāpēṣ ḥesed)*" rehearse the major themes and vocabulary of Exod 34:6-7,[101] in which YHWH reveals the divine self to Moses, stating, "YHWH, YHWH, a G–d merciful and gracious, slow to anger *(ʾerek ʾappayim),* and abounding in steadfast love and faithfulness *(wĕrab ḥesed wĕʾemet),* keeping steadfast love for the thousandth generation, forgiving iniquity and transgression and sin *(nōśēʾ ʿāwôn wāpešʿa wĕḥaṭ ṭāʾâ)* . . . ." Verse 19 emphasizes the return of YHWH's mercy by employing the verb *rḥm,* "to have/show mercy" (cf. Exod 34:6, *ʾēl raḥûm,* "a merciful G–d"). It metaphorically describes YHWH's treading iniquities underfoot and casting sins into the depths of the sea as an expression of the psalmist's confidence that YHWH will act on Israel's behalf. The concluding statement of the liturgy and the book in verse 20 emphasizes YHWH's fidelity to the covenant with the people of Israel by calling to mind YHWH's "faithfulness *(ʾemet,* literally, 'truth') to Jacob," "unswerving loyalty *(ḥesed)* to Abraham," and the promises "sworn to our ancestors from the days of old." This, of course, recounts the promises made by YHWH to Abraham (Gen 12; 15; 17) and to Jacob (Gen 28; 35) that they will become a great nation and possess the land of Israel in covenant with YHWH forever. Interpreters cannot be certain that the present forms of the chapters in Genesis that relate these promises were available to Micah or the writer of this liturgy, but certainly some form of these traditions were extant

---

[101] Cf. Fishbane, *Biblical Interpretation* 349–50.

in either oral or written form at the time that it was composed. In essence, the author of Mic 7:7-20, and indeed of the entire book of Micah, emphasizes YHWH's faithfulness to the covenant with Israel as the basis for the claim that YHWH will intervene to turn the present situation of punishment and calamity into one of restoration, power, and security. The concluding reference to "the days of old" refers back to the similar reference at the end of verse 14 to tie together the Mican motif of YHWH as the shepherd who guides Israel through punishment and restoration with the references to Israel's past traditions of the Exodus and the promises to the ancestors. In essence, the writer looks to YHWH's faithfulness to Israel in the past as the basis for the claim that YHWH will remain faithful to Israel in the present and the future.

FOR FURTHER READING

COMMENTARIES

Allen, Leslie. *The Books of Joel, Obadiah, Jonah and Micah*. The New International Commentary on the Old Testament. Grand Rapids: Eerdmans, 1976.

Hillers, Delbert. *Micah*. Hermeneia. Minneapolis. Fortress, 1984.

Mays, James Luther. *Micah: A Commentary*. Old Testament Library. Philadelphia: Westminster, 1976.

Renaud, B. *Michée, Sophonie, Nahum*. Sources bibliques. Paris: Gabalda, 1987.

Rudolph, Wilhelm. *Micha–Nahum–Habakuk–Zephanja*. Kommentar zum Alten Testament XIII/3. Gütersloh: Gerd Mohn, 1975.

Simundson, Daniel J. "The Book of Micah: Introduction, Commentary, and Reflections," *The New Interpreter's Bible. Volume VII: Introduction to Apocalyptic Literature, Daniel, The Twelve Prophets*, ed. Leander E. Keck et al. Nashville: Abingdon, 1996.

Smith, Ralph L. *Micah–Malachi*. Word Biblical Commentary 32. Waco: Word, 1984.

Vuilleumier, René. "Michée," *Michée, Nahoum, Habacuc, Sophonie*. By René Vuilleumier and Carl-A. Keller. Commentaire de l'ancien Testament XIb. Neuchâtel: Delachaux et Niestlé, 1971.

Wolff, Hans Walter. *Micah: A Commentary*. Translated by Gary Stansell. Continental Commentaries. Minneapolis: Augsburg, 1990.

STUDIES

Beyerlin, Walter. *Die Kulttraditionen Israels in der Verkündigung des Propheten Micah*. Forschungen zur Religion und Literatur des Alten und Neuen Testaments 72. Göttingen: Vandenhoeck & Ruprecht, 1959.

Hagstrom, David Gerald. *The Coherence of the Book of Micah: A Literary Analysis*. SBL Dissertation Series, 89. Atlanta: Scholars Press, 1988.

King, Philip J. *Amos, Hosea, Micah—An Archaeological Commentary*. Philadelphia: Westminster, 1988.

Lescow, T. "Redaktionsgeschichtliche Analyse von Micha 1–5," *ZAW* 84 (1972) 46–85.

Lescow, T. "Redaktionsgeschichtliche Analyse von Micha 6–7," *ZAW* 84 (1972) 182–212.

Luker, Lamontte M. "Beyond Form-Criticism: The Relation of Doom and Hope Oracles in Micah 2–6," *Hebrew Annual Review* 11 (1987) 285–301.

Mason, R. *Micah, Nahum, Obadiah*. Old Testament Guides. Sheffield: JSOT Press, 1991.

Renaud, B. *La Formation du livre de Michée. Tradition et actualisation*. Études bibliques. Paris: Gabalda, 1977.

Shaw, Charles S. *The Speeches of Micah: A Rhetorical-Historical Analysis*. Journal for the Study of the Old Testament Supplement Series 145. Sheffield: JSOT Press, 1993.

Wagenaar, Jan Aart, *Oordeel en Heil. Een Onderzoek naar Samenhang Tussen de Heils-en Onheilsprofetieën in Micha 2–5/Judgement and Salvation. A Study into the Relationship between the Oracles of Hope and the Oracles of Doom in Micah 2–5*. Ph.D. dissertation. Utrecht: University of Utrecht, 1995.

Willi-Plein, Ina. *Vorformen der Schriftexegese innerhalb des Alten Testaments*. Beiheft zur Zeitschrift für die alttestamentliche Wissenschaft 123. Berlin and New York: Walter de Gruyter, 1971.

Willis, John T. "The Structure of the Book of Micah," *Svensk Exegetisk Årsbok* 34 (1969) 5–42.

Wolff, Hans Walter. *Micah the Prophet*. Translated by Ralph D. Gehrke. Philadelphia: Fortress, 1981.

NAHUM

NAHUM

Overview

The book of Nahum is the seventh book in both the Masoretic and the Septuagint versions of the Book of the Twelve. The superscription of the book presents no explicit information concerning its historical setting, but it identifies the contents of the book as "an oracle concerning Nineveh, the book of the vision of Nahum the Elkoshite."[1] Nineveh was established as the capital city of the Assyrian empire during the reign of Sennacherib (705–681 B.C.E.) until the city fell to a combined assault by the Babylonians and Medes in 612 B.C.E. The book of Nahum is designed to refute the view that YHWH is powerless or unjust, particularly in light of Assyria's destruction of the northern kingdom of Israel in the late-eighth century and the imposition of its rule over Judah and Jerusalem throughout most of the seventh century B.C.E.[2] It presupposes the destruction of Nineveh, either as an actual or an anticipated event, and points to Nineveh's downfall as an act of YHWH that demonstrates YHWH's power and justice as the true master of all creation. It follows Micah in the Masoretic version of the Book of the Twelve. It therefore points to the ultimate downfall of Assyria following Micah's presentation of YHWH's plans to restore Judah and Jerusalem as a dominant force at the center of the nations following the punishment of Judah and Jerusalem just as Samaria and Israel were punished. Nahum's announcement of the downfall of Nineveh marks the beginning of that

[1] For overviews of critical discussion concerning the book of Nahum, see Mason, *Micah, Nahum, Obadiah* 57–84; Spronk, *Nahum* 1–18; Kevin J. Cathcart, "Nahum, Book of," *ABD* IV:998-1000.

[2] For the following assessment of the structure and purposes of the book of Nahum, see Marvin A. Sweeney, "Concerning the Structure and Generic Character of the Book of Nahum," *ZAW* 104 (1992) 364–77.

process, and the following books of Habakkuk, Zephaniah, Haggai, Zechariah, and Malachi present the various stages by which the rest of the process will be realized. Nahum follows Joel, Obadiah, and Jonah, all of which are concerned with various issues pertaining to the nations in the Septuagint version of the Book of the Twelve. Jonah presents YHWH's willingness to show mercy to a repentant Nineveh, but the placement of Nahum after Jonah indicates that Nineveh failed to follow through and suffered the consequences as a result. Again, Nahum precedes Habakkuk, Zephaniah, Haggai, Zechariah, and Malachi in the LXX sequence of the Twelve. It thereby marks the beginning of punishment against the nations and the purging of Jerusalem prior to its restoration over the nations at the end of the sequence.

Apart from the contents of the book, nothing is known of the prophet Nahum. He is not mentioned elsewhere in the Hebrew Bible. The name is derived from the root *nḥm*, which means "to comfort, have compassion," and apparently is related to the name Nehemiah which is derived from the same root. The superscription of the book identifies Nahum as an Elkoshite, a gentilic name that is derived from the place name Elkosh. Elkosh is likewise never mentioned elsewhere in the Bible nor is the site known. It has been variously identified as the Galilean village of Elcesai or Hilkesi, perhaps the modern site of El-Kauzeh, by Jerome. The Greek name of the town Capernaum, located on the western shore of the Kinneret or Sea of Galilee, is derived from the Hebrew expression *kĕpār nāḥûm*, "village of Nahum," but there is no definitive identification of the town with the prophet or Elkosh. The modern Turkish town of Al-Qush, located near the modern city of Mosul, next to the site of ancient Nineveh, is also identified with the prophet. Other potential locations for Elkosh include a site in the territory of southern Judah or Simeon and Beit Jibrin, a modern Syrian site near Begabar. Nahum is frequently identified as a so-called "cult prophet" of the Jerusalem Temple, in large part because he condemns Judah's enemies rather than Judah itself, but such a contention is based upon a very narrow view of the social role of prophets that maintains that true prophets in the pre-exilic period would only speak messages of judgment against Israel and Judah. Prophets are not defined by their criticism of Israel or Judah; they are defined by their ability to speak on behalf of YHWH regardless of whether they criticize or support Israel and Judah. Nahum may well have been a cult prophet, but this role does not dictate the contents of his message.[3]

---

[3] For the contention that Nahum is a cult prophet, see esp. Jörg Jeremias, *Kultprophetie und Gerichtsverkündigung in der späten Königszeit Israels*, WMANT, vol. 35 (Neukirchen-Vluyn: Neukirchener, 1970) 11–55.

Although the superscription provides no explicit information concerning the setting of Nahum's prophecy, the book refers both to the fall of Thebes (Hebrew, *No-Amon;* see Nah 3:8-10), which took place in 663 B.C.E., as well as to the fall of Nineveh. Many scholars have therefore attempted to argue that the setting of the book must be placed in relation to the Assyrian conquest of Thebes, which established Assyrian control over Egypt and represented the apex of Assyrian power in the world.[4] The book of Nahum would therefore emerge as a diatribe against the Assyrians that would express the prophet's bitterness and hope for the downfall of the city. There are no grounds for such a contention, however, as the purpose of the reference to the conquest of Thebes is clearly retrospective and comparative. The prophet refers back to a known event as a basis for making his claims about the significance of Nineveh's collapse. Indeed, he portrays Thebes as a city surrounded by the waters of the Nile that provided protection. Although the Nile did run through Thebes, such a description appears to relate much more closely to Nineveh's situation in which the waters of the Khusur canal ran through the city and were used to fill the moats that provided additional protection for the city's walls and ramparts. Although the accounts of Nineveh's destruction by Diodorus Siculus, who indicated that Nineveh was destroyed by a flood, are not entirely trustworthy, control of the water system would have been a key factor in the Babylonian/Median siege and assault against Nineveh. Given the very powerful fortifications of this 1800 acre site, the ability to control the flow of water into the moats would give the attackers an advantage that would enable them to undermine the walls or to scale them, and take the city by frontal attack.[5]

The ability to point to the downfall of the city, whether real or anticipated, is a key element in the prophet's rhetorical strategy to convince his audience that YHWH is indeed the powerful and just ruler of all creation who punishes Nineveh for its abuse of other nations. Following the superscription of the book in Nah 1:1, the balance of the book is presented as the prophet's *maśśāʾ,* "oracle, pronouncement," in which he attempts to convince his audience to abandon their doubts about YHWH's impotence or injustice and recognize YHWH as the cause of Nineveh's demise. The prophet employs elements of the disputation

[4] For discussion, see Mason, *Micah, Nahum, Obadiah* 59–61.

[5] See Amélie Kuhrt, *The Ancient Near East, c. 3000–330 B.C.* (New York: Routledge, 1998) 540–6; David Stronach and Stephen Lumsden, "UC Berkeley's Excavations at Nineveh," *BA* 55 (1992) 227–33 (note esp. the discussion of Halzi gate, which was clearly refortified in anticipation of an assault and is the site where the corpses of over a dozen defenders of the city were found where they fell in battle).

genre, an argumentative speech form in which the speaker challenges a contention for the audience and attempts to persuade them to adopt a counter-thesis,[6] to present the oracle as a refutation speech concerning Judah's and Assyria's perception of Yhwh's impotence. The address forms indicate that the oracle comprises three basic parts. The initial second person masculine plural address to Judah and Assyria in Nah 1:2-10 challenges their low estimation of Yhwh's power. It first presents a partial acrostic in verses 2-8 that asserts Yhwh's power and justice in taking vengeance against enemies, and follows with a rhetorical question in verses 9-10 that likewise asserts Yhwh's power and will to punish enemies. The second person feminine singular address to Judah in Nah 1:11–2:1 [NRSV: 1:11-15] asserts that the end of Assyrian oppression is an act of Yhwh. The initial statement in verse 11 asserts that Judah has misperceived Yhwh, verses 12-14 presents speeches by Yhwh concerning the end of Assyrian oppression and the destruction of the Assyrian king, and Nah 2:1 [NRSV: 1:15] calls upon Judah to celebrate the cessation of evil or worthlessness in her midst. Finally, the address in Nah 2:2–3:19 [NRSV: 2:1–3:19], first to Nineveh in Nah 2:2–3:17 [NRSV: 2:1–3:17] (second person feminine singular) and then to the Assyrian king in Nah 3:18-19 (second person masculine singular) in Nah 2:2–3:19 [NRSV: 2:1–3:19], explicitly identifies the fall of Nineveh as an act of Yhwh that was brought about to punish Assyria for its abusive treatment of other nations.

Clearly, the prophet's rhetorical strategy depends upon the ability to point to Nineveh's fall as a demonstrable event that has already taken place or is imminent. This would indicate that the book of Nahum is to be dated to 612 B.C.E., either immediately before or after the actual fall of Nineveh to the Babylonians and Medes. From the standpoint of the book of Nahum, the fall of Nineveh represents an act of justice in which the oppressor has finally been stopped and punished for its crimes. Insofar as Yhwh is the one who brings such justice about, Yhwh emerges as the true power of the world.

The Superscription: 1:1

The superscription for the book of Nahum appears in Nah 1:1. It is structurally and generically distinct from Nah 1:2–3:19 in that it serves as an introduction that identifies the following material in terms of its

---

[6] Sweeney, *Isaiah 1–39* 519; A. Graffy, *A Prophet Confronts His People*, AnBib, vol. 104 (Rome: Pontifical Biblical Institute, 1984); D. F. Murray, "The Rhetoric of Disputation: Re-examination of a Prophetic Genre," *JSOT* 38 (1987) 95–121.

genre, subject matter, and author, i.e., "An oracle concerning Nineveh, the book of the vision of Nahum the Elqoshite."[7] Many commentators note the dual nature of the superscription and argue that it is the result of redactional activity in which an early reference to "an oracle *(maśśāʾ)* concerning Nineveh" has been specified by the addition of the reference to "the book *(seper)* of the vision *(ḥāzôn)* of Nahum the Elqoshite."[8] There is a certain ambiguity to the term *maśśāʾ*, "oracle, pronouncement" as it is a technical term for a prophetic oracle but scholars have had difficulty in defining its precise nature. The term appears throughout prophetic literature (Isa 13:1; 14:28; 15:1; 17:1; 19:1; 21:1, 11, 13; 22:1; 23:1; 30:6; Jer 23:33, 34, 36, 38; Ezek 12:10; Nah 1:1; Hab 1:1; Zech 9:1; 12:1; cf. 2 Kgs 9:25), and appears to be derived from the verb *nśʾ*, "to lift up," which refers to "lifting up" or "raising" the voice to deliver a prophetic oracle (see Num 23:7, 18; 24:3, 15, 20, 21, 23). Weis' recent study of the *maśśāʾ* argues that it is a type of prophetic discourse that attempts to explain how YHWH's actions are manifested in human affairs, although it seems to have no specific structural or literary characteristics.[9] The specification of the "oracle concerning Nineveh" as "the book of the vision of Nahum the Elqoshite" adds two other generic terms, "book" *(seper)* and "vision" *(ḥāzôn)*. The term *seper* refers generally to a "book" or "scroll" and appears to have little impact on the characterization of Nahum other than as a self-contained entity or discrete "book" that was composed independently of other writings. The term *ḥāzôn* appears elsewhere in prophetic superscriptions Isa 1:1; Obad 1; cf. 2 Chr 32:32), and functions generally as a generic term for prophetic activity and experience (e.g., Isa 29:7; Jer 23:16; Ezek 12:24; Hos 12:11 [NRSV: 12:10]; Mic 3:6; Hab 2:2; Dan 1:17; 9:24; Ps 89:20 [NRSV: 89:19]; Prov 29:18). Overall, the term appears to include both visual and auditory experience. It may be related to the interpretation of dreams (1 Sam 3:1; Isa 29:7; Dan 1:17), although it characterizes the contents of entire prophetic books (Isa 1:1; cf. Isa 2:1). Its inclusion in the superscription for Nahum may indicate an interest in explicating the meaning of the semi-acrostic psalm in Nah 1:2-8, in which the psalm constitutes the *maśśāʾ* and the rest of the book constitutes the *ḥāzôn*, which explains the meaning of the psalm in relation to the fall of Assyria. Neither the *maśśāʾ*

---

[7] See Gene M. Tucker, "Prophetic Superscriptions and the Growth of the Canon," *Canon and Authority*, ed. G. W. Coats and B. O. Long (Philadelphia: Fortress, 1977) 56–70.

[8] E.g., Seybold, *Nahum, Habakuk, Zephanja* 17–8; Renaud, *Michée, Sophonie, Nahum* 274–5.

[9] Richard D. Weis, "The Genre *Maśśāʾ* in the Hebrew Bible" (Ph.D. diss., Claremont Graduate School, 1986).

nor the *ḥāzôn* has a specific literary structure, but appears as an under-lying concern or pattern in texts that display a variety of structures. In the present instance, the following material in Nah 1:2–3:19 conveys the *maśśāʾ* or *ḥāzôn* within a refutation speech that points to the down-fall of Nineveh as an act of YHWH. The *maśśāʾ* therefore functions as part of an effort to convince the audience to abandon views of YHWH's im-potence.

The superscription specifies that the book is concerned with Nineveh, but it provides no chronological information. Nineveh was established as the capital of the Assyrian empire from the reign of Sennacherib (705–681 B.C.E.) until the fall of the city—and the Assyrian empire—to the Babylonians and Medes in 612 B.C.E.[10] It replaced the older capital city of Assur, apparently to provide the Assyrian kings with a more favorable geographical position from which to rule the westward ex-panding empire. It is identified with Tel Kuyunjik, located on the east bank of the Tigris River across from modern Mosul, which placed it along the major north-south trade route in the region so that it straddled the major east-west land route at the foot of the Kurdish mountains. Sennacherib rebuilt the city with a massive imperial palace, a major processional way, and a system of aqueducts and canals to irrigate his extensive gardens. The city was heavily fortified with a massive wall and towers that enclosed the entire 1800 acre site.

The prophet Nahum is not mentioned elsewhere in the Hebrew Bible. Likewise, the name Nahum is not attested elsewhere in the He-brew Bible, although the LXX reads the name Rehum in Ezra 2:2 as Naoum, the Greek equivalent of Nahum. The name is derived from the root *nḥm*, which means "to comfort, have compassion," and appears to be related to the name Nehemiah which is derived from the same root. The designation of Nahum as the "Elqoshite," *hāʾelqōšî*, employs a gen-tilic form that apparently refers to a place name, Elqosh or Elkosh, which is not mentioned elsewhere in the Bible.[11] The site of Elqosh is not known, but it has been identified with various locations. Jerome identifies it with the Galilean village of Elcesi or Hilkesei, perhaps to be identified with the modern site of el-Kauzeh. Likewise, the Greek name Capernaum, located on the western shore of the Kinneret/Sea of Galilee, is derived from the Hebrew, *kĕpār nāḥûm*, "village of Nahum." The modern Turkish town, "Al-Qush," located near Mosul, is also identi-fied with the prophet. Other locations identified with Elqosh include a site in the southern part of Judah or Simeon and Beit Jibrin, near Be-gabar in modern Syria.

[10] See A. Kirk Grayson, "Nineveh," *ABD* IV:1118-9.
[11] See Yoshitaka Kobayashi, "Elkosh," *ABD* II:476.

Although the superscription supplies no date for the oracle, the prophet's portrayal of Nineveh's downfall suggests that the oracle was written in relation to the fall of the city in 612 B.C.E., either shortly before or shortly after the event. Some interpreters date the book in relation to the fall of Thebes to Assyria in 667 or 663 B.C.E. based on the reference to Thebes' downfall in Nah 3:8,[12] but the rhetorical structure of the book indicates that Thebes is mentioned only as a comparison to the fall of Nineveh. As the following commentary demonstrates, Nah 1:2–3:19 is formulated as a refutation to those who maintain that YHWH is powerless, and it makes its argument by asserting that YHWH is responsible for the downfall of Nineveh. Insofar as the force of the argument depends upon the ability to point to the actual downfall of Nineveh, whether it is imminent or already accomplished, the book must be dated near to 612 B.C.E.

Maśśāʾ Proper:
Refutation Speech concerning Judah's and
Assyria's Perception of YHWH's Impotence: 1:2–3:19

The main body of the book appears in Nah 1:2–3:19, which is formulated as a prophetic refutation speech.[13] The refutation is a component of the larger disputation genre, an argumentative rhetorical form which is designed to examine contrasting points of view and to make a decision as to which represents the better position, point of view, or option for action.[14] Examples of the genre appear in the various speeches of Job, in which the reasons for Job's suffering are examined; Gen 31:36-43, in which Jacob challenges Laban's attempts to accuse him of wrongdoing; and especially in the prophetic literature where a prophet argues against a prevailing viewpoint and attempts to persuade the audience to adopt an alternative view (e.g., Isa 8:16–9:6 [NRSV: 8:16–9:7]; 40:12-17; Ezek 18:1-20; Mic 2:6-11; Hag 1:2-11; Mal 1:2-5; 1:6–2:9; 2:10-16; 2:17–3:7; 3:8-12; 3:9-24). The disputation genre generally includes three components as part of its basic "deep" or "conceptual" structure: the

[12] E.g., Spronk, *Nahum* 12-3; Keller, *Michée, Nahoum, Habacuc, Sophonie* 102–5.

[13] See Marvin A. Sweeney, "Concerning the Structure and Generic Character of the Book of Nahum," *ZAW* 104 (1992) 364–77.

[14] For discussion of the disputation genre, see Adrian Graffy, *A Prophet Confronts His People: The Disputation Speech in the Prophets*, AnBib, vol. 104 (Rome: Pontifical Biblical Institute, 1984); D. F. Murray, "The Rhetoric of Disputation: Re-examination of a Prophetic Genre," *JSOT* 38 (1987) 95–121.

statement of the thesis or proposal that is to be challenged; the statement of the counter-thesis or alternative proposal for which the speaker
argues; and the refutation or argumentation in which the speaker attempts to challenge the initial thesis and argue on behalf of the counter-
thesis.

Nahum 1:2–3:19 is designed to challenge and refute the notion that
YHWH is powerless by pointing to the fall of Nineveh as an act of YHWH.
By arguing this point, the prophet is able to demonstrate that YHWH is
indeed powerful and that YHWH is just insofar as Nineveh's demise is an
act of punishment for Nineveh's past actions of oppression against Israel. Because of its shifting address forms, uncertainties concerning the
meaning of the term Belial in Nah 1:11 and 2:1 [NRSV: 1:15], the presence
of the partial acrostic in Nah 1:2-8, and various philological problems
in the first chapter, the structure of the book has been very difficult to
assess.[15] Close attention to the address forms and the rhetorical forms
and functions of the various statements in chapter 1, however, points to
a basic three-part literary structure that conveys the basic refutational
form of the book. Nahum 1:2-10 constitutes an address directed to both
Judah and Assyria that employs the partial acrostic hymn in Nah 1:2-8
to challenge the prevailing view that YHWH is powerless to punish enemies. Nah 1:11–2:1 [NRSV: 1:11-15] constitutes an address to Judah in
which the prophet asserts that the end of Assyrian oppression is an act
of YHWH. Finally, Nah 2:2–3:19 [NRSV: 2:1–3:19] constitutes addresses to
both Assyria and the Assyrian king in which the prophet asserts that the
fall of Nineveh is an act of YHWH that is intended to punish Nineveh for
its oppressive treatment of Israel.

Address to Judah and Assyria Challenging
Their Low Estimation of YHWH: 1:2-10

Nahum 1:2-10 constitutes the first major component of Nahum's
maśśāʾ, in which the prophet addresses both Judah and Assyria and
challenges their view of YHWH's powerlessness. In order to make this
challenge, the prophet employs a hymn in verses 2-8 that extols YHWH's
power to punish enemies throughout the entire cosmos and a rhetorical question in verses 9-10 that builds upon the hymn to demand that
the audience reconsider its view of YHWH. Judah and Assyria are not
explicitly mentioned as the addressees for the prophet's speech, but

---

[15] For discussion of the problems in establishing the structure of Nahum, see
Coggins, *Nahum, Obadiah, Esther* 6–8.

they apparently are the subjects of the second masculine plural address forms that are employed in this passage. They are mentioned explicitly in the following addresses to Judah in Nah 1:11–2:1 [NRSV: 1:15] (see esp. Nah 2:1 [NRSV: 1:15]), which employs second person feminine singular address forms throughout, and to Assyria in Nah 2:2–3:19 [NRSV: 2:1–3:19] (see esp. Nah 2:9 [NRSV: 2:8]; 3:1, which refer to Nineveh and the bloody city, and Nah 3:18, which refers to the king of Assyria), which employ second person feminine address forms for Nineveh and second masculine singular address forms for the king of Assyria.

The passage is demarcated initially by the appearance of the hymn in verses 2-8 and by the very clear relationship between the question in verses 9-10 concerning YHWH's power and the portrayal of that power in the hymn, i.e., once verses 2-8 portray YHWH's power to punish enemies, the question asks the audience what it thinks of YHWH now that YHWH's capacity to punish is evident. Whereas the question is formulated as a second person masculine plural address, the following address to Judah in Nah 1:11–2:1 [NRSV: 1:11-15] is formulated with second feminine singular address forms. Nahum 1:11–2:1 [NRSV: 1:11-15] attempts to demonstrate that Judah's past view of YHWH's powerlessness is wrong by announcing the end of Judah's affliction.

The hymn in verses 2-8 asserts YHWH's power and capacity to punish enemies throughout the cosmos. It is generally recognized as a partial acrostic composition because each of its major stanzas begins with a successive letter of the Hebrew alphabet from *Aleph* to *Kaph*. There are problems with this view, however, because the sequence of letters is not consistent throughout the entire hymn, i.e., the stanza beginning with *Aleph* is much longer than the other stanzas and seems to emphasize words that begin with *Nun; Daleth* is missing in the sequence; and *Zayin* and *Yodh* do not appear as the first letter of their respective stanzas. Many have attempted to reconstruct a full alphabetic acrostic hymn, but the present text simply does not provide the necessary evidence for such a reconstruction.[16] Nevertheless, the alphabetical sequence does appear in verses 2-8, despite the above-mentioned problems, but no one has ever successfully explained why an acrostic that ranges only from *Aleph* to *Kaph* should appear, why words with the letter *Nun* should be emphasized at the outset, and why the disruptions in the sequence appear.

The stanza beginning with the letter *Aleph* appears in verses 2-3a, "A jealous and avenging G–d is YHWH (*ʾl qannô wĕnōqēm yhwh*) . . ." The *Aleph* appears in the initial word in the stanza, "G–d (*ʾl*), and the letter

[16] For full discussion of the issue, see Michael H. Floyd, "The Chimerical Acrostic of Nahum 1:1-10," *JBL* 113 (1994) 421–37.

Nun appears in the second qualification of G–d/Yhwh as "avenging *(wĕnōqēm,* literally, 'and avenging')." The letter *Nun* also appears at the beginning of each of the next three statements concerning Yhwh's power, "Yhwh is avenging *(nōqēm yhwh)* and wrathful"; "Yhwh takes vengeance *(nōqēm yhwh)* on his adversaries"; and "and rages *(wĕnôtēr)* against his enemies." The *Nun* also plays a prominent role in the last statement of the initial stanza, "Yhwh is slow to anger, but great in power, and Yhwh will by no means clear the guilty *(wĕnaqqēh lōʾ yĕnaqqeh yhwh)."* The significance of this emphasis on *Nun* is unknown, although many scholars observe that it is also the first letter of the names Nineveh and Nahum. It may indicate that Yhwh's wrath against enemies is directed against this city in the book of Nahum.

It is also noteworthy that the statement in verse 3a, "Yhwh is slow to anger, but great in power, and Yhwh will by no means clear the guilty," appears to be drawn from the statement of Yhwh's attributes to Moses in Exod 34:6-7,

> Yhwh, Yhwh, a G–d merciful and gracious, slow to anger, and abounding in steadfast love and faithfulness, keeping steadfast love for thousands, forgiving iniquity and transgression and sin, yet by no means clearing the guilty, but visiting the iniquity of the parents upon the children and the children's children, to the third and fourth generation."[17]

This statement was made by Yhwh to Moses at the time that Yhwh revealed the divine self to Moses following the Golden Calf incident at Sinai. In the Exodus narrative, it serves as a statement of Yhwh's mercy and justice, and thereby explains the capacity for judgment against those in Israel who abandoned Yhwh for an idol as well as Yhwh's capacity to show fidelity to those who show fidelity to Yhwh. The Nahum version of this statement is clearly shortened, and represents an attempt to interpret the statement in relation to the rhetorical needs of Nahum, i.e., it emphasizes Yhwh's power and capacity for justice against an enemy but it does not include the statements concerning Yhwh's mercy. This is in contrast to the version of the statement that appears in Jon 4:2, which emphasizes Yhwh's mercy because divine mercy is a major concern of the book of Jonah. Essentially, the book of Nahum (like Jonah) borrows, rereads, and modifies a well-known statement from tradition to make a point about Yhwh's character, i.e., Yhwh maintains fidelity to Israel and that fidelity is expressed through Yhwh's punishment of Nineveh following a period which brought Nineveh or the Assyrians to carry out punishment (cf. Isaiah 5-12).

---

[17] See Fishbane, *Biblical Interpretation* 347.

Now that the time of punishment is over, it is time for Nineveh to be punished in turn.

The letter *Beth* begins the statement in verse 3b, "in whirlwind *(bĕsûpâ)* and storm is his way, and the clouds are the dust of his feet." In addition to providing the second letter of the alphabet, this statement introduces Yhwh's role as master of the cosmos or the natural world by calling up the natural imagery of a whirlwind and storm to convey Yhwh's power and capacity for destruction. Such images appear frequently in texts that portray Yhwh's punitive action against enemies or those deemed guilty (e.g., Isa 29:6; Hos 8:7; Ps 83:16 [NRSV: 83:15]; Job 9:17; 27:20). The cloud of dust at his feet conveys the image of an approaching chariot, horses, or army as well as the metaphor of wind (cf. Isa 5:28).

The letter *Gimmel* begins the statement in verse 4a, "He rebukes *(gô'ēr)* the sea and makes it dry, and he dries up all the rivers. The verb "rebuke" *(g'r)* frequently appears in contexts that describe Yhwh's defeat or control of the sea (Ps 106:9), the nations (Isa 17:13; Ps 9:6 [NRSV: 9:5]), Satan (Zech 3:2); the locusts that threaten Jerusalem (Mal 3:11), etc. The specific reference to the sea recalls the motif of Yhwh's creation of the heavens and the earth that begins with the sea (Genesis 1), as well as the mythological traditions that portray creation as Yhwh's defeat of the sea or sea monsters (Psalms 74; 104; Job 38; Isa 27:1) or Yhwh's deliverance of Israel in relation to the control of the sea (Exodus 15; Isaiah 11; 51). In all cases, the sea represents chaos in the world and Yhwh's defeat or control of the sea represents the institution of order in nature or human society.

One would expect the letter *Daleth* to appear at the beginning of verse 4b, but the letter *Aleph* appears instead, "Withered *('umlal)* are Bashan and Carmel, and the bloom of Lebanon fades *('umlāl)*." Various attempts have been made to emend the initial *'umlal* to *dālĕlû*, "languish," but there is no textual evidence for such an emendation. The initial *'umlal* appears to be a reduplication of the final word of the statement, but no secure explanation for this feature has emerged. The Bashan and the Carmel are the names of the fertile hill country of the Golan heights and the hilly ridge that extends south from modern Haifa along the Mediterranean coast. The flower of Lebanon likewise employs the imagery of the fertile and forested Lebanon mountain range, known in antiquity for its majestic trees. Again, these images testify to Yhwh's role as creator and thus as master of the natural world as a basis for the contention that Yhwh is able to defeat enemies.

The letter *He* begins the statement in verse 5a, "The mountains *(hārîm)* quake before him, and the hills melt." The image is that of earthquake, which once again testifies to Yhwh's role as creator and master of the natural (and human) world.

The letter *Waw* begins the statement in verse 5b, "and the earth heaves *(wattiśśāʾ hāʾāreṣ)* before him, the world and all who live in it." The image continues the prior metaphor of earthquake, and points to its effects on the world's inhabitants. The statement thereby explicitly combines YHWH's role in relation to both nature and the human world.

The letter *Zayin* appears at the beginning of the second word in the rhetorical questions of verse 6a, "before his indignation *(lipnê zaʿmô)* who can stand? And who can endure the heat of his anger?" This represents a slight disruption in the alphabetical acrostic sequence, but it appears to serve as a rhetorical device that calls attention to the rhetorical questions. The questions of course assert that no one can stand before YHWH's wrath, and provide further testimonies to YHWH's power in the world.

The letter *Ḥeth* appears at the beginning of the statement in verse 6b, "His wrath *(ḥămātô)* is poured out like fire, and by him the rocks are broken in pieces." This image portrays a volcano eruption, and builds upon the prior imagery of earthquake to portray once again YHWH's natural power.

The letter *Ṭet* appears at the beginning of verse 7a, "Good *(ṭôb)* is YHWH, a stronghold in a day of trouble." This statement introduces a seeming contradiction in relation to the prior images of destructive earthquakes and volcanoes by portraying such threats to the natural and human worlds as good. The statement represents an attempt to define some sense of moral order in a world that can be shattered so easily, i.e., such disasters represent YHWH's power and capacity to punish those who act contrary to the divine will. The image of YHWH as a protective fortress conveys the sense of protection for those who do live in accordance with YHWH's wishes.

The letter *Yod* appears as the second letter of the first word in verse 7b-8aα, immediately following the conjunction and prior to the participle, "and he knows *(wĕyōdēʿa)* those who take refuge in him, even in a rushing flood." Again, the statement stresses the image of divine protection for those who turn to YHWH. Natural imagery appears once more in the reference to the rushing flood. Such an image alludes to the sudden flooding of a wadi, a dry stream bed in the summer that suddenly becomes a rushing torrent in times of rain. It also alludes to the flood tradition (Genesis 6–9) in which such a natural phenomenon as flooding is portrayed as a moral agent of punishment against those who are evil. Again, it testifies to YHWH's power and capacity for justice.

The letter *Kaph* introduces the final statement of the acrostic in verse 8aβ-b, "a full end *(kālâ)* he will make of his adversaries (literally, 'her place'), and will pursue his enemies into darkness." This statement constitutes the primary rhetorical goal of the acrostic hymn, i.e., the assertion that Y{\sc HWH} will destroy enemies and therefore that Y{\sc HWH} is indeed powerful and just. Most scholars emend the phrase "her place *(mĕqômāh)*" to "his adversaries *(bĕqomāyw)*" based upon the readings of the Greek versions of this text, which presuppose very similar Hebrew consonants. The {\sc MT} reference to "her place" apparently refers to the place of Nineveh which will be completely destroyed.

Having laid out Y{\sc HWH}'s capacity for power and punishment in the partial acrostic of verses 2-8, verses 9-10 then pose a question to the audience of the book, "what do you reckon unto Y{\sc HWH}?" The {\sc NRSV} incorrectly translates, "why do you plot against Y{\sc HWH}? *(mah-tĕššĕbûn ʾel-yhwh),*" based on the assumption that this text is directed against Israel's enemies and a misinterpretation of the preposition *ʾel,* "unto." Although it presupposes that the addressees include both Judah and Assyria, it is doubtful that this text was composed for an Assyrian reading or listening audience; rather it was composed for a Judean audience and it is intended to have its rhetorical impact upon its Judean readers or listeners. The question essentially asks, "what do you think about Y{\sc HWH}?" or "how do you evaluate Y{\sc HWH}?" and appears to be designed to challenge doubts about Y{\sc HWH}'s power and justice in the aftermath of the assertions made by the partial acrostic hymn. This intent becomes clear in the following material in verse 9aβ, which asserts that Y{\sc HWH} will make an end (i.e., complete destruction), and that no adversary will rise up twice. This assertion is reinforced in turn by the *kî* ("because, for") clause in verse 10, which metaphorically portrays Y{\sc HWH}'s enemies entangled like thorns or incapacitated like drunks; in either case, they are unable to stand against Y{\sc HWH}. The statement emphasizes the letter *Samekh* in its formulation, "for like thorns they are entangled, like drunks they are drunk *(kî ʿad-sîrîm sĕbuʾîm ûkĕsobʾām sĕbûʾîm).*" Because *Samekh* follows the previously mentioned *Nun,* this has prompted unsuccessful attempts to reconstruct the acrostic in this verse as well. After reading or hearing this portrayal, one is intended to come to the conclusion that Y{\sc HWH} is powerful and just, and that Y{\sc HWH} will act against Nineveh.

Address to Judah Asserting that the End of Assyrian Oppression is an Act of Y{\sc HWH}: 1:11–2:1 [{\sc NRSV}: 1:11-15]

Nahum 1:11–2:1 [{\sc NRSV}: 1:11-15] constitutes the prophet's address to Judah that asserts that the end of Assyrian oppression is an act of Y{\sc HWH}. It is demarcated by its consistent use of second person feminine singular address forms to address in Judah (see esp. 2:1 [{\sc NRSV}: 1:15]; cf.

1:11, 12-13), which contrasts with the second person masculine plural address forms employed for Judah and Assyria in Nah 1:2-10. This also contrasts with the use of second feminine address forms to refer to Assyria in Nah 2:2–3:17 [NRSV: 2:1–3:17]. The second masculine address form in Nah 1:14 is directed to the Assyrian king (cf. Nah 3:18-19, which also employs second masculine address forms in reference to the Assyrian king) to report YHWH's command concerning his upcoming demise. The unit is syntactically independent from the preceding material in Nah 1:2-8 and the following material in Nah 2:2–3:19 [NRSV: 2:1–3:19]. Overall, it focuses on YHWH's pledge to deliver Judah from Assyrian oppression, whereas Nah 1:2-10 focuses on YHWH's power to punish oppressors and Nah 2:2–3:19 [NRSV: 2:1–3:19] focuses on YHWH's punishment of Nineveh and the Assyrian king. Again, its argumentative character is evident in the initial assertion in verse 11 that Judah has misjudged YHWH, its report in verses 12-14 of YHWH's statements concerning the end of Judah's oppression and the demise of the Assyrian king, and its concluding command to Judah in Nah 2:1 [NRSV: 1:15] that calls upon Judah to celebrate the end of its suffering.

The initial statement by the prophet that Judah has misjudged YHWH appears in Nah 1:11. The interpretation of this passage has been complicated by the appearance of the participial phrase, *yōʾēṣ bĕlîyāʿal*. Because the referent for the participle *yōʾēṣ* is unclear, it may be translated as "counselor," "counsel," or "counseling." Likewise, the term *bĕlîyāʿal* has been problematic because of tendencies to read the term in relation to its later use as a reference to a personified evil figure, Satan or the like, in the late-Second Temple period and beyond. But various studies of the term in texts prior to the late-Second Temple period demonstrate that the term does not refer to a personified figure, but to more generalized concepts of evil, disorder, or worthlessness.[18] The phrase *yōʾēṣ bĕlîyāʿal* would therefore have to mean, "worthless counsel," especially because it appears as a parallel to the term *rāʿâ*, "evil," in verse 11. The verse therefore reads, "from you has gone forth thinking about YHWH evil, worthless counsel," or in more idiomatic English, "evil thinking, worthless counsel, has gone forth from you about YHWH." The verse then constitutes the thesis that he intends to dispute within the context of the disputation genre, viz., the people think ill of YHWH and the prophet intends to demonstrate that YHWH indeed has acted on their behalf.

---

[18] For discussion of the term and bibliography, see Theodore Gastor, "Belial," *IDB* 1:357; idem, "Belial," *Encyclopaedia Judaica* 4:428-9; B. Otzen, "*Bᵉlîyāʿal*," *TDOT* 2:131-6; Theodore Lewis," "Belial," *ABD* I:654-6; and S. D. Sperling, "Belial," *DDD²* 169–71.

His argumentation for this contention appears in verses 12-14, which constitute the prophet's report of YHWH's statements concerning the end of Judah's oppression in verses 12-13 and the demise of the Assyrian king in verse 14. Verses 12-13 begin with the messenger formula, *kōh ʾāmar yhwh*, "thus says YHWH," which identifies the following statement as a speech by YHWH. The first part of YHWH's speech in verse 12aα⁴⁻⁷β presents many difficulties, but the NRSV correctly grasps its intention to state that Judah's oppressors will be cut off and pass away even though they are well equipped and numerous. This intention is clear especially from the second half of the verse in which YHWH states, "although I have afflicted you, I will afflict you no more." It is likewise clear from YHWH's following statement in verse 13 in which the Deity pledges to break the yoke and the bonds of the oppressor from upon Judah. This passage may presuppose Isa 10:5-34, which condemns Assyria for oppressing Israel with rod and staff. It may also have influenced the prophet Jeremiah when he appeared in the streets of Jerusalem wearing a yoke and bonds to symbolize his contention that Judah must submit to Babylon (see Jeremiah 27–28).

The prophet's report of YHWH's address to the Assyrian king appears in verse 14. It begins with a report formula, "and YHWH has commanded concerning you," which is syntactically joined to verses 12-13 by the initial conjunctive *waw*. As noted above, the address form shifts to a second person masculine singular, which clearly refers to a party other than the second feminine singular forms addressed to Judah. Based upon the analogy of the second masculine singular forms in Nah 3:18-19, the address appears to be directed to the Assyrian monarch. YHWH's statement includes three basic components. The first asserts that the monarch's name will no longer be perpetuated. This effectively entails the complete demise of the monarch as he would have no sons to carry on his legacy. As in most cultures, this is a fundamental issue in the ancient Near East as indicated by Abraham's concern for descendants (see Genesis 15) and the need to establish a line of descent and inheritance (cf. Num 27:1-11; 36:1-12, which take up the issue of inheritance by daughters in cases where no son is available). The second asserts that the king's idols will be cut off from the house of his god, effectively ending any divine support that he may have anticipated and asserting YHWH's power over the Assyrian gods. The third announces the death of the Assyrian king, and states that he will die because he has disparaged YHWH. Again this points to the Isaian tradition in which the Assyrian king is condemned for blaspheming against YHWH (see Isa 10:5-34; 36-37). It is noteworthy that Isa 37:36-38 indicates that the Assyrian king Sennacherib was defeated by YHWH after his blasphemous assertions, and that he was murdered by his own sons in the temple of his god, Nisroch. It appears that Nahum's statements build upon the Isaian oracle in Isa 10:5-34. Insofar as Isaiah 36–37 is a later composition from the seventh century B.C.E., it is possible that this narrative presupposes Nahum's statements. In any case, the present form of Nahum employs the Isaian tradition to assert that YHWH's promises of deliverance to Judah articulated in Isaiah have now come to pass.

Having concluded his argument that YHWH will bring Assyria's oppression of Judah to an end, the prophet then calls upon Judah to celebrate in Nah 2:1 [NRSV: 1:15]. Although this verse is not syntactically connected to Nah 1:11, 12-14, it is clear that it is to be read as a part of this section because of its continuing use of the second person feminine address forms in reference to Judah and because it brings the issue of *bĕlîyāʿal* or "worthlessness" from Nah 1:11 to a resolution by declaring that "worthlessness" will never again pass through Judah as it will be entirely cut off. Although the NRSV understands this statement to refer to the cessation of invasion, the meaning of *bĕlîyāʿal* as "worthlessness" indicates that it refers to the end of any sort of trouble for Judah. The prophet's announcement begins with his portrayal of a messenger of good tidings who approaches on the mountains. Such a scene clearly pertains to Jerusalem which is built on a lengthy mountain ridge extending from north to south. Such a messenger would be visible to the lookouts of the city who surveyed the surrounding territory in antiquity for signs of travelers, threats, messengers, etc. The command to celebrate the festivals and pay the vows indicates the resumption of normal cultic practice to honor YHWH. The three primary holidays of the nation, Passover, Shavuot, and Sukkoth, celebrate not only the various stages of the agricultural year, but YHWH's acts on behalf of Israel as well. All Israelite men are required to appear before YHWH at the Temple on these holidays, and they are not to come empty-handed, i.e., they are to bring offerings to the Temple by which to honor YHWH (see Exod 23:14-19; 34:18-26; Deut 16:1-17). Insofar as these festivals recount YHWH's deliverance of Israel from Egypt at the Exodus, YHWH's revelation of the Torah to Israel at Sinai, and YHWH's guidance of Israel through the wilderness, the offerings of Israel constitute an effort to thank YHWH for the benefits that YHWH grants to Israel (see esp. Deut 26:1-15, in which the Israelite farmer recounts YHWH's actions on behalf of Israel as he makes his offering at the altar). Vows were special offerings to YHWH made in thanks for some divine action on behalf of the nation or individuals or in anticipation of divine action.[19] Examples include Jacob's vow to accept YHWH as G–d at Beth El (Gen 28:20-22),

---

[19] See G. H. Davies, "Vows," *IDB* 4:792-3.

Hannah's vow of Samuel's service to YHWH if she is granted a son (1 Sam 1:11), the vow of the sailors if they are saved from shipwreck (Jon 1:6), and Israel's vow to devote all of Arad to YHWH (Num 21:1-3). Vows were not required, but once made, they were required to be paid (Deut 23:21-23). They could be paid either in the form of animal sacrifice (Lev 22:17-25) or in cash with set values for each type of animal (Leviticus 27). The vows of women could be canceled by their husbands or fathers if they acted on the day the vow was made (Numbers 30).

Many have noted that Nah 2:1 [NRSV: 1:15] shares a great deal of vocabulary and imagery with Isa 52:1, 7, which likewise state that "the uncircumcised and the unclean shall enter you no more," and "how beautiful upon the mountains are the feet of the messenger who announces peace . . ." Although some contend that the statement in Nahum is a later midrash that was composed on the basis of the Isaian text,[20] the very difficult syntax and vocabulary of the Nahum text indicates that it is original and that the Isaian text was composed in reference to Nahum. This would suggest that Second Isaiah's text indicated that the earlier prophecy had been fulfilled with the impending fall of Babylon to Cyrus. Second Isaiah's reference to the oppression of Israel by Egypt and by Assyria in Isa 52:4 demonstrates the prophet's dependence upon earlier tradition.

Address to Nineveh and the Assyrian King Asserting that the Fall of Nineveh is an Act of YHWH: 2:2–3:19

The third major component of Nahum's *maśśāʾ* appears in Nah 2:2–3:19 [NRSV: 2:1–3:19], in which the prophet addresses both Nineveh and the Assyrian king in order to argue that the fall of Nineveh is an act of YHWH. By utilizing Nineveh and the Assyrian king as its fictive addressees, this section serves the larger purpose of the prophet's refutation speech by attempting to convince its Judean audience that YHWH is indeed efficacious and that YHWH will bring Assyrian oppression to an end. The differing address forms indicate that the section is divided into two basic units. The second person feminine singular address forms in Nah 2:2–3:17 [NRSV: 2:1–3:17] and the explicit identification of Nineveh in Nah 2:9 [NRSV: 2:8] and the city of bloodshed in Nah 3:1 indicate that this text constitutes the prophet's address to Nineveh. The shift to second person masculine singular address forms and the explicit

---

[20] Jeremias, *Kultprophetie* 13–5.

identification of the Assyrian king in Nah 3:18-19 indicate that this text constitutes the prophet's address to the Assyrian king. Although the primary argument appears in the address to Nineveh, the address to the king is essential to the purposes of this composition in that it pits YHWH against the Assyrian king (cf. Isaiah 10; 36–37). Insofar as YHWH is responsible for the welfare of Jerusalem and the Assyrian king is responsible for Nineveh, the text portrays YHWH as the omnipotent figure over against the now unprepared and defeated Assyrian king.

THE PROPHET'S ADDRESS TO NINEVEH: 2:2–3:17 [NRSV: 2:1–3:17]

As noted above, the second person feminine address forms and the explicit mention of Nineveh identify Nah 2:2–3:17 [NRSV: 2:1–3:17] as the prophet's address to Assyria. The overall purpose of this section is to demonstrate that YHWH is responsible for the downfall of Nineveh. It is not entirely clear whether this passage presupposes the actual fall of Nineveh to the Babylonians and Medes in 612 B.C.E. or anticipates it. The references in Nah 2:7-9 [NRSV: 2:6-8] to the role of the opened river gates in the destruction of the city apparently corresponds to the description of Nineveh's fall by Diodorus Siculus, who reports that Nineveh was taken when the flood waters washed away portions of the city's defenses.[21] There are problems with this interpretation because archeological evidence provides no indication that Nineveh was destroyed by flood, but there is a great deal of evidence that the city was burned. It should be noted, however, that Nineveh's defenses included a series of moats that helped to protect the walls when filled with water.[22] Tampering with the flood control gates of the Khusur River which runs through the city may well have contributed to Nineveh's fall without leaving evidence of extensive flooding. This would suggest that the prophet was able to point to the actual fall of Nineveh as part of his larger effort to demonstrate YHWH's power and role in the matter. The appearance of statements by YHWH introduced by the formulaic announcement, "behold, I am against you," in Nah 2:14 [NRSV: 2:13] and 3:5-7 indicates that the prophet's speech comprises three major sub-units or stages in the argumentation. Nahum 2:2-14 [NRSV: 2:1-13] concentrates on describing the assault against Nineveh and its consequences, and concludes with YHWH's statement that identifies YHWH as

---

[21] History 2.26, 27; cf. Xenophon, Anabasis 3.4.12, who attributes the fall of the city to the fear of Zeus. For discussion, see Roberts, *Nahum, Habakkuk, Zephaniah* 65–6; Spronk, *Nahum* 94–6.

[22] See A. Kirk Grayson, "Nineveh," *ABD* IV:1118-9.

the cause of the assault. Nahum 3:1-7 constitutes a woe oracle directed against the city that points to its abusive treatment of nations as the reason for its punishment. Once again, YHWH's statement identifies YHWH as the cause of the city's demise. Finally, Nah 3:8-17 provides the argumentative component of the speech by comparing Nineveh's situation to that of Thebes, which was destroyed by the Assyrians in 663 B.C.E., and by contending that Nineveh's fate will be no different.

The prophet's initial portrayal of the assault against the city in Nah 2:2-14 [NRSV: 2:1-13] begins in verses 2-3 [NRSV: 1-2] with the statement that "a scatterer has come up against you" and portrayals of the various commands given by the Assyrian commanders to their troops to prepare for the defense of the city. The NRSV follows the commonly suggested emendation of *mēpîṣ*, "scatterer," to *mappēṣ*, "shatterer," which involves only a minor change in vowels and suggests the image of a battering ram. The LXX apparently presupposes *mappîaḥ*, "blowing/panting," as part of its effort to read the verse in relation to Nah 2:1 [NRSV: 1:15] and to portray the panting messenger who escaped affliction to enter the doomed city. Apparently, the LXX attempts to read this text as a threat against Israel. Nevertheless, there is no basis for such a change as the verb *pwṣ*, "to scatter," is employed in Gen 11:8 to portray YHWH's scattering of the nations after they built the tower of Babel and in Num 10:35 to portray YHWH's power to defeat enemies when the ark sets out, "Arise, O YHWH, let your enemies be scattered, and your foes flee before you." The use of this term therefore identifies YHWH as the source of the threat posed to the yet unidentified city. Verse 3a [NRSV: 2a] makes this identification explicit when it employs a *kî* clause to state that YHWH's restoration of "the majesty of Jacob as well as the majesty of Israel" is the cause of this threat. Again, LXX attempts to read this statement as a threat against Israel by stating that YHWH "has turned aside the pride of Jacob as the pride of Israel," but this represents a later interpretative attempt to transform the oracle into a portrayal of judgment against Israel. A second *kî* clause in verse 3b [NRSV: 2b] relates the reasons for YHWH's attempt to restore Israel, which has been ravaged and ruined. The verb *bqq*, translated by NRSV as "to ravage," actually means "to empty, depopulate," and recalls the Assyrian practice of deporting native populations. The portrayal of Israel's ruined branches may reflect Assyria's use of the Shephelah region and the coastal plain for olive oil production.[23] Apparently, many Israelites

---

[23] For Assyria's development of a major olive oil industry in the Philistine Shephelah, see Seymour Gitin, "Tel-Miqne-Ekron: A Type Site for the Inner Coastal Plain in the Iron Age II Period," *Recent Excavations in Israel: Studies in Iron Age Archaeology*, ed. S. Gitin and W. Dever, AASOR, vol. 49 (Winona Lake: Eisenbrauns, 1989) 23–58.

were relocated to this area so that their "branches" would have been ruined in order to support the growth and harvesting of olive trees to supply the needs of the Assyrian empire.

Verses 4-10 [NRSV: 3-9] then turn to a portrayal of the attacking army. Apparently, these verses contain a great deal of military imagery and technical terminology that is not fully understood in modern times. Verse 4a [NRSV: 3a] begins with a portrayal of the red shields and clothing of the attacking army. Some have speculated that this reflects soldiers spattered in blood during the course of the battle (cf. the imagery of Isa 63:1-6),[24] but these soldiers have only just begun their advance. More likely, they have reddened themselves as a means to terrify and undermine the morale of the defending soldiers who will imagine their own blood splattered all over the attacking troops. Verse 4b [NRSV: 3b] portrays the shining metal of the fittings of the chariots as the sun flashes off of their fittings. The NRSV translates the last words of the verse as a reference to their prancing chargers, the Hebrew phrase *wĕhabbĕrōšîm horʿālû* actually means "and the cypresses quiver," which may refer to the central draft pole to which the horses were harnessed.[25] Verse 5 [NRSV: 4] employs the imagery of torches and lightning to portray the chariots racing through the streets of the conquered city. Such imagery conveys both the speed of the marauding chariots and their destructive force as the city is set on fire by the conquering army. Chariots normally served as mobile platforms from which arrows were fired against the enemy, and it is likely that flaming arrows were used in an initial assault to set the enemy city on fire. Verse 6 [NRSV: 5] portrays the assault by the ground troops as the officers are given their orders, and soldiers rush the walls. The identity of the one who gives the order is not given; presumably this would be the general commander, but the anonymity of the statement, like that of the reference to "scatterer" in verse 2 [NRSV: 1], lends itself to a portrayal of YHWH as the one who gives the order. The portrayal of the soldiers' stumbling conveys the urgency of soldiers who carry weapons and equipment as they rush the walls of a heavily defended city, presumably under the covering fire of arrows from the chariots. The reference to the "mantelet," indicates the use of a woven shield or barrier that is employed to protect attacking soldiers from enemy arrows and stones. The meaning of the Hebrew term *sōkēk*, translated by NRSV as "mantelet," is uncertain, but it is derived from a root that means "to weave" and apparently refers to

---

[24] See the discussions in Roberts, *Nahum, Habakkuk, Zephaniah* 65; Spronk, *Nahum* 89.

[25] See M. A. Littauer and J. H. Crouwel, "Chariots," *ABD* I:888-92.

such shields that appear in various reliefs of assaults against a defended city.[26]

Verses 7-9 [NRSV: 6-8] employ the imagery of flooding waters to portray the overthrow of Nineveh. The three verses are linked together by conjunctive *waw*'s. Verse 7 [NRSV: 6] begins with the notice that the gates of the rivers are opened and the palace dissolves. Such a portrayal corresponds to the above-mentioned contention of Diodorus Siculus that Nineveh was taken after flood waters washed away parts of its defenses. Although there is no evidence of flooding on the site, the use of canals and moats to defend the city is well known, and it is likely that a key element in the strategy to take such a large and well-defended city as Nineveh would be to gain control of the water sources that fed the canals and moats and to use these waters as part of an effort to undermine the city's defenses. Verse 8 [NRSV: 7] represents one of the most difficult verses of the book in that it refers to a figure, *huṣṣab* in Hebrew, that is exiled and taken up as "her maidens" are led away.[27] Although the verbs and pronouns are clearly feminine, the term *huṣṣab* is masculine. The meaning of the term is uncertain. It is derived from the verb root *nṣb*, "to stand up, erect," and is generally taken as a reference to a statue or other installation that somehow represents the power and authority of the city of Nineveh. Ibn Ezra understood it as a reference to the Assyrian queen named Huzzab, but this interpretation has long been abandoned. Others maintain that the term refers to a statue of Ishtar, the patron goddess of Nineveh, which would have been pulled down and carted off as booty. Such a contention cannot be confirmed, although the reference to her handmaidens, priestesses or attendants, and their metaphorical portrayal as cooing doves beating their hearts (apparently a reference to beating wings, contra NRSV) would suggest the image of a statue of the goddess attended by cultic personnel. In any case, the reference apparently conveys Nineveh's now lost majesty as the conquerors exile the city that once exiled so many others. Finally, verse 9 [NRSV: 8] explicitly names Nineveh for the first time, and portrays it as a city that sits in a pool of water. This has prompted many to conclude that the city is destroyed by flood in keeping with verse 7 [NRSV: 6] and Diodorus, but the verse portrays the waters fleeing. It portrays the command to "Stop! Stop!" with none to turn back, which suggests an unsuccessful attempt to halt the onrushing waters; the portrayal of fleeing waters suggests that the water has been

---

[26] See *ANEP* 368, 372–3, which portray Assyrian assaults against walled cities. In both cases, bowmen fire from behind woven shields that apparently serve as the referents for the term "mantelet."

[27] For an overview of the discussion, see Spronk, *Nahum* 96–8.

drained from the moats. If the attacking army had gained control of the flood gates that controlled the flow of water into the moats, this would enable them to drain the moats and deprive the city of a principle means of defense. In keeping with the imagery of verses 4-6 [NRSV: 3-5], this would make a frontal assault by chariots and ground soldiers against the walls or embankments that surround the city possible, and facilitate the capture of the city.

Finally, the portrayal of the assault against the city concludes in verse 10 [NRSV: 9] with the commands to plunder the silver, gold, and treasure of the city.

Verses 11-14 [NRSV: 10-13] portray the terror of the defenders of the city and its king as they realize that YHWH is against them. Verse 11 [NRSV: 10] begins with a three-part alliterative phrase that conveys the terror of the defenders, *bûqâ ûmĕbûqâ ûmĕbullāqâ*, "devastation, desolation, and destruction." Each term is based upon the root *bqq* or *blq*, and forms a formulaic trio analogous to the phrase *hinnēh yhwh bôqēq hāʾāreṣ ûbôlĕqāh*, "behold, YHWH is emptying the land and devastating it," in Isa 24:1. Apparently, the alliteration aids the rhetorical impact of the prophet's portrayal of complete devastation. The following portrayal of faint hearts, trembling knees, quaking loins, and pale faces clearly conveys the stark terror of the city's inhabitants as Nineveh is overrun. Verses 12-14 [NRSV: 11-13] are sometimes considered as an independent unit from verses 2-11 [NRSV: 1-10] because of the imagery of lions and the use of the rhetorical question form, but they build upon the statement in verse 11 [NRSV: 10] by portraying the inability of the Assyrian king to do anything to protect the city. The use of lion imagery is particularly pertinent to the present context because the Assyrian kings customarily portrayed themselves in massive palace reliefs as lion hunters as a means to convey their power, bravery, and skills as warriors.[28] Of course, such large reliefs were meant to have an impact on the Assyrian population—as well as upon foreign visitors—and the book of Nahum is able to take that image and turn it against the Assyrian monarchs as a means to contend that they are unable to stand against YHWH. The initial rhetorical question in verse 12 [NRSV: 11], "where is the lion's refuge?" refers to the king and his palace, a central feature of the city of Nineveh in which Sennacherib built his palace as the center of the city and the destination of its processional way. The rhetorical question of course asserts that king and palace are nowhere to be found. The imagery then employs lions, young lions, and cubs once again to assert ironically that the palace of the Assyrian kings is now actually overrun by wild lions and their cubs, i.e., the king is no

[28] See *ANEP* 184, 185.

longer able to defend the city and the lions that he formerly hunted now have free run over his own home and no one frightens them away. Whereas the king once hunted lions, the lions now kill game, tear it apart for their cubs, and store it in their own caves and dens on the very location where the Assyrian king lived. The turnabout is now complete.

The passage concludes in verse 14 [NRSV: 13] with the prophet's portrayal of YHWH's statement, "behold, I am against you . . . *(hinĕnî ʾēlayik)*." This is an example of the so-called *Herausforderungsformel* or "challenge formula," in which one party calls another out to battle or a duel (see 1 Sam 17:14-54). It is frequently employed by the prophets to convey YHWH's words of punishment against various parties (see Jer 21:13; 50:31; 51:25; Ezek 5:8-9; 13:8-9).[29] In the present case, it conveys YHWH's intention to punish Nineveh. It also functions rhetorically to identify YHWH for the first time as the power that attacks the city, identified previously only as a "scatterer" in verse 2 [NRSV: 1] or the one who commands the officers to begin the assault in verse 6 [NRSV: 5]. It closes off this unit so that the next unit in Nah 3:1-7, likewise closed by the "challenge formula," may proceed. The oracular formula with full reference to the name, YHWH of Hosts, identifies YHWH as the speaker. YHWH's following statement indicates that YHWH will destroy the chariots and young lions or warriors of Nineveh so that they will no longer gather prey nor will their messengers be heard again. These last statements are especially important because they convey the Assyrian penchant for conquest and the collection of tribute as messengers are sent regularly for such purposes by the Assyrian monarch. If the messenger of the Assyrian king was not given an adequate answer or payment, the army would not be far behind.

The second major component of the prophet's address to Nineveh appears in Nah 3:1-7 in which a woe oracle directed against the city constitutes the basis for charging that the city's own misconduct against other nations is the reason for its demise. This segment is demarcated by the initial "woe" oracle *(hôy)* form in verse 1 and by the appearance of the statements based on the "challenge" formula *(Herausforderungformel)* in verses 5-7 that conclude the section in a manner analogous to that of Nah 2:2-14 [NRSV: 2:1-13]. The rhetorical question directed to Nineveh in verse 8 marks the beginning of the next sub-unit of the prophet's address.

The first part of this section appears in verses 1-3, which employs the "woe" oracle form to portray Nineveh's demise as the city is overrun by an invading army. The "woe" oracle is a form of address that

---

[29] See Ronald M. Hals, *Ezekiel*, FOTL, vol. 19 (Grand Rapids: Eerdmans, 1989) 359.

begins with the particle *hôy*, "woe!" to convey a sense of warning concerning approaching danger from invaders (e.g., Zech 2:10 [NRSV: 2:6]) or punishment for some wrongdoing (e.g., Isa 5:8-24; Amos 5:8-20; Hab 2:6-20).[30] Nineveh is not explicitly named until verse 7, but the prior reference to the city in Nah 2:9 [NRSV: 2:8] makes it clear that Nineveh is the addressee. The initial woe address implicitly levels an accusation against Nineveh by referring to it as "city of bloodshed, utterly deceitful, full of booty—no end to the plunder." Insofar as the initial "woe" statement is an address form, the prophet thereby effectively accuses Nineveh of murder, dishonesty, and theft. The Hebrew term *dāmîm*, literally "blood," generally refers to the shedding of blood by violence or murder (see Gen 4:10, 11; 2 Sam 3:28; 16:8; 2 Kgs 9:26; Isa 1:15; Hab 2:8, 17), and *kaḥaš* is commonly employed for lying (Hos 7:3; 10:13; 12:1 [NRSV: 11:12]; Ps 59:13 [NRSV: 59:12]). The term *pereq*, "booty," is derived from a root that means "to tear apart, away," and thus conveys the violence inherent in the taking of booty. The term *ṭerep*, "plunder," is likewise derived from a root that means "to tear apart," and is generally employed to describe lions or other carnivores tearing apart their prey. These images combine to portray the actions of the city that has acted as a conqueror and assaulted and plundered others through the course of its rise to power.

Verses 2-3 turn the tables against Nineveh and its past abuse of others by portraying the conquering army rushing through its streets. Verse 2 focuses on the imagery of enemy chariots, including the crack of the whip, the rumbling of chariot wheels, and the images of horses running and chariots bouncing along as the victorious enemy dashes through the streets of the vanquished city. Verse 3 employs the image of a horse rearing up (Hebrew, *pārāš maʿăleh*, literally "a horseman going up"; cf. NRSV, "horsemen charging"), followed by references to "a flashing sword" and "glittering spear." Such images convey not only the visual effect of the sun's effects on shining metal weapons, but their swift movements as the enemy soldiers cut down the doomed people of the city. The concluding image of the many corpses strewn about or piled in the streets so that one can only stumble about them testifies to the effectiveness of the conquering army and conveys the grim reality of a city that has been overcome.

Verses 4-7 then turn to the reasons for these scenes of bloodshed by stating initially that Nineveh's own "harlotry" and "sorcery" against other nations is the cause for such suffering, which indicates that the conquest of the city is to be construed as punishment for wrongdoing.

---

[30] Sweeney, *Isaiah 1–39* 543.

The use of the motif of harlotry is a relatively common means in prophetic literature to convey the charge that the nation has abandoned
YHWH, especially since Israelite tradition sometimes portrays Israel as
the bride that YHWH found and married in the wilderness (see Hosea
1–3; Jeremiah 2; Ezekiel 16). The image generally represents the nation's turn to other gods and its entering into relationships with other
nations rather than relying solely on YHWH for sustenance and protection.
In the present instance, Nineveh is accused of engaging in harlotry in
the course of "selling" other nations (*mōkeret;* cf. NRSV, "enslaving"),
which apparently refers to the Assyrian practice of deporting elements
of conquered populations from their homelands to foreign territories
much as one would transport a slave from one location to another (cf. 2
Kings 17).[31] The reference to sorcery likewise conveys Nineveh's allegiance to foreign gods, e.g., Assur or Ishtar, and polemecizes against
their native religious practices by portraying them as forms of witch-
craft or sorcery. The prophet presents YHWH's statements in verses 5-7,
as indicated by the first person speech forms and the oracular formula
that identifies YHWH of Hosts as the speaker. As noted above in the discussion of Nah 2:14 [NRSV: 2:13], the "challenge" formula, "Behold, I am
against you," identifies YHWH as the one who brings about the punishment and thereby testifies to YHWH's power and role as the master of
creation and nations at large. The imagery continues the prior portrayal of Nineveh's fall to an invading army. At this point, verse 5 turns
to the treatment of women by a conqueror by metaphorically portraying Nineveh as a woman who is exposed before her captors, presumably to be raped. The Assyrians were also known to have forced male
captives to march without clothing as a means to humiliate and control
them.[32] Images of humiliation follow as YHWH states the intention to
throw "dung" (*šiqquṣîm,* cf. NRSV, "filth") on the captive city and to
make it a spectacle. YHWH portrays the reactions of others to Nineveh's
humiliation in verse 7 by indicating that no one who sees Nineveh's
sorry state will mourn for her; presumably because the other nations
have suffered considerably at Nineveh's hands and will hardly take
pity on her in her own moment of degradation.

The third portion of the prophet's address to Nineveh appears in
Nah 3:8-17 in which he compares Nineveh's fate to that of Thebes,
which Assyria conquered in 663 B.C.E., and argues that Nineveh's experience will be no different. As in the woe oracle of verses 1-7, there is a

[31] See Bustenay Oded, *Mass Deportations and Deportees in the Neo-Assyrian Empire*
(Wiesbaden: Harrassowitz, 1979).

[32] See *ANEP* 358; cf. Isa 7:20.

heavy use of irony here in that the suffering inflicted by Nineveh upon others is now to be inflicted upon her. This segment of the prophet's address is demarcated at the beginning by the rhetorical question directed to Nineveh. The second masculine singular forms used to address the Assyrian king in verses 18-19 mark the beginning of the next unit.

The prophet's citation of the prior conquest of Thebes in verses 8-10 is key to the argumentative strategy of this text. Thebes, referred to as No-Amon, i.e., a transliteration of its Egyptian name, "city of (the god) Amon," in the Hebrew text, was the principal city of Egypt from 711–525 B.C.E., especially during the reign of the Twenty-Fifth Sudanese dynasty.[33] It was located along both sides of the Nile about seven hundred kilometers south of the Mediterranean Sea, and it was known for its extensive temples and role as sometime capital and major administrative center throughout the history of ancient Egypt. These features indicate that Thebes was very similar to Nineveh in that it was a city that straddled its major river and functioned as its nation's capital. The Assyrians sacked the city in 663 B.C.E. as part of their campaign of conquest against Egypt, although they were only able to hold Egypt for a short period as the new Twenty-Sixth dynasty, apparently an early ally of the Assyrians, ultimately reestablished native rule. Nevertheless, the fall of Thebes marked the high point of the Assyrian empire during the course of its two-century history.

Although some interpreters understand the reference to Thebes as an indication that Nahum was composed about the time of the city's fall, the citation of Thebes' downfall is not intended to represent a contemporary event as there was little reason to think that Nineveh would ever suffer a similar fate in the early seventh century or that YHWH would play any role in bringing such an event about. Rather, the citation of Thebes' downfall provides the rhetorical ammunition to argue not only that Nineveh would fall, but that YHWH would be responsible for that fall. The later references in verse 14 to Nineveh's trampling in the mud and seizing the brick mold allude to traditions of Israelite slavery in Egypt and indicate that Nineveh would now be forced into slavery by YHWH. Overall, the citation of Thebes' downfall contributes to the irony of Nineveh's demise—at the hands of YHWH.

The prophet's initial rhetorical question, "are you better than Thebes/No-Amon?" establishes the analogy between Nineveh and Thebes and serves as an assertion that indeed Nineveh is no different

[33] See Donald B. Redford, "Thebes," *ABD* VI:442-3; for discussion of the Egyptian dynasties discussed here, see William W. Hallo and William Kelly Simpson, *The Ancient Near East: A History* (New York: Harcourt, Brace, Jovanovich, 1971) 285ff.

than Thebes. It will suffer the same fate, and the proof of that contention is found in the threat that is now posed—or about to be posed—against Nineveh. The prophet's question continues by laying out the parallels between the two cities. Thebes sits on the Nile and the prophet states that water surrounds her just as Nineveh sits on the Khusur canal and is surrounded by water. Of course, this is an indication that the prophet's images are based on those of Nineveh; whereas Nineveh employed moats filled with water as part of its defenses, Thebes was not similarly defended as the Nile simply ran through the center of the city. The prophet's statements presuppose that he is immediately familiar, either by direct experience or by the reports of others, with the defenses of Nineveh and the means by which it did—or would—fall, but he is not similarly familiar with Thebes. The references to Cush, i.e., Ethiopia or Sudan, Egypt, Put, and the Libyans, reflect the eclectic character of Egypt during the time of the Twenty-Fifth dynasty. The Twenty-Fifth dynasty was Cushite, and preferred to rule Egypt from Thebes which was closer to their own homeland. Libyan tribes were also an important component of the empire at this time, and had previously ruled Egypt during the periods of the Twenty-Second and Twenty-Third dynasties (940–730 B.C.E.). Put apparently refers to another Libyan group or perhaps to Somalia.[34] According to Gen 10:6 and 1 Chr 1:8, Put is the third son of Ham, son of Noah, and brother of Cush, Egypt, and Canaan. Apparently, the Assyrians had assistance from the Libyans and Put during their campaign of conquest against Egypt as indicated by the Libyan names of the succeeding Twenty-Sixth dynasty and the location of their capital in the western delta city of Sais. The Twenty-Sixth dynasty was put into power by the Assyrians as presumably loyal vassals who would control Egypt on behalf of Assyria. Verse 10 indicates the atrocities that Thebes would have experienced at the time of her conquest, i.e., her people were exiled and taken into captivity, her babies were dashed to pieces by the conquering soldiers, lots were cast for her captives, and her officials were bound in fetters.

Although verse 11 shifts back to a depiction of Nineveh's suffering and dazed state at the time of its downfall, the paired particles *gam*, "also," that introduce the two halves of the verse establish continuity with the depiction of Thebes' downfall because they form a parallel with the paired *gam* that introduces the first two phrases of verse 10. Having established the analogy between Thebes and Nineveh, verse 11 goes on to employ the metaphor of drunkenness to portray Nineveh's dazed, confused, and desperate state as she tries to hide and seek refuge

---

[34] See David W. Baker, "Put," *ABD* V:560.

from her enemies. Verse 12 shifts to a metaphor of fig trees to portray Nineveh's defenses. Just as one may shake a fig tree at a time when its branches are filled with the ripe first fruits of the season so that a fresh fig falls right into one's mouth, so implicitly the defenses of Nineveh will be easily shaken and devoured. Verse 13 shifts to a metaphor of women, implying that Nineveh's defenders will be like women rather than warriors and therefore unable to defend themselves effectively against the attacking army. As a result, the gates of the land are burst open as fire consumes the bars, presumably wooden, that hold the gates shut against the attacking hoards. Verse 14 portrays the desperate efforts of the defenders to shore up their defenses. They are commanded to draw water for the siege, to strengthen their defenses, to trample clay and take up the brick mold so that they can make bricks and thereby strengthen the walls. Ironically, Nineveh is reduced to making bricks, just as the Israelites made bricks for the Egyptians at the time of their enslavement in Egypt. The allusion to this Exodus motif aids in asserting that YHWH is the cause of Nineveh's suffering.

Verses 15-17 continue the depiction of Nineveh's demise with a metaphorical description of its people being cut down and scattered once the enemy forces have breached its defenses. Verse 15 begins with the relatively common metaphors of fire devouring the city and the sword cutting down the people, but it shifts to the image of the locust who will devour the land. Such an image is well known from Amos 7:1-3 and Joel 1–2, both of which employ the image of the locust devouring the land of Israel as a means to convey a threat against the nation. The locust plague is also the eighth major plague visited against Egypt at the time of the Exodus (Exod 10:1-20); in Ps 105:34-35, it is the penultimate plague (cf. Ps 78:46. See also Isa 7:18-19, which portrays the enemy soldiers who invade the land as flies or bees that settle everywhere). There is once again a note of accusation in verse 16, which states that Nineveh increased "its merchants more than the stars of the heavens," i.e., they sent traders and emissaries throughout the empire to enrich the homeland. Economic gain, after all, was the major motivation for Assyria's expansion throughout the eighth and seventh centuries, and it frequently prompted Assyria's abusive policies when its goals were challenged. But with the rising of the sun, the many locusts or grasshoppers that inundate the world will flee and disappear as they are wont to do on cold days at sunrise. It is no accident that YHWH is frequently portrayed with solar imagery as a G–d who defeats Israel's enemies (see Deuteronomy 33; Habakkuk 3; Psalm 104). Again, such imagery serves the prophet's argument that YHWH is the cause of Nineveh's downfall, and that it is to be construed as punishment for Assyria's abusive treatment of nations.

The Prophet's Address to the Assyrian King: 3:18-19

Although the prophet addresses himself primarily to Nineveh the city, the last two verses of the book are directed to the Assyrian king. The address to the king takes up once again the address to the king in Nah 1:14, and it points to the role of the king as the chief guarantor of Nineveh's security. Insofar as the prophet speaks on behalf of YHWH, his address to the monarch represents the direct confrontation of YHWH as master of the universe and the human king who would see himself in the same role (see esp. Isaiah 10; 36-37). In contrast to the second feminine address forms of Nah 2:2–3:17 [NRSV: 2:1–3:17], Nah 3:18-19 employs second person masculine address forms and names the Assyrian monarch explicitly in verse 18.

The prophet's address is a taunt in which he employs the metaphor of the shepherd, a common metaphor for monarchs in the ancient world because of the role that the shepherd plays in protecting and tending the sheep, i.e., the sheep are dependent upon the shepherd who in turn is responsible for their welfare (cf. 1 Samuel 16; Ezekiel 34). The prophet clearly contends that the Assyrian king has not done his job properly as his own shepherds and officers sleep. Because of their inattention, the flock or people of Nineveh are now scattered over the mountains and cannot be gathered, a major disaster for a shepherd who is responsible for his flock. In verse 19, the prophet contends that the king's wounds are mortal and cannot be healed. As a finale, he contends that everyone who hears about the king's situation will clap their hands, not in sympathy but in applause, as all will celebrate the downfall of this cruel tyrant who has brought suffering throughout the world. The final rhetorical question of the book, "for who has ever escaped your endless cruelty?" speaks to this concern and indicates that with the full turn of events, the oppressor now suffers and justice is finally done. At this point, the book of Nahum comes full circle by returning to the motif with which the book began in the first statements of its semi-acrostic introduction.

FOR FURTHER READING

COMMENTARIES

Coggins, Richard J. and S. Paul Re'emi. *Israel Among the Nations: Nahum, Obadiah, Esther*. International Theological Commentary. Grand Rapids: Eerdmans, 1985.

García-Treto, Francisco O. "The Book of Nahum: Introduction, Commentary, and Reflections," *The New Interpreter's Bible. Volume VII: Introduction to Apocalyptic Literature, Daniel, The Twelve Prophets*, ed. Leander E. Keck et al. Nashville: Abingdon, 1996.

Renaud, B. *Michée–Sophonie–Nahum*. Sources Bibliques. Paris: J. Gabalda, 1987.

Roberts, J. J. M. *Nahum, Habakkuk, and Zephaniah: A Commentary*. Old Testament Library. Louisville: Westminster/John Knox, 1991.

Rudolph, Wilhelm. *Micha–Nahum–Habakuk–Zephanja*. Kommentar zum Alten Testament XIII/3. Gütersloh: Gerd Mohn, 1975.

Seybold, Klaus. *Nahum, Habakuk, Zephanja*. Zürcher Bibelkommentare AT 24, 2. Zürich: Theologischer Verlag, 1991.

Smith, Ralph L. *Micah-Malachi*. Word Biblical Commentary, 32. Waco: Word, 1984.

Spronk, Klaas. *Nahum*. Historical Commentary on the Old Testament. Kampen: Kok Pharos, 1997.

Vuilleumier, René and Carl-A. Keller. *Michée, Nahoum, Habacuc, Sophonie*. Commentaire de l'ancien Testament XIb. Neuchâtel: Delachaux et Niestlé, 1971.

STUDIES

Cathcart, Kevin J. *Nahum in the Light of Northwest Semitic*. Biblica et Orientalia, 26. Rome: Biblical Institute, 1971.

Jeremias, Jörg. *Kultprophetie und Gerichtsverkündigung in der späten Königszeit Israels.* Wissenschaftliche Monographien zum Alten und Neuen Testament, 35. Neukirchen-Vluyn: Neukirchener, 1970.

Mason, R. *Micah, Nahum, Obadiah.* Old Testament Guides. Sheffield: JSOT Press, 1991.

Schulz, Hermann. *Das Buch Nahum.* Beiheft zur Zeitschrift für die Alttestamentliche Wissenschaft, 129. Berlin and New York, 1973.

Seybold, Klaus. *Profane Prophetie. Studien zum Buch Nahum.* Stuttgarter Bibelstudien, 135. Stuttgart: Katholisches Bibelwerk, 1989.

Sweeney, Marvin A., "Concerning the Structure and Generic Character of the Book of Nahum," *Zeitschrift für die Alttestamentliche Wissenschaft* 104 (1992) 364–77.

HABAKKUK

HABAKKUK

Overview

The book of Habakkuk is the eighth book in the sequence of both the Masoretic and the Septuagint versions of the Book of the Twelve. In both cases, it follows Nahum which argues that the downfall of Nineveh is an act of YHWH, and it precedes Zephaniah which calls upon the people of Jerusalem and Judah to return to YHWH and thereby avoid the punishment that will otherwise come if they continue to identify with pagan gods. The two superscriptions of Habakkuk provide no information concerning the historical setting or concerns of the book, but simply identify the contents either as "The pronouncement which Habakkuk the prophet saw" (Hab 1:1) or as "The prayer of Habakkuk the prophet concerning Shigionoth" (Hab 3:1). The contents of the book, however, focus especially on the threat posed to Jerusalem or Judah by the emergence of the Chaldeans or the Neo-Babylonian empire following its victory over Egypt at Carchemish in 605 B.C.E.[1] Thus, Habakkuk's placement between Nahum and Zephaniah addresses Jerusalem's and Judah's situation in the period between the fall of Assyria and the Babylonian exile. The book wrestles with the question of divine righteousness insofar as it identifies YHWH as the one who sent the Babylonians against Judah in the first place. Like Nahum, it therefore maintains that YHWH controls world events and employs nations for divine purposes. Whereas Nahum celebrates YHWH's defeat of a major enemy, Assyria, as an expression of divine justice, Habakkuk contends that YHWH raises the Babylonians as a threat to Judah for the purpose of punishment but that the Babylonians will ultimately fall

---

[1] For overviews of critical discussion concerning the book of Habakkuk, see Marvin A. Sweeney, "Habakkuk, Book of," *ABD* II:1-6; Rex Mason, *Zephaniah, Habakkuk, Joel* 60–96; and Jöcken, *Das Buch Habakuk*.

because they have acted unjustly in carrying out YHWH's purpose. This prepares for Zephaniah, which calls upon the people to make their decision to observe YHWH's requirements or suffer punishment if they refuse to do so. Although Zephaniah does not name YHWH's agent of punishment, its placement following Habakkuk indicates that Babylonia will fill this role.

The Hebrew Bible provides no information concerning the prophet Habakkuk other than the contents of his book. The name is not mentioned elsewhere in the Bible. It may be based upon the Hebrew root *ḥbq*, "to clasp, embrace," which has prompted later medieval kabbalistic tradition to identify him with the son of the Shunammite woman whose birth the prophet Elijah announced by saying that she would "embrace" a son in the coming year (2 Kgs 4:16). The name may in fact be derived from the Akkadian term *ḥabbaqūqū* or *ḥambaqūqū*, which refers to a type of garden plant. The Greek rendition of the name, *ʾambakoum*, appears to resemble the Akkadian term. The lack of information about the prophet has prompted a great deal of speculation concerning his identity and dates in later literature. The apocryphal Bel and the Dragon identifies him as "Habakkuk, the son of Jesus, of the tribe of Levi" (Bel 1:1 = LXX Dan 14:1). The Levitical identification probably presupposes Habakkuk's station at his "watchpost" (*mišmeret;* Hab 2:1), a term used elsewhere to refer to the priestly "watches" or periods of active service in the Temple (1 Chr 23:32; Neh 12:9). The pseudepigraphical Lives of the Prophets likewise places him in the exile, but identifies him as a member of the tribe of Simeon (Life of Habakkuk 1–9). This is probably because the imagery of YHWH's theophany in Habakkuk 3 relates to the Negev or southern desert areas beyond Judah (Josh 19:1-9). The midrashic historical work *Seder ʿOlam Rabbah* places him in the reign of Manasseh, presumably because of the violence and the breakdown of Torah and law mentioned in Hab 1:2-4. Clement of Alexandria states that Jeremiah, Ezekiel, Jonah, and Daniel are contemporaries of Habakkuk during the period of Babylonian exile, apparently because of the mention of the Chaldeans in Hab 1:6.

Scholarly discussion of the date of Habakkuk has produced a wide range of possibilities from the time of Sennacherib's invasion of Judah in 701 B.C.E. to Alexander's conquest of the Near East in 332–323 B.C.E. The key element in the discussion is the reference to the Chaldeans (*kaśdîm*) in Hab 1:6 which refers to the Neo-Babylonian empire founded by Nabopolassar in 625 B.C.E. The Neo-Babylonians were responsible for the downfall of Assyria in the late-seventh century. Under the rule of Nebuchadrezzar, the son of Nabopolassar, (605–562 B.C.E.), the Neo-Babylonian empire defeated Egypt at Carchemish in 605 B.C.E. and emerged as the dominant power in the ancient Near East. Nebuchadrezzar later destroyed Judah, Jerusalem, and Solomon's Temple in 587/6 B.C.E., brought an end to the active rule of the house of David, and exiled large numbers of Judeans to Babylonia during the course of invasions of Judah in 598/7, 587/6, and 582 B.C.E. Although most scholars agree in dating Habakkuk to the period prior to the Babylonian exile, the precise dating of the book and the nature of Habakkuk's message continue to provoke dispute. Many scholars maintain that the prophet's protests against the influence of the "wicked" refers to Judeans who reject YHWH's justice or Torah (Hab 1:2-4). Haak maintains, for example, that Habakkuk was an opponent of King Jehoiakim of Judah (609–598 B.C.E.), who argued that the Babylonians were brought by YHWH to punish the errant king and his supporters.[2] Such a contention creates problems, however, because the Chaldeans are later identified as the "wicked who swallow the righteous" (Hab 1:13; cf. Hab 1:12-17). Haak and others have argued that Habakkuk's prophecies were first directed against Judah and later reapplied to Babylon.[3]

It seems best, however, to argue that the "wicked" refers to Babylonia throughout the book.[4] Habakkuk originally protested to YHWH concerning the evil brought about by the emergence of Babylon as an enemy to Judah, and was subsequently surprised to learn that YHWH was responsible for the rise of Babylon. This provides the opportunity for Habakkuk to address the question of theodicy or the righteousness of G–d in which he asks how G–d can look upon evil or be silent when the treacherous or wicked swallow the righteous (Hab 1:13).[5] The issue is seemingly resolved when YHWH declares that the wicked will ultimately fall as a result of his excessive greed (Hab 2:4, 5). The woe oracles in Hab 2:5-20 and the psalm in Habakkuk 3 testify to YHWH's role in bringing down the oppressor and point to the manifestation of YHWH's justice. Such a reading points to the debate that would have taken place in Judean society beginning in 605 B.C.E. when Judah became a vassal of Babylon. Judah and Babylon had been allied against Assyria during the reign of Hezekiah (see Isaiah 39; 2 Kgs 20:12-19), and King Josiah of Judah died at the hands of Pharaoh Necho of Egypt in 609 B.C.E. in an effort to stop the Egyptians from moving north to Haran to support the Assyrians against the Babylonians (2 Kgs 23:28-30).

---

[2] Haak, *Habakkuk* 107–49; cf. Roberts, *Nahum, Habakkuk, Zephaniah* 81–5.

[3] E.g., Jeremias, *Kultprophetie* 55–110.

[4] See Sweeney, "Structure, Genre, and Intent in the Book of Habakkuk," *VT* 41 (1991) 63–83; idem, "Habakkuk, Book of."

[5] See also, Gowan, *The Triumph of Faith in Habakkuk*; Keller, *Michée, Nahoum, Habacuc, Sophonie*, and others who emphasize the concern with theodicy in Habakkuk.

Many in Judah would have felt betrayed by the Babylonians who treated Judah as a hostile vassal rather than as a trusted ally. Habakkuk appears to have been among them, prompting his questions to Yhwh concerning Yhwh's righteousness in bringing about the Babylonian oppressors in the first place.

The question of Habakkuk's vocation has also prompted a great deal of discussion. Many scholars follow Mowinckel who argues that Habakkuk was a cultic prophet stationed in the Temple.[6] This contention is based upon the frequent appearance of liturgical language in the book, such as the terminology of the complaint psalms in Hab 1:2-4 and 1:12-17 or the liturgical psalm in Habakkuk 3. Jeremias likewise points to the reference to the prophet's "watchpost" *(mišmeret)*, which corresponds to the term employed for the priestly "watches" or obligations for cultic service in the Temple (Neh 13:30; 2 Chr 7:6; 8:14; 35:2; cf. Isa 21:8).[7] It is likely that Habakkuk was a Temple-based oracle diviner or prophet much like Isaiah (see Isa 37:14-35/2 Kgs 19:14-34), Jeremiah (Jeremiah 7), or Ezekiel (see Ezekiel 3-6; n.b., the exile forced Ezekiel to prophesy in Babylon rather than in the Temple). As a Temple prophet, Habakkuk would be expected to present his oracles in a liturgical setting.[8] Others maintain that Habakkuk was a visionary without cultic connections,[9] that he came from a wisdom background,[10] or that he was simply an individual concerned with the events of his day.[11] None of these views represents a serious challenge against the contention that Habakkuk was a cultic prophet. Visionary activity is an important component of Temple-based oracular prophecy, and many prophets have a wisdom background as a part of their basic education.[12] For the most

[6] Sigmund Mowinckel, *Psalmenstudien I–VI* (Kristiana: Dybwad, 1921–24) 3.27-9. See also Széles, *Wrath and Mercy* 3–9; Eaton, *Obadiah, Nahum, Habakkuk, and Zephaniah* 81–4.

[7] *Kultprophetie* 103–7.

[8] See R. J. Tournay, *Seeing and Hearing G–d with the Psalms: The Prophetic Liturgy of the Second Temple in Jerusalem*, JSOTSup, vol. 118 (Sheffield: JSOT Press, 1991) and esp. David L. Petersen, *Late-Israelite Prophecy: Studies in Deutero-Prophetic Literature and in Chronicles*, SBLMS, vol. 23 (Missoula: Scholars Press, 1977) 55–87, who argues that the earlier role of the Temple prophetic singers was undertaken by the Levites in the Second Temple period.

[9] Rudolph, *Micha–Nahum–Habakuk–Zephanja* 193–4.

[10] Gowan, *The Triumph of Faith.*

[11] Keller, *Michée, Nahoum, Habacuc, Sophonie* 141–2.

[12] For a full discussion of oracular divination or prophecy in Israel and the ancient Near East, see Frederick H. Cryer, *Divination in Ancient Israel and Its Near Eastern Environment: A Socio-Historical Investigation*, JSOTSup, vol. 142 (Sheffield: JSOT Press, 1994).

part, arguments against Habakkuk's cultic connections depend on the excision of cultic references from the book as later additions or reworkings of earlier prophetic material.

The literary form and composition of the book has also prompted a great deal of discussion, especially since Habakkuk 3 constitutes a psalm or hymnic composition with its own superscription and literary characteristics. Because the psalm in Habakkuk 3 differs so markedly in form from the presentation of the dialogue between Habakkuk and YHWH in Habakkuk 1–2, many scholars have argued that Habakkuk 3 is an independent composition that originally had nothing to do with Habakkuk's material in the first two chapters.[13] This view was reinforced by the discovery of the Habakkuk Pesher or commentary at Qumran (1QpHab) which includes only chapters 1–2. Nevertheless, Habakkuk 3 appears together with Habakkuk 1–2 in the major manuscripts of the Twelve Prophets from the Judean wilderness, including the Wadi Murabbaat Minor Prophets Scroll (Mur88) and the Greek Minor Prophets Scroll from Nahal Hever (8HevXIIgr). Furthermore, there are affinities between Habakkuk 3 and Habakkuk 1–2 despite their differences in form. Both include superscriptions that identify each as works of Habakkuk (Hab 1:1; 3:1); both are concerned with YHWH's "work" (Hab 1:5; 3:2); both are concerned with the threat posed to the people by foreign invaders (Hab 1:5-17; 2:5-20; 3:12-14, 16); and both anticipate YHWH's actions to overthrow the enemy threat.[14]

The literary structure of the book comprises two basic parts, as indicated by the superscriptions in Habakkuk 1:1 and 3:1 and the distinctive forms of Habakkuk 1–2 and 3.[15] Habakkuk 1–2 constitutes "the pronouncement *(maśśāʾ)* of Habakkuk the prophet" (Hab 1:1). The prophet pronouncement or *maśśāʾ* is a typical prophetic form in which the prophet attempts to delineate YHWH's actions in the world.[16] Following the superscription in Hab 1:1, the pronouncement appears in Hab 1:2–2:20 in the form of a dialogue report between YHWH and Habakkuk.[17] The prophet initially raises a complaint to YHWH in Hab

---

[13] See Hiebert, *G–d of My Victory* 129–49.

[14] Cf. Hiebert, *G–d of My Victory* 129–49, who considers Habakkuk 3 to be an earlier composition that now functions as YHWH's response to the prophet's complaints in chapters 1–2.

[15] Széles, *Wrath and Mercy* 7–9; Sweeney, "Structure, Genre, and Intent."

[16] Sweeney, *Isaiah 1–39* 534–5.

[17] Contra. Michael H. Floyd, "Prophetic Complaints about the Fulfillment of Oracles in Habakkuk 1:2-17 and Jeremiah 15:10-18," *JBL* 110 (1991) 397–418, who maintains that this material constitutes a complaint rather than a dialogue, but he misses the significance of the reporting forms in Hab 2:1-20.

1:2-4 concerning the breakdown of justice and Torah in Judean society as the wicked oppress the righteous. YHWH's response to Habakkuk in Hab 1:5-11 is somewhat startling as YHWH claims to be the one who brought the Chaldeans to oppress the land in the first place. Habakkuk then renews his complaint to YHWH in Hab 1:12-17 by demanding to know how YHWH can stand silently by while such evil is manifested in the world. Finally, the prophet reports YHWH's second response in Hab 2:1-20 in which YHWH claims that the wicked one will ultimately fall as a result of his greed and the prophet presents a series of woe oracles in the form of a taunt song that announces the downfall of the oppressor as punishment for the crimes of plundering, extortion, bloodshed, and rape.

The second major portion of the book then follows in Habakkuk 3 in the form of "the prayer of Habakkuk concerning Shigionoth" (Hab 3:1). The term Shigionoth is not well understood, although the appearance of the term in Ps 7:1 indicates that it refers to a lamentation or a situation of distress. Following the superscription in Hab 3:1, Hab 3:2-19a constitutes the prayer or petition of the prophet to YHWH to manifest divine power in the world in order to defeat the enemies that threaten the nation and creation at large. The petition proper appears in Hab 3:2. The prophet's report of YHWH's theophany or the manifestation of YHWH's presence in the world follows in Hab 3:3-15, including a description of YHWH's approach in verses 3-7 and an address to YHWH in verses 8-15 that portrays YHWH's victory over the chaos elements and the nations that threaten both creation and Israel. The psalm concludes in Hab 3:16-19a with an expression of the psalmist's confidence in YHWH's deliverance. Finally, Hab 3:19b constitutes instructions to the choirmaster concerning the musical presentation of the psalm.

The Pronouncement *(maśśāʾ)* of Habakkuk: 1:1–2:20

The first major portion of the book of Habakkuk appears in Hab 1:1–2:20, which presents the "pronouncement," *maśśāʾ*, of the prophet. The term *maśśāʾ* is derived from the verb root *nśʾ*, "to lift up," and frequently translated as "burden." Such a translation hardly conveys the oracular nature of the form, however, especially since the verb *nśʾ* is sometimes employed to describe the act of prophetic or oracular speech. Consequently, the term *maśśāʾ* refers to a prophetic speech form that is uttered when the prophet "lifts up" his or her voice to speak or to pronounce the word of YHWH (see Num 23:18; 24:3, 15, 20, 21, 23; Isa 14:4). The specific genre *maśśāʾ* or prophetic pronouncement is a type of

prophetic discourse in which the prophet attempts to delineate how
YHWH's actions are manifested in human affairs.[18] The form has no
characteristic structure, but is identified by its contents and the designation of the text as *maśśāʾ* (see Isa 13:1; 14:28; 15:1; 30:6; Nah 1:1; Zech
9:1; 12:1; Mal 1:1). The *maśśāʾ* is analytical in character in that it examines past and present events in order to draw conclusions about YHWH's
activity and purposes in the world. In the present instance, the designation *maśśāʾ* appears in the superscription in Hab 1:1, and it is followed by the body of the *maśśāʾ* in Hab 1:2–2:20. The appearance of a
second superscription in Hab 3:1 marks the beginning of the second
major component of the book. Habakkuk's *maśśāʾ* addresses the question of theodicy.[19] It presents the report of a dialogue between the
prophet and YHWH in which the prophet pleads for deliverance from
invading Babylonian troops that pose a threat to Judah.[20] In the course
of the interchange with the Deity, the prophet learns that YHWH in fact
is the one who raised up the Babylonians to dominate the world in the
first place. The issue of divine righteousness is resolved when YHWH
announces that the Babylonian oppressor will ultimately fall as a result
of his own greed in swallowing and oppressing other nations.

The Superscription for the maśśāʾ: 1:1

The superscription for the prophet's *maśśāʾ* or pronouncement appears in Hab 1:1. Although it appears at the beginning of the book of
Habakkuk, it does not formally introduce the book of Habakkuk as a
whole. Instead, it introduces only Hab 1:2–2:20 because a second superscription in Hab 3:1 introduces the second major component of the
book in Habakkuk 3. As a formal superscription, Hab 1:1 is structurally
and generically distinct from the material that it introduces in that its
role is to introduce and identify the material that follows.[21] It identifies

[18] Sweeney, *Isaiah 1–39* 534–5; Richard D. Weis, "Oracle," *ABD* V:28-9; idem, "A
Definition of the Genre *Maśśāʾ* in the Hebrew Bible," (Ph.D. diss., Claremont Graduate School, 1986).

[19] See also Donald Gowan, *The Triumph of Faith in Habakkuk* (Atlanta: John Knox,
1976).

[20] For a full discussion of the form of Habakkuk 1–2, see Marvin A. Sweeney,
"Structure, Genre, and Intent in the Book of Habakkuk," *VT* 41 (1991) 63–83; idem,
"Habakkuk, Book of," *ABD* III:1-6.

[21] Gene M. Tucker, "Prophetic Superscriptions and the Growth of the Canon,"
Canon and Authority, ed. G. W. Coats and B. O. Long (Philadelphia: Fortress, 1977)
56–70.

the material in Hab 1:2–2:20 as "The Pronouncement *(maśśāʾ)* that Habakkuk the Prophet saw." As noted above, *maśśāʾ* is a generic term that designates a type of prophetic discourse in which the prophet attempts to delineate divine actions in human affairs. Although the *maśśāʾ* is generally recognized as a form of discourse, Hab 1:1 employs the verb *ḥzh*, "to see, envision," to describe the prophet's apprehension of Yhwh's actions. This presents little problem in the Hebrew verb *ḥzh* and its derivatives, e.g., *ḥāzôn*, "vision," is characteristicaly employed to refer to both visual and auditory experiences of divine revelation or prophetic experience (see Isa 29:7; Jer 23:16; Ezek 12:24; Hos 12:11 [NRSV: 12:10]; Mic 3:6; Hab 2:2; Dan 1:17; 9:24; Ps 89:20 [NRSV: 89:19]; Prov 29:18). It may be employed in reference to dreams (1 Sam 3:1; Isa 29:7; Dan 1:17) as well as in superscriptions to characterize the contents of entire prophetic books or portions thereof (Isa 1:1; 2:1; Obad 1; Nah 1:1; cf. 2 Chr 32:32).

The identification of Habakkuk as "the prophet" *(nābîʾ)* employs the general designation for a prophet, which includes the roles of "seer" *(rōʾeh;* see 1 Sam 9:9; Isa 30:10); "visionary" *(ḥōzeh;* see 2 Kgs 17:13; Isa 29:10); and one who "prophesies" *(nbʾ;* see 1 Sam 10:11; 19:20; 1 Kgs 22:18; Amos 7:12-13, 15-16); "pronounces" *(nśʾ;* see Num 23:7, 18; Isa 14:4); or "speaks" *(dbr;* see Deut 18:18-22; Jer 23:16) the word of Yhwh or of other gods. In the present instance, Habakkuk's designation as "the prophet" aids in establishing the credibility of the following material. Many identify Habakkuk as a cultic prophet who served in the Jerusalem Temple.[22] Such a view is based on the appearance of liturgical speech or song forms throughout the book (e.g., Hab 1:2-4; 3:1-19), the reference to the prophet's watch station in Hab 2:1 which is analogous to those of the Temple priests and Levites (see Neh 13:30; 2 Chr 7:6; 8:14; 35:2), and the extensive use of technical vocabulary for prophecy or oracular speech (e.g., *maśśāʾ,* "pronouncement"; *ḥāzâ,* "to have a vision"; *nābîʾ,* "prophet").

Apart from the present prophetic book, the prophet Habakkuk is otherwise unknown in the Hebrew Bible. The name is derived from the verb root *ḥbq,* "to clasp, embrace," which has prompted later medieval kabbalistic speculation that Habakkuk is to be identified with the son of the Shunammite woman whom the prophet Elijah prophesied that she would embrace some day as a result of her providing him with food even though she had little for herself (2 Kgs 4:16; Zohar 1:7; 2:44-45). The apocryphal Bel and the Dragon identifies him as, "Habakkuk, the son of Jesus, of the tribe of Levi," a contemporary of Daniel at the

---

[22] E.g., Jeremias, *Kultprophetie;* Széles, *Habakkuk and Zephaniah;* Haak, *Habakkuk among the Prophets.*

time of the Babylonian exile (Bel 1:1 = LXX Dan 14:1). The 1st century C.E. pseudepigraphical Lives of the Prophets follows Bel in this identification although it assigns him to the tribe of Simeon (Life of Habakkuk 1–9). The 2nd–3rd century C.E. midrashic history *Seder Olam Rabbah* places him in the reign of Manasseh (S. Olam Rab. 20). The 2nd century C.E. church father Clement of Alexandria identifies him as a contemporary of Jeremiah, Ezekiel, Jonah, and Daniel in the period of the Babylonian exile (Str 1:21). Most scholars view the name as a derivation from the Akkadian *ḫabaqūqū/ḫambaqūqū,* which refers to a type of garden plant.

Scholars have proposed a wide variety of dates for the prophet, ranging from the time of Sennacherib's invasion of Judah in the late-eighth century B.C.E. to the time of Alexander the Great's conquest of the Near East in the latter part of the fourth century B.C.E. Most scholars note the reference to the Chaldeans or Neo-Babylonians in Hab 1:6, which points to the late-seventh century B.C.E. when the Babylonians first began to pose a threat against Judah. This would refer to the period following the death of King Josiah in 609 B.C.E. at the hands of Pharaoh Necho of Egypt (see 2 Kgs 23:28-30), which forced Judah into the Egyptian political orbit. Egypt was an enemy of Babylon at this time and following the Babylonian defeat of Egypt at Carchemish in 605 B.C.E., the Babylonians took control of Judah, which was ruled by the pro-Egyptian monarch Jehoiakim ben Josiah (606–598 B.C.E.). A series of revolts by Judah against Babylon in 598–7, 588–7, and 582 B.C.E. saw the exile of King Jehoiachin and many prominent Judeans, the ultimate destruction of Jerusalem and Solomon's Temple, the destruction of the Judean state, and the exile of many additional Judeans to inaugurate the period of the Babylonian exile. As Judah had been previously allied with Babylon during Hezekiah's eighth-century revolt against Sennacherib (see Isaiah 39/2 Kgs 20:12-19) and during the reign of Josiah who died trying to stop the Egyptians from supporting Assyria in its last stand against Babylon, many in Judah felt betrayed by Babylonia's treatment of Judah as a vassal state in the aftermath of Babylonia's victory over Egypt.

The Pronouncement *(maśśāʾ)* Proper: Report of a Dialogue between Habakkuk and YHWH: 1:2–2:20

The pronouncement *(maśśāʾ)* proper appears in Hab 1:2–2:20. It is formulated as a report of a dialogue between the prophet and YHWH in which the prophet poses successive complaints to YHWH concerning the threat posed to Judah by the rise of the Chaldeans or Neo-Babylonian empire and receives Yhwh's answers. Although the exchange begins simply as a presentation of Habakkuk's words to Yhwh and Yhwh's response to the prophet without a narrative framework, the prophet's first person statements in Hab 2:1-2aα in which he reports Yhwh's response to him following a wait upon his watch station indicates that the entire section constitutes the prophet's own first person report of his dialogue with Yhwh. The shifts in speakers and addressees throughout the text indicates that it comprises four basic sub-units in which Habakkuk and Yhwh alternatively speak. The first is Hab 1:2-4, in which the prophet presents a complaint to Yhwh concerning the oppression of the righteous by the wicked. The second is Yhwh's response to Habakkuk in Hab 1:5-11 in which Yhwh states that Yhwh is the one who has established the Chaldeans. The third is Hab 1:12-17 in which Habakkuk presents a renewed complaint to Yhwh demanding to know how Yhwh can stand by as the Chaldeans carry out their atrocities. The fourth is Hab 2:1-20 in which Habakkuk reports Yhwh's second response, which includes Yhwh's statements that the oppressor will ultimately fall victim to his own greed and the prophet's explication of this response with a series of woe oracles that point to the ultimate downfall of the oppressor.

HABAKKUK'S FIRST COMPLAINT TO YHWH CONCERNING OPPRESSION OF THE RIGHTEOUS BY THE WICKED: 1:2-4

Habakkuk 1:2-4 constitutes the prophet's first complaint to Yhwh. It is demarcated by its first person address form, which indicates that the prophet is the speaker, and its explicit identification of Yhwh as the party addressed by the prophet. The speech employs the typical vocabulary of the complaint psalms to demand action from Yhwh concerning the oppression of the righteous by the wicked.[23] The prophet begins in verse 2 with a two-fold plea to Yhwh for deliverance. The first, "O Yhwh, how long shall I cry for help, and you will not listen," employs the stereotypical phrase *ʿad-ʾānâ*, "how long?" that appears in contexts of complaint to demand how long a situation is to be endured (see Pss 13:2, 3 [NRSV: 13:1, 2]; 62:4 [NRSV: 62:3]; Job 18:2; 19:2; cf. Exod 16:28; Num 14:11; Josh 18:3; Jer 47:6). The use of the verb *šwʿ*, "to cry out for help," likewise typically appears in such situations of distress in

---

[23] For discussion of the complaint psalms, see Erhard Gerstenberger, *Psalms Part I, with an Introduction to Cultic Poetry*, FOTL, vol. 14 (Grand Rapids: Eerdmans, 1988) 11–4.

which someone pleas for deliverance (see Pss 5:3 [NRSV: 5:2]; 18:7, 42 [NRSV: 18:6, 41]; 22:25 [NRSV: 25:24]; 28:2; 31:23 [NRSV: 31:22]; 30:3 [NRSV: 30:2]; 88:14 [NRSV: 88:13]; 119:147; Job 30:20; 36:13; 38:41; Isa 58:9; Jon 2:3 [NRSV: 2:2]; Lam 3:8). The prophet's reference to YHWH's failure to respond indicates the intensity and desperation of the situation, and provides motivation to the Deity whom the prophet presumes to be just. The second statement runs parallel to the first, and reinforces the initial plea, "or cry to you, 'violence!' and you will not save?" The verb *z'q*, "to cry out," likewise appears typically in situations of appeal to YHWH for deliverance from threat (see Judg 3:9; 1 Sam 7:8; 12:8, 10; Mic 3:4; Jer 11:11; Pss 22:6 [NRSV: 22:5]; 107:13, 19; 142:6 [NRSV: 142:5]; Jon 1:14). The term *ḥāmās*, "violence," appears commonly to describe situations of oppression or wrongdoing (Mic 6:12; Zeph 1:9; Prov 10:6, 11; Amos 3:10; Jer 6:7; 20:8; Ezek 45:9; Isa 60:18; Pss 55:10 [NRSV: 55:9]; 7:17 [NRSV: 7:16]; 73:6). Again, the prophet's accusation that YHWH does not deliver is intended to motivate a presumably just Deity to a situation of urgent need.

Verses 3-4 then turn to the key issue of the prophet's complaint, i.e., the manifestation of evil against the righteous that threatens to overturn moral world order. He begins with the rhetorical questions of verse 3a in order to assert that YHWH forces him to see wrongdoing and trouble in the world. Verse 3b follows immediately with the statements that destruction and violence are before the prophet as well as strife and contention. Verse 4, which begins with the particle *'al-kēn*, "therefore," points to the basic issue underlying the presence of evil in the world, i.e., it threatens the moral world order.[24] The translation in the NRSV, "so the law becomes slack and justice never prevails," does not convey this concern adequately. The Hebrew term *tôrâ*, translated here as "law," actually means, "instruction," and generally refers to divine instruction that is intended to create or maintain order in the world of creation. Examples of such "Torah" include the entire Five Books of Moses or Torah that has come to embody the basis for divine revelation in Judaism (Ezra 3:2; 7:6; Neh 8:1, 3, 18; 9:3; Pss 19:8 [NRSV: 19:7]; 119:1, 18, 29); the instruction of parents to their children (Prov 1:8; 6:20, 23; 3:1; 4:2; 7:2), sages to their disciples (Prov 13:14; 28:4-7, 9), wives to their husbands (Prov 31:26); instruction in the proper use of ritual in the Temple that stands as the center of creation and cosmic order (Exod 13:9; 16:4; Lev 6:2, 7, 18 [NRSV: 6:9, 14, 25]; 7:1, 7, 11; Deut 17:11; Ezek 43:12); the various law codes that lay out the basic legal principles for a just society (Exod 24:12; Josh 24:26; Deut 1:5; 28:61); and the "custom,"

[24] Cf. M. D. Johnson, "The Paralysis of Torah in Habakkuk i 4," *VT* 35 (1985) 257–66, who notes that the establishment of Chaldea is not the answer to the prophet's question, but points instead to the cause of the problem.

"manner," or "essential nature" of human beings (2 Sam 7:19). Likewise, the Hebrew term *mišpāṭ*, translated here as "justice," more properly refers to "law" in general (Jer 8:7; Isa 58:2; 42:4; 51:4), which embodies the basic principles of justice. The final clause of the passage in verse 4b begins with a *kî*, "for," to express the consequences of such a situation, i.e., "the wicked surround the righteous—therefore judgment comes forth perverted. The term *maktîr*, literally "surrounds," refers to the domination of the righteous by the wicked or to the triumph of the wicked over the righteous. The Hebrew term *mišpāṭ* appears once again behind the NRSV's "judgments," and is best translated as "justice" in the present case, i.e., "therefore, justice comes forth perverted." Protection against the perversion of justice due to all is a basic concern of Israelite law (see Exod 23:6-8), even when it means siding with the rich over against the poor (Exod 23:3; 22:20-23 [NRSV: 22:21-24]) or siding with a foreigner against an Israelite (Exod 23:9). Each person in Israelite society can expect justice as a fundamental right, no matter what their station in life might be (n.b., Nathan's condemnation of King David for adultery with Bath Sheba, the wife of a foreigner, in 2 Samuel 12). Habakkuk does not identify the righteous or the wicked at this point, but it is clear that the moral order of his world has been compromised by the violence, wrongdoing, and strife that he has seen.

Yhwh's Response to Habakkuk:
Yhwh Has Established the Chaldeans: 1:5-11

Yhwh's response to Habakkuk's complaint appears in Hab 1:5-11, although the second person masculine plural address forms might indicate that the speech is addressed to the entire nation of Judah as well as to the prophet. Yhwh is not explicitly named as the speaker, but appears to be the only candidate behind the first person statement of verse 6a, "for behold, I am establishing the Chaldeans . . ." The basic elements of the response appear in verses 5-6, in which Yhwh announces the establishment of the Chaldeans. Yhwh's speech begins in verse 5a with the command to look at the nations and see what is taking place. This command is especially important for establishing the character of the prophetic *maśśāʾ* as an example of the prophet's role in analyzing human events in order to deduce Yhwh's actions in the world. The initial statement conveys the astonishing nature of the conclusion to which the prophet comes—or which Yhwh announces—and verse 5b continues that sense of astonishment with Yhwh's announcement that Yhwh is undertaking "a great deed/work" that the audience would never believe even if it was told. The bombshell comes in verse

6, i.e., Yhwh is responsible for bringing the Chaldeans to dominate the entire earth. Based upon the reading of the verse in the Habakkuk Pesher (1QpHab; a commentary on Habakkuk 1–2) from Qumran, the Hebrew term *kaśdîm* is sometimes emended to *kittîm*, a term used in reference to the Greeks or Romans.[25] There is no basis for such an emendation, however, as Qumran Bible manuscripts frequently alter the biblical text so that it conforms to their own ideology or understanding of the scriptures. The term *kaśdîm* is apparently a Hebrew rendition of the Akkadian term *kaldû* (or the earlier *kašdû*) used in reference to the land of Chaldea, located along the banks of the Tigris and Euphrates Rivers at the head of the Persian Gulf. The Chaldeans revolted against Assyria at the death of Assurbanipal in 627 B.C.E., and ultimately destroyed the Assyrian empire by 609 B.C.E. The Neo-Babylonian empire dominated much of the Near East during the reigns of Nabopolassar and Nebuchadrezzar from 609 B.C.E. through its submission to the Persian monarch Cyrus in 539 B.C.E., long after the death of Nebuchadrezzar. The astonishing nature of Yhwh's revelation entails the fact that Judah and the Chaldeans had long been allies; Hezekiah had allied with the Chaldean prince Merodach Baladan in an effort to oppose Sennacherib in 705 B.C.E. (see Isaiah 39), and King Josiah of Judah died in 609 attempting to prevent the Egyptians from reaching Haran in time to support the last remnants of the Assyrian army against the Babylonians. When Babylon defeated the Egyptians at Carchemish in 605 B.C.E. and took control of Judah, they treated the country as a hostile vassal state rather than as a trusted ally, no doubt in part because of the presence of the pro-Egyptian Jehoiakim on the Judean throne. Nevertheless, many in Judah would consider this to be a betrayal by a past ally, although there were also many in Judah, such as the prophet Jeremiah, who favored alliance with Babylon (see Jeremiah 27–28). Yhwh's description of Babylon in verse 6 as "a fierce and impetuous nation" that marches to the ends of the earth to dominate the homes of others indicates the sense of threat and betrayal felt by many in Judah, apparently including the prophet Habakkuk, at their treatment by the Babylonians.

Clearly, Yhwh's action brings evil against Judah, and there is no clear rationale for such a move on Yhwh's part, i.e., Yhwh does not accuse Judah of wrongdoing or characterize the rise of Babylon as a punishment. This highlights the issue of theodicy, i.e., is G–d in fact responsible for evil that afflicts the righteous? From Habakkuk's standpoint, that is certainly the case. The issue is highlighted by Yhwh's own description in verses 7-11 of the terror inspired by the Babylonians.

[25] For discussion, see Roberts, *Nahum, Habakkuk, Zephaniah* 92; Haak, *Habakkuk* 37–8.

YHWH describes them in verse 7 as dreadful and fearsome. The NRSV translation of the second half of the verse, "their justice and dignity proceed from themselves," indicates arrogance on the part of the Babylonians, which is correct in and of itself. Nevertheless, the phrase also indicates that the Babylonians are establishing their own "law" (*mišpāṭ*) and "dominance" (*śĕ'ēt*) in the land. The term *mišpāṭ*, "law," was discussed above. The term *śĕ'ēt*, "dominance," is used elsewhere to describe the preeminent or dominant position of one party over another, such as that of Cain over Abel (Gen 4:7); Reuben over his brothers (Gen 49:3); or YHWH over anyone (Job 13:11). The new order imposed by Babylon contrasts markedly with the perverted world order described by Habakkuk in verse 4—and YHWH claims responsibility for it. YHWH describes the menacing Babylonian cavalry in verse 8, whose horses are faster than leopards and more fearsome than hungry wolves when darkness descends. The second half of the verse portrays the charging or leaping horsemen, who fly like eagles as they range through the land and overcome their opposition. Verse 9 portrays the violent aims of the Babylonian army, as their massed ranks face forward, enabling them to advance and take countless captives. The Hebrew expression *mĕgammat pĕnêhem qādîmāh*, literally, "the troop of their faces is forward," is difficult, but apparently describes the ranks of Babylonian soldiers facing forward as they engage in combat.[26] Verse 10 portrays the confidence and arrogance of the Babylonians as they laugh at kings and princes who prove to be no challenge to them. The same applies to fortifications. The statement, "and heap up earth to take it," refers to the standard military practice of the time of employing prisoners of war to pile dirt against the walls of a fortified city in order to form a ramp by which the attacking soldiers might bring up weapons and heavy equipment so that they will be able to attack over the wall and overcome the city. The Assyrians used this tactic to take Lachish in 701 B.C.E., and the Romans later used it to take Masada from its Zealot defenders in 73–74 C.E.[27]

The final statement of YHWH's speech in verse 11 portrays the rapid movement of the Babylonians as they sweep by opposition, but it shifts to a portrayal of their own self-confidence and—from a Judean perspective—blasphemy as they incur guilt by worshiping their own strength as divine. By placing this statement in the Deity's mouth, Habakkuk highlights the issue of theodicy, because YHWH claims to have brought this very situation about.

---

[26] See Roberts, *Nahum, Habakkuk, Zephaniah* 93; Haak, *Habakkuk* 43–5.

[27] See David Ussishkin, "Lachish," *ABD* IV:114-26, esp. 121–23; Ehud Netzer, "Masada," *NEAEHL* 3:973-85, esp. 983–4.

HABAKKUK'S SECOND COMPLAINT TO YHWH
CONCERNING THE EVIL NATURE OF THE CHALDEANS: 1:12-17

Habakkuk's second address to YHWH in Hab 1:12-17 renews of his complaint and advances the argument in the aftermath of the revelation that YHWH is responsible for bringing about the Babylonian threat. YHWH is explicitly named as the addressee in verse 12, and the first person subject and second person masculine singular address forms indicate that the prophet speaks once again to YHWH. Habakkuk's speech focuses especially on the issue of theodicy by demanding to know how YHWH can tolerate such a situation. The prophet employs a combination of rhetorical questions and blunt assertions in verses 12-13 to characterize YHWH as a supposedly righteous and eternal G–d and to demand why YHWH allows this situation to take place and continue. The first rhetorical question in verse 12α, "are you not from old?" essentially asserts YHWH's eternal character as creator of the universe, and implies that YHWH neither dies nor changes. Why then should this righteous creator suddenly allow such evil to take place? YHWH's eternal character is highlighted once again in the succeeding assertion of verse 12aβ, "O YHWH, my G–d, my Holy One, you shall not die." The Hebrew text actually reads *lōʾ nāmût*, "we shall not die," instead of the expected *lōʾ tāmût*, "you shall not die." This is apparently one of the so-called *Tiqqunei Soferim*, "corrections of the scribes."[28] Ancient Jewish scribal practice allowed for the modification of biblical texts that were theologically offensive or that portrayed YHWH in disparaging terms. For example, Gen 18:22 indicates that Abraham was still standing before YHWH, but the text actually should read that YHWH was still standing before Abraham because YHWH was part of the group that was departing for Sodom. But such a statement suggests that Abraham is somehow superior to YHWH because YHWH seeks Abraham's attention. The modification presents Abraham as one who seeks the audience of YHWH instead, and thereby eliminates a potential disparagement of YHWH. According to the tradition, there are eighteen such corrections in the Bible, but the various lists preserved in Rabbinic literature actually identify more than eighteen instances. In the present case, Habakkuk's statement, "you shall not die," is true, but such a statement from a human being suggests the possibility that YHWH might die, an assertion that disparages YHWH in the eyes of the scribes who transmitted this text. Verse 12a then asserts the prophet's view of YHWH as a just G–d who appoints the Babylonians for justice and punishment, i.e.,

---

[28] C. McCarthy, "Emendations of the Scribes," *IDB[S]* 263–4; E. J. Revell, "Scribal Emendations," *ABD* V:1011-12.

Habakkuk claims that such a terrible army must have been brought by
Yhwh to punish the people for some wrongdoing. He continues this
line of thought in verse 13a with the assertion that Yhwh's eyes are too
pure to look upon evil and that Yhwh is incapable of looking upon
wrongdoing, presumably without putting a stop to the situation. But
having made these claims, Habakkuk returns to the fundamental
enigma of the situation with his rhetorical question in verse 13, "why
do you look on the treacherous, and are silent when the wicked swallow those more righteous than they?" Indeed, this is the very question
of theodicy that is asked in modern times in the aftermath of the Shoah
when G–d and much of the world, including governments, churches,
banking concerns, and corporations, stood by silent as six million Jews
and others were murdered by the Nazis, with a great deal of assistance
by people from the various nations that had been conquered by Ger-
many. That question was posed twenty-five hundred years ago by the
prophet Habakkuk, and it still has not been answered adequately.

The prophet continues in verses 14-17 with a renewed description
of Babylon's unstoppable conquest of the world. He employs the metaphor of a fisherman who uses his nets and hooks to sweep the sea clean
of fish and other creatures. Such imagery is especially appropriate because the Babylonian mythology employs similar imagery, e.g., Marduk employs a net to defeat Tiamat in portraying the establishment of
created world order.[29] Likewise, similar imagery is applied to Yhwh in
Job 40:25–41:26 [NRSV: 41:1-34] in describing Yhwh's subduing of the
chaos monster Leviathan as part of the process by which Yhwh established creation. The text suggests some elements of the overturning of
the created order, however, in that human beings are now considered
as the fish of the sea or crawling things—this is not the world that
Yhwh created, but a distortion of that world. Verse 15 portrays the use
of hooks and nets to take these helpless creatures, and again emphasizes the laughter of the Babylonians as they flaunt any sense of justice
in their conquest of the earth. The element of blasphemy appears once
again in verse 16 as the Babylonians sacrifice to their nets and burn incense to their seines on account of the rich "harvest" that they have
caught with no acknowledgment of Yhwh who made their success possible in the first place.

Finally, the prophet once again poses the essential question of theodicy in verse 17, "is he then to keep on emptying his net and destroy-
ing nations without mercy?" The answer is obviously no—at least in
the prophet's mind. Again, this is a rhetorical question that actually

---

[29] See the Enuma Elish, or Babylonian account of creation, *ANET* 60–72; cf.
Roberts, *Nahum, Habakkuk, Zephaniah* 104.

makes an assertion. In this case, however, there is an underlying question: is YHWH going to stop this?

HABAKKUK'S REPORT OF YHWH'S SECOND RESPONSE: THE EVIL WILL FALL: 2:1-20

The prophet's report of YHWH's second response appears in Hab 2:1-20. In contrast to the previous three sections which simply quote the words of Habakkuk or YHWH, this section is formulated as a first person speech by the prophet. He describes the situation in which he receives YHWH's response, quotes the response itself, and then adds his own lengthy comments to explicate the meaning of YHWH's response in relation to the expected downfall of the Babylonians. Habakkuk does not address YHWH per se as he did in Hab 1:2-4 and 1:12-17; instead, he speaks about YHWH in the third person and thereby addresses the reader or his own listening audience. The basic structure of the passage includes two major parts: the prophet's report of the setting in which he receives YHWH's response in verse 1 and the prophet's report of YHWH's response together with his own explanatory oracles in verses 2-20.

The prophet states in verse 1 that he stands at his "watchpost" and takes his station on the "rampart" to keep watch for YHWH's response. The Hebrew term *mišmeret*, "watchpost," has a very specialized meaning in relation to priestly service in the Temple, which suggests that Habakkuk serves in some cultic function as a prophet or oracle diviner based in the Temple.[30] The term appears frequently in reference to holy offices and functions of the priests and Levites, including their divisions for service (Neh 12:9), their basic offices or positions (2 Chr 7:6; 8:14; 35:2), their sacred duties (Lev 8:35; 22:9; Ezek 44:8, 16; 48:11; Zech 3:7; Neh 12:45), and specific functions in relation to sacrifice (Num 18:5; Ezek 40:46), the priestly offerings (Num 18:8), the tent of meeting (Num 18:4; 1 Chr 23:32), the Temple (Ezek 40:45; 44:14, 15), purity (Neh 12:45), etc. The term is also used generally in relation to a simple guard or watch (1 Sam 22:23; 2 Kgs 11:5, 6, 7), such as a prison situation (2 Sam 20:3), but it also appears metaphorically in relation to an oracular context in which a prophet expects to receive a divine message based upon the observation of approaching riders (Isa 21:8). Although this use of the term is ambiguous, the tent of meeting or the Temple elsewhere appear to be the setting of oracular divination in which a prophet such

---

[30] Cf. Jeremias, *Kultprophetie* 104–7, who points to the prophet's watchstation as evidence that he serves as a cultic prophet in the Temple.

as Moses or Isaiah receives divine revelation (Exod 34:29-35; Isa 37:14-35/2 Kgs 19:14-34; cf. also the portrayal of Balaam in Numbers 22–24, who performs specified sacrifices in preparation for his delivery of oracles concerning Israel).[31] The reference to the "rampart" is somewhat problematic because the Hebrew term *māṣôr* generally refers to a siege-work (Deut 20:20; Mic 4:14 [NRSV: 5:1]; Ezek 4:2, 7). Although the term is usually derived from the root *ṣwr*, "to confine, besiege," it may also be derived from *nṣr*, "to guard." In later times, *māṣôr* comes to refer to a rampart in general (Zech 9:3). The oracular context of this situation is clear from the prophet's statement that he stands watch "to see what he (YHWH) will say to me." The prophet's parallel statement, "and what he will answer concerning my complaint," actually reads "and what I will answer concerning my complaint." Although this passage is not listed among the *Tiqqunei Sopherim* or "Corrections of the Scribes," many have speculated that this is a correction based upon the view that YHWH should be the subject of the verb in keeping with the Syriac reading of this verse.[32] YHWH is hardly required to answer the prophet's complaint and therefore the statement was modified so that the prophet would have to answer to YHWH concerning the complaint that he leveled against the Deity. Unfortunately, there is no secure evidence for this claim as the Peshitta is a very late textual version. It should be noted that the reading can be construed to refer to the prophet's anticipation of another statement to YHWH after he hears YHWH speak. The term "complaint," *tôkaḥat*, generally refers to correction or rebuke (e.g., Pss 39:12 [NRSV: 39:11]; 73:14; Prov 29:15; Ezek 5:15; 25:17), reproof (Prov 1:23; 27:5; 3:11; 5:12), and argumentation (Ps 38:15 [NRSV: 38:14]; Job 13:6; 23:4). Here, the term indicates Habakkuk's rebukes or complaints directed against YHWH, especially in Hab 1:12-17 in which YHWH is explicitly named.

The prophet then reports YHWH's response and his own oracular elaboration on that response in verses 2-20. The narrative introduction in verse 2 indicates the report of YHWH's response in verses 2-4 and the conjunctive particle, *wĕ'ap-kî*, "moreover," introduces the prophet's explication in verses 5-20.

The prophet's report of YHWH's response begins with the speech formula in verse 2aα, "Then YHWH answered me and said." The speech itself begins with the Deity's instructions to the prophet in verses 2aβ-3 concerning the need to record the vision and to wait for its fulfillment. The practice of writing oracular visions and interpreting them was a

---

[31] For a full discussion of oracular divination in Israel and the ancient Near East, see Cryer, *Divination in Ancient Israel and its Ancient Near Eastern Environment*.

[32] E.g., Hiebert, "Habakkuk," 639; Haak, *Habakkuk* 54.

common activity of oracle diviners in the ancient Near East,[33] and such a practice appears to underlie Isaiah's recording of the oracular significance of the birth of his son Maher-shalal-hash-baz in Isaiah 8. It also appears to reflect the recording of the ten commandments on two tablets by the Levitical prophet or oracle diviner Moses (Exodus 24; 34). Indeed, the writing of the prophetic books in the Bible at large may well be the result of such a concern. The phrase, "so that a runner may read it," does not convey adequately the meaning of the Hebrew *lĕmaʿan yārûṣ qôrēʾ bô*, literally, "so that the one reading/proclaiming it may run/hurry." Apparently the phrase refers to the passing of the recorded vision to a runner or a herald who will read or proclaim the message publicly,[34] much as the herald of good tidings in Isa 40:9-11; 52:7-10; and Nah 2:1 [NRSV: 1:15] announces the restoration of Jerusalem and Judah. The book of Isaiah contains several instructions to read the book in order to await its fulfillment (e.g., Isa 34:16-17; 29:11-12; 8:16-18). Verse 3 emphasizes that the fulfillment of this vision will not be immediate—indeed, the Babylonian empire did not fall to Persia until 539 B.C.E., some sixty-six years after Babylon defeated Egypt to become the suzerain of Judah. Although the term "appointed time" *(môʿēd)* frequently refers to festivals (Hos 9:5; 12:10 [NRSV: 12:9]; Lam 2:7, 22; Deut 31:10; Lev 23:2), it also refers generally to an appointed time when some important event will take place, such as the time of YHWH's return when Sarah bears a son (Gen 18:14), Jonathan's meeting with David (1 Sam 20:35), the place where the men of Ai would meet Israel in battle (Josh 8:14), or the time when the Shunammite woman would bear a son (2 Kgs 4:16). In the present case, the term refers to the time of the projected downfall of Babylon. The phrase, "it speaks of the end, and does not lie," has also been the subject of a great deal of discussion due to uncertainties in the meaning of its vocabulary, but it simply states assurance that the oracle will be fulfilled. The following phrases in verse 3b, which call for patience in awaiting its fulfillment, function similarly.

The basic statement of the vision appears in verse 4.[35] It has been extensively discussed, especially because of the role it plays in Paul as a prooftext for the principle of justification by faith (see Rom 1:17; Gal 3:11; cf. Heb 10:38-39). The NRSV translation, "Look at the proud! Their spirit is not right in them, but the righteous live by their faith," reflects the influence of Protestant theological concerns. The Hebrew term

---

[33] See Cryer, *Divination*, for discussion of the role played by writing in professional practice of ancient divination.

[34] Cf. Hiebert, "Habakkuk," 641.

[35] See my "Structure, Genre, and Intent," 74–7, for discussion of this verse.

ʿuppĕlâ, "proud," is derived from the root ʿpl, which means "to swell up" and appears in Num 14:44 where it means "to act presumptuously, arrogantly, or heedlessly." It refers to one who is proud, but it more likely indicates one who is arrogant. The phrase, "their spirit is not right in them," lōʾ yāšĕrâ napšô, means literally, "not straight in him is his life." Indeed, the phrase is constructed around the feminine singular noun nepeš, "throat, life," frequently mistranslated as "soul" under the influence of the NT, which also provides the antecedent for ʿuppĕlâ, "arrogant." The term nepeš sometimes functions elliptically as a reference to an individual person so that together, these phrases mean "behold, he is arrogant, his life is not stable/secure," i.e., the Babylonian is going to die as a result of his arrogance. The second part of the phrase, "but the righteous shall live by their faith," obviously contrasts the righteous with the arrogant figure mentioned in the first half of the statement. The term ʾĕmûnâ, is frequently translated as "faith" under the influence of the NT, but it refers more generally to "constancy," "stability," or "reliability." In this case, such constancy relates to the reliance of the righteous on YHWH. In contrast to the Babylonian who will perish because of his arrogance, the righteous will live as a result of his reliance on YHWH. In keeping with the principles laid down in verses 2-3, the righteous must now wait for YHWH to act against Babylon at the appointed time.

Verses 5-20 then present the prophet's explication of the meaning of YHWH's oracle to him, including an explanatory statement in verse 5 that employs the metaphor of drunkenness to explain the impending downfall of the Babylonians and the prophet's presentation of a taunt song in verses 6-20 which lays out the reasons for the impending fall of Babylon. The third person references to YHWH in verses 13, 14, 16, and 20 indicate that Habakkuk is the speaker in the section devoted to the taunt song. The identity of the speaker in verse 5 is far more ambiguous, although its syntactical features and explanatory character indicate that the prophet—and not YHWH—is the speaker here as well.

Verse 5 begins with the particle, wĕʾap-kî, "moreover," which joins verse 5 to the preceding presentation of YHWH's oracular speech but does so by indicating syntactic disjunction as well. When following a statement introduced by hinnēh, "behold," which introduces Hab 2:4, it indicates a statement that reinforces the preceding statement, i.e., "how much more so . . ." (e.g., Prov 11:31; 15:11; 17:7; Job 9:14; 1 Sam 14:30; 1 Kgs 8:27). The particle wĕʾap-kî therefore clearly serves the explanatory character of verse 5, which suggests that the verse represents the prophet's attempt to illustrate the meaning of YHWH's oracle. He employs the metaphor of wine or drunkenness to make the point about the impending downfall of the arrogant mentioned in verse 4. It begins by stating that "wine is treacherous, the arrogant do not endure." Some have attempted to follow the Habakkuk pesher from Qumran by reading *hôn,* "wealth," in place of MT *hayyayin,* "the wine," which involves only a minor difference in the consonantal text, i.e., *hwn* versus *hyyn* (see NRSV). The reading of "wealth" apparently serves the attempt to portray the motivations of the "wicked priest," which the Qumran scroll reads as the object of Habakkuk's condemnation, but it destroys the character of the metaphor that appears throughout verse 5. The following phrase, "the arrogant (man) will not endure," appropriately portrays the effects of drinking excessive wine, i.e., he will not be able to stand for long. The second half of the verse, "they open their throats wide as Sheol; like Death they never have enough," portrays the boundless capacity for drink that one might have at the beginning of the drinking festivities that ultimately lead to the collapse of the drinker as the wine works its effects. The English translation of the phrase masks a pun with verse 4 in that the Hebrew word *nepeš* means both "throat" in verse 5 and "life" in verse 4. The reference to Sheol or the underworld opening its mouth to swallow the living builds upon this pun by pointing to the ultimate death of the Babylonian oppressor for swallowing more nations than he can chew. This principle is made explicit in the last phrases of verse 5 that portray the gathering of all the nations by the arrogant conqueror. Basically, the prophet employs these metaphors to assert that Babylon's excessive greed and arrogance in the oppression of other nations will lead ultimately to its downfall when it is unable to absorb all of the nations that it has taken.

The prophet's presentation of a taunt song in which he presents the nations' derisive singing and celebrating at the fall of their oppressor then follows in verses 6-20. The nations condemn the oppressor for his various acts of plundering, extortion, bloodshed, and rape, and thereby identify the reasons for which the oppressor must be condemned. The presentation of the song itself appears in verse 6-17 and the prophet's commentary on the song, in which he points to the emptiness of Babylonians idolatry in comparison to the power of YHWH in the Temple, then follows in verses 18-20.

The prophet begins the presentation of the taunt song in verse 6a with an introduction that identifies the genre of the material that follows, "shall not everyone taunt such people and, with mocking riddles, say about them . . . ?" The form of the rhetorical question of course actually constitutes an assertion that everyone should indeed engage in such ridicule against the oppressor. The Hebrew term *māšāl,* "taunt," refers generally to a song or poetic composition (Num 21:27-30; 1 Kgs 5:12 [NRSV: 4:32]; Pss 49:5 [NRSV: 49:4]; 78:2), such as a proverb (1 Sam 10:12; Ezek 12:22; Prov 1:1; 10:1; 25:1) or parable (Ezek 17:2; 21:5 [NRSV:

20:49]; 24:3), in which one thing metaphorically portrays another. It is frequently employed in prophetic literature to refer to a prophetic discourse or oracle that relies on metaphor or figuration (e.g., Num 23:7, 18; 24:3, 15, 20, 21, 23; Isa 14:4; Mic 2:4). Whereas *māšāl* can indicate a poetic or figurative composition in general, *mĕlîṣâ*, "mocking," is unambiguous in its meaning. It is derived from the root *lyṣ*, "to scorn," and clearly refers to the denigration of the oppressor, although the term is also used in reference to enigmatic interpretation (Gen 42:23; Job 33:23; Isa 43:27; cf. *mĕlîṣâ* in Prov 1:6). The term *ḥîdâ*, "riddle," simply refers to perplexing or enigmatic sayings or riddles, such as those posed to Solomon by the Queen of Sheba to test his intelligence (1 Kgs 10:1), the riddle posed by Samson in Judges 14, the allegories posed by Ezekiel in Ezekiel 17, or the obscure speech which YHWH does not employ in speaking to Moses in Num 12:8. The prophet's introduction is syntactically dependent on the following song, indicating its role as the introduction.

The song itself appears in verses 6b-17 in the form of four "woe" speeches, which are designed to address the Babylonian oppressor by laying out the crimes of which he stands accused. Following the typical form of the "woe" oracle, each begins with the particle *hôy*, "woe!" followed by a verbal statement that conveys the actions for which the addressee is condemned.[36] Such series of woe oracles appear elsewhere in Isa 5:8-25; 28-33, and they appear individually in Amos 5:18-20; Isa 1:4; 3:11; 10:5; Nah 3:1; and Hab 3:1. Although addressed to the oppressor, the woe form is also designed to catch the attention of the prophet's audience.

The first woe oracle of the series appears in verses 6b-8 which accuses the addressee of plundering that which is not his own. The basic accusation is made in the introductory woe statement of verse 6b. The reference to "goods taken in pledge" (*ʿabṭîṭ*) refers to goods or cash that has already been deposited with a creditor as surety for a loan or debt of some sort; it might also refer to tribute paid by a vassal nation to a suzerain (Deut 15:6) in return for protection from enemies. Deuteronomy 24:10-13 forbids the creditor from taking such a pledge forcibly from a debtor, and requires that the garment pledged by a poor person be returned at sundown so that the poor debtor will have something to sleep in during the period in which he repays the loan. Verses 7-8 then applies the basic Israelite legal principle of reciprocity (i.e., an eye for an eye, Exod 21:22-25; Lev 24:13-23; Deut 19:21) to the oppressor who engages in such actions. The oppressor can expect his own creditors to

[36] For an overview of the woe form, see Sweeney, *Isaiah 1–39* 543, and the bibliography cited there.

rise against him in order to take booty from him. It is unlikely that Babylon was in debt in this period, but the statement metaphorically portrays the impetus to revenge that the victims of oppression will seek from their oppressor. This is a lesson that the Babylonians should well have known; they rose up against the Assyrians in the late seventh century B.C.E. and destroyed them as a result of Assyrian oppression of Babylon. Verse 8 renews the initial accusation of verse 6a in an effort to identify the cause of Babylon's ultimate downfall, "because you have plundered many nations, all that survive of the peoples shall plunder you—because of human bloodshed, and violence to the earth, to cities and all who live in them." Babylon has brought such terror to the world, and as a basic principle of justice can expect to receive the same. This refrain concludes the first woe oracle, and it will conclude the last woe oracle in the series (see verse 17b), thereby forming a literary "envelope" that encloses all four woes.

The second woe oracle of the series appears in verses 9-11 which accuses the addressee of engaging in extortion to build his own house. The woe address begins with the statement, "woe for you who get evil gain for your houses." The Hebrew term *beṣaʿ*, "evil gain," and the verbal forms of the root *bṣʿ*, "to cut off, gain by violence," are commonly employed in reference to unjust gain or gain made by violence, extortion, plunder, etc. (noun: Judg 5:19; Mic 4:13; Exod 18:21; 1 Sam 8:3; verb: Ps 10:3; Prov 1:19; Ezek 22:27). The use of the term here clearly presupposes the payment of tribute demanded by the Babylonians as they asserted their hegemony over nations, such as Judah, that came under their control. The following reference to setting your nest on high to keep it safe from harm employs the metaphor of a bird's nest to portray the efforts of the addressee to employ such extorted gain to secure his own dwelling. During the Neo-Babylonian period, and especially during the reign of Nebuchadrezzar, the city of Babylon was rebuilt into a magnificent capital city with major palaces for the king, the hanging gardens of Babylon, a processional way through the city, and the ziggurat Entemenanki which served as the focal point for the Akitu New Year celebration.[37] It was at the temple located at the top of the Entemenanki that the Babylonian king received the tablets of destiny that authorized his kingship for another year. Verse 10 then levels the accusation against the addressee that he has brought shame on his own house by cutting off so many other peoples. The last phrase of the verse, "you have forfeited your life," means literally, "your life (i.e., 'you') have incurred sin," or more colloquially, "you are guilty." The *kî*,

[37] See Laurie E. Pearce, "Babylon," *HBD* 97–9; Jean-Claude Margueron, "Babylon," *ABD* I:563-5.

"for, because," statement in verse 11 metaphorically portrays the stones and rafters of the house crying out because of the guilt of the addressee. In this case, the prophet thereby employs the well-known image of the king's palace or perhaps other public buildings in Babylon, as a symbol of accusation for the treatment of Judah and other nations that had fallen to Babylonian rule.

The third woe oracle in the series, which appears in verses 12-14, accuses the addressee of bloodshed. The initial woe address in verse 12 essentially accuses the addressee of building a city with blood and a town with iniquity. This of course would recall the previous references to the building activity of the addressee, apparently to be identified with the rebuilding of Babylon during the Neo-Babylonian period. Verses 13-14 challenge the ideology of the Neo-Babylonian empire by asserting that YHWH—and not the Babylonian god Marduk—is ultimately responsible for Babylon's greatness. According to Babylonian mythology, Marduk, the city god of Babylon, gained the right to rule the entire world by defeating the chaos monster Tiamat.[38] In order to commemorate Marduk's victory, the Entemenanki was built to represent the center of the cosmos from which creation and Babylon's role at the center of the nations would be renewed annually. Overall, the Neo-Babylonian rebuilding of Babylon featured the Entemenanki at the center of the city and thereby symbolized Babylon's preeminent role among the nations. Following the rhetorical question in verse 12a that asserts that all of this comes ultimately from YHWH, verse 12b asserts that the nations' labor is for nothing because it only serves as a means to support the power of the Babylonian empire. As the present series of woe oracles—and indeed the entire book of Habakkuk—asserts that Babylon will fall, such labor is of course pointless. Verse 14 reinforces this perspective by pointing to the knowledge of YHWH's glory that fills the entire earth. The term "glory" *(kābôd)* generally refers to the presence of YHWH in the wilderness tent and tabernacle (Exod 29:43; 40:34, 35) or the Temple in Jerusalem (1 Kgs 8:11; 2 Chr 5:14; 7:1, 2, 3; Ezek 11:23; 43:4, 5). The claim that knowledge of YHWH's glory permeates creation stands as a counterpoint to the Babylonian claim that Marduk is the sovereign of creation. The phrase also appears in Isa 11:9 to make similar claims for YHWH's role as sovereign over creation and the nations at large.

---

[38] See the Enuma Elish, or the Babylonian epic of creation that was recited at the time of the Akitu or New Year's festival in Babylon that commemorated Marduk's victory of Tiamat, the establishment of order in creation, and the establishment of Babylon at the center of the nations (Pritchard, *ANET* 60–72; see also Jacob Klein, "Akitu," *ABD* I:138-40).

The fourth and final woe of the series appears in verses 15-17 which accuses the addressee of drunkenness and rape. The initial woe statement in verse 15 employs the metaphor of forced drunkenness to accuse the addressee of disabling his neighbors in order to look upon their nakedness. The combined metaphors of drunkenness and wrath point to a very threatening situation. This is basically a metaphor for rape and humiliation that points to the treatment of captives by the conqueror who allows his troops to roam unchecked through the streets of the conquered city, plundering, killing, and raping the population as they like. Verse 16 then turns to the fate of the conqueror who will fill himself with contempt rather than with glory for such actions. It points to the reversal of the conqueror's situation in that the cup of the right hand of YHWH will ultimately come around to the oppressor, and result in his own humiliation. The reference to YHWH's "right hand" recalls the motif of YHWH's power to employ the right hand against the enemies of Israel (Exod 15:6, 12; Pss 20:7 [NRSV: 20:6]; 77:11 [NRSV: 77:10]; 98:1; 78:54; 18:36 [NRSV: 18:35]; Isa 41:10; 62:8). Interestingly, the metaphor of drunkenness returns to the portrayal of the ultimate downfall of the oppressor in the prophet's initial explanation of YHWH's oracle in verse 5, where he stated that the oppressor would fall after having drunk too much wine and consumed too many nations. The concluding *kî*-clause in verse 17 refers to "violence of Lebanon" and "the destruction of animals" that will overwhelm the conqueror. Babylon was known for stripping the forests of Lebanon to supply wood for Nebuchadrezzar's building projects.[39] That and the reference to the destruction of animals points to Babylon's role as an enemy of creation in general (cf. Deut 20:19-20, which prohibits the destruction of trees during siege, perhaps as a means of protecting creation and the land's capacity to provide food for its inhabitants). The final refrain, "because of human bloodshed and violence to the earth, to cities and all who live in them," points to the threat posed to the human elements of creation. It also replicates the refrain that appeared at the conclusion of the first woe oracle in the series (see verse 7b), and thereby forms a conclusion for the four woe oracles in verses 6-17.

The prophet's summation or explanatory comments on the taunt song then follow in verses 18-20. This section points to the oppressors' idolatry and failure to recognize YHWH (cf. Hab 1:11, 16; see also 2:13a) as the root cause for the atrocities outlined in the taunt song. The summation begins with the rhetorical question in verse 18 that asserts the

[39] See Pritchard, *ANET* 307, for a translation of Nebuchadrezzar's Wadi-Brisa inscription in which he recounts his efforts to transport cedar from Lebanon to Babylon for use in the construction of his palace.

worthlessness of idolatry. Basically, the question asserts that an idol cannot possibly benefit its own creator. Reliance on such a cast image results in reliance on a lie because it is only a silent object that is fashioned with his own hands. Verse 19 continues this theme by presenting a woe statement, like those of the preceding woe series, that ridicules one who fashions wood or silent stone into an idol and then calls upon it to awaken and to teach its maker (cf. the satire against the idol maker in Isa 44:9-20). Such a creation is nothing but an object overlaid with silver and gold with no breath or life force within. The final statement in verse 20 points once again to YHWH as the ultimate power of the universe by calling for silence throughout the entire earth as YHWH's presence is manifested in the holy Temple (in Jerusalem), the true center of creation in the universe according to the prophet. Such a call for silence appears also in Zeph 1:7; Zech 2:17 [NRSV: 2:13]; and Ps 46:11 [NRSV: 46:10], and appears to accompany a theophany in which YHWH's presence is manifested in the Temple. Priests performing the sacrifices and other rituals of the Temple worked in silence before YHWH's presence, indicated by the opening of the doors of the Temple to expose the Holy of Holies where the ark resided (see 1 Kgs 8:1-11), because human voices are not able to replicate the divine speech of the angels who serve YHWH in the heavenly realm. The metaphor of silence indicates a demonstration of respect for YHWH, and conveys the "otherness" of holy divine speech by the angels who praise YHWH in the heavens.[40]

The Prayer/Petition by Habakkuk to YHWH: 3:1-19

The second major component of the book of Habakkuk appears in Habakkuk 3, which constitutes the prophet's prayer or petition to YHWH.[41] The chapter presents a psalm in which the psalmist petitions YHWH for mercy or assistance in defeating the enemies that threaten the nation Israel. It is demarcated initially by the superscription in Hab 3:1, which identifies the following material as "the prayer of the prophet Habakkuk according to Shigionoth." The psalm itself follows in verses 2-19a, and the concluding instruction to the choirmaster in verse 19b closes the chapter.

[40] For discussion, see Israel Knohl, *The Sanctuary of Silence: The Priestly Torah and the Holiness School* (Minneapolis: Fortress, 1995).

[41] In addition to the commentaries, see Theodore Hiebert, *G–d of My Victory: The Ancient Hymn in Habakkuk 3*, HSM, vol. 38 (Atlanta: Scholars Press, 1986).

The authorship of this chapter is disputed as many scholars maintain that the hymnic forms and technical vocabulary of the psalm indicate that someone other than the prophet Habakkuk must be the author.[42] Likewise, the absence of this chapter in the Qumran pesher of Habakkuk and the existence of the Barberini Greek version of chapter 3 alone, an alternative to the Septuagint with affinities to the Palestinian Syriac text, the Peshitta, and Coptic and Latin textual versions from Africa, has reinforced the claims of those who maintain that Habakkuk 3 represents a composition independent from Habakkuk 1–2. Nevertheless, the superscription in Hab 3:1 identifies this chapter as "the prayer of the prophet Habakkuk," and Habakkuk 3 appears together with Habakkuk 1–2 in both the Muraba'at and the Greek Nahal Hever Minor Prophets scrolls from the Judean wilderness. Furthermore, the major concerns of the psalm, i.e., the petition to Yhwh to make Yhwh's work known (cf. Hab 1:5), the appeal by the psalmist to protect the nation against invading enemies, and the psalmist's confidence that Yhwh will do so, correspond to those of Habakkuk 1–2.[43] If Habakkuk was indeed a cultic prophet who was responsible for the performance of liturgical works in the Temple, he could easily have composed Habakkuk 3.[44]

The superscription: 3:1

The superscription for the psalm appears in verse 1. In keeping with the generic characteristics of superscriptions, it introduces and identifies the following material so that it stands as a distinct structural and generic unit within the chapter as a whole.[45] It identifies the following material as "the prayer of Habakkuk the prophet according to Shigionoth." The term *těpillâ*, "prayer," is a general term that designates prayer or human attempts to address Yhwh directly (e.g., 2 Sam 7:27; 2 Kgs 19:4/Isa 37:4; Jon 2:8 [NRSV: 2:7]). It frequently appears in the superscriptions of the psalms, such as Pss 17:1; 86:1; 90:1; 102:1; 142:1,

[42] For a brief overview of the discussion, see Sweeney, "Habakkuk, Book of" *ABD* III:1-6, esp. 4–5.

[43] See also Hiebert, *G–d of My Victory* 129–49, who argues that Habakkuk 3 represents Yhwh's response to the problems posed by the prophet in Habakkuk 1–2.

[44] For arguments that Habakkuk was a cultic prophet, see Jeremias, *Kultprophetie* 55–127.

[45] Gene M. Tucker, "Prophetic Superscriptions and the Growth of the Canon," *Canon and Authority*, ed., G. W. Coats and B. O. Long (Philadelphia: Fortress, 1977) 56–70.

and in reference to the Davidic psalter (Ps 72:20). The reference to
Habakkuk the prophet corresponds to the identification of the prophet
in the initial superscription of the book in Hab 1:1, although it does not ·
state specifically whether Habakkuk is the author or the singer of the
psalm (or both). The reference to Shigionoth *(šigyōnôt)* has been particularly problematic. The precise meaning of the term is uncertain. Although some derive it from the root *šgh,* "to go astray," and understand
it as a reference to a wild song with rapid changes in rhythm, there is
little basis in the present context for such a view. The singular form of
the term, *šiggāyôn,* appears in the superscription for Psalm 7, "A *Shig-
gayon* of David, which he sang to Yʜᴡʜ concerning Cush of Benjamin,"
which is formulated as a psalm of lamentation. The Akkadian term,
šegu, likewise refers to a song of lament, although the equation of this
term with *šigyōnôt* is contested.[46] Nevertheless, the psalm in Habakkuk
3 presupposes a situation of distress in which the psalmist petitions
Yʜᴡʜ for relief from enemies. It therefore seems best to understand
šigyōnôt as a reference to such a situation of distress. If indeed the term
is derived from the root *šgh,* it would then refer to a situation in which
things have gone wrong and need to be set right.

The Prayer/Petition Proper: 3:2-19a

The prayer or petition proper of the prophet appears in verses 2-
19a. The psalm is demarcated initially by the first person singular references to the psalmist or singer in verses 2, 7, 14, 16, 18-19a, which
contrasts with the third person perspectives of the superscription in
verse 1 and the instruction to the choirmaster in verse 19a. Although it
employs the genre of theophany report in verses 3-15, it must be identified as a petition on the basis of the appeal to Yʜᴡʜ for relief from distress
that is made in verses 2 and 16. The structure of the psalm/petition
comprises three basic parts. The initial petition to Yʜᴡʜ in verse 2 is
characterized both by its first person speaker's perspective and by its
second person singular address to Yʜᴡʜ, in which the psalmist calls
upon Yʜᴡʜ to make Yʜᴡʜ's work known. Although the first person
speaker's perspective continues throughout in verses 3-15, these verses
are no longer addressed to Yʜᴡʜ, but instead present a third person
theophany report in which Yʜᴡʜ appears and engages in combat
against the enemies of the nation and its king. Both the first person
speaker's perspective and the third person references to Yʜᴡʜ con-

---

[46] See Sweeney, "Structure, Genre, and Intent," 78, for references.

tinue in verses 16-19a, but these verses renew the initial petition, specifying it in relation to the anticipated defeat of the nation that threatens the psalmist's own nation, and express the psalmist's confidence that Yhwh will indeed act to defeat the attacking nation and thereby remove the threat. Finally, the instruction to the choirmaster in verse 19a returns to the objective perspective of the superscription and concludes the chapter.

INTRODUCTION:
THE PSALMIST'S PETITION TO YHWH TO MANIFEST DIVINE POWER: 3:2

The petition to Yhwh to manifest divine power appears in verse 2. This verse serves as the introduction to the psalm as a whole and defines its basic concerns, although the reason for the psalmist's petition does not become clear until the following material which portrays the nations that threaten the nation and its king. The psalmist is the speaker in this verse, as indicated by the first person singular subject, and the petition is addressed directly to Yhwh, as indicated by the initial reference to Yhwh's name and the second person singular address forms that appear throughout the verse. The psalmist begins by referring to Yhwh's reputation, "O Yhwh, I have heard of your renown, and I stand in awe, O Yhwh, of your work." By referring to Yhwh's reputation, the psalmist establishes a basis by which Yhwh will respond to the following petition, i.e., Yhwh has acted in the past and can be expected to act again. The reference to Yhwh's "work" employs the same Hebrew term, *pōʿal* (here, *pāʿŏlĕkā*, "your work") as Hab 1:5, which indicates that the psalmist's appeal for action by Yhwh relates to Yhwh's earlier claims to action in the Deity's initial response to the prophet's complaint of injustice. The petition proper follows, "in our own time revive it; in our own time make it known." The phrase, "in our own time," reads literally, "in the midst of years (*bĕqreb šānîm*)," and apparently refers to the manifestation of Yhwh's actions in the temporal framework of human history. Such an appeal would call upon the Deity, the infinite master of all creation whose heavenly dwelling exists outside of the finite bounds of time, to enter into the finite human realm in order to intervene on behalf of the oppressed people of Israel. The imperative, "revive it," literally, "make it live (*ḥayyêhû*)," apparently refers to Yhwh's previously mentioned action or work, which must be metaphorically "brought to life" or enacted in order to see Yhwh's intentions through to completion. The parallel with the imperative, "make it known," likewise attests to the meaning of the term as an appeal or petition to Yhwh to take action. Although Yhwh's intentions are not stated, the prophet's earlier *maśśāʾ* in Habakkuk 1–2 and the present psalm implicitly anticipate the manifestation of YHWH's proper justice or Torah in the world (e.g., Hab 1:4, 7; 2:4). The final phrase of the verse, "in wrath may you remember mercy," returns to the initial attempt to appeal to YHWH's reputation as it calls upon YHWH to exercise mercy as well as wrath in manifesting proper justice in the world. Such a statement apparently presupposes that the attacking nations were brought about by YHWH for punishment, but once the punishment is accomplished, mercy must come back into play so that the nation might continue.

THE THEOPHANY REPORT: 3:3-15

The report of a theophany then appears in verses 3-15 in order to depict YHWH's anticipated actions against the enemies that threaten Israel and its king. A theophany report is a genre of biblical literature, generally poetic in form, that depicts an appearance or manifestation of YHWH in the temporal world.[47] It is frequently associated with military situations in which YHWH defeats the enemies that threaten Israel and the general order of creation. Although it is frequently associated with military victories, the setting of the genre is probably to be located in the Temple, where YHWH is symbolically manifested or enthroned in the Holy of Holies to represent the meeting of heaven and earth at the center of creation. Theophany reports generally contain two basic elements: a portrayal of YHWH's approach and a portrayal of natural upheaval together with reactions of fear or awe. Examples of theophanies appear throughout the Hebrew Bible, such as Deut 33:2; Judg 5:4-5; Amos 1:2; Mic 1:3-4; Ezek 1:4-28; Pss 68:8-9 [NRSV: 68:7-8]; 97:2-5.

The portrayal of YHWH's approach appears in verses 3-7. This section is identified both in its thematic content, which portrays YHWH's approach and the reactions to it, and its third person descriptive perspective. The appearance of a first person singular pronoun in verse 7 indicates that the psalmist is the speaker. Overall, these verses employ the imagery of the rising sun to depict YHWH's manifestation in the world and YHWH's advance to meet the enemies of Israel. Such a depiction draws upon the traditions of creation where the emergence of light, the first element to be created, begins the process of setting the world of creation in order. Such imagery is manifested in the Temple as well. The Temple faces east so that the doors of the Temple might be

---

[47] Sweeney, *Isaiah 1–39* 541; Jörg Jeremias, *Theophanie. Die Geschichte einer alttestamentlichen Gattung*, WMANT, vol. 10 (Neukirchen-Vluyn: Neukirchener, 1965).

opened at sunrise to allow the light to enter the darkened Holy of Holies where the ark symbolizing YHWH's throne or presence in the world resides. As the light streams into the Holy of Holies, the entire process of creation is symbolically inaugurated once again. In order to understand the interrelation of the creation of the natural world and the issue of Israel's security from enemies and place within creation, the reader must recall that the story of creation does not end in Genesis 11, but continues throughout the entire Pentateuch in which the people of Israel are formed as a nation and brought from Egyptian slavery to the promised land.

Verse 3a begins the description of YHWH's approach by stating that G–d comes from "Teman" and "Mount Paran." Teman is the name for Yemen in modern Hebrew. The term *têmān* is derived from the root *ymn*, which means "right" and is employed to refer to the "south," the direction that is at one's right hand when facing toward the east. It apparently refers generally to the south (Exod 26:18; Ezek 47:19), the southern quadrant of the sky (Job 39:26), the south wind (Ps 78:26; Cant 4:16), or to some southerly or southernmost land (Josh 15:1). The term is frequently associated with the land of Edom (Amos 1:12; Obad 9; Jer 49:7, 20; Ezek 25:13; Josh 12:3; 13:4) or its eponymous ancestor Esau (Gen 36:15; 1 Chr 1:36). Such an identification is noteworthy because other theophanic texts associate YHWH's theophany with the sunrise that appears over Edom or Seir, immediately east of Jerusalem and the land of Israel (see Deut 33:2; Judg 5:4-5). The reference to Mount Paran likewise indicates an association with Seir, as indicated by its parallel use with Seir in Deut 33:2. It is also identified as the home of Ishmael (Gen 21:21), whose daughter Esau married (Gen 28:6-9), so that it is frequently identified with the Arabah that runs from the Dead Sea to the Gulf of Aqaba (1 Kgs 11:18) or the general wilderness region south of Israel through which the people traveled on their journey from Egypt to the promised land (Num 12:16; 10:12; 13:2, 26. Deuteronomy 33:2 also associates it with Sinai as well as with Seir. The meaning of the term Selah *(selâ)* is unknown, but it apparently functions as a technical term to indicate a musical interlude or some other musical device.

Verses 3b-4 continue to employ the metaphor of sunlight to depict the presence and approach of YHWH. Verse 3b begins by relating how YHWH's "glory" covers the heavens, and YHWH's "praise" fills the earth. The term, *hôd*, "glory," generally denotes YHWH's majesty, splendor, vigor, and authority in general. It is frequently associated with the imagery of the sun or light in general (Pss 8:2 [NRSV: 8:1]; 96:6; 104:1; 145:4 [NRSV: 145:3]; 148:13; Job 37:22; 40:10), again, as a manifestation of YHWH's first act of creation. The term *těhillâ*, "praise," reflects the songs and hymns that would be sung in the Temple to mark YHWH's manifestation once again at sunrise (e.g., Psalm 104). Verse 4 relates the brightness and rays of light that emanate from the divine appearance, and testify to the divine power that is hidden within the metaphor of light.

Verses 5-7 then shift to the metaphor of earthquake to express the divine power mentioned in verse 4 and to provide the basis for the depiction of the reactions to YHWH's manifestation in both the natural and the human world. The initial portrayal of "pestilence" and "plague" recalls the plagues visited by YHWH upon the Egyptians at the time of the Exodus in which pestilence or cattle disease *(deber)* was the fifth plague visited upon Egypt (Exod 9:1-7). The term, "plague," *rešep*, does not indicate one of the Egyptian plagues in the book of Exodus, although it is employed to refer to the thunderbolts sent by YHWH against the flocks of the Egyptians in Ps 78:48. Although Resheph refers to flame or pestilence in the Hebrew Bible (see also Deut 32:24), it was also the name of a Canaanite god of pestilence who brought about fever, and appears throughout western Asia from the third millennium on.[48] Resheph appears in Egyptian reliefs to depict the Pharaoh's striking at enemies, and Mesopotamian accounts of the flood portray various gods advancing before the flood waters to set the earth on fire.[49] Verse 6aα then correlates the reaction of both the natural and the human realms. YHWH stands or stops, and the earth shakes as in an earthquake; YHWH looks, and the nations tremble. The balance of verse 6 then focuses on natural imagery as the mountains are shattered and the eternal hills brought down as YHWH advances along the ancient pathways. The identity of these pathways is not clear, but they may be identified with the course of the sun as it travels across the heavens. Verse 7 then returns to the human world as the psalmist describes the tents of Cushan and the tent curtains of Midian shaking and trembling like the mountains and hills. Both of these place names portray the south. The name Cushan appears only here in the Hebrew Bible, although it is generally considered to be a derivative of the name Cush, which refers to Ethiopia or upper Egypt throughout the Hebrew Bible. The term Midian is the common designation for the Syrian and Arabian deserts and the nomadic people who inhabited them. Midian is a son of Abraham and his concubine Keturah who was expelled together with Ishmael to the east (Gen 25:1-2, 6). The Midianites roamed far from their homeland, and were to be found in the Sinai as well. Moses fled to Midian from Egypt, and there encountered Jethro, a priest of Midian (Exodus 2–3). Moses married Zipporah, Jethro's daughter. The equation of Cushan and Midian in

---

[48] See P. Xella, "Resheph," *Dictionary of Deities and Demons in the Bible,* ed., K. van der Toorn, B. Becking, P. van der Horst (2nd edition; Leiden: Brill, 1999) 700–3.

[49] See, e.g., the account of the flood in the Gilgamesh Epic (Pritchard, *ANET* 94).

this text is apparently relevant to Numbers 12, where Miriam condemns Moses for marrying a Cushite woman. Miriam's challenge to Moses is likely based on the fact that Moses, the Levite, married a foreign woman, which might be construed as a violation of the laws of priestly purity in marriage (see Lev 21:1-15; cf. Exod 34:11-16; Deut 7:1-6). Although Zipporah is clearly Midianite and not Ethiopian, this passage has played a major role together with Numbers 12 in the contention that Moses' wife, and perhaps Moses himself, was black. It should be noted, however, that present-day Bedouin are very dark-skinned, and the contention that ancient Bedouin or Midianites were similarly dark-skinned is likely.

Verses 8-15 shift from a third person report of YHWH's approach to a second person singular direct address to YHWH that relates YHWH's combat against the natural forces and the nations that threaten creation and the nation of Israel. The portrayal of this combat, which is heavily influenced by mythological themes, constitutes the second major component of a theophany by portraying the effects of YHWH's manifestation on the world at large. Again, the first person singular reference in verse 14 indicates that the psalmist continues to function as the speaker.

The psalmist begins this portion of the psalm by addressing rhetorical questions to YHWH that portray YHWH's rage against the rivers and the sea. The motif of YHWH's combat against rivers and sea recalls older mythological motifs, both in the Hebrew Bible and in pagan cultures, in which YHWH or the principle god, such as Baal in Canaan or Marduk in Babylonia, make war against various chaos monsters that are associated with water. Thus, YHWH battles the sea (Psalm 93), rivers (Isa 11:10-16), and sea monsters, such as Leviathan (Psalms 74; Job 38; Isa 27:1) or Rahab (Isa 51:9-11), to establish order in the natural world and to protect Israel. The sea and flooding rivers represent threats to life on dry land, and frequently symbolize threats posed to a nation by attacking armies (e.g., Judges 5; Isa 17:12-14; Pss 46:1-3; 93:3-4). The motif of a flooding river recalls the wadis of Israel (or the American southwest). Normally, the wadi is a dry streambed during the summer, but it quickly becomes a raging torrent when the sudden rains of winter fill it to form a flash flood. Likewise, Baal battles the sea monster Lothan, apparently an Ugaritic representation of the later Leviathan, and Marduk battles Tiamat for similar purposes in relation to their respective cultures.[50] The portrayal of YHWH's riding a chariot and driving horses in battle against these forces recalls the imagery of the sun and the depiction of YHWH riding through the heavens in a chariot to defeat enemies (see Psalms 68; 104; cf. Psalm 18/2 Samuel 22).

[50] See C. Uehlinger, "Leviathan," *DDD*[2] 511–5; B. Alster, "Tiamat," *DDD*[2] 867–9.

Verse 9 shifts from rhetorical questions to simple assertions in portraying YHWH's bow directed against enemies. The reference to a naked bow apparently indicates a bow that is unwrapped, strung, and ready for action. The second part of the statement reads literally, "oaths (the) arrows spoke." Although difficult, this statement apparently indicates the metaphorical fulfillment of YHWH's oaths to destroy the enemy. Again, the notation Selah in the middle of the verse is a technical term that indicates a musical interlude or other instruction to the performers of the psalm. The motif of rivers appears once again as YHWH employs rivers to split the earth and subdue the foe. The appearance of this theme recalls YHWH's use of the sea to defeat the pursuing Egyptians in Exodus 15 or the use of the wadi Kishon to defeat Sisera's forces in Judges 5. Verses 10-11 then portray the reaction of the natural world to YHWH's attack. The mountains saw and fled, much like an enemy army sees a superior force and flees before it is too late. The rain waters likewise "passed by," and the deep gave its voice, apparently a cry of alarm, at the sight of YHWH. The sun raised its hands, perhaps to strike the enemy as the sun is identified with YHWH. The imagery of the moon standing still likewise seems to be supportive of YHWH's efforts to defeat the foe, much as the sun and the moon stood still at Gibeon to enable Israel's full defeat of the southern coalition of Canaanite kings (Joshua 10). The imagery of the lighted arrows and the flashing, gleaming spear recalls once again the solar imagery with which YHWH is portrayed.

Verses 12-14 then turn to a portrayal of YHWH's combat against the nations that threaten Israel. The transition appears in verse 12 which speaks of YHWH's treading the earth and trampling the nations in anger. Verse 13 emphasizes that YHWH's combat against the nations is intended to defend the nation Israel from attack by stating to YHWH, "you have come forth to save your people, to save your anointed." The reference to "your anointed" indicates the king, and demonstrates that this psalm is to be read in relation to the pre-exilic monarchic period. The graphic imagery of crushing the head, etc., is typical of ancient near-eastern mythological combat accounts. The NRSV translation, "laying it bare from foundation to roof," apparently attempts to read this phrase in relation to "the wicked house," but it should be read in relation to the "crushed head," literally, "laying bare the foundation until the neck." The "wicked house" is simply a metaphorical reference to the enemy nations that threaten Israel. Again, the notation, Selah, indicates a musical interlude or other technical instruction for the performance of this psalm. The graphic war imagery returns in verse 14 with the reference to the arrows that pierce the head. The NRSV has difficulties in translating the following statement, which reads literally, "his princes come like a whirlwind to scatter me, their gloating is as if (they are ready) to devour the poor who were in hiding." Apparently, this statement employs the metaphors of whirlwind and eating—as well as the image of frightened people attempting to hide—to reiterate the threat posed to the people by the attacking nations.

The theophany report closes in verse 15, which returns to the initial mythological theme from verse 8 of YHWH's trampling the sea with horses. Again, this image recalls YHWH's chariot racing through the heavens at dawn in pursuit of the darkness that symbolizes Israel's and YHWH's enemies.

CONCLUSION:
EXPRESSION OF CONFIDENCE BY THE PSALMIST: 3:16-19A

The psalmist's prayer concludes in verses 16-19a, which express the psalmist's confidence that YHWH will respond to the petition and strike down the enemies that threaten the nation. Such an expression of confidence implicitly reiterates the initial petition which the entire psalm is designed to convey. Again, this section is a first person speech by the psalmist, but there is no indication of the addressee. The initial statement, "I hear," recalls the initial statement of verse 2 in which the psalmist states, "O YHWH, I have heard of your renown." The following images of quivering lips, rotten bones, and trembling are expressions of the psalmist's own fear and anxiety while waiting for YHWH to act. Verse 16 explicitly states that the psalmist waits for "the day of calamity" when YHWH will strike down "the people that come up to attack us," demonstrating once again that the psalm presupposes that Israel is threatened by enemy nations. Verses 17-19a return to natural imagery to express the psalmist's confidence that YHWH will act on Israel's behalf. The fig tree, vine, olive tree, fields, flock, and herd express the natural bounty that YHWH provides to the people in the land of Israel (cf. Deut 14:22-29; 18:3-8; 26:1-15). Interestingly, the blessings that YHWH will provide to the people when they observe YHWH's covenant include both the bounty of harvest and flock as well as protection from enemies (Deut 28:1-14; Lev 26:3-13) and the curses include the withdrawal of these blessings (Deut 28:15-68; Lev 26:14-33). The psalmist's final statements in verses 18-19a express joy and confidence in YHWH and YHWH's capacity and willingness to deliver the people. The concluding metaphor likens the psalmist to a deer who jumps and leaps across the tops of the mountains in joy and freedom.

Instruction to the Choirmaster: 3:19b

Verse 19b is a technical notation to the choirmaster that the psalm is to be performed with stringed instruments (see 1 Chr 15:16-24, esp. verse 21 which notes the Levites who were to lead the performance of psalms in the Temple with lyres).[51] Similar notations appear in fifty-five Psalms (e.g., Psalms 4; 6; 54; 61; 76). Like the Psalms, Habakkuk 3 was apparently intended to be performed as part of the Temple liturgy.

---

[51] For discussion of prophetic involvement in the Temple liturgy, see R. J. Tournay, *Seeing and Hearing G–d with the Psalms: The Prophetic Liturgy of the Second Temple in Jerusalem*, JSOTSup, vol. 118 (Sheffield: JSOT Press, 1991).

FOR FURTHER READING

COMMENTARIES

Eaton, J. H. *Obadiah, Nahum, Habakkuk and Zephaniah: Introduction and Commentary.* Torch Bible Commentaries. London: SCM, 1961.

Hiebert, Theodore. "The Book of Habakkuk: Introduction, Commentary, and Reflections," *The New Interpreter's Bible. Volume VII: Introduction to Apocalyptic Literature, Daniel, The Twelve Prophets,* ed. Leander E. Keck et al. Nashville: Abingdon, 1996.

Keller, Carl-A. and René Vuilleumier. *Michée, Nahoum, Habacuc, Sophonie.* Commentaire de l'ancien Testament XIb. Neuchâtel: Delachaux et Niestlé, 1971.

Roberts, J. J. M. *Nahum, Habakkuk, and Zephaniah: A Commentary.* Old Testament Library. Louisville: Westminster/John Knox, 1991.

Rudolph, Wilhelm. *Micha–Nahum–Habakuk–Zephanja.* Kommentar zum Alten Testament XIII/3. Gütersloh: Gerd Mohn, 1975.

Seybold, Klaus. *Nahum, Habakuk, Zephanja.* Zürcher Bibelkommentare AT 24, 2. Zürich: Theologischer Verlag, 1991.

Smith, Ralph L. *Micah-Malachi.* Word Biblical Commentary, 32. Waco: Word, 1984.

Széles, Mária Eszenyei. *Wrath and Mercy: Habakkuk and Zephaniah.* International Theological Commentary. Grand Rapids: Eerdmans, 1987.

STUDIES

Gowan, Donald E. *The Triumph of Faith in Habakkuk.* Atlanta: John Knox, 1976.

Haak, Robert D. *Habakkuk.* Vetus Testamentum Supplements, 44. Leiden: Brill, 1992.

Hiebert, Theodore. *G–d of My Victory: The Ancient Hymn in Habakkuk 3.* Harvard Semitic Monographs, 38. Atlanta: Scholars Press, 1986.

Jeremias, Jörg. *Kultprophetie und Gerichtsverkündigung in der späten Königszeit Israels.* Wissenschaftliche Monographien zum Alten und Neuen Testament, 35. Neukirchen-Vluyn: Neukirchener, 1970.

Jöcken, Peter. *Das Buch Habakuk. Darstellung der Geschichte seiner kritischen Erforschung mit einer eigenen Beurteilung.* Bonner Biblische Beiträge, 48. Bonn: Peter Hanstein, 1977.

Mason, Rex. *Zephaniah, Habakkuk, Joel.* Old Testament Guides. Sheffield: JSOT Press, 1994.

Sweeney, Marvin A., "Structure, Genre, and Intent in the Book of Habakkuk," *Vetus Testamentum* 41 (1991) 63–83.

ZEPHANIAH

ZEPHANIAH

Overview

Zephaniah is the ninth book in both the Masoretic and the Septuagint traditions of the Book of the Twelve. It follows Habakkuk, which is concerned with the emergence of Babylonia and its subjugation of Judah, and it precedes Haggai, which takes up issues pertaining to the construction of the Second Temple and the potential restoration of the Davidic monarchy. This would suggest that the scenario of destruction and punishment outlined in the book should be read in relation to the Babylonian destruction of Jerusalem and the Temple and the exile of the people of Judah. The chronological and theological implications of Zephaniah's placement in the Book of the Twelve, particularly its association with the Babylonian exile, apparently play a role in influencing the interpretation of the book. Many interpreters read Zephaniah as a post-exilic scenario of YHWH's eschatological judgment and restoration of the entire world, in which Israel and then the nations are to be judged and punished in preparation for the restoration of Jerusalem and Israel as the center for praise of YHWH by all the peoples of the earth. Various motifs within Zephaniah, including the initial statements concerning the punishment of all creation and humanity, the Day of YHWH as a day of sacrifice and theophany, the judgment against the nations, the restoration of Israel's exiles, and world-wide praise of YHWH by the nations, contribute to this interpretation.

Nevertheless, there is considerable evidence that the book is designed to be read in relation to the pre-exilic reign and reform program of King Josiah of Judah (ca. 640–609 B.C.E.). The superscription of the book identifies the historical setting of Zephaniah's career as the reign of Josiah.[1] According to the biblical accounts in 2 Kgs 21:19–23:30 and 2 Chr 33:21–35:26, Josiah came to the throne at the age of eight as a result of the

---

[1] For discussion of Josiah's reform and its relationship to prophetic literature, including Zephaniah, see my *King Josiah of Judah: The Lost Messiah of Israel*.

assassination of his father Amon in a failed palace conspiracy that was put down by "the people of the land." By his twelfth (2 Chr 34:3) or eighteenth year (2 Kgs 22:3), Josiah initiated a program of religious reform and national restoration based upon a Torah scroll that was discovered during the course of Temple renovations. Because of the correspondence between Josiah's reforms and the requirements of Deuteronomy, particularly the emphasis upon only one legitimate worship site for the people (see Deuteronomy 12), most scholars identify the Torah scroll as an early form of Deuteronomy. Zephaniah's call for the people to purify themselves from pagan religious practice and economic abuse appears to presuppose Josiah's reform measures. Many have argued that Zephaniah must be placed early in Josiah's reign prior to the reform insofar as his oracles presuppose the continued presence of pagan features, but the exhortational character of Zephaniah's oracles indicates that the book is designed to demonstrate the prophet's support for Josiah's reform program insofar as he calls upon the people to abandon improper practice and to seek YHWH (see esp. Zeph 2:1-3).

This, of course, has implications for assessing the literary structure and presentation of the book. Many interpreters argue that Zephaniah is organized according to a three-part eschatological scheme of 1) punishment against Israel (Zeph 1:2–2:3); 2) punishment against the nations (2:4-15); and 3) restoration of Jerusalem and Israel among the nations (Zeph 3:1-20). These motifs clearly underlie the theological or conceptual outlook of the book, especially insofar as Zephaniah portrays the Day of YHWH as a day of sacrifice in which the death and destruction of a sacrificial animal plays a role in human atonement for wrongdoing and thereby aids in restoring the relationship between YHWH and human beings. Nevertheless, this pattern does not constitute the literary structure of the book. As the following commentary demonstrates, the rhetorical, syntactical, and lexical features of the book point to a two-part structure that is based in the prophet's exhortation to the people to "seek YHWH." In this scenario Zeph 1:2-18 constitutes the announcement of the Day of YHWH, and Zeph 2:1–3:20 constitutes the exhortation to seek YHWH, i.e., to support the reform program of King Josiah with its goals of restoring proper worship of YHWH in Jerusalem, the restoration of the kingdom of Israel, and just treatment for the common people of Judah/Israel.

The Superscription: 1:1

The superscription for the entire book of Zephaniah appears in Zeph 1:1. It is generically and structurally distinct from the rest of the book in that it is designed to introduce and identify the following material in Zeph 1:2–3:20.[2] In contrast to the presentation of the oracular speech forms that are reported throughout the balance of the book, the superscription in Zeph 1:1 appears in a third person narrative form that identifies the following material as "the word of YHWH that was unto Zephaniah . . ." In addition, it provides information on Zephaniah's ancestors, identifying him as "the son of Cushi, the son of Gedaliah, the son of Amariah, the son of Hezekiah," and it specifies the time that YHWH's word came to him, viz., "in the days of Josiah son of Amon, King of Judah." It is very similar in form to the superscriptions in Hos 1:1; Joel 1:1; Mic 1:1; LXX Jer 1:1, and it appears to be a variant of the narrative formula, "and the word of YHWH was unto X," that appears so frequently throughout prophetic literature (e.g., Jer 1:4, 11, 13; Ezek 3:16; 6:1; Jon 1:1; 3:1; Zech 4:8; 6:9, etc.). Zephaniah 1:1 is not a part of YHWH's word to Zephaniah; it precedes it. It thereby stands as the first major component of the book, and Zeph 1:2–3:20 constitutes the second.

Zephaniah's genealogy is somewhat unusual in that it traces the prophet's line back through four generations. Biblical tradition does not identify his father, Cushi, although many interpreters have speculated that he is of Ethiopian ancestry. The term *kûšî* is a gentilic form that is commonly applied to people from Ethiopia (i.e., Cush in biblical literature; see e.g., Jer 13:23; Amos 9:7; Zeph 2:12), and perhaps from Midian (see Hab 3:7; cf. Num 12:1). It is unlikely that the inclusion of the name in Zeph 1:1 is intended to point to Zephaniah's ethnic or racial background insofar as Cushi appears as a proper name in Jer 36:14, and Cush appears as a proper name in Ps 7:1. As Keller notes, the question probably stems from the European preoccupation with race.[3] Zephaniah's grandfather, Gedaliah, and his great-grandfather, Amariah, both bear very common Judean names, but nothing specific is known about them. Many have speculated that his great-great-grandfather, Hezekiah, is the late-eighth century king of Judah who revolted against the Assyrian king Sennacherib (see 2 Kings 18–20; Isaiah 36–39; 2 Chronicles 29–32). This might account for the unusual genealogy of four generations, but there is no explicit indication that this Hezekiah was in fact the king. In any case, no son of King Hezekiah by the name of Amariah is identified in biblical tradition.

---

[2] See Gene M. Tucker, "Prophetic Superscriptions and the Growth of the Canon," *Canon and Authority*, ed. George W. Coats and Burke O. Long (Philadelphia: Fortress, 1977) 56–70.

[3] René Vuilleumier and Carl-A. Keller. *Michée, Nahoum, Habacuc, Sophonie.* Commentaire de l'ancien Testament XIb. (Neuchâtel: Delachaux et Niestlé, 1971) 187, n. 2.

Zephaniah's Exhortation to Seek Yhwh: 1:2–3:20

The body of the book in Zeph 1:2–3:20 appears as a lengthy discourse by the prophet that is designed to persuade its audience to seek Yhwh. Although many oracles employ first person singular pronouns that can only be understood in reference to Yhwh (e.g., "I will surely destroy all from upon the face of the earth . . . and I will cut off humanity from upon the face of the earth . . .," Zeph 1:2-3), the frequent appearances of the oracular formula, *nĕʾūm yhwh*, "utterance of Yhwh" (Zeph 1:2, 3) and other third person references to Yhwh throughout the structural framework of the passage (e.g., "Silence from before the L–rd Yhwh, for the day of Yhwh is near!" Zeph 1:7; "and it shall come to pass on the day of the sacrifice of Yhwh," Zeph 1:8) demonstrate that the book presents the prophet as the speaker who quotes Yhwh's words to his audience. The identity of the audience is apparently the people of Judah and Jerusalem (Zeph 1:4), here identified as "the worthless nation" (Zeph 2:1), "the humble of the land" (Zeph 2:3), "the terrifying, defiled, oppressing city" (Zeph 3:1), and "the daughter of Zion/ Israel/the daughter of Jerusalem" (Zeph 3:14). Although others are also addressed, such as "the inhabitants of the sea coast" (Zeph 2:5) and "the Cushites" (Zeph 2:12), they must be considered as secondary addressees within a discourse that is designed to persuade the people of Jerusalem and Judah to adhere to the prophet's message.

Overall, the theme of the "Day of Yhwh" permeates the entire discourse.[4] The motif appears frequently in the prophetic books where it conveys Yhwh's judgment against Israel (Amos 5:18-20; Joel 1–2), the land or world at large (Isa 2:6-22), Babylon (Isaiah 13), Edom and the nations that are enemies of Zion (Isaiah 34; Obad 1–21), or Egypt and its allies (Ezekiel 30). It appears to be rooted in traditions concerning Yhwh's deliverance of the people of Israel from their enemies, but as the examples from Amos, Joel, and Isaiah 2 demonstrate, it can be directed against Israel or Judah as well. The imagery employed here portrays the day as a time of sacrifice (Zeph 1:7, 8) in which Yhwh will act to destroy those who have acted improperly. It should be born in mind that the practice of sacrifice in ancient Israel and Judah (and indeed in the ancient Near East generally) employed the death or destruction of the sacrifice as a means of purification and restoration; hence the destruction of the sacrifice plays a role in restoring the relationship between the divine and the human realms. This pattern seems to underlie the entire discourse insofar as it looks to the destruction of the wicked

---

[4] For discussion of the Day of Yhwh, see A. J. Everson, "Day of the L–rd," *IDB[S]* 209–10.

as the means to purify Jerusalem/Judah and to restore the relationship with YHWH.

The exhortational character of the discourse is evident from its two-part structure and the linguistic features of its components. The core of the discourse, and indeed of the entire book, is the exhortational appeal in Zeph 2:1-3, which employs masculine plural imperative verbs to call upon the audience for action, viz., "Gather yourselves and assemble, O worthless nation"; "Seek YHWH, all you humble of the land"; "Seek righteousness, seek humility." The motivations for the proposed actions presuppose explicit threats, "before a decree (of punishment) is born"; "before the fierce anger of YHWH comes upon you"; "perhaps you shall be hidden in the day of YHWH's wrath." Essentially, the specific content of the exhortation to seek YHWH is conveyed throughout the rest of the book, which calls for the expunging of pagan religious practice and economic abuse, and which points to the defeat of various nations as evidence that YHWH is acting. But the prophet's discourse does not begin with the exhortation in Zeph 2:1-3 per se. Instead, the first major section in Zeph 1:2-18 announces the Day of YHWH as a means to identify the problems that the prophet or YHWH seeks to rectify and thereby to motivate the audience for the exhortation that follows. Likewise, the exhortation itself does not stand alone. It appears as the second major section of the discourse in Zeph 2:1–3:20 with a presentation of evidence that YHWH is acting and the projected outcome of that action, viz., the Philistine cities are being destroyed (Zeph 2:4). This in turn will lead to the punishment of a variety of nations that stand as obstacles to Judah and the policies of its king Josiah (Zeph 2:5-15) prior to the projected restoration of Jerusalem/Judah/Israel that will proceed from its current downtrodden state. By the end of the discourse, Jerusalem/Israel sings and exults as its enemies are defeated, its king YHWH is in its midst, and its outcasts are restored. Clearly, the projected scenario of cleansing, punishment, and restoration is designed to motivate the audience to accept the prophet's message.

Prophetic Announcement of the Day of YHWH: 1:2-18

Many interpreters maintain that Zeph 1:2–2:3 constitutes the first major textual block of the prophet's oracles in that both Zeph 1:2-18 and 2:1-3 take up the theme of the Day of YHWH. Nevertheless, several features of Zeph 1:2-18 and 2:1-3 demonstrate that 1:2-18 forms a distinct textual unit that prepares the audience for the exhortation in 2:1-3, but that 2:1-3 introduces an entirely new section.

Fundamentally, the generic character and contents of Zeph 1:2-18 contrast markedly with those of 2:1-3. Zephaniah 1:2-18 contains a great deal of material formulated in a first person address form that presupposes YHWH as the speaker (1:2-4[5a], 8aβ-9, 10aβ-11, 12aβ-13, and 17) and an unspecified audience, most likely the people of Jerusalem and Judah (see 1:4; cf. 1:12). These speeches by YHWH are encased in third person language by the prophet who speaks about YHWH in various forms, viz., the oracular formulas in 1:2b, 3β and the third person references to YHWH in 1:5b-6, 7-8aα, 10aα, 12a, 14-16, 17aβ, 18. With the exception of Zeph 1:7, which employs a direct address to the audience, "Silence from before the L–rd YHWH, for the Day of YHWH is near," the language is third person proclamation language that is designed to make an announcement to an audience. In the present form of the text, Zeph 1:2-18 appears as a speech by the prophet in which he quotes YHWH as part of a general proclamation of the Day of YHWH. Overall, the quotations of YHWH lend force to the proclamation by demonstrating that the decision to bring about the Day of YHWH is indeed YHWH's. Nevertheless, the full rhetorical impact of this proclamation is not completely clear at this point. By proclaiming the Day of YHWH, the speech either addresses the righteous in Jerusalem/Judah in order to inform them of the fate of the wicked, or it addresses the people of Jerusalem/Judah in general in order to convince them to choose righteousness and thereby to avoid being included among the wicked who will be punished. In contrast to the proclamatory language of Zeph 1:2-18, the language of Zeph 2:1-3 is clearly exhortational in that it is clearly designed to prompt its audience to make a decision. As noted above, the passage employs second person plural imperatives to address its audience directly. It does not quote YHWH, but refers to YHWH only in the third person. It does not proclaim the Day of YHWH; rather the Day of YHWH serves as the premise by which the prophet demands a decision from the audience.

In addition to the distinctive generic characteristics and contents of Zeph 1:2-18 and 2:1-3, the syntactical interrelationships of the two passages must also be considered. There is no overt syntactical conjunction between Zeph 1:2-18 and 2:1-3. Zephaniah 1:2-18 stands entirely by itself as a generically and syntactically coherent textual unit that proclaims the Day of YHWH. Zephaniah 2:1-3, on the other hand, is joined to Zeph 2:4 by the particle *kî*, "for, because." Many interpreters have argued that this is an example of an emphatic *kî* that is designed to introduce an entirely new unit,[5] but such an assertion does not consider

---

[5] E.g., James Muilenburg, "The Linguistic and Rhetorical Usages of the Particle ‫כי‬ in the Old Testament," *HUCA* 32 (1961) 135–60.

the normal conjunctive force of the particle. When it is read in relation to 2:3, Zeph 2:4 provides concrete motivation for the audience to accept the prophet's exhortation to seek YHWH, viz., the Philistine cities have fallen, and this provides concrete evidence that YHWH is acting to bring about the Day of YHWH against Jerusalem and Judah proclaimed in Zeph 1:2-18. The following announcements of punishment against the nations begin with the announcement directed against the Philistines in Zeph 2:5-7. These announcements provide further support for the exhortation in Zeph 2:1-3 in that they present additional evidence that the Day of YHWH is taking place and that the people must make their choice to seek YHWH or suffer the consequences.

In sum, Zeph 1:2-18 announces the Day of YHWH, whereas the following material beginning in Zeph 2:1 exhorts the people to seek YHWH and provides evidence as to why they should do so.

ZEPHANIAH'S PROCLAMATION OF YHWH'S ORACULAR SPEECHES: 1:2-6

Within the larger framework of the proclamation of the Day of YHWH in Zeph 1:2-18, verses 2-6 form a distinctive textual sub-unit in which the prophet conveys YHWH's initial oracular speeches prior to the full announcement of the Day of YHWH in verses 7-18. Zephaniah 1:2-6 contains two oracular speech reports by the prophet in which he quotes YHWH, and provides further information that identifies YHWH as the speaker or elaborates upon the meaning of what YHWH has said. Overall, Zeph 1:2-6 conveys YHWH's announcements of punishment against those people of Jerusalem and Judah who are engaged in syncretistic worship of pagan deities.

The first oracular speech report appears in verses 2-3a. It includes three first person statements by YHWH that employ the verb *ʾāsēp*, "I will destroy, bring to an end," in which YHWH outlines plans to bring punishment that will affect all of creation. The initial statement appears in verse 2, and constitutes the basic statement of the sequence in which YHWH announces punishment against all the land. The oracular formula, *nĕʾūm yhwh*, "utterance of YHWH," clearly identifies the announcement as an oracular statement conveyed by the prophet. The initial verbs of the statement, *ʾāsōp ʾāsēp*, have provoked considerable discussion because of the difficulties in their grammatical forms. The verb *ʾāsōp* is an infinitive absolute form of the verb root *ʾsp*, "to gather," which conveys emphasis when placed prior to the following verb. The problem is that infinitive absolutes normally appear before finite forms of the same verb root, but *ʾāsēp* is a first person singular *hiphil* imperfect form of the root *swp*, "to destroy, bring to an end." The infinitive absolute *ʾāsōp* therefore requires the corresponding form of the root *ʾsp*, viz., *ʾeʾĕsōp* or the cohortative form *ʾōsēp*, "I will gather" (cf. *ʾāsōp ʾeʾĕsōp*, "I will surely gather," in Mic 2:12). Scholars have attempted various emendations, but none has proved convincing. It should be noted that a similar construction appears in Jer 8:13, *ʾāsōp ʾăsîpēm*, "I will surely destroy them," in which the infinitive absolute of *ʾsp*, "to gather," is combined with a first person singular *hiphil* imperfect of *swp*, "to destroy," with a third person masculine plural suffix pronoun. This would suggest that, despite the grammatical difficulties with the phrase, it constitutes an idiomatic and emphatic expression for destruction. In any case, it should be noted that the root *ʾsp* is employed for gathering the harvest,[6] and thereby conveys the cutting or destruction of the plants in the field as they are gathered at harvest time.

The next two statements by YHWH specify the first. Verse 3aα states that YHWH will destroy "human beings" and "cattle," and verse 3aβ states that YHWH will destroy "birds of the heavens" and "fish of the sea." Many scholars note that the three statements by YHWH in verses 2-3a take up language from the account of creation in Genesis 1 in an overall portrayal of the reversal or destruction of creation, and therefore argue that this passage portrays a post-exilic vision of eschatological destruction. The decision to view this imagery as a post-exilic scenario depends to a large extent upon the assignment of Genesis 1 to the post-exilic P stratum of the Pentateuch, but such a view is unnecessary. It is not unusual for prophets to refer to the disruption of the natural world in their efforts to point to failings in the human realm (see Hosea 4:1-19; Amos 7:1-6; Jer 4:23-26, 27-31; Isa 24:1-13). Furthermore, account must be taken of the reference to "this place" in verse 4, which is generally recognized as a reference to the Temple as the site for Zephaniah's prophesying. Throughout the monarchic period and beyond, the Temple in Jerusalem was viewed as the center of creation insofar as its imagery was designed to symbolize the Garden of Eden and its altar is identified elsewhere as the "navel" or "bosom" (*ḥêq*; Ezek 43:13-17) which stands at the center of the newly created world in Ezekiel 47–48.[7] The Temple was conceived of as the source of agricultural and animal fertility as well as the source of well-being for humans in Judean society insofar as the annual harvest and produce of the flock were brought to the Temple for sacrifice. The use of verb *ʾsp*, "to gather," in verse 1 calls to mind this role, and the following verses 3b-6 presuppose a cultic or Temple context insofar as they are concerned

---

[6] E.g., Exod 23:10, 16; Lev 23:39; 25:3, 20; Deut 11:14; 16:13; 28:38; Isa 17:5; Jer 40:10, 12; Ruth 2:7.

[7] See Jon D. Levenson, "The Temple and the World," *JR* 64 (1984) 275–98.

with cultic apostasy. Overall, the reversal of creation portrayed in these verses presupposes the perversion of the Temple by cultic apostasy.

The last statement in the sequence, verse 3aβ, "and causing the wicked to stumble," is generally recognized as a gloss. It is not formulated as a first person statement by YHWH, but it employs a feminine plural *hiphil* participle (*wĕhammakšēlôt*, "and causing to stumble") for which "the wicked" serves as direct object (*ʾet-hārĕšāʿîm*). The participle has no clear antecedent that would serve as subject as the terms for "human," "birds," and "fish," are all masculine. It disrupts the syntax of the verse, and introduces the reference to "the wicked" abruptly without explanation. It appears to be a marginal comment written at an early time, that found its way into the body of the text.

The second oracular speech report appears in Zeph 1:3b-6, which focuses on the punishment of syncretistic elements within Jerusalem and Judah. It includes a sequence of three statements, each of which begins with a first person *waw-consecutive* perfect verb for which YHWH is the speaker. Again, third person references to YHWH throughout the passage indicate that the prophet conveys YHWH's statements. The first is the basic statement of the series in verse 3b, in which the prophet conveys YHWH's stated intention, "and I will cut off humankind from the face of the earth." The oracular formula at the end of the verse demonstrates that the prophet is the speaker who quotes YHWH. The second statement of the series follows in verse 4a in which YHWH specifies that this punishment is directed specifically against Judah and the inhabitants of Jerusalem. The use of the phrase, "and I will stretch forth my hand," is a common motif that expresses YHWH's judgment. It appears in relation to the motif of YHWH's, Moses', and Aaron's outstretched hand in the Exodus plague traditions (Exod 7:19; 8:1, 2 [NRSV: 8:5, 6]; 9:22; 10:12, 21, 22; 14:16, 21, 27). It also appears in the Isaiah traditions where the statement, "and his hand is stretched out still" conveys YHWH's judgment against Israel (Isa 5:25; 9:11, 16, 20 [NRSV: 9:12, 17, 21]; 10:4) and a similar statement is directed against the sea and Canaanites/Tyrians (Isa 23:11). The motif is employed to convey judgment against Babylon in Jer 51:25, and in Ezekiel it is employed against idolaters (Ezek 6:14; 14:9, 13), YHWH's unfaithful wife Jerusalem (Ezek 16:27), and nations such as Ammon (Ezek 25:7), Edom (Ezek 25:13; 35:3), and Philistia (Ezek 25:16). The final statement in the sequence appears in Zeph 1:4b-6, in which YHWH specifies that the judgment is directed against syncretists who have given worship or allegiance both to YHWH and to pagan gods. It begins with YHWH's statement, "and I will cut off from this place the remnant of Baal, the name of the idolatrous priests with the priests . . ." The reference to "this place" may indicate any general place, the city of Jerusalem, the land of Judah, etc., but the term *māqôm*, "place," is frequently employed as a technical term for the site of Y<small>HWH</small>'s altar or Temple (e.g., Deut 12:5, 14; 14:23, 25; 15:20; 16:2, 6; 17:8; 18:6, etc.; Josh 9:27; Neh 1:9; 1 Kgs 8:29, 30, 35, etc.). The use of the term for Temple or altar in Deuteronomy is especially important insofar as an early form of Deuteronomy, with its command for the establishment of only one "place" or Temple/altar for the worship of Y<small>HWH</small> is a key feature of Josiah's reform, which the book of Zephaniah addresses. Such a reference to the Temple sets the context for the problems of cultic syncretism that appear throughout verses 4b-6.

The reference to "remnant of Baal" has provoked a great deal of discussion in that the term "remnant" suggests some previous reform activity that has failed insofar as only a remnant of Baal is left. But the term also suggests an ongoing program of cultic purification that has already begun among the people and is now directed against the cultic functionaries or priests who represent such syncretistic practice. The reference to "the idolatrous priests" *(hakkĕmārîm)* is somewhat enigmatic in that scholars are not entirely certain what the term means. It is noteworthy, however, that such "idolatrous priests" are removed from the cities of Judah by Josiah during the course of his reform (2 Kgs 23:5), and the Akkadian term *kamâru* means "to lay prostrate, overthrow," which suggests that the term could be an Akkadian loan word that refers to cultic functionaries. It is paired with the usual Judean term for priests *(hakkōhānîm)*. Some consider this reference to be a gloss, but the appearance of the term here aids in conveying the imagery of syncretistic practice among Judean priests.

Verses 5-6 continue to specify the targets of Y<small>HWH</small>'s judgment with a sequence of direct object phrases that are linked by conjunctive *waw,* "and." The third person references to Y<small>HWH</small> in verses 5b-6, however, make it clear that the prophet and not Y<small>HWH</small> is now the speaker. Nevertheless, the use of the conjunction and the direct object markers tie verses 5-6 syntactically into Y<small>HWH</small>'s speech in verse 4b. The phrase, "and those who worship upon the rooftops to the host of heaven" (verse 5a) portrays a form of worship or celebration that appears also in Isa 22:1. Here it is directed to "the host of heaven," a reference to the worship of astral deities that was particularly common in Mesopotamia as well as in Syria-Israel-Philistia. The "host of heaven" were also targeted in Josiah's reform (2 Kgs 23:4, 5). Likewise, the phrase, "and those worshiping who are sworn to Y<small>HWH</small> and who are sworn by their king" has attracted attention because the Lucianic Greek versions and the Peshitta read the phrase "by their king" *(bĕmalkām)* as a reference to the Ammonite deity Milcom who is also the target of Josiah's reforms (2 Kgs 23:13). But such a reading is unnecessary as the earliest Septuagint manuscripts read the word in reference to "their king."

Furthermore, Milcom is hardly singled out but appears together with Ashtoret of Sidon and Chemosh of Moab in the account of Josiah's reform (2 Kgs 23:13). The issue centers around the difficulty of understanding the simultaneous reference to "those sworn to YHWH" and "those sworn by their king." The interrelationship of the Davidic king and YHWH is very clear in the tradition. Judean religious thought identifies the Davidic king as the "son" of YHWH (Pss 2:7; 89:26-27; 2 Sam 7:14), and relates David's efforts to build a Temple for YHWH to YHWH's choice of David and Zion (Psalm 132, cf. Psalm 110). Exodus 22:27 [NRSV: 22:28] forbids cursing G–d and reviling the ruler *(nāśîʾ)*, and 1 Kgs 21:10 relates an incident in which Naboth is tried by the Israelite King Ahab for treason because he has "cursed G–d and the king *(melek)*." Isaiah 8:21 relates the frustration of the people who abandon YHWH's Torah in a time of distress and "curse its king and its G–d." Zephaniah 1:5 presupposes the very close interrelationship between YHWH and the king in Judean thought, and it employs the image of those sworn to/by YHWH and king to convey its portrayal of syncretism within Jerusalem and Judah as such persons also give worship to Baal and the host of heaven. Note that in ancient Judah and the Near East in general, it is the kings who build Temples. Likewise, it is King Josiah who carries out the reform of Temple practice; just as YHWH legitimizes the king, so the king tends to YHWH (Psalm 132). The final statement of the objects of YHWH's punishment appears in verse 6, which summarizes the passage with the statement, "and those who turn aside from after YHWH; and who have not sought YHWH and have not inquired of him." The reference to "inquiry" employs the verb root *drš*, which refers to oracular inquiry of YHWH through Judean cultic officials. In sum, the passage refers to those Jerusalemites and Judeans who are obligated to adhere to YHWH, but seek out other gods.

ZEPHANIAH'S ANNOUNCEMENT OF THE DAY OF YHWH: 1:7-18

The discourse shifts in verses 7-18 with the prophet's explicit announcement of the Day of YHWH. Zephaniah is still clearly the speaker, as indicated by the third person references to YHWH throughout the passage, although he continues to quote YHWH's statements concerning the punishment of the people. Although the passage begins with a reference to the Day of YHWH as a cultic sacrifice, the focus of concern shifts from cultic matters to the conduct of government officials and those engaged in economic exchange and the pursuit of wealth. It includes two basic components in verses 7-13 and 14-18, as indicated by the syntactically independent introductory announcements concerning the coming or "near" Day of YHWH in verses 7 and 14.

The first component appears in verses 7-13, in which the prophet conveys YHWH's announcements concerning the significance of the Day of YHWH as a day of sacrifice for those whom YHWH intends to judge. The passage begins with the prophet's command for silence in verse 7, "Silence from before the L—rd YHWH, for near is the Day of YHWH; for YHWH has prepared a sacrifice, he has sanctified his invitees." Although the term *has*, "silence!" functions as an imperative verb, it appears to be an onomatopoeic particle that is to the analogous English term "hush!" Similar examples of the expression appear elsewhere in Hab 2:20, "And YHWH is in his Temple; silence from before him all the earth!" and in Zech 2:17, "Silence all flesh from before YHWH for he has awakened from his holy refuge!" In both cases, the formula, "silence from before YHWH/him," presupposes the setting of the Temple, and apparently functions as a call to silence in preparation for some liturgical representation of YHWH's action in the world. The representation of the Day of YHWH as a day of sacrifice is therefore particularly pertinent in Zeph 1:7 in that the cultic action of sacrifice represents YHWH's intentions to bring judgment against those who have acted improperly. A reading of the procedures for conducting the Temple sacrifices in Leviticus indicates that the sacrifices are carried out in silence; the priests do not speak as they carry out the slaughter of the animal, the preparation for the altar, and the disposal of its non-sacrificial portions.[8] The Levitical choirs would sing hymns or psalms (see 1 Chronicles 16) in conjunction with the Temple sacrifices, but the priests engaged in the sacrifice itself would remain silent throughout the procedure. The reference to YHWH's sanctification of those whom YHWH has called or invited is deliberately enigmatic. Those who are called to the sacrifice might be understood as guests who will partake in the sacrificial meal as Moses, Aaron, and their companions do at Sinai (Exod 24:9-11) or as Saul does by Samuel's invitation at Ramah (1 Sam 9:13, 22-24). But the following announcements of punishment against various officials and people of means suggests that those invited might also become the victims of the sacrifice! The portrayal of the poured-out blood and entrails of YHWH's human victims later in verses 17-18 certainly suggests that this is the case.

A series of statements introduced by a future time formula, "and it shall come to pass on that day/at that time," then follows in verses 8-9,

---

[8] See Israel Knohl, *The Sanctuary of Silence: The Priestly Torah and the Holiness School* (Minneapolis: Fortress, 1995).

10-11, and 12-13 in which the prophet quotes YHWH's statements of intention to punish infidel government officials and traders.

Verses 8-9 begin with the prophet's statement, "and it shall come to pass on that day," immediately prior to the quote of YHWH's first person announcement of punishment against government officials. The statement, "and I shall visit punishment upon the officials," employs the common verb *pqd*, "to attend to, visit, muster," which signifies official or authorized examination by a legitimate authority, in this case, YHWH. Here, it signifies examination of those placed in positions of authority and the consequent punishment of those who fail to measure up to YHWH's expectations. The term "officials" (*śārîm*) is the common term employed for those who are appointed to some office, such as tribal chieftains, military officers, administrative figures who work under the authority of a king, or other persons who are appointed to positions of responsibility.

The reference to the "sons of the king" is particularly enigmatic in that Josiah's sons could hardly have been considered as adults who would have been subject to YHWH's punishment by the time of his reform. Josiah was eight years old when he assumed the throne. He would have been fourteen when his son Jehoiachin was born (see 2 Kgs 24:8 which reports that Jehoiachin was twenty-five years old when he began to reign after Josiah's death at the age of thirty-one), and sixteen when Jehoahaz was born (see 2 Kgs 23:31 which reports that Jehoahaz was twenty-three when he began to reign after Josiah's death). If Josiah's reforms began either in the twelfth (2 Chr 34:3) or eighteenth (2 Kgs 22:3) year of his reign, his sons would have been either six and four or twelve and ten respectively. In either case, they would have been minors at the beginning of Josiah's reform, and would hardly constitute appropriate targets for YHWH's punishment. It is noteworthy, however, that ancient Near Eastern treaty language typically employs the metaphors of "father" and "son" to express the relationship between a suzerain monarch and his vassals (cf. Ps 2:7; 2 Sam 7:14, which employs the same language to define the relationship between YHWH and the Davidic king). This provides a context for understanding the references to "the seventy sons of Ahab" in 2 Kings 10:1 and the seventy sons of Jerubaal (Gideon) in Judg 9:2, 5. Insofar as the ruling council of elders in Israel normally constitutes seventy (Exod 24:1, 9) and the king's sons often act in an administrative capacity (see 1 Kgs 22:26-27), some have suggested that "the sons of the kings" refers to the king's officials as well. Both Judges 9 and 2 Kings 10 make it clear that the seventy sons of the king are biological sons as well; it may be that the sons of the king are included here, despite their minority, because they represent the ruling elite of the government who are subject to YHWH's examination as well. The exhortational character of the prophet's discourse indicates that those named for examination or punishment have the opportunity to correct their actions. It is noteworthy that the king is not named in this passage; after all, Josiah sponsored the reform.

The reference to "those who wear foreign garments" has also attracted the attention of interpreters. Although some understand the term *malbûš nokrî*, "foreign garment," to be a reference to some sort of cultic vestment that might represent syncretistic worship, 1 Kgs 10:5 indicates that the term *malbûš* indicates some sort of a formal garment that may be worn by government officials in a state ceremony (cf. Job 27:16, where it refers simply to a garment of uncertain nature).

Verse 9 constitutes a second first person statement by YHWH that begins with the verb, "and I will examine/visit punishment upon." The target here is "those who leap over the threshold" and "those who fill the house of their master(s) with violence and deceit." The reference to leaping over the threshold has suggested to many interpreters that the verse condemns cultic apostasy insofar as the term "threshold" *(miptān)* appears in 1 Sam 5:4, 5 in reference to the threshold of the sanctuary of the Philistine god Dagon. The notice in 1 Sam 5:5 that no one treads upon the threshold of Dagon would then explain the "leaping" over the threshold in Zeph 1:9. In this case, "the house of their master," would refer to YHWH's Temple in Jerusalem insofar as the plural of majesty (literally, "masters") would be employed for the Deity. In this case, the term for "leap" is a simple *qal* form of *dlg*, not the usual intensive *piel* form that means "leap," and signifies only "stepping over." The term *miptān* is commonly employed for the threshold of the Temple in Jerusalem (see Ezek 9:3; 10:4, 18; 46:2; 47:1), but it does not appear to be a technical term in any sense because it is also qualified by reference to the Jerusalem Temple or to Dagon's temple. It would seem that the expression here means simply those who enter their master's house, whether that of the king or of YHWH, to bring in violence and deceit. The terms for "violence" *(ḥāmās)* and "deceit" *(mirmâ)* are commonly employed for wrongdoing by force (e.g., Gen 16:5; Amos 3:10; Hab 1:2, 3) and economic deception (e.g., Hos 12:8; Amos 8:5; Mic 6:11; Prov 11:1; 20:3). Both therefore convey the abuse of power or the failure to exercise responsibility.

Verses 10-11 begin with the prophet's introduction, "and it shall come to pass in that day, utterance of YHWH," which identifies the following quote by YHWH. No first person language appears in this statement; it merely announces the fear and consternation of the traders or merchants who will suffer punishment. Such attention to commercial interests would be particularly important during Josiah's reforms as the Assyrian empire had established the Shephelah and Philistine regions as a major center for trade and the production of olive oil.[9] Insofar as Josiah's reforms take place during the course of Assyria's collapse, these statements might well be directed against those who were engaged in trade with or on behalf of Assyria. YHWH's statement identifies outcry and wailing from several quarters of the city of Jerusalem and its environs, including the "Fish Gate," the "Mishneh," the "hills," and the "Maktesh." The Fish Gate was apparently situated on the north or the west side of the city (2 Chr 33:14; Neh 3:3; 12:39), which would provide the closest access to the Mediterranean sea coast from which fish would be brought to Jerusalem for sale. The Mishneh is the "second" quarter of the city that was established on the western hill overlooking the Temple mount and the city of David, probably in the late-eighth century by Hezekiah to accommodate northern Israelites and Judeans who were moving to Jerusalem for protection in the aftermath of the Assyrian destruction of the northern kingdom of Israel. It is generally viewed as the wealthier section of the city, and perhaps a major commercial area. The prophetess Huldah, whom Josiah consulted upon finding the Torah scroll in the Temple, lived in this area (2 Kgs 22:14; 2 Chr 34:22). The "hills" are not specified, but Jerusalem is surrounded by hills that readily echo noise. The Maktesh is derived from the Hebrew word for "mortar," based on the verb root *ktš*, "to pound," and likely refers to a "mortar"-shaped depression in the Jerusalem landscape. The most likely candidate is the Tyropoean Valley, which lies between the City of David/Temple mount and the hill on which the Mishneh was built. This area also served as a major commercial area in ancient times. The commercial motif continues in the final statements that express the motivation for the outcry in these quarters. The demise of "the people of Canaan" refers to the Canaanites not as an ethnic or a religious group, but employs the term as a designation for traders or merchants (cf. Isa 23:8; Job 40:30 [NRSV: 41:6]; Prov 31:24). Canaan after all controlled the sea trade routes and coastal ports employed throughout antiquity by the Phoenicians as well as the coastal plain through which the highways between Syria/Asia Minor and Egypt passed. This was the same area developed by the Assyrians in the seventh century B.C.E. as a major center for trade and the production of olive oil to supply the needs of the empire. The reference to the people of Canaan as merchants is confirmed by the parallel reference to the demise of "those who handle/bear silver" at the end of the verse.

---

[9] See Seymour Gitin, "Tel Miqne-Ekron: A Type Site for the Inner Coastal Plain in the Iron Age II Period," *Recent Excavations in Israel: Studies in Iron Age Archaeology*, ed. Seymour Gitin and William G. Dever, AASOR, vol. 49 (Winona Lake, IN: Eisenbrauns, 1989) 23–58.

The third element of the series in Zeph 1:12-13 again begins with the prophet's introduction, "and it shall come to pass in that time," prefixed to a statement by Yнwн. Essentially, this statement sums up the preceding insofar as it identifies those to be judged as infidels, and announces the loss or destruction of their wealth and property. Yнwн states the intention to search out "those who linger over their lees/wine," and say that "Yнwн does not do good, and he does not do evil." The reference to the wine indicates the idleness of those who make such statements, and indicates that they are wealthy enough to have the leisure for drinking. The choice of the word for wine, *šimrêhem*, "their lees," employs the root *šmr*, "to watch, observe." Here it refers to wine that is watched while it ferments, but the root is frequently used in relation to the observance of Yнwн's commands or teachings which suggests a deliberate pun for "those who coagulate/stall over their observances." The result of this drunkenness is a statement that Yнwн is powerless or incapable of doing either good or evil (cf. Isa 5:11-12, 18-23; Hab 2:5). Yнwн's statement concludes with the assertion that their wealth and homes will be plundered, and that they will neither dwell in their homes nor drink the wine of their vineyards. The irony of the situation is clear in that—Yнwн brings about judgment against wealthy infidel drunks who will lose their homes and wine because they believe Yнwн to be impotent.

The second component of the prophet's announcement of the Day of Yнwн appears in Zeph 1:14-18, in which he lays out the consequences of the day. This section is syntactically independent of Zeph 1:2-6, and it includes two basic elements that are joined together by a *waw-consecutive* perfect verb in verse 17, "and I shall afflict." The first element in verses 14-16 comprises the prophet's description of the Day of Yнwн in third person announcement language. Verse 14 begins the section by renewing the announcement previously made in verse 7 that the Day of Yнwн is near. It continues with statements that the Day of Yнwн is rapidly approaching, and that it is a day of bitterness in which warriors shriek, perhaps as a cry of battle or perhaps in terror. As noted above, whereas the Day of Yнwн frequently expresses Yнwн's vengeance against the enemies of Judah or Israel, it can be employed ironically in the prophets to designate a day of Yнwн's punishment against Judah or Israel rather than deliverance from a threat (cf. Amos 5:18-20). This latter understanding of the Day of Yнwн is evident in verses 16-17, which employ a series of five paired metaphors to describe the day. It is initially identified as a day of wrath (verse 15a), and then as a day of "trouble and stress," "destruction and devastation," "darkness and gloom," "cloud and dark cloud," and "Shofar and trumpet blast." The terms adequately convey the distress of the situation, and several have

specialized meanings. The term "destruction" *(šōʾâ)* conveys total devastation and is now employed in modern Hebrew as the term for the
Holocaust or destruction of European Jewry in World War II. The images of "darkness" *(ḥōšek),* "gloom" *(ʾăpēlâ),* "cloud" *(ʿănān),* and "dark
cloud" *(ʿărāpel)* typically appear in theophanic descriptions of YHWH's
manifestation in the world (Exod 19:16; 20:18; Deut 4:11; 1 Kgs 8:12;
Nah 1:3; Ps 97:2; 2 Chr 6:1; cf. Isa 8:22-23; Joel 2:2), and likely convey the
darkness of the Holy of Holies in the Temple where the Ark of the Covenant is kept behind a veil so that no light can enter. Likewise, the reference to the Shofar *(šôpār)* and the "trumpet blast" *(tĕrûʿâ)* accompany
theophanic descriptions of the Deity (Exod 19:16; Joel 2:1), and likely
represent the sounding of Shofar and trumpet in the Temple at the New
Year (Num 29:1; cf. Lev 23:24; Num 10:10) and Jubilee year (Lev 25:9) as
well as a call to arms against enemies (Judg 3:27; Josh 6:4-5; cf. Isa
27:13). Verse 16b concludes the description of the Day of YHWH with a
statement that the Day is directed against the fortifications and corner
towers that are designed to protect the people (cf. Isa 2:6-21), again, an
expression of irony analogous to that of Zeph 1:13.

Verses 17-18 then describe the impact of the Day on its victims. This
section begins with a first person statement by YHWH, "and I will afflict
humanity so that they will go as the blind," but the balance of the passage is formulated in third person language and constitutes speech by
the prophet. Verses 17aβ-18 provides motivation for YHWH's statement
as indicated by the introductory *kî,* "because they have sinned against
YHWH." Some consider this phrase to be a gloss because it interrupts
YHWH's speech, but the reference to YHWH in verse 18 demonstrates
that the prophet is speaking here, too. Returning to the sacrificial motif
that begins in verse 7, the prophet describes the spilling of blood like
dust and entrails like dung balls undoubtedly conveying the graphic
imagery of animals being slaughtered for sacrifice. Returning to the imagery of verses 11 and 13, he states that even their silver and gold will not
be able to save them. In verse 18, the prophet sums up the entire passage by returning to the initial motif of world-wide destruction in 1:2-3
by describing the Day of YHWH's wrath as a day when all the land will
be consumed and all of its inhabitants will suffer complete destruction.

Zephaniah's Prophetic Exhortation to Seek YHWH Proper: 2:1–3:20

Zephaniah 2:1–3:20 constitutes the primary unit of Zephaniah that
calls upon its audience to seek YHWH. As noted above, the exhortational character of the unit, particularly Zeph 2:1-3, distinguishes it

from the announcement of the Day of YHWH in Zeph 1:2-18. It is joined
to Zeph 2:4 and the following material by the causative *kî* that begins
the verse and thereby portrays the destruction of the four Philistine
cities as the demonstration that the Day of YHWH is indeed taking
place. Although the oracles against the nations in Zeph 2:5-15 begin
with an introductory *hôy*, "woe!" which generally marks the beginning
of a new unit, the continued theme of destruction directed against the
Philistine sea coast followed by the other nations indicates that Zeph
2:5-15 is designed to follow upon Zeph 2:4. It thereby provides further
elaboration on the theme of the Philistine downfall as a motivation for
the exhortation to seek YHWH. The following material in Zeph 3:1-20,
likewise introduced by *hôy*, turns the audience's attention to Jerusalem
and Judah and thereby brings the point of the prophet's address home.
He outlines a scenario of Jerusalem's own guilt and punishment, recalling that of the nations, and thereby prepares the audience for the
impending restoration of Zion and Israel when the nations will acknowledge YHWH's sovereignty, the exiled people of Judah/Israel will
return, and Israel will be restored among all the peoples of the earth.

Furthermore, just as Zeph 2:1-3 is formulated as a second person
masculine plural address to its audience, the people of Jerusalem and
Judah, so Zeph 2:4–3:20 is dominated by second person masculine
plural address forms. Although this section frequently identifies its addressees as the Philistines (Zeph 2:5); Cush (Zeph 2:12); Daughter of
Zion/Jerusalem (Zeph 3:7; 11-13), the references to the Philistines and
Cush quickly shift to third person references and the feminine singular
references to the Daughter of Zion shift to masculine plural forms (see
Zeph 3:8, 14, 19-20). This demonstrates that the primary addressees are
not Philistia, Cush, or Daughter of Zion in these passages; they are only
secondary addressees included in the discourse for rhetorical effect.
The primary addressees are the people of Jerusalem/Judah/Israel, as
indicated by the masculine plural address forms that constitute a literary envelope around the passage in Zeph 2:1-3 and 3:19-20 as well as
the masculine plural forms in Zeph 3:8, 14.

ZEPHANIAH'S EXHORTATION ADDRESS: 2:1-3

The basic exhortation address appears in Zeph 2:1-3.[10] The passage
contains two exhortation statements, formulated with masculine imperative plural verbs followed by motivation statements, that are de-

---

[10] See A. Vanlier Hunter, *Seek the L–rd! A Study of the Meaning and Function of the
Exhortations in Amos, Hosea, Isaiah, Micah, and Zephaniah* (Baltimore: St. Mary's Semi-
nary and University, 1982).

signed to call upon the audience to seek Y<small>HWH</small> and thereby avoid the projected punishment on the Day of Y<small>HWH</small>.

The first begins with the dual command, "Be gathered and assemble, O worthless nation!" The choice of verbs is unusual in that they are two variant forms of the same root, *qšš*, "to gather straw." The first is a reflexive *hithpael* form, "gather yourselves," and the second is a simple *qal* form "gather," i.e., "assemble." Because interpreters have had difficulties in understanding why the prophet should call upon the people to gather straw, there have been many suggestions to emend either or both of the verbs but none have been convincing. Indeed, the use of *qšš* is entirely appropriate here, in that the entire discourse began in Zeph 1:2-3 with variations of the verb *ʾsp*, "to gather," which is employed for the gathering of the harvest prior to presenting it at the Temple for sacrifice. Many have speculated that Zephaniah's discourse is formulated for delivery at a major Temple holiday, such as Shavuot (Pentecost) or more likely Sukkoth (Tabernacles), when the harvest of grain and fruits are brought into the Temple respectively. It was noted above that the discourse presents the Day of Y<small>HWH</small> as a day of sacrifice for those who have acted improperly in Judah by engaging in syncretistic worship, economic abuse, and collaboration with Assyria. Insofar as the verbs *ʾsp* and *qšš* convey the harvest and gathering of grain and its chaff, they likewise convey the prophet's/Y<small>HWH</small>'s portrayal of the audience as part of the rhetorical strategy to call upon them to return to Y<small>HWH</small>. Y<small>HWH</small> is gathering in the harvest. The people can choose to be chaff, and thereby be discarded as worthless, or they can seek Y<small>HWH</small> and be spared. Hence, although the root *qšš* is normally applied to the gathering of straw, its use for the assembly of the people here provides an appropriate pun that aids the prophet in his rhetorical goals.

This imagery is reinforced by the designation of the people as "worthless nation." The term for worthless, *lōʾ niksāp*, is unusual because it is based upon the verb root *ksp* that normally means "to long for, desire" (Gen 31:30; Ps 84:3 [N<small>RSV</small>: 84:2]). Its use here is quite appropriate, however, in that the root also stands as the base of the noun *kesep*, "silver," and thereby provides an appropriate play of words on those who "bear silver" (Zeph 1:11), and who are condemned by the prophet in the initial address of Zeph 1:2-18. In the present instance, the term for "undesirable" becomes "worthless" and further indicates that their wealth will not save them on the Day of Y<small>HWH</small> (Zeph 1:18).

The imagery is further reinforced by the three motivating statements in Zeph 2:2, each of which begins with the particle *bĕṭerem*, "before," which indicates that the audience had better decide quickly before the consequences are at hand. The first reads, "before the decree is born, like chaff a day passes." The term "decree," clearly conveys the

judgmental character of the Day of YHWH, and the term "chaff" reinforces the agricultural imagery of sacrifice as the useless chaff of the
grain that blows away and is lost. The second and third statements are
explicit in that they both call upon the audience to act before the wrath
of YHWH comes upon them.

The second exhortation statement is much more direct, "Seek
YHWH, all you humble of the land who do his (YHWH's) justice; seek
righteousness, seek humility . . ." It is at this point that the prophet's
rhetorical goal is clear; he asks the audience to "seek," i.e., adhere to,
YHWH. In identifying the audience as "the humble of the land," he
invokes the image of poverty or at least contrasts the audience with
wealthy wrongdoers identified in Zeph 1:2-18. In this manner, he asks
the audience to identify with the poor who do YHWH's law, i.e., who do
what YHWH expects or what is just. The term *mišpāṭ* conveys both "law"
and "justice." It is noteworthy, therefore, that the people of the land
brought Josiah to the throne after his father Amon was assassinated in
a palace coup. Josiah's reform gave greater economic rights to the poor
in the laws of Deuteronomy, and Zephaniah asks the people to identify
with the poor rather than the rich in supporting Josiah's reform. The
motivating statement to these exhortations is simple, "perhaps you will
be hidden on the day of YHWH's wrath."

Zephaniah's Explanatory Address: 2:4–3:20

Zephaniah 2:4–3:20 provides the basis for the prophet's exhortation
to seek YHWH in Zeph 2:1-3 by explaining how YHWH's purposes will
be worked out in relation to world events and in relation to Jerusalem/
Judah/Israel. As noted in the discussion of the literary structure of
Zephaniah 2–3 above, the prophet's portrayal of the downfall of the
Philistine cities in Zeph 2:4 constitutes the primary basis for the exhortation, and the successive announcements of upcoming punishment directed against the nations (Zeph 2:5-15) and punishment followed by
restoration for Jerusalem/Judah/Israel (Zeph 3:1-20) demonstrate how
the destruction of the Philistine cities initiates a process in which YHWH
will see to the downfall of Judah's enemies and the restoration of Israel
to its center in Jerusalem.

THE EXHORTATION BASIS: 2:4

Zephaniah 2:4 plays a key role in the exhortation address in that it
provides evidence that the prophet's announcement of an impending

Day of YHWH that will see the sacrificial purification of Jerusalem and Judah, the downfall of Judah's enemies, and the restoration of Israel and Judah in Zion will actually take place. Linked to the exhortation address in Zeph 2:1-3 by an explanatory *kî*, Zeph 2:4 identifies four Philistine cities that are targeted for destruction. The list includes Gaza, Ashkelon, Ashdod, and Ekron. The fifth Philistine city, Gath, is believed to have been destroyed by the Assyrians in the late eighth century to such an extent that it never regained its standing and faded into obscurity.[11] The verse demonstrates the use of paronomasia to associate the names of the cities with similar sounding verb roots that describe their respective fates. The verse reads, "For Gaza (*ʿazzâ*) will be abandoned (*ʿăzûbâ*; root *ʿzb*), and Ashkelon (*ʾašqĕlôn*) shall become a desolation (*šĕmāmâ*; root *šmm*); they shall drive out (*yĕgārĕšûhā*; root *grš*) Ashdod (*ʾašdôd*) by noon, and Ekron (*ʿeqrôn*) shall be uprooted (*tēʿāqēr*; root *ʿqr*)." By capturing the ear of the audience in this fashion, the verse better enables a speaker to make a lasting impression on the audience and convey the message.

The choice of the Philistine cities and the order of their presentation likewise serves the exhortational purposes of the passage in relation to its historical setting. During the mid-seventh century, the Assyrians had made the Philistine plain the commercial center of their western empire. The port cities of Gaza, Ashkelon, and Ashdod clearly played key roles in facilitating sea trade in the eastern Mediterranean, especially with Egypt, and in providing ocean access to land-locked areas such as Judah and northern Israel. The existence of trading colonies, such as the Greek colony at Yavneh Yam/Mesad Hashavyahu supports this scenario.[12] The Assyrians were also able to turn Ekron into a major industrial center for the production of olive oil in sufficient quantities to serve the needs of the entire empire, and they moved large numbers of the population of Philistia, Israel, and Judah to the region in order to carry out the agricultural and processing tasks that were necessary for such a large scale operation. Indeed, those local authorities who took part in the Assyrian trading apparatus, such as officials in the royal house of David under Manasseh and other members of the Judean upper class, could be expected to profit handsomely, and it is such persons in Judah whom Zephaniah appears to target in Zeph 1:2-18.

Nevertheless, the Assyrian trade hub in Philistia began to be threatened in the mid-seventh century as the Assyrian empire weakened and challengers began to step forward. Based upon statements made by the

---

[11] n.b., Gath also does not appear in Amos 1:6-8, the oracle against the Philistines.
[12] See Jane C. Waldbaum, "Early Greek Contacts with the Southern Levant, ca. 1000–600 B.C.: The Eastern Perspective," *BASOR* 293 (February 1994) 53–66.

fifth-century Greek historian Herodotus (*History* I.105), scholars have postulated an invasion of the region by the Scythians, a horse-mounted nomadic people from the Caucassus steppes.[13] Although evidence for such an invasion is otherwise lacking, Herodotus does point to incursions into the region by the Egyptian pharaoh Psammetichus (Psamtek, r. 664-609), who is said to have bribed the Scythians to leave the region after they plundered the Temple of Aphrodite at Ashkelon. Herodotus also reports that Psamtek engaged in a twenty-nine year siege of Ashdod (*History* II. 157). The increasing Egyptian presence in the region during the reign of Josiah is undisputed, as Psamtek's son Necho is named as the Pharaoh who killed Josiah at Megiddo in 609 B.C.E. With regard to the emerging Egyptian presence, the order of the Philistine cities in Zeph 2:4 is significant, in that they are presented in the order that one would encounter them from south to north, i.e., from the direction of Egypt. Furthermore, given the previous conquest of Egypt by the Assyrians, the emergence of a revitalized Egypt in the mid-seventh century could be interpreted as a threat to Assyria. After all, it was only in 616 B.C.E. that Egypt's alliance with Assyria against Babylonia became clear. During the early years of Josiah's reign, the emergence of Egypt and its overrunning the Philistine plain would be interpreted by Zephaniah as evidence that Yhwh had begun to make good on the promise that Assyria would be punished for its actions against Israel.

The Oracles against the Nations 2:5-15

The oracles against the nations in Zeph 2:5-15 are introduced by the particle *hôy*, "woe!" which typically serves as a means by which a prophet captures the attention of an audience in order to warn of upcoming disaster. The woe oracle form appears either in single oracles (e.g., Amos 5:18-20; Isa 1:4; Nah 3:1) or in series (e.g., Isa 5:8-24; 28-33; Hab 2:6-20). Here, it introduces a series of oracles directed against various nations, including the Philistines (Zeph 2:5-7), Moab and Ammon (Zeph 2:8-11), Cush/Ethiopia (Zeph 2:12), and Assyria (Zeph 2:13-15). Some have suggested that the selection of these nations indicates a desire to present Yhwh's eschatological judgment against all the nations of the earth, insofar as they represent the four cardinal directions of the compass, i.e., west (Philistia), east (Moab and Ammon), south (Cush/Ethiopia), and north (Assyria). But this fails to note that eschatology is

---

[13] See Henri Cazelles, "Zephaniah, Jeremiah, and the Scythians in Palestine," *A Prophet to the Nations: Essays in Jeremiah Studies*, ed. Leo G. Perdue and Brian W. Kovacs (Winona Lake, IN: Eisenbrauns, 1984) 129–49.

not portrayed in this passage, and that the nations presented do not represent all the principal nations of the earth or even the farthest known locales. Egypt is not mentioned, and although one would travel north to reach Assyria from Judah, known countries farther to the "north," such as Elam or Medea (see Isaiah 22), are not mentioned. Instead, the countries chosen are of particular concern to Judah in the seventh century B.C.E.

The oracle against the Philistines is particularly important in that the Philistines were a traditional enemy of Israel and Judah from the earliest days of the Judges, and they were a primary factor in stimulating the origins of the monarchy in Israel. By the seventh century, they were relatively pacified and had been known to ally with Judah and Israel on various occasions. As noted above, the Assyrians had turned the Philistine coastal plain into a major trade and industrial area, and had moved large numbers of Israelites and Judeans to the area in order to support its activities. The presence of a Hebrew-inscribed ostracon at the trading colony in Yavneh Yam, in which a worker asks for the return of his garment from his employer, testifies to the presence of Israelite/Judean exiles in this region.[14] Likewise, the discovery of characteristic four-horned altars at Tel Miqne (Ekron) also points to the presence of Israelite/Judean exiles.[15] Insofar as the book of Zephaniah calls for the return of dispersed or exiled Israelites and Judeans to Zion (see Zeph 3:10, 19-20), those who were taken by the Assyrians to Philistia would be among the first who would come to mind.

It is noteworthy that the oracle calls for judgment against "inhabitants of the sea coast" and "the nation of Kerethites/Cretans," in that this points to the role of the region in sea trade in the eastern Mediterranean with Crete and other locales. The reference to Judah as "the remnant of Judah" that will dwell in the abandoned houses of Ashkelon has provided evidence to some interpreters that this must be a post-exilic composition. This is unwarranted, however, in that archeological surveys of the region have demonstrated that Judah's population diminished during the course of the seventh century, and that it moved away from the Shephelah or the rolling hills that border Philistia in order to concentrate in the central hills around Jerusalem and further to the east and south.[16] This was due in part, no doubt, to Judah's subju-

[14] For a translation of the text, see Pritchard, *ANET* 568.

[15] Seymour Gitin, "Incense Altars from Ekron, Israel, and Judah," *Eretz Israel* 20 (1989) 52*–67*.

[16] See Israel Finkelstein, "The Archaeology of the Days of Manasseh," *Scripture and Other Artifacts: Essays on the Bible and Archaeology in Honor of Philip J. King*, ed. Michael D. Coogan et al. (Louisville: Westminster John Knox, 1994) 169–87.

gation to Assyria during this period and Assyrian movement of the local population into the Philistine plain to support its trade and industrial activities. Zephaniah clearly looks to the reversal of this situation in which Judah will become the dominant presence in the aftermath of the Philistine destruction. The interpretation of the final statement of verse 7, "for YHWH their G–d will visit punishment upon them, and will return their captivity/restore their fortune," is disputed. Some read the phrase *wĕšāb šĕbûtām (qere; šĕbîtām, ketib)*, "and they will return their captivity," whereas others read, "and they will restore their fortune." In either case, the phrase conveys the restoration of Judah and its domination of the Philistine plain in the aftermath of Assyria's collapse.

The oracle against the Moabites and Ammonites in Zeph 2:8-11 functions in a manner analogous to that against the Philistines. During the course of the ninth and eighth centuries B.C.E., both Ammon and Moab occupied territory that had formerly been the territory of the Israelite tribes of Manasseh, Gad, and Reuben. The Assyrian invasions of the late eighth century B.C.E. had sealed this situation, in that the Assyrians stripped the Trans-Jordanian lands and their populations from Israel and left them to Ammon and Moab respectively. The statement that the Ammonites and Moabites "had shamed my people and expanded their border," in verse 8 clearly envisions such a situation. With the impending collapse of Assyria, the time had come for Judah (and Israel) to reassert these claims. It is therefore noteworthy that the reference to "the shame of Moab" employs the term *ḥerpâ*, "shame," that is normally applied to portray violent rape at a time of conquest (Lam 5:1; Neh 1:3; Job 16:10), and "the revilings of the Ammonites" obviously conveys such imagery.

After having outlined the crimes of Ammon and Moab in verse 8, the prophet reports YHWH's statements of punishment in verse 9 beginning with the particle *lākēn*, "therefore," to convey the following actions as the consequence of their deeds. YHWH employs an oath formula to swear that "Moab will become like Sodom and the sons of Ammon (will become) like Gomorrah." The oracle employs the imagery of the Dead Sea region, with its characteristic thorny nettles and salt pits to convey the devastation that Ammon and Moab will suffer. Again, the references to "remnant of my people" and "the remainder of a nation" that will plunder and possess them does not require a post-exilic scenario, but merely refers to the fact that Israel/Judah had been diminished by the forced loss of their land and population to Ammon and Moab. In the concluding verses 10-11, the prophet recapitulates the earlier themes of YHWH's speech by noting that the pride of Moab and Ammon will be replaced by shame as the people of YHWH reclaim their lands. The result will be acknowledgment of YHWH's power in relation to the other gods of the earth, and their worship of YHWH from the farthest reaches or coastlands of the earth. This last statement apparently looks back as well to the oracle concerning the Philistines and the sea coast in Zeph 2:5-7.

The oracle against Cush in Zeph 2:12 is a very short address by YHWH, first to the Cushites and then to the audience at large, concerning YHWH's intent to slay Cush by the sword. Interpreters have argued that Cush here refers either to Ethiopia or to the Midianite tribes that inhabit the Sinai or the Negev wilderness to the south of Judah. Ethiopia is the more likely referent as the identification with Midian depends on Hab 3:7, where Cushan is presented as a parallel to Midian. It is not entirely clear that Cushan is equivalent to Cush. The appearance of Cush/Ethiopia presents difficulties to many interpreters, however, who are unable to explain Zephaniah's interest in Ethiopia during the latter seventh century. An Ethiopian dynasty, the Twenty-Fifth, ruled Egypt during the latter part of the eighth century and the early seventh century, but it was overthrown by Psamtek in 664 B.C.E. Indeed, Psamtek's overthrow of the Ethiopians likely explains the presence of this oracle in Zephaniah as the prophet apparently viewed the resurgent Egyptian empire as a sign of YHWH's action in the world to defeat Assyria and restore Jerusalem/Judah. As noted above, the Egyptians were involved in the destruction of the Philistine cities mentioned in Zeph 2:4, 5-7, and threatened to overthrow Assyrian hegemony in the Syro-Israelite region. Egypt had once been subject to Assyria, and under Psamtek had overthrown Egyptian rule. At some time during the years 625–616 B.C.E., the Egyptians ultimately allied with Assyria against Babylon, but this was not evident during the early years of Josiah's reform.

The oracle against Assyria appears in Zeph 2:13-15 in the form of a speech by the prophet as the climax of the oracles against the nations. Whereas the previous oracles were directed against nations that controlled Israelite/Judean territory or populations or whose demise signaled YHWH's action in the world, Zeph 2:13-15 is directed against Judah's major oppressor. It employs a version of the "outstretched hand" formula (see Zeph 1:4) to convey judgment against the "north," the direction in which one would travel to Assyria from Israel or from which the Assyrians would approach. The oracle targets the Assyrian capital Nineveh (cf. Nahum) for destruction, and portrays the desolation of the city as a dry wilderness with various forms of wildlife, including flocks or herds, scavenger birds in the capitals, and owls or lizards in the windows and thresholds. The prophet's summary appraisal of Nineveh's condition in verse 15 includes a characterization of the once secure city, "This is the exultant city which sits securely, saying in her heart, 'I and no other,'" later appears in Isa 47:8 in reference to Babylon. This portrayal of Nineveh's security and self-confidence contrasts markedly with the devastation that it will experience as a result of YHWH's judgment, when people will pass by hissing and gesturing with their hands in contempt and dismissal. The downfall of Nineveh and Assyria demonstrates YHWH's power and precedes the restoration of Jerusalem, Judah, and Israel.

The Oracles concerning Jerusalem and Israel: 3:1-20

The oracles concerning Jerusalem and Israel in Zeph 3:1-20 convey the basic theological program that underlies the exhortation of the book of Zephaniah in that they outline the process by which YHWH will restore Jerusalem and Israel. Overall, this passage begins by describing Jerusalem's present desolate state as a result of the failures of its leaders (verses 1-4), continues by describing YHWH's punishment of Israel's oppressors and gathering of Israel's exiles (verses 5-13), and concludes by announcing to Jerusalem and Israel that the time of restoration is nearly at hand (verses 14-20). The passage begins with an introductory *hôy*, "woe!" oracle concerning Jerusalem that suggests continuity with the oracles against the nations in Zeph 2:5-15 that likewise began with *hôy*. In this manner, the passage draws its audience into a scenario of punishment against Jerusalem that might be expected by a population that had experienced the realities of Assyrian rule and the effects of an attempted coup d'etat against the Davidic monarchy during the course of the seventh century B.C.E. But a clear shift takes place in the midst of the passage that indicates YHWH's plans to overcome Israel's enemies and to restore the nation. By presenting the material and arguing in this fashion, the book provides a rationale for Jerusalem's suffering during the Assyrian period and builds the basis in the audience for the acceptance of the exhortation to seek YHWH and thereby to support Josiah's reform in the post-Assyrian age.

Nevertheless, these motifs do not constitute the literary structure of the chapter. The passage begins with a prophetic announcement of salvation for Jerusalem in Zeph 3:1-13. This announcement is defined by its introductory *hôy*, "woe!" and its formulation as the prophet's announcement about Jerusalem throughout. It contains a lengthy first person speech by YHWH in verses 6-13 concerning YHWH's plans to punish the nations, to gather them for praise, and to establish the remnant of Israel, but this speech is incorporated into the prophet's speech as indicated by the oracular formula, "utterance of YHWH," in verse 8aα and the formulation of verses 1-5 as a third person speech by the prophet that introduces YHWH's words. Zephaniah 3:14-20 is formulated very differently as the prophet's direct address to Jerusalem and Israel in which he summons them to rejoice because of their upcoming restoration by YHWH.

Zephaniah's Announcement of Salvation for Jerusalem: 3:1-13

As noted above, Zeph 3:1-13 presents the prophet's address about Jerusalem and YHWH's plans to restore it from its present downcast state. Although it contains a first person speech by YHWH in verses 6-13, the formulation of the introductory material in verses 1-5 and the oracular formula in verse 8aα demonstrates that the prophet conveys YHWH's speech in the context of his own.

The literary structure of the prophet's address includes two major components. The first is the "woe" oracle of Zeph 3:1-4. "Woe" oracles are typically employed by the prophets to announce a warning of an impending disaster or a judgment that is now being realized. In the present instance, the prophet's speech is directed against the city of Jerusalem and its leaders, although the city is never explicitly named. Following the initial "woe" statement in verse 1, charges of wrongdoing are leveled against the city and its leaders in verses 2-4. Although verse 5 is also formulated as a speech by the prophet, it introduces a new theme of YHWH's justice and restoration that provides an introduction to the quotation of YHWH's speech in verses 6-13.

The "woe" oracle in verses 1-4 begins with a typically formulated "woe" statement in verse 1 addressed to "the rebellious, defiled, oppressing city." This designation is deliberately ambiguous in that it leaves the audience in suspense concerning the identity of the city addressed and thereby captures its attention. The city is not named, and the introductory "woe" stands in continuity with the introductory "woe" of the preceding oracles against the nations. This would perhaps suggest that the oracle addresses a foreign city such as Nineveh, in that Nineveh and Assyria were the objects of the last foreign nation oracle in Zeph 2:13-15. The terminology employed to characterize the city continues to be ambiguous in that it suggests double entendre. The first term, *mōrᵓâ,* "rebellious," is derived grammatically from the verb root *mrh,* "to rebel," but the appearance of the letter ᵓalep is somewhat unusual. Its presence suggests that the word could be read as otherwise unattested forms of the verb *yrᵓ,* "to fear," i.e., *hiphil* "menacing" (cf. the noun form, *môrâᵓ,* "fear") or *hophal* "feared." The second term, *nigᵓālâ,* "defiled," is a *niphal* participle derived from the root *g*ʾl, "to defile, pollute," but the more common meaning ascribed to the root is "to redeem," i.e., "redeemed," in the present context. The final term, *hāʿîr hayyônâ*, "the oppressing city," employs a participle form of the verb *ynh*, "to oppress," but the term *yônâ* also means, "dove," and suggests an image of gentleness and vulnerability. Altogether, the referents for the city, "menacing/feared, defiled, oppressing," could refer to Nineveh, which would follow from the oracle against Assyria in Zeph 2:13-15; the referents, "rebellious, defiled, oppressing," could refer to a sinful Jerusalem depicted in verses 1-4; or the referents, "rebellious, redeemed, dove," could refer to the emergence of a redeemed Jerusalem depicted in verses 1-20. By employing such ambiguous terminology, the oracle keeps the audience open to several interpretations, all of which are employed in a scenario of Jerusalem's wrongdoing, oppression by Assyria, and redemption by YHWH.

The ambiguity begins to resolve itself in the description of the city's actions in verses 2-4. The first statement in verse 2a, "it did not listen (to a voice), it did not take direction," could apply either to Nineveh or to Jerusalem, although a variant of this statement is later employed in Jer 7:28 in reference to Judah. By verse 2b, it becomes clear that Jerusalem is the referent, "it did not trust in YHWH; unto its G–d it did not draw near." Verses 3-4 then employ metaphorical images to portray the officials of Jerusalem as irresponsible, incompetent, and dishonest. A similar portrayal using much the same imagery and vocabulary appears in Ezek 22:25-29. The officers are described as "roaring lions," an image which employs the lion as the symbol of Judah that roars over its prey or victims (cf. Amos 1:2), in this case, the people of Judah who are placed under their care. The judges are portrayed as "evening wolves who strip the meat from the bones of their victims by morning." The image appears again in Hab 1:8. The term for "evening" (*ʿereb*) is sometimes read as "Arab," or "steppe," but the intent of the depiction is clear insofar as the wolves, however they are qualified, devour what comes under their control. The prophets are frivolous, treacherous, and unreliable; the priests profane sanctity and do violence to or pervert Torah (instruction). In both cases, the prophets and priests do exactly the opposite of what their positions require. Altogether, the oracle assigns blame for Jerusalem's sorry state to the leaders who have failed to fulfill their responsibilities on behalf of the city and its people.

Following the woe oracle concerning Jerusalem, Zeph 3:5-13 then shifts to the prophet's announcement of YHWH's righteous acts on behalf of Jerusalem/Israel. Although the core of the passage is a first person speech by YHWH to Jerusalem/Israel in verses 6-13, the third person announcement language in verse 5 and the oracular formula in verse

8aα[4-5] demonstrate that it is a speech by the prophet in which he quotes YHWH. Because verse 5 appears in third person form and because it continues the third person feminine singular references to Jerusalem, many scholars maintain that it must be considered a part of the woe oracle in verses 1-4 rather than as the prophet's introduction to verses 6-13. But several considerations demonstrate that it provides the introductory framework for YHWH's speech. First, whereas verses 1-4 constitute a woe oracle that addresses the wrongdoing of Jerusalem and its officials, verse 5 shifts to a concern with YHWH's righteous acts and their positive outcome. Second, YHWH's speech in verses 6-13 likewise focuses on YHWH's righteousness on behalf of Jerusalem/Israel, including the defeat of nations hostile to Jerusalem/Israel, the gathering of nations and the dispersed of Israel, and the restoration of the remnant of Israel in security. Third, no syntactical conjunction joins verse 5 to verses 1-4; rather, verse 5 abruptly introduces YHWH as the subject, whereas Jerusalem is the subject of verses 1-4. The introduction of YHWH's name at this point identifies YHWH as the speaker of verses 6-13 and thereby establishes the introductory role of verse 5.

Zephaniah 3:5 focuses on YHWH's righteousness in the midst of Jerusalem and the motif of light, which symbolizes YHWH's justice (cf. Isa 2:2-4, 5; 51:4-5; Hos 6:5; Ps 37:6), as a means to demonstrate that YHWH will bring about a just and positive outcome from the problems outlined in verses 1-4. By focusing on YHWH's righteousness that "comes to light" every morning, the prophet employs the cosmic imagery of the sunrise to symbolize and convey the sense of order, continuity, and fidelity inherent in YHWH's justice. The prophet's report of YHWH's speech in verses 6-13 then illustrates this principle.

Zephaniah 3:6-13 constitutes Zephaniah's report of YHWH's salvation oracle to Jerusalem and Israel. Apart from the previously mentioned oracular formula in verse 8aα, the first person perspective indicates that YHWH is the speaker throughout. YHWH describes past actions against the nations in verses 6-7. Verse 6 alludes to previous statements in the book; it employs the verb *hikratî*, "I have cut off" (cf. Zeph 1:3, 4), as well as references to the destruction of corner towers (cf. Zeph 1:16) and streets that are emptied of inhabitants (cf. Zeph 2:5) to express the punishment of the nations. In verse 7, YHWH relates statements made to Jerusalem, "indeed, you will fear me, you will take instruction," that take up language from Zeph 3:2 to convey YHWH's intent to carry out all that YHWH has promised. The statement in verse 7aβ, "and her refuge, all that I have appointed for her, shall not be cut off," is a disputed reading. The Septuagint reads *mĕʿônāh*, "her refuge," as *ex ophthalmōn autēs*, "from her eyes," which only requires a slight change in the vowels from the MT to *mĕʿênêhā*. The verse would then read, "and all that I have appointed for her shall not be cut off from her eyes." Both readings convey Yнwн's actions on behalf of Jerusalem, but they employ somewhat different imagery to do so. The verse concludes with Yнwн's statement that, despite Yнwн's actions, the people of Jerusalem persisted in corrupt action.

Following the retrospective view of verses 6-7, Zeph 3:8-13 then shifts to Yнwн's future actions on behalf of Jerusalem and Israel. This section begins with the particle *lākēn*, "therefore," to indicate that Yнwн's future actions follow as a consequence from those outlined in verses 6-7. Yнwн begins with a command to the people, "wait for me," and continues by stating plans to arise as a witness, to gather nations and kingdoms in justice, to pour out wrath upon the nations, and to consume all the earth in zealousness. The first verb employed for "gathering" the nations, *le'ĕsōp*, "to gather," is the harvest terminology of Zeph 1:2 (cf. 1:3; 2:1), and thereby aids in conveying the imagery of sacrifice that appears especially in Zeph 1:2-18. The Deity states that the goal of these actions is to give "pure speech" to the nations so that they will call upon the name of Yнwн and serve Yнwн as one (verse 10). The Deity further specifies that "my suppliants, worshipers," and "the daughter of my dispersed ones," will present an offering to Yнwн from beyond the rivers of Cush/Ethiopia. The terminology employed here indicates that Yнwн's worshippers are Judeans or Israelites who have been exiled from the land as far away as Ethiopia. This statement should not be at all surprising when one considers that Egypt, under the rule of the Twenty-Fifth Ethiopian dynasty, was one of northern Israel's and Judah's key allies in their attempts to revolt against Assyria during the late eighth century B.C.E. (see 2 Kgs 17:1-6; Hos 7:11; 12:1; Isaiah 18-20; 30-31) and many refugees would have fled to Ethiopia to escape the Assyrians (see Hos 9:3, 6). The terminology for the presentation of an offering is technical terminology for the presentation of an offering *(minḥâ)* at the Temple; it conveys the restoration of the people of Israel and Judah at the Temple in Jerusalem.

Verses 11-13 follow upon this scenario with Yнwн's statements concerning the future character of Israel as a result of the Deity's actions. This segment begins with the formula, "in that day," to signify the future time in reference to the "Day of Yнwн" articulated in Zeph 1:7-8 and 2:1-3. Essentially, these statements presuppose that the people have brought disaster upon themselves by wrongdoing, and that Yнwн will remove the causes for such wrongdoing from among them. Yнwн states that the people need no longer feel shame for their rebellion, because Yнwн will remove pride and haughtiness from the people in the "holy mountain," i.e., Zion or the site of the Temple (verse 11). Yнwн further states the intention to cause a humble and poor remnant of the people to remain in Jerusalem to take refuge in the name of YHWH (verse 12), and that the "remnant of Israel" will no longer do evil, lie, or deceive, but they will graze and lie down like sheep with none to make them afraid (cf. Isa 11:6-9). These last points are crucial to understanding the message of the book. First, they point to the concept of the remnant of Israel in the late seventh century B.C.E. as part of the larger ideology of Josiah's reform, insofar as Josiah envisioned the restoration of a restored and reunited Israel in the aftermath of Assyrian domination. Second, the restoration of Israel and Judah involved the purging of the ruling class that had cooperated with Assyria in its occupation of the land and had a hand in the assassination of Josiah's father Amon. Again, Josiah was placed on the throne by "the people of the land," and the laws of Deuteronomy, on which the reform is believed to have been founded, give far greater rights to the poor than other Israelite law codes. Third, the exhortational character of the book must be considered, as it aims to convince its hearers or readers that they should be a part of the poor and humble remnant of Israel that will be reestablished in Zion.

ZEPHANIAH'S SUMMONS TO JERUSALEM AND ISRAEL TO REJOICE: 3:14-20

This segment of the book is the prophet's summons to Jerusalem and Israel to rejoice at YHWH's deliverance. The text is formulated as a speech by the prophet directed to Jerusalem and Israel, although he quotes YHWH in verses 18-20. Nevertheless, the speech formula, "says YHWH," at the end of verse 20 demonstrates that the prophet is the speaker. This passage serves the exhortational character of the book as a whole in that it points forward to the realization of the promises of deliverance and restoration for Jerusalem, Judah, and Israel articulated throughout the book. In calling upon Jerusalem and Israel to rejoice, it essentially asks the audience to accept that the projected restoration will indeed take place.

The passage begins in verses 14-15 with the summons formulated in imperative verbs drawn from the hymnic tradition that call upon "the daughter of Zion" to sing aloud (*rānnî*, see Lev 9:24; Isa 12:6; 24:14; 54:1; Jer 31:7; Ps 35:27), "Israel" to shout (*hārî'û*, cf. 1 Sam 4:5; Isa 44:23; Pss 47:2 [NRSV: 47:1]; 66:1; 81:2 [NRSV: 81:1]; 95:1, 2; 98:4, 6; 100:1; Ezra 3:11, 13), and "the daughter of Jerusalem" to rejoice (*śimḥî*, 1 Sam 2:1; Pss 21:2 [NRSV: 21:1]; 32:11; 1 Chr 16:10) and to exult (*'ālzî*, cf. Hab 3:18; Pss 68:5 [NRSV: 68:4]; 149:5). Verse 15 provides the reason for praise in that YHWH has removed the judgments against the people, turned aside enemies, and is established as king in the midst of Jerusalem/Israel so that they need no longer fear.

Verses 16-20 then assure the audience by projecting the future re-joicing and restoration of the people. Verses 16-17 comprise an an-nouncement of assurance to Jerusalem introduced by the phrase, "in that day, it shall be said to Jerusalem," which directs the audience's attention to the future. A typical reassurance formula, "do not fear, O Zion, do not let your hands grow weak" (cf. Gen 15:1; 21:17; 35:17; Exod 20:20; Isa 7:4; 35:4; 40:9; 41:10; Jer 30:10; Joel 2:21; Hag 2:5; Ruth 3:11), is addressed to Zion because YHWH will be in Zion's midst to rejoice over the city. The statement, "he will be silent in his love," is frequently re-garded as a corrupt text. Although any number of emendations have been offered, the most likely reading is *yĕʾāraś*, "he will betroth (you)." The root *ʾrś*, "to betroth," sounds somewhat like *ḥrš*, "to be silent." Marriage is sometimes employed to express the relationship between YHWH and Israel or Jerusalem in the prophetic traditions (see Isaiah 54; Jeremiah 2; Hosea 1-3), and Jerusalem is addressed in this passage as the "daughter of Zion/Jerusalem" with feminine singular forms. It is possible that the reference here was modified in order to protect the sanctity of YHWH from an anthropomorphic characterization. The root *ḥrš* also means "to plow," and is sometimes employed figuratively for sexual relations (see Judg 14:18).

Finally, verses 18-20 cite YHWH's final statements concerning the re-moval of Jerusalem's shame, its deliverance, and the gathering of its exiles for recognition and praise of YHWH in all the earth. The initial phrase *nûgê mimmôʿēd* has caused tremendous difficulties to transla-tors; it likely refers to the appointed afflictions or punishments that YHWH is now "gathering" (*ʾāsaptî*, "I have gathered") as they were a "burden" and a "shame" upon the people (verse 18). YHWH further states the intention to "do" or "deal with" Jerusalem's oppressors, to deliver the "lame," and to gather the "outcast" or the exiles. The purpose of these actions is so that the people will constitute a "praise" and a "name" in all the earth, i.e., so that they will provide a basis by which YHWH will be praised and recognized throughout the entire world (verse 19). In the final verse, YHWH repeats the intention to "bring" and "gather" the people in the future, and to appoint them for "name" and "praise" among all the peoples of the earth. Insofar as this last statement repeats and clarifies verse 19, many have seen it as an explanatory gloss. It ex-plicitly states YHWH's intention to "return your captivity/restore your fortunes" (cf. Zeph 2:7) as the projected outcome of YHWH's actions. It thereby makes it very clear that the restoration of exiled Israelites and Judeans is a primary goal of the program here articulated and a pri-mary basis for Zephaniah's exhortation.

FOR FURTHER READING

COMMENTARIES

Bennett, Robert A. "The Book of Zephaniah: Introduction, Commentary, and Reflections," *The New Interpreter's Bible. Volume VII: Introduction to Apocalyptic Literature, Daniel, The Twelve Prophets*, ed. Leander E. Keck et al. Nashville: Abingdon, 1996.

Berlin, Adele. *Zephaniah*. Anchor Bible 25A. New York: Doubleday, 1994.

Renaud, B. *Michée–Sophonie–Nahum*. Sources Bibliques. Paris: J. Gabalda, 1987.

Roberts, J. J. M. *Nahum, Habakkuk, and Zephaniah: A Commentary*. Old Testament Library. Louisville: Westminster/John Knox, 1991.

Rudolph, Wilhelm. *Micha–Nahum–Habakuk–Zephanja*. Kommentar zum Alten Testament XIII/3. Gütersloh: Gerd Mohn, 1975.

Seybold, Klaus. *Nahum, Habakuk, Zephanja*. Zürcher Bibelkommentare AT 24, 2. Zürich: Theologischer Verlag, 1991.

Széles, Mária Eszenyei. *Wrath and Mercy: A Commentary on the Books of Habakkuk and Zephaniah*. International Theological Commentary. Grand Rapids: William Eerdmans; Edinburgh: Handsel, 1987.

Vuilleumier, René and Carl-A. Keller. *Michée, Nahoum, Habacuc, Sophonie*. Commentaire de l'ancien Testament XIb. Neuchâtel: Delachaux et Niestlé, 1971.

STUDIES

Ball, Ivan J., Jr. *Zephaniah: A Rhetorical Study*. Berkeley: BIBAL, 1988.

Ben Zvi, Ehud. *A Historical-Critical Study of the Book of Zephaniah*. Beiheft zur Zeitschrift für die alttestamentliche Wissenschaft 198. New York: Walter de Gruyter, 1991.

Edler, Rainer. *Das Kerygma des Propheten Zefanja.* Freiberger Theologische Studien 126. Freiburg, Basel, Vienna: Herder, 1984.

Irsigler, Hubert. *G-ttesgericht und JHWHtag. Die Komposition Zef 1,1-2,3, untersucht auf der Grundlage der Literaturkritik des Zefanjabuches.* Arbeiten zu Text und Sprache im Alten Testament 3. St. Ottilien: EOS, 1977.

Kapelrud, Arvid S. *The Message of the Prophet Zephaniah: Morphology and Ideas.* Oslo: Universitetsforlaget, 1975.

Krinetzki, Günter. *Zefanjastudien. Motiv-und Traditionskritik + Kompositions-und Redaktionskritik.* Regensburger Studien zur Theologie 7. Frankfurt am Main: Peter Lang, 1977.

Mason, Rex. *Zephaniah, Habakkuk, Joel.* Old Testament Guides. Sheffield: JSOT Press, 1994.

Ryou, Daniel Hojoon. *Zephaniah's Oracles against the Nations: A Synchronic and Diachronic Study of Zephaniah 2:1–3:8.* Biblical Interpretation Series 13. New York: E. J. Brill, 1995.

Sabottka, Liudger. *Zephanja. Versuch einer Neuäübersetzung mit philologischem Kommentar.* Biblica et Orientalia 25. Rome: Biblical Institute Press, 1972.

Seybold, Klaus. *Satirische Prophetie. Studien zum Buch Zefanja.* Stuttgarter Bibelstudien 120. Stuttgart: Katholisches Bibelwerk, 1985.

Sweeney, Marvin A. "A Form-Critical Reassessment of the Book of Zephaniah," *The Catholic Biblical Quarterly* 53 (1991) 388–408.

Weigl, Michael. *Zefanja und das "Israel der Armen."* Österreichische Biblische Studien 13. Klosterneuburg: Österreichisches Katholisches Bibelwerk, 1994.

HAGGAI

HAGGAI

Overview

The book of Haggai is the tenth book of both the Masoretic and the Septuagint versions of the Book of the Twelve. It is set in the second year of King Darius of Persia, 520 B.C.E. (Hag 1:1; 1:15b–2:1; 2:10), which is the year in which construction of the second Temple in Jerusalem began under Zerubbabel ben Shealtiel, governor of Judah, and Joshua ben Jehozadak, the high priest (cf. Ezra 3). The book presents the oracles of the prophet Haggai, who argued that the people must begin construction of the Temple in order to carry out the will of YHWH and to realize the manifestation of YHWH's sovereignty in the world. Haggai follows upon the book of Zephaniah in both MT and LXX which anticipates Jerusalem's punishment and restoration, so that Haggai points to the time when the restoration would begin. It precedes the book of Zechariah, which also points to the cosmic significance of the building of the second Temple but looks well beyond the building of the Temple itself to the future and describes in detail the process by which YHWH will defeat the forces of evil in the world and institute divine sovereignty from Jerusalem.

Relatively little is known of the prophet Haggai. The narrative introduction to the book simply identifies him as "Haggai the prophet (*haggay hannābîʾ*)," and places him in the second year of Darius, 520 B.C.E. The name Haggai means "my festival." Similar forms of the name appear as Haggith, the wife of David and mother of Adonijah (2 Sam 3:4; 1 Kgs 1:11; 2:13; 1 Chr 3:2); Haggiah, a Levite descended from Merari (1 Chr 6:30); and Haggai, one of the sons of Gad and grandsons of Jacob (Gen 46:16; Num 26:15). The range of dates provided in the book of Haggai, including the first day of the sixth month (1 Ellul; Hag 1:1), the twenty-fourth day of the sixth month (24 Ellul; Hag 1:15b); the twenty-first day of the seventh month (21 Tishri; Hag 1:15b–2:1); and the twenty-fourth day of the ninth month (24 Kislev; Hag 2:10, 18, 20) indicate a very narrow time frame from the late summer to the onset of winter in the year 520 B.C.E.

Haggai is mentioned together with Zechariah in the accounts of the building of the second Temple in the time of Zerubbabel in Ezra 1–6 (see Ezra 5:1; 6:14). The tradition reports that both prophets were actively prophesying in support of the efforts by Zerubbabel ben Shealtiel and Jeshua ben Jozadak (an Aramaic variation of the name Joshua ben Jehozadak) to reconstruct the Temple in Jerusalem. According to the account of the book of Ezra, Tattenai, the governor of the Persian province "Beyond the River," which would likely have included Samaria and perhaps Judah as well, an official named Shethar-bozenai and other associates sent a letter to King Darius of Persia in an apparent attempt to block construction of the Temple or at least to determine whether or not it was authorized by the Persian monarch Cyrus the Great as claimed. Upon receiving confirmation from Darius that the rebuilding of the Temple had indeed been authorized by Cyrus, Tattenai, Shethar-bozenai, and their associates gave assistance so that the Temple was completed in the sixth year of Darius.

The book of Haggai must be read in relation to events from the early reign of Darius (522–486 B.C.E.).[1] The first two years of his reign saw a series of insurrections within the Persian empire that challenged his rule and that of the Achaemenid dynasty. The first Achaemenid monarch was Cyrus the Great (559–530 B.C.E.), who had united the Median and Persian empires, and subsequently conquered the Babylonian empire. This victory came with the help of a Babylonian general Gobryas, who apparently also made it possible for Cyrus to enter Babylon peacefully and be declared by the priests of Marduk to be the legitimate king of Babylon in 539 B.C.E. Upon ascending to the Babylonian throne, Cyrus decreed that various peoples exiled by the Babylonians, including the exiled Judeans, could return to their homelands and rebuild their temples and cities (see 2 Chr 36:22-23; Ezra 1:1-4).[2] A first attempt to return to Jerusalem under the leadership of Sheshbazzar apparently failed.[3] Little was done during the reign of Cyrus' son

---

[1] For an overview of the historical setting of Haggai, see Mason, *Haggai, Zechariah, Malachi* 7–16.

[2] For a translation of the Cyrus cylinder which records Cyrus' decree for such repatriation, see Pritchard, *ANET* 315. See also Amélie Kuhrt, "The Cyrus Cylinder and Achaemenid Imperial Policy," *JSOT* 25 (1983) 83–97, who points out that this version of the decree applies to cities located within the former Babylonian home country.

[3] See Ezra 1; 5. For discussion, see Blenkinsopp, *Ezra-Nehemiah* ad loc.

Cambyses. Cambyses conquered Egypt in 525 B.C.E., but he died unexpectedly near Mt. Carmel in Israel in 522 B.C.E. He was succeeded by Darius, a military commander and member of the Achaemenid family. Although Darius was not a direct descendant of the royal line, he was able to gain the support of Cambyses' army, returned to Media, and executed Gaumata, who had instigated a revolt in the aftermath of Cambyses' death. Revolt then broke out throughout the empire, particularly in Babylonia, as various elements of the empire sought to free themselves from Achaemenid rule. By 520 B.C.E., Darius had been able to quell most of the revolts, except in Egypt, and he took measures to secure his hold on the empire. Some maintain that Darius' authorization to build the Temple in Jerusalem was calculated to gain the support of Judah during the time when he was struggling to secure his throne, but the decision appears to be entirely in keeping with prior Persian policy. In the aftermath of the revolts, however, one of Darius' principle tactics was to revise the earlier practice, instituted by Cyrus, of allowing native governors to administer the various satrapies that comprised the Persian empire. Under Darius, the native governors were replaced with ethnic Persian governors whose loyalty was directed exclusively to the king.

Haggai's prophecy appears to presuppose this historical background. As noted above, the narrative date formulas that appear within the book place the prophet's oracles in the second year of Darius, which would correspond to the period when the Persian monarch was defeating the last of the revolts against his rule. Haggai's statements that YHWH is "shaking" the heavens, the earth, and all the nations, and that the nations will bring silver and gold to the new Temple to acknowledge YHWH's sovereignty (Hag 2:6b-9) apparently refer to the revolts against Darius in 522–520 B.C.E. Likewise, Haggai's statements that YHWH will overthrow the throne of the kingdoms, destroy the strength of the nations, overturn chariots, horses, and riders, and set the swords of men against each other must also refer to the revolts against Darius. From Haggai's perspective, the building of the new Temple inaugurated the time when YHWH would act to overthrow Persia and to establish YHWH's own sovereignty throughout the world. Zerubbabel, the grandson of Jehoiachin (1 Chr 3:17-19), the last Davidic monarch who was taken into exile by Nebuchadnezzar (2 Kgs 24:8-17; cf. 25:27-30), would be designated as YHWH's "signet ring." Insofar as the signet was a symbol of royal authority in the ancient world, Zerubbabel would effectively be installed as the new Davidic king who would rule as YHWH's designated monarch in Jerusalem. In short, the reconstruction of the Temple pointed to the restoration of the Davidic monarch and the kingdom of Judah as the symbol for YHWH's world-wide sovereignty. The absence of Zerubbabel in the narrative concerning the completion of the Temple in the sixth year of Darius (Ezra 6:13-22) suggests to many scholars that Zerubbabel was removed from office by Darius or otherwise disappeared.[4] Although the matter is far from settled—some maintain that Zerubbabel's absence is hardly noteworthy in the Ezra narrative—Haggai's oracles suggest the very real possibility that Zerubbabel was ultimately considered to be a threat against Darius' rule over Judah.

The overall form of the book of Haggai is a narrative that reports or presents the oracles delivered by YHWH to the prophet in a succession of dates from the first day of the sixth month (1 Ellul), through the twenty-first day of the seventh month (21 Tishri), and to the twenty-fourth day of the ninth month (24 Kislev). Three major narrative date formulas mark the three major structural blocks of the book. Thus, Hag 1:1-15a presents the oracle delivered by YHWH to Haggai on 1 Ellul, 520 B.C.E.; Hag 1:15b–2:9 presents the oracle delivered by YHWH to Haggai on 21 Tishri, 520 B.C.E.; and Hag 2:10-23 presents the two oracles (see also Hag 2:20) delivered by YHWH to Haggai on 24 Kislev, 520 B.C.E. Although the overall form of the book is a narrative, the oracles of YHWH to Haggai appear in the form of disputational speeches and instructions to the prophet. The overall intent of the oracles appears to be the motivation of Zerubbabel, Joshua, and the people to undertake construction of the Temple. The first narrative in Hag 1:1-15a relates an oracle in verses 2-11 that is directed through Haggai to Zerubbabel ben Shealtiel and Joshua ben Jehozadak. It calls upon them to commence construction on the Temple. The oracle contends that the heavens have withheld rain and that the crops have been poor because the Temple has not yet been built. Verses 12-15a report their compliance with YHWH's instructions by the twenty-fourth day of Ellul. The second narrative in Haggai 1:15b–2:9 presents YHWH's instructions to Haggai to speak to Zerubbabel, Joshua, and the people. According to verses 2-9, Haggai is to argue against the contention made by some of the people that the new Temple will not be as glorious as that of Solomon (cf. Ezra 3:10-13). He contends that once the Temple is built, YHWH will shake the heavens and the earth so that the nations will come to Jerusalem with silver and gold to acknowledge YHWH's sovereignty. Not only will

---

[4] For discussion of the problem posed by Zerubbabel, see Coggins, *Haggai, Zechariah, Malachi* 11–4. The problems is related to identification of Joshua ben Jehozadak as the royal figure by whose throne a priest will stand in Zech 6:9-15. Many presuppose that Zerubbabel was originally the subject of this prophecy, but that Joshua's name was substituted after Zerubbabel was removed from office or killed. See the discussion of this passage in the commentary on Zechariah below.

the glory of the new Temple surpass that of the old, but its reconstruction will inaugurate a new era of peace. The third major narrative in Hag 2:10-23 reports two oracles from YHWH to Haggai on the same day. Verses 10-19 give YHWH's instructions to Haggai to inquire of the priests concerning the status of consecrated meat that is touched by unclean food or persons. When the priests declare such meat to be unclean, Haggai makes a comparison to the impure state of the people's sacrifices, i.e., as long as the Temple does not stand and serve as an agent for sanctifying the people, their offerings to YHWH must be considered unclean. At this point, Haggai is to reiterate the argument that the people's failure to build the Temple is the cause of the poor crop harvests that they have suffered. Once the Temple is rebuilt, YHWH will bless the land which will in turn produce bounteous crops. Verses 20-23 then relate YHWH's instructions to Haggai to speak to Zerubbabel and to inform him that he has been designated as YHWH's "signet ring." As noted above, the signet ring is the symbol of royal authority in the ancient world. Zerubbabel's designation as YHWH's signet therefore indicates that he is to be established as YHWH's regent, i.e., Zerubbabel will reign as the new Davidic monarch in Jerusalem once the Temple is rebuilt.

Narrative concerning People's Compliance with YHWH's Instructions through Haggai to Build the Temple (1 Ellul): Haggai 1:1-15a

The first major component of the book of Haggai appears in Hag 1:1-15a, which relates the people's compliance with YHWH's instructions through the prophet Haggai to build the Temple in Jerusalem. Although most prophetic books begin with a superscription which identifies the following material as the words, oracles, or activities of the prophet (cf. Isa 1:1; Jer 1:1-3; Hos 1:1; Joel 1:1; Amos 1:1; Obad 1; Mic 1:1; Nah 1:1; Hab 1:1; Zeph 1:1; Mal 1:1), the book of Haggai is clearly formulated as a narrative which presents Haggai's oracles concerning the building of the Temple and the role of Zerubbabel ben Shealtiel as the "signet ring" of YHWH.[5] In this regard, it is analogous to Ezekiel, Jonah, and Zechariah, which are also formulated as narratives and thereby lack formal superscriptions even though each begins with a reference to the initial date of the prophet's activities (Ezek 1:1; Zech 1:1) or the initial transmission of the word of YHWH (Jon 1:1). As is the

[5] See the discussion in Petersen, *Haggai and Zechariah 1–8* 32–6.

case in Ezek 1:1 and Zech 1:1 (cf. Jon 1:1), the reference to the date in
Hag 1:1 does not function in relation to the entire book, but only in relation to the initial oracles and activities of the prophet. The narrative is
clearly demarcated at the beginning by the narrative date formula in
Hag 1:1, which dates the transmission of YHWH's oracle through Haggai to the first day of the sixth month of the second year of the reign of
King Darius of Persia, i.e., the first day of Ellul in the year 520 B.C.E. The
narrative closes with a reference to the date of the people's compliance
with this instruction on the twenty-fourth day of the sixth month, i.e.,
the twenty-fourth day of Ellul. The initial date formula in Hag 1:1 and
the concluding date formula in Hag 1:15a aid in binding the unit
together as a coherent whole. The narrative date formula in Hag 1:15b–
2:1 is parallel to that of Hag 1:1 and marks the beginning of the next
major unit of Haggai.

The narrative structure of Hag 1:1-15a comprises two basic parts:
verses 1-11 relate the transmission of YHWH's instructions to Zerubbabel
ben Shealtiel, the governor of Judah, and Joshua ben Jehozadak, the high
priest, by means of the prophet Haggai, and verses 12-15a relate the compliance of the people with these instructions. By reporting the people's
compliance with YHWH's instructions through Haggai to build the
Temple in Jerusalem, Hag 1:1-15a lays the foundation on which the following oracles concerning YHWH's granting of glory to the Temple and
land (Hag 1:15b–2:9) and YHWH's promises to bless the people and appoint Zerubbabel as the divine "signet ring" (Hag 2:10-23) may proceed.
Haggai 1:1-15a thereby functions as the initial narrative in a sequence
that is designed to point to the future glory of the Temple and blessing of
the people in which the Davidic monarchy will ultimately be restored.

The narrative report concerning the transmission of YHWH's instructions to Zerubbabel and Joshua through Haggai in Hag 1:1-11 in
turn comprises two basic sub-units: verses 1-2 relate the basic instruction that it is time to build the Temple, and verses 3-11 relate a more detailed disputational speech that is designed to convince the people that
the time to build the Temple has come. Each sub-unit is marked by the
appearance of an example of the YHWH word transmission formula in
verses 1b and 3 respectively. The YHWH word transmission formula[6]
typically includes a form of the verb *hyh*, "to be," a reference to the
děbar-yhwh or "word of YHWH," an appearance of the preposition *ʾel*,
"to, unto," which indicates to whom the divine word is directed, and
an appearance of the infinitive construction *lēʾmōr*, "saying," which introduces the following quotation of YHWH's word. In both cases, the
formula introduces the instructional material, indicates that it is trans-

---

[6] See Sweeney, *Isaiah 1–39* 546–7.

mitted "by (literally, 'by the hand of') Haggai the prophet," and identifies it as a word of YHWH through the prophet Haggai.

Haggai 1:1-2 sets the basic theme of the initial report of the transmission of YHWH's instructions by identifying the date of the transmission, the generic character of the instruction as "word of YHWH," the major parties involved, and the content of the instruction. The reference to the second year of "Darius the King" indicates that the year is 520 B.C.E. since Darius ruled the Persian empire during the years 522–486 B.C.E.[7] Although he was not a descendant of either Cyrus (559–530 B.C.E.) or his son Cambyses (530–522 B.C.E.), he was a distant relative of his predecessors and a military commander who took control of the throne upon the death of Cambyses who left no heir. Darius' first year was marked by widespread revolt, which he put down by mid-521 B.C.E. His strategy for putting down the revolt included rewarding those who remained loyal to the Achaemenid dynasty, such as the province of Judah which was able to rebuild the Temple in Jerusalem with Darius' support (cf. Ezra 6). The reference to "the sixth month, on the first day of the month" indicates the first day of Ellul (ca. late-August through early-September), which would precede the seventh month (Tishri) in which the New Year (Rosh ha-Shanah), the Day of Atonement (Yom Kippur), and the festival of Booths or Tabernacles (Sukkoth) are celebrated. There is no particular significance to the month of Ellul itself, although the first day would mark the appearance of the new moon (cf. Num 28:11-15). Insofar as Sukkoth is the time when the Temple altar is dedicated (cf. Ezra 3:1-7; 2 Chr 7:8-10; cf. 1 Kings 8) and perhaps when priests are ordained (cf. Exodus 29; Leviticus 8), the transmission of YHWH's instructions at the beginning of the sixth month might be intended to see to the beginning of work on the Temple prior to festival season of the seventh month and the ceremonies that would attend to the preparation of the altar for the year and the ordination of priests (see Exodus 29; Leviticus 8). The identification of Haggai as the prophet through whom the instruction is transmitted corresponds to the notices in Ezra 5:1 and 6:14 that Haggai and Zechariah ben Iddo were prophesying support of the reconstruction of the Temple during the early reign of Darius. Both Zerubbabel ben Shealtiel and Joshua ben Jehozadak are known from the book of Ezra as well. Zerubbabel is apparently the grandson of King Jehoiachin, the last monarch of the Davidic line who was deported to Babylon in 597 B.C.E. and replaced on the throne by his uncle, Zedekiah (cf. 2 Kgs 24:8-17). According to 2 Kgs 24:27-30, Jehoiachin was released from prison by King Evil-merodach of Babylon, but he remained in Babylon and never

---

[7] For discussion of Darius, see T. Cuyler Young, Jr., "Darius," *ABD* II:37-8.

returned to Judah. 1 Chronicles 3:17-19 identifies Shealtiel as the son of
Jehoiachin, although it identifies Zerubbabel as the son of Pedaiah, another of Jehoiachin's sons. His name is apparently a variant of the
Babylonian name, *zēr-bābili*, "seed of Babylon,"[8] which would indicate
some assimilation on the part of the exiled Jewish community into the
Babylonian culture. Such assimilation would hardly be unusual for the
third generation as indicated by the evidence of the Murashu archives
in Babylonia and the experience of many other immigrant groups in
other cultures.[9] According to Ezra 2:2 and Neh 7:7; 12:1, Zerubbabel
was among those who led exiled Jews back from Babylonia to Judah,
and Ezra 3:2, 8; 5:2 identifies him together with Jeshua ben Jozadak as
the major figure involved in the reconstruction of the Temple. There is
some question concerning his title as "governor" *(peḥâ)*, as the sources
in Ezra and Nehemiah are unclear as to whether or not Judah was a
separate province from Samaria,[10] although it seems likely that Darius
would have granted Judah such status in return for its support during
the initial years of his reign when he faced revolt in the empire. Joshua
ben Jehozadak, known as Jeshua ben Jozadak in Ezra 2:2; 3:2, 8, 9; 5:2;
Neh 7:7; 12:1, is identified as the high priest. According to 1 Chr 6:14-
15, Jehozadak was the son of the high priest Seraiah who was killed by
Nebuchadnezzar at Riblah following the destruction of Jerusalem (2
Kgs 25:18-21; Jer 52:24-27). Jehozadak was then taken into exile. Ezra
7:1 identifies Ezra as the son of the high priest Seraiah, which would
make Joshua ben Jehozadak a nephew of Ezra, but the problems with
the chronology of Ezra and Nehemiah and the information presented
in Ezra 7:1 raise questions about this identification.[11] Zechariah 3:1-10
portrays the cleansing of Joshua ben Jehozadak at the time of his ordination, and Zech 6:10-15 identifies him as the royal figure who will
build the Temple and sit on the royal throne. Many argue that Zerubbabel was originally intended as the figure portrayed in Zech 6:10-15,
however.[12]

[8] See Bryan E. Beyer, "Zerubbabel," *ABD* VI:1084-6.

[9] The Murashu archives are a group of Babylonian legal documents that record
the business transaction of the Murashu family during the latter part of the fifth
century B.C.E. Among their many clients were Jews living in Babylonia, many of
whom gave their children Babylonian names. For discussion, see Matthew W.
Stolper, "Murashû, Archive of," *ABD* IV 927–8.

[10] See Petersen, *Haggai and Zechariah 1–8* 45–56; Meyers and Meyers, *Haggai and
Zechariah 1–8* 13–6.

[11] See esp. Joseph Blenkinsopp, *Ezra-Nehemiah: A Commentary*, OTL (Philadelphia:
Westminster, 1988) 135–6.

[12] See my commentary below on Zechariah 6 and R. J. Coggins, *Haggai, Zechariah,
Malachi*, OT Guides (Sheffield: JSOT Press, 1987) 46–8.

The presentation of the oracle in verse 2 begins with an example of the messenger formula, "thus says Yhwh Sebaoth (*kōh ʾāmar yhwh ṣĕbāʾôt lēʾmōr*)," which identifies the following statement as an oracle from Yhwh. The oracle itself, "these people say the time has not yet come to rebuild Yhwh's house," constitutes the initial element of a disputation speech in which a thesis is put forward so that it may be disputed or challenged.[13] Disputation speeches generally include three elements: a statement of the thesis to be disputed, a statement of the counter-thesis, and the argumentation itself. In this case, the prophet will challenge the assertion of his opponents that the construction of the Temple must be delayed. The following oracular material in verses 3-11 will argue against this notion and make the case that now is precisely the time to begin construction.

The presentation of the detailed disputation in verses 3-11 is designed to convince the people that the time to build the Temple has come. It begins with an example of the Yhwh word transmission formula that introduces the following material and identifies it as "the word of Yhwh (that) came by the prophet Haggai." Once again, the oracle employs the basic form of the disputation speech, but the text is organized in a two-part structure that emphasizes Yhwh's commands to begin work. Verses 4-6 begin the disputation by pointing to the relatively dismal produce of food, drink, and clothing in the land as a basis for challenging the notion, initially articulated in verse 2, that nothing should be done about building the Temple. The sub-unit begins with a rhetorical question that asserts that the people can no longer sit around in their own homes while the Temple lies in ruins. The question plays to a sense of responsibility that would have been felt by the people to rebuild the Temple in two major respects. First, it suggests that the people are doing relatively little in that they have the time to sit at home. Although the NRSV translates, "Is it a time for you yourselves to sit . . . ?" but the Hebrew phrase *hăʿēt lākem ʾattem lāšebet* suggests that the people have the time, "Do you indeed have time to sit . . . ?" Second, the expression "in your panelled houses" (*bĕbātêkem sĕpûnîm*) is somewhat enigmatic in that the term *sĕpûnîm* can mean "panelled" or "roofed" (literally, "overlaid"), but it adequately conveys the contrast between the people who dwell in secure houses and the Temple that lies in ruins. Basically, the question conveys the sentiment that it is time to quit sitting around and that the Temple must be built.

Verses 5-6 begin in verse 5a with an emphatic "and now" (*wĕʿattâ*), which conveys the urgency of the situation, and an example of the messenger formula, which emphasizes once again that the following

---

[13] For discussion of the disputation form, see Sweeney, *Isaiah 1–39* 519.

message comes straight from YHWH. The oracle itself in verses 5b-6 is designed to prompt the audience to consider the reason why the produce of the land has been so poor. It begins with the idiomatic statement *śîmû lĕbabkem ʿal darkêkem,* literally, "set your hearts upon your ways," translated in the NRSV as "consider how you have fared." Basically, the statement is designed to prompt the audience to stop and consider the circumstances. This provides the opportunity to introduce the main theme of this particular segment of the oracle, i.e., the people have not realized sufficient produce from the land to supply their needs. Verse 6 presents a series of contrasts beginning with the general statement, "you have sown much and harvested little." It then moves to the specific categories of the needs for life, i.e., food, drink, and clothing. In each case, the verse begins by stating the need, and then by pointing to the inadequate satisfaction of that need, i.e., "you eat, but you never have enough (literally, 'eating, but no satiety'); you drink, but you never have your fill (literally, 'drinking, but there is no drunkenness'); you clothe yourselves, but no one is warm (literally, 'clothed, but there is no warmth')." The verse then employs the very familiar metaphor of a bag or purse with a hole in it to describe the loss of income, i.e., "you that earn wages earn wages to put them into a bag with holes (literally, 'he who is paid is paid unto a pierced bag')." The metaphor is just as apt today as it was in Haggai's time! Altogether, the oracle describes the grave circumstances of the people and bolsters the contention that something must be done to rectify things.

Having made the point that the people can no longer sit around doing nothing, the passage turns in verses 7-8 to a discussion of what must be done. Verses 7-8 are demarcated by the introductory messenger formula in verse 7a, which parallels that of verse 5a, and the closing YHWH speech formula, "says YHWH" *(ʾāmar yhwh)* at the end of verse 8. Once again, the combination of formulas emphasizes that this instruction comes directly from YHWH. Again the formulaic idiom, "consider how you have fared" (cf. verse 5b), calls upon the audience to consider its situation. This time, however, instead of pointing to the problems faced by the people, the passage points to constructive action. Verse 8a cryptically relates in imperative form what the people must do, "go up to the mountain, and bring wood and build the house." Although the NRSV translates, "go up to the hills," the Hebrew word *hāhār* is singular and refers to "the hill" or "the mountain" on which the Temple is located. Furthermore, the use of the term "the house" *(habbayit)* for the Temple employs a standard term for the Temple, but it is also the term used in verse 4 to describe the people's houses, thereby aiding in establishing the contrast between the people's homes and the current state of the Temple. Verse 8bβ then relates the results if the people build the

Temple, i.e., Yʜwʜ will be pleased and honored. The first person for-mulation of this statement again emphasizes Yʜwʜ as the source of this command. Furthermore, the statement, "I will be honored," employs the verb root *kbd* which stands at the base of the noun *kābōd*, "glory, honor," which describes the divine presence in the Temple (cf. Exod 40:34; 1 Kgs 8:11). Verse 8 thereby expresses the counterthesis of the dis-putation, i.e., it is time to build the Temple and to restore the glory of Yʜwʜ.

Verses 9-11 then return to the initial theme of the disputation, i.e., that the people are realizing very little produce from the land, as a means to bolster the argument that it is time to act. In this case, the pas-sage argues that the continued ruined state of the Temple is the reason why Yʜwʜ has caused the land to yield so little. Verse 9 points to the circumstances of the present, but it adds the proviso that Yʜwʜ is ac-tively involved in the people's deprivation. Verse 9a reiterates the in-ability of the people to provide themselves with food by stating that they looked for much, but the little that they brought to the Temple was blown away by Yʜwʜ. This calls to mind the fact that Temples are built on the sites of threshing floors in which the grain brought by the people as offerings is threshed and prepared for consumption (cf. 2 Sam 24:18-25; 1 Chr 21:18–22:1). The standard means to thresh grain in the ancient world is to crush it, thereby separating the wheat from the chaff, and the wind then carries away the chaff and leaves the heavier grain. Verse 9b then presents a rhetorical question together with a statement of the oracular formula, "says Yʜwʜ Sebaoth." The question is simply, "Why?" i.e., why does this happen? Why do the people not have enough to sup-port themselves? The answer reiterates the initial premise of verse 4 and points to the cause, "Because my house lies in ruins, while all of you hurry off to your own houses."

Verses 10-11 then pins the blame for the poor harvest squarely on the people and relates the consequences of their failure to build the Temple. Verse 10a employs an emphatic *ʿal-kēn ʿălêkem*, "therefore be-cause of you . . .," to make the point. The balance of the verse plays upon the verb *klʾ*, "to withhold," i.e., "the heavens have withheld the dew, and the earth has withheld its produce," implicitly charging that the people have withheld their labor in declining to build the Temple. In verse 11, Yʜwʜ employs first person language to indicate that Yʜwʜ is in full control of the cosmos and deliberately withholds the produce of the earth on account of the ruined state of the Temple, "I have called for a drought on the land and the hills, etc." The use of the term "drought," *ḥōreb*, presents a pun on the term "ruins" (literally, 'ru-ined'), *ḥārēb*, used in verse 9 (see also verse 4) to describe the current state of the Temple. The drought will affect the "grain," "new wine," and "oil," generally listed as the basic or staple agricultural products of the land (cf. Deut 18:4) as well as everything else that grows from the earth. The passage concludes by stating that the drought will affect humans and animals as well as all of their work. Essentially, these statements emphasize YHWH's role as master of all creation and as a judge who withholds the bounty of nature as a punishment for inappropriate human action.

Verses 12-15a then relate the compliance by Zerubbabel, Joshua, and the people with the divine instructions that are conveyed in verses 1-11. This compliance report is particularly important to understanding the structure and message of the book as a whole. It cannot be construed as an independent section within the book as some interpreters have attempted to argue.[14] The *waw-consecutive* narrative form and the contents indicate that it follows directly from the report of the conveyance of YHWH's instructions through Haggai in verses 1-11. Furthermore, the reported compliance demonstrates that the primary purpose of the book is not to report Haggai's oracles concerning the actual building of the Temple; rather, the building of the Temple constitutes the presupposition on which the following oracle reports in Hag 1:15b–2:9 and 2:10-23 proceed. These oracles look forward to the recognition of YHWH and the Temple by the nations and to the downfall of the throne of the kingdoms, i.e., Persia, and the reinstitution of Davidic kingship in Jerusalem. The concern with the future implications of the building of the Temple thereby constitutes the primary goal of the book.

Verse 12 basically reports the compliance of Zerubbabel, Joshua, and the people with YHWH's instructions. The full names of both Zerubbabel and Joshua and Joshua's title are given once again (cf. verse 1), apparently to establish without question that they carried out YHWH's instructions. The people are also included, apparently to signify the unified and absolute compliance of the entire community. They are called "the remnant of the people" (*šĕʾērît hāʿām*), which draws on the language employed by the prophets, particularly by Isaiah, to describe the future Jewish community that will be established in Jerusalem following the exile (cf. Isa 37:4, 32/2 Kgs 19:4, 31; Jer 23:3; 31:7; Zeph 2:7, 9; 3:13; see also Isa 10:20, 21, 22; 11:11, 16). It also identifies Haggai fully by both name and title once again (cf. verse 1) to make the same point. Beuken has argued that this concern with the names and titles, the affinities with the book of Chronicles, and other features, indicate that the narrative framework of Haggai was composed in a Chronistic milieu,[15] that was concerned with recording the events per-

---

[14] E.g., March, "Haggai," 719–21; Petersen, *Haggai and Zechariah 1–8* 55–60.
[15] Beuken, *Haggai-Sacharja 1–8* esp. 42–8.

taining to Haggai's career and the reconstruction of the Temple and with polemicising against the Samaritan community. Others point to theocratic circles that were concerned with the reality of G–d's rule in the present as opposed to visionary groups who looked forward to divine intervention.[16] Indeed, such a theocratic setting appears likely, although the dichotomy between prophetically-oriented visionaries and theocratic circles can hardly be maintained.[17] To a certain extent, the distinction is based upon an old Protestant theological polemic against the priesthood of the Roman Catholic Church (and of Judaism) and its identification with the role of the prophet. As Cook's recent study indicates, millennial groups tend to identify with their central religious institutions and establishments, and the apocalyptic literature in the Hebrew Bible draws heavily upon priestly language.[18] It would appear that visionary circles in Persian-period Judaism would in fact have been located within priestly circles. In the present case, the presentation of Haggai's oracles and the expectation for the restoration of YHWH's world-wide sovereignty and Davidic rule would reflect the thinking of the early-Persian period Jerusalem priesthood concerning the significance of the restoration of the Temple. The book of Haggai, with its careful recording of the compliance of Zerubbabel ben Shealtiel the governor, Joshua ben Jehozadak the high priest, and the remnant of the people, would look forward to realization of this new world order once the Temple was complete. Furthermore, it explicitly states that the people "feared YHWH," i.e., they accepted YHWH as their G–d and submitted to YHWH's requirements accordingly. The book of Haggai serves as the documentation for their obedience and their expectation.

Verse 13 reiterates Haggai's role as "the messenger of YHWH" (*malʾak yhwh*), which apparently corresponds to his earlier identification as "Haggai, the prophet" (*haggay hannābîʾ*). The term "prophet" is generally employed throughout the Bible, but the term "messenger" is frequently applied to divine figures or angels (see Gen 19:1, 15; 28:12; Exod 23:20, 23; 1 Kgs 19:5, 7; Mal 3:1), although it can be used for prophets and other emissaries as well (1 Kgs 13:18; Gen 32:3). The term "message of YHWH" (*malʾăkût yhwh*) again emphasizes that the role of

---

[16] R. A. Mason, "The purpose of the 'editorial framework' of the book of Haggai," *VT* 27 (1977) 413–21.

[17] Cf. Paul Hanson, *The Dawn of Apocalyptic: The Historical and Sociological Roots of Jewish Apocalyptic Eschatology* (Fortress: Philadelphia, 1975), who argues for such a distinction as the basic component of his views concerning the origins of apocalyptic.

[18] Stephen L. Cook, *Prophecy and Apocalypticism: The Postexilic Social Setting* (Minneapolis: Fortress, 1995).

the prophet is simply to serve as YHWH's emissary to the people. Haggai conveys YHWH's message as, "I am with you" (*ʾănî ʾittĕkem*), and the following oracular formula identifies it as such once again. The formula "I am with you" is derived from the typical form of the priestly or prophetic oracle of reassurance or salvation that is delivered to convey YHWH's support in a time of crisis.[19] The oracle normally appears with the formula, "do not fear," followed by some expression of divine favor such as the formula presented here. Examples of the form appear in Isa 41:10; 43:5; Jer 30:10-11.[20] The appearance of the form, lacking the formula "I am with you," in Isa 37:5-7 and 7:4-9 suggests that it was delivered in response to a situation of oracular inquiry or threat in which some indication of divine protection was sought. In the present case, the use of this formula in Haggai indicates that perhaps Haggai was sought out for oracular inquiry in order to determine whether or not it was propitious to begin construction of the Temple, although it is entirely possible that Haggai acted on his own.

Verse 14 then states that YHWH "stirred up the spirit" of Zerubbabel, Joshua, and the people to begin the work on the Temple. Once again, full names and titles are given to emphasize the complete compliance of the community and their leaders. The expression "to stir up the spirit" (*hāʿîr rûaḥ*) typically appears in prophetic texts (Jer 51:11; cf. Isa 51:9, 17; 52:1), the work of the Chronicler (1 Chr 5:26; 2 Chr 21:16; 36:22-23) and in Ezra (Ezra 1:5) to describe YHWH's motivation of various individuals or groups to undertake action. The report in verse 14b that they "came" and "did" the "work" employs the term *mĕlāʾkâ*, "work," which can refer to any occupation, but is employed elsewhere to describe the work on the Temple (1 Kgs 5:30); the Tabernacle and its furnishings (Exod 36:2); and general priestly service (2 Chr 29:34).

Finally, verse 15a indicates that the work began on the twenty-fourth day of the sixth month, i.e., 24 Ellul. That would suggest that it took some three and a half weeks to organize so that the work might begin. Some have tried to suggest that this date formula should be placed before Hag 2:15,[21] but there is no textual evidence for such a transposition. Indeed, the three and a half week delay does not indicate lack of decisive action on the part of the people; rather, it indicates a reasonable amount of time to prepare for such a massive undertaking.

[19] For discussion of the Oracle of Salvation and the Reassurance Formula, see Sweeney, *Isaiah 1–39* 526, 547.

[20] Petersen, *Haggai and Zechariah 1–8* 57–8.

[21] E.g., Wolff, *Haggai* 59–63.

Narrative concerning Haggai's oracle to Zerubbabel and Joshua promising the future glory of the Jerusalem Temple: 1:15b–2:9

The second major component of the book of Haggai appears in Hag 1:15b–2:9, which relates the transmission through Haggai of YHWH's oracle to Zerubbabel and Joshua concerning the future glory of the Jerusalem Temple. This unit is clearly demarcated at the outset by the narrative date formula in Hag 1:15b–2:1, which is formulated as a parallel to the much longer date formula in Hag 1:1. Like Hag 1:1, the formula notes the transmission of the oracle "in the second year of King Darius" in verse 15b. Although the versification of the passage associates Hag 1:15b with Hag 1:15a, the concluding function of verse 15a hardly requires a repetition of the notice concerning the second year of King Darius. The following reference in Hag 2:1 that places the oracle "in the seventh month, on the twenty-first day of the month" does require a reference to the year of the king, however, to place the precise date of the new oracle. The introduction of a new date formula in Hag 2:10 likewise requires a reference to the year of the king in order to establish properly the date of the following oracle, but the reference to a second oracle on the same date in Hag 2:20 requires no such reference as the year of the king is noted in Hag 2:10. Indeed, the date formula in Hag 2:10 marks the beginning of a new unit and thereby demonstrates that Hag 2:9 concludes the unit begun in Hag 1:15b. The formula in Hag 2:1 continues a contracted form of the statement in Hag 1:1b, "the word of YHWH came by the prophet Haggai saying . . ." Once again, the YHWH word transmission formula indicates that the following material constitutes an oracle by YHWH to the prophet. Haggai 2:1 omits the references to Zerubbabel and Joshua as their names and titles appear in verse 2 as part of YHWH's instruction to the prophet.

Overall, the date formula in Hag 1:15b–2:1 constitutes a narrative introduction to the instruction by YHWH to Haggai in Hag 2:2-9 that the prophet should deliver an oracle to Zerubbabel and Joshua concerning the future glory of the Temple. The dating of this instruction to the twenty-first day of the seventh month in the second year of Darius, i.e., the twenty-first day of Tishri in 520 B.C.E. is noteworthy for several reasons. First, it clearly establishes a chronological sequence with the reference to the first day of Ellul in 520 B.C.E. in Hag 1:1 and the twenty-fourth day of Ellul in Hag 1:15a, i.e., this oracle follows chronologically upon the first oracle and its fulfillment. Second, the oracle is delivered during the period in which Darius fights off challenges in the larger Persian empire to his accession to the throne in the aftermath of the death of Cambyses. During this period, Darius needed desperately to court allies in his efforts to establish his control over the empire, and support for the reconstruction of the Temple in Jerusalem would likely insure the continued allegiance of Judah to his (and Achaemenid) rule. As noted in Ezra 3:8-13, the foundation for the Temple was laid in the second year following the arrival of Zerubbabel and Joshua in Jerusalem, and according to Ezra 6:1-22, the Temple was completed in the sixth year of Darius following the king's intervention against attempts by Tattenai, the Persian governor of the region, and his allies to block construction of the new edifice. Third, the twenty-first day of Tishri marks the seventh day of the festival of Sukkoth, which is the eve of the eighth day on which a complete rest or Shabbaton is observed. Thus, the oracle is presented during the course of the observance of Sukkoth, which would be the time that the Torah is read to the people every seventh year (Deut 31:9-13) thereby reminding them of their obligations in relation to the covenant with YHWH. It would also mark the second anniversary of the dedication of the altar at the site of the Temple, insofar as Ezra 3:1-7 indicates that the altar was erected in the seventh month (in the year of Zerubbabel's and Joshua's arrival, i.e., 522 B.C.E.) and commenced operation for the festival of Sukkoth. The anniversary of the construction of the altar and the role of Sukkoth in relation to the reading of the Torah would provide an appropriate setting for efforts to renew the construction of the Temple. The foundation of the Temple had been laid in the second month of the second year after the arrival of Zerubbabel and Joshua (Ezra 3:8), but Ezra 3:12-13 relates that some of the people who remembered Solomon's Temple wept aloud at the sight of the new foundations. Most interpreters understand this to be an expression of disappointment that the new Temple would not match the splendor of the previous structure.[22] Insofar as Hag 2:3 suggests that some among the people would regard the new Temple "as nothing," it would appear that the present oracle is intended to motivate the people to undertake construction of the Temple despite such doubts (cf. Hag 1:1-15a, which takes up the people's reluctance to build the Temple). The oracle suggests that the new Temple would ultimately surpass the glory of the former structure when all the nations of the earth would acknowledge YHWH's sovereignty over all creation (Hag 2:6-9).

Following the narrative introduction in verses 15b–2:1, Hag 2:2 begins the quotation of YHWH's statement to the prophet with an instruction formula that calls upon the prophet to speak the following oracle in verses 3-9 to Zerubbabel and Joshua. Both figures are identified by name, patronymic, and office, i.e., "governor Judah" and "high priest,"

---

[22] See Blenkinsopp, *Ezra-Nehemiah* 101.

as in Hag 1:1. Such identification reinforces the formal and public character of the oracle so that the officials addressed by YHWH are clear. In addition to Zerubbabel and Joshua, YHWH's instruction also identifies "the remnant of the people *(šĕʾērît hāʿām)*" as a third addressee. The meaning of this term is debated as some interpreters understand it as a reference to the decimated Jewish community which returned to Jerusalem following the exile.[23] The term must also be related to earlier prophetic statements concerning the restoration of "a remnant of Israel" following the period of punishment in the Assyrian and Babylonian periods (cf. Isa 37:4, 32/2 Kgs 19:4, 32; Mic 2:12; 5:6, 7 [NRSV: 5:7, 8]; 7:18; Jer 23:3; 31:7; Zeph 2:7, 9; 3:13; Zech 8:6, 11, 12). As Koch has demonstrated, the restored Jewish community under Ezra regarded itself as "the remnant of Israel" (cf. Ezra 9:14) that would be reestablished in accordance with the views of Isaiah.[24] The use of the term, "remnant of the people," suggests that the restoration of the Temple under Zerubbabel and Joshua and its implications for the restoration of the nation and its king is viewed already in Haggai as the fulfillment of earlier prophecy.

The oracle that Haggai is instructed to deliver to Zerubbabel and Joshua appears in Hag 2:3-9. It is formulated as a disputation speech[25] that is intended to overcome doubts about the rebuilding of the Jerusalem Temple and to encourage Zerubbabel and Joshua to undertake the task because it will result in the world-wide recognition of YHWH's glory and sovereignty.

The oracle comprises two major components. The first appears in verse 3 as a set of rhetorical questions that are designed to counter the premise that the new Temple will not match the former glory of Solomon's Temple (cf. Ezra 3:12-13). The first question in verse 3a asks for those who have seen the glory of the former Temple in relation to the current proposed structure. It thereby calls for the identification of those who would challenge the importance of the current building and prepares for the counter-argument of the disputation that will follow in subsequent verses by focusing the response on those persons who raised the lamentation in the first place. The second set of questions in verse 3b begins by asking those who had seen the former Temple how they view the current structure. The initial question is followed immediately by the rhetorical question, "is it not in your sight as nothing?" which succinctly states the views of those who would downplay the

---

[23] See Meyers and Meyers, *Haggai, Zechariah 1–8* 49, 34.

[24] Klaus Koch, "Ezra and the Origins of Judaism," *Journal of Semitic Studies* 19 (1974) 173–97.

[25] For discussion of the disputation form, see Sweeney, *Isaiah 1–39* 519.

importance of the proposed structure. The question clearly lays out the premise that is to be challenged by the disputation at large, i.e., the new Temple lacks the glory of the former Temple of Solomon. The underlying premise therefore is that the community should not rally to the support of the new construction.

The second part of the oracle in verses 4-9 is explicitly designed to counteract the premise articulated in verse 3. It begins with exhortational statements to Zerubbabel, Joshua, and the people in verses 4-5 to undertake the construction of the new Temple, and it continues in verses 6-9 with a lengthy elaboration upon the reasons why they should do so. The exhortation to undertake the work begins initially with the phrase, "and now (*wĕʿattâ*)," which accentuates the contrasts between the past glory of Solomon's Temple and the current doubts concerning the new structure. More importantly, it focuses the audience's and the reader's attention on the current situation and the need to commence construction. A series of three occurrences of the imperative verb *ḥăzaq*, "take courage," is directed successively to the addressees of the oracle, Zerubbabel, Joshua, and the people, in language reminiscent of that directed by Joshua to the people of Israel at the outset of the conquest of the land of Canaan (Josh 1:6, 7). The introduction of the oracular formula, *nĕʾum yhwh*, "says YHWH," following the statement to Zerubbabel and the people respectively, highlights the fact that these exhortations come directly from YHWH even though they are transmitted by Haggai the prophet. Together, the three imperatives provide the exhortational basis for the fourth imperative in the series, *waʿăśû*, "work (literally, 'and do [it]')," which is addressed to Zerubbabel, Joshua, and the people collectively. This command constitutes the primary rhetorical goal of the passage and indeed of the entire book, to call upon the parties addressed to undertake the construction of the new Temple. Verses 4b-5, introduced by a causative *kî*, "because," then provide the basic reason why Zerubbabel, Joshua, and the people should undertake the construction of the Temple, i.e., because YHWH supports them in their efforts and will see to the success of the program. This statement is formulated with elements of the typical reassurance oracle or priestly/prophetic oracle of salvation. As noted in the discussion of Hag 1:13, the initial statement, "because/for I am with you," constitutes one of the typical elements of the form, and functions as reassurance to the addressee that YHWH indeed will act on the addressee's behalf (cf. Isa 41:10; 43:5; Jer 30:10-11). This formula appears in various contexts. It is generally delivered in response to a situation of oracular inquiry (see e.g., Isa 37:5-7; 7:4-9), and it functions as a means to encourage its addressees to have confidence in the face of adversity. The appearance of the oracular formula, "says YHWH of Hosts," further reinforces the contention that YHWH will act on behalf of the building by reiterating that these statements come directly from YHWH. Verse 5a, which refers to the covenant made by YHWH with the people at the time of the exodus from Egypt, is problematic in that it is absent in the LXX and presumed by many to be a later addition to the text. Although it is translated, "according to the promise that I made with you when you came out of Egypt," it is in fact an awkward formulation that functions as the direct object of the command, "work/and do," i.e., "and do . . . the thing/covenant that I cut/made with you when you came out of Egypt." The language is idiomatic, viz., "the thing that I cut with you," refers to "the covenant that I made with you," but overall, it calls upon the people to build the Temple because that was part of the terms of the covenant made by YHWH with the people at the time of the Exodus. Readers must bear in mind that YHWH brought the people out of Egypt so that they might undertake a three-day journey to worship YHWH (cf. Exod 3:18; 5:1). Furthermore, YHWH commanded Israel to construct the tabernacle in the wilderness, which served as a surrogate Temple until the arrival in the promised land (see Exodus 25–30; 35–40), and the song of the sea indicates that the goal of Israel's journey from Egypt was YHWH's sanctuary (Exod 15:17). Verse 5bα continues the reassurance with the statement, "(and) my spirit abides (literally, 'stands') among you," which articulates YHWH's presence among the people. Finally, the reassurance formula ʾal tîrāʾû, "do not fear," the basic element of the priestly or prophetic oracle of salvation,[26] concludes this initial statement of YHWH's support for the building of the Temple.

Verses 6-9 then provide an extended elaboration concerning YHWH's plans for the Temple and the world once the new Temple is completed. Overall, these verses provide the fundamental counter-argument against the premise that the new Temple will lack the glory and significance of Solomon's former structure. The argument is based upon the future promise of glory, wealth, and peace for the new Temple in contrast to the circumstances of the present that apparently show so little promise in the eyes of the people. The passage begins with a causative *kî* that relates these verses to the preceding material. The *kî* in turn is followed by an example of the prophetic messenger formula that aids in validating the promises of future glory as a statement by YHWH. The difficult phrase in verse 6aβ, ʿôd ʾaḥat mĕʿat hîʾ means literally, "yet one, it is a little/few."[27] The NRSV correctly conveys the intention of the phrase with the translation, "in a little while," which expresses the

[26] Ibid., 526, 527.
[27] See Rudolph, *Haggai—Zecharja 1–8—Zecharja 9–14—Maleachi* 41.

hopeful anticipation of the promise that is being held out to the people. The phrase suggests that the prophet and other supporters of Temple construction seek just a little more time from the people to complete the project and realize its potential. The promises per se follow in verses 6b-9. YHWH's statement, "(and) I am shaking the heavens and the earth and the sea and the dry land" employs the theophanic imagery of an earthquake that encompasses all of creation to express the cosmic implications of the reconstruction of the Temple and YHWH's action in the world. The shaking of both "the heavens and the earth" and "the sea and the dry land" indicates that YHWH's actions affect all of creation. Although the NRSV translates this passage with future verbs, the use of the participle *marʿîš*, "shaking," suggests that YHWH's action is presently taking place. Such a statement would relate well to the current upheaval "shaking" the Persian empire as various factions in the empire were rising in revolt against Darius. The use of cosmic or theophanic language would likewise relate well to the role of the Temple as the center of the natural world or cosmos as well as of the human world.[28] The *waw-consecutive* perfect verbs of verse 7, however, explicitly point to the future orientation of YHWH's promises, and the content of the verse indicates the shift from the cosmic to the human realm. The earthquake-like "shaking" of the nations will prompt them to bring their treasure and to fill the new Temple with glory. The term "treasure" (*ḥemdat*) literally means "desire" and refers to "desirable" or "precious" goods, such as Hezekiah's treasures (2 Chr 32:27) or the "precious vessels" taken by Nebuchadnezzar from Solomon's Temple in Jerusalem (2 Chr 36:10; cf. Nah 2:10 [NRSV: 2:9]). Indeed, the reference to "the precious vessels" taken by Nebuchadnezzar suggests that Haggai envisions the return of the plunder taken from Jerusalem and the Temple at the time of the Babylonian destruction of the city. The portrayal of the nations coming to acknowledge YHWH at Jerusalem and bringing their wealth corresponds to various portrayals of such a scene in the literature of the late-exilic or early-Persian period, e.g., Isa 2:2-4; 60:1-22; Zech 8:20-23. The portrayal would likely correspond to idealized scenes of subject nations bringing offerings to the court of the Persian monarch to acknowledge his sovereignty. In a time of revolt against Darius, such a portrayal of the nations in relation to YHWH could well suggest that YHWH and the Temple would succeed where Darius and the empire might fail. The concluding speech formula at the end of verse 7, "says (*ʾāmar*) YHWH of Hosts," reinforces the con-

---

[28] For discussion of the theophanic language of this passage, see Jeremias, *Theophanie* esp. 68–9. For discussion of the Temple as cosmic center of creation, see Jon D. Levenson, "The Temple and the World," *JR* 64 (1984) 275–98.

tention that these promises come directly from YHWH. Verse 8 then states the claim by YHWH that the silver and the gold that are brought to the Temple belong exclusively to G–d, i.e., the wealth brought by the nations is to be considered as sacred offerings to YHWH as a means to acknowledge YHWH's sovereignty over all the world and the nations (cf. Isa 23:18). In this respect, the Israelite/Judean practice of bringing offerings to YHWH at the Temple is extended to the entire world and includes silver and gold. Silver and gold are brought by the exiles as well to restore the Temple and provide ornamentation or crowns for the new priests and perhaps a king (Ezra 1; Zech 6:9-15) in a manner analogous to that described for the building of the tabernacle in the wilderness (Exod 25:1-9). Once again, the concluding oracular formula at the end of verse 8 certifies this as a statement by YHWH. Verse 9 then contains two statements concerning the projected results of YHWH's theophanic action and the response of the nations. Verse 9a states that the glory of the new Temple will be greater than that of the former, and thereby addresses the perceptions of the people that the new Temple does not compare to Solomon's Temple. The concluding speech formula again certifies this as a statement by YHWH. Finally, verse 9b promises peace for "this place," i.e., the Temple, and thereby builds upon the tradition of Jerusalem as the city of peace and the Temple as the source of peace for the city and the world (n.b., the name Jerusalem, *yĕrûšālayim*, is generally construed as a derivation from the phrase "possession of peace" *[yĕrûš šālēm]* or "foundation of peace/Shalem" *[yĕrû šālēm]*).[29] The concluding oracular formula again stresses that these promises stem directly from YHWH.

Narrative concerning Haggai's oracles promising the restoration of fecundity to the land and the Davidic monarchy: 2:10-23

The third and final component of the book of Haggai appears in Hag 2:10-23, which presents YHWH's instructions to Haggai to deliver two oracles concerning YHWH's promise of fecundity to the land in verses 10-19 and YHWH's promise to Zerubbabel that he will reign as YHWH's "signet ring" or as the new Davidic monarch. The unit begins with another example of the narrative date formula that continues the sequence begun in Hag 1:1 and 1:15b–2:1. The narrative date formula in Hag 2:20 is clearly tied to that of Hag 2:10 by the repetition of the

[29] See Brown, Driver, Briggs, 436.

same date, the twenty-fourth day of the ninth month in the second year of Darius, and the notice that the word of YHWH came to Haggai "a second time." The two date formulas thereby point to the two major sub-units of this section, i.e., the presentation of Haggai's oracle concerning YHWH's blessing the agricultural produce of the land in verses 10-19 and the presentation of the oracle concerning YHWH's promise of kingship to Zerubbabel in verses 20-23.

The narrative presentation of YHWH's instructions to Haggai in verses 10-19 begins with a narrative date formula that includes the prophetic word transmission formula and identifies the twenty-fourth day of the ninth month of the second year of Darius as the date for the oracle. Most interpreters miss the significance of this date, which is the twenty-fourth day of Kislev, i.e., the day prior to the beginning of the observance of Hanukkah.[30] This is not surprising because the eight-day observance of Hanukkah, which begins on the twenty-fifth of Kislev, was not inaugurated until 164 B.C.E. when the Hasmonean priest, Judah the Maccabee, and his followers rededicated the Temple in Jerusalem to the worship of YHWH following its desecration by the Seleucid Syrian monarch, Antiochus IV (r. 176–163 B.C.E.), who had turned the Temple into a shrine for the Syrian-Greek god Zeus.[31] The eight-day celebration of the festival traditionally recalls the eight days that the meager supply of oil for the eternal light burned in the Temple at the rededication (bShabbat 21b), but it also recalls the time required to dedicate an altar (cf. Ezek 43:13-27; Exod 29:37; Lev 8:33, 35; 1 Kgs 8:62-66; 2 Chr 7:8-10; Ezra 3:1-7; 1 Macc 4:36-59; 2 Macc 10:1-9). Although the origins of the Hanukkah celebration are in fact not entirely clear, there is no evidence that the festival was celebrated in the time of Haggai or that a dedication of the altar took place at this time. Indeed, Ezra 3:1-7 places the dedication of the altar in the festival of Sukkoth during the seventh month (Tishri) of the first year of the return under Zerubbabel and Joshua, i.e., 15-23 Tishri, 522 B.C.E. It is possible that the Maccabean rededication of the Temple altar on the twenty-fifth of Kislev was somehow understood as a fulfillment of Haggai's prophecy, especially since 1 Macc 4:44-46 indicates that the Maccabees stored the stones of the profaned altar until such time as a prophet should come and tell them what to do.

The presentation of the oracle in verses 11-19 begins with an example of the messenger formula in verse 11a, "Thus says YHWH of Hosts," to identify the following material as YHWH's statement to Hag-

---

[30] See, e.g., March, "Haggai," 726–27, who states that "There was nothing special about the date—no appointed festival, no special moment in Israel's history" (726).

[31] For discussion of Hanukkah, s.v., "Hanukkah," *Encyclopaedia Judaica* 7:1280-8.

gai. Verse 11b indicates that the oracle constitutes Yhwh's instruction to Haggai to make an inquiry to the priests. One of the primary functions of the priests is to instruct the people in Yhwh's requirements concerning sacred action, including both cultic and moral action (see Lev 10:10-11; Deut 33:10; Jer 18:18; Ezek 7:26; Hos 4:4-6; Mic 3:11). The NRSV translates the command *šĕʾal-nāʾ . . . tôrâ*, "ask . . . for a ruling," but this clouds their role in the proper interpretation of Yhwh's Torah or instruction concerning sacred matters. Interestingly, verbal syntax of the presentation of Haggai's request in verses 12-14 does not portray a proposed request; rather it presents a narrative report of a request that has already taken place. Fundamentally, the question posed to the priests concerns the distinction between sacred food that is fit for presentation on the altar or ritual consumption and food that is unfit for sacred use, and the means by which sacred food might become unfit by contact with other profane food. The distinction is expressed by the terms *qōdeš*, "holy, consecrated," and *ṭāmēʾ*, "unclean, impure." Such sacred food might include meat from those animals that are fit for human consumption and that is properly slaughtered and prepared, i.e., from which the blood has been fully and properly removed (see Leviticus 11; 17; Deut 14:3-21; 15:19-23). Basically, the question in verse 12 posits that sacred meat is carried in a garment, and it comes into contact with some profane food that has not been properly prepared for sacred use, such as bread, stew, wine, oil, etc. The ruling of the priests is that such meat is no longer sacred because it has come into contact with non-sacred food, i.e., the sacred character of the meat is compromised because of its contact with profane food. Haggai then asks in verse 13 whether such meat becomes impure if a ritually impure person touches it. Such a person might be one who has consumed profane food, engaged in sexual activity, had some disease or bodily discharge, has engaged in some immoral action, or has come into contact with the dead and has not been purified by bathing properly in water (see Leviticus 11-21). The priests' ruling is that sacred meat becomes impure if touched by someone who is impure. Finally, Haggai makes a statement in verse 14 that the condition of the people must be considered as an analogy to the priests' ruling concerning the sacred character of the meat that was the subject of his questions in verses 12-13. Just as sacred meat becomes impure if it comes into contact with profane food or an impure person, so the offerings and deeds of the people to Yhwh must be considered impure. The people have not been properly purified by the presence of the Temple, and all that they touch must therefore be considered impure or unfit for sacred use on the altar until the people are properly sanctified. The oracular formula in verse 14 certifies that the statement of analogy stems directly from Yhwh. In short, the question posed to the priests constitutes a symbolic action that functions as an argument for the reconstruction of the Temple.

Having completed the presentation of YHWH's instruction to carry out the inquiry to the priests, Haggai then turns in verses 15-19 to a two-part statement, each of which begins with the formula, "consider (what will come to pass) from this day on," that explains the past difficulties of the community in producing sufficient food. Basically, the prophet argues that YHWH sent blight and diseases against the crops of the people because they had failed to build the Temple and thereby failed to consecrate their offerings properly. The section begins with the statement in verse 15aα¹, "and now (wĕʿattâ)," in order to distinguish the past experience of the people from the future blessing that they will experience once the Temple is built. The first statement in verses 15aα²⁻³ points to the scant agricultural harvest that the people have reaped prior to the building of the Temple. The NRSV translation of verse 16 begins with the question, "how did you fare?" but the Hebrew phrase *mi-hyōtām* means literally, "from their being," which expresses the former state of affairs. The verse should read, "in the past, one expected (literally, "came unto") a bundle of twenty, but there were ten."[32] The numbers refer to the expected yield of grain versus the actual yield, i.e., one might expect twenty measures from the seed planted, but the yield was only ten measures. The same situation applies to the wine vat, i.e., whereas one would expect fifty measures of wine, only twenty were actually produced. The prophet quotes YHWH in verse 17, stating that YHWH deliberately struck the people and their produce with "blight," "mildew," and "hail." Despite these plagues, YHWH states, "yet you did not return to me," i.e., the people did not build the Temple and therefore did not properly worship YHWH. The concluding oracular formula identifies this as a word from YHWH.

Verses 18-19 give YHWH's promise of blessing now that the process of rebuilding the Temple has begun. Again, the passage begins with the statement, "consider from this day on," and it specifies that "this day" is the twenty-fourth day of the ninth month (24 Kislev) when the foundation of the Temple was laid. According to Ezra 3:8-13, Zerubbabel and Joshua "made a beginning" in the second month, and Ezra 3:10 suggests that the laying of the foundation of the Temple might have taken place at that time, although most scholars agree that the Ezra narrative presents a telescoped version of events that are placed in the

---

[32] For discussion of the translation of this statement, see Meyers and Meyers, *Haggai, Zechariah 1–8* 60; Petersen, *Haggai, Zechariah 1–8* 86, 90. Most scholars emend the statement to *mah-hĕyîtem*, "how were you," in relation to the LXX reading of the verse (see also Rudolph, *Haggai—Zecharja 1–8—Zecharja 9–14—Maleachi* 45).

reign of Cyrus (cf. Zech 4:9, which places the laying of the foundation in the time of Zerubbabel, but does not specify the date).[33] In verse 19, the people are asked to consider the seed in the barn, the vine, the fig tree, the pomegranate, and the olive tree. The question is rhetorical in that it asks whether these items produce nothing; it therefore asserts that they will indeed produce great quantities of produce in the future now that work on the Temple has begun. YHWH's final statement in verse 19, "from this day on, I will bless you," underscores this point.

Haggai 2:20-23 then constitutes a second narrative presentation of an oracular instruction by YHWH to Haggai concerning YHWH's promise of kingship to Zerubbabel. The sub-unit begins in verse 20 with a narrative date formula that resumes that of verse 10. Like Hag 2:10, it includes the prophetic word transmission formula and states that the date is again the twenty-fourth day of the ninth month (24 Kislev), but it also indicates that the word of YHWH came to Haggai a second time on that day. Again, verse 21a demonstrates that the oracle is formulated as an instruction by YHWH to Haggai who commissions the prophet to speak an oracle to Zerubbabel. Zerubbabel's full name and title as governor of Judah is included in keeping with the formal nature of the address forms in the book of Haggai. Given the nature of the following oracle, it is essential to identify precisely to whom the oracle is addressed. Verse 21b employs a statement that is nearly identical to that of verse 6b to indicate that YHWH is shaking the heavens and the earth. Again, the theophanic language of earthquake draws upon the role of the Temple as cosmic center to convey the cosmic significance of YHWH's coming announcement concerning the Persian empire and Zerubbabel. In verse 22, YHWH announces plans "to overthrow the throne of the kingdoms" and "to destroy the strength of the kingdom of the nations." When read in relation to the early years of Darius' reign, these statements indicate the expectation that the Persian empire is about to be overthrown as Darius is forced to fight off various challenges to the throne. It articulates the belief that YHWH is indeed acting in the world to overthrow the Persian empire and to manifest YHWH's own sovereignty over the world in Jerusalem and the new Temple. In this respect, it builds upon the previous tradition of Deutero-Isaiah, who identified the Persian monarch Cyrus as YHWH's messiah and Temple builder (see Isa 44:28; 45:1), but it indicates that the period of Persian rule is now coming to an end as YHWH's true kingdom is manifested in the world. The references to the overthrow of chariots, horses, and their riders, and the portrayal of combat among comrades points to the internal warfare within the Persian empire during the early years

---

[33] Blenkinsopp, *Ezra-Nehemiah* 100.

of Darius. Verse 23 presents a series of statements by Y<small>HWH</small> that designate Zerubbabel as Y<small>HWH</small>'s "signet ring." The verse begins with the *bayyôm hahû>,* "in that day," formula that appears typically in the prophetic books as an indication of future action.[34] The first of three occurrences of the oracular formula then follows to certify that this is indeed a statement by Y<small>HWH</small>. Y<small>HWH</small>'s first statement is that Zerubbabel ben Shealtiel will be taken as Y<small>HWH</small>'s "servant." It is noteworthy that the designation "servant" or "servant of Y<small>HWH</small>" is applied to a select cadre of noteworthy figures in the Hebrew Bible, e.g., the patriarchs (Exod 32:13; Deut 9:27); Abraham (Gen 26:24; Ps 105:6); Isaac (Gen 24:14); Jacob (Ezek 28:25); Moses (Exod 14:31; Num 12:7; Deut 34:5); Joshua (Josh 24:29); Caleb (Num 14:24); Job (Job 1:8); David (2 Sam 3:18; 7:5); Hezekiah (2 Chr 32:16); Eliakim (Isa 22:20); the messianic "Branch" who will build Y<small>HWH</small>'s Temple (Zech 3:8; 6:12); the Levitical singers (Pss 113:1; 134:1); the prophets (2 Kgs 9:7); Israel (Isa 41:8; 43:10); Deutero-Isaiah's servant (Isa 42:1; 52:13), and others. In this case, Zerubbabel's royal status as the grandson of King Jehoiachin and his role as Temple builder appears to be especially important to his designation as Y<small>HWH</small>'s servant. Y<small>HWH</small>'s designation of Zerubbabel as "signet ring *(hôtām)"* is particularly important to his royal identity as well. The signet ring of the Persian monarch was the ultimate symbol of royal authority and power in the Persian empire (see Esth 3:10; 8:2). It was used essentially to produce the signature of the king;[35] documents that were affixed with the royal seal, impressed by the king's signet ring, carried the force of law in the Persian empire equivalent to the word of the king himself. 1 Kings 21:8 indicates that Jezebel used Ahab's signet ring to write letters in the name of the king as part of her plan to have Naboth executed. Jeremiah 22:24 raises the possibility that King Jehoiachin could have been understood as Y<small>HWH</small>'s signet, although the passage denies that this is the case for the exiled monarch. Y<small>HWH</small>'s designation of Zerubbabel as "signet" demonstrates that Zerubbabel would rule as Y<small>HWH</small>'s designated monarch, i.e., Zerubbabel would rule as Y<small>HWH</small>'s representative on earth, much as the Davidic king traditionally was conceived as the son or designated representative of Y<small>HWH</small>'s royal authority (see Psalm 2; 2 Samuel 7). Y<small>HWH</small>'s concluding statement, "for I have chosen you," likewise indicates Zerubbabel's royal status in keeping with the tradition that Y<small>HWH</small> had chosen David as designated ruler (1 Sam 10:24; 16:8, 9, 10; 2 Sam 6:21; 1 Kgs 8:16/2 Chr

---

[34] For discussion of this formula, see now DeVries, *From Old Revelation to New* 38–63.

[35] For a general discussion of seals and signets, see Bonnie Magness-Gardiner, "Seals, Mesopotamian," *ABD* V:1062-1064.

6:6; 1 Chr 28:4, 5; 29:1; 2 Chr 6:5, etc.). When read in relation to the revolts in the Persian empire against Darius' rule, this statement indicates Haggai's expectation of and support for the restoration of the Davidic monarchy (and thus for the restoration of an independent Judean state) as a result of the rebuilding of the Temple. Zerubbabel's role as Davidic scion and Temple builder effectively marked him as YHWH's messiah or anointed Davidic monarch. Once the Persian empire fell, YHWH's sovereignty in the world would be manifested with the reestablishment of the Temple and the royal house of David in Jerusalem that would be acknowledged by all the nations of the world.

FOR FURTHER READING

COMMENTARIES

Amsler, Samuel with André Lacoque and René Vuilleumier. *Aggée, Zacharie, Malachie*. Commentaire de l'ancien Testament, XIc. 2nd edition. Geneva: Labor et Fides, 1988.

March, W. Eugene. "The Book of Haggai: Introduction, Commentary, and Reflections," *The New Interpreter's Bible. Volume VII: Introduction to Apocalyptic Literature, Daniel, The Twelve Prophets*, ed. Leander E. Keck et al. Nashville: Abingdon, 1996.

Meyers, Carol L. and Eric M. Meyers. *Haggai, Zechariah 1–8*. Anchor Bible, 25B. Garden City: Doubleday, 1987.

Mitchell, Hinckley G. with John Merlin Powis Smith and Julius A. Bewer. *A Critical and Exegetical Commentary on Haggai, Zechariah, Malachi, and Jonah*. International Critical Commentary. Edinburgh: T. and T. Clark, 1912.

Petersen, David L. *Haggai and Zechariah 1–8*. Old Testament Library. Philadelphia: Westminster, 1984.

Redditt, Paul L. *Haggai, Zechariah, Malachi*. New Century Bible Commentary. London: Marshall Pickering; Grand Rapids: William Eerdmans, 1995.

Reventlow, Henning Graf. *Die Propheten Haggai, Sacharja und Maleachi*. Das Alte Testament Deutsch, 25, 2. Göttingen: Vandenhoeck & Ruprecht, 1993.

Robinson, Theodore H. with Friedrich Horst. *Die Zwölf Kleinen Propheten*. Handbuch zum Alten Testament, 14. 3rd edition. Tübingen: J. C. B. Mohr (Paul Siebeck), 1964.

Rudolph, Wilhelm. *Haggai–Sacharja 1–8–Sacharja 9–14–Maleachi*. Kommentar zum Alten Testament, XIII/4. Gütersloh: Gerd Mohn, 1976.

Smith, Ralph L. *Micah–Malachi*. Word Biblical Commentary, 32. Waco: Word: 1984.

Wolff, Hans Walter. *Haggai: A Commentary*. Translated by Margaret Kohl. Continental Commentaries. Minneapolis: Augsburg, 1988.

STUDIES

Beuken, W. A. M., S.J. *Haggai–Sacharja 1–8. Studien zur überlieferungsgeschichte der frühnachexilischen Prophetie*. Studia Semitica Neerlandica, 10. Assen: Van Gorcum, 1967.
Coggins, R. J. *Haggai, Zechariah, Malachi*. Old Testament Guides. Sheffield: JSOT Press, 1987.
Hanson, Paul. *The Dawn of Apocalyptic: The Historical and Sociological Roots of Jewish Apocalyptic Eschatology*. Philadelphia: Fortress, 1975.

ZECHARIAH

ZECHARIAH

Overview

The book of Zechariah is the eleventh book in both the Masoretic and Septuagint versions of the book of the Twelve. The date formulas of the book indicate that it is set in the second and fourth years of the reign of King Darius of Persia (r. 522–486 B.C.E.; see Zech 1:1, 7; 7:1) at the time that the construction of the second Temple commenced under the Persian-appointed Judean governor Zerubbabel ben Shealtiel, the grandson of King Jehoaichin of Judah, and the priest Joshua ben Jehozadak (cf. Ezra 3). The book presents an account of the visions of Zechariah concerning the significance of the reconstruction of the Temple, and it looks forward to the time when YHWH will remove the corrupt "shepherds" or leaders of the people, here understood as a reference to the Persian monarchs, in order to manifest divine sovereignty over the cosmos and nations at large from Zion. The book follows Haggai, which calls upon the people of Judah to support Temple reconstruction in anticipation of the nations' recognition of YHWH at Zion and YHWH's establishment of Zerubbabel as the divine "signet" or world ruler on YHWH's behalf. It precedes the book of Malachi, which reaffirms YHWH's commitment to the covenant with the Jerusalem priesthood and the people of Israel/Jacob, and anticipates the time when YHWH will send a divine "messenger," i.e., the prophet Elijah, to bring about the purification of the priesthood and nation at large.

The present form of the book of Zechariah is clearly intended to be read in relation to the reconstruction of the Jerusalem Temple in the early years of King Darius I of Persia.[1] Zechariah is mentioned together

---

[1] For an overview of the historical setting of the book, see Coggins, *Haggai, Zechariah, Malachi* 7–16.

with Haggai in Ezra 1–6 as one of the two prophets who called upon the people of Jerusalem and Judah to support the efforts of Zerubbabel and Joshua ben Jehozadak to rebuild the Temple in Jerusalem in the second year of King Darius I of Persia. Although King Cyrus of Persia had earlier authorized the return of Jews from Babylonia to Jerusalem as early as 539 B.C.E. (2 Chr 36:22-23; Ezra 1:1-11), apparently little had been accomplished apart from the laying of the Temple's foundation under the leadership of an obscure figure known as Sheshbazzar (Ezra 5:6-17). Following the unexpected death of Cyrus' son and successor Cambyses in 522 B.C.E., the Persian empire was plunged into civil war as Cambyses left no clear heir to the throne. Darius, a military commander under Cambyses and a member of Achaemenid royal family, took control of the Persian army, rushed back to Media, and executed a pretender to the throne named Gaumata who had mounted a revolt upon hearing of Cambyses' death. As revolts broke out throughout the empire, Darius was compelled to campaign extensively during the first years of his rule. Many speculate that his grant of permission to Zerubbabel and Joshua to return to Jerusalem to rebuild the Temple was motivated by Darius' interest in building a base of support for himself in Judah as he put down the various challenges to his rule. As a result of Darius' authorization, Zerubbabel and Joshua returned to Jerusalem in 522 B.C.E. with a large group of supporters. They commenced work on the Temple in 520 B.C.E., and the work was completed in 515 B.C.E. when the new Temple was dedicated (see Ezra 2–6).

Zechariah is identified as "the son of Iddo" in Ezra 5:1 and 6:14, which indicates that he was a priest as well as a prophet. Iddo is identified in Neh 12:4 as one of the priests and Levites who returned to Jerusalem with Zerubbabel and Joshua ben Jehozadak in 522 B.C.E., and Neh 12:16 identifies Zechariah as the head of the priestly house of Iddo. Indeed, various aspects of the book indicate his priestly background. The account of his visions in Zech 1:7–6:15 emphasize the concerns of a priest, i.e., the construction and significance of the altar in Zech 2:1-4 [NRSV: 1:18-21]; the ordination ceremony of Joshua ben Jehozadak as high priest in Zech 3:1-10; the image of the Menorah or Temple lampstand and its significance for Zerubbabel and Joshua in Zech 4:1-14; the flying scroll in Zech 5:1-4, which symbolizes the reading of Torah to the people from the Temple; the woman in the Ephah in Zech 5:5-11 which symbolizes the purification of the community; and the vision of the "Branch" or messianic figure in Zech 6:1-15 who is identified as the priest Joshua ben Jehozadak. Likewise, the question concerning the need for continued mourning and Zechariah's answer in Zechariah 7–8 reflects a typical example of priestly Torah in which questions concerning ritual purity or cultic observance are posed to a priest who then gives a response concerning correct holy procedure (see Hag 2:10-19). Finally, the symbolic action in Zechariah 11:4-17, in which Zechariah takes a position as a shepherd to dramatize YHWH's intention to remove the Persian monarchy reflects the role of a priest who cares for sheep that are presented to the Temple for sacrifice and the support of the Temple staff.

Zechariah 1:1, 7, however, identifies Zechariah as "the son of Berechiah, the son of Iddo," which would make Iddo his grandfather rather than his father. Many speculate that this indicates some confusion in Zechariah's genealogy, but the designation of Berechiah as his father appears to be a deliberate attempt to associate the prophet with the figure of Zechariah ben Jeberechiah, one of two men named as witnesses to the birth of the prophet Isaiah's son, Maher-shalal-hash-baz ("the spoil speeds, the prey hastens"), who is intended to serve as a sign of the ultimate downfall of the Assyrian empire in fulfillment of Isaiah's prophecies (see Isa 8:1-4). The name Berechiah is simply a minor grammatical variant of the name Jeberechiah, and the identification is apparently intended to point to Zechariah's book as a representation of the fulfillment of Isaiah's prophecies at the time of the building of the second Temple and beyond. Whereas the book of Isaiah looked to the downfall of the Assyrian and Babylonian empires as a prelude to the restoration of YHWH's sovereignty in Zion or the Jerusalem Temple as a result of Persian rule, the book of Zechariah points to the reconstruction of the Temple as the catalyst for the downfall of the Persian empire and the realization of YHWH's sovereignty over the nations from Zion. The book of Isaiah calls upon its audience to read the book in anticipation of the fulfillment of Isaiah's prophecies (see Isa 34:16-17; 29:11-12; cf. 8:1–9:6, esp. 8:16). The book of Zechariah alludes extensively to passages from the book of Isaiah to make the point that Isaiah's prophecies are about to achieve their fulfillment. In addition, Zechariah cites other prophetic books, such as Jeremiah, Ezekiel, Hosea, Amos, and Haggai, in an effort to establish Zechariah's continuity with earlier prophetic tradition and as a means to support his own contentions. Jeremiah 23 and 33 are frequently cited as these chapters point to a future royal Davidic figure identified as the "Branch" (cf. Zechariah 3; 4; 6; see also Isa 11:1-16). They also take up concerns with false prophecy and the downfall of "shepherds" that appear to be major concerns of Zechariah (see esp. Zechariah 11).

Given Zechariah's extensive citation of Isaiah and other prophetic books, it would appear that the authors of Zechariah were early readers of Isaiah and sought to cast Zechariah as the witness to the fulfillment of Isaiah's message. This is clear at the outset of the book in which YHWH, through Zechariah, calls for the people to return from their evil ways and deeds unlike their ancestors who refused to heed similar calls from the "former prophets," e.g., Isaiah (see Isa 1:2-31). It is also clear in Zechariah 7–8, which alludes extensively to Isaiah 1 and especially to Isaiah 2. The former focuses on explaining that Jerusalem and Judah suffer punishment for their failure to observe YHWH's will, and the latter presents Isaiah's vision of the nations streaming to Jerusalem, turning their swords into plowshares and their spears into pruning hooks, in order to hear the word of YHWH and to learn YHWH's Torah once the entire earth has been punished for arrogance and pride. But although Zechariah cites Isaiah, the book also disagrees with aspects of Isaiah's scenario. Isaiah views the punishment of the world as a divine process that is applied to both Israel and the nations, and Isa 2:5 indicates that Jacob/Israel is invited to join the nations at Zion as they go there to recognize YHWH's sovereignty. Likewise, Isaiah affirms the rule of the Persian monarch Cyrus as YHWH's anointed Temple builder (Isa 44:28; 45:1), and essentially identifies YHWH's purposes with the rise of the Persian empire throughout the book. Zechariah, on the other hand, views Judah in contention with the nations, and portrays Jerusalem's and Judah's conflict with the nations as an essential part of the process by which the nations will come to Zion at the festival of Sukkoth in order to recognize YHWH's sovereignty from Zion (see Zechariah 14). In keeping with this scenario, Zechariah anticipates the downfall of the Persian empire.

Overall, Zechariah's scenario appears to agree much more with that of Micah, who portrays the rise of a Davidic monarch as the agent who will carry out YHWH's punishment of the nations and ultimately bring them to Zion to hear YHWH's word and learn YHWH's Torah. Indeed, Zech 8:20-23 cites the Mican version of the "swords into plowshares" passage (Mic 4:1-5) rather than the Isaian version (Isa 2:2-4) in order to make this point. Furthermore, the criticism leveled against YHWH's shepherd(s) in Zechariah 9–14 for taking improper care of YHWH's flock seems not to allude to corrupt Judean leadership, but to Persian leadership instead. Indeed, the designation of the corrupt shepherd as "my (worthless) shepherd" in Zech 11:17 and 13:7 employs the same term used to describe Cyrus in Isa 44:28 when Cyrus is designated as YHWH's Temple builder and immediately thereafter as Messiah (Isa 45:1). It is likely no accident that Mic 2:12-13 portrays YHWH as the one who will lead the people of Israel, as a shepherd leads the flock, into the punishment of exile and back again to restoration (see also Micah 4–5). In reading Isaiah's vision, the authors of Zechariah appear to have been heavily influenced by Micah as well as by other prophetic writings, particularly Jeremiah.

Although Zechariah is clearly presented as a single book, questions concerning its authorship and overall interpretation have been raised throughout the history of Jewish and Christian interpretation of the book.[2] Matthew 27:9-10, for example, cites Zech 11:13 concerning the payment of thirty shekels of silver, but incorrectly ascribes it to Jeremiah. Modern critical scholars have observed major differences between chapters 1–8 and 9–14, or even between chapters 9–11 and 12–14. Most notably, Zechariah 1–8 presents the visions of the prophet Zechariah concerning the reconstruction of the Temple together with chronological statements concerning his activities in Zech 1:1, 7; 7:1. Zechariah 9–14, on the other hand, presents two sections of material, each of which is introduced by a superscription based on the term *maśśā²*, "oracle, pronouncement" (see Zech 9:1; 12:1). Each section then respectively presents an apocalyptic scenario of the return of Jerusalem's king and the removal of the corrupt shepherds (Zechariah 9–11) and YHWH's combat from Zion against the nations in which the Mount of Olives splits, day and night come to an end, and the nations ultimately submit to YHWH and celebrate the festival of Sukkoth (Zechariah 12–14). Zechariah 9–14 lack any reference to Zechariah, or indeed to any other identifiable figure. As a result, many interpreters argue for the presence of a Deutero-Zechariah and possibly a Trito-Zechariah in Zechariah 9–14 (or 9–11; 12–14) in addition to the work of the original prophet in chapters 1–8. The reference to the Greeks in Zech 9:13 prompted many scholars to speculate that these chapters may presuppose the conquest of the Near East by Alexander the Great in 333–323 B.C.E., but the portrayal of a confrontation between Jews and Greeks in the verse contradicts the generally warm reception that Alexander received in Jerusalem.[3] Interpreters are increasingly coming to recognize that these chapters apparently presuppose the period of the Persian empire with its long history of conflict between the Persians and the Greeks from the time of Darius' initial campaigns against Thrace and Macedonia in 516 B.C.E. through Alexander's campaigns beginning in 334 B.C.E.[4] Furthermore, the question of authorship is hardly settled as material

[2] See esp. Coggins, *Haggai, Zechariah, Malachi* 40–51, 60–72; Brevard S. Childs, *Introduction to the Old Testament as Scripture* (Philadelphia: Fortress, 1979) 472–87.

[3] For a brief account of Alexander's relations with Judea and Jerusalem, see "Alexander the Great," *Encyclopaedia Judaica* 2:577-80.

[4] See the comments by Petersen, *Zechariah 9–14 and Malachi* 3–6. For a detailed discussion of Persian history during this period, which encompasses the entire period of Achaemenid conflict against various Greek kingdoms and alliances, see M. A. Dandamaev, *A Political History of the Achaemenid Empire* (Leiden: Brill, 1989).

from Zechariah 9–14, for example, the first person account of the prophet's symbolic action concerning the shepherds in Zech 11:4-17, may well be derived from Zechariah, and Zechariah 1–8 clearly reflects the work of an editor other than Zechariah in Zech 1:1-6; 1:7; and 7:1–8:23.[5] Furthermore, various later additions or modifications appear to have been made to the vision reports in Zech 1:14b-17; 2:10-17 [NRSV: 2:6-13]; 3:8-10; 4:6aβ-10a; and 6:9-15.

Although the authorship of the book of Zechariah is in question, it is clearly designed to be read as a single work that depicts both the visions and the oracles or pronouncements of the prophet Zechariah.[6] The overall structure of the book appears to be defined in relation to the chronological statements in Zech 1:1, 7; and 7:1, and the overall generic contents of the book. Thus, Zech 1:1-6 presents the introduction to the book in which the narrator identifies the following material as the word of YHWH to Zechariah ben Berechiah ben Iddo in the eighth month of the second year of Darius (Heshvan or November/December, 520 B.C.E.) and then presents a statement by YHWH to the prophet that calls upon the people to return to YHWH so that the relationship between YHWH and the people might be restored. The balance of the book then presents the visions of the prophet in Zechariah 1:7–6:15 and the oracles or pronouncements of the prophet in Zechariah 7:1–14:21, each of which is introduced once again by the narrator's statement of the dates when YHWH's word came to the prophet.[7] The visions are dated to the twenty-fourth day of the eleventh month (Shebat, January/February) of Darius's second year (519 B.C.E.). They are cast as first person accounts by the prophet himself, who presents a total of eight visions, each of which takes up various aspects of the process and significance of Temple reconstruction, the ordination of Joshua ben Jehozadak, and the designation of Joshua as the "Branch." The presentation of the "oracles" or "pronouncements" is dated to the fourth day of the ninth month (Kislev, November/December) of Darius' fourth year (518 B.C.E.). They are introduced by a question posed to Zechariah in Zechariah 7–8 concerning the need for continued mourning for the loss of the Temple now that it is to be rebuilt. Zechariah's answer states that the times for

[5] See esp. Coggins, *Haggai, Zechariah, Malachi* 25–32.

[6] For discussions of the relationship between Zechariah 1–8 and 9–14 and the overall structure of the book as a whole, see Coggins, *Haggai, Zechariah, Malachi* 60–72; R. A. Mason, "The Relation of Zechariah 9–14 to Proto-Zechariah," *Zeitschrift für die alttestamentliche Wissenschaft* 88 (1976) 226–39; Childs, *Introduction to the Old Testament as Scripture* 475–86; Mike Butterworth, *Structure and the Book of Zechariah*, JSOTSup, vol. 130 (Sheffield: Sheffield Academic Press, 1992); Edgar Conrad, *Zechariah*, Readings (Sheffield: Sheffield Academic Press, 1999).

[7] See now Conrad, *Zechariah*, who arrives at a similar structure.

mourning are to be considered as a time for rejoicing as the nations will now recognize YHWH in Jerusalem as the Temple is rebuilt. The actual pronouncements in Zechariah 9–11 and 12–14 then spell out the process by which this scenario is to take place. First the "worthless shepherds," i.e., the Persian monarchs are to be removed as the true king returns to the land in Zechariah 9–11, and second, YHWH will defeat the nations that threaten Zion so that they will come to Zion at Sukkoth to recognize YHWH as the world-wide sovereign in Zechariah 12–14.

Introduction to the Book of Zechariah: Narrative concerning YHWH's Call through Zechariah for the People's Return: 1:1-6

The first major component of the book of Zechariah is Zech 1:1-6, which relates YHWH's call for the people's return. This concern underlies the entire book of Zechariah, which is designed to demonstrate the world-wide significance of YHWH's action in reestablishing the Temple in Jerusalem for the people of Israel/Judah, the nations, and the cosmos at large. The passage therefore serves as the introduction to the book of Zechariah. It is formulated as a narrative which relates YHWH's oracle to Zechariah in which the call is made. Although many prophetic books begin with a superscription which identifies the following materials as the words, oracles, and actions of the prophet (cf. Hos 1:1; Joel 1:1; Amos 1:1; Obad 1; Mic 1:1; Nah 1:1; Hab 1:1; Zeph 1:1; Mal 1:1; Isa 1:1; Jer 1:1-3), Zechariah is analogous to the prophetic books of Ezekiel, Jonah, and Haggai, which are also formulated as narratives. It begins with a reference to the transmission of the word of YHWH to Zechariah (cf. Jon 1:1) and the date on which that transmission took place in the eighth month of the second year of King Darius, i.e., in the month of Heshvan (October–November), 520 B.C.E. (cf. Ezek 1:1; Hag 1:1). The narrative concerning this oracle continues through verse 6. The appearance of a similar date formula for the transmission of another oracle by YHWH in Zech 1:7 marks the beginning of the next major component of the book of Zechariah. Although successive date formulas appear in Zech 1:7 and 7:1, the absence of a conjunction in Zech 1:7 and the presence of one in Zech 7:1 demonstrates that Zech 1:7–6:15 and the material introduced by Zech 7:1 are to be read together as two structural components of a larger unit within the book. At the same time, the three date formulas establish a chronological progression of oracles throughout the book during the eighth month of Darius' second year (Zech 1:1), the twenty-fourth day of the eleventh month in Darius'

second year (Zech 1:7), and the fourth day of the ninth month in Darius'
fourth year (Zech 7:1).

The narrative structure of Zech 1:1-6 is quite simple in that the dated
transmission formula of verse 1 introduces the quotation of YHWH's
words to Zechariah in verses 2-6. The Hebrew text mentions only the
month and the year in which the oracle is delivered. The eighth month
of the Jewish calendar, Heshvan, generally begins at some time in October and concludes in November. The Hebrew text does not mention
the day of the month, but the Syriac Peshitta version of the book adds
bḥd byrḥ, "on the first of the month." No other versions specify the day,
but the Peshitta translator apparently reasoned that the absence of a
reference to the day in a context that takes special care to specify days
elsewhere (see Zech 1:7; 7:1; cf. Hag 1:15; 2:10, 20; esp. 1:1; 2:1) must
indicate the first day of the month. The second year of Darius, the
Achaemenid monarch who ruled the Persian empire from 522 through
486 B.C.E., would be 520 B.C.E. As noted in the commentary on Haggai,
this would have been the time that Darius was putting down the various revolts that challenged his reign throughout the empire. Thus, the
oracle is placed following Haggai's first two oracles on the first day of
the sixth month (Elul; Hag 1:1-15a) and the first day of the seventh
month (Tishri; Hag 1:15b–2:9) of Darius' second year, and prior to the
two oracles delivered by Haggai on the twenty-fourth day of the ninth
month (Kislev; Hag 2:10-19; 2:20-23) in the same year. The sequence of
Zechariah's oracles therefore begins prior to Haggai's announcement
that Zerubbabel will serve as YHWH's "signet," which indicates that he
will serve as YHWH's chosen monarch in Jerusalem, but Zechariah's
subsequent oracles extend well beyond that time and make no overt
claims for Zerubbabel's kingship. Although it is possible that Zechariah
initially saw Zerubbabel as a potential Davidic monarch, the present
form of the book makes no such claim (see below on Zech 6:9-15).

The attention to the date and the specification of the identity of the
prophet in verse 1 indicates a "chronistic" literary style, like that of
Haggai, which would have been characteristic of post-exilic priestly
circles.[8] Although the YHWH word formula, *hāyâ dĕbar-yhwh ʾel*, "the
word of YHWH was unto," is characteristically employed to indicate the
transmission of a divine oracle to a prophet,[9] Zechariah must be identi-

---

[8] See especially Beuken, *Haggai-Sacharja 1–8* 84; cf. Coggins, *Haggai, Zechariah,
Malachi* 25–31; R. A. Mason, "The purpose of the 'editorial framework' of the book
of Haggai," *VT* 27 (1977) 413–21; idem, "The Prophets of the Restoration," *Israel's
Prophetic Tradition,* ed. R. Coggins, A. Phillips, and M. Knibb (Cambridge: Cambridge University Press, 1982) 137–54, esp. 144–6.

[9] Sweeney, *Isaiah 1–39* 546–7.

fied as a Zadokite priest as well as a prophet. Ezra 5:1 and 6:14 identify Zechariah ben Iddo as a prophet who, together with Haggai, called for the rebuilding of the Temple in Jerusalem at the time of the return to Jerusalem of Zerubbabel ben Shealtiel, grandson of King Jehoiachin of Judah who was exiled by Nebuchadnezzar (2 Kgs 24:8-17; 1 Chr 3:17-19), and Joshua ben Jehozadak, grandson of the high priest Seraiah who was killed by Nebuchadnezzar (2 Kgs 25:18-21; 1 Chr 5:40-41). According to Neh 12:4, Iddo was one of the priests who accompanied Zerubbabel and Jeshua (i.e., Joshua ben Jehozadak) on their return to Jerusalem, and Neh 12:16 names Zechariah as the head of the priestly house of Iddo. Some suggest that the placement of Zechariah in the days of Joiakim, son of Jeshua, might refer to a later priest with the same name,[10] but Zechariah ben Iddo would have been of the same generation as Joiakim ben Jeshua.

The identification of Zechariah in verse 1 as "the son of Berechiah son of Iddo" raises questions in that it suggests that the prophet Zechariah is in fact the grandson of Iddo. This identification is particularly significant in relation to Isa 8:2, which identifies "Zechariah ben Jeberechiah" as one of the two men engaged by the prophet Isaiah to serve as witnesses for the writing of the name Maher-shalal-hash-baz which was subsequently given to the prophet's son. Insofar as Berechiah *(berekyāhû)* is a variant of the name Jeberechiah *(yĕberekyāhû)*, many have supposed that there is some association between the prophet Zechariah and the figure mentioned in Isa 8:2.[11] The association is generally considered to be accidental or mistaken, but the book of Zechariah makes extensive use of the book of Isaiah. It is striking that in the same context as the mention of Zechariah ben Jeberechiah, Isa 8:16–9:6 calls for the sealing of testimony and torah among Isaiah's disciples so that the prophet might wait for YHWH, who hides the divine face from the house of Jacob. The prophet's children serve as signs and portents from YHWH, and the prophet looks forward to the emergence of a righteous monarch who will establish the Davidic throne in a time of peace (Isa 9:1-6). Elsewhere throughout the book of Isaiah, references are made to a future reading of the book of Isaiah at a time when the prophet's promises will be realized (see Isa 28:11-12; 30:8; 34:16-17; cf. 40:8b; 55:11). Indeed, the identification of the prophet as Zechariah ben Berechiah ben Iddo may well be deliberate in that the prophet and priest is presented as a witness to the fulfillment of the prophecy of Isaiah. The book of Isaiah looks forward to the time when YHWH will

[10] See the comments by Blenkinsopp, *Ezra-Nehemiah* 339.

[11] E.g., Meyers and Meyers, *Haggai, Zechariah 1–8* 92; Hanhart, *Sacharja* 19–20; Mitchell, *Zechariah* 81, 108.

cease to hide the divine face from Jacob (Isa 8:16–9:6), thereby restoring the people to the land of Israel and rebuilding both Jerusalem and the Temple (Isa 44:21-28; 45:1-7; 48:1-21). Those promises were about to be realized in the time of Zechariah; in the following material he makes explicit reference to the restoration of Jerusalem and the Temple (Zech 1:16-17); the role of the Davidide Zerubbabel in the building of the Temple (Zech 4:1-14); and the streaming of the nations to Zion to seek YHWH as stated in the book of Isaiah (Zech 8:20-23; cf. Isa 2:2-4). The following discussion of the "former prophets" in verses 2-6 and the extensive use made of earlier prophetic tradition, particularly of Isaiah, throughout the rest of the book also supports the contention that the authors of the book of Zechariah identify the prophet with the witness mentioned by Isaiah. In the time of the priest/prophet Zechariah, the promises made by YHWH and sealed in the time of Isaiah were about to be realized.

YHWH's oracle to Zechariah follows in verses 2-6. The statement, "and you shall say to them (NRSV, 'therefore say to them')" indicates that it is formulated as YHWH's instruction to the prophet to speak to the people. Apart from this phrase, however, the passage presents a transcript of what the prophet is to say to the people. As noted by Beuken, the prophet's speech to the people is formulated as a typical Levitical sermon in which Zechariah is to call upon them to return to YHWH.[12] The Levitical sermon generally addresses its audience in second person form, makes reference to past tradition (particularly to YHWH's commands or Torah), employs exhortation and parenetic forms in an attempt to persuade the audience to repent from some course of action or to return to YHWH.[13] Typical examples of the form appear in 2 Chr 15:1-7; 19:6-7; 20:15-17; 30:6-9; 32:7-8a (cf. Deut 20:1-9; Josh 1:1-11; Jer 7:1-26). The use of such a form is hardly surprising when one considers that Zechariah is a priest as well as a prophet.

Overall, the sermon is designed to persuade the people that the time of YHWH's anger is over and that it is therefore time to return to YHWH and, by implication, begin the process of rebuilding the Temple.

---

[12] Beuken, *Haggai-Sacharja 1–8* 88–115.

[13] For discussion of the Levitical sermon, see Gerhard von Rad, "The Levitical Sermon in I and II Chronicles," *The Problem of the Hexateuch and Other Essays* (London: SCM 1984) 267–80. See also his *Studies in Deuteronomy*, SBT, vol. 9 (London: SCM, 1953), in which he discusses sermonic forms in relation to Deuteronomy as well. More recently, R. A. Mason, *Preaching the Tradition: Homily and Hermeneutics after the Exile* (Cambridge: Cambridge University Press, 1990), has correctly challenged von Rad by pointing out that the sermon form is not inherently Levitical. The form must be understood simply as a sermon that is employed in a Levitical or priestly context.

An underlying premise of the sermon is that YHWH's anger against the people and, thus, YHWH's punishment of them in the form of exile and destruction of the first Temple, was justified because of their ancestors' previous rejection of YHWH and YHWH's commands. The initial premise of the sermon is stated in verse 2, "YHWH was very angry with your ancestors." This statement speaks to the concern held by many in the period of the exile and the early Persian period that YHWH was indeed angry with the people and that YHWH's anger had prompted the Babylonian exile and destruction of Jerusalem and the Temple. The question to be addressed, however, was whether or not YHWH was still angry. By stating this premise at the outset, the prophet would bring this fundamental concern out into the open and prepare the basis for the assertion that YHWH was ready to put anger aside if the people would return. This strategy becomes evident in verse 3 in which YHWH instructs the prophet to tell the people that YHWH will return to them if they will return to YHWH. As noted above, verse 3 begins with an explicit notice of YHWH's instruction to the prophet. This is followed by the messenger formula, which identifies the following statements as the exact words of YHWH. The primary goal of YHWH's, and thus the prophet's, exhortation is the appeal, "return to me *(šûbû ʾēlay)*." The verb *šûb*, "return," is commonly employed in calls for repentance, and it is a standard feature of Levitical sermons which call upon the people to return to YHWH (Hos 6:1; 14:2 [NRSV: 14:1]; Amos 4:6, 8, 9; Isa 9:12 [NRSV: 9:13]; 10:21; Jer 3:7; 1 Kgs 8:33, 48; 2 Chr 15:4; 30:9). The appeal, however, does not specify what exactly is meant by a return to YHWH, but the later references to YHWH's words and statutes suggests a general paradigm of obedience to YHWH or acceptance of YHWH as sovereign G–d. An example of the oracular formula, "says YHWH of Hosts *(nəʾum yhwh ṣəbāʾôt)* reinforces the early validation that this is a word from YHWH. The following statement, "and I will return to you," expresses YHWH's willingness to reciprocate so that the relationship will indeed be mutual, thereby signaling an end to YHWH's anger and punishment against the people. Fundamentally, the restoration of such a mutual relationship would revisit the ideology of the pre-exilic era in which the people of Israel, through the Davidic monarch and the Temple in Jerusalem, would enjoy a binding covenant relationship that would ensure YHWH's worship and Israel's security. Again, the speech formula, "says YHWH of Hosts *(ʾāmar yhwh ṣəbāʾôt)*" emphasizes that this is indeed YHWH's word.

Having established the general premises and goals of the appeal, the sermon turns in verses 4-6 to more specific elements of the proposed restoration of the relationship. In doing so, it establishes a sense of continuity between the people of Zechariah's generation and those of the pre-exilic period by holding up the people's ancestors and the pre-exilic prophets as examples of negative behavior, thereby pointing to the consequences of such action, and calling upon the people to re-ject those past models of actions for the future. Verse 4 calls upon the people not to be like their ancestors who did not listen to YHWH and YHWH's prophets. The verse lays out a scenario in which the people were warned to repent from evil actions by YHWH's prophets, and thereby assigns ultimate responsibility for the Babylonian exile to the people themselves rather than to YHWH. In this manner, YHWH/the prophet addresses a primary concern of the audience which would have some doubts as to whether YHWH's anger had indeed abated or whether YHWH was even capable of bringing about the proposed restoration of the Jerusalem Temple. The statement, "do not be like your ancestors," is formulated very similarly to 2 Chr 30:7 in which Hezekiah calls upon the people of Israel to observe Passover in Jeru-salem. The reference to "the former prophets *(hannĕbîʾîm harišōʾnîm)*" clearly calls to mind the many prophets who called upon the people to change or suffer punishment from YHWH in pre-exilic times, and aids in establishing the case that the people, and not YHWH, are ultimately re-sponsible for their fate. The expression "the former prophets *(hannĕbîʾîm harišōʾnîm)*" now designates the first part of the second major portion of the Hebrew Bible, "The Prophets," in Judaism (i.e., Joshua; Judges; Samuel; Kings). Verse 4 contains a quotation from the prophets, identi-fied by the characteristic messenger formula, that calls upon the people to "return from your evil ways and from your evil deeds *(šûbû nāʾ middarkêkem hārāʿîm ûmaʿăllêkem [qere] hārāʿîm)*." Such language is char-acteristic of the prophet Jeremiah (Jer 15:7; 18:8, 11; 25:5; 26:3; 35:15; 36:3, 7; 44:5; 23:14, 22) and the Deuteronomistic historical work (1 Kgs 8:35; 13:33; 2 Kgs 17:13), with which Jeremiah is frequently associated.[14] Again, the association with Jeremiah points to the language of the Levitical sermon in that Jeremiah was an Elide priest. Beuken relates the statement that "they did not hear or heed me *(wĕlōʾ šāmĕʿû wĕlōʾ hiqšîbû ʾēlay)* to typical forms of Chronistic language (Neh 9:16-17, 29; 2 Chr 25:16, 20; 35:22 [cf. Dan 9:6]; cf. 2 Chr 24:19).[15] The concluding oracular formula again validates this statement as a word from YHWH.

Verse 5 then poses the rhetorical questions, "Your ancestors, where are they? And the prophets, do they live forever?" The answers are ob-viously that the ancestors and the prophets are now long dead and gone. By directing this question to the audience, however, YHWH or the

[14] See Beuken, *Haggai-Sacharja 1–8* 97, nn. 3, 4 for these citations, which he draws from William Holladay, *The Root Shûbh in the Old Testament* (Leiden: Brill, 1958) 80.

[15] Beuken, *Haggai-Sacharja 1–8* 98.

prophet will prompt their listeners or readers to conclude that the circumstances of the past are now gone as well, and that the new situation presents an opportunity to restore the relationship between YHWH and the people that had been disrupted throughout the period of the Babylonian exile. Verse 6 then follows up with statements concerning the responsibility of the ancestors for their fate as a means to prompt the contemporary audience to ponder its own response to the proposal. Verse 6a employs another rhetorical question to assert that the ancestors were overtaken by YHWH's words and statutes as commanded by the prophets. Once again, the sermon blames the people for their own suffering, and highlights the role of the prophets in delivering YHWH's warning to the people. Of course, this serves as a subtle reminder to the audience that they should heed the words of Zechariah, YHWH's present prophet. Verse 6b concludes by placing a statement of responsibility in the mouths of the ancestors, i.e., "YHWH of Hosts has dealt with us according to our ways and deeds, just as he planned to do." The English word "planned" suggests that YHWH planned punishment all along regardless of the actions of the people, but the Hebrew verb *zāmam* is best rendered as "proposed," which indicates the propositional nature of the punishment. In any case, verse 6b indicates that the ancestors themselves recognized that they themselves were to blame for their misfortunes, which of course suggests to the present audience that they are capable of taking appropriate action to avoid such a catastrophe. They simply need to obey YHWH, and do what the prophet asks of them.

Narrative Presentation of YHWH's words to Zechariah: 1:7–14:21

Following the introductory narrative in Zech 1:1-6 concerning YHWH's call for the people's return, Zech 1:7–14:21 constitutes the second major structural component of the book of Zechariah as a whole. Zechariah 1:7–14:21 employs a narrative form to present an account of the transmission of YHWH's words to the prophet Zechariah. This concern is evident in the initial statement of the block in Zech 1:7, "On the twenty-fourth day of the eleventh month, the month of Shebat, in the second year of Darius, the word of YHWH came to the prophet Zechariah son of Berechiah son of Iddo; and Zechariah said . . ." It is also evident in Zech 7:1, which employs another date formula to follow upon the first, "In the fourth year of King Darius, the word of YHWH came to Zechariah on the fourth day of the ninth month which is Chislev." The absence of a syntactical connector at the beginning of

Zech 1:7 clearly identifies this statement as the introduction to a new structural block within the book of Zechariah. The appearance of syntactical connector at the beginning of Zech 7:1, *wayĕhî bišnat ʾarbaʿ*, "and it came to pass in the fourth year . . . ," and its later date relative to Zech 1:7 indicate that the block beginning in Zech 7:1 is subsumed structurally to Zech 1:7 so that Zech 1:7–14:21 form a single unit with two major components concerned with the transmission of YHWH's word to Zechariah on two successive dates. Zechariah 1:7–6:15 relates YHWH's word to Zechariah on the twenty-fourth day of Shebat in 520 B.C.E. in the form of eight visions. Zechariah 7:1–14:21 relates YHWH's word to Zechariah on the fourth day of Chislev in 518 B.C.E. The form of this second block includes two reports concerning the transmission of YHWH's words to Zechariah in Zech 7:1-7 and 7:8–14:21 that are identified by third person references to Zechariah, viz., "the word of YHWH came to Zechariah." Although first person references to the transmission of YHWH's word to Zechariah, viz., "the word of YHWH of Hosts came to me, saying," appear in Zech 7:8; 8:1(?); and 8:18, these notices are subsumed structurally to the third person notices that characterize the whole as a third person report in which the words of the prophet are included. The two blocks of material in Zechariah 9–11 and 12–14, each of which is introduced by the syntactically independent superscription, *maśśāʾ*, "an oracle (pronouncement),"[16] must be included as part of the third person report of the transmission of YHWH's word to Zechariah beginning in Zech 7:8. Although the material in chapters 9–11; 12–14 was likely composed independently from that in chapters 7–8, they now function as oracles that explain how YHWH's statements concerning the restoration of Zion transmitted to the prophet in Zech 7:8–8:21 will be realized in the world.

Narrative concerning the Transmission of YHWH's
Word to Zechariah on the Twenty-fourth of Shebat, 520 B.C.E.:
The Visions of Zechariah: 1:7–6:15

Zechariah 1:7–6:15 constitutes a narrative report concerning the transmission of YHWH's word to Zechariah on the twenty-fourth day of the eleventh month, i.e., Shebat, in the second year of the reign of King Darius of Persia, i.e., 520 B.C.E. The twenty-fourth day of Shebat would place this transmission sometime in late-January through late-February,

---

[16] For discussion of the *maśśāʾ*, "pronouncement, oracle," see Sweeney, *Isaiah 1-39* 534–5; R. D. Weis, "Oracle," *ABD* V:28-9.

some three and one half months following the transmission of YHWH's initial word to Zechariah in Zech 1:1-6 and exactly two months following the transmission of YHWH's last words to Haggai in Hag 2:10-19 and 2:20-23. There appears to be no particular significance to this date, although Deut 1:3 states that Moses began his last speech to the people of Israel, in which he "repeated" YHWH's Torah to them, on the first day of the eleventh month, immediately prior to his death and the conquest of the land of Israel under Joshua. Again, the date formula appears together with an example of the YHWH word transmission formula,[17] which validates the following material as the word of YHWH, and the full identification of Zechariah the prophet as the son of Berechiah and the grandson of Iddo. As indicated above, this pedigree identifies Zechariah as a Zadokite priest and as the witness to fulfillment of the prophet Isaiah's prophecies as stated in Isa 8:2. In any case, the date and the images of the reconstruction of the altar (Zech 2:1-4 [NRSV: 1:18-21]), the measurement of the city (Zech 2:5-17 [NRSV: 2:1-13]), the ordination of Joshua ben Jehozadak (Zech 3:1-10), etc., indicate that it appears to be quite early in the process of Temple reconstruction. The structure of this block of material is determined by the initial third person date formula in Zech 1:7 and the successive presentation of eight first person vision reports by Zechariah in Zech 1:8-17; 2:1-4 [NRSV: 1:18-21]; 2:5-17 [NRSV: 2:1-13]; 3:1-10; 4:1-14; 5:1-8; 5:9-11; and 6:1-15, all of which are concerned with some aspect of the inauguration of service at the site of the soon-to-be-constructed Temple.

THE REPORT OF THE FIRST VISION:
YHWH'S HORSES PATROLLING THE EARTH: 1:8-17

Zechariah 1:8-17 introduces the sequence of visions that constitute YHWH's word to Zechariah on the twenty-fourth of Shevat, 520 B.C.E. Zechariah's account of his first vision is formulated as a first person report. Overall, the prophet recounts his encounter with a "man" riding a horse, who is later identified as YHWH's "messenger" or "angel," and who informs the prophet of the significance of the vision of horses hidden in a glen of myrtles. By the end of the prophet's report, it becomes clear that this vision signifies YHWH's decision to restore Jerusalem or Zion and to rebuild the Temple.

Verse 8 begins with the syntactically independent verb *rā'îtî*, "I saw," which marks the beginning of the sequence of visions throughout Zech 1:8–6:15, in that all of the subsequent visions begin with some

[17] See Sweeney, *Isaiah 1–39* 546–7.

form of the syntactical conjunction *waw*. The prophet begins his account of the first vision in verse 8 with a simple statement concerning the setting of his vision at night and a description of what he sees. The nighttime setting of the vision suggests the possibility of a dream with which many prophetic visions are associated (Num 12:6; Joel 3:1 [NRSV: 2:28]; Job 33:15; Dan 2:1, 2; cf. Deut 13:2, 4 [NRSV: 13:1, 2]; Jer 23:27, 28; 27:9; 29:8; Zech 10:2; see also Gen 20:3; 31:10, 11, 24; 37:5, 6; 40:5, etc.), although no specific reference is made to a dream (but see Zech 4:1). The prophet describes a man riding upon a red horse standing in the midst of a glen of myrtle trees with horses of red, sorrel, and white standing behind him. This statement presents several issues, particularly in relation to the significance of the colors of the horses and the glen of myrtles, that are relevant for interpreting the significance of the vision as a whole. The identification of the glen of myrtle trees is of paramount importance in that there is a correspondence between the flowers of the myrtle and the horses that are described in the vision. The common myrtle *(myrtus communis)* is native to the eastern Mediterranean region, particularly to the damp plains of the banks of the Jordan River, the Dan Valley, the upper Galilee, the Golan, and Mt. Carmel.[18] It has two names in Hebrew, *ʿēṣ ʿābôt* (Lev 23:40; Neh 8:15) and *hadas* as employed in the present text (Neh 8:15); the latter name stands as the base for the Hebrew name of Esther, i.e., Hadassah (Esth 2:7). The myrtle is an evergreen shrub that grows to a height of approximately 2 meters, and its dense branches produce olive-shaped leaves that grow in opposite pairs, although groupings of three or four leaves may also be produced. It blossoms in the summer, and its flowers are white and sometimes rose colored. Its berries are blackish-blue. Myrtles play a role in ancient mythologies in that their evergreen character prompts statements that their long roots reach to the depths of the subterranean waters so that they are always supplied with water.[19] The use of the term, "glen," *mĕṣulâ*, may suggest this role as well.[20] It is a *hapax legomenon* of uncertain meaning, although it may be derived from the root *ṣll* which means "to grow dark" or "to shadow," from which the meaning "glen" is derived.[21] Interpreters note, however, that it may be

---

[18] For discussion of the myrtle, see Harold N. Moldenke and Alma L. Moldenke, *Plants of the Bible* (New York: Ronald Press, 1952) 143–5; Michael Zohary, *Plants of the Bible* (Cambridge: Cambridge University Press, 1982) 119; and "Myrtle," *Encylcopaedia Judaica* 12:728-9.

[19] Klaus Seybold, *Bilder zum Tempelbau. Die Visionen des Propheten Sacharja*, SBS, vol. 70 (Stuttgart: Katholisches Bibelwerk, 1974) 70.

[20] Ibid., 67–9.

[21] BDB, 853, 846–7.

closely associated with the root *ṣwl*, which stands at the base of *ṣûlâ*, "ocean deep" (Isa 44:27), and *mĕṣôlâ*, "depth, deep" (Exod 15:5; Neh 9:11; Mic 7:19; Jon 2:4 [NRSV: 2:3]; Zech 10:11; Job 41:23). The myrtle's aromatic branches made it useful in betrothal rites, remedies of various sorts, and as a decorative plant for royal gardens and palaces. In Jewish tradition, the myrtle is one of the "four species" of plants that are waved as part of the Lulav at the festival of Sukkoth (Lev 23:40; Neh 8:15) to symbolize the rebirth of creation in the fall at the time when the rainy season of Israel begins. It appears likewise in Isa 41:19 and 55:13 as one of the symbols of the rebirth of creation at the time when YHWH will bring the exiled people of Israel back to Jerusalem, rebuild the Temple, and manifest divine sovereignty over the entire natural and human world. It is noteworthy, therefore, that Sukkoth is the time when Solomon dedicated the first Temple (1 Kgs 8:65-66; 2 Chr 7:8-10), Jeroboam dedicated the altar at Beth El (1 Kgs 12:32, n.b., the northern festival was in the eighth month, but it was analogous to the Judean Sukkoth), and Zerubbabel and Joshua ben Jehozadak dedicated the altar of the second Temple (Ezra 3:1-7). The seven day dedication ceremony for the altar and the ordination of priests fits well with the seven day celebration of Sukkoth (see Exod 29:35-37; cf. Leviticus 8). The colors of the horses, red, sorrel, and white, appear to correspond to the colors of the myrtle's flowers, and the setting in February indicates the time immediately prior to the spring time when the myrtle can first be expected to flower. The use of three colors may also be relevant as the three-leaved branches tend to be preferred for use in the Lulav at Sukkoth (bSuk 12a). Furthermore, the leaves are shaped like eyes, and appear to stand behind the role of the horses as YHWH's patrols that are sent to search out the earth. Altogether, the imagery of the myrtle suggests that the site of myrtle grove or glen near the site of the Temple may well have prompted this vision of the horses sent by YHWH to patrol the earth. Certainly, the role of the myrtle at Sukkoth as a symbol of rebirth and new creation would fit well with the role of the Temple as the center of creation and the cosmos.

The prophet begins an interchange with the "man" on the horse by asking, "what are these, my lord?" which of course provides the occasion for an explanation. A figure who is identified as "the angel who talks with me" gives his answer, but the repeated reference in verse 10 to "the man who was standing among the myrtle trees" suggests that the "man" and the "angel" are two different figures. Nevertheless, verse 11 combines the two descriptions as "the angel of YHWH who was standing among the myrtle trees," and thereby demonstrates that the "man" and the "angel" are one and the same. The use of the term *malʾāk*, "messenger, angel," identifies him as a divine emissary. Such figures appear frequently in apocalyptic literature to guide their charges in the course of a vision and to explain the significance of what is seen (cf. Ezek 8:2; Dan 10:5).[22] He states to Zechariah that he will show the prophet what these things are. "The man standing among the myrtle trees" then begins to provide the explanation in verse 10 by stating that "they (the horses) are those whom YHWH has sent to patrol the earth." The term "patrol," *lĕhithallēk,* means literally, "to move to and fro," and by inference signifies that their role is to patrol or keep watch on behalf of YHWH. In verse 11, the horses themselves answer the angel by stating that they have been sent to patrol the earth and that the earth "remains at peace" (*yōšbet wĕšōqāṭet,* literally, "still and quiet"). The image of horses patrolling the earth on behalf of YHWH corresponds to the historical reality of the horse-mounted messengers that were employed extensively throughout the Persian empire to facilitate communications between the king and his satraps and to provide the king with information as to the state of affairs throughout the empire.[23] During the latter part of the second year of Darius, 520 B.C.E., the various revolts that had broken out following the death of Cambyses in 522 B.C.E. had been put down. It would appear that this time of quiet is understood in the prophet's vision as the time when YHWH would begin to act.

The vision shifts in verses 12-17 to YHWH's statements that will provide a full explanation of the purpose of this vision. Verse 12 begins with a presentation of the angel's question to YHWH, "O YHWH of Hosts, how long will you withhold mercy from Jerusalem and the cities of Judah with which you have been angry these seventy years?" The question deliberately alludes to both Isaiah and Jeremiah in an effort to address issues concerning the time of Israel's exile that are raised in these respective prophetic books. The question, "how long? (*ʿad mātay),*" for example, is frequently identified as a characteristic element in an individual or communal psalm of lament in which the petitioner requests that YHWH bring an end to a situation of strife (Pss 6:4 [NRSV: 6:3]; 13:2-4 [NRSV: 13:1-3]; 79:5; 80:5 [NRSV: 80:4]; 90:13),[24] but it also appears in Isaiah's address to YHWH at the time of his inaugural vision in which YHWH informs the prophet that Israel is to be punished (Isaiah 6). After YHWH states that Isaiah's task is to "make the mind of this people dull, and stop their ears, and shut their eyes, so that they may not look with their eyes, and listen with their ears, and comprehend with their

---

[22] For discussion of apocalyptic literature, see John J. Collins, *Daniel, with an Introduction to Apocalyptic Literature,* FOTL, vol. 20 (Grand Rapids: Eerdmans, 1984) 2–24.

[23] Petersen, *Haggai, Zechariah 1–8* 144–5.

[24] Ibid., 146.

minds, and turn and be healed" (Isa 6:10), the prophet asks, "how long, O YHWH?" (Isa 6:11a). The response in Isa 6:11b-13 indicates that the punishment will last "until cities lie waste" and "until YHWH sends everyone away" until only a tenth of the population survives that will then form the basis of a restored Judah. Isaiah 6 of course includes Jerusalem and the cities of Judah, and Isaiah 36–37 portrays the Assyrian devastation of the cities of Judah (Isa 36:1) and its siege of Jerusalem. Likewise, Jeremiah 39 portrays the destruction of Jerusalem by the Babylonians, and Jer 25:11 and 29:10 state that the period of Judah's service or exile to Babylon will last for seventy years, after which time YHWH will act to restore the exiled people and the Temple to the city of Jerusalem. The rebuilding of the Temple by Zerubbabel and Joshua ben Jehozadak may have been timed to coincide with Jeremiah's statements; after all, the destruction of the Temple took place in 587 B.C.E. and its reconstruction during the years 520–515 would coincide with the period stated in Jeremiah. Under such circumstances, the prophet Zechariah ben Berechiah ben Iddo would be a witness to the fulfillment of the prophecies of both Isaiah (cf. Isa 8:2) and Jeremiah concerning the time of Jerusalem's and the Temple's restoration following the period of exile that was stated in both prophetic books.

The initial response of YHWH in verse 13 indicates that YHWH answers with "gracious and comforting words" (*děbārîm ṭôbîm děbārîm niḥumîm*, literally, "good words, comforting words"). The reference to "comforting words" also alludes to Isaiah, in which Second Isaiah begins in Isa 40:1 with the statement, "comfort, comfort (*naḥămû naḥămû*), my people," as a means to announce that the period of Israel's exile to Babylon has come to an end and that it is time to return to Jerusalem to restore the Temple. YHWH's full statement then follows in verses 14-17, which points to the role of this vision in relation to the decision to rebuild the Temple. Verse 14aα introduces the speech of the angel to Zechariah in verses 14aβ-17 which transmits YHWH's oracles. Overall, the angel's speech constitutes two instructions to the prophet in verses 14aβ-16 and 17 to "proclaim (*qĕrā'*)" the messages that follow each instruction. The first instruction in verses 14aβ-16 calls upon the prophet to deliver two interrelated oracles, each of which is introduced by the messenger formula, "thus says YHWH of Hosts." The first oracle in verses 14aβ-15 presents YHWH's statement in verses 14b-15 immediately following the appearance of the messenger formula. YHWH speaks in the first person, and begins by stating divine "jealousy" or "zeal" on behalf of Jerusalem and Zion. Various forms of the root *qn'*, "to be jealous/zealous," are often employed to describe YHWH's special relationship with and concern for Jerusalem and the people of Israel/Judah (Isa 9:6 [NRSV: 9:7]; 37:32=2 Kgs 19:31; Isa 42:13; 59:17; 63:15; Exod 34:14; Deut

4:24; 6:15). In the present context, it indicates that YHWH's anger against Jerusalem and the people has abated (cf. Zech 1:2), and that it is now directed against "the nations that are at ease." This description of the nations calls to mind the role of the nations that were called upon to punish Israel/Judah and Jerusalem in prior prophetic books, but it suggests that these nations have not yet received the punishment due to them as indicated in the various collections of oracles against the nations (Isaiah 13–23; 34; 47; Jeremiah 46–51; Ezekiel 28–32; Zeph 2:4-15; Nahum; Obadiah). YHWH specifies that the divine anger against the nations is "great," and indicates that the reason for such anger may be found in the nations' efforts to make the disaster worse. This calls to mind the role of Assyria in the book of Isaiah, which was called by YHWH to punish Israel and Judah, but whose king blasphemed against YHWH by likening YHWH to the various deities of the nations that Assyria had conquered and thereby prompted YHWH's wrath (see Isa 10:5-11:16; 36–37). This initial concern with YHWH's zeal for Zion and wrath against the nations leads to the second oracle in verse 16. The verse begins with *lākēn*, "therefore," which indicates that it is presented as a consequence of the previous oracle. It, too, begins with the messenger formula which identifies it as a statement by YHWH. Here YHWH states explicitly the primary concern and goal of the entire vision and indeed of the visions of Zechariah as a whole, "I have returned to Jerusalem with compassion; my house shall be built in it." The following appearance of the oracular formula reinforces the validation of this statement as a word of YHWH. The following statement, "and the measuring line shall be stretched out over Jerusalem," offers an interesting combination of puns and allusions. The term *qāw*, "measuring line," is sometimes employed as a metaphor of destruction against a party that is condemned by YHWH (2 Kgs 21:13; Isa 34:11; Lam 2:8), including Zion in Isa 28:17. At the same time, the term is employed in relation to marking off land for possession (Isa 34:17) or in reference to the building or restoration of the Temple and its fixtures (1 Kgs 7:23; 2 Chr 4:2; Ezek 47:3; cf. Jer 31:39). The *Qere* form of the term, *qwh*, may constitute a pun in that the root *qwh* stands at the base of *tiqwâ* and *miqweh*, both of which mean, "hope" (see Hos 2:17 [NRSV: 2:15]; Jer 31:17; 29:11; 14:8; 17:13; Ezra 10:2; 1 Chr 29:15). In any case, the message is clear: YHWH has returned to Jerusalem and the Temple will be rebuilt.

The second instruction to the prophet in verse 17 reiterates this message. It is clearly linked to the preceding by the introductory statement, "proclaim further" (*ʿôd qĕrāʾ*, literally, "again, proclaim"), and by the following messenger formula. YHWH's message is unequivocal in its support for the restoration of Jerusalem and Judah. YHWH states that "my cities," i.e., the cities of Judah that were destroyed by foreign invasion (cf. verse 12 above) will "overflow" with "prosperity" or "good-ness," thereby reiterating a theme that appears in Hos 14:5-8; Joel 4:18-21 [NRSV: 3:18-21]; Amos 9:11-15, and elsewhere. The oracle concludes with two more unequivocal statements, apparently by the angel speaking on behalf of YHWH, "YHWH will again comfort Zion and again choose Jerusalem." The language of comfort of course relates to that of Isa 40:1 as noted above in reference to verse 13, and the choice of Jerusalem reiterates the motifs of YHWH's choice of Abraham (Neh 9:7), David (1 Kgs 8:16=2 Chr 6:6); Jerusalem/Zion (Isa 14:1; Ps 132:13; 2 Chr 6:6; Zech 2:16 [NRSV: 2:12]; 3:2); and the people of Israel (Deut 7:7; Isa 44:1; Ezek 20:5). By stating YHWH's comfort for and choice of Jerusalem/Zion, the oracle emphasizes that the time of punishment is ended (Isa 40:1-2), and that Jerusalem will resume its place as the site of YHWH's revelation to Israel/Judah and the world at large (cf. Isa 2:2-4).

THE REPORT OF THE SECOND VISION:
THE FOUR HORNS AND THE FOUR ARTISANS: 2:1-4 [NRSV: 1:18-21]

The narrative presentation of Zechariah's second vision appears in Zech 2:1-4 [NRSV: 1:18-21], which portrays the four horns that scattered the people of Israel, Judah, and Jerusalem and the four artisans who come to cast down the horns of the nations that have inflicted this punishment upon Judah. The repetition of formulae for the prophet's visionary experience and his questioning of the angelic figures concerning the significance of the visions in verses 1-2 [NRSV: 18-19] and 3-4 [NRSV: 20-21] suggests the possibility that these segments might constitute two vision reports, but the close parallels in the contents of the visions and their interrelationship indicates that they are to be read as one.

The first portion of the vision appears in verses 1-2 [NRSV: 18-19], which begin with the formula, "and I looked up and saw . . . *(wā'eśśā' 'et-ʿênay wā'ēre' wĕhinnēh)*." The vision of the four horns has been the subject of various explanations, including animal horns, horns in the ground, the horns of a war helmet, and the horns of the Temple altar in Jerusalem.[25] The term "horn" *(qeren)* is frequently employed as a symbol of power or strength (e.g., Pss 75:11 [NRSV: 75:10]; 92:11 [NRSV: 92:10]; 112:9), such as that of Hannah (1 Sam 2:1), YHWH's king (1 Sam 2:10; Ps 89:25 [NRSV: 89:24]), Moab (Jer 48:25), Israel's enemies (Lam 2:17), or Israel itself (Lam 2:3). Deuteronomy 33:17 depicts Joseph's power by employing the image of the first-born bull or wild ox, whose horns

---

[25] Ibid., 162.

gore his enemies and drive them away. Likewise, the prophet Zedekiah ben Chenaanah makes horns of iron and dons them symbolically to "chase" the enemies of King Ahab and thereby to predict his victory over the Arameans at the upcoming battle at Ramoth-Gilead (1 Kings 22). The term may also denote rays or flashes of lightning that serve as YHWH's weapons to defeat enemies (Hab 3:4). The number four must also be considered, however, as the portrayal of four horns relates specifically to the four horns of the typical Israelite altar (Amos 3:14; Jer 17:1; Ezek 43:15, 20; Ps 118:27; Exod 27:2; Lev 4:7; 1 Kgs 1:50, 51; 2:28). Again, the horns depict YHWH's power, and the number four represents the four cardinal directions to indicate that YHWH's power is manifested throughout the whole of creation.[26] It would appear that Zechariah's vision is based upon the image of the Jerusalem Temple altar that was built at the time that Zerubbabel and Joshua ben Jehozadak returned to Jerusalem in 522 B.C.E. (Ezra 3:1-7). Like the preceding image of the horses hidden in the myrtle glen, the reconstruction of the altar would signal YHWH's plans to realize the restoration of Jerusalem and to manifest divine sovereignty in the world at large. The prophet asks the angel who speaks with him to explain the significance of the vision. The angel simply states that "these are the horns that have scattered Judah, Israel, and Jerusalem." The verb "scattered," *zērû*, relates to the setting of the altar and Temple as a site for processing the grain offerings of the people as the verb *zrh* also means "to winnow" (see Ruth 3:2; Isa 30:24; cf. 2 Sam 24:18-25; 1 Chr 21:18–22:1, which identifies the threshing floor of Araunah/Ornan as the site of the Jerusalem Temple). In this respect, it depicts the process of YHWH's judgment against the people as a process of winnowing in which grain is crushed and thrown up into the wind to separate the grain from the chaff (cf. Isa 41:14-16; Jer 4:11; 15:7). The identification of the four horns of the altar as those that scattered and thus punished the people is consistent with the perspective of the book of Zechariah as a whole which identifies YHWH as the one who brought about Israel's punishment in the first place and is now acting to bring about the restoration (see Zech 1:1-6).

The second portion of the vision in verses 3-4 [NRSV: 20-21] mirrors the presentation in verses 1-2 [NRSV: 18-19] insofar as it also employs the image of the four horns that scattered Judah. It differs in several significant respects so that it points both to YHWH's prior punishment of Israel and to YHWH's present actions against the nations that oppressed the people in carrying out this punishment. The passage be-

---

[26] On the cosmic significance of the Temple, see Jon D. Levenson, "The Temple and the World," *JR* 64 (1984) 275–98; idem, *Sinai and Zion: An Entry Into the Jewish Bible* (Minneapolis: Winston, 1985) esp. 111–42.

gins with the formula, "then Yhwh showed me . . . *(wayyarᵊēnî yhwh),"* which might seem to duplicate the initial vision formula of verse 1 [NRSV: 18]. Nevertheless, the identification of Yhwh as the one who shows the prophet this vision is important because it points to Yhwh as the source of the visions shown to the prophet by the angel. It thereby serves as a device that allows the prophet (and thus the reader) to probe behind the significance of the initial vision, which points to Yhwh's punishment of the people, to point to Yhwh's present action of restoration. In this instance, the prophet sees four artisans *(ḥārāšîm).* The correspondence in the number four naturally points to an association between the artisans and the previously mentioned four horns. The term *ḥārāš* denotes workers in metal (1 Sam 13:19; Hos 8:6), wood (2 Sam 5:11; 2 Kgs 12:12), and stone (2 Sam 5:11; Exod 28:11), and it is employed to describe both Bezalel ben Uri ben Hur and Oholiab ben Ahisamach, the artisans who were commissioned by Yhwh and Moses to build the wilderness tabernacle and all of its furnishings (Exod 35:30-35; 38:22-23). Of course, this would also include construction of the altar with four horns (Exod 27:1-8; 38:1-8). The term is also employed to describe the artisans who rebuilt the altar on the site of the Temple at the time of Zerubbabel's and Joshua ben Jehozadak's return (Ezra 3:7). The prophet requests in verse 4 that Yhwh explain to him the significance of this vision. Yhwh's response begins with reference to the four horns which scattered Judah, although the qualification, "so that no head could be raised," is added to indicate the excessive force with which the punishment was carried out (cf. Isa 10:5-34). The explanation then shifts to the artisans themselves who come "to terrify them." The term "to terrify" employs the *hiphil* form of the verb *ḥrd,* which also appears in contexts that describe the excessive force of the Assyrians or other nations that struck against Israel at Yhwh's bidding (Isa 10:29) or the fear that they will experience when Yhwh comes to punish them (Isa 19:16; 32:11). The participle form frequently appears in the formulaic statement that none shall terrify the people in a time of peace (e.g., Lev 26:6; Jer 30:10; Ezek 34:28; Mic 4:4; Zeph 3:13; Isa 17:2). The referent for "them" is uncertain as it is formulated as a masculine pronoun *(ᵓōtām),* but "horns" is a feminine plural *(qĕrānôt).* It seems most likely that "them" anticipates the following masculine plural term for the "nations" *(gôyîm)* that threaten Israel. The explanation of the vision continues with the statement that the task of the artisans is "to strike down the horns of the nations that lifted up their horns against the land of Judah to scatter it." This, of course, entails a reversal of the image of Yhwh's punishment of Israel as symbolized by the initial presentation of the four horns. But it also identifies the four horns with the artisans who built them, and thereby signals that the horns of the altar, which symbolize Y<small>HWH</small>'s power throughout the world, also symbolize Y<small>HWH</small>'s actions to restore the people of Israel, Judah, and Jerusalem now that the period of punishment is over.

THE REPORT OF THE THIRD VISION:
YHWH'S WALL OF FIRE AROUND JERUSALEM AND THE MESSAGE
FROM YHWH'S ANGEL TO ZECHARIAH: 2:5-17 [NRSV: 2:1-13]

Zechariah 2:5-17 [NRSV: 2:1-13] constitutes the third vision report of the prophet Zechariah. Although most scholars argue that verses 10-17 [NRSV: 6-13] comprise a secondary addition to the original vision report in verses 5-9 [NRSV: 1-5],[27] the latter verses are subsumed structurally into the speech by the second angel to Zechariah that begins in verse 8 [NRSV: 3]. Verses 10-17 [NRSV: 6-13] contain examples of the oracular formula in verses 10a, 10b, and 14b [NRSV: 6a, 6b, 10b] together with a messenger formula in verse 12a [NRSV: 8a] that identify Y<small>HWH</small> as the speaker of these words. Nevertheless, the third person references to Y<small>HWH</small> in verses 13b, 15a, 15b, 16, and 17 [NRSV: 9b, 11a, 11b, 12, and 13], and the repeated occurrences of the term *šĕlaḥānî,* "he has sent me," demonstrate that Y<small>HWH</small> cannot be the speaker of these words, unless they are understood to be the quotations of statement that Y<small>HWH</small> expects another party to speak. The reference to "me" in this phrase cannot refer to Y<small>HWH</small>. Y<small>HWH</small> is not sent by anyone, and the appearances of the phrase in verses 13b and 15b [NRSV: 9b and 11b] explicitly identifies Y<small>HWH</small> as the one who has "sent me." The reference can then only be to the prophet Zechariah who is instructed by Y<small>HWH</small>/the angel to state that Y<small>HWH</small> has sent him. The angel thereby instructs Zechariah to speak Y<small>HWH</small>'s oracles and to add his own statements that elucidate Y<small>HWH</small>'s words.

The vision report begins with the formulaic statement analogous to Zech 2:5 [NRSV: 2:1] in which the prophet states, "I looked up and saw a man with a measuring line in his hand." The vision is reminiscent of Amos 7:7-9 in which Amos saw Y<small>HWH</small> with a plumbline in the divine hand that was to symbolize Y<small>HWH</small>'s "measuring" the "straightness" or moral character of Israel as part of a divine decision to bring judgment upon Israel. A "measuring line" *(hebel middâ)* is simply a device employed to measure the boundaries of land that are to be assigned as the

---

[27] E.g., Reventlow, *Haggai, Sacharja und Maleachi* 48–50; Amsler, *Zacharie 1–8* 73; Petersen, *Haggai, Zechariah 1–8* 174; Petitjean, *Les oracles* 89–94. Cf. Hanhart, *Sacharja* 120–37; Redditt, *Haggai, Zechariah, Malachi* 59; Meyers and Meyers, *Haggai, Zechariah 1–8* 172.

inheritance or the property of a tribe or an individual (cf. Mic 2:4-5; Amos 7:7; Deut 32:9; 1 Chr 16:18=Ps 105:11; Josh 17:5, 14; 19:9; Ezek 47:13; Deut 3:4, 13, 14; 1 Kgs 4:13). In the present case, the measuring line must be understood in reference to the reconstruction of the Temple and perhaps also to rebuilding within the city of Jerusalem itself. The reconstruction of the Temple would certainly require measurements to determine its overall structure and continuing measurements to ensure that the structure was properly built and structures within the city would require similar measurement. Again in characteristic form, the prophet asks for an explanation of the vision. In this case, however, his question to the angel is, "where are you going?" The response is that the angel intends to measure Jerusalem to determine "its width" *(rāḥbāh)* and "its length" *(ʾārkāh)*. It is noteworthy that the terms *rōḥab*, "width," and *ʾōrek*, "length," appear elsewhere in the Hebrew Bible in relation to the measurements of the wilderness tabernacle and its furnishings (Exod 25:10, 17; 26:2, 8; 27:1, 9, 12, 13, 18; 38:1), Solomon's Temple and palace (1 Kgs 6:2, 3, 20; 7:6, 27); and the future city of Jerusalem and the Temple in Ezekiel's vision (Ezek 40:5, 11; 41:1, 5, 7, 9, 12; 45:1, 3, 5). Overall, this terminology appears primarily in contexts that are concerned with the construction or reconstruction of Jerusalem and the Temple so that it is fitting to portray measurements in relation to the reconstruction of the Temple and the city here. It would appear that Zechariah's vision is based in the images of Temple and city reconstruction at the time of Zerubbabel's and Joshua ben Jehozadak's return to Jerusalem (see Ezra 3:1-7; 6:13-15).

Verse 7 [NRSV: 3] introduces a new figure in the scene, i.e., another angel who meets the first angel that speaks with Zechariah. It is not clear who this second angel is, but verses 8-17 [NRSV: 4-13] indicate that he comes to deliver a new set of instructions from YHWH that the first angel is to transmit to the prophet. Verse 8aα [NRSV: 4aα] contains a speech formula that identifies the following material as the speech of the second angel to the first, and verse 8aβ [NRSV: 4aβ] constitutes the second angel's instruction statement, "run, say to that young man, . . ." The reference to "that young man" *(hannaʿar hallāz)* clearly refers to Zechariah.

The speech that the first angel is to transmit to Zechariah appears in verses 8b-17 [NRSV: 4b-13], and the syntax of the speech indicates that it comprises five main components in verses 8b-9, 10, 11-13, 14-16, and 17 [NRSV: 4b-5, 6, 7-9, 10-12 and 13]. Each begins with a syntactically independent statement and, with the exception of the last segment in verse 17 [NRSV: 13], is identified formulaically as an oracle or word of YHWH. Altogether, the speech that Zechariah is to be instructed to speak maintains that Jerusalem is to be restored, that the exiles are to return to

Jerusalem from Babylon, that YHWH has sent the prophet to make this announcement, that YHWH will dwell in the midst of the people and the nations of the world, and that all flesh in the world is to remain silent as YHWH is roused in YHWH's holy habitation.

The first statement in verses 8b-9 [NRSV: 4b-5] announces YHWH's restoration of the city of Jerusalem. The oracular formula in verse 9aα [NRSV: 5aα] identifies the whole as a statement by YHWH that is to be delivered by the prophet. The section begins with the statement that "Jerusalem shall be inhabited like villages without walls." The term *pĕrāzôt*, here translated as "villages without walls," generally indicates small, unfortified hamlets that dot the countryside in contrast to the major fortified cities of a land (cf. Ezek 38:11; Esth 9:19). The image would fit Jerusalem during this period as the city remained unfortified due to the destruction wreaked by the Babylonian army when they conquered the city in 587/6 B.C.E. Indeed, the city walls of Jerusalem were not rebuilt until the time of Nehemiah, ca. 445 B.C.E. (Nehemiah 2–6). This does not mean that the city was completely without walls, however, as the Babylonians apparently only destroyed enough of the wall to leave the city indefensible. The point of the image in the present context, however, is that so many people and cattle will settle in the city that there will be insufficient space to contain them all within the confines of the city's former boundaries and that they will spill out over the countryside as a sign of the city's restoration and tremendous population. Verse 9 [NRSV: 5] follows with YHWH's first person statement that YHWH will constitute "a wall of fire" all around the city and "glory" in its midst. The wall of fire, of course symbolizes YHWH's protection, and the reference to "glory" *(kābôd)* employs the common term to represent the Divine Presence in the Temple (e.g., Exod 24:16, 17; 40:34, 35; 1 Kgs 8:11=2 Chr 5:14; Ezek 1:28; 8:4; 9:3; 10:19; 11:22; 43:2, 4, 5; 44:4; Isa 6:3). Petersen correctly points to the analogy of the Persian royal city of Pasargadae, which was built without walls and which contained a large number of fire altars to represent the presence of the Persian god Ahura Mazda.[28] Insofar as Ahura Mazda brought order to the cosmos and to the human world, including the Achaemenid dynasty, Pasargadae represented cosmic stability conceived as the stability of Persian rule. It would seem that Jerusalem is here conceived in somewhat similar terms as a city that represents the divine sovereignty of YHWH over the cosmos and the human world. The restoration of YHWH's presence or "glory" to Jerusalem is thus presented as an analogy to Ahura Mazda's presence in Pasargadae and thus to Persian imperial power.

[28] Petersen, *Haggai, Zechariah 1–8* 171.

Although the role of verses 10-17 [NRSV: 6-13] within the present framework is disputed,[29] they must be considered as a part of the second angel's speech to the first angel beginning in verse 8 [NRSV: 4]. As noted above, verse 10 [NRSV: 6] must be considered as the second major component of this speech. Verse 10 [NRSV: 6] is a syntactically independent presentation of an oracular statement by YHWH that is transmitted as part of the second angel's speech. The two appearances of the oracular formula at the end of verses 10a and 10b [NRSV: 6a and 6b] respectively identify it as such, and validate each as a word from YHWH. Although the oracular formulas also identify each half verse as a statement by YHWH, the causative *kî* at the beginning of verse 10b [NRSV: 6b] links the two parts of the verse together. Verse 10 [NRSV: 6] begins a sequence in verses 10, 11-13, 14-16, and 17 [NRSV: 6, 7-9, 10-12 and 13] that lays out the anticipated results of the announcement in verse 9 [NRSV: 5] that YHWH has restored Jerusalem as a city that requires no walls for defense, i.e., it is now time for those who were exiled to Babylon to return to Jerusalem and take up residence in the city. Verse 10 [NRSV: 6] constitutes YHWH's appeal to the exiles to flee the city of Babylon, and thereby looks forward to their return to Jerusalem. Verse 10a [NRSV: 6a] begins with a double occurrence of *hôy hôy*, translated by the NRSV as, "up, up!," which warns the people to flee from "the land of the north." Normally, the particle *hôy*, "woe!," introduces the prophetic "woe" oracles, but its use here indicates its role in relation to warning or instigation. The command to flee from "the land of the north" very clearly refers to Babylon, to which one would travel by a northern route although it lay directly east from Judah across the Arabian desert. By referring to Babylon as "the land of the north," the statement recalls an earlier prophetic tradition in Jeremiah that identified "the foe from the north" as the enemy that would carry Judah off into exile (cf. Jer 1:14-19; 4:5–10:25) and maintains that the punishment envisioned by Jeremiah is now at an end. The reference to YHWH's scattering the people like "the four winds of the heavens" calls to mind the image of the four horns of the altar and the four artisans in Zech 2:1-4. The four horns of the altar, of course, symbolize the four cardinal points of the compass that are frequently identified as the four winds in biblical and general ancient Near Eastern thought.[30] The image thereby recalls the role of the Temple as cosmic center, i.e., YHWH as sovereign of the cosmos called for Judah's exile and now calls for the exiles to return home. Such a call recalls the role of Cyrus as king of Babylon, likewise conceived in Babylonian

---

[29] See Meyers and Meyers, *Haggai, Zechariah 1–8* 172; Petersen, *Haggai, Zechariah 1–8* 174.

[30] Meyers and Meyers, *Haggai, Zechariah 1–8* 164.

thought as the center of the cosmos, who decrees that Jews and other exiled peoples could return to their homelands (2 Chr 36:22-23; Ezra 1:1-4).[31]

The second major segment of the angel's speech appears in verses 11-13 [NRSV: 7-9], which specify that the call in verse 10 [NRSV: 6] refers to the people of Jerusalem who have been exiled to Babylon, and point to YHWH as the source for this call. Although it is related to verse 10 [NRSV: 6] in form, verses 11-13 [NRSV: 7-9] are syntactically independent from the preceding statement. Verses 12a, 12b, and 13 [NRSV: 8a, 8b and 9] constitute three explanatory clauses that are linked to verse 11 [NRSV: 7] by introductory *kî's*. As the following discussion demonstrates, these statements are formulated as speech by YHWH, but it is quite clear that the second angel is actually the speaker who speaks on behalf of YHWH.

Verse 11 [NRSV: 7] constitutes a repeated call to the exiles to flee from Babylon, but the identities of the people and Babylon are made explicit. Like verse 10 [NRSV: 6], the call is introduced by the particle *hôy*, "Up!" but it is directed to "the daughter of Zion," a common personification of the city of Jerusalem. The second half of the verse specifies that "the daughter of Zion" "inhabits the daughter of Babylon," i.e., that the exiled people of Jerusalem now live in Babylon. Like Jerusalem, Babylon is personified as "daughter Babylon" to highlight the interrelationship and contrast between the two cities. Such an image draws heavily upon that of the book of Isaiah which frequently portrays Jerusalem and Babylon as women who suffer various misfortunes and restorations (see Isa 3:25–4:1; 49:18; 52:1-2; 54; see also Isaiah 47), and calls upon the exiles to leave Babylon for Jerusalem (Isa 48:20; 49:8-13; 51:9-11; 52:11-12).

The first *kî* clause that explains this statement appears in verse 12a [NRSV: 8a]. It begins with a version of the messenger formula that identifies YHWH as the speaker, but the contents of the statement make it clear that the second angel actually speaks on behalf of YHWH. The statement is very problematic in that the initial *ʾaḥar kābôd šělāḥanî* has defied interpretation.[32] The Hebrew translates literally, "after/behind glory (he) has sent me." Most interpreters consider the verse to be corrupt, and tend to follow the LXX which treats the noun *ʾaḥar*, "after, behind," as a variant of the preposition *ʾaḥărê*, "after," i.e., "after (his) glory sent me" (NRSV). Such a view fails to recognize that the expression *ʾaḥar kābôd* is a cryptic reference to YHWH much like *ʾehyeh*, "I am," cryp-

---

[31] See also the Cyrus cylinder (Pritchard, *ANET* 315–6), in which Cyrus decrees that various nations exiled by the Babylonians could return to rebuild their homelands and temples.

[32] See esp. Hanhart, *Sacharja* 117–8, for discussion of this verse.

tically functions as a designation for YHWH in Exod 3:14.[33] When Moses asks YHWH the divine name in Exod 3:13, YHWH does not state the divine name, but simply provides the formula, "I am who I am," *ʾehyeh ʾăšer ʾehyeh,* in response to Moses' question. The verb *ʾehyeh,* "I am," provides a pun on the name YHWH which associates the divine name with the verb, *hyh,* "to be, exist." YHWH follows up this initial statement in Exod 3:14 with "Thus you shall say to the Israelites, 'I am has sent me to you.'" The phrase "I am has sent me" reads in Hebrew *ʾehyeh šělāḥanî,* which provides a parallel with *ʾaḥar kābôd šělāḥanî* in Zech 2:12 [NRSV: 2:8]. The term *ʾaḥar kābôd,* "after/behind glory," would then refer to Moses' vision of YHWH in Exod 33:12–34:9 in which YHWH revealed the divine presence or "glory," *kābôd,* to Moses but only allowed Moses to see YHWH's "back," *ʾāḥôr,* a variant of *ʾaḥar,* "after, behind, back." The reference in Zech 2:12 [NRSV: 2:8] thus refers to YHWH as the "back of glory," which Moses saw in his initial revelation at Mt. Sinai. The statement, "the back of glory (i.e., YHWH) has sent me," thus indicates that YHWH has sent the angel on YHWH's behalf to the nations that plundered Jerusalem. The reason for such a an action would be to announce that the time has come for the nations to submit to YHWH at Jerusalem now that Jerusalem is to be reestablished as YHWH's sanctuary in the cosmos (see verses 13, 14-16 below [NRSV: 9, 10-12]). Again, such a message corresponds well to Isaiah, which portrays YHWH's punishment and restoration of Jerusalem as a sign of YHWH's sovereignty over the nations and cosmos at large (Isa 2:2-4, 6-21; 42:1-9; 45:9-14; 49:1-26; 51:1-11; 60-62).

Verse 12b [NRSV: 8b] then provides a rationale for YHWH's actions with another *kî* clause, "for (contra NRSV, 'truly') one who touches you touches the apple of his eye." By referring to Jerusalem as "the apple of his (i.e., YHWH's) eye," the angel signals that his task is one of punishment and subjugation, i.e., the nations are to be punished for their treatment of Jerusalem and compelled to submit to YHWH for their actions. This becomes clear in verse 13 [NRSV: 9], which presents yet another *kî* clause to explain the situation. Although NRSV translates, "see now, I am going to raise my hand . . . ," the passage should read, "for I am raising my hand . . ." The verse describes a scenario in which the nations that plundered Jerusalem will in turn be plundered by their own servants. The verb employed to describe the raising of YHWH's hand, *mēnîp,* is borrowed from the sphere of the Temple sacrificial ritual. The verb *nwp* is normally translated, "to wave, move to and fro, besprinkle," and is employed to describe the presentation of the priests'

---

[33] See also Ps 73:24, which employs the phrase *ʾaḥar kābôd* in a similar fashion (Hanhart, *Sacharja* 118).

share of sacrificial meat at the altar (see Lev 23:11; Exod 29:26; Lev 7:30; 8:29; 9:21; 10:15; Num 6:20; 8:11; etc.). It is also employed in Isa 11:15 and 19:16 to describe YHWH's actions against the nations that threaten Israel. In short, YHWH will act to offer the nations as a sacrifice to Jerusalem, i.e., the nations will now serve YHWH at Jerusalem. The appearance of the formula, "then you will know that YHWH of Hosts has sent me," at the end of verse 13 [NRSV: 9] certifies that YHWH makes this promise and validates the second angel as the messenger who transmits this statement on YHWH's behalf (cf. Zech 2:15 [NRSV: 2:11]; 4:9; 6:15).

The third major segment of the second angel's speech appears in verses 14-16 [NRSV: 10-12], which call upon Zion to rejoice at the restoration of YHWH's presence in her midst. The passage begins in verse 14a [NRSV: 10a] with feminine singular imperatives that call upon "the daughter of Zion" to "sing" (ronî) and "rejoice" (śimḥî) with language that is once again reminiscent of Second Isaiah (see Isa 42:11; 44:23; 49:13; 52:8, 9; 54:1; 61:7; cf. Isa 9:2 [NRSV: 9:3]; 12:1; 24:14; 26:19; 35:2, 6; 66:10).

The reason for Zion's rejoicing is spelled out in verses 14b-16 [NRSV: 10b-12], which begin with an explanatory kî clause in verse 14b [NRSV: 10b] followed by specifications in verses 15 and 16 [NRSV: 11 and 12]. Verse 14b [NRSV: 10b] is formulated as an oracular statement by YHWH, as indicated by the presence of the oracular formula at the end of the verse, in which YHWH states, "for lo, I will come and dwell in your midst." This statement establishes the return of YHWH's presence to the city of Jerusalem which is symbolized by the reconstruction of the Temple (see Psalm 132 for YHWH's residence in the Jerusalem Temple). Verses 15 and 16 [NRSV: 11 and 12], both of which are joined syntactically to verse 14b [NRSV: 10b] by waw-consecutive perfect verbal constructions, then state YHWH's relationship to the nations at large and to Judah and Jerusalem respectively as part of the overall scenario of YHWH's manifestation of cosmic sovereignty in Zion.

Verse 15 [NRSV: 11] comprises a sequence of four statements that are concerned with the role of the nations. The first states that "many nations shall join themselves to YHWH on that day." It employs imagery and language from the book of Isaiah, including the reference to "many nations" (gôyim rabbîm; see Isa 2:4, which mentions YHWH's arbitration between gôyim, "nations," and ʿammîm rabbîm, "many peoples") and the verb nilwû, "they will be joined" (see Isa 56:6, which states that foreigners will "be joined," nilwîm, to YHWH). Such a scenario corresponds to the overall outlook of Isaiah which envisions the nations coming to Zion together with Israel/Jacob to acknowledge YHWH's world-wide sovereignty (see Isa 2:2-4; 25:6-10; 56:1-8; 60-62; 66:18-24). The second states that "they shall be my people," which employs the old formula by which YHWH established a relationship with the people of Israel (see Exod 6:6-7; Lev 26:12; Deut 26:17-19; 27:9; 28:9; 29:12 [NRSV: 29:13]; 2 Sam 7:24; Hos 1:9; 2:1 [NRSV: 1:10]; Jer 7:23; 11:4; 24:7; 31:1, 33; 32:38; Ezek 11:20; 14:11; 36:28; 37:23, 27; Zech 8:8). In essence, YHWH states the intention to formulate a covenant with the nations much like that formed with Israel, although the following statements make it clear that Jerusalem and Judah will continue to stand at the center of that relationship. Thus, the third states that YHWH will continue to dwell in the midst of Zion, and the fourth indicates that Zion will thereby know that "YHWH of Hosts has sent me unto you." This statement is addressed directly to Zion with second person feminine language, but the third person reference to YHWH and the repeated occurrence of the above-discussed *šĕlāḥanî*, "has sent me," (see Zech 2:12 [NRSV: 2:8]) indicates that the angel speaks on YHWH's behalf. Once again, the appearance of the angel serves as a sign or confirmation of YHWH's statements.

Verse 16 [NRSV: 12] includes two statements that focus on the continuing role of Judah and Jerusalem at the center of the nations. Verse 16a [NRSV: 12a] states that YHWH will "inherit Judah as his portion in the holy land." Much like the tribes of Israel were assigned their inheritances of land at the time of the conquest under Joshua (see Joshua 13–23), so YHWH will designate the land of Judah as YHWH's own special inheritance that will function as "holy land." Such a statement indicates that just as the Temple serves as a sacred precinct at the center of Israel, so Judah will serve as a sacred precinct among the nations at large. Likewise, just as the priests and Levites serve as sacred officials among Israel within the Temple, so the people of Israel will serve as a sacred people at the center of the nations at large (cf. Zech 8:20-23 below and Exod 19:6, which designates Israel as "a priestly kingdom and a holy nation" to YHWH). Judah's holy status is acknowledged in YHWH's statement in verse 16b [NRSV: 12b] that YHWH "will again choose Jerusalem." YHWH's choice of Jerusalem mirrors YHWH's choice of David as king (1 Sam 16:8; 2 Sam 6:21; 1 Kgs 8:16=2 Chr 6:6), Israel as the "chosen people" (Deut 7:7; Isa 44:1; Ezek 20:5), and it corresponds to other statements concerning YHWH's choice of Jerusalem or Zion as the divine dwelling place or the site of the Temple (2 Chr 6:6; Isa 14:1; Ps 132:13; see also Zech 1:17; 3:2).

Finally, verse 17 [NRSV: 13] constitutes the fourth major component of the angel's speech in verses 8b-17 [NRSV: 4b-13]. The command should read literally, "Be silent, all flesh, before YHWH; for he has roused himself from his holy dwelling." The command to "all flesh," i.e., all people, to be silent appears elsewhere in Zeph 1:7 and Hab 2:20 where it functions in the context of theophany. In Zeph 1:7, the command to silence appears in the context of a text that takes up the theme of sacrifice on the "Day of YHWH," in which YHWH's destruction of those who are wicked within Judah is portrayed as a Temple sacrifice. In Hab 2:20, the command for silence appears at the end of along sequence of woe oracles that condemn Babylon as the wicked oppressor of Judah (Hab 2:5-20). Insofar as the priests perform the Temple rituals in silence, it would appear that the command for silence before YHWH presupposes a Temple ritual in which YHWH's presence is manifested. Such a ritual would likely include any major sacrifice offered at the Temple in that the Temple ritual symbolically addresses YHWH and presupposes divine presence in the Temple. In the case of Zech 2:17 [NRSV: 2:13], the call for silence before YHWH as YHWH's presence is manifested in "his holy dwelling" symbolizes the restored presence of YHWH in the restored Jerusalem Temple.

THE REPORT OF THE FOURTH VISION:
THE ORDINATION OF JOSHUA BEN JEHOZADAK FOR SERVICE
AT THE JERUSALEM ALTAR: 3:1-10

Zechariah 3:1-10 constitutes the fourth vision report of the prophet Zechariah. This chapter is frequently considered to be a secondary addition to an original sequence of seven vision reports because its form differs so markedly from that of the other vision reports in Zechariah.[34] The introductory formula of the passage, "then he showed me *(way-yarʾēnî)*," varies from the usual formula in Zechariah, "and I looked up and saw *(wāʾeśśāʾ ʿênay wāʾereʾ)*," and its variants. Furthermore, the vision report lacks the usual questions and answers of the other vision reports because the significance of the vision is evident as no puzzling symbol that requires interpretation by the angel appears. The emphasis on the high priest Joshua ben Jehozadak in a context that looks forward to the "branch *(ṣemaḥ)*," a clear reference to Zerubbabel as a royal figure, would help to prepare the reader for the eighth vision of the sequence in Zech 6:1-15 in which the high priest Joshua rather than Zerubbabel assumes the role of the monarch. Many scholars also consider Zech 3:8-10 to be an even later addition to Zech 3:1-7.[35] The reasons for such a position include the formally independent call to attention in verse 8 that introduces the passage and its affinities with other later passages in the prophetic corpus that take up the issue of the

---

[34] See Petersen, *Haggai, Zechariah 1–8*, 187–8, for a summation of issues.

[35] Meyers and Meyers, *Haggai, Zechariah 1–8* 222; Petitjean, *Les oracles* 161–206 (with bibliography).

"branch," such as Jer 23:5-6; 33:14-26; Isa 4:2-6, and the "stone" that is associated with the high priest's turban, e.g., Exod 28:9-12, 17-21, 36-38. Although both of these passages in chapter 3 may well be considered in relation to the compositional history of Zechariah, they play a key role in the present form of the book because of the association of priestly ordination with the dedication of the Temple altar during the seven days of Sukkoth (cf. Exod 29:35-37; Lev 8:31-36) and they present Joshua and his colleagues as "signs" for the future coming of the "branch" which in turn points to Zechariah 9-14.

The overall form of the passage is a vision report that relates the ordination of Joshua ben Jehozadak. Ordination rites for the priests appear in Exodus 29 and Leviticus 8–9. Basically, they call for a ceremony in which the priest is washed in water at the entrance to the Temple, dressed in clean or pure holy garments, including the tunic, robe of the ephod, the ephod itself, the breastpiece, the turban, and the diadem of the turban, and anointed with oil. The priest officiates over a sacrifice of one young bull and two rams in which the blood of the bull and one lamb are employed to sanctify the altar and the blood of the other ram is employed to sanctify the lobe of his right ear, thumb, and big toe, as well as the altar. The bull and the first ram are burned entirely on the altar, and the right thigh of the second ram is presented by the priest together with the entrails and bread as his own ordination. The breast of the ram is then presented as the priest's portion to be eaten only by the priest. This ordination ceremony is repeated for seven days to complete the ordination of the priest and the sanctification of the altar. Insofar as the dedication of the altar is associated with the festival of Sukkoth (1 Kgs 8:1-66; 2 Chr 5:2–7:10; Ezra 3:1-7), the ordination of the priests also appears to take place at this time. On the eighth day at the conclusion of the festival, the priest officiates at the altar on behalf of the people (Leviticus 9).

The identification of this scene as a report or vision concerning the ordination of Joshua is sometimes disputed.[36] One reason is that Joshua appears already to be recognized as high priest, but the above-mentioned ordination ceremonies indicate that the ordination of the priest takes place in conjunction with the sanctification of the altar. Although Joshua may already have been recognized as high priest prior to his return to Jerusalem by virtue of his birth, he could not have been fully ordained until the ordination ceremony at the altar in Jerusalem had been completed. A second reason is that the description of Joshua's garments and turban appears to differ from the description of the priest's garments and turban in Exodus 29, but Zechariah 3 appears

---

[36] See the discussion in Meyers and Meyers, *Haggai, Zechariah 1–8* 213–22.

merely to employ a generalized description of the garments and turban rather than the detailed description in Exodus 29 and Leviticus 8–9. The third reason is that the form of Zechariah's vision report appears to have affinities with various examples of the prophetic call narratives rather than with a priestly ordination ceremony. The chapter indicates that Joshua stands between the angel and Satan and others are also standing about, which suggests the setting of YHWH's royal court as described in prophetic visionary scenes such as 1 Kings 22 or Isaiah 6. Both passages describe YHWH sitting on the divine throne with the royal divine court arrayed around the throne. The prophet appears to be a member of the audience that appears before YHWH, and either witnesses the proceedings (1 Kings 22) or participates in them (Isaiah 6), much as Zechariah does as indicated by his speaking role in verse 5. Although YHWH's throne is not described here, YHWH's presence is certainly indicated. Because these visions deal with prophetic rather than priestly calls, the vision concerning Joshua must not refer to his ordination. But such a view overlooks Zechariah's role as both priest and prophet. Zechariah 3 indicates that he has a view of the royal court of YHWH, and that view provides him with insight concerning the ordination of Joshua ben Jehozadak as priest at the Jerusalem altar.

The structure of the passage follows a three-part narrative sequence in verses 1-2, 3-5bα, and 5bβ-10 in which the narrative portrayal of the scene introduces presentations of statements by the key figures. The first component appears in verses 1-2. Here, an unnamed party shows Zechariah the scene of Joshua ben Jehozadak standing between the angel of YHWH and Satan (verse 1), which introduces YHWH's statement to Satan (verse 2). The second component appears in verses 3-5bα, which begins with the description of Joshua standing before the angel in filthy garments (verse 3). This introduces presentations of statements by the angel to those standing around Joshua (verse 4), and a statement by Zechariah calling for the dressing of Joshua in a clean turban and garments (verse 5a-bα). A reference to the angel of YHWH standing in verse 5bβ introduces the report of his transmission of YHWH's oracular statement (verses 6-10). Although verses 8-10 are sometimes considered to be secondary, they constitute a part of the oracular statement by YHWH in verses 7-10 that is transmitted by the angel.

Verses 1-2 describe the initial scene of Joshua's ordination for service at the altar in verse 1 with YHWH's statement or rebuke to Satan in verse 2. Verse 1 begins with the previously mentioned statement, "and he showed me," which provides no indication of the subject of the verb. The context, however, suggests that the subject is "the angel " (verse 3) or "the angel of YHWH" (verses 5, 6), who appears in the vision and speaks on YHWH's behalf. This angel would likely be identified with the first angel who has served as guide for Zechariah throughout the vision sequence, and who was instructed by the second angel in Zech 2:7-17 [NRSV: 2:3-13] to speak to "that young man" (Zech 2:8 [NRSV: 2:4]), i.e., to Zechariah. The prophet sees Joshua, who is described as "the high priest" *(hakkōhēn haggādôl)*. The title "high priest" is elsewhere applied to Joshua in Hag 1:1, 12, 14; 2:2, 4; Zech 3:8; 6:11. The term is also applied to Jehoiada (2 Kgs 12:11 [NRSV: 12:10]); Hilkiah (2 Kgs 22:4; 23:4; 2 Chr 34:9); Eliashib (Neh 3:1, 20; 13:28); and in the Pentateuch for Aaron and his successors (Lev 21:10; Num 35:25, 28; Josh 20:6), and it eventually becomes the standard term in Rabbinic Hebrew. Elsewhere, biblical literature employs the term, "the head priest" *(hakkōhēn hārōʾš)* for Seraiah (2 Kgs 25:18; Jer 52:24); Amariah (2 Chr 19:11); Jehoaiada (2 Chr 24:11); Azariah (2 Chr 26:20; 31:10); and Aaron (Ezra 7:5) or "the anointed priest" *(hakkōhēn hammāšîaḥ;* Lev 4:3, 5, 16; 6:15 [NRSV: 6:22]). "The angel of YHWH" *(malʾak yhwh)* apparently refers to the angel who speaks with Zechariah. The reference to "Satan," literally, "the accuser" *(haśśātān),* is frequently misconstrued as the devil figure of later Christian and Jewish literature and theology. The verb root *śtn* simply, "to oppose, to act as an adversary," and this meaning of the term appears to underlie the use of the noun form in 1 Sam 29:4; 2 Sam 19:23 [NRSV: 19:22]; 1 Kgs 5:18 [NRSV: 5:4]; 11:14, 23, 25; and Ps 109:6. The term applies to a heavenly figure in Job 1-2, in which the Satan challenges Job's righteousness, and in 1 Chr 21:1, which personifies YHWH's anger in 2 Sam 24:1 as the Satan figure. The angel sent by YHWH to block Balaam's path may also contribute to the use of the term in relation to a heavenly figure although the term is used to describe the angel simply as an adversary (Num 22:22, 32). The emergence of the Satan figure as a heavenly foe in the early Persian period may presuppose the practice of both the Neo-Babylonian and the Achaemenid rulers to employ spies and informers to keep them apprized of activities throughout the empire that might challenge the throne.[37] It also appears to have been influenced by Persian concepts of theological dualism in which the Satan figure came to represent the figure of Angra Mainyu or Ahriman, the Persian god of evil, who opposed Ahuramazda, the supreme god of order in the universe. In any case, the Satan figure here appears to be a part of YHWH's heavenly court who stands together with the "angel of YHWH" at Joshua's ordination. Whereas the Satan's role is to accuse Joshua, the angel's role is to invest him with pure garments that will help to enable him to assume his priestly role (see verses 3-5).

[37] See Victor Hamilton, "Satan," *ABD* V:985-9, and esp. A. L. Oppenheim, "The Eyes of the L–rd," *JAOS* 88 (1968) 173–80.

The presentation of YHWH's speech of rebuke to Satan appears in verse 2. It is introduced by a standard narrative speech formula, "and YHWH said." YHWH's "rebuke" of the Satan figure appears to function as the rejection of an attempt to allow Joshua to serve as priest. Given the propensity of the Neo-Babylonian and Achaemenid dynasties to employ informers against those who might challenge the throne,[38] the present statement appears to be modeled on a court scene in which an informer's challenge to a king's appointment is rejected. YHWH is here described as the one "who has chosen Jerusalem," which rehearses the terminology employed for YHWH's choice of Israel (Deut 7:7; Ezek 20:5); Jerusalem (2 Chr 6:6; Ps 132:13); David (2 Sam 6:21; 1 Kgs 8:16); and the priests (Deut 18:5; 21:5; 1 Chr 15:2; 2 Chr 29:11; Ps 105:26), in the Davidic/Zion tradition of YHWH's unconditional covenant. The association of YHWH's choice of Jerusalem as the site of the Temple with the service of the priests apparently underlies the decision to reject Satan's accusations and to proceed with Joshua's ordination for priestly service. The final question in YHWH's statement, "Is not this man a brand plucked from the fire? *(hălô' zeh 'ûd muṣṣāl mē'ēš)"* employs terminology drawn from Amos 4:11 (cf. Isa 7:4), in which the "brand plucked from the fire" is employed to describe those who survived YHWH's punishments against Israel. The image represents one who has suffered, but survived, and applies to Joshua as one who has suffered exile to Babylonia, but has survived to return home to Jerusalem in order to reinstitute holy service at the rebuilt altar and Temple.

Verses 3-5bα relate the statements made by the angel and Zechariah, and indirectly by YHWH, that initiate the change of garments that constitute an essential element of the priestly ordination. The passage begins in verse 3, which begins with a simple conjunction followed by an emphatic mention of the name Joshua to signal the beginning of a new sub-unit in chapter 3. The verse describes the circumstances of the situation, i.e., Joshua is clothed in filthy garments and stands before the angel. The expression "filthy garments" *(běgādîm ṣô'îm)* highlights the contrast between Joshua's "impure" state prior to the ordination and his new state of ritual "purity" that will be symbolized by his donning the pure priestly vestments. The term *ṣō'î*, "filthy," is derived from *ṣō'â*, "filth," which is elsewhere used to describe human vomit (Isa 28:8) or excrement (2 Kgs 18:27/Isa 36:12). It is also related to *ṣē'â*, "filth," which describes the excrement that defiles the camp of the Israelite army (Deut 23:14) or that pollutes Ezekiel's food (Ezek 4:12). The term appears to be an extreme description of filth, but it highlights the purification of Joshua. Verse 4 then presents the angel's statements to

---

[38] See esp. Oppenheim, "The Eyes of the L–rd."

both those standing before him in the heavenly court (verse 4a) and to Joshua (verse 4b). Verse 4 does not specify that the angel is the speaker; his identity is clear only from the end of verse 3 which relates that Joshua stands before him. Apparently, the angel serves as majordomo in the royal court, perhaps akin to the role of the officer appointed over the king's house (cf. Isa 36:3/2 Kgs 18:18). The role of this angel develops into the figure of Metatron in later Jewish mystical literature of the Second Temple and Talmudic periods.[39] He calls upon those standing before him to remove the filthy garments from Joshua, which prepares him for the purification of priestly ordination as specified in Exod 29:4 and Lev 8:6. The angel then speaks to Joshua in verse 4b, stating that he has removed Joshua's "guilt," and that he should now clothe himself with the "festal apparel." The removal of "guilt" (ʿāwōn) is symbolized by the washing and donning of purified priestly vestments in the ordination ceremony; it essentially refers to the physical cleansing and moral purification that is expected of a priest who serves upon the altar. The term, "festal apparel" (maḥălāṣôt), appears elsewhere only in Isa 3:22, where it is one of the fine garments worn by the ladies of Jerusalem. The term is derived from the root, ḥlṣ, "to draw off," and is generally understood as a reference to some sort of formal outer robe or cloak that can be taken off and put aside to reveal a second set of garments underneath. Because it applies to both the garments of the high priests and to the garments of women, maḥălāṣôt is apparently a generic term that can be applied generally to such an outer garment. Although the term does not appear in Exodus 29 or Leviticus 8, it apparently corresponds either to the "tunic" (kuttōnet) or the "robe of the ephod" (mᵉʿîl hāʾēpōd) with which the priest is dressed in Exod 29:5 and Lev 8:7. Because the mᵉʿîl appears to cover the kuttōnet in Lev 8:7, it is more likely that the latter is the case. Verse 5 presents Zechariah's statements, apparently directed to those standing before Joshua and the angel, that the "clean turban" (ṣānîp ṭāhôr) should be placed upon Joshua's head. Many scholars have attempted to emend the initial first person speech formula, "and I said" (wāʾōmar), to a third person statement, "and he said (wayyōʾmer), based upon the reading of the Vulgate,[40] but this is entirely unnecessary. Zechariah is a priest as well as a prophet and has every right to be a part of a priestly ordination ceremony. Again, the terminology for the turban differs from that of Exod 29:6 and Lev 8:9, both of which use miṣnepet instead of ṣānîp. Both terms, however, are derived from the same root, ṣnp, "to wrap,

---

[39] Gershom Scholem, "Metatron," *Encyclopaedia Judaica* 11:1443-6; see also, Carol Newsom, "Angels," *ABD* I:248-53.

[40] See BHS note; Hanhart, *Sacharja* 170–2.

wind." The term *ṣānîp* is employed for a royal turban in Isa 62:3 and for a woman's headdress in Isa 3:23, whereas *miṣnepet* is used primarily for the turban of the high priest (Exod 28:37; 29:6; 39:28, 31; Lev 8:9; 16:4), except in Ezek 21:31 [NRSV: 21:26] where it is used to describe a royal turban. It may be that the term *ṣānîp* is the generic term, whereas *miṣnepet* is a technical term.

The statement in verse 5bβ that "the angel of YHWH was standing by" (*ûmalʾak yhwh ʿōmēd*), literally, "and the angel of YHWH was standing," has been judged by most scholars to be a misplaced sentence fragment at the conclusion of verse 5.[41] It actually appears to be a statement of circumstance, much like verse 3, which describes the action of the angel of YHWH and introduces the presentation of his speech in verses 6-10.

Verse 6 is a speech formula that introduces the angel's transmission of YHWH's oracle to Joshua. The verb "assured" (*ʿwd*) generally appears in legal contexts where it refers to legal testimony (Deut 4:26; 30:19; 31:28), and generally means "to admonish, warn, enjoin."[42] Its use here indicates that YHWH's oracle is intended to affirm Joshua's status as high priest provided that he meets the conditions stated therein. The oracle from YHWH appears in verses 7-10. An example of the prophetic messenger formula in verse 7aα[1-4], "Thus says YHWH of Hosts," introduces YHWH's words to the priest. The oracle per se comprises two basic components: a commission to serve as high priest in verse 7aα[5]-b and an announcement in verses 8-10 concerning the significance of the ordination of Joshua and his colleagues.

The commission in verse 7aα[5]-b states the conditions by which Joshua will serve as high priest. The statement employs a typical protasis-apodosis form, much like those found in biblical legal materials, which states a set of conditions in the protasis and set of results in the apodosis (see, e.g., the slave law in Exod 21:1-11). The protasis is generally introduced by a conditional particle, such as *ʾim*, "if," *kî*, "because, when," or *ʾăšer*, "when," and the apodosis generally employs a *waw-consecutive* verbal form. The present case is problematic, however, in that verse 7aβγ employs two occurrences of the conjunctive particle *wĕgam*, "and also," (i.e., "and you also shall rule my house and also you shall have charge of my courts") which make it difficult to decide if this phrase serves as a condition of the protasis or as a resulting privilege for Joshua in the apodosis.[43]

The initial statement in verse 7aα[5-11], "if you will walk in my ways and keep my requirements," is clearly part of the protasis or the state-

---

[41] But see Hanhart, *Sacharja* 172.

[42] So Petersen, *Haggai and Zechariah 1–8* 203.

[43] Ibid., 203–8.

ment of the conditions that Joshua must meet to serve as high priest. Both parts of the statement begin with the conjunctive particle *wĕʾim,* "and if," in keeping with the typical formulation of protases in the Hebrew Bible. The condition that Joshua "walk in my ways" is a typical statement of the conditions expected of Israel or selected individuals in Deuteronomy and the Deuteronomistic History (e.g., Deut 8:6; Josh 22:5; Judg 2:22; 1 Kgs 2:3; 2 Kgs 21:22). It essentially means that Joshua must observe Yhwh's commands. The second condition that Joshua "keep my requirements," *ʾet-mišmartî tišmōr,* means literally, "observe my charge." The term *mišmeret,* "charge, watch," refers to the specific duties or charge of priestly service in the sanctuary or at the altar of the Temple (see Lev 8:35; 22:9; Num 1:53; 3:7, 38; 18:5; Ezek 40:46; 44:15).

The conclusion of the commission in verse 7b, "and I will give you the right of access among those who are standing here," clearly constitutes the apodosis or the role and privileges that Joshua will enjoy as a result of meeting Yhwh's conditions. The "right of access," *mahlĕkîm,* apparently refers to the high priest's right of access to the Holy of Holies in the Jerusalem Temple. The term appears only here in relation to this specialized meaning, but it appears to refer to the exclusive right of the high priest to enter the Holy of Holies in the Jerusalem Temple to appear before Yhwh as the representative of the Jewish community to make atonement for the people's sins on Yom Kippur or the Day of Atonement (see Leviticus 16). Overall, the high priest possessed a degree of sanctity that surpassed that of other priests,[44] i.e., he alone deals with the sin offerings whose blood is brought into the sanctuary (Lev 4:3-21), he may not come into contact with the dead even to mourn for his closest relatives, he does not leave the sanctuary, and he may marry only a virgin of his own kin (Lev 21:10-15). The other priests were also considered holy, but they were not permitted to appear in the Holy of Holies, to take care of the sin offerings in which blood was brought into the sanctuary, and they were permitted to mourn for their closest relatives and to marry the widows of other priests (see Leviticus 21). Essentially, verse 7b indicates that if Joshua meets Yhwh's conditions, he will serve as high priest.

The above comments have implications for considering whether verse 7aβγ serves as part of the protasis or as part of the apodosis for Yhwh's commission to Joshua. The statement identifies two activities, i.e., that Joshua "shall rule my house," and "have charge of my courts." The first statement, "and also you shall rule my house," *wĕgam ʾattâ tādîn ʾet-bêtî,* begins with an emphatic use of the independent pronoun

[44] See esp. Menahem Haran, "Priests and Priesthood," *Encyclopaedia Judaica* 13:1069-86.

ʾattâ, "you," which highlights Joshua as the addressee and suggests
that the statement differs from the protasis in verse 7aα[5-11]. Furthermore, the statement that "you shall judge my house," may be taken as
a reference to the normal judicial activities of the priests (see Deut 17:8-
13; Ezek 44:24), but the use of the verb *dîn* in relation to *ʾet-bêtî*, "my
house," suggests a more specialized role. The parallel use of "my
house" with "my courts" indicates that "my house" refers to YHWH's
Temple. The verb *dîn* normally takes people or law cases at its object,
not the Temple itself. Because the Temple itself can hardly be judged, it
would seem that the expression refers to the administration or rule of
the Temple in Jerusalem, an activity that the high priest would ultimately carry out. Likewise, the statement that Joshua will "have charge
of my courts," *tišmōr ʾet-ḥăṣērāy*, literally, "shall watch my courts," suggests supervision of the Temple courts, which points ultimately to the
role of the high priest. Although other priests will share in these functions, they are ultimately responsible to the high priest. Verse 7aβγ
must refer to the special role of the high priest as the chief supervisor of
YHWH's Temple and courts. It therefore stands as part of the apodosis of
YHWH's commission to Joshua in that it points to his ultimate responsibility for the care of the Temple and thus to his ultimate privilege of access to the Holy of Holies.

The second part of YHWH's oracle to Joshua in verses 8-10 states the
significance of his appointment as high priest. The passage begins with
a call to attention directed to Joshua and his colleagues sitting before
him. The call to attention notably addresses him with his title, "Joshua,
high priest," to signify his newly acquired status as a result of the ordination process that is portrayed in the preceding verses. The reference
to Joshua's "colleagues" sitting before him has prompted some discussion.[45] The term *rēʿa* generally refers to a "friend," "neighbor," "companion," or "colleague," based on the meaning of the verb root *rʿh*,
which means, "to associate with." Such association might suggest that
the term refers to Joshua's priestly colleagues, but there is no evidence
that the priests gathered in such an assembly with the high priest at
their head. It might also suggest that the term refers to the major non-
priestly leaders of the restoration Judean community who helped to
place Joshua as high priest. In order to decide this question it is necessary to consider their role as an "omen of things to come" in relation to
"the branch" and the significance of the stone in relation to the removal
of the guilt of the community must be considered.

The introductory *kî*, "because, for," indicates that verse 7b is designed to serve as an explanatory clause for the call to attention in verse

---

[45] Petersen, *Haggai and Zechariah 1–8* 208–10.

7a. It thereby explains the significance of Joshua and his "colleagues" as an omen concerning Yнwн's bringing of the "branch." The term "branch," ṣemaḥ, is a very clear reference to the coming of a royal Davidic figure as indicated by the "branch" or "shoot" imagery of Isaiah 11, which points to the coming of a righteous Davidic monarch, and that of Jer 23:5-6 and 33:14-26, which employ the term "branch" as a designation for the future Davidic monarch of a restored land of Israel. One must also consider the fact that the name Zerubbabel is derived from the Akkadian term *zēr bābili*, "seed/branch of Babylon." Insofar as Zerubbabel was the grandson of King Jehoiachin, the designation of "branch" as the future Davidic monarch must clearly take his role as the potential king of a restored Judean state into consideration. It would seem that the term "branch" here points to the reestablishment of the Davidic monarchy or at least to the fulfillment of the oracles in Isaiah 11 and Jer 23:5-6; 33:14-26. The designation of Joshua's colleagues as an "omen," *môpet*, must also be considered, especially in relation to the role of Isaiah's sons in Isa 8:18 as "signs and omens" *(lĕʾōtôt ûlĕmôpĕtîm)* for Yнwн's future actions on behalf of Zion to bring a righteous Davidic monarch (Isa 8:16–9:6; see also Ezek 12:6 in which Yнwн declares that Ezekiel himself, through his symbolic actions, shall be an omen to the people of Israel). Insofar as Isa 8:1-4 designates Zechariah ben Jeberechiah as a witness to that time and the book of Zechariah identifies the prophet with this figure by use of the name Zechariah ben Berechiah ben Iddo, it would seem that the prophet is intended to serve as a witness to the fulfillment of Isaiah's oracles. Isaiah looks for a future righteous Davidic monarch; and Zechariah witnesses to the time of the fulfillment of Isaiah's oracle. The "branch" represents that fulfillment. It would seem then that Zechariah must be one of the colleagues who sits before Joshua. Zechariah is not only a prophet, but a priest as well. Furthermore, Ezra 3:2 takes care to mention that Joshua returned to Jerusalem in the company of "his brothers the priests." The high priest may not leave the sanctuary (Lev 21:12) and only priests are permitted within the sanctuary itself (Ezek 44:6–45:5). It therefore stands to reason that the term "colleagues" must refer to Joshua's priestly colleagues, such as Zechariah, who sit before the high priest in deliberation.

It is noteworthy, therefore, that priests play a key role in anointing Israelite monarchs at crucial periods of transition. Thus, Samuel, who is not a Levite but who functions as a priest, anoints both Saul (1 Sam 9:1–10:16) and David (1 Samuel 16). Zadok, assisted by the prophet Nathan, anoints Solomon (1 Kings 1), and Jehoiada crowns Joash (2 Kings 11). Furthermore, Deut 17:14-20 asserts that the king is to be supervised by the Levitical priests. This does not appear to be an exclusive right as the people of the land sometimes step in to designate the king, such as Joash, who is actually anointed by the people of the land (2 Kgs 11:12), Azariah/Uzziah (2 Kgs 14:21), Josiah (2 Kgs 21:24), and Jehoahaz (2 Kgs 23:30). It would seem that the lines of authority for designating the king were not entirely clear, but the designation of Joshua as the "branch" in Zechariah 6 suggests that the priests in this period played a major role in deciding who should exercise royal power, and chose to designate one of their own. Such a designation is especially noteworthy because it conflicts with Haggai's designation of Zerubbabel as YHWH's signet (Hag 2:20-23), and indicates that there was controversy concerning the designation of the king at the time of the rebuilding of the Temple. Indeed, the designation of a non-Davidic figure as king is entirely in keeping with the presentation of the book of Isaiah, which portrays Cyrus as YHWH's anointed (Isa 44:28; 45:1) and by the end of the book asserts that YHWH is the true king (see Isa 66:1; cf. 2:2-4). As high priest, Joshua would in fact represent YHWH's kingship. Interestingly, Jer 33:14-26 points to the "branch" in relation to both the Davidic promise and to the Levitical priests.

Verses 9-10, which also begin with an introductory *kî*, constitute a second explanation of the significance of Joshua's ordination as high priest. In this case, the explanation focuses on the engraved stone which apparently corresponds to the rosette that is fastened to the turban of the high priest in Exod 28:36-38. Although Petitjean argues that the stone must refer to the setting of a ritual cornerstone at the building of the Temple,[46] the description of the stone in the present passage corresponds closely to the description of the rosette on the high priest's turban in Exod 28:36-38. As noted above, Joshua is dressed with a clean/pure turban in verse 5. Because the stone is affixed to the high priest's turban, it may be described as "before Joshua" just as Exod 28:37 states that the rosette "shall be on front of the turban." It is engraved, just as Exod 28:36 indicates that the rosette is engraved with the words, "Holy to YHWH." Finally, it serves as a sign that YHWH will remove the guilt of the land in one day just as the rosette in Exod 28:38 indicates that Aaron will take upon himself the guilt incurred by the people of Israel.

A major problem remains. Zechariah 3:9 describes this object as a "stone" (*ʾeben*) whereas Exod 28:36 designates it as a "rosette of pure gold" (*ṣîṣ zāhāb ṭāhôr*), which would suggest a different object. Nevertheless, the relationship between the stone and the high priest's turban appears to be determinative. An explanation for the discrepancy in terminology appears to be the author's use of Isaiah 28, in which YHWH states the intention to lay a "tested," "precious," and "sure" "foundation

---

[46] Petitjean, *Les oracles* 179–84.

stone" in Zion (verse 16). Although the Isaian text clearly refers to a foundation stone used in building, it is understood metaphorically in relation to proper leadership in the nation. In this regard, it is noteworthy that Isaiah 28 begins with references to "the proud garland of the drunkards of Ephraim . . . which is on the heads of those bloated with rich food, of those overcome with wine." The reference clearly employs the imagery of crown, and it employs the term *ṣîṣ*, "flower," to describe its fading beauty, i.e., "the fading flower *(ṣîṣ)* of its glorious beauty." The passage goes on in verses 5-6 to describe YHWH as a "garland of glory," a "diadem *(ʿăṭeret)* of beauty," and a "spirit of justice" that will designate "the one who sits in judgement" over the people. The image of the "crown/diadem" *(ʿăṭeret)* is explicit, and the language draws upon Isa 11:1-16, which portrays the righteous Davidic monarch as a sprouting branch. Insofar as the book of Isaiah ultimately designates YHWH, and not the Davidic monarch, as king (Isa 66:1) and the "crown" in Isa 28:5-6 is identified in relation to the "stone" of Isa 28:16, it would seem that the language pertaining to the stone and the turban in Zech 3:9 draws upon both Exod 28:36-38 and Isa 28:1, 5-6, 16 to describe the stone on Joshua's turban and to identify him in relation to the "branch" who will serve as righteous ruler. Zechariah 6:9-15 employs specific references to "crowns" *(ʿăṭārôt)* in verses 11 and 14 and to the designation as "branch" *(ṣemaḥ)* in naming Joshua ben Jehozadak as the righteous monarch who will wear the crown on his head, sit on the throne, and build the Temple. Again, the designation of Joshua for this role is entirely in keeping with the outlook of the book of Isaiah which identifies YHWH as the ultimate king (Isa 66:1) and Zechariah ben Jeberechiah as the witness (Isa 8:2). It also calls to mind the presentation of the "branch" in Jer 33:14-26 in relation to both the Davidic monarch and the Levites. Joshua's designation as the high priest constitutes the "omen" of YHWH's future righteous rule through "the branch."

The reference to "the seven facets," literally, "the seven eyes" *(šibʿâ ʿênāyim)* "on a single stone" must be read in relation to the metaphorical portrayal of the seven-branched Temple lampstones as the eyes of YHWH in Zech 4:2, 10. Joshua's ordination as high priest would have taken place at the entrance to the Temple (see Exod 29:4; Lev 8:3), whether under construction or completed, and among the major fixtures within the Temple is the lampstand, with seven lights (cf. Exod 25:31-39). The stone on Joshua's turban is understood to be a shining object, as the rosette in Exod 28:36-38 is made of pure gold, that will reflect the seven lights of the Temple lampstand within the Temple, before which he is ordained.

Finally, the statement in verse 10 indicates that at the time that the guilt of the people is removed (verse 9), the people will invite each other to sit under their respective vines and fig trees. This is clearly an image of peace in the world that is drawn from Micah 4:4, where the image of people sitting under their vines and fig trees concludes the image of YHWH's judging the nations and bringing peace, which recapitulates the same image in Isa 2:2-4. Such an image corresponds to the image of the "branch" in Jer 23:5-6 and to the more lengthy descriptions of the righteous and peaceful rule of the Davidic "branch" figure in Isa 11:1-10. It also corresponds to the portrayal of peace by the Assyrian Rab Shakeh in Isa 36:16. Joshua's ordination as high priest signals the time when such peace will be realized.

THE REPORT OF THE FIFTH VISION:
THE TEMPLE LAMPSTAND AND THE LAYING OF THE FOUNDATION
BY ZERUBBABEL: 4:1-14

Zechariah 4:1-14 constitutes the fifth vision report by the prophet. The passage begins in a somewhat unusual manner with the statement, "(and) the angel who talked with me came again, and wakened me, as one is wakened from sleep." This varies from the customary formula, "I looked up and I saw," which plays a role in most of the other vision reports in Zechariah. The translation of the Hebrew phrase, *wayyāšāb hammalʾāk haddōbēr bî wayʿîrēnî kěʾîš ʿāšer-yēʾôr miššěnātô*, is contested as some understand the verb *wayyāšāb*, literally, "and he returned," to indicate repeated action, i.e., "and the angel who talked with me again awakened me," whereas others understand it as a reference to the angel's return, i.e., "and the angel who talked with me returned and awakened me . . ." The former translation presupposes that Zechariah had been sleeping and that he was awakened during the course of his visions. Visionary experience is sometimes portrayed as a dream experience elsewhere in the Hebrew Bible (cf. Num 12:6; Deut 13:2-6 [NRSV: 13:1-5]; 1 Samuel 3; Isa 29:7; Jer 23:23-40; 31:26; Zech 10:2). Such an understanding might build upon the reference to the prophet's vision of a man riding a red horse in the night in Zech 1:8, but there is no clear reference to the prophet sleeping in this vision. The latter translation presupposes that the angel was elsewhere, and returned to awaken Zechariah so that the visions could continue. Zechariah 3 indicates that the angel did not depart as he was with Zechariah and had just shown him the vision of Joshua's ordination. The phrase must therefore be understood as a reference to the angel's returning his attention from Joshua to Zechariah and awakening him for the next vision. The reference to the angel's awakening Zechariah must be understood metaphorically as indicated by the simile that compares the prophet's awakening to that of a man awakened from sleep. It refers simply to a turn in the prophet's attention from one vision to the next. The passage is presented as a first person report by the prophet, and continues until the introduction of the next vision report in Zech 5:1.

Following the opening statement in verse 1, the overall form of verses 2-14 is a presentation of a conversation between the angel and Zechariah concerning the vision of the Temple lampstand and Yhwh's oracle concerning the laying of the Temple foundation stone by Zerubbabel. The conversation opens in verse 2a with Zechariah's report of the angel's stereotypical question to the prophet, "What do you see?" Zechariah's response to the angel follows in two successive reports in verses 2b-3 and 4. In verses 2b-3, Zechariah states that he sees a lampstand *(měnôrâ)* made entirely of gold, and he proceeds to describe its overall structure and components. The first is "its bowl on top of it," which is rendered in the NRSV as "a bowl on top of it," a minor and unnecessary emendation of *wěgullāh,* "and its bowl," to *wěgullâ,* "and a bowl." The "bowl" on top of the menorah refers to the main basin of the lampstand in which olive oil is collected so that it can feed the wicks of the various "lamps" that are then described. Although modern readers might think of a lampstand with candles akin to modern versions of the Hanukkah menorah, ancient lamps used wicks saturated with oil instead of candles.

The prophet's description of the menorah includes seven lamps that are upon the bowl and the seven "lips" *(mûṣāqôt)* that are upon each of the lamps. The term *mûṣeqet* has caused some confusion as it has been taken to mean either "pipe" or "casting."[47] The meaning of the term as a "pipe" is derived only from the present context, where it would refer to a channel for oil from the main basin. But the term is derived from the verb root *yṣq,* "to pour out," which refers either to the pouring out of oil or to the "casting" of metal. Insofar as ancient lamps use wicks, they do not "pour out" their oil; rather the term must refer to the cast metal/gold construction of the menorah. The NRSV understands the term as "casting" and renders it as "lip" to refer to the thick lip-like edge of each lamp basin in which a wick is placed and fed by oil from the main basin. The entire menorah therefore includes forty-nine "lamps" or wicks, which is based on the double reference to "seven" in verse 2bβ, *šibʿâ wěšibʿâ mûṣāqôt lanērôt ʾǎšer ʿal-rōšāh,* literally, "seven and seven lips to the lamps which are on its top." The double reference to seven indicates a distributive sense, which requires a meaning of seven "lips" for each of the seven lamps, i.e., "seven lips each for the lamps

---

[47] For discussion, see Petersen, *Haggai and Zechariah 1–8* 221–3; Meyers and Meyers, *Haggai, Zechariah 1–8* 235–8.

which are on its top."[48] The relationship between this menorah and those mentioned elsewhere in biblical tradition is not entirely clear.[49] The tabernacle menorah described in Exod 25:31-40 and 37:17-24 includes a central shaft with six branches, three to each side. Each of the six branches includes a molded construction of three almond blossom-shaped cups with calyx and petals, and the central shaft includes a molded construction of four almond blossom-shaped cups with calyx and petals. This suggests that each branch includes multiple wicks, but it is not clear that seven wicks are intended (see also Num 8:1-4, which refers to the seven lamps of the Menorah). The reference to the seven "lips" for each lamp in Zech 4:2 may refer to the cast metal or molded work that is applied to each of the seven lamps, i.e., the "cups, calyxes, and petals" that form one piece with each of the seven "branches" of the Menorah. Many argue that the lampstands mentioned in Zechariah 4 and Exod 25:31-40; 37:17-24 differ from the ten lampstands in Solomon's Temple because Solomon's lampstands included only a single shaft with no branches. But 1 Kgs 7:49 describes them only as "lampstands" (*měnōrôt*) with no reference to the details of their construction.

Zechariah's description of the lampstand continues in verse 3 with a reference to the two olive trees that stand respective to the right and left of the lampstand. At one level, the two olive trees symbolize the olive oil that is used in the lampstand so that the lights burn perpetually (cf. Exod 27:20-21; Lev 24:1-4). They would therefore represent the central role of the Temple in relation to the fertility of the land that produces the olive oil and in relation to the creation of light each evening as the lamps are lit by the priest so that they burn throughout the night (see also Exod 30:7-8). At another level, however, verse 14 below indicates that the two olive trees represent the two major authority figures of the post-exilic Jewish community, i.e., the king and the priest, both of whom are anointed with olive oil (1 Sam 16:3; 1 Kgs 1:39; Ps 89:21 [NRSV: 89:20] for the king and Exod 28:41; 29:29; Lev 7:36; Num 35:25 for the priest). Joshua ben Jehozadak clearly served as the priest, and Zerubbabel, as a descendant of the last Davidic king Jehoiachin, represented the potential restoration of the Davidic monarchy. Just as the

---

[48] For a discussion of distribution in biblical Hebrew, see Bruce K. Waltke and M. O'Connor, *An Introduction to Biblical Hebrew Syntax* (Winona Lake: Eisenbrauns, 1990) section 7.2.3.

[49] See Petersen, *Haggai and Zechariah 1–8* 216–24 and Meyers and Meyers, *Haggai, Zechariah 1–8* 229–38 for discussion of the menorah or lampstand. In addition to the commentaries, see Carol Meyers, "Lampstand," *ABD* IV:141-3; "Menorah," *Encyclopaedia Judaica* 11:1355-67.

olive oil represents the fertility, light, and stability of creation, so the king and the priest represent the stability of the people of Israel. The longevity of the olive tree—some live as long as one thousand years—contributes to its role as a symbol of stability and permanence in both the natural and the human worlds.[50]

Verse 4 presents a second speech by the prophet in which he asks the angel to explain the meaning of the lampstand and the olive trees. The angel answers initially in verse 5 with a rhetorical question, "Do you not know what these are?" to which Zechariah replies, "No, my lord." The use of this rhetorical technique highlights the significance of the vision, and draws the reader's attention to the explanation which follows in verses 6-10.

The angel's explanation in verses 6-10 has been the subject of a great deal of discussion because many scholars maintain that verses 6aβ-10a are a secondary addition to an original text in which the angel answered the prophet's question by stating that the lampstand and olive trees represented the seven "eyes of Yʜwʜ which range through the whole earth" (verse 10b).[51] Verses 6aβ-10a are distinguished from the present context by the introductory formula, "This is the word of Yʜwʜ to Zerubbabel," which identifies the following material in verses 6b-10a as oracular material concerning Zerubbabel and his role in the building of the Temple. Indeed, the passage includes two major segments in verses 6aβ-7 and 8-10a respectively. The first is an oracle directed to Zerubbabel. The initial statement of the oracle, "Not by might, nor by power, but by my spirit, says Yʜwʜ of Hosts," is somewhat enigmatic. The terms "might" and "power" are clearly contrasted with "spirit." Both suggest physical or military power, which may be relevant in relation to the expectations for Zerubbabel articulated by Zechariah's colleague Haggai. Haggai envisions Zerubbabel as Yʜwʜ's "signet," or authority figure in relation to Yʜwʜ's plans "to overthrow the throne of the kingdoms" (Hag 2:20-23). As noted in the commentary to Haggai, these statements indicate an interest in restoring Zerubbabel to the Davidic throne and Judah as an independent state free from Persian control. The language in Hag 2:20-23 suggests the possibility of military overthrow of Persian rule, especially since it refers explicitly to the destruction of the strength of the kingdoms of the nations and the overthrow of their chariots, horses, and riders by the sword. The oracle in Zech 4:6b, however, envisions a very different scenario in which Yʜwʜ's "spirit" rather than military might will be the operative

---

[50] Meyers and Meyers, *Haggai, Zechariah 1–8* 238–9.

[51] See Petersen, *Haggai and Zechariah 1–8* 224, 238; Petitjean, *Les oracles* 207–67. Cf. Beuken, *Haggai–Sacharja 1–8* 258–82.

agent for change. The reader must recall that Zerubbabel's and Joshua's return to Jerusalem and the reconstruction of the Temple took place during the early years of the reign of the Persian monarch Darius I (reigned 522–486 B.C.E.) during which he was forced to put down numerous revolts against his rule. Whereas Haggai sees this as an opportunity for the overthrow of Persian rule over Judah, Zechariah apparently envisions a different scenario, yet to be specified, in which Zerubbabel's leading role in the reconstruction of the Temple will not entail the military overthrow of the Persian empire. Instead, YHWH's "spirit" will be employed to undertake the necessary action.

The rhetorical question in verse 7, "what are you, O great mountain?" seems clearly to be a metaphorical reference. It has been widely discussed and identified as Joshua ben Jehozadak, Tattenai the regional administrator from Samaria who attempted to block Temple construction (see Ezra 4–6), the difficulties that Zerubbabel will face in Temple reconstruction, and the piled-up ruins of the first Temple. The last proposal seems to be the most likely referent for the metaphor. It corresponds well to the following statements that the mountain will become a plain, i.e., the pile of building stones will be gradually reduced to a level plain as the work progresses, and that Zerubbabel will bring out the top stone, presumably to commence the building process. As a Davidic scion, Zerubbabel would play a special role in Temple reconstruction as he would emulate the actions of his ancestor Solomon who built the first Temple and thereby initiated the relationship between the house of YHWH and the dynasty of King David (see Psalm 132, which identifies David's efforts to find a home for YHWH as the basis for YHWH's promise of a dynasty for David; cf. 2 Samuel 7). Petersen points to the analogy between Zerubbabel's actions here and those mentioned in texts from ancient Mesopotamia and Seleucid Syria in which a cultic singer or builder of a new Temple removes a brick from the old temple and sets it aside with appropriate offerings so that it might be used in the construction of the new temple and thus play a role in establishing the continuity between the two shrines.[52] Insofar as Zerubbabel carries out this role in Zechariah 4, he establishes the continuity of the two Temples and the house of David. The reference to the shouts of "grace, grace to it" (*ḥēn ḥēn lāh*) follows. The Hebrew term *ḥēn* actually signifies favor, and indicates divine favor for the reconstruction of the Temple. In this sense, the shout of "favor, favor," is analogous to the shout of the

---

[52] Petersen, *Haggai and Zechariah 1–8* 239–44; idem, "Zerubbabel and Temple Reconstruction," *CBQ* 36 (1974) 366–72. Cf. Antti Laato, "Zechariah 4, 6b-10a and the Akkadian royal building inscriptions," *ZAW* 106 (1994) 53–69, who extends the analogy even further.

people, "long live King Solomon" (1 Kgs 1:39), at the anointing of the new king (cf. 2 Kgs 11:12 concerning the anointing of King Jehoash or Joash of Judah).

The presentation of the second oracle then follows in verses 8-10a which is directed to the angel who speaks with Zechariah. This is evident from the YHWH word transmission formula in verse 8 which states, "moreover the word of YHWH came to me saying . . . ," and identifies the following material as an oracle from YHWH. Insofar as the angel is identified in verse 6 (cf. verse 5) as the speaker of the entire oracle sequence in verses 6-11, the reference to "me" indicates that he is the one to whom this oracle is addressed. The initial *waw-consecutive* formation, here translated as "moreover . . . ," indicates that the oracle is intended to build upon the first oracle in verses 6aβ-7. The oracle proper follows in verses 9-11. It begins in verse 9aα with the statement, "the hands of Zerubbabel have founded this house," which is entirely in keeping with the portrayal of Zerubbabel as Temple builder in the preceding oracle; indeed, the statement in verse 9aα confirms this role. The following statements, however, are problematic. Verse 9aβ states, "his hands shall also complete it." This points to a major problem with regard to the figure of Zerubbabel in that Ezra 3 clearly notes Zerubbabel's role, together with that of Joshua ben Jehozadak, in the foundation of the Temple during the second year of Darius' reign, but Ezra 6 does not mention Zerubbabel at all in its account of the completion and dedication of the Temple in the sixth year of Darius' reign. Indeed, Zerubbabel's absence from this account has sparked a great deal of controversy concerning his fate.[53] His absence in Ezra 6 is especially problematic because he is also absent from Zechariah 6, which points to the crowning of a royal figure who will sit on the throne with a priest beside him, but identifies Joshua ben Jehozadak as the figure rather than Zerubbabel. Many interpreters speculate that he was removed from power, killed, or imprisoned by the Persians when they learned that he might become the ruling Davidic monarch of a newly independent Judean kingdom (see especially Hag 2:20-23), but there is no secure proof for such a contention. Others suggest that he was simply omitted from the account and continued in his role as governor of Judah because the marriage of Zerubbabel's successor, Elnathan, to Zerubbabel's daughter Shelomith (cf. 1 Chr 3:19), indicates the continuity of the Davidic line in the office of governor. This contention is based upon a late sixth-century seal found in Jerusalem that reads, "belonging

---

[53] See R. J. Coggins, *Haggai, Zechariah, Malachi* 11–5, 46–8, for an overview of the issue.

to Shelomith, maidservant of Elnathan the governor."[54] The reference to Shelomith, however, proves nothing as the name is hardly unusual for this period and it is unlikely that Zerubbabel's successor would refer to his predecessor's daughter as "maidservant" if indeed he had exercised power by virtue of his marriage to her. In this regard, it is important to note that the verse claims that Zerubbabel's hands "shall . . . complete it," i.e., the Temple. There is no evidence that Zerubbabel completed the Temple. The following statement in verse 9b, "Then you will know that YHWH of Hosts has sent me to you," points to Zerubbabel's accomplishment of his task as the sign that the angel who speaks with Zechariah indeed was sent by YHWH to both the prophet and the people. Although the meaning of the two references to "you" in verse 9b is not clear in English, the first reference to "you" is singular in Hebrew and therefore refers to Zechariah, and the second reference to "you" is plural and therefore refers to the people at large. Finally, verse 10a provides a motivating statement that contrasts the relatively minor beginnings of the reconstruction of the Temple with the greatness of its projected outcome, i.e., "For whoever has despised the day of small things shall rejoice and shall see the plummet in the hand of Zerubbabel." Some see the "plummet" (hā'eben habĕdîl), literally, "the tin stone," as a leveling tool used by Zerubbabel at the commencement of Temple reconstruction (see LXX, which reads *ton lithon ton kassiterinon*, "the stone/plummet of tin") or as a metallic tablet used as a foundation deposit for the new structure, but scholars have been unable to come to agreement concerning the significance of this object.[55]

Clearly, several aspects of these statements remain enigmatic, and must be considered further. First, the verb "to complete," is a *piel* form of the root *bṣ'*, "to cut off, gain by violence." When used in the *piel* form, it refers to the completion of YHWH's work on Mt. Zion in punishing the arrogant boasting of the Assyrian monarch (Isa 10:12); the completion of YHWH's previously planned work against Jerusalem in bringing punishment (Lam 2:17); and the oppressive gain of Israel's corrupt rulers (Ezek 22:12). In short, the term refers not to the completion of the Temple, but to the accomplishment of some violent and punitive act. When read in relation to the expectations of Haggai, such an act would be the reestablishment of the Davidic monarchy and the overthrow of Persian rule.

---

[54] See Meyers and Meyers, *Haggai, Zechariah 1–8* 9–13; idem, "The Shelomith Seal and Aspects of the Judaean Restoration: Some Additional Reconsiderations," *Eretz Israel* 17 (1985) 33–8.

[55] For discussion see Hanhart, *Sacharja* 252; Petersen, *Haggai and Zechariah 1–8* 243–4.

Second, if Zerubbabel does not complete this action, then the angel's credentials as a messenger of YHWH are invalid, i.e., Zerubbabel's accomplishing his action, whatever it might be, validates the angel's identity as YHWH's messenger. Indeed, the credibility of this oracle, and the entire oracle sequence to Zechariah, is in question at this point. Clearly, this issue is unresolved if this statement is read solely in relation to its present literary context or even in relation to Zechariah 1–8. But the reader must consider this oracle in relation to the literary context of the book of Zechariah as a whole. Zerubbabel failed to reconstitute the Davidic dynasty, and biblical sources suggest that he also did not complete the reconstruction of the Temple. Although the material in Zechariah 9–14 is generally considered to be much later additions to Zechariah 1–8, they point to a potential resolution to the problem in that they appear to outline the fulfillment of the promises articulated in the present oracles concerning Zerubbabel. Throughout Zechariah 9–14, reference is made to the future Davidic monarchy. Zechariah 9:9-10 calls for the people to rejoice because the king will come to them riding upon a donkey and establishing his dominion from sea to sea. Zechariah 12 looks forward to the "Day of YHWH" in which YHWH's victory over the nations will be realized, and "the house of David shall be like G–d, like the angel of the L–rd," at the head of the inhabitants of Jerusalem (Zech 12:8). Zechariah 13 points to the future cleansing of the house of David and the inhabitants of Jerusalem by a fountain opened in Jerusalem. Zechariah 14 points to YHWH's battle against the nations in which the Mt. of Olives will split in two to reveal a valley between its two halves. When YHWH becomes king over all the earth (Zech 14:9), the whole land shall be turned into "a plain from Geba to Rimmon south of Jerusalem" (Zech 14:10), and Jerusalem shall be secure as the nations come to Jerusalem at the festival of Sukkot each year to acknowledge YHWH's sovereignty.

Reading Zech 4:6-10 in relation to Zechariah 9–14 also appears to clarify some important aspects of the "plummet" in the hands of Zerubbabel. As noted above, the term "plummet" in verse 10 is the Hebrew expression *hāʾeben habĕdîl*, literally, "the tin stone." The term *bĕdîl*, "tin," is especially noteworthy because it is a passive noun construction from the root *bdl*, "to be divided, separate," and therefore means "that which is separated" in reference to "alloy, tin, dross." It is noteworthy that the expression refers to a plummet nowhere else in the Hebrew Bible; rather it refers simply to tin together with other metals in Num 31:22 and Ezek 22:18. In Isa 1:25, however, it is employed metaphorically in reference to the smelting of Jerusalem to remove its impurity and thereby to extract its "alloy" or "tin" as the remnant of the people that will survive YHWH's punishment or process of purification.

In this regard, it is noteworthy that Zechariah 13 employs the same metaphor of smelting as part of a process to purify the House of David and the people of Jerusalem "to cleanse them from sin and impurity" (Zech 13:1) and to remove two-thirds of the people as dross so that the remaining third may be refined as silver or gold to serve as YHWH's people (Zech 13:7-9). The figure of the stone also enters into the picture in Zechariah 12 in which YHWH states that Jerusalem will become a "heavy stone" for the nations that they will be unable to lift and that will therefore play a role in YHWH's granting victory over the nations to Judah and the House of David. It would appear that the "plummet in the hands of Zerubbabel" from Zech 4:10 anticipates some of the imagery of YHWH's actions toward Judah and the House of David, i.e., granting victory over the nations and the purification of Jerusalem and the Davidic monarchy.

Insofar as the overall scenario in Zechariah 9–14 appears to build upon specific elements of the oracles in Zech 4:6aβ-10a, i.e., the figure of the Davide Zerubbabel, the transformation of the mountain into a plain, the significance of the foundation of the Temple, the "completion" of Zerubbabel's hands, and the validation of the angel as the messenger of YHWH, the smelting of the people and the monarchy, and the use of the stone against the nations, it would appear that Zechariah 9–14, at least in part, is designed to point to the fulfillment of this oracular material. Although Zech 4:6aβ-10a may originally have envisioned Zerubbabel's restoration of the Temple as a signal for the restoration of the house of David and the overthrow of Persian rule, in the present form of the book, such a restoration is suspended until a far more distant future when YHWH would come to bring punishment upon the nations and restore the house of David and the city of Jerusalem to their intended roles in a world ruled by YHWH.

Finally, the statement in verse 10b, "these seven are the eyes of YHWH which range through the whole earth." As noted above, this statement appears to have been the angel's original response to Zechariah's question in verse 4 concerning the meaning of the image of the menorah with the two olive trees at its side prior to the insertion of the material in verses 6aβ-10a. Although the later material seems clearly to relate to Zechariah 9–14, the significance of verse 10b must be considered as well, both in relation to Zechariah's original question and in relation to the images presented in verses 6aβ-10a. When considered in relation to the preceding images of the menorah and the olive trees, the explanation that these are the eyes of YHWH clearly presupposes that the seven lamps of the menorah must represent the presence of YHWH in the Temple and the world at large insofar as the Temple symbolizes the center of the universe from which creation proceeds. Because the menorah illumines the Temple and the world at large so that all can be seen, it symbolically represents YHWH's eyes that see all that takes place in the world (see 2 Chr 16:9, which also describes YHWH's eyes ranging throughout the world; cf. Ezek 1:18 in which the rims of the wheels of YHWH's throne chariot are metaphorically portrayed as eyes; see also Job 34:21; Pss 14:2; 66:7; Prov 15:3). Thus, the lighting of the menorah would symbolize the restoration of YHWH's Presence to the site of the new Temple much as the descent of YHWH's glory in the form of fire and smoke symbolized YHWH's presence in the wilderness tabernacle (Exod 40:34-38). The restoration of YHWH's presence to the Temple in this chapter clearly looks forward to the role that YHWH's presence will play in the scenario of punishment, purification, and restoration articulated throughout Zechariah 9–14. But whereas verse 10b answers Zechariah's question in verse 4, "what are these, my lord?" in relation to the menorah, it does not answer the question entirely because it does not explain the two olive trees. To a certain extent, the references to Zerubbabel in verses 6aβ-10a addresses this concern because as a royal figure he would be anointed with olive oil, but this additional material does not answer the question fully because it does not account for *two* olive trees. This prepares the way for Zechariah's two questions in verses 11-12.

Zechariah 4:11 presents the first of the prophet's questions, "what are these two olive trees on the right and the left of the lampstand?" and Zech 4:12 presents the second, "what are these two branches of the olive trees, which pour out the gold through the two golden pipes?" The first question merely asks about the significance of the symbol that was not addressed in the angel's first response to Zechariah's question in verses 5, 6-10, i.e., he only explained the significance of the menorah, but he did not deal fully with the two olive trees especially since his focus on Zerubbabel would not explain the significance of two olive trees. Interestingly, earlier Canaanite and Egyptian representations of the goddess Kadesha or Asherah, generally symbolized by the presence of a sacred tree, would represent her flanked by the gods Resheph (plague, death) and the ithyphallic Min (fertility, life) to represent the interplay of death and life in the world of creation or nature.[56] The menorah, which is clearly modeled on the imagery of the tree, appears to draw upon this motif but portrays the figures responsible for life or death in the world in relation to the two olive trees, which as noted above symbolize continuity and stability in the world as the olive tree can live up to a thousand years and continually regenerates its trunk even as its center becomes hollow. Indeed, shoots that will eventually

[56] See Pritchard, *ANEP* 470–4, with discussion on pages 304–5.

produce their own fruit will grow from the base of the older tree, which may symbolize the two smaller olive trees beside the larger "tree" of the menorah. The second question points to the two "branches" of the olive trees which pour out the oil through the two golden pipes. The exact purpose of the two "branches" and "pipes" is uncertain, but they appear to be designed as a device that will either feed olive oil to the main menorah or that will drain olive oil from the main menorah to symbolize the fertility engendered by the presence of YHWH in the Temple. In either case, the imagery of the "branches," *šibbǎlîm*, literally, "ears of grain/fruit" (Gen 41:5; Isa 17:5; Ruth 2:2) or "branch of a stream" (Judg 12:6; Ps 69:16 [NRSV: 69:15]; Isa 27:12) must be understood in relation to the produce of the trees and thus their capacity to produce food and stability in the world. The oil that they produce is metaphorically described as "gold" (cf. NRSV which renders the term as "oil" but adds a note that in Hebrew the term is "gold") so that it relates to the overall imagery of the gold-plated menorah.

The angel's answer to Zechariah's questions appears in verses 13 and 14. Verse 13 presents his first response in the form of a rhetorical question, "do you not know what these are?" to which Zechariah responds, "No, my lord." As in verse 5, the rhetorical question highlights the prophet's own question and builds anticipation in the reader for the coming answer. The answer itself is presented in verse 14 in which the angel states that the two olive trees represent "the two anointed ones who stand by the lord of all the earth." Although they are not identified by name, the reference to "the two anointed ones," literally, "the sons of oil" *(běnê hayyiṣhār)*, clearly refers to both the royal figure, Zerubbabel, and the priestly figure, Joshua ben Jehozadak, as both kings and priests are anointed with olive oil in ancient Israel (1 Sam 16:3; 1 Kgs 1:39; Ps 89:21 [NRSV: 89:20] for the king and Exod 28:41; 29:29; Lev 7:36; Num 35:25 for the priest). Both figures are instrumental in the reconstruction of the Temple, the city of Jerusalem, and the nation of Israel.

THE REPORT OF THE SIXTH VISION:
THE FLYING SCROLL: 5:1-4

Zechariah 5:1-4 constitutes the sixth vision of the prophet Zechariah. This brief passage begins with a version of the customary introduction to the vision reports of the prophet, "Again, I looked up and saw . . ." In this case, the vision is a "flying scroll," *měgillâ ʿāpâ*. The structure of the passage is quite simple. Following Zechariah's first person statement in verse 1 that he has seen the "flying scroll," the prophet's report of his dialogue with the angel in verses 2-4 takes up the meaning of this symbol.

There is relatively little precedent for the vision of a flying scroll. Most interpreters point to the scroll given by YHWH to Ezekiel at Ezekiel's commissioning in Ezek 2:1–3:11. In Ezekiel's vision, the scroll represented the word of YHWH that the prophet was to eat (cf. Jer 15:16) so that he could internalize the divine message that he was to deliver to the people of Israel. The specific contents of Ezekiel's scroll would therefore presumably constitute the contents of the prophetic message that appears throughout his book. Other analogies include the scroll of Jeremiah's prophecies that was written by his scribe Baruch and burned by King Jehoiakim in Jeremiah 36 and "the scroll of the book" that is equated with YHWH's Torah in Ps 40:8-9 [NRSV: 40:7-8]. Although the scrolls mentioned for Ezekiel and Jeremiah suggest that Zechariah's scroll should somehow be identified specifically with his prophetic message, the details of the dialogue between Zechariah and the angel indicate that the scroll is to be identified in general with YHWH's Torah.

The dialogue begins with the presentation of the angel's stereotypical question to Zechariah, "What do you see?" Zechariah reports his answer in first person form by stating that he has seen a flying scroll and its length is twenty cubits and its width ten cubits. The cubit is the standard unit of measure in the ancient Near Eastern world.[57] The standard cubit is based on the length of a man's forearm from the elbow to the fingertip and is roughly equivalent to eighteen inches, and the Babylonian royal cubit is approximately three finger widths longer. Based upon the standard cubit, the measure of the scroll in Zechariah's vision would therefore be approximately thirty feet by fifteen feet, which would constitute a scroll far too large to be of any practical use. The exaggerated size of the scroll may be understood in relation to the visionary context in which it is portrayed, but scholars have noted that its dimensions correspond precisely to several features of the Jerusalem Temple.[58] According to 1 Kgs 6:3, the vestibule of the Temple, i.e., the entry court that stands before the main chamber of the Temple, measures twenty by ten cubits. Likewise, 1 Kgs 6:23-28 indicates that the combined measurements of the two cherubim placed in the Holy of Holies of the Temple, i.e., the inner or third chamber of the Temple where the ark of the covenant resides, measures twenty by ten cubits. The measure of each wing of the cherubim is five cubits for a combined total of twenty cubits for the two of them, and their height is ten cubits.

[57] For discussion, see Marvin A. Powell, "Weights and Measures," *ABD* VI:895-908.

[58] See B. C. Ollenburger, "Zechariah," 774.

The correspondence in the measurement of Zechariah's flying scroll, the vestibule for the Temple, and the cherubim of the Holy of Holies must be considered. As winged creatures, the images of the cherubim lend themselves to the motif of flight, and they stand guard over the ark of the covenant (1 Kgs 6:19) where the tablets of the covenant, given by YHWH to Moses at Mt. Sinai, are stored (Exod 25:16; 40:20; 1Kgs 8:9; cf. Exod 31:18). The tablets of the covenant formed the basis for the Torah of Moses that Moses wrote and gave to the Levites who carried the ark of the covenant as well as to the elders of Israel at the conclusion of his speeches to the people in the book of Deuteronomy (Deut 31:9). Deuteronomy 31:9-13 stipulates that the Torah is to be read to the people "every seventh year, in the year of remission, during the festival of booths (Sukkoth), when all Israel comes to appear before YHWH your G–d at the place that he will choose, you shall read this Torah before all Israel in their hearing" (Deut 31:10). According to Josh 8:30-35, Joshua copied the Torah of Moses on stones, and read the Torah to all Israel assembled before the ark of the covenant at Mt. Ebal and Gerizim in Shechem. Although Deuteronomy refers only to the "place" that YHWH will choose, later tradition clearly understands the "place" to refer to the Temple in Jerusalem. Thus, when Josiah read the Torah to all the people, he did so at the Temple in Jerusalem (2 Kgs 23:2). Josiah's location by the pillar (2 Kgs 23:3), the place designated for the king to stand (see 2 Kgs 11:14), clearly designates the vestibule of the Temple as the place where he read the Torah to the people. According to 1 Kgs 7:15-22, Solomon built the two bronze pillars, Jachin and Boaz, to be placed on either side of the vestibule of the Temple (1 Kgs 7:21). It would seem from this example that the vestibule of the Temple, from which one can see into the Temple where the Holy of Holies and the ark of the covenant were located, was the place where the Torah was normally to be read to the people on every seventh Sukkoth. Although Ezra later reads the Torah to the people on a platform outside the Water Gate on the eastern side of the city outside of the Temple area, he does so prior to Sukkoth on the first day of the seventh month (Rosh ha-Shanah or the New Year) so that all of the people may hear, whether they are able to enter the Temple or not (see Neh 8:1-12). This would have enabled him to prepare the people for the observance of Sukkoth which followed (Neh 8:13-18).

The measurements of the flying scroll and their correspondence to the measurements of both the Temple vestibule, where the Torah was normally read to the people every seventh Sukkoth, and the cherubim which guarded the ark of the covenant where the tablets of the covenant were kept, suggest that the scroll is somehow to be identified with YHWH's Torah. This contention is further supported by the angel's final statements to Zechariah in verses 3-4 concerning the meaning of the flying scroll. According to the NRSV, the angel states in verse 3, "This is the curse that goes out over the face of the whole land; for everyone who steals shall be cut off according to the writing on one side, and everyone who swears falsely shall be cut off according to the writing on the other side." There are tremendous problems with this translation. The first is the statement that those who steal or swear falsely shall be "cut off" (*niqqâ*). The Hebrew term *niqqâ* does not mean "to be cut off," but refers to someone who is acquitted of a crime or who remains free or exempt from punishment (see Exod 21:19; Num 5:28; 1 Sam 26:9) or from oaths (Gen 24:8, 41; cf. Num 5:19). The root *nqh* means "to be empty, clean," and this sense stands behind Isa 3:26 in which the women of Jerusalem sit "desolate" because they have been emptied or cleaned out of all that they have. Otherwise, the juridical sense of innocence or exemption is conveyed by this term. This is especially important to consider in relation to the "curse," *ʾālâ*, that is mentioned at the outset of the passage. The term *ʾālâ* means literally "oath," and refers to the blessings or penalties that will result depending on whether or not one observes the terms of the oath to which one has sworn. Such blessings and curses follow the legal section of Deuteronomy (Deuteronomy 28; see also Deut 29:18, 19, 20, etc., where the term *ʾālâ* refers to the penalties for failing to observe the covenant). The term also appears in relation to the testing of a woman suspected of marital infidelity (Num 5:21, 23, 27), in relation to the covenant curses envisioned by Jeremiah (Jer 29:18; 42:18; 44:12), or any public oath (Lev 5:1; Gen 24:41). This is especially pertinent in that the angel's statement in verse 3 appears to relate the problem that YHWH's oracle in verse 4 is intended to address, i.e., the curses or penalties envisioned by the Torah in cases of wrongdoing, e.g., theft or false oaths, are not being enforced. In this instance, the Hebrew text must be translated differently from the NRSV. The parallel phrases *kol-hannōgēb* and *kol hannišbāʿ* do not refer to crimes mentioned on one side of the scroll or the other, but to hypothetical crimes, i.e., "all who steal" and "all who swear (falsely, see verse 4 below)." The use of the phrase *mizzeh kāmôhā niqqâ* in each case refers to the exemption of each perpetrator of a crime, i.e., "from this (the previously mentioned crime) according to it (the scroll) he is exempt." The image of the flying scroll is intended to convey a situation in which the normal systems of law that ensure order in a society have broken down, i.e., those who do wrong are not being punished for their crimes. Prior to the arrival of Joshua ben Jehozadak the high priest and Zerubbabel the governor, this is precisely the situation that early Persian period Jerusalem faced. Insofar as the Temple, the high priest, and the governor are the symbols and agents of the enforcement of civil law in Judah, the arrival of the high priest and governor and the reconstruction of the Temple inaugurates the time when such lawlessness will come to an end.

The angel's statement in verse 4, presented as an oracle of YHWH, expressly states that such lawlessness will end. The oracular formula, "says YHWH of Hosts" *nĕʾum yhwh ṣĕbāʾôt*, identifies the statement as an oracle of YHWH. YHWH begins with the statement, "I have sent it out," in reference to the "scroll" or "curse/oath," both of which are feminine nouns which correspond to the feminine pronouns of YHWH's statement. YHWH continues by stating that "it shall enter the house of the thief, and the house of anyone who swears falsely by my Name, and it shall abide in that house and consume it, both timber and stones." Overall, the scroll and the oath are perfect metaphors to express the punishment that those who commit such crimes will suffer now that the rule of law has been restored in Jerusalem. The reader must bear in mind that, until the arrival of Joshua and Zerubbabel, Jerusalem lay undefended with no central authority as a result of the Babylonian destruction of the city. Indeed, this would signal a first attempt to restore order as, later, Nehemiah undertook measures to restore order, but only after rebuilding the walls of the city to ensure its protection (Nehemiah 1–13).

THE REPORT OF THE SEVENTH VISION:
THE WOMAN IN THE EPHAH: 5:5-11

Zechariah 5:5-11 constitutes the prophet's report of his seventh vision concerning the ephah which is sent to Shinar (Babylon) with a woman inside. An ephah is a standard measure of volume in the Hebrew Bible roughly equivalent to 20.8 quarts or less than two thirds of a bushel.[59] Such measures could be carried in baskets, jars, or other containers depending upon the nature of the material. Again, the basic form of the narrative is a first person account of a vision by the prophet in which conversation takes place between Zechariah and the angel concerning the meaning of the symbols described by the prophet. In the present case, the narrative includes two components. Verses 5-8 present the angel's instruction to Zechariah to observe the ephah and the subsequent discussion concerning its meaning; and verses 9-11 present the prophet's observation of the two flying women who take up the ephah for transport to Shinar and the ensuing discussion with the angel concerning the significance of this act.

[59] Powell, "Weights and Measures."

Verses 5-8 begin with the prophet's report in verse 5 that the angel who was speaking with him "went out" (*wayyēṣēʾ*; NRSV translates "came forward"), which indicates that he came out of the Temple itself where the menorah stood and from which the Torah was read to the people. Such a move is hardly surprising when considered in relation to the following image of the woman in the ephah. Insofar as she represents wickedness (verse 8), she cannot remain in the Temple itself as she would defile the holy precinct. The angel approaches Zechariah in order to instruct him to look up and see what is coming out; presumably she is coming out of the Temple as the efforts at reconstruction would undoubtedly entail the purification of the site for holy service.

Verse 6a relates the prophet's stereotypical question upon seeing the various visions, i.e., "what is it?" It continues with the report of the angel's three-part explanation in verses 6b-8aα. The first two parts of the explanation in verses 6b state that "this is a basket coming out" and that "this is their iniquity in all the land." There are problems with both of these translations. As the NRSV notes, the term "basket" should actually read ephah with the Hebrew; apparently the NRSV rendered the term as "basket" so that the reader might understand the type of container that would be used to hold an ephah measure of grain or other material. As noted above, a jar or other container could have served just as well. The second statement deserves closer attention. The NRSV translation "their iniquity" accepts the LXX's rendition of the Hebrew term *ʿênām*, "their eye," as *hē adikia autōn*, which presupposes that the underlying Hebrew text reads *ʿăwōnām*, "their iniquity." The change from *ʿênām* to *ʿăwōnām* requires only a very minor orthographic change of the middle letter *yod* to *waw*, which appear to be very similar in the Aramaic square script employed for Hebrew beginning in the Second Temple period. Overall, the LXX reading appears to suit the context well, especially since the woman in the ephah is defined as wickedness and would therefore represent the iniquity of the people that is being removed. But the question remains, why would the MT read "their eye" in place of the commonly accepted LXX reading "their iniquity?" The answer appears to lie in the deliberate contrast that the text makes between the woman in the ephah which is being expelled from the sanctuary and the preceding images of the menorah and the flying scroll, which represent the reinstitution of YHWH's presence in the Temple together with the symbols of YHWH's sovereignty and authority, i.e., the high priest, the king, and the Torah. Floyd has already noted the satirical presentation of the woman in the ephah in contrast to the preceding images of YHWH's authority.[60] Whereas

---

[60] Michael H. Floyd, "The Evil in the Ephah: Reading Zechariah 5:5-11 in Its Literary Context," *CBQ* 58 (1996) 51–68.

the menorah represents the "eyes of YHWH which range through the whole earth" (Zech 6:10), the woman in the ephah represents "their eye in all the land." Although the referent for "their" is not specified, it would have to refer to the Persian authorities who ruled Judah from Babylon, to which the woman in the ephah is about to be sent (see verse 11 below; n.b., Shinar is Babylon, cf. Gen 10:10; 11:2).

Verse 7 continues the second part of the angel's explanation by pointing to the leaden cover which was lifted up from its place on the ephah to reveal a woman sitting inside. The "leaden cover," literally "a round cake of lead" *(kikkar ʿōperet)* apparently served as a heavy weight to weigh down the contents of the ephah and to seal its contents inside. The woman has been the subject of a great deal of misogynistic interpretation in that she has been taken to represent the sin of Eve by which all humanity suffers (Genesis 3) or the impurity of the holy community which is commanded to avoid contact with a woman prior to approaching holy ground (see Exod 19:15). Indeed, the Hebrew text of Zechariah suggests no such interpretation; it is derived from the above reading of "their iniquity" in verse 6 of the LXX version of this text. Instead, the image of the woman must be read in relation to other prophetic texts which suggest that the Temple became the site for the worship of the Queen of Heaven and Tammuz during the period of the exile (Jeremiah 44; Ezekiel 8). The Queen of Heaven is frequently identified with the Mesopotamian goddess Ishtar, represented by Venus or the Morning Star, who was the goddess of fertility, passion, and war.[61] According to the Babylonian myth, "the Descent of Ishtar to the Netherworld," Ishtar was the consort of the shepherd god, Tammuz, who died and went to the netherworld leaving the earth devoid of life and fertility. In order to restore fertility to the world, Ishtar descended into the netherworld to recover the dead Tammuz and bring him and the world back to life. The myth explains the seasonal cycles of the Near East; i.e., during the six months that Tammuz is in the netherworld, the earth suffers its dry season when nothing grows, but during the six months that Tammuz is alive, the rains come and the earth lives. According to Jeremiah 44 and Ezekiel 8, many Judeans turned to the worship of these deities, or at least engaged in a native Judean form of such goddess worship, when it became apparent that the Babylonians were going to defeat Judah and thus YHWH. It would appear that the reconstruction of the Temple by Zerubbabel and Joshua ben Jehozadak in

[61] See Philip C. Schmitz, "Queen of Heaven," *ABD* V:586-8; William J. Fulco, "Ishtar," *ABD* III:521-2; for translations of the earlier Sumerian myth of "the Descent of Inanna to the Netherworld" and "the Descent of Ishtar to the Netherworld, " see Pritchard, *ANET* 52–7, 106–9.

the late sixth century would have been the occasion for such worship to come to an end.

Verse 8 concludes with the third part of the angel's explanation of the significance of the vision of the woman in the Ephah and a report of his thrusting her back into the ephah and thrusting the leaden cover back onto the mouth of the ephah. The angel defines her as "wickedness," and then takes action to expel her from the community. Insofar as she represents a goddess figure, she is defined as wickedness in contrast to YHWH. Although worship of such figures is well known in Judaism throughout the pre-exilic, exilic, and early post-exilic periods, it would be considered syncretistic and thus contrary to the monotheistic teachings of Judaism.[62]

Several satirical aspects of this presentation must be noted in addition to the previously mentioned contrast between the "eyes of YHWH" in the vision of the menorah (Zech 4:10) and "their eye," i.e., the eye of the Persian/Babylonian rulers of Judah in verse 6.[63] First, whereas the menorah, high priest, king (Zerubbabel), and Torah scroll are portrayed as becoming established in Zechariah 3; 4; and 5:1-4, the woman in the ephah is being expelled. The use of the verb *šlk*, "thrust, expel," in verse 8 highlights this aspect of the angel's actions. Second, her definition as "wickedness" is designed to discredit such worship, even though it had been practiced in Judah throughout the period of the exile, and apparently constituted an important component of Judean folk religion. Third, the use of the term *kikkar*, "rounded cake," to describe the lead lid of the ephah is fraught with irony. The term is also used to describe one of the types of cakes offered at the altar during the course of the priestly ordination ceremony (Exod 29:23; *kikkar leḥem*, translated in NRSV as a "loaf of bread"). Cakes are also prepared for the Queen of Heaven (Jer 7:18; 44:19), but a different term is employed to describe them. Fourth, the ephah is empty except for the woman. As a province of the Persian empire, Judah would be expected to send an annual tax or tribute back to its Persian rulers, generally in the form of grain or other types of agricultural produce that might be carried in an ephah container. In this case, no grain is sent back to Shinar; only the woman representing the Babylonian goddess figure. Such a move

[62] For discussion, see William G. Dever, "The Silence of the Text: An Archaeological Commentary on 2 Kings 23," *Scripture and Other Artifacts: Essays on the Bible and Archaeology in Honor of Philip J. King*, ed. M. D. Coogan, J. C. Exum, and L. E. Stager (Louisville: Westminster John Knox, 1994) 143–68; Mark S. Smith, *The Early History of G–d: YHWH and the Other Deities in Ancient Israel* (New York: Harper and Row, 1990).

[63] See esp. Floyd, "The Evil in the Ephah."

would reflect Judean sentiments that the building of the Temple heralded the restoration of an independent Judean state.

The second portion of this vision report begins with the standard introductory formula, "then I looked up and saw . . ." In this case, however, the formula introduces a new episode rather than an entirely new vision. Again, the satirical viewpoint of the first part of the vision plays a role in the imagery of the second. The prophet sees two women with wings like a stork going out and lifting the ephah into the air. Although the NRSV states that the two women were "coming forward," the Hebrew verb *yôṣĕ'ôt*, "going out," indicates that they were leaving the Temple precincts. Insofar as the two women have wings, they are portrayed in imagery that would suggest the two cherubim who guard the ark of the covenant in the holy of holies. Rather than guard the contents of the Temple, however, they are actively engaged in removing the woman in the ephah from the Temple which highlights her diminished status in relation to the preceding images of the scroll, the king, the menorah, and the priest. They are portrayed as women because they bear the woman in the ephah. Furthermore, the description of the women's wings "like the wings of a stork" hints at irony as well. The Hebrew term for "stork," *ḥăsîdâ*, closely resembles the noun *ḥāsîd*, "pious, faithful one," and thereby mocks the faithfulness of those who had worshiped the Queen of Heaven during the period when the Temple lay in ruins.

Verse 10 reports the prophet's question as to where the two women are taking the ephah. Verse 11 relates the angel's answer that they are taking it to the land of Shinar where a "house" or temple will be built for it and it will set down there on a base or pedestal. As noted above, Shinar is the land where Babylon is located (see Gen 10:10; 11:2). During much of the Persian period, Babylon served as the administrative capital for the western portions of the Persian empire, which would include Judah, during the reigns of Cyrus (539–530 B.C.E.) and Cambyses (530–522 B.C.E.).[64] It was also one of the major centers of revolt against Darius in the early years of his reign, and the revolts against him may well have sparked Judean efforts to break free of Persian control at this time. Indeed, the sending of the woman/goddess in the ephah would lend itself to such a scenario. After the revolts were successfully put down, Darius reorganized the administrative structure of the empire and built a new capital at Persepolis, although the Persian royal court continued to employ other cities as additional capitals, including Susa, Ecbatana, and Babylon, in order to control the vast empire. The place-

---

[64] For an overview, see Pierre Briant, "Persian Empire," *ABD* V:236-44.

ment of the ephah on a pedestal in a temple indicates that it is to be revered as a god—in Shinar. This adds to the satirical portrayal of the woman in the ephah in relation to the Judean symbols of divine and royal authority previously mentioned in Zechariah's visions. Once again, the removal of the woman in the ephah represents the reestablishment of YHWH's Temple, Torah, priesthood, and kingship and the end of foreign rule.

THE REPORT OF THE EIGHTH VISION:
THE FOUR CHARIOTS: 6:1-15

Zechariah 6:1-15 constitutes the eighth and final vision report of the prophet Zechariah. The report begins with a typical variation of the introductory formula for the reports, "And again I looked up and saw . . ." The report focuses on the image and significance of four chariots, each with a set of different colored horses, which represent the four winds that patrol the earth on behalf of YHWH. Following the conclusion of the report proper in verse 8, verses 9-15 present an oracle to the prophet in which YHWH calls for the crowning of a figure called "the branch" who shall build the Temple of YHWH. This oracle report must be read together with the vision of the four chariots because the crowning of the branch and the projected building of the Temple constitute the reason that the chariots must patrol the earth. Furthermore, the motifs of the colored horses that patrol the earth and the building of the Temple recall the motifs of the first vision report in Zech 1:7-17, and indicate that the projected building of the Temple is about to take place. Zechariah 6:1-15 thereby rounds out and concludes the prophet's vision reports in Zech 1:7–6:15 by pointing to the crowning of the branch and the building of the Temple as signs of the ultimate restoration of Zion. The date formula in Zech 7:1 marks the beginning of the next major unit of the book of Zechariah in chapters 7–14.

The prophet's report of the vision of the four chariots in verses 1-8 includes two major components in verses 1-6 and 7-8 in which Zechariah first describes the movements of the chariots and then receives some explanatory comment from his angelic guide. Whereas verses 1-6 relate the initial emergence of the four chariots and their significance, verses 7-8 relate their movement throughout the earth and thus the inauguration of the process in which the Temple is rebuilt and YHWH's sovereignty is manifested in the world.

The first portion of the prophet's vision report in verses 1-6 begins in verses 1-3 with his description of the emergence of the four chariots from between the two mountains of bronze and the colors of the horses that accompany each of the chariots. The image of the chariot is frequently employed in biblical literature to portray the means by which YHWH moves through the heavens.[65] Although the term chariot does not appear in Ezekiel's visions of YHWH's throne-chariot in Ezekiel 1–3 and 10–11, it is clear that the image of the cherubim who bear the wheeled throne of YHWH through the heavens is based upon the portrayal of the ark of the covenant, which is conveyed by a cart with wheels in some traditions (see 2 Samuel 6; cf. 1 Samuel 6; contra 1 Chronicles 15). Indeed, 1 Chr 28:18 refers to "the golden chariot of the cherubim that spread their wings and covered the ark of the covenant of YHWH." Other traditions portray YHWH as a warrior who drives horses and chariots against the enemy (Hab 3:8; Isa 66:15; Ps 68:17; cf. 2 Kgs 6:17; 7:6) or as the rider of the heavens (Ps 68:33) who is mounted on cherubim or the wind (Ps 18:11 [NRSV: 18:10]; 2 Sam 22:11) and whose chariot is equated with the clouds (Ps 104:3). Likewise, a chariot and horses of fire carried the prophet Elijah to heaven (2 Kgs 2:11).

Although YHWH is clearly not mounted in any of the four chariots described in this vision, they signify divinely ordained movements from the heavens. This is clear from the references to the two mountains of bronze from which the chariots emerge. The identification of these mountains is sometimes disputed, but they must be equated with the two pillars of bronze, Jachin and Boaz, that were placed at the entrance to the Temple of Solomon (1 Kgs 7:15-22; 2 Chr 3:15-17). Insofar as the Temple represents the center of the cosmos and the place where heaven and earth are conjoined,[66] the pillars at the entrance to the Temple define the entryway both to the Holy of Holies of the Jerusalem Temple and to the heavenly throne of YHWH. They likely symbolize the "foundations of the world" (Ps 18:16 [NRSV: 18:15]; 2 Sam 22:16) or the "foundations of the earth" (Ps 82:5; Mic 6:2; Isa 24:18; Jer 31:37; Prov 8:29) on which the security of creation is based. Although Jachin and Boaz were broken into pieces and carried off as booty at the time of the Babylonian destruction of the Jerusalem Temple (2 Kgs 25:13; Jer 52:17-23), the bronze columns would still serve as a symbol of YHWH's heavenly Temple on which the earthly Temple was based. In this present context, the emergence of the chariots from between the mountains of bronze represents the beginning of divine action in the world.[67] It is

---

[65] See also the Mesopotamian cylinder seal in Pritchard, *ANEP* 689, which depicts the weather god in his chariot receiving offerings.

[66] See Levenson, "The Temple and the World"; idem, *Sinai and Zion*.

[67] See also the two Mesopotamian cylinder seals in Pritchard, *ANEP* 683, 685, which portray the ascent or release of the sun god Shamash from between the two mountains to symbolize the inauguration of the day and the renewal of creation.

noteworthy that the image of the two mountains anticipates the split of the Mount of Olives into two portions in Zech 14:1-5 when YHWH defeats the nations that threaten Jerusalem and finally restores the city as the holy center of the earth.

The prophet's description of the four chariots and their horses in verses 2-3 notes that each chariot is accompanied by horses of a different color. Thus, the first chariot has red horses, the second chariot has black horses, the third chariot has white horses, and the fourth chariot has "dappled gray" horses. This last term is problematic as the Hebrew text reads *sûsîm běruddîm ʾămuṣṣîm*. The term *běruddîm* apparently refers to "spotted" horses as the root *brd* is related to the term for "hail," which suggests the general shape of stones or spots. The term *ʾămuṣṣîm*, however, creates difficulties because it is derived from the root *ʾmṣ*, "to be strong," and appears in verse 7 as an apparent reference to the "strong steeds" that pull the chariots. Although some scholars maintain that the term has been misplaced here from verse 7 by scribal error or that it is a textual corruption for *ʾădummîm*, "red" (cf. verse 2) that is designed to suggest spotted red horses,[68] the term can be read as a reference to the "spotted strong horses" of the fourth chariot. There have been numerous attempts to speculate concerning the significance of the colors of the horses, e.g., they represent the colors of sunset or various moral qualities, etc.,[69] but they seem merely to indicate a natural range of colors that might have been found among horses. It is noteworthy that they correspond roughly to the colors of the horses that are mentioned in the first vision (Zech 1:8), i.e., "red" (*ʾădummîm*) and "white" (*lěbānîm*). Zech 1:8 employs *śěruqqîm*, "sorrel, mottled," in place of *běruddîm*, "spotted," in Zech 6:3, and the color "black" (*šěḥōrîm*) does not appear in Zech 1:8 at all. Nevertheless, the two visions form a sort of frame at the beginning and end of the vision sequence in Zechariah. Whereas Zech 1:7-17 portrays the different colors of horses hidden in the myrtles awaiting the time when the Temple would be built, Zech 6:1-8 portrays the different colors of horses, now attached to chariots, emerging from the heavenly Temple to range through the earth as the process of Temple reconstruction commences.

Verses 4-6 relate Zechariah's request that the angel explain the significance of these symbols followed by the angel's reply. The report of

---

Shamash also serves as the god of wisdom in Mesopotamian tradition. He is the god who gives law to King Hammurapi (see Pritchard, *ANET* 164; idem, *ANEP* 246, 515).

[68] See the discussions in Hanhart, *Sacharja* 383–5; Meyers and Meyers, *Haggai, Zechariah 1–8* 322; and Petersen, *Haggai and Zechariah 1–8* 263.

[69] For a brief survey, see Petersen, *Haggai and Zechariah 1–8* 269.

the prophet's request in verse 4, "what are these, my lord?" is identical
to his requests in Zech 1:9 and 4:4 and analogous to those in Zech 2:2, 6
[NRSV: 1:19; 2:2]; 4:12; 5:6, 10. The report of the angel's response in
verses 5-6 begins in verse 5 with his statement that the chariots are to
be identified with the four winds of the heavens that are departing
after having presented themselves before the lord of all the earth. The
four winds of heaven have already appeared in the context of the third
vision in Zech 2:10 [NRSV: 2:6] where they symbolize YHWH's power to
exile the people of Jerusalem and Judah to the north. In the earlier vision, YHWH calls for the exiled people to return home to Zion from their
place of exile to the north in Babylon. Whereas Zech 2:5-17 [NRSV: 2:1-
13] anticipates the time when the return from exile will take place, the
present context indicates that the time is at hand. In this respect, the
four winds of heaven represent and embody YHWH's power to act for
both punishment and deliverance in the world, much as the four winds
play a role in bringing about the punishment of Elam (Jer 49:36) or in
bringing the dead bones of Ezekiel's vision back to life (Ezek 37:9).
They play a similar role in Mesopotamian traditions concerning the
creation of the cosmos in which the four winds enable Marduk to defeat the chaos goddess Tiamat, and thereby to establish his and Babylon's sovereignty over the entire world.[70] In Dan 8:8 and 11:4, the four
winds represent the four cardinal directions, and thereby symbolize
the entirety of the earth. Such symbolism is inherent in the present context as well with regard to the previously mentioned role of the Temple
as the center of the cosmos. The four winds, which symbolize YHWH's
world-wide power in creation, now prepare to move throughout the
world as the commencement of the rebuilding of the Temple signals
the manifestation of YHWH's sovereignty throughout the cosmos. The
angel describes the movements of the chariots in verse 6, i.e., the chariot with black horses goes to the north, the chariot with white horses
goes to the west, and the chariot with the spotted horses goes to Teman
in the south. Although verse 6 states literally that the white horses
"have gone out after them," the term *ʾaḥărêhem*, "behind them," refers
to the west; when one faces the sun in the east, the west is behind.
Teman refers to Edomite territory in the south (Jer 49:7, 20; Amos 1:12;
Obad 9), and apparently functions elsewhere as a general designation
for the south (Hab 3:3; Ezek 25:13). The term refers to Yemen, in the
southern Arabian peninsula, in modern Hebrew. Most interpreters
note that the chariot with the red horses is not mentioned here, and that
no chariot travels to the east. YHWH is often portrayed metaphorically
as the sun that rises in the east (Deut 33:1-2; Judg 5:4-5; Hab 3:3; Psalm

[70] See Pritchard, *ANET* 66–7.

104), and the Temple faces the east to catch the morning sun as it rises over the Trans-Jordan. No chariot need therefore be sent to the east as YHWH is identified with this region. Perhaps the chariot with the red horses is identified with YHWH's chariot, and its place is to remain at the newly reestablished Temple. This would be in keeping with the lead role played by the man riding the red horse in Zech 1:8 who serves as spokesman for the other riders hidden in the myrtle grove.

The second major component of the prophet's vision report in verses 7-8 relates the movement of the chariots, here labeled "steeds" (*ʾămuṣṣîm*), as they begin their patrol of the earth. The passage begins with the prophet's portrayal of the movement of the steeds, just as verses 1-6 began with the prophet's description of the chariots and their horses. The use of the term "steeds" (*ʾămuṣṣîm*) focuses especially on the horses rather than on the chariots and aids in relating this vision to the initial vision of the horsemen in Zech 1:7-17. Following his description of the departure of the steeds and their intent to patrol the earth, the prophet relates the angel's command that they commence their patrol and their compliance with that command in verse 7. The mission of the steeds to patrol the earth corresponds to that of the horsemen in Zech 1:7-17 (see esp. Zech 1:10). Again, this image reflects the Achaemenid Persian practice of employing riders to maintain communications throughout the empire and to keep the king apprised of any problems or important developments that might arise.[71] In verse 8 the prophet reports the angel's shouted communication to him that those going to the north, i.e., the black horses, have set YHWH's spirit to rest in the north. Although the angel states literally, "my spirit," he speaks on behalf of YHWH, which apparently entitles him to use the first person as though YHWH were the actual speaker (cf. Zech 4:8-10a in which it is clear that the angel speaks a word from YHWH as if it was his own). The angel's statement that YHWH's spirit is at rest in the north must be read in relation to the many statements in prophetic tradition that YHWH will bring an enemy from the north to punish Israel, Judah, or Jerusalem (see Isa 14:31; Zeph 2:13; Jer 1:14, 15; 6:1, 22; 15:12; 46:20, 24; 47:2; Ezek 26:7; 38:6, 15; 39:2) and that those exiled to foreign lands will return to Jerusalem from the north (Jer 3:18; 16:15; 23:8; 31:8; Isa 43:6; 49:12). Although Israel's and Judah's enemies, such as Assyria and Babylon, technically lay to the east, the Arabian desert made it extremely difficult to journey from Mesopotamia westward into the land of Israel. All Mesopotamian invaders therefore approached Israel from the north, as this route provided greater support (and important military, political, and economic objectives) for large armies. The use of the

---

[71] See Oppenheim, "The Eyes of the L–rd."

verb "to give rest" *(hēnîḥû)* draws upon the typical language employed for YHWH's giving rest from enemies to Israel, David, etc., from enemies (Isa 28:12; 2 Chr 14:5; Deut 12:10; 25:19; Josh 23:1; 2 Sam 7:1, 11; 1 Chr 22:9; etc.). When considered in relation to the beginning of the horses' patrols throughout the earth, such a statement indicates that the time of YHWH's anger has come to an end as the process for the rebuilding of the Temple and the manifestation of YHWH's sovereignty in Jerusalem is now taking place. Again, such a concern harks back to the first vision in Zech 1:7-17 in which all the earth is at peace and YHWH's anger against Judah and Jerusalem has come to an end as the Temple is about to be rebuilt. The beginning of the chariots' or horses' patrol signals the reinauguration of YHWH's sovereignty at the building of the Temple.

Zechariah's report of YHWH's oracle to him concerning the crowning of the "branch," here identified as Joshua ben Jehozadak, and the building of the Temple appears in Zech 6:9-15. Many scholars view this report as a secondary addition to the vision report in Zech 6:1-8 because of its different generic identity,[72] but the oracle complements the vision in that it points to the crowning of Joshua and his role in Temple reconstruction as the impetus for the chariots' movement out of the "heavenly gates" of the Temple to begin their world-wide patrol on YHWH's behalf. Scholars have also noted that the designation of the high priest Joshua ben Jehozadak as the figure to be crowned raises a host of problems, especially because one would expect that Zerubbabel, the Davidic grandson of Jehoiachin who would be eligible to reestablish the Davidic monarchy in Jerusalem on YHWH's behalf (cf. Hag 2:20-23), would be the figure to be crowned.[73] Indeed, various features of the present text point to such a conclusion: crowns are generally given to kings (and queens; see Jer 13:18; Ezek 21:30-31[NRSV: 21:25-26]; cf. Isa 28:1); the designation "branch" *(ṣemaḥ)* is generally reserved for a royal figure rather than for a priest (Jer 23:5; 33:15; cf. Isa 11:1-16; Ps 132:17; Hos 8:7), and the figure of the "branch" is differentiated from that of Joshua in Zech 3:8; kings are expected to build Temples rather than priests (cf. 2 Samuel 6; 24; 1 Kings 6–8; Isa 44:28; 1 Chronicles 15–16; 2 Chronicles 3–7; cf. Ezra 3–5, which highlights the roles of both Zerubbabel and Joshua in rebuilding the Temple; see also the role of the kings in reforming Temple practice, e.g., Asa, 1 Kgs 15:9-15/2 Chr 14:1-8; Joash, 2 Kgs 12:4-16/2 Chr 24:1-14; Hezekiah, 2 Kgs

[72] See esp. Petitjean, *Les oracles* 268–71.

[73] E.g., Robert P. Carroll, *When Prophecy Failed: Cognitive Dissonance in the Prophetic Traditions of the Old Testament* (New York: Seabury, 1979) 162–8. For an overview of the discussion, see Coggins, *Haggai, Zechariah, Malachi* 47–8.

18:3-8/2 Chronicles 29–31; Josiah, 2 Kgs 22:3–23:27/2 Chronicles 34–35); and the notice that council of peace shall exist between the "branch" who sits on his throne and the priest who sits on his own throne suggests a differentiation between the two roles. It seems likely that Zerubbabel was in fact the figure to be crowned in an earlier version of this text, but he was replaced by Joshua ben Jehozadak as the book of Zechariah went through its process of editing and recomposition during the centuries following the building of the second Temple when the Davidic monarchy failed to be reestablished and the Jerusalem priesthood emerged as the ruling figures of Judah. In the present form of the text, the oracle in Zech 6:9-15 legitimizes the rule of the Jerusalem priesthood through Joshua ben Jehozadak, and points forward to the time when YHWH will be recognized as the true sovereign of the world. Insofar as the book of Zechariah appears to have initially posited a Davidic monarch, but later points to YHWH as sovereign, it presents an understanding of kingship similar to that of the final form of the book of Isaiah which also points to righteous Davidic rule (see Isa 8:23–9:6; 11:1-16) but ultimately identifies first Cyrus (Isa 44:28; 45:1) and later YHWH (Isa 66:1-2) as the true righteous monarch (cf. Isa 32:1-9).

The prophet's oracle report begins with an example of the YHWH word transmission formula in verse 9, which identifies the following material as an oracle from YHWH to Zechariah. The oracle itself appears in verses 10-15. It comprises both a set of instructions from YHWH to the prophet to crown Joshua ben Jehozadak and to speak an oracle to him concerning his role as YHWH's "branch" in verses 10-13 and the angel's instructions to the people at large concerning the disposition of the crowns and the significance of the rebuilding of the Temple in verses 14-15.

YHWH's instructions to Zechariah in verses 10-13 include a chain of seven basic commands, each introduced by a second person verb, concerning the crowning of Joshua as the "branch." The first statement appears in verse 10a to "take" something from the exiles, specifically from Heldai, Tobiah, and Jedaiah. Although the statement does not specify what is to be taken, verse 11 indicates that silver and gold are the desired objects. Many have noted that the initial verb, *lāqôḥ*, "take," is an infinitive absolute rather than an imperative form, but infinitive absolutes may introduce a chain of commands as an emphatic imperative.[74] The identities of Heldai, Tobiah, and Jedaiah are uncertain, but Tobiah and Jedaiah appear to be common names for Levites. Thus, an earlier Tobiah was a Levite sent by King Jehoshaphat to teach Torah to

---

[74] See Gesenius, Kautzsch, Cowley, *Gesenius' Hebrew Grammar* (Oxford: Clarendon, 1910) 113bb.

the people of Judah (2 Chr 17:8-9) and another Tobiah was head of a priestly family in Zerubbabel's time that was unable to prove its priestly lineage (Ezra 2:60; Neh 7:62). Indeed, Tobiah is the name of a long line of priests who later came to prominence during the second Temple period.[75] Jedaiah is the name of several Levitical figures or families that accompanied Zerubbabel on his return to Jerusalem (Neh 12:6, 7; Ezra 2:36 and Neh 7:39). Heldai is otherwise unknown during this period, although an earlier Heldai was one of David's captains (1 Chr 27:15). It would appear that these three men are prominent figures among the exiles who returned with Zerubbabel, and that they are enlisted to provide the gold and silver that will play a role in authorizing another returned exile, either Zerubbabel in an earlier edition of the oracle or Joshua ben Jehozadak in the present edition, to begin the process of building the Second Temple. The second command in verse 10bα employs the second person pronoun *'attâ*, "you," to stress that "you shall come on that day." The pronoun apparently refers to the prophet Zechariah and emphasizes his role, as both prophet and priest, to crown Joshua as the "branch." Such a role would be analogous to that of Samuel who anointed both Saul and David as king (see 1 Sam 9:1–10:16; 16); the priest Zadok who anointed Solomon (1 Kgs 1:38-40); or the priest Jehoiada who crowned and anointed Jehoash (2 Kgs 11:12; 2 Chr 23:11). The third command in verse 10bβ calls upon Zechariah to enter the house of Josiah ben Zephaniah, who also comes from Babylon. Nothing is known of this man, although his name corresponds to that of the great reforming king of Judah, Josiah ben Amon (2 Kings 22–23), and the name of his father corresponds to that of the prophet who supported Josiah's reforms (Zephaniah 1–3). The fourth, fifth, and sixth commands in verse 11 make it clear that Zechariah is to "take" silver and gold from the house of Josiah ben Zephaniah, to "make" crowns, and to set the crown/crowns on the head of Joshua ben Jehozadak the high priest. The plural form of the nouns *'ăṭârôt*, "crowns," indicates that more than one crown is to be made. It is clear that only one crown may be set on the head of Joshua ben Jehozadak, but verse 14 makes it clear that the crowns are to be given to the four figures mentioned in verse 10, although the names of some of them are different. It would appear that these four figures are to be designated somehow as associates of Joshua. Insofar as the crowns are to be given to these men, it is noteworthy that the command in verse 11b never specifies that Zechariah is to place *the crown* on the head of Joshua. The phrase *wĕśamtā bĕrō'š* never specifies a pronoun referring to "crowns" as the object of the verb; rather, the name "Joshua ben Jehozadak the high

[75] "Tobiads," *Encyclopaedia Judaica* 15:1178-80.

priest" appears to be the object of the verb in the syntactical structure of the sentence. It would therefore read, "and you shall place Joshua ben Jehozadak the high priest at (the) head," i.e., at the head of the four figures who have been named in verse 10. Such a reading would require that *běrōʾš*, generally understood as "on the head of (Joshua)" be translated as "at the head" or "in front," a rendering which the preposition *bě*, "in, at, by," permits. It would also reflect Joshua's position as High Priest in that he stands before others (cf. Zech 3:4, 7). Because the name Joshua is never equated with the "branch" in the following oracle in verses 12-13, it could be that Joshua here is intended only to serve as the head of the delegation that will designate the "branch" as the figure who will build Yʜᴡʜ's Temple.

The seventh instruction of the series appears in verses 12-13, which begin with the instruction to Zechariah, "say to him," literally, "and you shall say to him." This is followed immediately by an example of the prophetic messenger formula, "Thus says Yʜᴡʜ of hosts," which identifies the following material in verses 11b-12 as an oracle or statement by Yʜᴡʜ. The oracle includes two basic components. The first in verse 11b begins with the statement, "Here is a man whose name is Branch." As noted above, the term "branch" (*ṣemaḥ*) is frequently applied to the righteous Davidic monarch anticipated in prophetic literature (see Jer 23:5; 33:15; Zech 3:8; cf. Isa 11:1-16). It is especially noteworthy in that the name Zerubbabel is apparently derived from the Akkadian name *zēr-bābili*, which means "branch/seed of Babylon."[76] It is also noteworthy that the statement, *hinnēh ʾîš šěmô*, "Behold a man; Branch is his name," does not necessarily refer to Joshua ben Jehozadak. Indeed, the statement is addressed to him in third person form rather than as a second person address, and it could easily refer to another person, such as Zerubbabel, who is brought to his attention during the course of the crowning ceremony. The following statements, "he shall branch out in his place, and he shall build the temple of Yʜᴡʜ," appear to designate a royal figure rather than a priestly figure. Again, the use of the verb *ṣmḥ* would apply to a royal figure (Isa 11:1-16), as would the role of Temple builder.

The second part of the oracle in verse 13 employs the independent pronoun *hûʾ*, "he," as a means to emphasize the role of the "Branch" figure. Again, the emphatic third person form suggests that the verse applies to someone other than Joshua ben Jehozadak. It repeats the role of the "Branch" as Temple builder, and it emphasizes that he "shall bear royal honor," and "sit and rule on his throne." All of these are attributes of a king, not a priest. The term *hôd*, here translated as "royal

[76] Bryan E. Beyer, "Zerubbabel," *ABD* VI:184-5.

honor," means "glory" or "splendor," and frequently refers to the majesty of a king (Ps 45:5 [NRSV: 45:4]; 21:6 [NRSV: 21:5]; 1 Chr 29:25; Dan 11:21; Jer 22:18; cf. Ps 104:1 which portrays YHWH's splendor as king). Likewise, sitting and ruling on his throne describes the action of a king (e.g., Deut 17:18; 2 Sam 3:10; 7:16; 1 Kgs 2:45; 8:20; Isa 9:6 [NRSV: 9:7]; Ps 89:5 [NRSV: 89:4]; etc.; cf. 2 Sam 12:1-15; 1 Kgs 3:16-28), although the high priest may also sit on a throne (1 Sam 1:9; 4:13, 18), as may honored guests (2 Kgs 4:10), a governor (Neh 3:7), or a judge (Ps 94:20). Indeed, verse 11b states, "and there will be a priest upon his throne *(wĕhāyâ kōhēn ʿal-kisʾô)*." The NRSV translation, "There shall be a priest *by* his throne," suggests that the priest shall stand by the throne of the branch figure in keeping with the portrayal of Deut 17:14-20 in which the priests stand by the king and provide him with a copy of the Torah. The preposition *ʿal* can suggest the meaning of "by," but it more commonly means "upon," which indicates that the priest sits upon his own throne rather than stands by that of the branch. Certainly the concluding statement of the oracle that "peaceful understanding," literally, "council of peace *(ʿăṣat šālôm)*," shall exist between "the two of them" presupposes the existence of two authority figures in the community. Likewise, 1 Chr 29:22 points to the anointing of both Solomon as king and Zadok as high priest, both of whom serve as the major authority figures in the viewpoint of the Chronicler.

The angel's instructions to Zechariah concerning the disposition of the previously mentioned crowns and the ultimate return of those who will build the Temple of YHWH appear in verses 14-15. The section is very clearly demarcated from verses 10-13 by the appearance of the initial noun, "and the crowns *(wĕhāʿăṭārōt)*," which breaks the *waw-consecutive* verbal chain that holds verses 10-13 together. The passage includes two basic parts. Verse 14 focuses on the crowns, and states that they shall be for Helem, Tobiah, Jedaiah, and Hen ben Zephaniah as a "memorial" in the Temple of YHWH. There are several major problems with this statement. The first is that the feminine plural noun "crowns *(ʿăṭārōt)*" does not agree grammatically with the feminine singular verb *tihyeh,* "(it) shall be." Many have suggested that the noun be emended to the singular *ʿăṭeret,* "crown" (see NRSV; LXX), which would require a change in the vowels but leave the consonantal text intact.[77] This would produce a grammatically coherent text, but it provides no explanation as to why the plural noun "crowns" would have been introduced in the first place. Insofar as the "crowns" are to be given to the four figures mentioned subsequently in the verse (cf. verse 10), it would make sense

---

[77] For full discussion, see Hanhart, *Sacharja* 407–9; Meyers and Meyers, *Haggai, Zechariah 1–8* 349–53.

that the noun be plural so that each man would receive a crown, but the verb *tihyeh* and the singular noun *zikārôn*, "memorial, remembrance," require that "crown" be singular. In keeping with the reading of verses 10-13 offered above, it seems possible that the text originally read the singular noun *ʿăṭeret* to designate the crown that Joshua ben Jehozadak was to give to the "Branch," Zerubbabel, but the term was changed to a plural and read in relation to the four men mentioned later in the verse following the failure of Zerubbabel's to be recognized as king in Judah. The names of the four men also present problems in that two of them have been changed from those given in verse 10.[78] The name Heldai is now read as Helem, which involves a minor textual change from *ḥeldāy* to *ḥelem*. The name Heldai and its variants are frequently changed to other names in the Hebrew Bible.[79] The reason for such a change is unclear, but it may have something to do with the fact that *ḥeled* means "mold" in later Hebrew,[80] and a major variant of the expression, *ḥōled*, means "weasel" (see Lev 11:29). Helem, on the other hand, means "strong." The substitution of Hen (*ḥēn*) for Josiah (*yōʾšîyâ*) also poses problems. Some have argued that *lĕḥēn*, "for Hen," should be read as a corrupted form of the Neo-Assyrian term *laḥḥinu* or the cognate Aramaic term *lĕḥēn*, which refers to an administrative official responsible for the distribution of grain.[81] Such an explanation does not account satisfactorily for the appearance of the pronoun *lĕ*, "for," before each of the four names in the sequence. The reason for the change is unknown, although it is noteworthy that *ḥēn* means "grace, favor," and Josiah is the name of one of the last great Davidic monarchs who reformed the Temple, but was killed by the Egyptians prior to completing his full program of national and religious restoration. Perhaps there was some concern that Josiah ben Zephaniah would be confused with King Josiah ben Amon, and the appellation Hen was introduced to alleviate the situation. Finally, the term *zikārôn*, here translated as "memorial," also means "remembrance." It does not generally refer to a memorial for the dead, but to a remembrance or symbol for some great event, such as the Passover (Exod 12:14), the crossing of the Jordan (Josh 4:7), or the stones of the High Priest's ephod which represent the tribes of Israel (Exod 28:12, 29; 39:7). This last reference is particularly important as the High

---

[78] For discussion, see Hanhart, *Sacharja* 411–2; Meyers and Meyers, *Haggai, Zechariah 1–8* 340–3.

[79] E.g., David's hero, Heled/Heldai, in 1 Chr 11:30; 27:15 is identified as Heleb in 2 Sam 23:29. See Petitjean, *Les oracles* 275–7, for a full discussion.

[80] See Jastrow, *A Dictionary of the Targumim* 464.

[81] See Aaron Demsky, "The Temple Steward Josiah ben Zephaniah," *IEJ* 31 (1981) 100–2.

Priest's ephod was to contain two stones as a remembrance for the sons of Israel. It may be that the crowns have somehow been equated with these stones, especially since they are set in a "signet (ḥôtām)" (Exod 39:6), the term employed to designate Zerubbabel as monarch in Hag 2:23. They might thereby understood in reference to the crowning of the high priest. This is speculative, however, and it is more likely that the crowns are placed in the Temple by the four men designated here as a symbol of the Davidic monarchy, i.e., the crowning of the "Branch."

The second statement in verse 15 is much less complicated. It begins with a reference to "those who are far off" who shall come and build the Temple. This, of course, envisions the return to Jerusalem of all Jews exiled by Assyria and Babylon who will then participate in the re-construction of the Temple. The return of the exiles is explicitly linked to the restoration of the Davidic monarch or "branch" in prior pro-phetic literature (Isa 11:1-16; Jer 23:5-8; cf. Jer 33:14-26). The return of the exiles then becomes a sign that "YHWH of Hosts has sent me to you." In this case, "me" indicates that the speaker is the angel. The ref-erence to "you" is no longer masculine singular as in verses 10-13, but masculine plural, which indicates that this statement is addressed to the entire people. The same applies to the concluding statement of the oracle, "this will happen if you diligently obey the voice of YHWH your G-d." The exhortational nature of this last statement is particularly noteworthy, because it presupposes a need for continued observance of YHWH on the part of the people so that the full range of promises en-gendered by the reconstruction of the Temple might be realized. This applies not only to the restoration of the entire Jewish people to the land of Israel, but to the restoration of the Davidic monarchy as well. Although the oracle in Zech 6:9-15 looks forward to the crowning of the "Branch" or Davidic monarch, it has not yet taken place. In this regard, the oracle looks forward to Zechariah 9–14, which point to the coming of the king to Jerusalem (Zech 9:9-10), but points ultimately to YHWH as the monarch who delivers Jerusalem from its enemies (Zechariah 14).

Narrative concerning the Transmission of YHWH's Word to Zechariah on the Fourth of Kislev, 518 B.C.E.: The Pronouncements of Zechariah: 7:1–14:21

Zechariah 7:1–14:21 constitutes a narrative report concerning the transmission of YHWH's word to Zechariah on the fourth day of the ninth month, i.e., Kislev, in the fourth year of King Darius of Persia, i.e., 518 B.C.E. The fourth day of Kislev would place the transmission of

YHWH's word at some point between mid-November and mid-December, nearly two years after the date given for the transmission of Zechariah's visions in Zech 1:7. There is no particular significance to this date, which is about a month and a half after the conclusion of Sukkoth. The introductory formula employs a modified version of the YHWH word transmission formula,[82] which validates the following material as the word of YHWH. In contrast to the formula in Zech 1:7, Zechariah's full name is not given. The abbreviated form of Zechariah's name and the introductory *waw-consecutive* formation, "and it came to pass *(wayĕhî),*" indicate that Zech 7:1 is structurally dependent upon Zech 1:7 so that Zech 1:7–6:15 and 7:1–14:21 form the two basic components of the larger block in Zech 1:7–14:21. Whereas Zech 1:7–6:15 relates Zechariah's visions, Zech 7:1–14:21 relates Zechariah's pronouncements.

The structure of Zech 7:1–14:21 is based upon the two appearances of the YHWH word transmission formula in Zech 7:1 and 7:8, which state that "the word of YHWH came to Zechariah." Although three other examples of the YHWH word transmission formula appear in Zech 7:4; 8:1; and 8:18, they must be considered as structurally subordinate to Zech 7:1 and 7:8. Zechariah 7:1 and 7:8 are clearly the work of a writer other than Zechariah, who relates the words of the prophet and the events in which he is involved and who sets the presentation of the entire book by similar introductory statements about Zechariah in Zech 1:1 and 1:7. Zechariah 7:4 and 8:18 are clearly autobiographical, as indicated by the use of the formula, "and the word of YHWH of Hosts came to me," and thereby constitute parts of the presentation introduced by the book's narrator in Zech 7:1 and 7:8 respectively. Contrary to the translation presented in the NRSV, the formula in Zech 8:1 provides no indication to whom the word of YHWH came, i.e., "and the word of YHWH of Hosts came, saying," which likewise indicates that it is a part of the narrator's presentation beginning in Zech 7:8. Although Zechariah 9–11 and 12–14 are generally considered to be independent compositions from a time later than that of the prophet Zechariah,[83] they, too, must be considered components within the basic structure defined by the narrator's introductions in Zech 7:1 and 7:8. Each is introduced respectively in Zech 9:1a and 12:1a by the formulas, "a pronouncement/oracle, the word of YHWH concerning . . . *(maśśāᵓ dĕbar yhwh bĕ/ʿal . . .),*" which have played a key role in establishing the independent character of these textual blocks. Nevertheless, the generic identification of the following material that is inherent in each provides no indication of the setting or the addressee of the pronouncement that

---

[82] Sweeney, *Isaiah 1–39* 546–7.
[83] Cf. Coggins, *Haggai, Zechariah, Malachi* 60–72.

would establish them as structurally independent blocks in relation to
Zech 1:1; 1:7; or 7:1. In the absence of such independent information,
Zechariah 9–11 and 12–14 must be considered as structurally subordinate in the first instance to Zech 7:1, which provides the necessary information concerning the setting of the following oracular material,
and in the second instance to Zech 7:8, which provides the introduction
to a major thematic block concerned with the restoration of Jerusalem
and Judah within Zech 7:1–14:21. Ultimately, Zechariah 9–11 and 12–14
form a component of the textual sub-unit introduced by the YHWH
word transmission formula in Zech 9:18; whereas Zech 8:18-23 indicates that the nations will ultimately recognize YHWH in Jerusalem,
Zechariah 9–11 and 12–14 provide a detailed scenario of the process by
which this recognition will take place.

The structure of Zech 7:1–14:21 comprises two basic components,
each of which includes its respective sub-units. Zechariah 7:1-7 introduces the entire block with its statement concerning the date of the
transmission of YHWH's word to Zechariah and the initial question
posed to the prophet concerning the need to continue a seventy-year
practice of imploring YHWH and mourning for the loss of the Temple.
Whereas verses 1-3 relate this question, verses 4-7 state the prophet's
initial response that such a practice is unnecessary. Zechariah 7:8–14:21
then relates YHWH's words to Zechariah which look forward to the time
when YHWH's sovereignty will be restored in Jerusalem. A sequence of
three reports concerning the transmission of YHWH's word to the
prophet outline YHWH's call for moral action on the part of the people
(Zech 7:8-14), YHWH's pledge to restore Jerusalem and Judah (Zech 8:1-
17), and YHWH's pledge that the former practice of mourning will be
turned to joy as the nations recognize Judah and YHWH in Jerusalem
(Zech 8:18–14:21). As noted above, Zech 8:18-23 introduces this theme,
and Zechariah 9–11 and 12–14 present it in detail with a pronouncement concerning intentions to act against the nations on Judah's behalf
(Zechariah 9–11) and a second pronouncement that projects YHWH's
defeat of the nations and restoration of Jerusalem (Zechariah 12–14). In
this regard, Zech 8:18–14:21 provide the prophet's final answer to the
initial question in 7:1-7 concerning the need for continued mourning.

INTRODUCTION TO ZECHARIAH'S PRONOUNCEMENTS:
CONCERNING THE NEED FOR CONTINUED MOURNING FOR THE
DESTRUCTION OF THE TEMPLE: 7:1-7

Zechariah 7:1-7 introduces the presentation of Zechariah's pronouncement by relating the initial query concerning the need to con-

tinue the seventy-year old observance of mourning for the loss of the Temple at the time of the Babylonian destruction of Jerusalem (cf. 2 Kings 25; Jeremiah 52). As noted above, verse 1 indicates that the query and the responses took place on the fourth of Kislev, the ninth month, in the fourth year of King Darius' reign (518 B.C.E.). The passage includes two basic components, each of which begins with a variation of the YHWH word transmission formula.

Verses 1-3 relate the question concerning the need for continued mourning observances. The YHWH word transmission formula appears in verse 1 together with the notice concerning the date. It seems clear that the formula does not identify the request by Sharezer, Regem Melech, and their men as the word of YHWH. The formula therefore serves as an introduction to the entire sequence of oracles reported to have been given by YHWH to the prophet throughout the balance of the unit in Zechariah 7–14 so that both the question and the responses are dated to 4 Kislev, 518 B.C.E. In this manner, the text indicates that the prophet's pronouncements are to be read as statements of YHWH's future action against the nations and on behalf of Jerusalem and Judah.

The report in verses 2-3 of the delegation sent from Beth El to inquire about the continuation of mourning practices for the destroyed Temple has prompted a great deal of discussion concerning the proper reading of the names in verse 2. A literal reading of verse 2 would be, "and Beth El sent Sharezer, Regem Melech, and his men to entreat the favor of YHWH." The first problem arises in relation to the identity of the party who sent the delegation. The text identifies Beth El rather than a person as the party who sent the delegates. Because of the prevailing view that an individual should be the subject of the verb *wayyišlaḥ*, "and he sent," attempts have been made to read the names *bêt ʾēl*, "Beth El," and *šar ʾeṣer*, "Sharezer," as a single name, i.e., Beth-El Sharezer, based upon the occurrence of a known Babylonian name, Bit-ili-sar-usur.[84] The term *shar* in Akkadian means "king," the term *usur*, means "to protect." When used together with the name of a deity, these terms commonly form the basis of many Babylonian names, e.g., Nergal Sarezer, "may Nergal protect the king," (Jer 39:3). In this case, Beth El, the name of the former northern Israelite sanctuary used by the Assyrians and later conquerors as a center for the religious administration of the land of Israel (see 2 Kgs 17:24-28), would serve in place of the name of the deity (cf. Gen 35:7 where Jacob names the site of his vision of G–d, *ʾēl bêt ʾēl*, "G–d of Beth El"). Such a reading is impossible in the

[84] For discussion, see Meyers and Meyers, *Haggai, Zechariah 1–8* 382–4; Petersen, *Haggai and Zechariah 1–8* 281; Hanhart, *Sacharja* 463–5; Rudolph, *Haggai–Sacharja 1–8–Sacharja 9–14–Maleachi* 135–40.

present form of the text, however, because the following name, Regem Melech begins with a conjunctive *waw*, which ties it to Sharezer, and thereby would produce a plural subject for the singular verb *wayyišlaḥ*, "and he sent." Instead, only *bêt ʾēl* can serve as the subject of the verb. Some might object that a place name such as Beth El must function grammatically as a feminine singular noun, but Beth El is an exception that functions as a masculine singular noun (see Amos 5:5). Although the reading might be considered somewhat awkward, a delegation sent from Beth El to make an inquiry concerning religious practice is in keeping with the role identified above for Beth El as a religious administrative center for the land of Israel. Although 2 Kgs 17:24-28 indicates that the Assyrians established Beth El in this role, there is no indication that Beth El ceased to function in this role during the periods of Babylonian and Persian rule until the time that the city was destroyed ca. 480 or 460 B.C.E.

The second problem relates to the reading "Sharezer, and Regem Melech, and his men," in that there are apparently two antecedents for the pronoun "his." This might lend further support to the above discussed proposal to read Beth El Sar Ezer as a single name, but "his" may refer directly to Regem Melech, i.e., "Sharezer and Regem Melech and his men" rather than "Sharezer, Regem Melech, and his men." The third problem relates to the use of Babylonian names for men who seem clearly to function as Israelites or Judeans insofar as they apparently are interested in the proper observance of Judean religious practice. Indeed, the name Sharezer is the name of one of Sennacherib's sons who assassinated him in the Temple of Nisroch (Isa 37:38; 2 Kgs 19:37). It should hardly be surprising that Jews in this period would adopt Babylonian names during the period when they had been exiled to Babylonia and perhaps assimilated to some extent into its culture. Zerubbabel, after all, is a Babylonian name of the grandson of Jehoiachin, the last monarch of the Davidic line. Finally, the name Regem Melech is sometimes read as Rab Mag, a common designation for a high Mesopotamian official that is reflected in the Syriac version of the Bible.[85] Such a reading is unnecessary, however, as Regem Melech means "spokesman of the king." It is more likely an official title for Sharezer that is read in the present form of the text as the personal name of a second individual.

The expression "to entreat the favor of YHWH" (*lĕḥallôt ʾet-pĕnê yhwh*) is commonly employed to designate a request made to YHWH for some benefit, but it appears here to indicate simply an inquiry concerning proper practice. Verse 3a indicates that the request is directed to the

[85] Hanhart, *Sacharja* 465.

priests and prophets of the Jerusalem Temple. It appears to be an example of a Torah question typically posed to the priests in order to determine proper religious practice (Hag 2:11-13; cf. Isa 1:11; Ezek 45:8b-9).[86] The question itself, "Should I mourn and practice abstinence in the fifth month as I have done for so many years?" again indicates a request made by one person, and lends support to the contention that Sharezer is the principle figure sent at the head of the Beth El delegation. The mourning and abstinence would be in commemoration of the destroyed Temple, and the occasion for the question at this would be the recognition that the Temple was being rebuilt. In such a case, is mourning still appropriate? The reference to "the fifth month" is particularly pertinent because this would be the month of Av. The ninth day of Av is a day of mourning and fasting in Judaism as tradition indicates that both the first and the second Temple were destroyed on the ninth day of Av.[87] Other disasters, such as the expulsion of Jews from Spain in 1492 took place on this date as well, which contributes to the overall character of the day as a day of disaster.

Zechariah 7:4-7 relates the prophet's initial response to the inquiry made by Sharezer and company in verses 1-3. Zechariah's response does not answer the question concerning the need for continued mourning for the Temple per se, but it poses a series of rhetorical questions[88] that are designed to provoke thought on the proper means for human action in relation to the loss—and the upcoming rebuilding—of the Temple that prepares the reader for the scenario of restoration in Zech 7:8–14:21. The unit begins in verse 4 with a version of the YHWH word transmission formula that both identifies the following material as an oracle from YHWH and identifies Zechariah as the speaker. The use of the first person pronoun, "unto me," indicates that these verses are autobiographical and that they stand in tension with the third person portrayal of Zechariah in verses 1-3. Clearly, some editing has taken place in this chapter as statements by the prophet have been placed in a third person narrative context in which the third person reference to Zechariah in verse 1 provides the only antecedent to the first person reference to the prophet in verse 4.

Zechariah's initial answer to Sharezer's question then appears in verses 5-7 in the form of three rhetorical questions that subtly suggest or introduce what YHWH does indeed require. Verse 5a constitutes YHWH's initial instruction to the prophet that he is to deliver his answer to all the people of the land and the priests, which indicates that the

[86] Sweeney, *Isaiah 1–39* 527–8.
[87] See "Av, Ninth of," *Encyclopaedia Judaica* 3:936-40.
[88] Sweeney, *Isaiah 1–39* 537.

delivery of this oracle is to be understood as a public event in which all of the people assembled at the site of the Temple will witness. Indeed, the second masculine plural formulation of the first two questions indicates that they are not addressed only to Sharezer, but to the people at large. The two questions appear as a contrasting pair in verses 5b and 6 that are joined by a conjunctive *waw*, "and." Both are formulated with an initial temporal statement that defines the circumstances to which the question is posed. The first question in verse 5b asks whether or not the people indeed fasted and lamented during the fifth and seventh months on YHWH's behalf for seventy years. The reference to the fifth month of course indicates the above-mentioned fast on the ninth of Av for the destruction of the Temple. The reference to the seventh month must indicate the fast held at the observance of the murder of Gedaliah ben Ahikam ben Shaphan, who had been appointed as governor of Judah by the Babylonians following the destruction of Jerusalem and the Temple. According to Jer 41:1-3 and 2 Kgs 25:25, Gedaliah was assassinated in the seventh month (Tishri). Later Rabbinic tradition sets the date as the third day of Tishri (bRosh ha-Shanah 18b).[89] Although one might suppose that the prophet refers to Yom Kippur, the day of atonement, on the tenth day of Tishri (the seventh month) following Rosh ha-Shanah or the New Year on 1 Tishri (see Lev 23:26-32; 16; Num 29:7-11), the reference to seventy years and the statement in Zech 8:19 that the fasts will be turned into days of rejoicing indicates that he refers to fasts that are associated with the fall of the Temple and the exile. The reference to seventy years indicates the time that the Temple lay in ruins from 587/6 B.C.E. until the present in 517/6 B.C.E., two years following the initiation of Temple reconstruction (cf. Zech 7:1, "the fourth year of Darius," and Zech 1:7, "the second year of Darius"). It also calls to mind the statements in Jer 25:11-12; 29:10 (cf. Zech 1:12), in which Jeremiah indicates that the exile will last for seventy years. By asking whether the people indeed fasted for YHWH during these seventy years raises the question as to whether or not the fasts satisfy YHWH's requirements or expectations. Although many interpreters understand this question as an attack on the fasts themselves or against ritual action in general, the later call for justice and moral action in verses 8-14 indicates that such practice is intended to have an impact on people's lives as well. It is worth recalling that the practice of fasting at Yom Kippur does not ensure forgiveness in and of itself. Forgiveness is granted in Judaism only when one changes one's actions and asks forgiveness both from G–d and from those who were wronged. The second question in verse 6 complements the first by offering a contrast-

---

[89] See "Gedaliah," *Encyclopaedia Judaica* 7:351-2.

ing scenario, i.e., when you eat and drink, do you not eat and drink for yourselves? Just as eating and drinking have no impact on YHWH, so does fasting alone have no impact on YHWH. The goal of such practice is to have an impact on the self, which thereby prompts action that YHWH does require as articulated in verses 8-14.

The final rhetorical question in the sequence appears in verse 7. The absence of a syntactical connection to the preceding questions and its placement at the end indicates that this question conveys the primary point of the prophet's response. The question asserts that these words were previously proclaimed by YHWH through the former prophets at a time when Jerusalem, its surrounding cities, the Negev, and the Shephelah were at peace. The Negev is the southern Judean desert below Hebron and Beer Sheba, and the Shephelah is the southwestern region of rolling hills that form the border with Philistia and the coastal plain. Such a statement would point directly to Isa 1:10-17; Hosea 4; Mic 6:6-8; Amos 5; Jeremiah 7; and other passages in which the pre-exilic prophets questioned the practice of sacrifice or other forms of ritual action that were not accompanied by moral action. By raising this issue at the end of this oracle, the prophet prepares for the following material that calls for such moral action on the part of the people at the time that the Temple is about to be restored and YHWH's sovereignty manifested throughout the world from Zion.

The Presentation of Zechariah's Response to Sarezer: YHWH's Pronouncements concerning Jerusalem and Judah: 7:8–14:21

Zechariah 7:8–14:21 constitutes the presentation of Zechariah's response to Sharezer's earlier question concerning the need for continued mourning and fasting for the Temple now that it was about to be rebuilt. Whereas the prophet's earlier response in verses 4-7 focused on questioning the need or appropriateness for fasting alone, the present response emphasizes the need for justice on the part of the people as the Temple is rebuilt and YHWH's sovereignty is manifested throughout the world. The primary scenario of the impact of the restored Temple is expressed through the pronouncements of YHWH in Zechariah 9–11 and 12–14. Although these chapters were composed independently of Zechariah 7–8, they are now subsumed into the overall structure of the three reports of the transmission of YHWH's word to Zechariah in Zech 7:8-14; 8:1-17; and 8:18-23. Overall, this material presents Zechariah's answer to Sharezer. Whereas the rhetorical questions in Zech 7:3-4 question the need for mourning for the destroyed Temple, the following material points to the need for moral action on the part of the people to prepare them for the time when the Temple will be restored together with YHWH's sovereignty over the entire world. These sub-units of this section call for just action on the part of the people (Zech 7:8-14), point to YHWH's pledge to restore Jerusalem (Zech 8:1-17), and point to the time when the nations will recognize YHWH and Judah in Jerusalem (Zech 8:18–14:21). Indeed, the pronouncements in Zechariah 9–11 and 12–14 elaborate on the brief oracle concerning the nations' recognition of YHWH in Zech 8:18-23 by pointing to YHWH's intentions to punish the nations (Zechariah 9–11) and bring about the restoration of Jerusalem during the course of their defeat (Zechariah 12–14).

PRESENTATION OF ZECHARIAH'S BASIC RESPONSE:
ORACLE CALLING FOR MORAL ACTION ON THE PART OF THE PEOPLE: 7:8-14

Zechariah 7:8-14 constitutes a presentation of Zechariah's initial response to Sharezer's question concerning the need for continued mourning and fasting for the destroyed Temple of Solomon. Whereas verses 4-7 questioned the need for such practice, verses 8-14 point to the necessity for moral action on the part of the people to prepare themselves for the time when the Temple will be restored and YHWH's sovereignty manifested throughout the world. By pointing to the need for moral action, the prophet provides an explanation for YHWH's past anger against the people and the destruction of the first Temple and builds the basis for the future restoration of Judah's relationship with YHWH.

The section begins in verse 8 with a version of the YHWH word transmission formula. Once again, this formula identifies the following material as an oracle from YHWH delivered by the prophet. The third person reference to Zechariah is analogous to that of Zech 7:1 and other key structural statements in the book, i.e., Zech 1:1; 1:7, which points to the role of verse 8 as the introduction to a major structural component of Zechariah 7–14.

The oracle itself appears in verses 9-14, which are in turn introduced by an example of the prophetic messenger formula, "Thus says YHWH of Hosts," which indicates that the prophet is quoting YHWH's words and thereby lends further authority to the following statements in verses 9b-10. The response itself draws upon the language of prophetic and priestly Torah or instruction that attempts to define YHWH's expectations for human action.[90] Other examples appear in Isa 1:10-17;

---

[90] See esp. Beuken, *Haggai–Sacharja 1–8* 119–38 who focuses on the parenetic character of this material.

Hosea 4; Amos 5; Mic 6:6-8; and Jeremiah 7. Although some argue that such moral qualifications must be separated from ritual action, the so-called Temple entrance liturgies in Psalms 15 and 24 (cf. Isa 33:14-16) likewise call for such ethical action on the part of those who would enter the Temple and participate in its cultic activities.[91] Indeed, Zechariah calls for such action on the part of the Judean community as a means to qualify them for entry into the soon-to-be rebuilt Temple and participation in its cultic service. The instruction proper in verses 9b-10 appears in the form of an order,[92] which includes one pair each of positive commands for moral action and prohibitions against immoral acts. The initial pair of commands appears in verse 9b, based upon a pair of imperative verbs. The first in verse 9bα, "render true judgments," literally, "true judgment judge (*mišpāṭ ʾemet šĕpōṭû),*" calls for proper justice in the law court, in which the Temple will play a major role (cf. Exod 21:6; Deut 17:8-13; see also Exod 23:1-3, 6-9; Deut 16:18-21). The demand for justice is tempered by a call for mercy in verse 9bβ, "show kindness and mercy to one another," literally, "and fidelity and mercy do (*ʿăśû)* each to his brother." The term "fidelity," *ḥesed,* frequently refers to the responsibility to meet one's obligations in the context of a relationship (Mic 7:20; Deut 7:9, 12; 1 Kgs 8:23; 2 Chr 6:14; 2 Sam 7:15; 22:51; 1 Kgs 3:6; Isa 54:10). The term "mercy," *raḥămîm,* relates to the noun *reḥem,* "womb," and conveys the love and pity of a mother for her child. All three attributes mentioned in verse 9b, "truth" (*ʾemet),* "fidelity" (*ḥesed),* and "mercy" (*raḥămîm),* are listed as attributes of Yhwh in Exod 34:6-7. Verse 10 contains the paired prohibition, again based upon negative imperative verbs. Verse 10a calls upon the people not to oppress the widow, orphan, the alien, and the poor. Protection of widows and orphans constitutes a fundamental element of justice throughout the Bible and the ancient Near East.[93] Indeed, the prohibition against oppressing the alien and the poor appears repeatedly in Israelite law (Lev 19:33; Deut 24:14; 27:19; Jer 7:6; 22:3). The reference to "the alien," *gēr,* refers to foreigners who take up residence in Israel, and who are given equal protection under its laws (see Deut 1:16; 16:11, 14; 26:11; Lev 17:8, 10; 25:47). Care of the poor is likewise a basic obligation in Israel (Lev 19:10; 23:22; cf. Exod 23:10-13; Deut 15:7-18). The prohibition against oppression employs the verb *ʿšq,* which frequently refers to economic extortion of the poor and outsiders (Exod 22:29; Lev 5:23 [NRSV: 6:4]; Mal 3:5). Fundamental to Israelite and Judean notions of justice is

---

[91] Sweeney, *Isaiah 1–39* 520.

[92] Ibid., 526.

[93] See F. C. Fensham, "Widow, Orphan, and the Poor in Ancient Near Eastern Legal and Wisdom Literature," *JNES* 21 (1962) 129–39.

that those who are in need must be cared for and granted their rights. The sanctity of the Temple requires such action in addition to its ritual. The concluding prohibition against devising evil in your hearts against one another draws upon similar language in Ezek 38:10; Pss 35:4; 41:8; 140:3; Gen 50:20; Jer 48:2; Nah 1:11.

The prophet resumes his own comments in verses 11-14 with an explanation as to why YHWH became angry with the people and brought about the catastrophe in the first place. His comments provide a contrast with the preceding word from YHWH in that they articulate the people's rejection of YHWH's Torah or words rather than their implication of YHWH's call for justice in verses 9b-10. As noted above, verses 9b-10 relate to several prophetic traditions, but they relate especially to Isa 1:10-17, a prophetic Torah speech in which YHWH dismisses the importance of Israel's sacrifices, holidays, etc., and calls for the people to practice justice, plead for the widow and orphan, reject evil, etc., all of which are expressly mentioned in verses 9b-10. It is noteworthy, therefore, that verses 11-14 appear to relate closely to the language and images of the book of Isaiah. In verse 11, Zechariah states that the people's refusal to listen, their turning a stubborn shoulder, and their stopping up their ears from hearing were major causes for YHWH's anger (cf. verse 12b). The statement, "but they refused to listen," employs the *piel* form of the verb *m'n*, "to refuse," which appears in Isa 1:20, "but if you refuse and rebel, you shall be devoured by the sword," and the *hiphil* form of the verb *qšb*, "to listen," also appears throughout the book of Isaiah where it frequently appears in contexts that call upon the audience to pay attention to YHWH's or the prophet's words (Isa 28:23; 34:1; 48:18; 49:1; 51:4; cf. 10:30). The statement, "and (they) turned a stubborn shoulder," employs the adjective *sōreret*, "stubborn," which appears in Isa 30:1 and 65:2 to describe the rebellious people of Israel and in Isa 1:23 to describe their leaders. The statement, "and (they) stopped their ears in order not to hear," draws on a major motif from Isaiah's vision of YHWH in which YHWH tells him that his task is to prevent the people from hearing or seeing unless they repent and are saved from YHWH's punishment (Isaiah 6). The *hiphil* form of the verb *kbd*, "to stop, make heavy," appears in YHWH's instructions to the prophet in Isa 6:10, "make the mind of this people dull, and stop their ears, and shut their eyes."

Verse 12 continues to present the reasons for YHWH's anger against the people, and it continues to draw especially on the Isaiah tradition. The statement, "they made their hearts adamant in order not to hear the law (Torah) and the words that YHWH of Hosts had sent . . ." employs a variation of the hardened heart motif that appears in Isa 6:10 as well, "make the mind (literally, "heart") of this people dull." The term, "adamant," *šāmîr*, literally, "thorn," is a metaphorical portrayal of Israel's rebellion that draws upon a term characteristically employed in Isaiah (Isa 5:6; 7:23, 24, 25; 9:17 [NRSV: 9:18]; 10:17; 27:4; 32:13). The rejection of YHWH's Torah and words appears frequently throughout the prophets, but it is especially highlighted in Isa 1:10; 5:24; 8:16, 20; 24:5; cf. Isa 2:3; 42:4; 51:4, 7). The reference to YHWH's sending divine instruction by the hand of the prophets of course indicates Zechariah's interest in prior prophetic tradition as indicated at the beginning of the book (Zech 1:1-6), and aids in understanding Zechariah as a prophetic book that looks to the fulfillment of prior prophecy in relation to the building of the Second Temple in Jerusalem. The statement that "great wrath came from YHWH of Hosts" presents a standard interpretation of punishment in prophetic tradition, but it must be observed that such a statement constitutes a form of theodicy in that it seeks to explain evil by charging the people with sin rather than by arguing that somehow YHWH was unable or unwilling to protect the people from threat.

Verse 13 continues the prophet's explanation for YHWH's anger by stating that YHWH called to the people, but they did not listen. This statement reflects YHWH's statements in Isaiah 66:4, "when I called, no one answered, when I spoke, they did not listen," and Ezek 8:18, "and though they cry in my hearing with a loud voice, I will not listen to them." The prophet continues by quoting YHWH, "so when they call, I will not listen." The NRSV translation, "so when they called, I would not listen," misrepresents the tense of the verbs. Again, YHWH's statement relates to Isa 1:15, "when you stretch out your hands, I will hide my eyes from you; even though you make many prayers, I will not listen" (cf. Isa 8:17).[94] The concluding speech formula, "says YHWH of Hosts," identifies the preceding statements as a quote of YHWH.

Finally, verse 14 continues the quotation of YHWH's words as indicated by the first person form of the statement, "and I scattered them with a whirlwind among all the nations that they had not known . . ." YHWH's use of a whirlwind to punish people appears elsewhere in Hos 13:3; Isa 54:11; cf. Jon 1:11; see also Amos 1:14; Jer 23:19; 30:23; Isa 29:6; Ezek 13:11, 13; Ps 83:16 [NRSV: 83:15]). The image anticipates the reference in Zech 9:14 to YHWH's use of whirlwinds of the south in the context of protecting Ephraim and Jerusalem. The image of a pleasant land turned to desolation for those who pass by draws upon the covenant curse traditions that are especially well represented in Jeremiah (see Deut 28:37; 2 Kgs 22:19; Jer 5:30; 25:9, 11, 18, 38; 29:18; 42:18; 44:12, 22;

---

[94] For discussion of the hiddenness of YHWH and the problem of theodicy, see Walter Brueggemann, *Theology of the Old Testament: Testimony, Dispute, Advocacy* (Minneapolis: Fortress, 1997) 333–99, and the literature cited there.

cf. 49:13, 17 for Edom; 50:23; 51:37, 41 for Babylon). The notion of a "pleasant land" (ʾereṣ ḥemdâ) appears also in Jer 3:19 and Ps 106:24.

PRESENTATION OF SEVEN ORACLES CONCERNING YHWH'S
PLEDGE TO RESTORE JERUSALEM AND JUDAH:
EXHORTATION TO ACT ON BEHALF OF RESTORATION: 8:1-17

Zechariah 8:1-17 constitutes the prophet's (or the editor's) presentation of a sequence of seven oracles that take up YHWH's pledge to restore the relationship with Jerusalem and Judah following the period of judgment. Following the introductory version of the YHWH word transmission formula in verse 1, the seven instances of the introductory messenger formula identify the seven oracles in the sequence in verses 2, 3, 4-5, 6, 7-8, 9-13, and 14-15. The sequence begins with the premise of YHWH's jealousy and anger directed against Jerusalem which caused the punishment in the first place (verse 2), but it continues by positing YHWH's return to Jerusalem (verse 3) and the images of a city and nations that have been restored and cleansed (verses 4-5, 6, 7-8). It concludes with a call to the people to take responsibility for their own part in the restoration process (verse 9-13), and returns at the end to a summation of YHWH's stance toward the city to bring an end to the past punishment and to inaugurate the restoration. It is noteworthy that each of the seven oracles appears to take up statements from Zechariah's prior vision reports or from earlier prophetic works, such as Isaiah, Jeremiah, and Haggai. In this respect, the oracle sequence constitutes the prophet's summation or understanding of prophetic tradition in general concerning the causes for Zion's punishment and YHWH's intentions to restore the city once the punishment is complete. The concluding verses 16-17 then define the character of the entire unit in that they exhort the people to engage in the true and just moral action necessary to bring about YHWH's pledge for the restoration of Zion.

The YHWH word transmission formula in verse 1 introduces the entire unit, and identifies it as the word of YHWH.[95] This particular example of the formula is remarkable, however, in that it does not identify to whom the word of YHWH is transmitted. This may relate to the fact that many of the oracles in the sequence appear to be the prophet's summation of the works or message of other earlier prophets, as well as his own prior material, that are now about to achieve their own realization in his time.

[95] Sweeney, *Isaiah 1–39* 546–7.

Verse 2 constitutes the first oracle in the sequence. Following the initial messenger formula in verse 2aα, the balance of the verse presents a first person statement by YHWH concerning YHWH's past jealousy and anger concerning Zion. This statement constitutes the premise from which the following oracles proceed, i.e., YHWH's anger against Jerusalem explains its punishment, but the time for punishment has ended and the restoration has begun. This statement recapitulates the basic premise of Zechariah's first vision in which YHWH states divine jealousy concerning Jerusalem and Judah (Zech 1:14) as the basis for Jerusalem's punishment prior to the present restoration. The motif of divine jealousy for Jerusalem or Israel in general plays a particularly conspicuous role in Isaiah (see Isa 9:6 [NRSV: 9:7]; 37:32; 42:13; 59:17; 63:15). Divine jealousy appears frequently together with divine anger in Ezekiel as a means to express YHWH's anger against Jerusalem (Ezek 5:13; 16:38, 42; cf. Ezek 8:3) and against the nations for their mistreatment of Israel (Ezek 36:6; cf. Ezek 39:25). It appears that Zechariah presupposes Ezekiel's sense of divine jealousy and anger against Jerusalem and Israel as the basis for the punishment, but he also draws upon Isaiah's and Ezekiel's sense of divine jealousy, not against the nations who mistreat Jerusalem and Israel, but as a basis for YHWH's promise to restore the city and nation in the balance of the passage.

Verse 3 constitutes the second oracle. Following the messenger formula in verse 3aα, the balance of the verse presents YHWH's first person statement concerning the divine intention to return and to dwell in the midst of Jerusalem. YHWH's return to the city will result in Jerusalem's becoming known as "the faithful city" and "the holy mountain." The phrase, "the faithful city," *ʿîr-hāʾemet*, more properly reads "the city of truth." Although the terminology differs, it appears to draw upon Isa 1:21-26 in which YHWH announces the intention to purge Jerusalem from evil in order that it might once again be recognized as "the city of righteousness (*ʿîr haṣṣedeq*)" and "the faithful city (*qiryâ neʾĕmānâ*)." The designation of Jerusalem as YHWH's "holy mountain" clearly presupposes Ezekiel's understanding of Jerusalem as the sacred site of the Temple that is purged so that YHWH's holy presence might be restored as the Temple is reestablished (see esp. Ezekiel 1–11; 40–48). The concept of Jerusalem as YHWH's holy mountain permeates prophetic and later biblical literature (see Isa 11:9; 48:2; 52:1; Jer 31:23; Ezek 20:40; Joel 2:1; 4:17 [NRSV: 3:17]; Obad 16; Zeph 3:11; Neh 11:1, 18; Dan 9:16, 20, 24; 11:45). This refers to Jerusalem's status as the site for the Temple of YHWH. The oracle marks the point in the sequence in which YHWH's return to Jerusalem will initiate the process of restoration.

Verses 4-5 constitute the third oracle in the sequence. Again, the messenger formula appears in verse 4aα, and the balance of the passage presents the oracle proper. In this case, the oracle is a third person description of Jerusalem repopulated with old men and women once again sitting in the city's streets, staff in hand, while boys and girls play. Such an idyllic picture points to the fact that Jerusalem will be secure for all, from the very old to the very young, and calls to mind the portrayal of Jerusalem's future in Isa 65:20 in which babies will not die prematurely and the elderly will live to a full age. It is analogous to Jer 33:10-11 which states that the streets of Jerusalem will be filled with people and animals as well as the joyful voices of bridegroom, bride, and those who wish them well. It also plays upon Zechariah's third vision, which looks forward to the repopulation of Jerusalem (see Zech 2:8 [NRSV: 2:4]). The repopulation of Jerusalem, of course, follows directly from YHWH's previously mentioned return to the city.

Verse 6 constitutes the fourth oracle in the sequence. Following the initial messenger formula in verse 6aα, the oracle presents a first person statement by YHWH concerning the wondrous nature of the event, i.e., the restoration of Jerusalem, in the eyes of "the remnant of this people" and in YHWH's own eyes. Although the NRSV translates the verb *plʾ* as "it seems impossible," the verb conveys a sense of wonderfulness as well as impossibility, especially in relation to YHWH's power (see 2 Sam 1:26; Pss 119:18; 118:23). The concept of the remnant of the people of Israel underlies the messages of Isaiah (see Isa 4:3; 10:20, 21, 22; 11:11, 16; 28:5; 37:4, 31, 32; cf. Isa 6:12-13), Micah (Mic 2:12; 5:6, 7 [NRSV: 5:7, 8]; 7:18), and Zephaniah (Zeph 2:7, 9; 3:12, 13) in which the remnant describes those who survive YHWH's judgment to rebuild Jerusalem and Israel for the future. The notion is employed in Ezra 9:8, 14 (cf. 2 Chr 34:21) to describe the returned exiles of the post-exilic Jewish community. The notion that such a restoration will be wondrous to both the people and to YHWH indicates that the restoration of a land and people following such a catastrophe is a remarkable or unprecedented event in the ancient Near Eastern world. Deutero-Isaiah continually challenges the exilic Judean audience to recognize that only YHWH is capable of such remarkable actions (e.g., Isa 40:12-31; 41:1-10; 44:6-8). The oracular formula in verse 6bβ reinforces the prophet's contention that this is a statement by YHWH.

The fifth oracle in the sequence appears in verses 7-8. The messenger formula in verse 7aα introduces a first person statement by YHWH in which YHWH states the fundamental reconstitution of the relationship with Israel. YHWH begins in verse 7aβ-b with the statement, "I will save my people from the east and from the west country," which calls to mind Zechariah's prior statements concerning YHWH's dispersal of the people (Zech 2:10 [NRSV: 2:6]; 7:14) and the sending of chariots throughout the earth as YHWH begins the process of restoration (Zech

6:1-8). The role of Yʜwʜ as one who "delivers, saves *(môšîʿa)*" the people recalls Yʜwʜ's role in Isaiah (Isa 43:3, 11; 45:15, 21; 49:26; 60:16; 63:8), Hosea (Hos 13:4), Jeremiah (Jer 14:8; 15:20; 30:11; 42:11), the hymnic tradition (2 Sam 22:3; Pss 31:3 [ɴʀsv: 31:2]; 106:21), etc. The second statement conveys Yʜwʜ's intention to bring the people so that they might dwell in Jerusalem recalls the earlier oracle in verse 3 as well as the basic premise of the restoration of the exiles from Isaiah, (Isaiah 11; 34–35; 40–48), Ezekiel (Ezekiel 40–48), and Jeremiah (Jeremiah 30–33). Yʜwʜ's final statement in this oracle, "they shall be my people and I will be their G–d, in faithfulness and in righteousness, recapitulates the basic formula for the covenant relationship between Yʜwʜ and Israel (see Exod 6:7; Lev 26:12; 2 Sam 7:24; Jer 7:23; 30:22; 31:33; Ezek 11:20; 14:11; 37:23, 27; contra Hos 1:8).[96] The qualification that the relationship be established "in faithfulness and in righteousness" recalls Yʜwʜ's qualities in Exod 34:6 and the above-noted ideal for Jerusalem in Isa 1:21-26 (see above on verse 3).

Verses 9-13 constitute the sixth oracle of the sequence. Following the messenger formula in verse 9aα[1-4], the balance of the passage constitutes the longest oracle of the sequence. This is no accident as verses 9-13 appear to convey the basic intent of the sequence as a whole, i.e., to motivate the people to take action to rebuild the Temple with the expectation that Yʜwʜ is now bringing about the restoration. This intent is clear from the statement, "let your hands be strong," which both introduces and concludes the oracle in verses 9aα[5-6] and 13bβ. By calling upon the people to let their hands be strong, the prophet calls upon them to take action concerning the rebuilding of the Temple (see verse 9b). Scholars have noted that the oracle appears to present the similar message and perspective as that of Haggai, who in Hag 2:4 employs the verb *ḥzq*, "be strong" (ɴʀsv, "take courage") three times to exhort Zerubbabel, Joshua ben Jehozadak, and the people of the land to undertake the work of building the second Temple.[97] Likewise, Haggai points to the benefits of such reconstruction, i.e., the end of strife and recognition by the nations, Yʜwʜ's agricultural blessing, and better times for all as motivating factors.

In calling upon the people to undertake the work of Temple reconstruction, the oracle points both to the past difficulties suffered by the people in the land prior to the reconstruction of the Temple (verses

[96] For study of this formula, see Rolf Rendtorff, *Die "Bundesformel": Eine exegetisch-theologische Untersuchung*, SBS, vol. 160 (Stuttgart: Katholisches Bibelwerk, 1995).

[97] E.g., Petersen, *Haggai, Zechariah 1–8* 305; Meyers and Meyers, *Haggai and Zechariah 1–8* 419.

$9a\alpha^{5\text{-}6}$-10) and the future benefits that will follow from YHWH for their efforts (verses 11-13).

Following the exhortation to "let your hands be strong," verses $9a\alpha^{5\text{-}6}$-10 begin by pointing to the fact that the people have heard these words from the prophets who were speaking at the time when the foundation for the Temple was laid. Ezra 3:8-13 maintains that the foundation for the Temple was laid in the second year after the arrival of Joshua ben Jehozadak and Zerubbabel at the house of G–d. There is a great deal of confusion within Ezra as Ezra 5:16 attributes the laying of the Temple's foundation to Sheshbazzar, who was commissioned by Cyrus in 539 B.C.E. to rebuild the Temple (see Ezra 1:1-11; cf. Ezra 5:13-17). Although Ezra 3:8-13 may refer retrospectively to the laying of the Temple's foundation, it clearly posits that Joshua ben Jehozadak and Zerubbabel are undertaking the work of Temple reconstruction. No prophets are mentioned in relation to Sheshbazzar's work, although one cannot discount the notion that prophets may well have condoned his actions (see, e.g., Isa 44:24-48, who attributes Temple rebuilding to Sheshbazzar's patron, Cyrus). Both Haggai and Zechariah are explicitly mentioned in Ezra 5:1-2 as supporters of Temple reconstruction and again in Ezra 6:14 as the work is finished. Zechariah's reference to the prophets is easily construed as a reference to Haggai, and the correspondence between Zech 8:9-13 and the message of Haggai supports such a reading. The use of other prophets in this oracle, especially Isaiah, but Jeremiah and Ezekiel as well, must also be considered. As noted above, the book of Isaiah calls for Temple reconstruction, and the book of Ezekiel is organized to present the reestablished Temple in Jerusalem as the goal of the entire process of Jerusalem's and Israel's purification through the destruction of the city and the exile. Jeremiah points more vaguely to the fact that the Temple will not save the people from punishment (Jeremiah 7), but he does envision restoration once the punishment is complete (see esp. Jeremiah 30–33). The idiom, "from the mouth of the prophets," apparently refers to the written words of the prophets that are recorded by dictation (Jer 36:4, 6, 17, 18, 27, 32; 45:1),[98] which suggests that Zechariah knows the words of earlier prophets from having read or studied them in written form.

Verse 10, introduced by the causative *kî*, "because," then provides the motivation for the people to undertake the building of the Temple. Here, YHWH points to earlier days when neither human beings nor animals were properly paid for their work, there was no safety for those who came and went from the city, and YHWH claims to have set the people against each other. Certainly Haggai also points to such depri-

---

[98] Meyers and Meyers, *Haggai, Zechariah 1–8* 419.

vation and problems as he asks the people to consider how they have fared without having rebuilt the Temple, i.e., the land has produced little, there is not enough to drink, there is insufficient clothing, and wages disappear far too quickly (see Hag 1:5-6). One must also keep in mind that the city of Jerusalem remains undefended as the city walls have not yet been rebuilt, and the early years of Darius' reign were a time of revolt within the Persian empire against his rule.

The initial *wĕʿattâ*, "but now," in verse 11 signals the contrast between YHWH's actions in the past and those of the future as they are portrayed in verses 11-13. Verse 11 presents YHWH's statement of the basic principle of the oracle, "but now I will not deal with the remnant of this people as in the former days," followed by the oracular formula which identifies YHWH as the speaker. YHWH's statement continues in verse 12 with a rationalization for this principle introduced by causative *kî*, "for, because," which focuses on the agricultural bounty that the people can expect as a result of building the Temple. YHWH states that there will be a "sowing of peace," which contrasts with the statement in verse 10 that there was no peace for or "safety" for those who left or entered the city. The statements that the vine will yield its fruit, that the land will yield its produce, and the heavens shall give their dew provide a relatively full picture of the fertility of creation that will result from the people's efforts. In addition, the references to the produce of the land and the dew of the heavens replicate statements from Hag 1:10 concerning the withholding of these products because the Temple continues to lie in ruins. YHWH's statement, "and I will cause the remnant of this people to possess all these things," returns to the initial language of verse 11 to provide an inclusio for verses 11-12 that sums up the significance of the prior statements. Verse 13 then presents the overall results of YHWH's promises in verses 11-12 for the people. Although it is not represented in the NRSV translation, the introductory *wĕhāyâ*, "and it shall come to pass," clearly indicates that the verse results from what precedes. Furthermore, it provides an appropriate conclusion for the entire oracle in verses 9-13 as it takes up motifs and language from verses 9-10 as well as from verses 11-12. The initial statement contrasts the prior state of the people as a "cursing among the nations," with their projected state as "a blessing." The Hebrew term *qĕlālâ* normally means "curse," but the NRSV translation renders the term so that it presents a stylistic parallel with *bĕrākâ*, "blessing." The term *qĕlālâ* appears in Deut 11:26, 28; Jer 24:9; 25:18; 29:22; Neh 13:2, etc., as a typical term to describe the exiled and destitute state of the people as a result of their punishment and exile. Likewise, *bĕrākâ* describes the contrasting state of the people in Deut 11:26, 27, 29; Neh 13:2, etc., that will follow from their adherence to YHWH's will. In keeping with the conception of the

Temple as the center of all Israel as well as of all creation (cf. Ezekiel 40–48), Yhwh's statement is directed to both the house of Judah and the house of Israel. Yhwh's statement, "I will save you," reiterates the language of Yhwh's earlier statement in verse 7. The concluding statements, "Do not be afraid, but let your hands be strong," employ a combination of the typical reassurance formula in which Yhwh, a prophet, or another person, announces salvation or promises relief from an oppressor (e.g., Gen 15:1; 35:7; 26:24; Isa 7:4-9; 10:24-26; 37:6-7; 35:4; 40:9),[99] and the initial statement of the oracle in verse 9aα[5-6]. The formula, "let your hands be strong," thereby forms an inclusio for the entire oracle.

The seventh oracle in the sequence appears in verses 14-15. As in the previous cases, this oracle begins in verse 14aα[1-5] with the prophetic messenger formula, but it also includes an introductory *kî*, "for, because." The *kî* indicates that the oracle is not a free-standing sub-unit in the sequence like its predecessors, but that it is linked syntactically to the previous material so that it forms a sort of summation or conclusion to the entire sequence. This is evident from the contents of the oracle as well in that they summarize the major motifs and movement of the prior oracle in verses 9-13 and indeed of the entire sequence beginning in verse 2, i.e., Yhwh's prior anger against Jerusalem and Judah have given way to restoration. The oracle proper in verses 14aα[6-12]-15 constitutes a basic summary statement of this movement that contrasts Yhwh's past stance toward the people with the present stance. Interestingly, the contrasting statements, "just as I purposed to do evil to you . . . so I have purposed in these days to do good," draws upon the moral instruction to the people offered in Isa 1:16-17, "cease to do evil, learn to do good." Likewise, Yhwh's statement, "and I did not relent (lit., 'be comforted,' *wĕlōʾ niḥāmĕtî*)," draws upon similar language from Isa 1:24, "Woe, I will be avenged (lit., 'be comforted,' *ʾennāḥēm*) from enemies." Zechariah's reference to the past time "when your ancestors provoked me to wrath *(bĕhaqṣîp ʾăbōtêkem ʾōtî)*," also relates to Zech 1:2, "Yhwh was very angry with your ancestors *(qāṣap yhwh ʾăbōtêkem qāṣep)*," and thereby returns the reader to the initial concern or premise of the book as a whole. The appearance of the reassurance formula, "do not be afraid," reiterates the concluding statements of verse 13.

The final segment of Zech 8:1-17 appears in verses 16-17, which constitute the prophet's presentation of Yhwh's exhortation to the people that calls upon them to undertake the moral action necessary to reconstitute holiness within the community as the Temple is rebuilt. Its syntactically independent character and its placement at the conclusion

[99] Sweeney, *Isaiah 1–39* 547.

of the oracle sequence aid in establishing this section as the rhetorical goal of the entire sequence, i.e., to call upon the people to take action as the Temple is built. The first statement in verse 16a, "these are the things that you shall do," serves as a general introduction to the more specific statements that follow in verses 16b-17a. These statements are formulated as an order[100] in that they begin with a pair of positive commands and conclude with a pair of prohibitions. The positive commands call upon the people to speak what is true to each other and to render true judgments that lead to peace. This second command, of course, envisions truth and peace in the lawcourt, and thereby recalls the role of the Temple as a place where legal decisions are made within the community (see Exod 21:6; 22:8; Deut 17:8-13). It also reiterates the earlier commands concerning true justice in Zech 7:9-10. The prohibitions call upon the people to refrain from devising evil in their hearts against their neighbors and from making false oaths. The first reiterates the prohibition of Zech 7:10. The second reiterates a basic principle of the ten commandments (Exod 20:16; Deut 5:20), and it also bears upon the issue of false testimony in a court of law (see Exod 23:7; Deut 19:15-21). An oath may establish innocence in a legal or cultic matter (Exod 22:8; Num 5:21; 30:3); certainly a false oath renders one culpable of wrongdoing, and requires purification at the Temple (Lev 5:4-6). The concluding statement, "for all these are things that I hate," provides the basis for following YHWH's instructions, and it reiterates the language of Isa 1:14, "your new moons and appointed festivals, my soul hates." Finally, the oracular formula identifies this statement as an oracle from YHWH.

The last segment of Zech 7:8–14:21 begins with the YHWH word transmission formula in Zech 8:18, "and the word of YHWH of Hosts came to me, saying." The first person pronoun indicates that the prophet is the recipient of YHWH's word. As noted above, Zech 8:18-23 serves as an introduction to Zechariah 9–11; 12–14, which present in great detail the basic principles that are defined in Zech 8:18-23. Following the initial formula in verse 18, three successive oracles, each introduced by the messenger formula, appear in verses 19, 20-22, and 23.

The first oracle in verse 19 takes up the initial question concerning the appropriateness of continued mourning for the loss of the Temple in Zech 7:1-3. Zechariah 7:4-7 had not provided a direct answer to the question, but merely questioned whether or not the practice of fasting in fact was for YHWH. Zechariah 7:8–8:23 then point to YHWH's restoration of Jerusalem following the period of punishment, and Zech 8:19 finally presents an answer to the question posed by the delegation from

---

[100] Ibid., 526.

Beth El. By stating that the fasts of the fourth, fifth, seventh, and tenth months are to become seasons of joy, gladness, and cheerful festivals for the house of Judah, the oracle answers the question by asserting that fasting is no longer necessary and that rejoicing shall take its place at these times as the Temple is to be rebuilt. As noted above, the fasts of the fifth and seventh months refer respectively to the ninth of Av when the Temple was destroyed (see 2 Kgs 25:8-21, which dates the destruction to the seventh day of the fifth month and Jer 52:12-27, which dates the destruction to the tenth day of the fifth month) and the third of Tishri when Gedaliah, the governor of Judah, was assassinated in 582 B.C.E. (see 2 Kgs 25:22-26 and Jer 41:1-18, which dates the assassination to the seventh month). The fasts of the fourth and tenth months had not been previously mentioned. Jewish tradition maintains that these fasts also commemorate events surrounding the destruction of the Temple and the Babylonian exile. Thus, the tenth of Tevet, the tenth month, marks the beginning of the Babylonian siege of Jerusalem (see 2 Kgs 25:1-2; Jer 52:4-5, Ezek 24:1-2, which date the beginning of the siege to the tenth month), and the seventeenth of Tammuz, the fourth month, marks the Babylonian's breaching of Jerusalem's walls (see 2 Kgs 25:3-11; Jer 39:2-7; 52:6-11, which dates the Babylonian breaching of the walls to the fourth month).[101] The concluding command to love truth and peace reiterates the commands of Zech 7:9-10 and 8:16-17.

The second oracle appears in verses 20-22, which builds upon the motif of restoration and rejoicing at the building of the Temple in verse 19. Following the messenger formula in verse 20a, the oracle proper in verses 20b-22 constitutes three interrelated statements that portray the future when the nations of the world will come to Jerusalem to recognize YHWH. The first appears in verse 20b, which basically states that peoples and the inhabitants of many cities will come. The introductory particles, *ʿōd ʾăšer*, "yet, when," together with the imperfect verb, *yābōʾû*, "they shall come," convey a time still in the future when such an event will transpire. The pilgrimage of the nations to Zion is a well-known motif in prophetic literature from the exilic and early post-exilic period, i.e., Isa 2:2-4; Mic 4:1-5; Isaiah 43:1-7; 60–62; 66:18-24; Hag 2:1-9. As the following discussion demonstrates, this oracle draws heavily on Isa 2:2-4 and Mic 4:1-5. Some argue that the particle is to be understood retrospectively as well, i.e., "yet again."[102] Although it seems clear that nations would have come to Jerusalem to acknowledge YHWH and the Davidic monarch, e.g., during the reigns of David and Solomon when the Davidic empire comprised many foreign nations, the thrust of the

---

[101] See "Fasting and Fast Days," *Encyclopaedia Judaica* 6:1189-96.
[102] For a summary of options, see Petersen, *Haggai, Zechariah 1–8* 316.

oracle is to look forward and to see the acknowledgment of YHWH by the nations as the result of the reconstruction of the Temple in Jerusalem as the holy center of the cosmos.

The second statement appears in verse 21, which is related to verse 20b by the *waw-consecutive* construction, *wĕhālĕkû,* "and they shall come." The present statement builds upon the former by presenting a situation in which the inhabitants of one city will come and speak to the inhabitants of another. A quotation of their statement appears in verse 21aα[7-12]-b, "come, let us go to entreat the favor of YHWH and to seek YHWH of Hosts; I myself am going." This statement builds upon the initial question posed by the delegation from Beth El, which came to Jerusalem to entreat the favor of YHWH and to inquire about the practice of fasting (Zech 7:2-3). Indeed, the recognition of YHWH by the people of Beth El would be the first stage in recognition by the nations at large because Beth El is the former idolatrous royal sanctuary of the northern kingdom of Israel (1 Kings 12–13) that served as the religious center for the foreign inhabitants of the land brought in by the Assyrians following the destruction of northern Israel (2 Kings 17). The structure and wording of the statement likewise build upon that of the nations in Isa 2:2, "and many peoples shall come and say, 'Come and let us go up to the mountain of YHWH, unto the house of the G–d of Jacob,'" and the parallel statement in Mic 4:2, "and many nations shall come and say, 'Come and let us go up unto the mountain of YHWH and unto the house of the G–d of Jacob.'" The concluding statement, "I will go (*ʾēlĕkâ*) emphasizes the role of the individuals. When read in the context of mourning, it provides an interesting contrast to Micah's statement in Mic 1:8 concerning his mourning for Jerusalem and Judah, "for this I will lament and wail; I will go (*ʾēlĕkâ*) barefoot and naked; I will make lamentation like the jackals and mourning like the ostriches." Whereas Micah was compelled to mourn for his people and could only look forward to a time when things would change, Zechariah maintains that the time is about to come.

The third statement in verse 22 is likewise linked to the preceding statements by a *waw-consecutive* construction, *ûbāʾû,* "and they shall come." Overall, the statement merely reiterates the preceding verses by stating that "many peoples and strong nations shall come to seek YHWH of Hosts in Jerusalem and to entreat the favor of YHWH." The reference to "many peoples and strong nations (*ʿammîm rabbîm wĕgôyim ʿăṣûmîm*) employs the same terminology as Mic 4:3, "and he shall judge between many peoples and he shall arbitrate for strong nations from afar," whereas Isa 2:4 states, "and he shall judge between the nations and he shall arbitrate for many peoples." Although Zechariah is heavily dependent upon Isaiah, this oracle appears to depend especially upon

Micah. Certainly, the portrayals of YHWH's defeat of the nations in Zechariah 9–14 corresponds more closely to the violent treatment of the nations by YHWH in Micah 4–5 rather than the more peaceful relationship envisioned in Isaiah 40–55 (but cf. Isaiah 2; 13-27; 65-66).

The final oracle in the sequence appears in verse 23. Following the initial messenger formula, the oracle states that ten men from every language will take hold of a Jew by his garment and ask, "let us go with you, for we have heard that G–d is with you." This scenario, of course, builds upon the motif of YHWH's recognition by the nations, but it also returns to themes from Isaiah. The reference to ten men from all the languages, i.e., nations, should be read in relation to Isaiah 6, especially Isa 6:13. This is the inaugural vision of Isaiah in which the prophet is told YHWH's plans to punish and decimate the people of Israel. Verse 13 in particular notes that the people will be burned like a stump so that only one tenth will remain, and then they will be burned again to form the holy seed for YHWH's projected restoration. In Zechariah, the notion that Judah constitutes a remnant of one tenth apparently refers to Judah's relationship with the nations so that Jews will constitute the tenth that will lead to YHWH's recognition by the nations of the world. The reference to "the tongues of the nations (NRSV: 'nations of every language')" naturally recalls the story of the tower of Babel in which the nations of the world are distinguished by their different languages (Genesis 11), but it also relates to Isa 66:18, which speaks of YHWH's intentions to gather "all nations and all tongues" at Jerusalem to recognize YHWH's divine glory. Likewise, the statement that the nations have heard that "G–d is with you" recalls Isaiah's sign to King Ahaz, i.e., the child Immanuel, which means "G–d is with us" in Hebrew. Immanuel was to be born as a sign of YHWH's commitment to deliver Judah at the time of the Syro-Ephraimitic War (Isa 7:14; cf. 8:8). From the perspective of Zechariah, that time is at hand.

ZECHARIAH'S FIRST PRONOUNCEMENT:
CONCERNING YHWH'S JUDGMENT AGAINST THE SHEPHERDS: 9:1–11:17

Zechariah 9–11 constitutes the first of two "pronouncements" or "oracles" of the prophet. Although both Zechariah 9–11 and 12–14 were apparently composed by a writer or writers other than the prophet Zechariah, they are currently presented as the prophet's "pronouncements" concerning YHWH's future actions against the "shepherds" who controlled Judah (Zechariah 9–11) and the nations at large (Zechariah 12–14). Each is introduced by the superscription *maśśāʾ*, which identifies the following material as a "pronouncement" or "oracle" of the

prophet that is designed to express and explain the manifestation of
YHWH's actions in the world.[103] As noted above, Zechariah is named in
the introduction to the book as "Zechariah ben Berechiah ben Iddo"
(Zech 1:1), which identifies the prophet with Zechariah ben Jeberechiah,
the witness to the birth and significance of Isaiah's son, Maher-shalal-
hash-baz, "the spoil speeds, the prey hastens" (Isa 8:1-4). Furthermore,
Maher-shalal-hash-baz signifies the ultimate downfall of Damascus to
the king of Assyria and much of the material in Zechariah 9–11 and
12–14 appears to be heavily indebted to Isaiah (including the depiction
of the fall of Damascus and surrounding territories to an unnamed
king in Zech 9:1-8). It would therefore appear that the two pronouncements are designed to be read as earlier statements by Isaiah, witnessed by Zechariah ben Jeberechiah, that are to be fulfilled in the time
of Zechariah ben Berechiah ben Iddo. The two pronouncements appear
to depict the rise and ultimate downfall of Darius I and Persian control
over Jerusalem and Judah.

Zechariah 9–11 is concerned overall with YHWH's judgment against
the "shepherds" who had responsibility for the care of "the house of
Judah" (Zech 10:2, 3) and the inhabitants of the earth in general (Zech
11:4-6; cf. Zech 11:15-17). Although the identification of specific figures
behind these chapters is hotly debated in the commentaries, it appears
that they portray the Persian monarch Darius I (522–486 B.C.E.), who
initially supported the reconstruction of the Temple and thereby offered the prospect of peace and restoration to Jerusalem and Judah. But
Darius suffered a series of revolts from within the empire against his
rule and several major defeats in his wars against the Greeks that would
call the stability and continuity of Persian rule into question.[104] Against
such a background, Zechariah 9–11 emphasizes YHWH's dissatisfaction
with Darius' rule of Jerusalem and Judah and points to his ultimate
downfall.

Following the initial superscription, *maśśāʾ*, "pronouncement," in
Zech 9:1aα[1], the following material comprises three major sub-units
that are defined by a combination of form and content. Zechariah
9:1aα[2-5]-17 portrays the approach of the victorious king who will bring
peace and security to Jerusalem, Israel, and Judah, prior to his attack
against the Greeks. Zechariah 10:1-12 expresses YHWH's dissatisfaction
with the "shepherds" of the people and YHWH's intention to restore
Israel and Judah by returning their exiles. Zechariah 11:1-17 relates
YHWH's intention to overthrow the "worthless shepherd that abandons

---

[103] Weis, "Oracle," ABD V:28-9; idem, *A Definition of the Genre Maśśāʾ*.
[104] For discussion of the reign of Darius I, see Dandamaev, *A Political History of the
Achaemenid Empire* 103–81.

the flock" (verse 17). Overall, the three sub-units present a progressive scenario of early hopes surrounding the reign of Darius and the collapse of those hopes as Darius failed to insure stability within the Persian empire and suffered several major defeats at the hands of the Greeks.

THE PROPHET'S PORTRAYAL OF THE APPROACH OF THE VICTORIOUS KING: 9:1aα²⁻⁵-17

Zechariah 9:1aα²⁻⁵-17 presents the prophet's portrayal of the approaching king who will bring peace and security to Jerusalem, Israel, and Judah, and who will wage war against the Greeks. The passage is marked at the beginning by the appearance of the word of YHWH, which is directed against Hadrach, Damascus, and other locations, and is designed to demonstrate YHWH's protection of the Temple in Jerusalem. Although verse 9 begins with a syntactically independent set of imperatives that call upon Zion/Jerusalem to rejoice and shout at the approach of the victorious king, verses 9-17 are tied to verses 1-8 by their concern for the protection of the people (verses 15, 16-17) even as they are set for war against the Greeks. Zechariah 10:1, with its introductory imperative that calls upon the people to request rain from YHWH, begins an entirely new sub-unit that turns to a concern with YHWH's dissatisfaction against the so-called "shepherds" of the people who have neglected to take care of the "flock."

Verses 1aα²⁻⁵-4 present the effects of YHWH's word against Hadrach, Damascus, and other foreign territories that presumably threaten Jerusalem and Judah. Verse 1a states that "the word of YHWH is against the land of Hadrach and will rest upon Damascus." Hadrach is the name of a region in Aram/Syria located north/northeast of Damascus, and Damascus served as the capital of Aram until it was destroyed in 734 B.C.E. and later as the principal city of the region.[105] The NRSV translation, "and (it) will rest upon Damascus," is incorrect. The Hebrew should read, "the word of YHWH is against Hadrach and its resting place Damascus." The designation of Damascus as "its resting place (měnuḥātô)" employs a term that elsewhere designates Zion or the Temple as YHWH's resting place (Ps 132:8, 14; Isa 66:1; 1 Chr 28:2; 2 Chr 6:41; cf. Ps 95:11; Isa 11:10). Verse 1b provides the motive clause for such a statement, introduced by causative kî, "for to YHWH belongs the capital of Aram, as do all the tribes of Israel." The NRSV translation, "capital

---

[105] Meyers and Meyers, *Zechariah 9–14* 91–2; Petersen, *Zechariah 9–14 and Malachi* 43.

of Aram," follows the LXX, which presupposes Hebrew *ʿāwû ʾărām*, but the Hebrew reads *ʿên ʾādām*, "eye/spring of humankind." The differences between the two readings are the result of very minor orthographic differences in the Masoretic Hebrew text and the presumed Hebrew text underlying the LXX.[106] The MT reading may refer to an otherwise unknown location or, more likely, to YHWH's control of all humanity as well as of the tribes of Israel. Verse 2a adds the city of Hamath (modern Hama), located north of Damascus in the general vicinity of Hatarikka (Hadrach). Verses 2b-4 shift to a description of the Tyre and Sidon, both of which will be dispossessed by YHWH. They are designated as "very wise," undoubtedly because of their successful role in seafaring which made them very rich as a result of their commercial activities and trading colonies throughout the Mediterranean world. Tyre in particular, at least until the time of Alexander, was a heavily fortified island that generally had resisted conquest except for the Assyrian king Sennacherib, who built a navy and defeated Tyre in 701 B.C.E. Later, Alexander conquered the city in 333 B.C.E. by filling in the waterway between Tyre and the coast to create a bridge for his troops. The reference to YHWH's hurling its wealth into the sea presupposes its role as an island fortress and naval power.[107]

Verses 5-8 are formulated as a first person speech by YHWH that is conveyed by the prophet (see the statements by the prophet in verses 14-17, which are syntactically joined to YHWH's words in verses 5-13 so that the prophet thereby presents YHWH's words). Although these verses are generally viewed in association with verses 1aα²⁻⁵-4, they must be read together with verses 9-13, which also comprise first person speech by YHWH. Verses 5-8 begin with the syntactically independent statement, "Ashkelon shall see it and be afraid," and is concerned throughout with YHWH's intention to subdue Philistia and thereby protect the Temple in Jerusalem. The geography of Philistia and Judah is particularly important to consider as Philistia is located in the coastal plain to the west of Judah, whereas Judah constitutes the rolling hill country of the Shephelah and later higher hill country where Jerusalem is located. Control of Philistia not only threatens Judah, it also cuts off potential support from Egypt to the south and Phoenicia to the north. Basically, the geography of the region dictates that Philistia provides the easiest access to the hill country of Judah, and most invasions of the country therefore originate in Philistia. This was certainly the case in

---

[106] For discussion, see Rudolph, *Haggai–Sacharja 1–8–Sacharja 9–14–Maleachi* 168.

[107] For full discussion of Tyre's history, see H. J. Katzenstein, *The History of Tyre* (Jerusalem and New York: Schocken, 1973); H. J. Katzenstein and D. R. Edwards, "Tyre," *ABD* VI:686-92.

Sennacherib's invasion of Judah in 701 B.C.E. The four cities listed here, Ashkelon, Gaza, Ekron, and Ashdod, constitute the major Philistine cities after Gath's destruction by the Assyrian monarch Sargon II in 712 B.C.E. The same cities are mentioned in Zephaniah's oracle against the Philistines in Zeph 2:4-7. The reference to "a mongrel people" that will settle in Ashdod actually refers to a "bastard *(mamzēr)*" that will dwell in the city. The term *mamzēr* appears elsewhere in Deut 23:2, and generally refers to those born of forbidden marriages, such as incest (Leviticus 18; 20), a marriage between a priest and a divorced woman or a prostitute (see Lev 21:7-9) or the remarriage of a man and a woman after she has been married to another man (Deut 24:1-4). A close analogy appears in the contention of Gen 19:30-38 that the people of Moab and Ammon are descended from the incestuous union of Lot and his two daughters. The term may well refer to the mixed ethnicity of the people of Philistia, who apparently originated as a mixed population of peoples who came from Greece and the local Canaanite population and who frequently suffered invasion by foreigners due to their location on the seacoast. The reference to YHWH's smiting "the pride *(gā'ôn)* of the Philistines" employs language that is especially typical of Isaiah (Isa 2:10, 19, 21; 4:2; 13:11, 19; 14:11; 16:6; 23:9; 60:15). The references to YHWH's taking blood from its mouth and abominations from between its teeth metaphorically portrays Philistia as a dog chewing on the bones of some corpse. It is noteworthy, therefore, that excavations at Ashkelon have uncovered a large burial ground for the corpses of dogs and puppies. The role of dogs and puppies in Ashkelon is disputed— perhaps they had some cultic significance—but the presence of such a canine cemetery indicates that the Philistines were known for some association with dogs during the early Persian period that apparently underlies the present oracle.[108] The designation of the Philistines as a "remnant for our G–d," and their comparison to a clan in Judah and the Jebusites, indicates that Philistia will become an enclave within Judah. The Jebusites, after all, were the earlier Canaanite inhabitants of Jerusalem who remained after David conquered the city and made it his capital. YHWH's statement of the intent to encamp at the "house," i.e., Temple as a guard points to the role of Philistia as an access point for the invasion of Judah. YHWH's statement, "for now I have seen with my own eyes," testifies to the fact that this was known as the result of bitter experience.

Many scholars have argued that the itinerary of locations, Hadrach, Damascus, Hamath, Tyre, Sidon, Ashkelon, Gaza, Ekron, and Ashdod,

---

[108] Paula Wapnish and Brian Hesse, "Pampered Pooches or Plain Pariahs? The Ashkelon Dog Burials," *BA* 56 (1993) 55–80.

represents Alexander the Great's victorious campaign along the Mediterranean coast in 332 B.C.E. when he besieged and conquered the former island fortress of Tyre and the port city of Gaza.[109] The itinerary mentioned here, however, does not correspond to that of Alexander. Following his victory in 333 B.C.E. over Darius III (336-330 B.C.E.) at Issus along the northeastern Mediterranean coast, Alexander moved directly down the coast to Tyre, and did not pass through Damascus or other Syrian territories until after he had subdued Egypt and then returned north to confront Darius once again at Gaugamela in upper Mesopotamia in 331 B.C.E. He did send a lieutenant, Parmenion, to conquer Damascus and the surrounding area at this time, but the Zecharian text indicates an itinerary that begins in Syria rather than in Issus.[110] Instead, the itinerary appears to represent that of the Assyrian monarchs who invaded Judah and Israel in the late-eighth century B.C.E., especially as they are portrayed in the book of Isaiah. Isaiah 7 refers to Assyria's defeat of Damascus at the time of the Syro-Ephraimitic War (see also Isa 17:1-3), and the Assyrian monarch who threatens Jerusalem in Isa 10:5-34 specifically mentions Hamath and Damascus, among other Syrian/Aramean locations, as cities that had previously submitted to him (cf. Isa 36:19-20, which mention Hamath and Arpad). Sidon and Tyre were previously conquered by Sennacherib in 701 B.C.E.; indeed, Sennacherib's unprecedented defeat of Tyre was the primary cause of the collapse of the anti-Assyrian alliance put together by Hezekiah. The downfall of Tyre and Sidon is related in Isaiah 23. Following his conquest of Tyre, Sennacherib moved south to Philistia where he restored Padi, King of Ekron, to the throne after Hezekiah had imprisoned him prior to the revolt. Earlier, Tiglath-Pileser III (745–727 B.C.E.) had subdued Philistia and Aram, and Sargon II (721–705 B.C.E.) had subdued both Philistia and Hamath (cf. Isa 14:28-32).[111]

Many commentators point out that Hadrach is to be identified with the Aramean district Hatarikka, northwest of Damascus, that was created by Tiglath Pileser III as he advanced against Damascus in 738 B.C.E.[112]

[109] For references, see Petersen, *Zechariah 9–14 and Malachi* 4; Paul Hanson, *The Dawn of Apocalyptic* 289–90.

[110] See Martin Hengel, "The Political and Social History of Palestine from Alexander to Antiochus III (333–187 B.C.E.)," *The Cambridge History of Judaism. Volume II: The Hellenistic Age*, ed. W. D. Davies and L. Finkelstein (Cambridge: Cambridge University Press, 1989) 36.

[111] For an account of the Assyrian campaigns against Israel and Judah during the eighth century, see Herbert Donner, "The Separate States of Israel and Judah," *Israelite and Judaean History* 381–434.

[112] E.g., Petersen, *Zechariah 9–14 and Malachi* 43; Meyers and Meyers, *Zechariah 9–14* 91–2.

The name is unattested elsewhere in the Bible, and it disappears from ancient Near Eastern sources after 698 B.C.E. Many scholars have argued that mention of Hadrach in Zech 9:1 demonstrates that Zech 9:1-8 dates to the time of Isaiah in the late-eighth century.[113] The destruction of Damascus by Tiglath Pileser III in 734 B.C.E., the above-mentioned actions against Hamath, and Sennacherib's conquest of Tyre would likewise support this view. Nevertheless, such a contention is very difficult to prove. Certainly the reference to a confrontation with the Greeks in verse 13 suggests at least a much later context for the passage, but the references to cities attacked by the Assyrians in the late-eighth century point to some effort to depict the current situation of the late-sixth and early-fifth century B.C.E. in relation to the earlier period of Isaiah ben Amoz. In this regard, Darius I's efforts to subdue the revolts against his rule at the outset of his reign would then be read as a fulfillment of Isaiah's statements concerning the significance of the birth of his son, Maher-shalal-hash-baz in Isa 8:1-4, i.e., the wealth of Damascus and the spoil of Samaria would be carried away by the Assyrian king. Of course, the other cities mentioned here also figure prominently in Isaiah's oracles. Darius is known to have passed by Judah on his way to subdue revolt in Egypt in 519–517 B.C.E.[114] Although there is no mention of revolt in Syria/Israel at the outset of his reign, he would have passed through Syria and Philistia, and perhaps parts of Phoenicia, on his way to Egypt. This would suggest that YHWH's word was against the cities and territories listed here as Darius was recognized as the king who authorized the rebuilding of the Temple and who would thereby bring peace to Jerusalem and Judah. In reality, these cities and territories seem to have recognized that revolt against Darius was not in their interest, but his appearance in the region in 519–517 B.C.E. may well have been decisive in convincing them to remain quiet. Indeed, many have suggested that the disappearance of Zerubbabel, designated as YHWH's signet by Haggai (Hag 2:20-23), may have been the result of Darius' passage through the region.[115]

Verses 9-13 comprise the second part of YHWH's speech, but unlike verses 4-8 which constitute YHWH's depiction of the punishment to be suffered by the Philistine cities, these verses constitute a direct second person feminine singular address to Zion that calls upon the city to rejoice at the approach of its king. Overall, this address points to the approaching king as one who will see to the peace and security of Zion,

---

[113] For an overview, see Hanson, *The Dawn of Apocalyptic* 289.

[114] See esp. Dandamaev, *A Political History of the Achaemenid Empire* 141–6.

[115] E.g., A. T. Olmstead, *History of the Persian Empire* (Chicago: University of Chicago, 1948) 142.

but it contends that such peace will come as a result of the king's extending his dominion throughout the world. Such peace therefore calls for war against the Greeks.

The sub-unit begins in verses 9-10 with an initial imperative call to Zion/Jerusalem to "rejoice greatly" and "shout aloud." The use of the second person feminine singular imperatives *gîlî mĕʾōd* and *hārîʿî* draws from language commonly employed in the Psalms (for *gîl*, see Pss 13:5; 51:10 [NRSV: 51:8]; 14:7; 16:9; 32:11; 48:12 [NRSV: 48:11]; 53:7 [NRSV: 53:6]; 96:11; 97:1, 8; 149:2, etc.; for *hārîʿa*, see Pss 41:12 [NRSV: 41:11]; 47:2 [NRSV: 47:1]; 66:1; 81:2 [NRSV: 81:1]; 95:1, 2; 98:4, 6; 100:1) and in the book of Isaiah (for *gîl*, see Isa 9:2 [NRSV: 9:3]; 25:9; 29:19; 35:1, 2; 41:16; 49:13; 61:10; 65:18, 19; 66:10; for *hārîʿa*, see Isa 42:13; cf. Isa 15:4). Although Isaiah is sometimes concerned with the rejoicing of Jerusalem (Isa 65:18, 19; 66:10), most interpreters point to Zeph 3:14-20 for the closest analogy for an address to the "Daughter of Zion" concerning YHWH's presence as king in her midst, the overthrow of her oppressors, and the return of her exiles. The language differs somewhat, but both verbs from Zech 9:9 are present in Zeph 3:14 and 3:17. Overall, the parallel suggests that Zech 9:9-13 may have been written in relation to the earlier Zephanian text, perhaps as a reapplication of the oracle in a manner analogous to the use of Isaiah in verses 1-8 above.

The passage draws upon other traditions as well. The designation of Jerusalem as "the daughter of Zion *(bat-ṣîyôn)*" and "the daughter of Jerusalem *(bat-yĕrûšālaim)*" employs a common ancient Near Eastern and biblical convention that identifies cities as women or maidens and often personifies them in relation to their protective goddesses, e.g., Athena for Athens or Tyche for Tyre.[116] Biblical tradition, of course, does not recognize goddesses or deities other than YHWH and therefore simply personifies cities, particularly Jerusalem, as the daughter of Zion (Isa 1:8; 10:32; 16:1; 62:11; Mic 1:13; 4:8, 10, 13; Jer 4:31; 6:2, 23; Zeph 3:14; Zech 2:14 [NRSV: 2:10]; Ps 9:15 [NRSV: 9:14]; Lam 1:6; 2:1, 4; 4:22) or Jerusalem (2 Kgs 19:21/Isa 37:22; Mic 4:8; Zeph 3:14; Lam 2:13-15). The cause for the rejoicing is the approach of the righteous and victorious king. The description of the king as "humble and riding on a donkey, on a colt, the foal of a donkey" draws upon Gen 49:11, which employs similar language to portray the royal tribe of Judah, "binding his foal to the vine and his donkey's colt to the choicest vine, he washes his garments in wine and his robe in the blood of grapes." The reference to the garments washed in wine would signify the dying of garments

---

[116] Klaus Baltzer, "Stadt-Tyche oder Zion-Jerusalem," *Alttestamentlicher Glaube und Biblischer Theologie. Festschrift für Horst Dietrich Preuss*, ed. J. Hausmann and H.-J. Zöbel (Stuttgart: Kohlhammer, 1992) 114–20.

to obtain characteristically royal colors. YHWH's statements concerning the cutting off of chariots, horses, and bows of war from Jerusalem and Ephraim of course draws upon a long tradition concerning YHWH's protection of Zion (Psalms 2; 46; 47; 48; etc.), but it also draws upon the Isaian and Zephanian traditions that envision YHWH's action against the military might of the nations (Isaiah 2) and the restoration of exiles from both Judah and Israel to Zion (Isaiah 11; Zeph 3:14-20). The resulting peace for the nations will coincide with the establishment of the king's dominion "from sea to sea, and from the River to the ends of the earth." The "river" refers to Euphrates, which forms the southern boundary of Mesopotamia. This statement nearly replicates Ps 72:8, "May he have dominion from sea to sea, and from the River to the ends of the earth," which describes the authority granted by YHWH to the Davidic monarch (cf. Ps 89:26 [NRSV: 89:25]).[117]

Although many interpreters identify this king as Alexander, as noted above, the itinerary of the king negates such identification. It also negates identification of the king with a Davidic monarch, as a Davidic monarch would not have approached Jerusalem from Aram, Phoenicia, and Philistia—that is the approach of an invader or a foreign monarch —and he would not have threatened the cities unless he were to approach them from Jerusalem. Indeed, Zeph 3:14-20 points to YHWH as the king of Israel who will turn aside Jerusalem's and Israel's enemies, achieve victory, bring cause for rejoicing, and restore the exiles. The book of Isaiah also points to YHWH as the king who will likewise restore Jerusalem (Isaiah 65–66; cf. Isaiah 32, which does not identify the king), but the depiction of YHWH as king is preceded by various passages that point first to a Davidic monarch (Isa 9:1-6; 11:1-16) and then to the Persian king Cyrus (Isa 44:24-28; 45:1-7). The reference to hostilities against the Greeks in verse 13 below suggests that the king in verse 9 might be identified with Darius I, who fought to restore order within the Persian empire throughout his reign and mounted campaigns against the Greeks early in the fifth century. Such actions would have born the promise of peace for the empire had he been successful. Such identification would posit that the book of Zechariah's envisions Judah's monarch along much the same lines as the final form of the book of Isaiah as first a Davidic monarch (Isa 9:1-6; 11:1-16; Zechariah 4; 6; 12-13), then a Persian monarch (Isa 44:24-28; 45:1-7; Zechariah 9), and ultimately YHWH (Isaiah 65–66; cf. 32; Zechariah 14).

Verses 11-13 then constitute two statements by YHWH, each of which is introduced by the particle *gam*, "also," which ties these statements

---

[117] See the discussion by K. Larkin, *The Eschatology of Second Zechariah* (Kampen: Kok Pharos, 1994) 75–7.

syntactically to verses 9-10. The first in verses 11-12a addresses Zion directly with the feminine singular pronoun, "you," and announces to her that her "prisoners" are to be set free from "the waterless pit." YHWH's reference to "the blood of my covenant with you," apparently draws upon Exod 24:1-8, which also refers to "the blood of the covenant that YHWH has made with you" in relation to a covenant ceremony that seals the relationship between YHWH and Israel. Blood from sacrificial animals was dashed against the altar and upon the people as a symbol of the commitment of the people to follow YHWH's words and by YHWH to act on behalf of the people. Although interpreters stress the people's responsibility in the relation, YHWH is also responsible for the security of the people. As indicated by the statement in Zech 9:11-12a, YHWH is about to act on that commitment. The references to the release of Zion's prisoners from the waterless pit and their return to their stronghold apparently draws upon Isaiah 24, which portrays YHWH's destruction of the earth, the singing of the people from the coastlands of the sea, and the trapping of the inhabitants of the earth as prisoners in the pit as YHWH advances to punish the host of heaven. Although Isaiah 24 refers to the punishment of the earth at large, such a scenario is a part of the process in the book of Isaiah by which Zion is cleansed from her sins and prepared to serve as the site from which YHWH exercises world-wide sovereignty. The return of the exiles or prisoners to Zion is a major step in that process. The reference to "the prisoners of hope *(ʾăsîrê hattiqwâ)*" apparently draws upon passages such as Jer 31:17, which expresses hope for the future of Rachel when her children return, and Hos 2:17 [NRSV: 2:15], which defines the Valley of Achor as Petah Tikvah (door of hope) as YHWH's bride Israel returns. More pointedly, it alludes to Isa 8:17 in which the prophet states that he will "wait for YHWH who is hiding his face from the house of Jacob" and that will "hope *(qwh)* in him." From the perspective of Zechariah 9, that time has come.

The second statement appears in verses 12b-13, which announce the coming confrontation with the Greeks. YHWH declares to Zion that "today . . . I will restore to you double *(mišneh)*." Many interpreters relate this statement to Isa 61:7, which states at the time of the release of Zion's prisoners that Zion will receive a double portion from the nations because her shame was double.[118] It must be kept in mind that the repayment for a crime of theft is a double portion (Exod 22:3) and that Isa 40:2 states that Jerusalem had already paid double for her sins. From the perspective of Zech 9:12, YHWH will return the payment to

---

[118] See the discussion by Nicholas Ho Fai Tai, *Prophetie als Schriftauslegung in Sacharja 9–14* (Stuttgart: Calwer, 1996) 63–5.

Zion now that the time for restoration is at hand. Verse 13, introduced by a causative *kî*, "because, for," provides the explanation for these actions. Judah and Ephraim are in fact to prepare for war as YHWH will set the sons of Zion against the sons of Greece. In order to ensure the final peace, dominion of the king, and release of captives, YHWH has declared war on the Greeks. Just as the book of Isaiah successively identifies YHWH with the imperial power of Assyria (Isaiah 5), Babylon (Isaiah 39), and Persia (through Cyrus, Isa 44:24-28; 45:1-7; cf. the oracles against the nations in Isaiah 13–23, which portray YHWH's judgment against the nations that were incorporated into the Persian empire), so Zechariah 9 identifies YHWH with the purposes of the Persian monarch Darius I, who sought to defeat and conquer the Greeks in the early fifth century B.C.E.

Verses 14-17 then return to the third person descriptive language of the prophet, although the introductory conjunctive *waw* in verse 14 ties his statements to those by YHWH in verses 5-13. These verses draw upon theophanic traditions concerning YHWH's defeat of Israel's enemies (see Habakkuk 3; Psalms 18/2 Samuel 22; Psalms 77; 144), and they serve as the prophet's explanation or elaboration of YHWH's words in the preceding verses. The prophet's words include three basic statements, each of which begins with a variation of the name of YHWH. The first in verse 14a simply states that YHWH will appear over the people, and that YHWH's arrows will go out like lightning. The depiction of a god in the form of a sun disk or chariot leading the army is a common motif in Mesopotamian art,[119] and it is possible that such depictions influence the portrayal of YHWH riding a chariot through the heavens (see Psalm 68; Habakkuk 3; cf. 2 Samuel 22/Psalm 18; Ezekiel 1). YHWH's arrows are a common motif in theophanic texts (Pss 18:15 [NRSV: 18:14]/2 Sam 22:15; Hab 3:11; Pss 77:18 [NRSV: 77:17]; 144:6). The prophet's statement apparently builds upon YHWH's statement in verse 13a that metaphorically portrays Judah and Israel as YHWH's bow and arrow. The second statement appears in verse 14b in which the L–rd YHWH sounds the trumpet and marches off in the whirlwinds of the south (Teman). The sounding of the shofar or a trumpet made from a ram's horn also appears in theophanic texts (Exod 19:16, 19; 20:18), although it appears more frequently as a call to war (Josh 6:4, 5, 20; Judg 7:8, 16; Hos 8:1; Amos 3:6). The sounding of the shofar is a common event in cultic celebration (Pss 47:6 [NRSV: 47:5]; 81:4 [NRSV: 81:3]; 98:6; 150:3; 2 Chr 15:14). In Lev 25:9, it signals the beginning of the Jubilee year of release from debts. Zephaniah 1:16 refers to the day of YHWH as a day of shofar and shouting, and the sounding of trumpets at the conquest

---

[119] For examples, see Pritchard, *ANEP* 486, 514, 518, 531–2, 534, 536.

of Jericho has cultic connotations (Joshua 6). The reference to YHWH's marching in the whirlwinds of Teman recalls Hab 3:3 in which YHWH's march against the enemies begins in Teman. Teman, equated in modern times with Yemen, tends to be a general designation for the south, and may originally have designated the region of Edom (see Amos 1:12; Obad 9; Jer 49:7, 20; Ezek 25:13; cf. Gen 36:11, 15, 42; 1 Chr 1:36, 53).

The third statement in the sequence comprises verses 15-17 in which the prophet presents in some detail the scenario of YHWH's defeat of enemies, presumably the Greeks mentioned in verse 13. The statement is set off from the preceding statements in verses 14a and 14b by the absence of a conjunctive *waw* prior to the name YHWH which indicates its climactic character. The first statement in verse 15aα$^{1-4}$ focuses on YHWH's protection of the sons of Zion previously mentioned in verse 13. The use of the verb *gnn*, "to protect," appears elsewhere only in Isaiah (Isa 31:5; 37:35; 38:6), parallel texts in Kings (2 Kgs 19:34; 20:6), and Zech 12:8, always in reference to YHWH's protection of Zion. Verse 15aα$^{5-8}$-b then shifts to a metaphorical portrayal of the actions of the sons of Zion as they defeat the enemy. First they devour and trample the enemy slingers, and then they drink and shout as if they were drinking wine. The image draws especially on the earlier reference to "the blood of my covenant" in verse 11 in that it presupposes the shedding of blood. The verb *hāmû*, rendered in NRSV as "their blood" or "they shall drink," refers to growling or roaring boisterously from drinking wine (cf. Prov 20:1). Wine was normally drunk from a bowl in the ancient world, and the image is employed to describe the drinking of the wine by the victorious soldiers who then dash the wine against the corners of the altar. This image returns to that of the blood of the covenant in Exod 24:1-8, in which Moses places half of the sacrificial blood in basins to dash upon the people and the other half is dashed against the altar as a symbol for the conclusion of the covenant between YHWH and Israel. In this case, the image of the wine dashed against the altar symbolizes YHWH's previously mentioned pledge of protection. Verses 16-17 then return to YHWH's actions. Verse 16a presents a basic statement that YHWH will deliver the people like sheep on that day. Two explanatory clauses, each introduced by *kî*, then provide rationales for YHWH's action. The comparison of the people to "the jewels/stones of a crown" shining upon the land in verse 16b expresses obvious high regard for the people, but it also calls upon the image of the stones that adorn the crown or diadem of the high priest who would perform the sacrifice and blood rite at the altar of the Temple (cf. Exod 24:1-8; 28:36-38; see also Exod 29:6; 39:30; Lev 8:9; cf. Lev 21:12). The image would thereby build upon that of Joshua ben Jehozadak's crown in Zech 3:1-10, although the terminology differs. The rhetorical question, "for what is his goodness and what is his beauty" (contra NRSV, "what goodness and beauty are his"), is answered by the reference to grain and new wine that make the young men and women "flourish" or "bear fruit." The reference to YHWH's "goodness" employs the term *tûb*, which generally refers to goods or good things, but also refers to YHWH's beauty (Exod 33:19). The reference to YHWH's "beauty" employs the term *yĕpô*, which appears in Isa 33:17 in reference to the future king, "your eyes will see the king in his beauty, they will behold a land that stretches far away." In the present case, the "goodness" and "beauty" refer to the agricultural produce, grain and new wine, that make the young men and women flourish. This is an obvious reference to fertility of both land and people that will result from YHWH's and Jerusalem's victory, and presumably from the reestablishment of the Temple in Zechariah.

THE PROPHET'S PORTRAYAL OF YHWH'S ANGER AGAINST THE SHEPHERDS AND PLANS TO RETURN ISRAEL AND JUDAH FROM EXILE: 10:1-12

Zechariah 10:1-12 presents the prophet's portrayal of YHWH's anger against the "shepherds" together with YHWH's plans to expel the "shepherds," strengthen Israel and Judah, and restore the exiles to their homeland. There is continuity with the preceding material in that it develops YHWH's previously stated intentions to bring peace to the people who are portrayed as YHWH's flock (cf. Zech 9:11-17). Nevertheless, the initial imperative, "ask rain from YHWH . . ." constitutes a syntactical break from chapter 9 that introduces a new concern with YHWH's dissatisfaction with the "shepherds," i.e., the leadership that has ruled Israel and Judah, and the intention to remove that leadership so that YHWH's "flock," i.e., Israel and Judah, may be strengthened and restored. The opening imperatives of Zech 11:1-3, "Open your doors, O Lebanon . . .; Wail oaks of Bashan . . ." likewise build upon the statements in Zech 10:10 that speak of the exiles' return to Lebanon and Gilead, but these imperatives introduce a new section that describes in detail YHWH's removal of the old leadership of the people and the plans to install a new "shepherd" or leader for the people.[120]

The image of the shepherds in Zechariah 10 and 11 appears to draw especially upon Jer 23:1-40, which employ the metaphor of shepherds

[120] See Tigchelaar, *Prophets of Old and the Day of the End* 92–4, who discusses the role of the short poems in Zech 9:9-10; 10:1-2; and 11:1-3 in linking chapters 9–11 together.

to relate Y_HWH's intentions to remove the leadership of Judah that has "scattered" Y_HWH's flock and to install "shepherds" who will care properly for the "scattered" sheep (verses 1-4).[121] The passage goes on to discuss the restoration of a righteous Davidic figure called "the branch" who will bring security to Israel and Judah (verses 5-8) and to denounce the false prophets who have deluded the people by claiming that no calamity will befall them (verses 9-40). All of these elements are present in Zechariah 10 and 11, although the points of reference have changed. Whereas Jeremiah 23 envisions the "shepherds" who have failed to tend the "flock" properly to be the Judean monarchs who brought the country to ruin in the late-seventh and early-sixth century, Zechariah 10 and 11 envision the corrupt "shepherds" who scattered the people to be the Persian monarchs who failed to exercise their intended roles in bringing peace to the people. In this regard, the Zecharian passages also presuppose Isa 44:24-28 (cf. Isa 45:1-7), which designates King Cyrus of Persia as Y_HWH's Messiah, Temple builder, and "shepherd" (Isa 44:28), who will carry out Y_HWH's purpose. But as the Persian monarchs failed to live up to the role assigned to them in the work of Deutero-Isaiah, the Zecharian tradition pointed to the rise of a new "shepherd" who would supplant them and carry out Y_HWH's plans (see Zech 3:15-17 below; cf. Jer 23:5-8).

The overall form of the passage is based in the two-part pattern of the prophetic judgment speech which includes both grounds for punishment and the announcement of punishment proper.[122] In the present cases, verses 1-2 take up the grounds for punishment with the accusation that the shepherds have allowed the sheep to stray and verses 3-12 take up Y_HWH's plans to take action against the shepherds.

Verses 1-2 begin with the command in verse 1aα to "ask rain from Y_HWH in the season of the spring rain." This command is reinforced in verse 1aβ-b by the assertion that Y_HWH is the maker of storm clouds and showers of rain, who gives the grass of the field to everyone. By making these assertions, the passage gives reason to believe that Y_HWH is capable of granting the request. The command seems somewhat enigmatic because it seems to request the obvious, but this is precisely the point. By calling upon the audience to ask Y_HWH for rain at the time of the spring rains, the prophet calls upon the people to request from Y_HWH that which will come anyway. This provides the basis for the

---

[121] See esp. Tai, *Prophetie als Schriftauslegung* 100–3.

[122] Cf. Reventlow, *Die Propheten Haggai, Sacharja und Maleachi* 101, who identifies verses 1-2 as an example of a *Mahnwort*, "warning," which functions as the "reasons for judgment/punishment" in the larger prophetic judgment speech pattern (Sweeney, *Isaiah 1–39* 533–4).

following contention in verse 2a concerning the empty consolations of the teraphim, the diviners, and the dreamers, all of which represent different types of prophecy or divination in the ancient world.[123] Teraphim are household idols that represent pagan deities (see Gen 31:19; 1 Sam 15:23; 19:13-16; 2 Kgs 23:24; Hos 3:4). They could be placed in shrines (Judg 17:5; 18:14, 17, 20), and the Babylonian king is portrayed divining before them in preparation for his attack against Jerusalem (Ezek 21:21). Divination was very well known in ancient Israel and the larger Near East (see Deut 18:10, 14; 1 Sam 6:2; 28:8; 2 Kgs 17:17; Isa 2:6; 3:2; 44:25; Jer 27:9; 29:8; Ezek 13:9; 21:26 [NRSV: 21:23]; 22:28; Mic 3:7, 11), and generally involves oracular inquiry through inspection of livers, conjuring spirits from the dead, etc. Dream interpretation is also well known in the Bible and the ancient Near East (see Gen 28:12; 37:5, 6; 42:9; Judg 7:13; Dan 2:1, 3; Joel 3:1 [NRSV: 2:28]; Deut 13:2, 4, 6 [NRSV: 13:1, 3, 5]; Jer 23:25).[124] Basically, verse 2 contends that the teraphim, diviners, and dreamers are false prophets who had prophesied what would obviously come to pass. In keeping with the critique of false prophets in Jer 23:9-40, their message did not come from YHWH; rather it came from their own minds (see esp. Jer 23:16-17). As a result of this false prophecy, the people are left like sheep without a shepherd, i.e., they stray and become lost.

The reference to the shepherd in verse 2b is particularly important in relation to Jer 23:1-4 and its contention that the people have suffered scattering as a result of their incompetent "shepherds" or leaders and the similar image in Ezekiel 34 of a Israel as sheep who have no shepherd. Both passages point to YHWH's plan to establish a new Davidic shepherd over the people, and presupposes that the old shepherd(s) who led to the problem in the first place must also be Judah's earlier kings. But the reader must keep in mind Zechariah's interaction with the book of Isaiah as well as the other prophetic books, particularly Isaiah's contention that Cyrus the King of Persia would be YHWH's shepherd (Isa 44:24-28). Zechariah calls for a new shepherd to replace the old (Zech 11:15-17) and points to the rise of the house of David in chapters 12–14 (in keeping with Jeremiah 23 and Ezekiel 34) as YHWH defeats the nations that threaten Jerusalem and Judah. This would sug-

---

[123] For a survey of divination in ancient Israel and the ancient Near East, see Cryer, *Divination in Ancient Israel and Its Near Eastern Environment*.

[124] For a study of dream interpretation, see Jean-Marie Husser, *Le Songe et la Parole. Étude sur le rêve et sa fonction dan l'ancien Israël* (BZAW 210; Berlin and New York: Walter de Gruyter, 1994). An English translation, *Dreams and Dream Narratives in the Biblical World*, Biblical Seminar, vol. 63 (Sheffield: Sheffield Academic Press, 1999), is forthcoming.

gest that the earlier shepherd who had scattered the people must be identified in Zechariah with the Persian monarchs who had failed to carry out YHWH's purpose in reestablishing the Temple and YHWH's dominion over all the world (see Haggai and the visions in Zechariah 1–8).

As a result of the failure of the "shepherd(s)," verses 3-12 outline YHWH's plans to unleash the people of Judah in war and thereby to restore both the house of Judah and the house of Joseph that had been exiled to Assyria and Egypt. The basic statement of this plan appears in verse 3 in which YHWH states, "My anger is hot against the shepherds and I will punish the leaders." The term "leaders" reads literally "he-goats," but the term *ʿattûdîm*, "he-goats," refers metaphorically to the leaders of the flock (cf. Isa 14:9; Jer 50:8; Ezek 34:17). The second part of the verse specifically identifies YHWH's flock with the house of Judah, and it promises that YHWH will make the people into "a proud war horse." Clearly, the verse envisions that Judah will take action against the leaders who have led it astray.

Verses 4-12 then elaborate upon the implications of verse 3 by laying out a scenario according to which Judah will go to war against its enemies and by which both Joseph and Judah will be restored from their exiles in Assyria and Egypt. Verse 4 presents the somewhat enigmatic statement, "out of them shall come the cornerstone, out of them the tent peg, out of them the battle bow, and out of them every commander." This verse presents a chain of metaphors for leadership and warlike action. The term "cornerstone," *pinnâ*, generally refers to the cornerstone that supports a building (Job 1:19; Prov 7:12; 21:9/25:24; Jer 51:26), but it also appears frequently as a metaphorical reference to the people of Israel (Judg 20:2; 1 Sam 14:38; Isa 19:13), which is especially pertinent to the designation of Judah as the "house" of Judah in verse 3 (cf. Isa 28:16 which claims that YHWH is laying a cornerstone in Zion in a context that calls for new leadership for the people and decries the lies and falsehood that have been fed to the people). In similar fashion, the term "tent peg," *yātēd*, refers to the supporting element of a tent (Judg 5:26; Isa 54:2; Exod 27:19; 35:18; Isa 33:20), but it also refers metaphorically to a person of authority, such as Eliakim, who will replace the royal steward Shebna in Isa 22:23, 24, or to the secure position of the surviving remnant of the people in Ezra 9:8. The reference to the battle bow is hardly metaphorical, but it takes up earlier references in Zech 9:10 and 13 in which YHWH first states that the bow will be cut off from Ephraim, i.e., the threat of war will be removed from Ephraim by the approach of the king, and then states the intention to bend Judah like a bow and to arm Ephraim with a bow in preparation for war against Greece. In both Zechariah 9 and 10, the prophet apparently envisions a process of war that will lead ultimately to peace and restoration for Judah and Israel. The final statement of verse 4 employs the some enigmatic "commander." Normally, the Hebrew term *nôgēś* means "oppressor," and it is generally employed in reference to the oppressors of Israel, such as the Egyptian taskmasters (Exod 3:7; 5:6, 10), Assyrian oppressors (Isa 9:3 [NRSV: 9:4]), or one who requires payment from another (Deut 15:2, 3; 2 Kgs 23:35). The term can be used in reference to the rulers of the people, sometimes sarcastically (Isa 3:12) and sometimes in reference to a righteous ruler (Isa 60:17), although in both cases it presupposes an oppressive presence. The term appears in Zech 9:8 as a reference to the oppressors of YHWH's people, but it appears here in reference to Judah's oppression of YHWH's enemies.

A chain of *waw-consecutive* statements in verses 5-12 then builds upon verse 4 by presenting a scenario in which YHWH strengthens Israel/Joseph and Judah so that they can be restored. The passage includes two components in verses 5-6 and 7-12 in which the prophet introduces a statement by YHWH. The prophet begins in verse 5 with a simile that compares the people to warriors who trample the mud of streets in time of war, who fight because YHWH is with them, and who will overcome the enemy cavalry. The last reference to cavalry is particularly important in relation to the Exodus tradition, which figures prominently in this passage, in which YHWH defeats the horsemen of Egypt. It also figures in relation to the Persian empire which relied heavily on cavalry in its armies.[125] YHWH's first person statement in verse 6 concerning the intention to strengthen the house of Judah and to deliver the house of Joseph then follows. The reference to Joseph of course indicates the northern tribes of Israel, identified as Ephraim in Zech 9:10, 13, but together with the earlier reference to the battle bow in verse 4 it also alludes to the description of Joseph as a bowman who fights off his enemies in the blessing of Jacob (Gen 49:22-26). YHWH promises to return the people because divine compassion recalls the earlier Hosean tradition in which YHWH first denied compassion to Israel, employing the symbolic name of the prophet's daughter, Lo Ruhamah (No compassion; see Hos 1:6-7), but later instructs Jezreel to call his sister Ruhamah (Compassion) at the time when Israel and Judah will be restored on the day of Jezreel (Hos 2:1-3 [NRSV: 1:10–2:1]). YHWH's statement, "and they shall be as though I had not rejected them," is theologically problematic. The analogy of the restoration of Job's dead children indicates that one cannot reverse the effects of re-

---

[125] See the discussion of the Persian army, and especially the cavalry, in Muhammad A. Dandamaev and Vladimir G. Lukonin, *The Culture and Social Institutions of Ancient Iran* (Cambridge: Cambridge University Press, 1989) 222–37, esp. 224.

jection and exile even through restoration (Job 42:13-15). The modern experience of the Shoah likewise calls into question divine assertions of mercy in the aftermath of catastrophe.[126] Nevertheless, the statement must not be taken literally, but as a reference to YHWH's commitment to build toward the future once the exile is completed. In verse 6b, YHWH asserts the divine role of G–d of Israel, and promises to answer the people. This recalls YHWH's statements concerning the restoration of the divine relationship with Israel in Hos 2:23-25 [NRSV: 2:21-23], "on that day I will answer, says YHWH . . . and I will have pity on Lo-ruhamah and I will say to Lo-ammi, 'You are my people'; and he shall say, 'You are my G–d.'" The close parallels between the present Zecharian text and that of Hosea 1–2 suggest that the prophet sees the fulfillment of the earlier Hosean prophecy in his own time.[127]

The second component in verses 7-12 begins in verse 7aα with the prophet's comparison of the people of Ephraim to warriors. The wording differs slightly, but the language is basically parallel to that of verse 5. The balance of the prophet's statement in verse 7aβ-b describes Ephraim's rejoicing in YHWH as a result of their newly found strength. As in verses 5-6, the prophet's statement serves as an introduction to YHWH's first person statements in verses 8-12. YHWH's words are set off syntactically by the absence of a *waw* or other syntactical connector, but the Deity's words are themselves held together by *waw*s as well as by the first person perspective throughout. The speech focuses on YHWH's plans to restore the exiled people of Ephraim from Assyria and Egypt in a manner reminiscent of the oracles of Isaiah ben Amoz. YHWH begins with the statement, "I will signal for them and gather them in, for I have redeemed them, and they shall be as numerous as they were before." The verb, "I will signal," *'ešrĕqâ*, literally, "I will whistle," also appears in Isaiah's statements in Isa 5:26 and 7:18 that YHWH "will whistle for a people at the ends of the earth" and "will whistle for the fly that is

---

[126] For issues in reading the Bible in the aftermath of the Shoah/Holocaust, see Emil Fackenheim, *The Jewish Bible after the Holocaust: A Rereading* (Bloomington: Indiana University Press, 1990); Marvin A. Sweeney, "The Emerging Field of Jewish Biblical Theology," *Academic Approaches to Teaching Jewish Studies* (Lanham: University Press of America, 2000) 83–105; and Tod Linafelt, editor, *Strange Fire: The Hebrew Scriptures after the Holocaust* (New York: New York University Press; Sheffield: Sheffield Academic Press, 2000), forthcoming. For discussion on theological issues relating to the Shoah, see esp. Steven T. Katz, *Post-Holocaust Dialogues: Critical Studies in Modern Jewish Thought* (New York: New York University Press, 1985) and Zev Garber, *Shoah: The Paradigmatic Genocide. Essays in Exegesis and Eisegesis* (Lanham: University Press of America, 1994).

[127] See also Tai, *Prophetie als Schriftauslegung* 105–6.

at the sources of the streams of Egypt and for the bee that is in the land of Assyria" in order to bring punishment upon Israel and Judah.[128] Although Isaiah's statements pertain to the punishment of the people, Zechariah also draws upon Isaiah's statements of restoration by speaking of the "gathering" (Hebrew verb, *qbṣ*) and the "redemption" (Hebrew verb, *pdh*) of the exiles, e.g., "He (YHWH) will raise a signal for the nations, and will assemble the outcasts of Israel and gather the dispersed of Judah from the four corners of the earth" (Isa 11:12; cf. Isa 40:11; 54:7; 56:8; 66:18; Zeph 3:19, 20) and "Zion shall be redeemed by justice and those who repent by righteousness" (Isa 1:27; cf. Isa 35:10; 51:11). Jeremiah's statements concerning YHWH's restoration of Israel also seem to play a role, "He who scattered Israel will gather him and will keep him as a shepherd a flock. For YHWH has ransomed Jacob and has redeemed him from hands too strong for him" (Jer 31:10-11) especially because they also employ the motif of the shepherd as leader.[129] The statement, "and they shall be as numerous as they were before," literally, "and they shall be numerous (*wĕrābû*) as they were numerous (*rābû*)," likewise draws upon the language of Jeremiah's statements against Judah's shepherds, "then I myself will father the remnant of my flock out of all the lands where I have driven them, and I will bring them back to their fold, and they shall be fruitful and multiply (*wĕrābû*)." By his use of language, Zechariah signals his dependence on both the Isaian and Jeremian traditions in pointing to the reversal of Ephraim's subjugation to Egypt and Assyria.

Verse 9 continues along the same general lines with YHWH's reference to the scattering of the people among the nations, followed by the assertion that they will remember YHWH in faraway places and that they will live and return. The verb *wāšābû*, "and they shall return," connotes both return to the land and repentance, i.e., return to YHWH. YHWH makes an unequivocal pledge to return the people from the land of Egypt and to "gather" (*qbṣ*) them from Assyria, again employing terminology from Isa 11:10-16 (cf. Isa 27:12-13; 35:10; see also 52:3-6). Somewhat puzzling is YHWH's pledge to return the people to Lebanon and Gilead, but the mention of both of these names apparently indicates that the returning people will be so numerous (see verse 8) that they will strain the capacity of the land to hold them. Gilead, the region east of the Kineret/Sea of Galilee and the Jordan River, was considered to be a part of Israel where the tribes of Gad and Manasseh settled. Lebanon marks the northernmost reaches of the land of Israel (Deut 1:7; 3:25; 11:24; Josh 1:4; 13:5-6; 1 Kgs 9:19), and refers to the white,

[128] Ibid., 102–3.
[129] Ibid., 103–4.

snow-capped Lebanon mountain range (n.b., the name Lebanon derives from the root, *lbn,* "white") rather than to the coastal territory of the modern nation.[130] Verse 11 continues YHWH's description of the people's return to the land in terminology reminiscent of the Exodus tradition (cf. Isa 11:10-16 and 49:3-6, which are likewise dependent upon the Exodus tradition of the parting of the sea to enable the exiles to return from Assyria and Egypt). Although the NRSV begins with the statement, "they shall pass through the sea of distress," verse 11aα[1-3] reads literally, "and he (YHWH) will pass by/over the sea of distress." The balance of the verse refers to YHWH's smiting the waves of the sea, putting to shame the depths of the Nile, bringing down the pride of Assyria, and removing the scepter of Egypt. Clearly, these statements presuppose the traditions of YHWH's defeat of the sea at the Exodus, the time of creation, and the time of Israel's redemption from exile (Exodus 15; Psalms 74; 93; 104; Job 38; Isa 27:1; 43:1-21; 51:9-16). The reference to the downfall of the pride of Assyria draws explicitly upon the imagery and language of Isa 2:6-21 and 10:5-34 and the reference to the removal of the rod from Egypt likewise draws upon Isa 10:5-34 (see esp. verses 24-27). Verse 12 then sums up the entire sequence of verses 5-12 by returning to the prophet's initial references to the strengthening of the people in verses 5 and 7, i.e., "and I will make them strong in YHWH, and they shall walk in his name, says YHWH." Although the third person references to YHWH suggest that these are the prophet's words, the first person form indicates that the prophet once again presents YHWH's words. Many have noted the parallel with Micah 4:5, "For all the peoples walk, each in the name of its god, but we will walk in the name of YHWH our G–d forever and ever."[131] Just as Zech 8:20-23 alludes to Mic 4:1-5, so does the present statement. It would seem that the prophet looks to his own time for the fulfillment of Micah's statement as well.

THE PROPHET'S PORTRAYAL OF YHWH'S INTENTION TO OVERTHROW THE WORTHLESS SHEPHERD THAT ABANDONS THE FLOCK: 11:1-17

Zechariah 11:1-17 then shifts to the prophet's portrayal of YHWH's plans to remove the "shepherds" or the leaders who have failed to exercise proper rule over the people and to replace them with a "shepherd" who will show no compassion. Although the purposes of such a brutal shepherd are not made clear in the present context, the following

---

[130] Meyers and Meyers, *Zechariah 9–14* 222-3.

[131] E.g., Tigchelaar, *Prophets of Old and the Days of the End* 103.

scenario of YHWH's war against the nations from Zion indicates that the new shepherd may well be YHWH. Many interpreters associate Zech 11:1-3 with the preceding material in Zech 10:1-12 because of the common interest in YHWH's anger against the shepherds of the people (see Zech 10:3). Nevertheless, the introductory commands of Zech 11:1-3 that call for mourning at the demise of the shepherds and the following presentation by the prophet of YHWH's oracles concerning the removal of the shepherds indicates that Zech 11:1-17 forms a coherent unit. Whereas Zech 10:1-12 relates YHWH's dissatisfaction with the shepherds and plans to restore the people of Israel, Zech 11:1-17 relates the process by which the old corrupt leadership will be replaced by a much more threatening figure.[132] The introductory reference to the *maśśā'* or "pronouncement" in Zech 12:1 marks chapters 12–14 as an entirely new unit following chapters 9–11.

The passage begins with an allegorical call to mourn in verses 1-3.[133] The use of the arboreal imagery is intentional in that references to the great cedars and cypresses of Lebanon, the oaks of Bashan, and the thickets of the Jordan are frequently employed in the prophetic literature to express the majesty and power of rulers, often as they are about to fall (see Isa 2:6-21; 10:5-34; 14:3-23; Jer 21:11-14; 22:1-22; Ezekiel 17; 31; cf. Judg 9:7-21). Lebanon was well-renowned for its majestic cedars and cypress that were used in the construction of the Jerusalem Temple and the palace of the Davidic kings (see 1 Kings 6–7), and the Bashan (modern-day Golan) and the Trans-Jordan were also well-known for their trees and thick undergrowth (see Isa 2:13; Ezek 27:6). The passage begins with a series of three imperatives in verses 1, 2a, and 2b. The first calls upon Lebanon to "open its doors" so that fire may devour its cedars (verse 1). The second and third call upon the cypresses and the oaks of Bashan to wail because of the downfall of the trees. The allegorical nature of the passage becomes clear in the two concluding statements of verses 3a and 3b that depict the wailing of the shepherds because "their glory is despoiled (*šuddĕdâ*)" and the roaring of the lions because "the thickets of the Jordan are destroyed (*šuddad*)." The NRSV translation masks the double use of the verb *šdd*, "to destroy." This is important because the image of the roaring lion recalls the common association of the lion with the tribe of Judah and the house of David (Gen 49:9; Amos 1:2; 1 Sam 17:34-36) and because of the use of the verb *šdd* to portray the coming downfall of Zion's oppressor in Isa 33:1, "Woe, you destroyer (*šôdēd*), who yourself have not been destroyed

---

[132] Again, note Tigchelaar's discussion of the function of Zech 9:9-10; 10:1-2; and 11:1-3 in linking chapters 9–11 together (*Prophets of Old* 92–4).

[133] See Saebø, *Sacharja 9–14* 229–33.

(*šādûd*), you treacherous one, with whom no one has dealt treacherously! When you have ceased to destroy (*šôdēd*), you will be destroyed (*tûššad*); and when you have stopped dealing treacherously, you will be dealt with treacherously." A similar use of the verb *šdd* appears in Isa 21:2 to relate the downfall of the oppressor, "A stern vision is told to me; the betrayer betrays, and the destroyer destroys (*wĕhaššôdēd šôdēd*). Go up, O Elam, lay siege, O Media; all the sighing she has caused I will bring to an end." The use of this imagery suggests that the "trees" or the leaders who are to be destroyed are Jerusalem's or Judah's oppressors and that the "lion" who will be left to roar over their demise is Judah or the house of David. Certainly, such a scenario fits well with Zechariah 12–14, which describe YHWH's actions against the nations who threaten Judah and the continuing role of the house of David.

The prophet then presents an autobiographical account of YHWH's communications to him concerning the process by which the "shepherds" will be removed and replaced by another "shepherd" who will show no compassion. Overall, this passage draws heavily on earlier prophetic texts that metaphorically portray Israel's or Judah's monarchs as shepherds who have been irresponsible in caring for their "flocks" or people, and will therefore suffer punishment (Jer 23:1-8; 25:34-38; Ezek 34:1-31).[134] Because of the predominant use of this motif in Jeremiah and Ezekiel to condemn Israel's and Judah's leaders, many interpreters understand this passage to be a critique of Judah's leadership in the early Persian or Hellenistic periods. Others opt for an apocalyptic scenario in which the "three shepherds" (verse 8) might refer to a succession of Davidic monarchs, foreign empires who conquered Judah, or Jerusalem priests.[135] Nevertheless, the literary context in chapters 12–14 appears to call for an understanding of the "shepherds" as the foreign rulers of Judah and Jerusalem who will be punished for their threats against the city and its people. The earlier discussion of chapters 9–11, which points to the advance of a king from Mesopotamia who will place Judah in conflict with Greece, rules out a Hellenistic setting for these chapters and suggests an early Persian period setting. Likewise, earlier prophetic tradition in Isaiah, with which the book of Zechariah so frequently interacts, designates Cyrus as YHWH's shepherd and messiah who will rebuild Jerusalem and the Temple (Isa 44:28). It would therefore appear that the "shepherds" who are condemned in the present passage must refer to the Persian monarchs. The overall turmoil in the Persian empire at the outset of Darius'

---

[134] See, e.g., Tai, *Prophetie als Schriftauslegung* 118–23.

[135] For surveys of opinions, see Paul Redditt, "The Two Shepherds in Zechariah 11:4-17," *CBQ* 4 (1993) 676–86, esp. 676–9; Smith, *Micah–Malachi* 270.

reign, his difficulties in putting down the revolts mounted against him, YHWH's stated intention in Hag 2:20-22 to overthrow the throne of the kingdom of the nations, and the designation of Zerubbabel as YHWH's signet in Hag 2:23, suggest that many in Judah saw this as a sign of YHWH's dissatisfaction with the Persians and a prelude to the restoration of Davidic rule in Jerusalem. In such a scenario, the reference to the destruction of the three shepherds in one month in Zech 11:8 would refer to the demise of the first three Persian monarchs, Cyrus, Cambyses, and the anticipated downfall of Darius, prior to the rise of a figure who would act on YHWH's behalf.

Zechariah 11:4-17 comprises five major sections, which alternatively present the prophet's accounts of YHWH's communication to him and the prophet's performance of symbolic acts to illustrate YHWH's words.[136] The first appears in verses 4-6 in which the prophet relates YHWH's initial oracle concerning YHWH's condemnation of the shepherds. The passage begins in verse 4a with an autobiographical version of the messenger formula, "Thus said YHWH my G–d," which identifies YHWH as the speaker of the following material in verses 4b-6. YHWH's statement to the prophet appears in verses 4b-6 in the form of an instruction to the prophet that he should "shepherd the flock doomed to slaughter." The instruction proper appears in verses 4b-5, including both the basic instruction in verse 4b and a qualification in verse 5 that makes clear why YHWH gives this instruction to the prophet, i.e., their previous shepherds have little interest in the sheep other than to enrich themselves. The designation of the people as "the flock doomed to slaughter" apparently points to the role of the prophet as a priest who would serve at the altar of the Jerusalem Temple. Although there are doubts as to whether Zechariah ben Berechiah ben Iddo is the author of this passage, it reflects both the role of prophet, as YHWH communicates directly with him in typical prophetic forms of speech, and the supervision or care of sheep that are to be slaughtered or sacrificed at the Temple altar is a common task for priests of the Aaronide line (see 1 Chr 23:12-13; 24:1-19). The qualification of this command points to the activities of those who buy the sheep and slaughter them without incurring any guilt for the shedding of blood and those who sell the sheep while intoning a blessing for YHWH. The prophet's description of these activities presupposes the role of the priests who sell lambs to the people and bless them so that they might offer sacrifice at the altar and that of the people who are held to be guiltless as a result of making

---

[136] For a general discussion of the nature and significance of symbolic acts in prophetic literature, see W. D. Stacey, *Prophetic Drama in the Old Testament* (London: Epworth, 1990).

their sacrifices to YHWH. Although some might read this as an indictment of the Temple or priesthood, the concluding statement of verse 5b, "and their own shepherds have no pity on them," points to the overall concern of this statement. There is nothing inherently wrong with the practice of priests and the people at sacrifice; the absence of pity for the sheep is normal as they are to be sacrificed on behalf of and for the benefit of human beings. Rather, the statement employs the imagery of sacrificial sheep as a metaphor to point to the role of the "shepherds" who similarly have no pity for their own "flock," i.e., the people of Judah. YHWH's explanation of the meaning of this image appears in the first person statement of verse 6, which is introduced by causative *kî*, "for I will no longer have pity on the inhabitants of the earth . . ." YHWH's statement describes a scenario of conflict in which the people of the land will fall into the hands of their neighbors and their king without any deliverance from YHWH. This scenario of conflict between neighbors and the king fits very well with the early years of Darius' reign in which he was forced to put down revolts throughout the empire in order to secure his throne. The phrase, "and they shall devastate the earth," is also instructive in that it employs the verb *wĕkittĕtû*, "and they shall devastate," literally, "and they shall hammer," which is also employed in the scenario of world peace that is portrayed at the outset of the book of Isaiah, "they shall beat *(wĕkittĕtû)* their swords into plowshares, and their spears into pruning hooks; nations shall not lift up sword against nation, neither shall they learn war any more" (Isa 2:4; cf. Mic 4:3). Although this passage was earlier cited in Zech 8:18-23 in anticipation of future world peace, Zech 11:6 indicates that such a scenario is not yet to be realized. The appearance of the oracular formula in the middle of the verse further identifies this as a statement by YHWH.

Having relayed YHWH's instruction to him, the prophet then describes his own actions in response to YHWH's instruction in verses 7-12. Basically, he engages in a prophetic symbolic action to illustrate YHWH's word and to draw an analogy between his own actions in accepting a position as a shepherd for the Temple sheep and the role of the leaders of the people.[137] Although the initial first person verb of verse 7, "and I shepherded," might suggest the continuation of YHWH's first person speech in verses 4b-6, the NRSV correctly renders the *waw-consecutive* form of the verb *(wā'er'eh)* to indicate a shift in perspective from YHWH's first person statements of future action to the prophet's report of his own past actions in response to YHWH's instruction, i.e., "So, on behalf of the sheep merchants, I became a shepherd of the flock

---

[137] Ibid., 213–4.

doomed to slaughter." The term "sheep merchants" presupposes the reading of the LXX, which reads the otherwise incomprehensible MT Hebrew, *lākēn ʿăniyê haššōʾn*, literally, "therefore, the poor of the sheep," as *likna ʿăniyê haṣṣōʾn*, i.e., "the Canaanites/merchants of the sheep." The LXX reading requires only a minor repainting of the Hebrew vowels and the combination of two words into one. The MT reading may reflect an interest on the part of the scribe in dissociating the name Canaanite from a Temple activity. The term "Canaanite" sometimes refers to merchants in the Hebrew Bible (e.g., Zeph 1:11; Ezek 16:29) because of the heavy involvement of Canaanites or Phoenicians in commerce. The prophet then describes his taking of two staffs, a common instrument for shepherding sheep, and assigning symbolic names to each of them. The first is called *nōʿam*, "Favor," and the second is called *ḥōbĕlîm*, "Unity," according to the NRSV translation. The NRSV translation of *ḥōbĕlîm*, however, does not convey its full significance in this term. The basic meaning of the root *ḥbl* is "to bind, pledge," and the term must be understood in relation to the binding nature of the relationship between Israel and Judah that is presupposed in verse 14 below. The use of these staffs in shepherding the sheep then signifies the coming disruption in relationships in the following verses.

The prophet next describes in verse 8 his dismissal of three shepherds in one month and the enmity that results therefrom. In terms of the prophet's symbolic action, this dismissal apparently refers to his discharge of three shepherds of the Temple flocks over whom the prophet would have had charge as a Temple priest. We are not told the cause of the dismissal other than that the prophet had become impatient with them, and the resulting enmity is to be expected in the case of termination of employment without cause. Such enmity is part of the prophet's symbolic action, as it represents the enmity that will be created among the nations or peoples as indicated in verse 10 below. As noted above, the dismissal of the three shepherds may well represent the demise of three Persian monarchs, Cyrus, Cambyses, and now Darius, after YHWH had previously designated Cyrus as "shepherd," "messiah," and Temple builder (Isa 44:28). Following the dismissal of the three shepherds, the prophet then undertakes an action in verse 9 that can only be construed as a demonstration of complete irresponsibility in relation to the care of the flock, i.e., he ceases to serve as shepherd and lets the sheep fend for themselves so that they may die, be destroyed, and even devour each other. Having abandoned his role as shepherd, the prophet then breaks his staff "Favor" in verse 10 to symbolize the disruption in the relationship or covenant among the peoples or nations. The use of the term *ʾet kol hāʿammîm*, "all the peoples," reflects the language of Isa 2:2-4; Mic 4:1-5; and even Zech 8:18-23 in which "the peoples" or "many peoples" will flow to Zion to receive YHWH's Torah and learn war no more. Again, the prophet's actions indicate the complete reversal of such a scenario; they also indicate the prophet's refusal to continue the contract that he had made to shepherd the sheep.

The prophet acknowledges the disruption of the relationship of the nations in verse 11, and notes that the sheep merchants understood the prophet's action to be a symbolic act illustrating the word of YHWH. He then relates his request for the payment of his salary as shepherd, fully cognizant of the fact that his employers may not be willing to pay him on account of his actions. He gives them the choice, to pay or not as they see fit, and he reports that he was paid thirty shekels. Some have commented that this is a low wage,[138] but it should be noted that the annual Temple tax for an adult male is sixty shekels and for an adult female it is thirty shekels (Lev 27:3-4). In addition, Deut 22:19 specifies that one hundred shekels be paid to the father of a bride who is falsely accused of unchastity, which is presumably equivalent to the bride price at marriage (cf. Exod 22:16-17), and Exod 21:32 specifies that a penalty of thirty shekels be paid to someone who is gored by an ox. These amounts suggest that the payment of thirty shekels for such work is a considerable sum of money, especially for one who did not fulfill his contract. The reference to this sum as "a lordly price" certainly suggests that the prophet considered it to be a lot of money. The prophet relates YHWH's instructions to him in verse 13 to cast the money into the Temple treasury. The NRSV note indicates that it follows the Syriac text in referring to the "treasury," and that the MT Hebrew calls for the prophet to cast the money into "the potter." Although the term *yôṣēr* may be employed in reference to a potter (Isa 29:16; 41:25; Jer 18:4, 6), the term refers to one who "forms" or "fashions," and it frequently refers to YHWH's acts of creation (Gen 2:7, 8; Isa 27:11; 43:1, 21; 44:21; 45:7, 9, 11). The MT therefore indicates that YHWH instructs the prophet to throw the money to "the creator," i.e., to YHWH in the Temple. The term "treasury," *ʾôṣār* in Hebrew, is somewhat similar to *yôṣēr*. The absence of the term "treasury" in other versions suggests that MT presents the correct reading, and that the Syriac translator likely employed "treasury" to clarify a metaphorical reference.

The prophet then relates his breaking of the staff "Unity" or "Bonds" in verse 14. Like the breaking of the first staff, this signifies the disruption of a relationship, in this case between Israel and Judah. The relationship is described as "family ties" in the NRSV, because the term *ʾaḥāwâ* is derived from *ʾāḥ*, "brother." The term appears nowhere else in

---

[138] E.g., Rudolph, *Haggai–Sacharja 1–8–Sacharja 9–14–Maleachi* 209; Petersen, *Zechariah 9–14 and Malachi* 97.

the Bible. Again, the reference suggests the reversal of the vision of peace in Isa 2:2-4 as Isa 2:5 indicates that Jacob, i.e., the northern kingdom of Israel, is invited to join the nations who stream to YHWH at Mt. Zion. The breaking of the relationship between Israel and Judah may reflect the efforts of "the people of the land," i.e., those of Samaria or Israel, to prevent the rebuilding of the Jerusalem Temple (Ezra 4–6). Although the inhabitants of Samaria are described as the descendants of foreigners who were settled in the land following the destruction of Israel, 2 Kings 17 indicates that they were instructed in the proper worship of YHWH, and Ezra 4:1-5 suggests that they saw themselves as adherents of YHWH.

The prophet relates YHWH's final statements to him in verses 15-17. The speech formula appears in verse 15a, and YHWH's speech appears in verses 15b-17 in the form of a final instruction that is designed to illustrate the coming of a pitiless shepherd. The basic instruction appears in verse 15b in which YHWH instructs the prophet to take once again the worthless shepherd's implement. Although NRSV translates *kĕlî rōʿeh ʾĕwilî* as a plural expression, the form is clearly singular and refers to the just broken staff "Bonds." YHWH's explanation for this symbolic act appears in verse 16 introduced by a causative *kî*. YHWH states the intention to raise a new shepherd in the land who takes no concern for those who are perishing, the youth (NRSV renders "the wandering" with Syriac), those who are maimed, or those who are healthy. The basic cruelty of the new ruler is expressed metaphorically by referring to him as a lion or wild animal that tears apart its prey, i.e., he devours the flesh of fat sheep and even tears off their hooves. The new ruler hardly protects the sheep, but becomes a predator who destroys them. YHWH's final statement of the passage is a woe oracle that warns the worthless shepherd of the people about his coming demise.[139] The oracle is addressed to "my worthless shepherd who abandons the sheep," and thereby refers simultaneously to the worthless shepherd's implement that the prophet is asked to take once again (verse 15) and Isa 44:28 in which Cyrus is called "my shepherd" by YHWH. The adjective *ʾĕlîl*, "worthless," differs from the *ʾĕwilî* of verse 15, but corresponds to the term employed in Isaiah, Habakkuk, and Ezekiel to refer to worthless gods (Isa 2:8, 18, 20; 10:10, 11; 19:1, 3; 31:7; Hab 2:18; Ezek 30:13; see also Lev 19:4; Jer 14:14; Ps 96:5; 1 Chr 16:26). The oracle clearly refers to the present ruler who is to be deposed, not to the coming ruler who will show no mercy. The oracle states that a sword will cause his right arm to wither and his right eye to be blinded. This statement takes up the prophecy concerning Cyrus in which YHWH states

---

[139] For discussion of the woe oracle, see Sweeney, *Isaiah 1–39* 543.

the intention to grasp Cyrus's right arm so that he will subdue nations. It also relates to Isa 41:2 in which Y$_{HWH}$ describes the victor (i.e., Cyrus) who defeats enemies with the sword. The reference to the blinded right eye of the shepherd employs the verb *khh*, "to grow dim, faint," which is employed in Isa 42:4 to describe the persistence of Y$_{HWH}$'s servant in establishing justice in the earth, "he will not grow faint or be crushed until he has established justice in the earth." It would seem that this oracle deliberately takes up language used in reference to Cyrus or Y$_{HWH}$'s servant in Isaiah to portray a picture of Y$_{HWH}$'s shepherd who will suffer punishment as a result of his neglect for Y$_{HWH}$'s sheep.

ZECHARIAH'S SECOND PRONOUNCEMENT:
CONCERNING YHWH'S JUDGMENT AGAINST THE NATIONS
AND SOVEREIGNTY AT MT. ZION: 12:1–14:21

Zechariah 12–14 constitutes the second of the two "pronounce-ments" or "oracles" of the prophet in Zechariah 9–14. Although this material was very likely composed by an author other than Zechariah ben Berechiah ben Iddo, it presently constitutes an important compo-nent of the book that points to the ultimate outcome of the prophet's vi-sions and oracles concerning the rebuilding of the Temple in Jerusalem and related events. Like the first "pronouncement," Zechariah 12–14 is introduced by a superscription in Zech 12:1 that is based upon the term *maśśāʾ*, "oracle" or "pronouncement," i.e., "A Pronouncement, the word of Y$_{HWH}$ concerning Israel, utterance of Y$_{HWH}$, who stretches out the heavens and founds the earth and creates the human spirit within" (author's translation). The superscription characterizes the following material generically as a *maśśāʾ*, "oracle" or "pronouncement," which is fundamentally concerned with revealing the manifestation of Y$_{HWH}$'s actions in the world.[140] It then specifies this designation with two other formulas that are designed to identify the following material as genu-ine statements by Y$_{HWH}$. The first, "the word of Y$_{HWH}$ concerning Is-rael," employs a typical form for the identification of prophetic words (cf. Amos 1:1; Jer 1:1), and specifies that the following material relates to all Israel. The use of the oracular formula, *nəʾum yhwh*, "utterance of Y$_{HWH}$," likewise employs a typical form from the prophetic litera-ture.[141] The qualification of Y$_{HWH}$ in verse 1b employs hymnic particip-ial forms to recall Y$_{HWH}$'s attributes as the creator of the heavens, earth,

[140] For discussion of the *maśśāʾ* form, see Weis, "Oracle," *ABD* V:28-9; idem, "A Definition of the Genre *Maśśāʾ* in the Hebrew Bible"; Sweeney, *Isaiah 1–39* 534–5.
[141] Sweeney, *Isaiah 1–39* 546.

and humankind. The portrayal of YHWH as the One who stretches out the heavens appears elsewhere in the prophets, especially Deutero-Isaiah (Isa 42:5; 44:24; 45:12; 51:13; Jer 10:12; 51:15), the Psalms (Ps 104:2), and Job (Job 9:8). YHWH's role as the founder of the earth likewise appears in Pss 24:2; 78:69; 89:12; 102:26 [NRSV: 102:25]; 104:5; Prov 3:19; Isa 48:13; Job 38:4; and Isa 51:13, 16. The divine role in fashioning human beings appears in Gen 2:7, 8; Isa 43:7; and Pss 94:9; 33:15. Together, these qualifications establish YHWH's role as creator, and thereby point to the Jerusalem Temple traditions concerning YHWH's ability to carry out the cosmos-wide transformation that will result in the universal recognition of YHWH at Zion.[142]

As noted above, Zechariah 12–14 is especially concerned with explaining how the oracles in Zech 8:18-23 concerning the nations' recognition of YHWH and the people of Judah in Jerusalem will take place. Following the superscription to the unit in Zech 12:1, two major components follow, each of which is introduced by the particle *hinnēh,* "see!" or "behold!" in Zech 12:2 and 14:1. Both sections together lay out the sequence of events on the coming "Day of YHWH" when YHWH will defeat the nations and establish sovereignty on Zion. Zechariah 12:2–13:9 focuses on YHWH's actions to prepare for the restoration of the divine relationship with the people of the world, i.e., the purification of Judah, Jerusalem, the house of David, and the downfall of the shepherd by the sword. Zechariah 14:1-21 then relates YHWH's war against the nations from Zion and the subsequent recognition of YHWH by the nations at the festival of Sukkoth.

CONCERNING YHWH'S PREPARATION OF JUDAH, JERUSALEM, THE HOUSE OF DAVID, AND THE SHEPHERD FOR THE DAY OF YHWH: 12:2–13:9

Zechariah 12:2–13:9 constitutes a first person statement by YHWH concerning plans to prepare the world, particularly Judah, Jerusalem, the House of David, and the unnamed Shepherd or leader of the people of the world, for the Day of YHWH that will result in universal recognition of YHWH's sovereignty at Zion. The basic structure of the passage begins in verses 2-3 with a basic statement of YHWH's intentions to set in motion a series of conflicts that will initiate the process. This is followed by a series of statements in Zech 12:4-5, 6-7, 8-10, 11-14, and 13:1-

---

[142] For an analysis of Zech 12:1-8 and 14:1-5 in relation to the Temple traditions of YHWH's combat against Jerusalem and the nations, see Hanns-Martin Lutz, *JHWH, Jerusalem und die Völker. Zur Vorgeschichte von Sach 12, 1-8 und 14, 1-5*, WMANT, vol. 27 (Neukirchen-Vluyn: Neukirchener, 1968).

9, each introduced by the syntactically independent formula, *bayyôm hahû*ʾ, "in that day," that lay out the various stages of this process, including conflict between Jerusalem and the nations, Jerusalem and Judah, the diminishment of the house of David, the end of false prophecy, and culminating in the downfall of the "shepherd."

The portrayal of the process begins in verses 2-3 with YHWH's first person statement concerning the divine intentions to make Jerusalem into "a cup of reeling" and "a heavy stone" for the surrounding nations and even for Judah. Overall, this statement presupposes the status of Jerusalem, as the site of YHWH's Temple, as the center of creation from which holiness and YHWH's presence proceeds and permeates all of creation. The reference to the heavy stone may then play upon the image of the Temple foundation stone in Zechariah 4. YHWH's presence is signified through metaphors of power that draw upon associations with YHWH's holy presence and that induce drunkenness or pain in order to incapacitate the peoples of the world and enable YHWH to overcome them. The first is the "cup of reeling," *sap ra*ʿ*al*. Even when read in English, this term adequately conveys the imagery of drunkenness that points to the vulnerability of the nations, but the Hebrew expression, *sap ra*ʿ*al*, must also be considered in order to understand the full import of the metaphor. The usual term for "cup" is *kôs*, but the present text employs the term *sap*, "basin" or "bowl," which commonly designates the basins or bowls that are employed for sacred use in the Temple (1 Kgs 7:50; Jer 52:19). The term is also employed to describe the threshold or door sockets of the Temple (Amos 9:1; Isa 6:4; Jer 35:4; Ezek 40:6, 7; 2 Chr 3:7; 1 Kgs 14:17). The choice of this term therefore appears to be deliberate in order to convey the imagery of the Temple as an agent in the incapacitation of the nations that are arrayed against Jerusalem. The term *ra*ʿ*al* and the general imagery of a cup of reeling draws upon the imagery of Isa 51:17-23, in which Deutero-Isaiah calls upon Jerusalem to awaken after having drunk from the cup of YHWH's wrath. This image, of course, represents the opposite of that intended by Zech 12:2 in that Jerusalem is to end its time of incapacitation. The term *kôs hattar*ʿ*êlâ*, "cup of staggering," appears twice in verses 17 and 22 of the passage. The term *tar*ʿ*êlâ* is, of course, derived from the same root as *ra*ʿ*al*. This would suggest that Zech 12:2 is also designed as a reversal of the image of Isa 51:17-22, i.e., now that Jerusalem has awakened from its own punishment or drunkenness, it is time for the punishment of those who afflicted Jerusalem in the first place. Interestingly, the cup is also directed against Judah as Judah is the first entity outside of Jerusalem to be permeated by YHWH's holy presence, and thus stands as the conduit by which YHWH's holiness is conveyed to the nations as well.

The statement in verse 3, introduced by the formula, *wĕhāyâ bayyôm hahû²,* "and it shall come to pass in that day," is joined syntactically to verse 2 by the *waw-consecutive* verbal formation, and conveys a similar metaphor of incapacitation that is derived from terminology associated with the holy presence of YHWH. The verse describes Jerusalem as "a heavy stone," *²eben ma²ămāsâ,* for all the peoples. The term employed for "heavy," *ma²ămāsâ,* actually means "load" or "burden." Ironically, it sounds somewhat like the Hebrew word, *maśśâ²,* "oracle, pronounce-ment," which appears in the superscription for Zechariah 12–14 to convey YHWH's word to the prophet. The term is derived from the verb root *²ms,* "to carry a load," which also appears in Isa 46:1 to describe the nations burdened from carrying the images of their gods, i.e., "these things (i.e., the idols) you carry are loaded as burdens on weary ani-mals." The description of the nations "who grievously hurt" them-selves from lifting this stone also relates to pagan religious practice. The verb employed here, *śrt,* "to incise, cut," appears elsewhere only in reference to incisions made in the bodies of those who worship pagan gods (Lev 21:5; cf. 1 Kgs 18:28). Just as verse 2 employed metaphorical terminology of holiness to describe Jerusalem's role in incapacitating the nations, verse 3 employs metaphorical terminology of pagan wor-ship to describe Jerusalem's impact on the nations. The concluding statement that "all the nations of the earth shall be gathered against it (i.e., Jerusalem)," draws on similar images in Isa 17:12-14; Psalms 2; 46; 47; 48 concerning the nations that threaten Jerusalem.

The first of the successive *bayyôm hahû²,* "in that day," statements appears in verses 4-5. It builds upon the previous portrayal of Jeru-salem at the center of a siege laid by Judah and the nations by portray-ing the transformation of Judah from besieger to ally. Following the introductory *bayyôm hahû²* formula, the oracular formula identifies the following first person statements as an oracle from YHWH. YHWH's statement concerning the intention to smite the horses and riders of the besiegers with "panic," "madness," and "blindness," draws upon the language of the covenant curses in Deut 28:28 in which the same terms describe the afflictions of the people should they fail to observe YHWH's expectations.[143] YHWH also indicates the intention to "open my eye" (cf. NRSV, "keep a watchful eye") on Judah, which will recognize YHWH's power and join Jerusalem.

The second *bayyôm hahû²* statement appears in verses 6-7, in which YHWH once again employs first person speech forms to relate Judah's actions against the nations. YHWH's statement metaphorically portrays Judah as a "blazing pot on a pile of wood" and a "flaming torch among

[143] Tai, *Prophetie als Schriftauslegung* 164.

sheaves" to describe how Judah will ignite and consume the nations that threaten Jerusalem on the right and the left. Judah's actions will result in Jerusalem's security in its own place. Verse 7 indicates YHWH's intention to grant victory to Judah first in order to avoid magnifying the "glory" of the house of David and the city of Jerusalem over the people of Judah. The term *tip'eret*, "glory, beauty," is frequently employed to signify the presence of the Temple in Jerusalem (Isa 60:7; cf. 63:15; Ps 96:6), the ark (Ps 78:61), the apparel of the high priest (Exod 28:2, 40), and the crown of a monarch (Isa 28:5; cf. Prov 4:9; Isa 62:3; Jer 13:18; Ezek 16:12). It may also designate an attribute of YHWH (Ps 71:8; 1 Chr 29:11). The concern to honor Judah first and thereby to avoid magnifying Jerusalem and the house of David apparently prepares the reader for the following portrayal of mourning by Jerusalem and the house of David over that which they have pierced.

The third *bayyôm hahû'* statement in the series appears in verses 8-10 in which YHWH relates plans to teach compassion to Jerusalem and the house of David so that they might serve as adequate shepherds for the world once YHWH's war against the nations is complete and YHWH's sovereignty recognized. The verses presuppose the earlier portrayal in Zechariah 11 of the overthrow of the shepherds and the rise of a new shepherd who will show no compassion for the flock. In contrast to verses 2-3, 4-5, and 6-7, YHWH no longer speaks, rather the prophet speaks and describes YHWH's efforts to teach compassion to Jerusalem and Judah. He begins in verse 8 with a statement that YHWH will defend Jerusalem and elevate the status of "the feeblest among them." The NRSV does adequately render the Hebrew term *hannikšāl bāhem*, literally, "the one who has stumbled among them." The term picks up the language of the prophets who maintain that the people of Jerusalem and Judah (or Israel) were punished because they had stumbled (e.g., Isa 3:8; Jer 6:21; cf. Hos 4:5). By portraying the rise of those who had stumbled, the prophet presents the restoration of Judah from its previous punishment as the people are prepared by YHWH to assume their role at the center of the nations. Not only are those who stumbled likened to the house of David, the house of David is compared to G–d or at least to the angel of G–d, so that the dynasty might also assume its role at the center of the nations. The specification of "like G–d" with "like an angel of YHWH" apparently represents the efforts of a later scribe who sought to protect the sanctity of G–d in the text.

Verses 9-10 continue verse 8, but the introductory *wĕhāyâ bayyôm hahû'*, "and it shall come to pass in that day," both establishes the link syntactically and marks the beginning of a sub-unit within verses 8-10. YHWH speaks in the first person form once again and states the intention to destroy the nations that threaten Jerusalem. Verse 10 has been the subject of a great deal of discussion because of its portrayal of compassion by the house of David and Jerusalem over one who has been "pierced."[144] Various proposals have been put forward for understanding this statement in relation to the suffering servant of Isaiah (see esp. Isa 52:13–53:12), the slain king Josiah of Judah (see 2 Kgs 23:28-30; 2 Chr 35:20-27), Uriah the Hittite (2 Samuel 11), Zerubbabel, Gedaliah (Jeremiah 41), the prophet Jeremiah, Onias III, Judah the Maccabee, and others. The images of Josiah and Zerubbabel are particularly attractive, especially given the reference to Megiddo, the site where Josiah was killed, in verse 11 and the general concern with Zerubbabel in the book of Zechariah. Nevertheless, the reader must pay particular attention to YHWH's statement of intention to pour out "a spirit of compassion *(ḥēn)* and supplication *(taḥănûnîm)*" concerning "the one whom they have pierced *(dāqārû)*" and the earlier statements in Zechariah 11 concerning the lack of compassion for the sheep by the shepherds and sheep merchants. The term *ḥēn*, "favor, compassion," is the same term applied to the prophet's first staff in Zech 11:4-17 which he broke to symbolize the annulment of YHWH's covenant with the nations. The term *taḥănûnîm*, "supplications," indicates the supplications of human beings to YHWH for favor (see Pss 143:1; 28:2, 6; Jer 3:21; 31:9). The use of these terms is designed to contrast the attitude of the earlier shepherds or leaders, i.e., the Persians, whom YHWH had designated to rule the world and the attitude of Jerusalem and the house of David who would be placed at the center of the world once YHWH's warfare against the nations is complete.

The reference to "the one whom they have pierced" employs a term that normally describes one pierced by a sword or other weapon in battle (see Num 25:8; Judg 9:54; 1 Sam 31:4; Isa 13:15; Jer 37:10; 51:4), but the following statements that call for mourning like that for an "only child *(yāḥîd)*" or for a "firstborn *(bêkôr)*" draw upon the language of Genesis 22, which relates the binding of Isaac (see esp. Gen 22:2, where Isaac is described as Abraham's "only child"). Although the imagery of bitter mourning for the death of an only child or firstborn certainly conveys the bitterness and tragic dimensions of such a loss, the association with Abraham's near sacrifice of Isaac at Mt. Moriah also draws upon a tradition that is associated with the site of the Jerusalem Temple, identified in 2 Chr 3:1 as Moriah. Whereas the binding of Isaac indicates that Isaac was spared and the covenant thereby preserved, the present context points to the realization of such a death as the cata-

---

[144] See esp. the discussions by Otzen, *Studien über Deuterosacharja* 173–84; Hanson, *The Dawn of Apocalyptic* 357–8; Larkin, *The Eschatology* 161–5; Meyers and Meyers, *Zechariah 9–14* 337–40; Petersen, *Zechariah 9–14 and Malachi* 120–3.

lyst for the compassion that must be shown by YHWH's shepherds who have responsibility for the flock. Insofar as YHWH's sovereignty over the world will be manifested at Zion, Jerusalem and the house of David must develop the qualities necessary for YHWH's shepherds. The text does not identify the one who was pierced, but the following verses refer to mourning at Megiddo and suggest that the figure is somehow associated with King Josiah of Judah, who was killed by Pharaoh Necho at Megiddo just as the young monarch was restoring the kingdom of Judah following the collapse of Assyria (see 2 Kings 22–23; 2 Chronicles 34–35). The statement may also allude to the death of Zerubbabel, the Temple builder of Zechariah 4, who seems to have been displaced by Joshua ben Jehozadak in Zechariah 6.

Nevertheless, the reader should recognize that interpreters' conceptions of "the one whom they have pierced" may well be overly influenced by theological models that seek to associate the reference with the suffering servant of Isaiah, Josiah, and Zerubbabel in order to provide some analogy with the crucifixion of Jesus or a more general concern with vicarious suffering. Indeed, the Hebrew text of the statement does not identify the figure as an individual who is pierced. Rather, the text reads literally, "that/what they have pierced (ʾet ʾăšer dāqārû)," so that the relative particle ʾăšer, "that, what, which," may refer either to an individual or to a group. The current division of the NRSV translation violates the syntactical relationship between verses 9-10 by presenting verse 10 as the introduction to an entirely new unit. Although the following statements refer to an *individual* first born or only child, they do so only to provide a metaphor for understanding the notions of grief and compassion that are inherent in such a loss. When the statement is read in relation to its literary context in verses 9-10, the phrase must be read in relation to verse 9, which calls for the destruction of the nations that threaten Jerusalem. In stating the intention to pour out a spirit of compassion and supplication on the house of David and the inhabitants of Jerusalem, YHWH indicates an interest in promoting a sense of concern in the house of David and the people of Judah for those who are slain by YHWH among the nations. In this manner, the passage presents the preparation of the house of David and the city of Jerusalem for their roles at the center of creation when YHWH's sovereignty is manifested at Zion.

The fourth *bayyôm hahûʾ* statement in the series appears in verses 11-14, which relate the mourning that will take place in Jerusalem over those who are slain. The segment begins in verse 11 with a statement that the mourning in Jerusalem will be as great as that for Hadad Rimmon in the plains of Megiddo. The exact significance of the name Hadad Rimmon is not clear. Most interpreters take it as a reference to the Aramean storm god Hadad, who is frequently associated with the Canaanite/Phoenician storm god Baal.[145] If it is indeed a reference to Hadad, the mourning rites might then refer to his role in general ancient Near Eastern mythology in which the weather god or rain god is believed to have "died" and gone to the netherworld during the summer dry season when no rain falls. In order symbolically to prompt the rebirth of the rain god or his rise from the netherworld in the late summer and early fall when the rains are about to come, ancient worshipers apparently enacted mourning rites for the "dead" god that would play a role in prompting his rise from the netherworld. The basic pattern of the myth is apparent in the Sumerian versions of "the Descent of Inanna to the Underworld" or the Babylonian "Descent of Ishtar to the Netherworld" in which the goddess Inanna or Ishtar journeys to the netherworld in order to rescue the god Dumuzi or Tammuz from the dead so that he might bring fertility to the earth once again.[146] Although there are no clear associations with Hadad, his role is akin to that of Baal and Tammuz, and it appears likely that he, too, may have been conceived in such a role.[147] Because of the question as to whether Hadad would be conceived in this manner, some interpreters propose that Hadad Rimmon must refer to a place name mentioned by Jerome where some mourning rite is carried out.[148] Many point to the reference to "the valley of Megiddo," which designates the place where King Josiah of Judah was killed by Pharaoh Necho of Egypt in 609 B.C.E. (2 Kgs 23:28-30; 2 Chr 35:20-27; n.b. 2 Chr 35:22 likewise refers to the location of Josiah's death as "the valley of Megiddo"). Many note that 2 Chr 35:24-25 refer to the great lamentation that was made for Josiah by the people and by the prophet Jeremiah, and to the continued practice of mourning for Josiah by singing men and women as a "custom" (literally, "statute") "to this day." The reference to mourning in the valley of Megiddo and its associations with the Chronicler's presentation of Josiah's death certainly points to an interest in establishing an analogy for the mourning in Jerusalem with that for Josiah. Such an interest may be motivated by the potential loss of Zerubbabel during the course of Temple reconstruction, but the reader must keep in mind that conclusive evidence for the "killing" or "disappearance" of Zerubbabel is lacking.

Verses 12-14 then specify the mourning that will take place among the various families of Jerusalem. The emphasis on the separate mourn-

---

[145] See esp. Meyers and Meyers, *Zechariah 9–14* 343–4.

[146] Pritchard, *ANET* 52–7, 106–9.

[147] See Walter A. Maier III, "Haddadrimmon," *ABD* III:13.

[148] Ibid.

ing of each family reinforces the notion that such mourning is universally practiced in Jerusalem by each of the families that constitute the city. The reference to the mourning by the women of each family likewise points to the universal nature of the mourning in the city as women and men apparently mourn separately as indicated by the reference in 2 Chr 35:25 to both the male and female singers of funeral dirges (cf. Jer 9:16-21 [NRSV: 9:17-22]; 22:18-19; Ezek 32:16). Following a general statement of the mourning throughout the land by each family in verse 12a, verses 12b-13 specifies four families by name: the family of the house of David (verse 12bα), the family of the house of Nathan (verse 12bβγ), the family of the house of Levi (verse 13a), and the Shimei family (verse 13b). The reference to these families apparently designates the leading families of Jerusalem. The house of David of course refers to the royal family. The house of Nathan is somewhat problematic, although it likely refers to the family of Nathan the prophet who designated both David and Solomon as king (see 2 Samuel 7; 1 Kings 1–2). 2 Chronicles 29:25 identifies David's prophets, Gad and Nathan, as the authorities responsible for the musical role of the Levites in the Temple. Insofar as the Chronicler identifies the Levitical singers as prophets (1 Chr 25; 2 Chr 20; 29; 34:30; 35:15),[149] it would appear that the house of Nathan here designates the line of the prophets of Judah who were perceived to serve in the Jerusalem Temple. The house of Levi of course designates the priestly family. The reference to the Shimei family apparently designates a Levitical family that was also dedicated to the performance of Temple music (1 Chr 6:27; 25:17), although the name also designates the brother of Zerubbabel (1 Chr 3:19). Finally, verse 14 offers a concluding statement that all the remaining families (of Jerusalem) would likewise participate in the mourning.

The fifth *bayyôm hahû'* statement in the series appears in Zech 13:1-9. It begins with a statement concerning the purification, but two successive sub-units in verses 2-3 and 3-9, each introduced by the formula *wĕhāyâ bayyôm hahû'*, "and it shall come to pass on that day," focus especially on the removal of false prophesy. The concluding oracle against the shepherd in verses 7-9, which is structurally a part of the sub-unit in verses 3-9, indicates that the destruction of the shepherd, the further "refining" or punishment of the people, and the restoration of YHWH's relationship with the people constitutes the culmination of

---

[149] For discussion of the Levitical/prophetical temple singers, see David L. Petersen, *Late Israelite Prophecy: Studies in the Deutero-Prophetic Literature and in Chronicles*, SBLMS, vol. 23 (Missoula, MT: Scholars Press, 1977) 55–87; Raymond Tournay, *Seeing and Hearing G–d with the Psalms: The Prophetic Liturgy of the Second Temple in Jerusalem*, JSOTSup, vol. 118 (Sheffield: JSOT Press, 1991).

the unit. The previously noted identification of YHWH's "shepherd" with Cyrus and his successors suggests that the concern with false prophecy may be directed against earlier prophetic tradition, such as Isaiah, that identifies Cyrus as YHWH's shepherd and thereby legitimizes and accepts Persian rule. Instead, the present passage looks to the demise of the Persian monarchy as part of the scenario in which YHWH will manifest world-wide sovereignty at Zion.

Verse 1 calls for the purification of Jerusalem on the coming "Day of YHWH." It employs the imagery of a fountain or water that frequently serves as a purifying agent in cases of corpse contamination, sexual relations or discharges, disease, or contact with something that is considered impure (Lev 22:1-9; Numbers 19). Basically, impurity is the result of an action or state of being that disrupts one's relationship with the holy and renders one unfit to appear at the altar of the Temple, the holy center of creation. Purification by repentance, water (or fire or blood; cf. Lev 15:16; Num 31:23; Lev 14:25), and sacrifice are mandated in the tradition of the Jerusalem Temple when one becomes unclean by reason of moral or ritual action or a physical state of being, i.e., the water and sacrifice symbolically restore one to a state of purity following an action that places one outside of the realm of the holy. Solomon's molten sea (2 Kgs 7:23-26; 2 Chr 4:2-6) was designed to function as a *mikveh* or ritual bath in which priests could purify themselves for service at the Temple. Jerusalem itself was conceived to be a source of water, such as the spring Gihon where Solomon was anointed king (1 Kgs 1:32-40; cf. Gen 2:13 which identifies the Gihon with one of the rivers of Eden which flows around the whole land of Cush) or the waters that well up from Jerusalem to water all creation at the time when the Temple is restored (Ezekiel 47). As in Zech 12:7, the house of David and the inhabitants of Jerusalem are treated together to signify their place at the center of YHWH's creation and sovereignty.

The prophet then presents YHWH's oracular statement in verses 2-3 concerning the cessation of idols, prophets, and the impure spirit from the land. The standard formula, "and it shall come to pass on that day," introduces YHWH's statement together with the oracular formula, "oracle of YHWH of Hosts." The association of idols, prophets, and an impure spirit is clearly intended to address the issue of false prophecy. False prophecy would have been an extremely important issue in the period of the Babylonian exile and early-Persian period restoration because of continuing attempts to wrestle with the issue of the theological meaning of the destruction of Jerusalem and the Temple in 587/6 B.C.E. Jerusalem of course was conceived as the center of creation as well as of the nation Israel, and a great deal of earlier tradition testified to YHWH's promises to secure the city and the ruling house of David (2 Samuel 7;

Isaiah 7:1–9:6; 36-37; Psalms 2; 46; 47; 48; 110; 132). But the reality of both the destruction and the restoration of Jerusalem would have posed a considerable issue in relation to the interpretation of prophetic literature in relation to these events, i.e., at what point do the prophecies of weal for Jerusalem cease in relation to the destruction and at what point do the prophecies of judgment cease in relation to the restoration? Jeremiah's challenge of the prophet Hananiah, whose message that Jerusalem would be free of Babylon in two years, constitutes a challenge of the fundamental position of Isaiah that YHWH will deliver Jerusalem (see Jeremiah 27–28), and Jeremiah's condemnation of false prophets apparently was directed against those who proclaimed the security of the city and nation (cf. Jeremiah 23). Ezekiel's condemnation of the false prophets accuses them of idolatry and deception for maintaining that YHWH would protect the land despite sin and faithless action. In both cases, Jeremiah and Ezekiel maintain that one who speaks of YHWH's protection in a time of punishment must be a false prophet, but both books can point to restoration once the punishment is complete. Such a perspective reflects their identities as both prophets and priests who would see the punishment as a means of purification for the city and nation much like the sacrificial ritual of the Temple plays a similar role in relation to the purification of the people. The book of Zechariah, who is likewise identified as both prophet and priest, as a whole wrestles with this issue insofar as it points to the "former prophets" as those who spoke of both punishment for Jerusalem because of the charge that people had not observed YHWH's will (see Zech 1:2-6) and restoration for Jerusalem once the punishment was over (see Zechariah 7–8). The present context does not indicate the cause for the concern of false prophecy, but the concluding statements in verses 7-9 indicate that it revolves the issue of the shepherd who is to be punished.

In keeping with the commands concerning the identification and punishment of a false prophet in Deut 18:9-22, verse 3 calls for death as the punishment for false prophecy. It calls for the closest family members of such a prophet, i.e., father, mother, and children, to accuse the false prophet of lying in the name of YHWH and to undertake the punishment themselves. This is in keeping with Deut 21:18-21 that calls upon the parents of a rebellious son to take responsibility for the accusation and execution of their child. Such a procedure is meant to emphasize the severity and integrity of the accusation and the execution of punishment by ensuring that there is no doubt as to the charge, i.e., the parents and children would presumably be the last to accept the guilt of their own child or parent. The verb, *dqr*, employed to convey the execution as an act of "piercing" or "stabbing" the false prophet is the same verb that appears in Zech 12:10 to describe those that will be killed on the Day of Y{HWH} as part of Y{HWH}'s efforts to punish and purify the world at large.

Verses 4-9, introduced by the formula, "and it shall come to pass on that day," continue the emphasis on the destruction of false prophecy prior to the condemnation of Y{HWH}'s shepherd. Verses 4-6 draw upon a number of earlier traditions concerning the prophets and other figures to make their point that such prophets have indeed deceived the people.[150] Verse 4 emphasizes the shame of the prophets in conveying such visions while prophesying, and stipulates that such persons will not wear "a hairy mantle" in order to deceive. The "hairy mantle," *ʾadderet śēʿār*, takes up the "mantle" (*ʾadderet* worn by the prophet Elijah and passed on to Elisha when he was designated as Elijah's successor (1 Kgs 19:13, 19; 2 Kgs 2:8, 13, 14). Although Elijah's mantle is not described as "hairy," it clearly symbolizes his prophetic role. The designation of a "hairy mantle" appears in Gen 25:25, where it describes Esau's hairy body, and thereby calls to mind Jacob's deception of his father Isaac by disguising himself as Esau to obtain the blessing of the first born (Genesis 27). Because Isaac was blind, Jacob wore sheep's wool and Esau's garments to carry out the deception. The use of this tradition in Zechariah is clearly intended to demonstrate that a trusted figure, such as a prophet, might deceive just as the patriarch Jacob deceived his father Isaac. In order to make this point, it draws upon a tradition in which even a figure like Jacob, the eponymous ancestor of Israel, can represent a figure worthy of punishment.

Verse 5 continues the concern with false prophecy by drawing upon the traditions of Amos and Cain. In the first part of the verse, the false prophet states, "I am no prophet; I am a tiller of the soil." Such a statement draws upon Amos' response to Amaziah, the high priest at Beth El, who demanded that Amos return to Judah after condemning King Jeroboam ben Joash and Israel, "I am no prophet, nor a prophet's son; but I am a herdsman and a dresser of sycamore trees, and Y{HWH} took me from following the flock, and Y{HWH} said to me, 'Go, prophesy to my people Israel'" (Amos 7:14-15). The statement in Amos is intended to emphasize the credibility of Amos' prophetic message, and the statement in Zech 13:5 draws upon the tradition to emphasize the false prophet's lack of credibility. The reference to the prophet as a "tiller of the soil (*ʿōbēd ʾădāmâ*)" appears also in Gen 4:2 to describe Cain as "a tiller of the soil" in contrast to his brother Esau who is described as "a shepherd of sheep." Of course, Cain killed Abel in Genesis 4, and this

---

[150] See esp. the discussions in Tai, *Prophetie als Schriftauslegung* 210–37 and Ollenburger, "Zechariah," 829–34.

tradition reinforces the portrayal of false prophets as despicable characters worthy of punishment. The allusion is continued in the following statement, "for humankind has caused me to possess since my youth" (contra NRSV, "for the land has been my possession since my youth," which is based on an emendation of *ʾādām hiqnanî*, humankind has caused me to possess" to *ʾădāmâ qinyānî*, "the land has been my possession"; see BHS note). The phrase *ʾādām hiqnanî*, "Adam/humankind has caused me to possess," is frequently read in relation to Eve's statement in Gen 4:1 upon bearing Cain, "I have produced a man with the help of YHWH," because of the similarity of the verb *qnh*, "to acquire, produce," with the name Cain *(qayin)*. The association with Cain is all the more interesting in that, although the use of the tradition aids in justifying the punishment of false prophets, Cain's murder of the shepherd Abel prefigures the call for the killing of the shepherd in verses 7-9. It also relates to the portrayal of the shepherds to be condemned in Zech 11:5 as "those who buy them kill them." The verb *qnh* is employed here as well to describe the shepherds who buy and kill the sheep. It would appear that Zech 13:5 builds upon the earlier statement in Zech 11:5 to describe the false prophets like Cain as tillers of the soil who "possess/acquire/buy," and kill the shepherd. The prophet would thereby charge that such false prophets are ultimately responsible for the killing of the shepherd.

Finally, verse 6 points to the statement made by the false prophet concerning the wounds on his back (literally, "between your hands," i.e., the back or chest) that he received in the house of his friends. The term "my friends," *mĕʾahăbāy*, employs a *piel* form of the verb *ʾhb*, "to love," which elsewhere designates adulterous lovers (Jer 22:20, 22; 30:14; Ezek 16:33, 36, 37; Hos 2:7, 9, 12, 14, 15 [NRSV: 2:5, 7, 10, 12, 13]). This imagery apparently contributes to the portrayal of the false prophets as deceivers who are caught and punished for their actions.

The preceding comparison of the false prophets with the farmer Cain who killed his shepherd brother Abel prepares the reader for the oracle in verses 7-9 which calls for the killing of YHWH's shepherd. The oracle is formulated as the prophet's presentation of a first person oracular statement by YHWH in which YHWH calls upon the sword to "awaken" *(ʿûrî)* against "my shepherd" *(rōʿî)*. The use of this terminology is significant in that it points to the author's attempt to allude once again to the book of Isaiah in which the Persian monarch is called "my shepherd" by YHWH (Isa 44:28) and in which YHWH and Zion are respectively called upon to "awake" in order to prepare for the combat against chaos that will result in the return of the exiled people (Isa 51:9) and to prepare for the anticipated restoration. But whereas the book of Isaiah sees the Persian monarch Cyrus as YHWH's shepherd or harbinger of restoration, Zech 13:7-9 envisions an awakened sword that will strike YHWH's shepherd down. The close relationship between YHWH and the shepherd is signified by the use of the expression, "the man who is my associate," to describe the shepherd. The term *ʿămîtî*, here translated as "my associate," appears elsewhere only in Leviticus to describe a person from one's own people (Lev 5:21 [NRSV: 6:2]; 18:20). Such a designation draws upon the notion that YHWH's chosen monarch is to be designated as YHWH's son (Pss 2:7; 89:26-27; 2 Sam 7:14). Although this designation is applied to David, Cyrus clearly emerges as YHWH's chosen monarch in Isaiah 44:24-28 and 45:1-19. The presence of the oracular formula in verse 7aβ identifies this statement as an oracle from YHWH. The following statement in verse 7b calls for the striking down of the shepherd and the scattering of the sheep, and YHWH states the intention to turn against even the little ones of the flock.

Verse 8 points to the destruction that will take place throughout the entire land so that two thirds of its inhabitants will perish and only one third will survive. Interpreters frequently cite Ezekiel's symbolic action in Ezekiel 5 in which he cuts off his hair with a sword, divides it into three parts, and then employs the three parts to symbolize the fate of the people in which one third are burned in the city, one third are killed by the sword, and one third are scattered to the wind and pursued by the sword. Although Ezekiel's portrayal suggests the destruction of all three parts, the third that is scattered or exiled corresponds to the third that remains in Zech 13:8. This would suggest that Zechariah takes up Ezekiel's image, but employs it as an illustration of what will happen to the people of the land now that the Babylonian exile is over, i.e., when the shepherd or Persian monarch is killed, the entire land will suffer much as it did under the Babylonians. Once again, the oracular formula at the end of verse 8aα certifies this as a statement by YHWH.

Verse 9 then concludes the oracle with YHWH's statements concerning the overall purpose of this brutal scenario. YHWH states the intention to burn the surviving third in fire so that it can be refined like silver and tested like gold. At this point, the imagery returns to that of the book of Isaiah in which YHWH states the intention to smelt Jerusalem in order to remove the dross and purify it so that it will become a city of righteousness and faithfulness (Isa 1:21-26; cf. Mal 3:2-4). The statement in verse 9 also presupposes Isaiah's program of punishment in which even the surviving remnant of the punished people will be punished or burnt further in order to produce the "holy seed" from which the future of the restored people will grow (Isa 6:13). Once this process of refinement or purification is complete, YHWH is ready to recognize the people and restore the relationship with them. YHWH's statement in verse 9b, "They will call on my name, and I will answer them. I will say,

'They are my people'; and they will say, 'Yнwн is our G–d,'" draws upon the language of Hos 2:25b [NRSV: 2:23b] to signify the restoration of the relationship between the people and Yнwн. Overall, variations of this statement appear throughout the Hebrew Bible as examples of the so-called covenant formulary that signifies the relationship between Yнwн and the people of Israel (Lev 26:12; Jer 7:23; Ezek 36:28; Zech 8:8; cf. Deut 26:17-18; Ps 100:3; Isa 51:16; Gen 17:6).[151] The passage clearly presupposes a continued period of conflict and punishment for the people following the demise of the Persian king, but it posits that such suffering will ultimately lead to the final scenario of restoration in Zechariah 14.

CONCERNING YHWH'S RECOGNITION BY THE NATIONS AT ZION ON THE DAY OF YHWH: 14:1-21

Zechariah 14:1-21 constitutes the climactic unit of the entire book with the prophet's portrayal of Yнwн's recognition as universal sovereign by the nations at Zion on the day of Yнwн, identified here as the festival of Sukkoth. Like its counterpart in Zech 12:2–13:9, the passage begins with a statement introduced by the particle *hinnēh*, "behold, a day is coming for Yнwн," but the prophet is the primary speaker in this passage rather than Yнwн. The overall concern of the passage is to delineate the events that will take place on that day. As Petersen notes, the overall structure of the passage must take account of the frequent formulaic references to "in that day *(bayyôm hahû²)*" that appear throughout the chapter.[152] Nevertheless, the basic structure of the passage appears to be defined formally by the disjunctive clause in verse 12, "and this *(wĕzō²t)* shall be the plague with which Yнwн will strike all the peoples that wage war against Jerusalem," and thematically by the shift from Yнwн's actions concerning Jerusalem in verses 1-11 to Yнwн's actions concerning the nations in verses 12-21. Both passages focus on the events that will take place "in that day *(bayyôm hahû²)*," and both conclude respectively in verses 9b-11 and 20-21 with a section, introduced by the syntactically independent formula *bayyôm hahû²*, "in that day," that portrays Jerusalem's secure or holy status in relation to the manifestation of Yнwн's sovereignty in the city.

Verses 1-11 present Yнwн's actions in relation to Jerusalem "on that day." The prophet is the speaker throughout, although he apparently quotes Yнwн in verse 2a or perhaps in verse 2a+b. Verses 1-5 constitute

[151] For discussion of the covenant formulary, see Rendtorff, *Die "Bundesformel."*
[152] Petersen, *Zechariah 9–14 and Malachi* 137–9.

a series of statements by the prophet that portray YHWH's actions per se, and verses 6-11 constitute a series of statements that lay out the results of YHWH's actions "on that day," culminating in the recognition of YHWH's unity and the security of Jerusalem.

Verses 1-5 portray the disaster that will once again overtake Jerusalem as the city is prepared for YHWH's ultimate triumph. The unit begins with the prophet's second person address to Jerusalem concerning the coming day of YHWH in which he announces that the spoil of the city will be divided in its midst.[153] The use of the second person feminine singular pronoun suffixes indicates that the city of Jerusalem is the addressee of this statement. He then turns to a first person statement by YHWH concerning Jerusalem, although it is uncertain whether YHWH's statement appears only in verse 2a or in both verse 2a and 2b. YHWH's use of the verb *wĕʾāsaptî*, "and I will gather," helps to prepare the reader for the emphasis on the festival of Sukkoth because Sukkoth is the festival of the final harvest of the year in which the produce of the vineyards and olive trees is "gathered"; indeed, the festival is referred to as "the festival of ingathering *(ḥag hāʾāsip/ḥag hāʾāsîp)*" in Exod 23:16; 34:22.[154] Instead of harvest and celebration, the imagery is that of war in which the city is captured, the houses plundered, and the women raped. The statement apparently draws upon Isa 13:16 which presents similar imagery to depict the downfall of Babylon on the day of YHWH. The MT reads the *ketiv* or written form of the verb *tiššāgalnâ* with the less crude *tiššākabnâ*, "they were lain with," as the *qere* or read form.[155] Although the third person descriptive form of verse 2b makes it impossible to determine whether it is a part of YHWH's statement or a statement by the prophet, the half verse states that half of the city's population will be taken off into exile, but the remaining half will not be cut off from the city. The earlier reference in Zech 13:9 to Isa 1:21-26 with its image of the "smelting" of Jerusalem by fire as one smelts and purifies metal suggests that such destruction apparently represents a process of purification in which the population is reduced and purified in preparation for Jerusalem's role as the seat for YHWH's universal sovereignty (cf. Zech 7:9-10; 8:3, which also draw on Isa 1:21-26).

The prophet's third person portrayal of YHWH's actions clearly returns in verses 3-4 with his description of the splitting of the Mount of

---

[153] For discussion of the "Day of YHWH," see K. J. Cathcart, "Day of YHWH," *ABD* II:84-5; R. H. Hiers, "Day of the L–rd," *ABD* II:82-3; A. J. Everson, "Day of the L–rd," *IDB[S]* 209–10.

[154] For discussion of Sukkoth, see "Sukkot," *Encyclopaedia Judaica* 15:495-502.

[155] For discussion of *Qere/Ketiv*, see W. S. Morrow, "Kethib and Qere," *ABD* IV:24-30.

Olives into two as Yhwh battles against the nations.[156] As its name implies, the Mount of Olives was a major area for the cultivation of olive trees in antiquity, and therefore plays a major role in preparing the reader for the imagery of Yhwh's recognition by the nations at the festival of Sukkoth when the olive harvest is brought in. As it is the highest ridge in the vicinity of Jerusalem, situated immediately east of the city across the Kidron Valley, the Mount of Olives also serves as Jerusalem's main lookout point to warn of approaching danger from the Trans-Jordan region to the east or the hills of Judea and southern Samaria to the north. Verse 4 represents a rare use of anthropomorphic imagery to portray Yhwh's "feet" standing on the Mount of Olives "on that day" (cf. Ezek 1:27 which speaks metaphorically of Yhwh's "loins" and Exod 33:22-23 which refers metaphorically to Yhwh's "hand," "face," and "back"). It also notes the location of the Mount of Olives to the east of Jerusalem. Overall, this verse takes up the traditional theme of Yhwh's defense of Jerusalem from the enemy nations that threaten the city (cf. Psalms 2; 46; 47; 48), but it also takes up Yhwh's role as creator in that it emphasizes the transformation of the cosmos as the Mount of Olives splits into two halves so that each half moves to the north and south respectively to expose a great valley between them. Such imagery is not unlike that of the splitting of the Red Sea in the Exodus traditions (Exodus 14; 15), the splitting of the Jordan River in the conquest tradition (Joshua 3), and the road created through the wilderness so that the exiles could return home to Jerusalem in Isaiah (Isa 35:8-10; 40:3-4; 43:14-21).

The first person reference to "my mountains" (cf. NRSV which reads "the L–rd's mountain," but notes the proper reading of the Hebrew) indicates that Yhwh speaks once again in verse 5. Yhwh's statement is formulated as a second person masculine plural address to the people of Jerusalem who will flee from the catastrophe. Although the Hebrew, followed by NRSV, indicates that "the valley of the mountain shall reach to Azal," the term ʾāṣal, read here as a place name, apparently reflects the Hebrew ʾeṣel, "side,"[157] so that the statement actually should read, "the valley of the mountain shall reach to (each) side," i.e., of the two halves of the Mount of Olives. The reference to the earthquake in the days of Uzziah king of Judah is drawn from Amos 1:1, which refers to the earthquake in the days of Uzziah as a means to date the prophecy

---

[156] For discussion of the traditio-historical background of this passage in relation to Yhwh's defense of Jerusalem against the nations, see Lutz, *JHWH, Jerusalem, und die Völker.*

[157] Cf. Meyers and Meyers, *Zechariah 9–14* 426; Petersen, *Zechariah 9–14 and Malachi* 136.

of Amos. The passage may also presuppose the image of the desolation and twisting of the surface of the earth in Isa 24:1-13 (see esp. verse 1), which speaks of the beating of the land as one beats an olive tree at the end of the grape harvest (see esp. verse 13). Although the NRSV reads the concluding statement of the sub-unit in verse 5b as "then Yhwh my G–d will come, and all the holy ones with him," the Hebrew reads "with you" as the prophet's address to Jerusalem once again.

Verses 6-11 then present a series of five statements, each introduced by the verb *wĕhāyâ*, "and it shall come to pass," that progressively describe the resulting transformation of nature and the city of Jerusalem as Yhwh's sovereignty over all the earth is recognized. The culmination of this section in verses 9b-11 begins with the formula *bayyôm hahûʾ*, "in that day," and describes both Yhwh's unity and Jerusalem's security. The first statement in the sequence appears in verse 6, which relates the cessation of light so that cold and frost will result on that day. Such an act of course reverses the very first act of creation in Gen 1:3-5 in which light was first created in the midst of darkness. The last two words of verse 6 are very problematic text critically in that the Hebrew reads *yĕqārôt yĕqippāʾôn*, "the precious things will freeze/congeal." The meaning of the Hebrew text is uncertain at this point, and most interpreters follow the LXX, which reads *kai psuchē kai pagos*, "and cold and frost," which would correspond to Hebrew *wĕqārût wĕqippāʾôn*, a slight consonantal variation from the MT.[158] The second statement in the sequence in verse 7a builds upon the first in that it envisions one long continuous day, such as is known only to Yhwh, that is neither day nor night. Once again, the image reverses the first act of creation which produced the distinction between day and night. The third statement in verse 7b continues to build on the image by stating that it will be light at the time of evening, which appears to contradict the statement in verse 6 that "there will not be light," and contributes to the conclusion that verse 6 is somehow corrupted.

The image then shifts in verse 8 with another reference to what shall take place "in that day" parallel to that of verse 6. Verse 8 portrays "living waters" that shall flow out from Jerusalem into both the eastern and western seas in both summer and winter. Such a portrayal builds upon the tradition that Zion is a source of water that brings fertility and growth to the entire earth (see Ezekiel 47; Joel 4:18 [NRSV: 3:18]; Gen 2:10-14; Ps 46:4). This theme is especially pertinent in relation to the festival of Sukkoth as that is the time that the rainy season commences in Israel, and brings new life to the land at the end of the dry summer season. The eastern sea of course refers to the Dead Sea in which nothing

---

[158] See Lacoque, *Zacharie 9–14* 208; Rudolph, *Sacharja 9–14* 232.

can live and the western sea is the Mediterranean. The cessation of summer and winter again indicates the transformation of the natural order of the seasons as it is outlined in Gen 1:14.

Verse 9a then concludes the initial sequence of *wĕhāyâ* statements with "and YHWH will become king over all the earth." The testimony to YHWH's sovereignty over all the earth of course recalls YHWH's role as creator in Genesis 1. It also recalls the enthronement psalms in Psalms 93; 96; 97; and 99, which celebrate YHWH's role as King and creator as well as YHWH's protection of Jerusalem. Again, such language is crucial to the theme of Sukkoth in that Sukkoth completes the sequence of holidays in the seventh month of Tishri, including Rosh Ha-Shanah (New Year), Yom Kippur (Day of Atonement), and Sukkoth (Tabernacles) that celebrate YHWH's sovereignty over the entire world.

Finally, verses 9b-11 constitute the culmination of this section with a portrayal of YHWH's unity and Jerusalem's security. The NRSV erroneously connects verse 9b to verse 9a in its translation, but the syntactically independent *bayyôm hahûʾ*, "in that day," marks the beginning of a new sub-unit that sums up the import of the previous statements. The statement that "on that day YHWH will be one and his name one" reflects the Shema in Deut 6:4, "Hear O Israel, YHWH is our G–d, YHWH is one," which stands as the basic creedal statement of the Jewish worship service. This statement indicates YHWH's sovereignty over the world, and introduces verses 10-11 which in turn portray the transformation of Jerusalem from a place of threat into a place of safety. Overall, the image points to Jerusalem elevated above all the surrounding land in keeping with Isa 2:2-4 and Mic 4:1-5 which speak of Jerusalem's elevation above all the mountains and hills. The portrayal of the land transformed into a plain highlights Jerusalem's elevation, and builds upon the image of the mountain transformed into a plain in Zech 4:7. According to Zech 4:7, Zerubbabel's work in laying the foundation of the new Temple would result in such a transformation. The term for "plain" here is *ʿărābâ*, "Arabah," which is the name of the dry rift in the earth that forms the Jordan River Valley and extends south from the Dead Sea into the Gulf of Aqaba. Such an image further contrasts with the exalted Jerusalem. The mention of specific places, Geba to the north and Rimmon to the south, points to the ideal northern and southern boundaries of the territory of Judah, much as the Dead Sea to the east and the Mediterranean to the west point to ideal boundaries for Judah. Although Geba was formally a part of Benjamin's territory (Josh 21:17; 1 Chr 6:15), it is mentioned together with the southern city of Beer Sheba in 2 Kgs 23:8 to describe the territory in which King Josiah carried out his reforms. The site of Rimmon is not entirely certain, but it appears to have been a part of the territory of Simeon (Josh 19:7; 1 Chr

4:32; cf. Josh 15:32, which assigns it to Judah). Both Geba and Rimmon are settled towns in Judah and Benjamin during the time of Nehemiah (Neh 11:25-36). Basically, the references to Geba and Rimmon are intended to encompass all of the territory of Judah.

The references to the gates and other locations in Jerusalem are likewise intended to encompass all of the city itself.[159] The exact site of the gate of Benjamin is unknown, but its name indicates that it was situated on the northern side of Jerusalem so that it would give access to the road that leads to the territory of Benjamin. It is mentioned in Jer 37:13 as the gate from which Jeremiah attempted to leave the city to redeem family property in Anathoth (situated in the territory of Benjamin). It is also mentioned in Jer 38:7 as the place where King Zedekiah was sitting, and may be identified with the people's gate by which the kings of Judah enter the city (Jer 17:19) or with the upper Benjamin gate (Jer 20:2) or with the upper gate of the house of YHWH built by Jotham (2 Kgs 15:35). Some maintain that it is also to be identified with the post-exilic Muster or Inspection Gate (Neh 3:31) or the Sheep Gate (Neh 3:32) located near the northern or upper ends of the eastern wall. The reference is to "the former gate" or "the first gate." This would suggest the main gate on the east side of the city where the water system was located and where the Assyrian Rab Shakeh made his demands for the surrender of Jerusalem in the time of Hezekiah (2 Kings 18–19; Isaiah 7; 36–37). The mention of the term "place" may indicate that the gate no longer existed. That would certainly apply to the eastern gate that would have been destroyed by the Babylonians and continued to lay in ruins for some seventy years or more after the time of Zechariah until Nehemiah rebuilt the walls and gates of Jerusalem (Neh 2:11–6:19). The "corner gate" is mentioned in 2 Kgs 14:13; Jer 31:38; 2 Chr 26:9, and perhaps in 2 Chr 25:23. The "corner gate" apparently was located on the west side of the city close to the northern wall at some point near to the present day Jaffa Gate. The site of the tower of Hananel is unknown although the tower is mentioned in Jer 31:38; Neh 3:1; and 12:39. Scholars believe that it was located at the northwest corner of the Temple mount, west of the Benjamin gate. The king's wine presses are not mentioned elsewhere in the Bible, and their site is unknown. Meyers and Meyers place them on the south side of the City of David near to the King's pool (Neh 2:14) and the King's Garden (Neh 3:15) on the belief that this area, where the waters of the Siloam pool were gathered, would have been a suitable place for the gathering of grapes for wine presses.[160] The proximity of this area to the Emek Rephaim or

[159] See esp. the discussion in Meyers and Meyers, *Zechariah 9–14* 444–7.
[160] Ibid.

Rephaim Valley, which was known in antiquity as a rich agricultural area (see Isa 17:4-6), supports such a contention. Altogether, the mention of the various gates and other installations points to an effort on the part of the author of this passage to encompass the entire area of Jerusalem, perhaps at its greatest extent. The passage concludes in verse 11 with a statement that Jerusalem will be inhabited, that it will never again be subject to destruction, and that it will dwell in security. Overall, the passage points to the restoration of Jerusalem in its entirety.

Following the portrayal of YHWH's actions concerning Jerusalem in verses 1-11, Zech 14:12-21 then turns to a portrayal of YHWH's actions concerning the nations that points ultimately to their recognition of YHWH's world-wide sovereignty at Zion during the festival of Sukkoth. The passage begins with the indicative statement, "and this shall be the plague with which YHWH will strike all the peoples that wage war against Jerusalem," which disrupts the verbal sequence that holds verses 1-11 together. Like verses 1-11, verses 12-21 employ a similar sequence of statements introduced by *wĕhāyâ*, "and it shall come to pass" (verses 13, 16, 17), that form the first major segment of the passage in verses 12-19 and culminate in a statement introduced by the syntactically independent *bayyôm hahû*', "in that day," in verse 20 that introduces the second segment in verses 20-21. Overall, the passage combines the motifs of YHWH's plagues from the Exodus tradition, YHWH's defense of Jerusalem against the assault of the nations, the presentation of offerings at the Temple at the time of Sukkoth, and the sanctity of the Temple that emanates from the center to permeate all of creation. In this manner, the passage points to YHWH's defeat of the nations as the means by which they recognize YHWH's sovereignty at Zion and thereby sanctify the entire world.

The first segment of the passage in verses 12-19 relates the submission of the nations to YHWH at Zion. The segment begins with the above-mentioned statement in verse 12 that identifies the plague that YHWH will visit upon the nations that mass to attack Jerusalem. The use of the term "plague" points to the influence of the Exodus tradition in which YHWH visited plagues upon the Egyptians in order to demonstrate YHWH's power as creator and sovereign of the universe over against that of the Pharaoh of Egypt who was also considered a god by his own people. Although Egypt will figure prominently in verses 18 and 19 below, the plague is applied to all of the nations that attack Jerusalem, and thereby draws upon the traditions concerning YHWH's protection of Jerusalem from the assault of the nations (see Psalms 2; 46; 47; 48). The portrayal of the rotting flesh, eyes, and tongues of the nations that threaten Jerusalem picks up language from Isa 34:4 that depicts the rotting of the host of heaven from the nations that threatened

Zion and from Ezek 4:17; 24:23; 33:10; and Lev 26:39 that depict rotting or wasting away as a suitable punishment for iniquity. Interestingly, the Hebrew text employs the singular grammatical forms to depict the nations in verse 12b, "his flesh rots and he is standing upon his feet and his eyes shall rot in their holes and his tongue rots in their mouth." The depiction of the nations in singular form recalls the image of the Assyrian king in Isa 10:5-34, who stands on Mount Nob to shake his fist against Zion, only to be cut down like an over-ripe olive tree that is harvested. Indeed, the image of the withered tree follows immediately upon the portrayal of the rotting host of heaven in Isa 34:4.

Verses 13-15, introduced by the verb *wěhāyâ*, "and it shall come to pass," then turn to a portrayal of the consternation and panic that will grip the nations as a result of YHWH's plague, causing them to fight among themselves so that their wealth is gathered as spoil for presentation to YHWH in Jerusalem. The statement clearly presupposes the "day of YHWH" motif as mentioned in verse 13. Rather than portraying YHWH's combat against the nations, the nations raise their hands against each other which results in their defeat much as Gideon's surprise of the Midianites caused them to turn their swords against each other so that Gideon's victory was assured (Judg 7:19-25; cf. Isa 9:5 [NRSV: 9:4], which relates the "Day of Midian" to Israel's situation in the Assyrian period)." Verse 14a cryptically notes that Judah will also fight against Jerusalem like the nations, taking up the motif of Zech 12:1-7 which portrays Judah as an enemy of Jerusalem that is turned as a result of its witnessing YHWH's power to defend the city. Verses 14b-15 then outline the wealth or spoil of the nations that will be gathered and dedicated to YHWH at Zion. The use of the verb *wě'ussap*, "and it shall be collected/gathered," once again employs the verb *'sp* that is characteristically associated with the festival of Sukkoth. Rather than depicting the gathering of the grape and olive harvest, however, the gathering of the spoil of the nations relates to the Exodus tradition concerning the Egyptians who gave their gold, silver, and clothing to the departing Israelite slaves, much as the wealth of the nations here consists of gold, silver, and clothing (see Exod 12:35-36). Insofar as the Exodus is intended to bring the people to YHWH's sanctuary in the sight of the nations (Exod 15:13-18), the portrayal of the nations' spoil that is to be offered to YHWH at Sukkoth recapitulates the Exodus motif of YHWH's world-wide power and sovereignty. The portrayal of YHWH's plague against the horses, mules, camels, donkeys, and other animals of the nations indicates that these, too, are included in the spoil dedicated to YHWH.

Verse 16, once again introduced by the verb *wěhāyâ*, "and it shall come to pass," then portrays the remnant of survivors of the nations who come to Jerusalem year by year to worship YHWH at the festival of Sukkoth. YHWH's sovereignty over the entire world is signaled by the designation of YHWH as "the King, YHWH of Hosts," as well as by the nations' obeisance. The significance of their recognition of YHWH at Sukkoth relates not only to the issue of YHWH's sovereignty, but to the reconstruction of the Temple as well that plays such an important role in the presentation of Zechariah's visions in Zechariah 1–6. Insofar as Temples or altars in ancient Israel and Judah are dedicated at Sukkoth (Exod 29:36-37; 1 Kgs 8:65-66; 2 Chr 7:8-10; Ezra 3:1-7; cf. 2 Chr 29:20-36; 1 Macc 4:52-58), the offerings presented by the nations to YHWH at Sukkoth signify the full restoration of the Temple to its role as the holy center for all creation. In this manner, Zechariah 14 represents the full completion of the Temple anticipated by Zechariah in the first part of the book.

Verses 17-19, once again introduced by the verb *wĕhāyâ*, "and it shall come to pass," outlines the consequences for the nations that do not recognize YHWH's sovereignty in Jerusalem at Sukkoth. Verse 17 basically states that the nations that do not acknowledge YHWH will not receive rain. As noted above, Sukkoth marks the beginning of the rainy season in the fall and points to the Temple as the center from which the stability of the natural world proceeds. The modern reader must bear in mind the crucial importance of rain to an agriculturally-based subsistence economy; if there is no rain, there is no food and hence no life. Recognition of YHWH at Zion is clearly the key to the future in such a conceptualization. Verse 18 then turns to the consequences for Egypt if it does not acknowledge YHWH and thereby lacks rain, i.e., this will be a recapitulation of YHWH's plague against the nations that do not come to Jerusalem at Sukkoth. In this manner, the author of the passage points once again to this event as a recapitulation of the Exodus tradition. Finally, verse 19 identifies the failure to come to Jerusalem at Sukkoth as the "sin" (*ḥaṭṭaʾ*) of Egypt and the nations. The NRSV translation of the term *ḥaṭṭaʾ* as "punishment" presupposes that this is an action worthy of punishment.

Finally, verses 20-21 comprise the second part of Zech 14:12-21. As noted above, they begin with the syntactically independent *bayyôm hahûʾ*, "in that day," and portray the sanctification of the horses and cooking utensils of Judah and Jerusalem. In essence, this represents the transference of the Temple's holiness to the city of Jerusalem and the nation of Judah that surrounds the sacred center of the Temple at Zion. The labeling of the horses' bells as "holy to YHWH" recalls the inscription of the signet that is placed in the turban of the high priest, "Holy to YHWH" (Exod 28:36-38; 39:30-31) and alluded to in the description of Joshua ben Jehozadak's ordination ceremony in Zech 3:9. The designa-

tion "Holy to Yhwh" is applied to sacrifices offered or dedicated to
Yhwh at the Temple (Lev 23:20; 27:30, 32), silver and gold vessels dedicated to the Temple for holy use (Ezra 8:28), and spoils of holy war
(Josh 6:19). The designation of horses' bells as "Holy to Yhwh" recalls
the portrayal of the horses in Zechariah's first vision (Zech 1:8-17)
which patrolled the earth to proclaim the restoration of Zion. It is noteworthy that the Persian empire made extensive use of horses to ensure
communications throughout the empire and to keep the king informed
of events throughout the realm. In the scenario outlined in the book of
Zechariah, the horses would then become agents in enabling Yhwh to
exercise world-wide sovereignty. It is also noteworthy that the horses
of Zech 1:8 were hidden in a "glen *(měṣulâ)* of myrtles" and that the
horses' "bells" *(měṣillôt)* are inscribed. The similarity between the two
different but similarly formed terms aids in establishing the relationship between the horses sanctified to Yhwh at the end of the book and
those hidden at the beginning of the book as they commenced their patrols to announce the restoration of Zion. The reference to the "cooking
pots" *(sîrôt)* of Judah employs a rather common term, but the comparison to the "bowls" *(mizrāqîm)* of the altar (see Exod 27:3; Num 4:14;
1 Kgs 7:40, 45; Jer 52:18; Zech 9:15) indicates an effort to treat all the
cooking utensils of Jerusalem and Judah, and thus the food prepared in
Jerusalem and Judah, like the holy utensils and food prepared at the
Temple itself. This becomes a rather circumspect way of designating
Jerusalem and Judah as the holy center of the nations at large who will
come to sacrifice and eat from the holy food prepared in Jerusalem and
Judah. The final comment, that "there shall no longer be traders in the
house of Yhwh of Hosts in that day," indicates the full sanctification of
the Temple at the center of Jerusalem and Judah and at the center of the
nations. The NRSV translation "traders" masks the Hebrew term *kěnaʿănî*,
"Canaanite." Although the term Canaanite can refer to "merchants" or
"traders" (Zeph 1:11; Ezek 16:29; Prov 31:24; cf. Zech 11:7, 11), the
double entendre refers to the Canaanite people whom Israelite tradition charged with having polluted the land with pagan worship and
immoral practices (e.g., Exod 34:11-16; Lev 18:2-5, 24-30; 20:22-26; Deut
7:1-6; Ezra 9:1). It also relates to the oracle against Tyre, a major Phoeni-
cian/Canaanite city that engaged in extensive trade by sea, in Isaiah 23
whose merchandise will ultimately be dedicated to Yhwh (Isa 23:17-18)
at the end of seventy years when the exile comes to an end (cf. Zech
1:12; 7:5). Altogether, this passage indicates the full restoration of the
Temple.

FOR FURTHER READING

COMMENTARIES

Amsler, Samuel, André Lacoque and René Vuilleumier. *Aggée, Zacharie, Malachie*. Commentaire de l'ancien Testament, XIc. 2nd edition. Geneva: Labor et Fides, 1988.

Conrad, Edgar. *Zechariah*. Readings. Sheffield: Sheffield Academic Press, 1999.

Hanhart, Robert. *Sacharja*. Biblischer Kommentar, Altes Testament, XIV/7, 1-7. Neukirchen-Vluyn: Neukirchener, 1990–1998.

Meyers, Carol L. and Eric M. Meyers. *Haggai, Zechariah 1–8*. Anchor Bible, 25B. Garden City: Doubleday, 1987.

Meyers, Carol L. and Eric M. Meyers. *Zechariah 9–14*. Anchor Bible, 25C. New York: Doubleday, 1993.

Mitchell, Hinckley G., with John Merlin Powis Smith and Julius A. Bewer. *A Critical and Exegetical Commentary on Haggai, Zechariah, Malachi, and Jonah*. International Critical Commentary. Edinburgh: T. and T. Clark, 1912.

Ollenburger, Ben C. "The Book of Zechariah: Introduction, Commentary, and Reflections," *The New Interpreter's Bible. Volume VII: Introduction to Apocalyptic Literature, Daniel, The Twelve Prophets*, ed. Leander E. Keck et al. Nashville: Abingdon, 1996.

Petersen, David L. *Haggai and Zechariah 1–8*. Old Testament Library. Philadelphia: Westminster, 1984.

Petersen, David L., *Zechariah 9–14 and Malachi*. Old Testament Library. Louisville: Westminster John Knox, 1995.

Redditt, Paul L. *Haggai, Zechariah, Malachi*. New Century Bible Commentary. London: Marshall Pickering; Grand Rapids: William Eerdmans, 1995.

Reventlow, Henning Graf. *Die Propheten Haggai, Sacharja und Maleachi*. Das Alte Testament Deutsch, 25, 2. Göttingen: Vandenhoeck & Ruprecht, 1993.

Robinson, Theodore H., with Friedrich Horst. *Die Zwölf Kleinen Propheten*. Handbuch zum Alten Testament, 14. 3rd edition. Tübingen: J.C.B. Mohr (Paul Siebeck), 1964.

Rudolph, Wilhelm. *Haggai–Sacharja 1–8–Sacharja 9–14–Maleachi*. Kommentar zum Alten Testament, XIII/4. Gütersloh: Gerd Mohn, 1976.

Smith, Ralph L. *Micah–Malachi*. Word Biblical Commentary, 32. Waco: Word: 1984.

STUDIES

Beuken, W. A. M., S.J. *Haggai–Sacharja 1–8. Studien zur überlieferungs-geschichte der frühnachexilischen Prophetie*. Studia Semitica Neerlandica, 10. Assen: Van Gorcum, 1967.

Butterworth, Mike. *Structure and the Book of Zechariah*. JSOT Supplements, 130. Sheffield: Sheffield Academic Press, 1992.

Coggins, R. J. *Haggai, Zechariah, Malachi*. Old Testament Guides. Sheffield: JSOT Press, 1987.

Hanson, Paul. *The Dawn of Apocalyptic: The Historical and Sociological Roots of Jewish Apocalyptic Eschatology*. Philadelphia: Fortress, 1975.

Jeremias, Christian. *Die Nachtgeschichte des Sacharja*. Forschungen zur Religion und Literatur des Alten und Neuen Testaments, 117. Göttingen: Vandenhoeck & Ruprecht, 1977.

Lamarche, Paul. S. J. *Zacharie IX–XIV. Structure litteraire et messianisme*. Études bibliques. Paris: Gabalda, 1961.

Larkin, Katrina J. A. *The Eschatology of Second Zechariah. A Study of the Formation of a Mantological Wisdom Anthology*. Contributions to Biblical Theology and Exegesis, 6. Kampen: Kok Pharos, 1994.

Lutz, Hanns-Martin. *JHWH, Jerusalem und die Völker. Zur Vorgeschichte von Sach 12, 1-8 und 14, 1-5*. Wissenschftliche Monographien zum Alten und Neuen Testaments, 27. Neukirchen-Vluyn: Neukirchener, 1968.

Mason, R. A. *Preaching the Tradition. Homily and Hermeneutics after the Exile*. Cambridge: Cambridge University Press, 1990.

Niditch, Susan. *The Symbolic Vision in Biblical Tradition*. Harvard Semitic Monographs, 30. Chico: Scholars Press, 1980.

Otzen, B. *Studien über Deuterosacharja*. Copenhagen: Munksgaard, 1964.

Person, Raymond F. *Second Zechariah and the Deuteronomic School*. JSOT Supplements, 167. Sheffield: Sheffield Academic Press, 1993.

Petitjean, Albert. *Les Oracles du Proto-Zacharie*. Paris: Gabalda. Louvain: Éditions Impremerie Orientaliste, 1969.

Rignell, Lars Gösta. *Die Nachtgesichte des Sacharja. Eine exegetische Studie*. Lund: Gleerup, 1950.

Saebø, Magne. *Sacharja 9–14. Untersuchungen von Text und Form.* Wissenschaftliche Monographien zum Alten und Neuen Testament, 34. Neukirchen-Vluyn: Neukirchener, 1969.

Schöttler, Heinz-Günther. *G–tt inmitten seines Volkes. Die Neuordnung des G–ttesvolkes nach Sacharja 1–6.* Trierer Theologische Studien, 43. Trier: Paulinus, 1987.

Seybold, Klaus. *Bilder zum Tempelbau. Die Visionen des Propheten Sacharja.* Stuttgarter Bibelstudien, 70. Stuttgart: Katholisches Bibelwerk, 1974.

Tai, Nicholas Ho Fai. *Prophetie als Schriftauslegung. Traditions-und kompositionsgeschichtliche Studien.* Calwer Theologische Monographien, 17. Stuttgart: Calwer, 1996.

Tigchelaar, Eibert J. C. *Prophets of Old and the Day of the End. Zechariah, the Book of Watchers, and Apocalyptic.* Oudtestamentische Studiën, 34. Leiden: Brill, 1996.

Tollington, Janet E. *Tradition and Innovation in Haggai and Zechariah 1–8.* JSOT Supplements, 150. Sheffield: Sheffield Academic Press, 1993.

Willi-Plein, Ina. *Prophetie am Ende. Untersuchungen zu Sacharja 9–14.* Bonner Biblische Beiträge, 42. Köln: Peter Hanstein, 1974.

MALACHI

MALACHI

Overview

Malachi is the twelfth book in the sequence of the Book of the Twelve in both the Masoretic and Septuagint versions. It presents a series of speeches by a prophet identified only as Malachi, Hebrew for "my messenger," that is designed to persuade its audience to observe YHWH's requirements concerning the proper presentation of offerings in the Temple and proper marriage practices among the priests and the people. By focusing on this combination of cultic and moral issues, Malachi presents the means by which the priests and the people will sanctify themselves and the Temple. Malachi follows Haggai and Zechariah, which anticipate the reconstitution of the Jerusalem Temple as the holy center of Israel, the nations, and the cosmos at large, so Malachi calls upon its audience to take the action that is necessary for Jerusalem and the Temple to fill this role.

Some have argued that Malachi was composed to form a conclusion for the Book of the Twelve,[1] but the interrelationships between Malachi and the other books among the Twelve are based only on very broad thematic parallels. Thus, YHWH's stated hatred for divorce in Malachi 2:10-16 provides an important commentary on the divorce of Hosea and Gomer or YHWH and Israel in the book of Hosea in that it points to YHWH's commitment to maintain the relationship with Israel despite

[1] Erich Bosshard and Reinhold G. Kratz, "Maleachi im Zwölfprophetenbuch," *BN* 52 (1990) 27–46; James D. Nogalski, *Redactional Processes in the Book of the Twelve*, BZAW, vol. 218 (Berlin: Walter de Gruyter, 1993) 182–212; Paul L. Redditt, "Zechariah 9–14, Malachi, and the Redaction of the Book of the Twelve," *Forming Prophetic Literature. Essays on Isaiah and the Twelve in Honor of John D. W. Watts*, ed. J. W. Watts and P. R. House, JSOTSup, vol. 235 (Sheffield: Sheffield Academic Press, 1996) 245–68.

the tensions between them that appear throughout the Book of the Twelve. Nevertheless, there is no indication that it was composed for this role. Some have also argued that Malachi was composed as an appendix to the book of Zechariah, insofar as the superscription identifies it as a *maśśāʾ*, "oracle, pronouncement," like those that introduce Zechariah 9–11 and 12–14.[2] But the reference to "Malachi" in Mal 1:1, the relationship of both Zechariah 9–11 and 12–14 to Zechariah 1–8, and the relatively self-contained nature of Malachi indicate that it was composed independently.

Others have argued that the concluding references to the Torah of Moses and Elijah the prophet in Mal 3:22-24 [NRSV: 4:4-6] indicate that Malachi, or at least these sections of the book, were composed to form a conclusion for the Torah and the Prophets in the larger biblical canon.[3] But these statements are integral to the prophet's speech and argument in Mal 3:13-24 [NRSV: 3:13–4:6] in that they form the concluding exhortation of the unit, which constitutes the main thrust of the speech. Furthermore, the two figures are cited because they share many qualities, most importantly they both experienced revelation of Yhwh at Mt. Horeb/Sinai (Exodus 32–33; 1 Kings 19), and both therefore represent ideal figures who adhere to Yhwh's Torah. Insofar as Elijah never died according to biblical tradition, but ascended to heaven in a fiery chariot (2 Kings 2), he apparently is to be identified as "my messenger" (Malachi), who will come to prepare the way for Yhwh on the coming Day of Yhwh when Yhwh will judge the wicked and sustain the righteous. Although the concluding verses of Malachi might be read in relation to the Torah and the Prophets, there is little indication that they were composed with this role in mind.

Nothing is known of the prophet Malachi, and indeed, the Hebrew word *malʾākî* does not even constitute a proper name in Hebrew until long after the composition of the present book. The term means, "my messenger" or "my angel," and apparently functions as a reference to the messenger or angel that Yhwh intends to send to prepare the way for the coming "Day of Yhwh" in which the wicked will be judged and the righteous sustained (Mal 3:1). The term *malʾāk* refers both to human and divine messengers. Examples of human messengers include the messenger that Jacob sent before him to make inquiries of his brother

²For discussion of this point, see Hill, *Malachi* 12–5; see esp. the critical discussion of Brevard Childs, *Introduction to the Old Testament as Scripture* (Philadelphia: Fortress, 1979) 491–2.

³See Redditt, "Zechariah 9–14, Malachi, and the Redaction of the Book of the Twelve"; Petersen, *Zechariah 9–14 and Malachi* 232–3; Rudolph, *Haggai–Sacharja 1–8–Sacharja 9–14–Maleachi* 291.

Esau (Gen 32:4) or the messengers that Moses sent to King Sihon (Deut 2:26). The term also refers to prophets (Isa 42:19; Hag 1:13; 2 Chr 36:15, 16) and priests (Qoh 5:5 [NRSV: 5:6]); indeed, Mal 2:7 identifies the priests as the messengers of YHWH. Examples of divine messengers or angels include those sent by YHWH to guide Abraham's servant to Haran to find a wife for Isaac (Gen 24:7, 40), those sent to Sodom prior to its destruction (Gen 19:1, 15), the messenger sent to Moses in the burning bush (Exod 3:2), the messenger sent to guide Israel through the wilderness at the time of the Exodus from Egypt (23:20; 33:2; Num 20:16), the messenger who spoke with Zechariah throughout his visions (Zech 1:7–6:15), etc. The concluding reference to Elijah in Mal 3:23 [NRSV: 4:5] who is sent to prepare for the coming Day of YHWH (cf. Mal 3:1) indicates that he is to be identified as YHWH's messenger in the book of Malachi. The fact that he does not die and that he was a prophet indicates that he is later conceived to function as part of the heavenly court in which the prophets are said to have stood (see the experience of the prophet Micaiah ben Imlah in 1 Kings 22 or that of Isaiah in Isaiah 6). In later periods, human figures were identified with angelic figures, such as Enoch (who likewise does not die, but "walks with G–d" in Gen 5:22) who is identified as the angel Metatron in texts related to the Heikhalot mystical tradition of the late Second Temple and early Rabbinic periods.[4] The 12th century C.E. Reuchlin manuscript of Targum Jonathan, an Aramaic version of the Prophets that probably dates back to the late Second Temple or early Rabbinic period, identifies Malachi with "Ezra the Scribe" in the superscription of the book.[5] Such an identification makes a great deal of sense because of Ezra's efforts to organize the community around the practice of YHWH's Torah, including both the proper presentation of offerings at the Temple and proper marriage practices, at the time of his return to Jerusalem in the late-fifth or early-fourth century B.C.E. (see Ezra 7–10; Nehemiah 8–10; cf. Nehemiah 13).

Indeed, most scholars date Malachi to the period immediately prior to the return to Jerusalem of Ezra the scribe.[6] Ezra's dates are disputed; his return in the seventh year of the Persian King Artaxerxes (Ezra 7:7) is sometimes taken as 458 B.C.E., the seventh year of Artaxerxes I (reigned,

---

[4] See "Enoch," *Encyclopaedia Judaica* 6:793-5; P. S. Alexander, "Enoch, Third Book of," *ABD* II:522-6; C. Rowland, "Enoch," *DDD²* 301–4.

[5] Kevin J. Cathcart and Robert P. Gordon, *The Targum of the Minor Prophets*, Aramaic Bible, vol. 14 (Wilmington: Michael Glazier, 1989) 229.

[6] For discussion of research on Malachi, see R. J. Coggins, *Haggai, Zechariah, Malachi* 73–80; Julia M. O'Brien, "Malachi in Recent Research," *CR:BS* 3 (1995) 81–94.

465–424 B.C.E.), or as 398 B.C.E., the seventh year of Artaxerxes II (reigned, 404–358 B.C.E.), because of problems in relating his activities and reforms in relation to those of Nehemiah, who arrived in Jerusalem in the twentieth year of Artaxerxes (Neh 2:1), i.e., 445 B.C.E.[7] The situation described in Malachi, in which offerings were not properly presented at the Temple and Jewish men were married to pagan women, corresponds well to conditions in Jerusalem prior to the arrival of Ezra. Previous research on Ezra indicates that he acted in fulfillment of prophetic tradition, particularly that of Isaiah.[8] Insofar as Ezra's reforms addressed the very issues raised in the book of Malachi, it is quite likely that Malachi the prophet spoke in anticipation or support of Ezra's reforms.

The literary form of Malachi supports such a contention. Following the superscription in Mal 1:1, the body of the book in Mal 1:2–3:24 [NRSV: 1:2–4:6] is formulated as a parenetic address to the priests and the people that is designed to persuade them to provide proper reverence for YHWH. Parenesis is a rhetorical speech form that is designed to convince its audience to adopt a set of beliefs or to take action in relation to a specific goal. It employs both positive and negative elements, i.e., exhortation and threat, in order to facilitate its aims. Most scholars follow E. Pfeiffer, who argues that the literary form of Malachi is based in the appearance of six disputation speeches in which the prophet argues with his audience concerning proper observance of YHWH's expectations.[9] Pfeiffer's identification of the form is based on the appearance of three basic elements in each speech: a thesis statement attributed to the audience, a counterthesis advanced by the prophet, and a section of argumentation that is designed to support the prophet's counterthesis over against that of the audience. He identifies six major disputation speeches in the book: Mal 1:2-5 concerning YHWH's love for the people; Mal 1:6–2:9 concerning the mishandling of cultic matters; Mal 2:10-16 concerning lax marriage practices; Mal 2:17–3:5 concerning complaints about YHWH's justice; Mal 3:6-12 concerning the mishandling of Temple tithes; and Mal 3:13-21 [NRSV: 3:13–4:3] concerning doubts about YHWH's justice. Pfeiffer dismissed Mal 3:22-24 [NRSV: 4:5-6] as a secondary appendix to the book. Closer attention to the syntax and the persuasive goals of Malachi's sub-units points to a somewhat modified form of Pfeiffer's thesis in which the prophet presents an argument for greater observance of YHWH's Torah/Instruction or expectations in six basic speeches: Mal 1:2-5 argues that YHWH loves Israel and wishes

---

[7] For discussion of chronological issues in Ezra, see Joseph Blenkinsopp, *Ezra-Nehemiah*, OTL (Philadelphia: Westminster, 1988) 139–44.

[8] Klaus Koch, "Ezra and the Origins of Judaism," *JSS* 19 (1974) 173–97.

[9] E. Pfeiffer, "Die Disputationsworte im Buche Maleachi," *EvT* 12 (1959) 546–68.

to maintain the relationship; Mal 1:6–2:9 argues that the priesthood must honor YHWH properly with proper offerings at the Temple altar; Mal 2:10-16 argues that the people must sanctify themselves with proper marriage practices; Mal 2:17–3:7 argues that YHWH's messenger will come to establish justice when YHWH returns to judge the wicked and sustain the righteous; Mal 3:8-12 argues that the presentation of proper tithes at the Temple will bring YHWH's blessing; and Mal 3:13-24 [NRSV: 3:13–4:6] concludes the sequence by exhorting the people to observe YHWH's Torah. This last sub-unit defines the overall rhetorical goal and organization of the book as a parenetic address to the priests and people that is designed to elicit observance of YHWH's Torah as a basis for the sanctification of the Jerusalem Temple and the nation at large.

The Superscription: 1:1

The superscription for the entire book of Malachi appears in Mal 1:1. In keeping with the typical form of superscriptions, it is structurally and generically distinct from the following material in Mal 1:2–3:24 for which it serves as an introduction.[10] It identifies the balance of the book generically as "an oracle" (*maśśāʾ*), and further qualifies this designation by adding "the word of YHWH to Israel by Malachi." The reason for such a qualification appears to be an attempt to define the meaning of the term *maśśāʾ*. Although *maśśāʾ* is a technical term for a prophetic oracle that appears at various places in the prophetic corpus (Isa 13:1; 14:28; 15:1; 17:1; 19:1; 21:1, 11, 13; 22:1; 23:1; 30:6; Jer 23:33, 34, 36, 38; Ezek 12:10; Nah 1:1; Hab 1:1; Zech 9:1; 12:1; cf. 2 Kgs 9:25), its specific technical meaning and function is not well understood. The term is frequently translated as "burden," and it is derived from the verb root *nśʾ*, "to lift, carry." Apparently the meaning stems from the lifting up of one's voice when an oracular speech is made (e.g., see the use of the verb *nśʾ* to describe Balaam's oracular speech in Num 23:7, 18; 24:3, 15, 20, 21, 23). Weis' recent dissertation examines all usages of the term and argues that the *maśśāʾ* is a type of prophetic discourse that attempts to explain how YHWH's actions are manifested in the realm of human affairs.[11] The specification of the *maśśāʾ* as "the word of YHWH" apparently aids in defining the meaning of this term as an oracular utterance.

---

[10] See Gene M. Tucker, "Prophetic Superscriptions and the Growth of the Canon," *Canon and Authority*, ed. G. W. Coats and B. O. Long (Philadelphia: Fortress, 1977) 56–70.

[11] Weis, "A Definition of the Genre *Maśśāʾ* in the Hebrew Bible"; idem, "Oracle," *ABD* V 28–9.

The superscription further specifies that the oracle is delivered to Israel. Such a designation is noteworthy because, despite the absence of explicit chronological information, the book appears to address the situation of early Persian-period Judah or Yehud during the period after the Temple was rebuilt.[12] The former northern kingdom of Israel had been destroyed long before this period, but the return of Jews to Jerusalem in 522 B.C.E. under Zerubbabel and Joshua ben Jehozadak constituted an attempt to reinstitute both the Temple in Jerusalem and the people of Israel. Although the restoration of the Temple and Jerusalem appears to be largely a Judean matter, the returning exiles apparently saw themselves as the nucleus or remnant of the nation Israel at large and saw the reconstruction of the Temple as the first stage in restoring all of the tribes of Israel to the land (see Haggai and Zechariah, esp. Zechariah 12–14). Certainly, such a perspective is evident in the later return to Jerusalem by Ezra, who sees the people as "the holy seed" (Ezra 9:2) that has the potential to restore the remnant of Israel in keeping with the prophecies of Isaiah (Isa 6:13; 4:2-6; 10:20-26, etc.).[13] The emerging conflict between Samaria, the former capital of the northern kingdom and quite possibly the Persian administrative center for the region at this time, must also be considered.[14] The rebuilding of the Jerusalem Temple apparently threatened Samaritan interests as such a move would signal a Persian attempt to remove Judah/Yehud from Samaritan jurisdiction within the Persian system for administering territories that had been incorporated into the empire (see Ezra 3–6). By directing its oracle to Israel, the book of Malachi may well be intended to address Samaria as well as Judah/Yehud in an effort to establish the Jerusalem Temple as the holy center of all Israel. Such a move would certainly be in keeping with the expectation that the rebuilding of the Temple would signal YHWH's world-wide sovereignty and the restoration of all Israel to the land (see Isaiah 60–62; Haggai; Zechariah).[15] It would also explain the use of figures frequently associated with the northern tribes, such as Moses and Elijah, at the end of the book in Mal 3:22-24 [NRSV: 4:4-6].

The name Malachi is not attested elsewhere in the Hebrew Bible, and there is a great deal of doubt as to whether it is a proper name at

---

[12] For discussion of the date of Malachi, see Coggins, *Haggai, Zechariah, Malachi* 74–5; Hill, *Malachi* 51–84; Petersen, *Zechariah 9–14 and Malachi* 5–6; O'Brien, "Malachi in Recent Research," 87.

[13] See esp. Klaus Koch, "Ezra and The Origins of Judaism," *JSS* 19 (1974) 173–97.

[14] For discussion of the Persian administration of Judah, see H. G. M. Williamson, "Palestine, Administration of (Persian Administration)," *ABD* V:81-6.

[15] Cf. Jon D. Levenson, "The Temple and the World," *JR* 64 (1984) 275–98.

all.[16] The Hebrew term *malʾākî* is derived from the noun *malʾāk*, which generally refers to a "messenger" (e.g., Gen 32:4; Deut 2:26) and frequently designates a "messenger" or "angel" from Yhwh (Gen 19:1, 15; Exod 3:2; 1 Kgs 13:18; Zech 1:9; 12:8). Yhwh's *malʾāk* plays a special role in leading the people through the wilderness at the time of the Exodus as they approach the land of Israel (Exod 23:20-33; 32:34; 33:1-6; Num 20:16; n.b. in Exod 23:23; 33:2, Yhwh refers to the angel as *malʾākî*, "my angel"). Many have speculated that the name *malʾākî* is actually derived from Mal 3:1 in which Yhwh states "behold I am sending my angel *(malʾākî)* to prepare the way for me," which of course recapitulates the figure from the Exodus and entry into the land of Israel. It is noteworthy, however, that Mal 2:7 designates the priest(s) as Yhwh's *malʾāk*.[17] Elsewhere, the term *malʾāk* is used to describe prophets (Isa 42:19; 44:26; 2 Chr 36:15, 16; Hag 1:13; cf. Qoh 5:5). Apparently, the term designates the prophet whose words follow in Mal 1:2–3:21 [NRSV: 1:2–4:3], but his or her name is not given. The discussion of Mal 3:22-24 [NRSV: 4:4-6] below indicates that Elijah the prophet is to be identified with the messenger.

As noted above, the superscription does not provide chronological information. Nevertheless, the book clearly presupposes the existence of a governor (*peḥâ;* Mal 1:8), an Assyrian loan word employed to designate the governors appointed over Judah by the Babylonians (Jer 51:23, 57; Ezek 23:6, 12) and Persians (Neh 2:7; 5:14; Esth 3:12; 9:3; Hag 1:1, 14; 2:2, 21). It also presupposes that the Temple is standing and functional, and that there is dissatisfaction with the priesthood and its operations or questions as to whether the Temple is truly holy. These considerations suggest that the book addresses the situation of Judah in the early Persian period, following the reconstruction of the Temple under Zerubbabel and Joshua ben Jehozadak in 520–515 B.C.E. and prior to the return to Jerusalem of Ezra, who resanctified the Temple and the Jerusalem community, in either 424 or 398 B.C.E.

Finally, because of the similarities of the superscription to Zech 9:1 and 12:1, the anonymity of the prophet and his/her possible association with the angel who speaks with Zechariah, and the placement of Malachi following Zechariah, there has been speculation that the book of Malachi was composed to serve as the third *maśśāʾ* or oracular addition to the book of Zechariah.[18] Several features, however, speak against such a conclusion. First is the internal coherence of the book of Malachi in that it can stand as a self-contained composition. Second is the internal

---

[16] Hill, *Malachi* 135–6; Petersen, *Zechariah 9–14 and Malachi* 165–6.

[17] Cf. Mason, *Preaching the Tradition* 235–9.

[18] See Hill, *Malachi* 12–5, for discussion of this issue.

coherence of the book of Zechariah, especially since Zechariah 9–11 and 12–14 may now be read as coherent structural components of the book rather than as separate blocks that must be read independently from Zechariah 1–8. Third is the difference in the forms of the super-scriptions in Zech 9:1; 12:1; and Mal 1:1. In contrast to Zech 9:1 and 12:1, Mal 1:1 designates Malachi, "my messenger," as the agent through whom YHWH's message is delivered to Israel, whereas the Zecharian texts say nothing about this issue. In contrast to Zechariah 9–11 and 12–14, Malachi does not relate directly to the concerns or scenarios of the book of Zechariah. Rather than articulating an uninterrupted proc-ess by which the Temple will be reestablished as the holy center of crea-tion and the world at large, Malachi addresses problems within the Temple once it has already been reconstructed. Although the book of Malachi may have been placed after Zechariah to address reasons why Zechariah's scenario had not yet taken place, it appears to be an inde-pendently composed and self-contained composition.

Parenetic Address to the Priesthood and People Concerning Proper Reverence for YHWH: Sanctity of Temple and Nation: 1:2–3:21 [NRSV: 1:2–4:3]

The main body of the book of Malachi follows in Mal 1:2–3:21 [NRSV: 1:2–4:3], which is formulated as a parenetic address to the priesthood and people of Israel that calls upon them to maintain the sanctity of the Temple and the people so that YHWH might be properly revered. Paren-esis is a type of address to either an individual or a group that employs both admonition and exhortation in an attempt to persuade its audi-ence with reference to a goal.[19] In the present case, Mal 1:2–3:21 [NRSV: 1:2–4:3] addresses questions concerning YHWH's power and justice that are apparently being raised among the priesthood and people in an ef-fort to persuade them to provide proper reverence for YHWH in the Temple. It would appear that such questions were raised in the after-math of the reconstruction of the Temple, when the earlier promises made by Haggai and Zechariah concerning the nations' recognition of YHWH and the Temple and their restoration of the exiles of Israel and Judah had failed to materialize. Although the Persian empire began to suffer setbacks in this period, such as Darius' defeat by the Greeks at Marathon in 490 or Xerxes' defeat by sea at Salamis in 480, no material change in the fortunes of Judah or Jerusalem had yet taken place, and

---

[19] Sweeney, *Isaiah 1–39* 527.

certainly there was no influx of returning exiles or wealth that would point to the reconstruction of the Temple as a symbol of YHWH's world-wide sovereignty.

The book of Malachi is designed to convince its audience that YHWH indeed loves them and that YHWH will act on behalf of the righteous, i.e., those who honor YHWH properly, to overthrow the wicked. In a groundbreaking study of the literary form of Malachi, Pfeiffer points to the use of disputation forms in the book in which the prophet challenges the people's views of YHWH's lack of interest or power, and attempts to persuade them that YHWH does indeed care and will act on their behalf if they "return" to YHWH and provide YHWH with proper reverence.[20] Pfeiffer identifies three basic elements in the disputation: 1) the basic assertions or theses argued by the prophet; 2) the counter-assertions or countertheses of the opponents that the prophet wishes to challenge; and 3) a lengthy statement of consequences or results in which the prophet attempts to establish his point. Pfeiffer argues that the structure of the book comprises six basic disputations that reflect the prophet's arguments with his opponents: Mal 1:2-5 concerning YHWH's love for the people; 1:6–2:9 concerning mishandling of cultic matters; 2:10-16 concerning lax marriage practices; 2:17–3:5 concerning grumbles about YHWH's justice; 3:6-12 concerning mishandling of Temple tithes; and 3:13-21 [NRSV: 3:13–4:3] again concerning doubts about YHWH's justice. His work has since been refined by scholars who have noted that Malachi addresses both priests and people and that the basic purpose of the speeches is to instruct or persuade the audience.[21] Indeed, Mason points to the sermonic elements of Malachi[22] and Petersen notes that the speeches are analogous to Greek diatribes in which only one party speaks in an attempt to make a point.[23] There is an argumentative character to the book, but it does not presuppose open debate as Pfeiffer postulated. Instead, it is composed in the form of a sermon or diatribe that attempts to dismantle the views of those who doubt YHWH by asserting that the people themselves are to blame for YHWH's failure to act. In short, it attempts to persuade the people to take action themselves in the expectation that YHWH will respond in kind.

When these refinements are considered together with closer attention to the syntactical form of the surface structure of the text, a somewhat

---

[20] Egon Pfeiffer, "Die Disputationsworte im Buche Maleachi (Ein Beitrag zur formgeschichtliche Struktur," *EvT* 12 (1959) 546–68.

[21] See Petersen, *Zechariah 9–14 and Malachi* 29–34, for a summary of the discussion.

[22] Mason, *Preaching the Tradition* 235–9.

[23] Petersen, *Zechariah 9–14 and Malachi* 31–4.

different assessment of the literary form of Malachi emerges. Malachi is indeed formulated as a series of speeches in which the prophet attempts to persuade his audience that YHWH does indeed love Israel and that YHWH will act on Israel's behalf. At the same time, Malachi points to issues within the community that need to be addressed, particularly marriage practices and the presentation of offerings at the Temple, in an effort to persuade his audience that YHWH's failure to act is the direct result of the people's failure to honor YHWH properly. The argument is developed in five basic steps with a concluding exhortation. In Mal 1:2-5, the prophet argues that YHWH does indeed love Israel and that Edom's demise demonstrates what happens when YHWH does not love a nation. In Mal 1:6–2:9, the prophet accuses the priests of failing to honor YHWH properly and demands that they observe the covenant of Levi and provide proper offerings. In Mal 2:10-16, the prophet argues that the people must sanctify themselves with proper marriage practices. In Mal 2:17–3:7, the prophet accuses the people of wearying YHWH by questioning YHWH's justice, and calls upon them to return by arguing that YHWH will send a "messenger" to judge the wicked. In Mal 3:8-12, the prophet accuses the people of robbing YHWH, and calls upon them to present proper tithes at the Temple. Malachi 3:13-24 [NRSV: 3:13–4:6] constitutes the concluding exhortation in which the prophet accuses the people of speaking harsh words against YHWH by asserting that YHWH does not act on their behalf. He argues that YHWH has already recorded the righteous who will be spared when YHWH comes to judge the wicked on the Day of YHWH. Insofar as YHWH has already decided the matter, the passage serves as a motivation to the audience to be counted among those who are considered to be righteous. Employing a speech by YHWH, he asserts that YHWH remembers who is righteous and will come to punish the wicked. He calls upon the people to remember the Torah of Moses and promises that Elijah the prophet will come before the day of YHWH to turn parents and children to one another once again so that the land will not be cursed.

The Prophet's First Speech:
Argument that YHWH Loves Israel: 1:2-5

The prophet's first speech appears in Mal 1:2-5 and focuses on the assertion that YHWH loves Israel. The passage is clearly demarcated at the beginning by the prophet's presentation of YHWH's statement, "I have loved you," and it concludes in verse 5 with the prophet's assertion that "YHWH is great beyond all the borders of Israel." The presentation of YHWH's statement in verse 6 is syntactically independent from verses 2-5, and turns to the topic of the proper respect due to YHWH. Overall, Mal 1:2-5 is formulated as a disputation speech in which the prophet quotes YHWH and points to the experience of Edom to counter assertions that YHWH does not love Israel. It begins in verse 2aα with the above-mentioned quote in which YHWH asserts love for Israel, and it continues in verse 2aβ with the prophet's presentation of a counter-assertion that has been raised among the people, "but you say, 'how have you loved us?'" Thus, verse 2a sets out the parameters of the issue to be addressed. Verses 2b-5 then provide the prophet's argumentation by which he attempts to demonstrate that YHWH does indeed love the people.

The prophet's argumentation presupposes the destruction of Edom that took place from the initial Babylonian assaults against Edom in 552 B.C.E. during the reign of Nabonidus through the fourth and third centuries when the Edomites were displaced from their land by various Arab tribes, such as the Qedarites and later the Nabateans.[24] Although O'Brien argues that this passage presupposes Babylonian actions against Edom,[25] the clear references to continuing sacrifices at the Temple throughout the book demonstrate that this passage must be read in relation to the Persian period when the Arab threats to Edom's possession of the land began to materialize.

Verses 2b-3 begin with the prophet's quotation of a rhetorical question by YHWH, "is not Esau Jacob's brother?" The use of the rhetorical question of course functions as an assertion that Esau, the eponymous ancestor of Edom is indeed the brother of Jacob, the eponymous ancestor of Israel. This assertion draws upon the Jacob traditions in Genesis 25–35 in which Jacob competes with his first-born fraternal twin brother Esau for the rights of the first-born and the blessing of their father, Isaac, that will enable him to claim the covenant of his ancestors with YHWH. The appearance of the oracular formula, *nĕʾum yhwh*, "oracle of YHWH," lends divine authority to this statement and to the prophet's argument. YHWH's following statements then elaborate upon the significance of the relationship between Jacob and Esau or Israel and Edom. In the first instance, YHWH asserts, "I love Jacob, and Esau I hated." This plays upon the motif of sibling rivalry and competition that provides the foundation for the narratives concerning Jacob and Esau. It draws particularly on the assertions of Gen 25:28 that Isaac

---

[24] For a summary discussion of the history of Edom, see J. R. Bartlett, "Edom," *ABD* II:287-95.

[25] Julia M. O'Brien, *Priest and Levite in Malachi*, SBLDS, vol. 121 (Atlanta: Scholars Press, 1990) 113–33.

loved Esau whereas Rebekah loved Jacob and the role reversal initiated by Rebekah in which Jacob wins the blessing of the father despite his preference for Esau. The resulting statement in Gen 27:41 that Esau hated Jacob because of his father's blessing must also be considered. YHWH's statements in Mal 1:2-3 reiterate the role reversal and emotions of the Genesis narrative as preface to the contemporary experience of both nations, i.e., the descendants of the two brothers in the Genesis narrative. YHWH's statement continues by describing the desolation inflicted upon Esau which leaves his heritage as a desert fit only for jackals.

Verses 4-5 then point to YHWH's intentions to destroy Edom even if the Edomites attempt to rebuild. Verse 4aα begins with a conditional statement that quotes Edom, "If Edom says, 'We are shattered but we will rebuild the ruins,'" and then follows in verses 4aβ-5 with the prophet's presentation of YHWH's response to such an attempt. The prophet begins with the messenger formula, "thus says YHWH of Hosts," which reinforces the identity of YHWH as the speaker. YHWH then asserts that if the Edomites attempt to rebuild, then YHWH will tear down whatever they erect to ensure that their land remains desolate. This prompts a comparison of Edom's experience with that of Israel's. Whereas people will say that Edom is a wicked country with which YHWH is angry, the people of Israel will see YHWH's greatness even beyond the borders of their own land. The contrasting fates of the two nations during this period of course serves the prophet's argument, i.e., Edom is destroyed whereas Israel remains in its own land. Surely YHWH loves Israel; look at what happens to a nation that YHWH hates. By this means, the prophet asserts that YHWH's relationship with Israel continues and that assertions that YHWH does not love Israel must be cast aside.

The Prophet's Second Speech:
Argument that the Priesthood must Honor YHWH: 1:6–2:9

The prophet's second speech appears in Mal 1:6–2:9, in which he charges the priests with profaning YHWH's name by presenting improper offerings at the Temple altar. He then calls upon them to fulfill their cultic obligations by presenting proper offerings as defined in YHWH's Torah or instruction. The passage is demarcated initially in verse 6 by the prophet's presentation of a statement by YHWH, which states the principle that YHWH deserves honor and respect just as a father or master deserves honor and respect from sons and servants.

This statement is not joined syntactically to the preceding verses 2-5, and the issue of YHWH's honor continues through Mal 2:9 in which YHWH threatens to despise the priests for failing to observe YHWH's Torah properly. Malachi 2:10, which is not syntactically joined to the preceding material, introduces a new concern with the observance of proper marriage. The structure of Mal 1:6–2:9 is based on the prophet's attempt to establish the failure of the priesthood to honor YHWH properly in Mal 1:6-8. This text is followed by two sections in Mal 1:9-14 and 2:1-9, each of which begins with the conjunctive particle, *wĕʿattâ*, "and now," which respectively call upon the priests to implore YHWH's favor and to observe YHWH's commandment.

The prophet lays out the basic charges against the priests in Mal 1:6-8. He makes extensive use of rhetorical questions to make his point beginning with a basic statement of issues in verse 6a-bα. The discourse begins in verse 6a with YHWH's assertion that "a son honors a father and a servant his master" (contra NRSV). Such an assertion is designed as the first step in a rhetorical strategy to persuade the audience to accept the primary contention of the passage, that YHWH deserves the respect and honor of the priests, by first raising a principle that is universally acknowledged by the audience, that sons honor their fathers and servants respect their masters. Having established this principle at the outset, the prophet then turns in verse 6bα to a pair of rhetorical questions by YHWH that employ the metaphors of father and master to assert that YHWH indeed does not receive the requisite honor and respect from the priests. By stating the conditions, "if I am a father" and "if I am a master," YHWH establishes the metaphor, and by questioning "where is my honor?" and "where is my respect?" YHWH contends that proper honor and respect are not given. The concluding speech formula both establishes the identity of YHWH as the speaker and the priests as the addressee. It also contributes to the overall contention of the passages by identifying the priests as "the priests who despise my name."

The passage then challenges potential objections by presenting in verses 6bβ-7 two hypothetical statements of defense on the part of the priests together with YHWH's charges that negate any potential defense. Both are presented as questions on the part of the priests that ask for proof for these charges followed by YHWH's answers that provide the proof. The first appears in verses 6bβ-7aα in which YHWH quotes a question that might be posed by the priests, "and you say, 'how have we despised your name?' " YHWH answers immediately with the assertion that they have brought impure or improper food offerings to YHWH's altar. This would refer to meat that is not properly selected and slaughtered as well as other offerings, such as grain and wine, that are not properly prepared in accordance with the laws of kashrut (the Jewish dietary and sacrificial laws) as stipulated in YHWH's Torah (e.g., Leviticus 1–7; 11; 17; 22–23; 27; Deuteronomy 14). The second question and answer in verse 7aβ-b, "and you say, 'how have we defiled you?' By your saying that YHWH's table is despised," builds upon the first. The Temple is considered to be the holy center of creation, and its service, which calls for the proper presentation of pure, unblemished sacrificial animals and other choice foods to YHWH, is considered to be a symbolic representation of order and stability in creation. YHWH provides such food to human beings from creation as a means to support human life, and humans are thereby obligated to acknowledge YHWH's action by presenting choice examples in return. To disrupt that service in any way is to disrupt creation and thus to despise YHWH who creates order and stability in the world.

The passage concludes with three further rhetorical questions in verse 8 that are designed to establish the guilt of the priests in this matter. Verse 8a contains a pair of questions formulated to convey hypothetical situations, "and when you bring a blind (offering) to sacrifice, is there no evil? And when you bring a lame or sick (offering), is there no evil?" Once again, these questions point to the need to present animals without any defects to the altar—blindness, lameness, and sickness all mark defective offerings—as an offering should reflect the ideal of YHWH's creation rather than flaws. It further presupposes that the people are bringing the best of their herd or flock for sacrifice rather than animals that are sick or defective in some way. Having established this point, the prophet presents YHWH's last proposal and question in verse 8b, in which YHWH proposes to the priests that they try to present such offerings to the Persian-appointed governor of the province so that they will see whether or not he accepts such treatment. The answer is obviously that he will not. In effect, YHWH demands at least as much respect as the governor. The concluding speech formula certifies that YHWH is indeed the speaker.

Malachi 1:9-14 then turns to an elaboration of the charges made in verses 6-8. As noted above, the passage begins with the particle *wĕʿattâ*, "and now," which introduces a command to the priests to implore YHWH's favor so that YHWH will show favor. This presents a deliberate contrast with the prior command to bring defective offerings to the Persian-appointed governor of the land, and it is designed to demonstrate a similar result, i.e., YHWH will reject such overtures. This is clear in verse 9b where YHWH states that the priests are at fault (literally, "from your hands this has happened") prior to asking a rhetorical question that asserts that YHWH will not show favor. The YHWH speech formula at the end of verse 9 certifies this as a statement by YHWH. A second rhetorical question in verse 10a, "who among you will close the doors so that my altar will not be kindled in vain?" charges that no one among the priests will take responsibility to stop the improper sacrifices outlined in verses 6-8. The doors of course refer to the doors of the Temple structure itself (see 1 Kgs 6:31-36; Ezek 41:21-26) which remain open while the altar is in use to represent YHWH's presence in the Holy of Holies or the inner sanctuary (cf. 1 Kings 8; 2 Chr 5:2–7:11). Clearly, the prophet charges that the offering of improper sacrifice "before YHWH" dishonors YHWH and should be stopped.

Verses 10b-14 then turn to a sustained discourse on the reasons why YHWH has no desire to be treated in such a contemptuous manner, i.e., because YHWH is the great king among all the nations. The passage begins with YHWH's statement, certified by the presence of a speech formula in mid-statement, "I have no pleasure from you . . . and I will not accept an offering from your hands." The term "pleasure" (*ḥepeṣ*) also means "desire," and conveys YHWH's disinterest in such actions. The reasons are then spelled out in verses 11-14, beginning with the *kî* clause in verse 11aα, "for *(kî)* from the rising of the sun to its setting my name is great among the nations . . ." The statement continues with reference to the various offerings of incense, meat, and grain that are presented to YHWH throughout the world because YHWH is recognized and respected among the nations. Such a contention recalls YHWH's role as creator and sovereign of all the earth, a role which is symbolized by the Temple and its service, and indicates that although YHWH is revered throughout all the world, such reverence is not to be found at home in YHWH's own Temple. Verses 12-13 then return to specific charges against the priests. Verse 12 restates the basic charge with a second masculine plural statement directed to the priests, "and you profane it when you say 'the table of my L–rd is defiled, and its food is despised.'" There is a potential pun in the designation of YHWH's table as "defiled" because the Hebrew word *mĕgōʾāl* is based on the root *gʾl*, which means both "to be defiled" and "to be redeemed." Apparently, the relationship between these two meanings derives from the fundamental meaning of the root as "to be released," i.e., to be released from sacred service means to be defiled and to be released from threat means to be redeemed. The English translation, "and its food may be despised," hides a textual problem in the Hebrew, *wĕnîbô nibzeh ʾoklô*, literally, "and its fruit is despised its food." Apparently, two subjects *wĕnîbô*, "and its fruit," and *ʾoklô*, "its food," appear for the same verb. Because *nîb*, "fruit," is rarely used, particularly in relation to sacrifice, it would seem that *ʾoklô* was added to the text as a gloss to define *wĕnîbô*.[26]

[26] Contra. Rudolph, *Haggai–Sacharja 1–8–Sacharja 9–14–Maleachi* 259, who argues that *wĕnîbô* is a dittography for *nizbeh*.

YHWH then illustrates the contemptuous behavior of the priests in verse 13 by continuing with a second person address that initially charges them with stating how wearisome all of this is and then continues by portraying their "sniffing" at the whole matter and bringing improper sacrifices. Among the sacrifices are offerings that have been improperly taken from the people as well as those that are lame and sick. A final rhetorical question asserts that YHWH does not accept the grain offering "from your hand." Two occurrences of the speech formula again certify these as statements by YHWH.

The entire sequence concludes in verse 14 with YHWH's curse against those who cheat. The use of the term *ʾārûr*, "cursed," recounts the language of Deuteronomy 27 and 28:15-46 in which the Levites, under the supervision of Moses, charged the people to observe YHWH's Torah by reciting the various punishments that they would suffer if they failed to do so. The use of the term *nôkēl*, "cheat, one who deceives," indicates the prophet's evaluation of those who have appropriate male and female sheep in their flock and yet offer defective animals in sacrifice to YHWH. YHWH's concluding statement, "for I am a great king . . . and my name is feared/respected among the nations," recalls the language employed by the Assyrian, Babylonian, and Persian monarchs who conquered and ruled Judah from the eighth through the fourth centuries B.C.E. Again, the comparison with the Persian-appointed governor is germane as the prophet asserts that surely YHWH deserves greater recognition than the agents of foreign rule.

Malachi 2:1-9 likewise begins with the introductory particle, *wĕʿattâ*, "and now," in presenting the prophet's statement to the priests in verse 1 that "this command" is enjoined upon them. The immediate context does not specify what "this command" might be, but the larger context of Mal 1:6–2:9 makes it clear that the command is to present proper offerings to YHWH at the Temple altar and thereby to show YHWH proper respect or reverence as noted above.

The prophet's injunction in verse 1 then introduces his presentation of YHWH's speeches in verses 2-9 in which YHWH threatens the priests with punishment if they do not observe their own priestly covenant to honor YHWH properly and thereby to convey true Torah or instruction to the people. The presentation begins with YHWH's statement in verse 2 that warns the priests of the consequences of failing to honor YHWH. The statement is formulated as a first person speech by YHWH directed to a second person masculine plural audience that must be identified as the priests mentioned in verse 1. The speech formula in the first part of the verse indicates that the prophet presents YHWH's speech. YHWH's statement is also formulated conditionally, much like an example of case law (e.g., Deut 13:2-6) or more specifically the conditional statements in the blessings and curses of Deuteronomy that warn of the consequences for failing to observe YHWH's commandments (e.g., Deut 28:15, 46, 58).[27] It begins with a double protasis that states the possibility that the priests might not listen to YHWH or pay attention to YHWH's command to give honor to YHWH's name. The Hebrew idiom, "to lay upon the heart," means "to be careful," or "to pay (close) attention." The apodosis of the statement then defines the consequences of such neglect, i.e., YHWH will send a curse against the priests. The term *mĕʾērâ*, "curse," appears infrequently in biblical Hebrew, but it does appear among the covenant curses of Deuteronomy in Deut 28:20 (translated in NRSV as "disaster") in which Moses conveys the consequences for Israel if they fail to obey YHWH's commandments. Likewise, YHWH's statement, "and I will curse your blessings," recalls the contrast between the blessings and curses that the people may expect in Deuteronomy 28 depending upon whether or not they obey YHWH's commands. Indeed, the language of this passage appears to presuppose the entire covenant between YHWH and Israel as articulated in Deuteronomy,[28] especially since Deuteronomy assigns special responsibilities and privileges to the priests who are to guide the people (see Deut 12:13-19; 14:22-29; 17:8-13, 18, 18:1-8; 20:1-9).[29] The concluding statement of the verse, "and indeed I have cursed it because you are not careful" (cf. NRSV), reiterates the charge that the priests are not doing their job and are therefore responsible for any lack of "blessing" or agricultural produce that the people might suffer.

Having stated at the outset the basic principle of curse for failure to observe YHWH's commands, verses 3-9 then turn to a sermonic elaboration of this basic point. The prophet begins with YHWH's statement, "behold, I am rebuking the seed, and I will spread dung upon your face, the dung of your festival sacrifices." The NRSV misunderstands the use of the Hebrew word *zeraʿ*, "seed," as "offspring"; rather, the term refers to the agricultural produce of the land that will be cursed if the priests fail to act properly in teaching the people how to honor YHWH (cf. Deuteronomy 28). The text does not speak simply to the self-interest of the priests or their self-perpetuation as the NRSV translation implies.

---

[27] See especially Moshe Weinfeld, *Deuteronomy and the Deuteronomic School* (Winona Lake: Eisenbrauns, 1992) 59–157, for discussion of Deuteronomy's blessings and curses.

[28] Steven L. McKenzie and Howard M. Wallace, "Covenant Themes in Malachi," *CBQ* 45 (1983) 549–63.

[29] For discussion of the Deuteronomy's law code and the role of the priests, see my forthcoming *King Josiah of Judah: The Lost Messiah of Israel* (New York: Oxford University Press).

Again, it is the priests' responsibility to instruct the people in proper observance of YHWH's will so that the welfare of the people and the land might be ensured. The reference to spreading dung on the faces of the priests is a metaphorical expression of their lack of fitness to serve at YHWH's altar. Basically, the statement employs one of the most shocking images of ritual impurity to convey the failure of the priests to honor YHWH properly. In this respect, it is noteworthy that the "dung," or entrails of the sacrificial animal, is to be removed before the animal is brought to the altar for sacrifice (see Exod 29:14; Lev 4:11; 8:17; 16:27; Num 19:5) in order to ensure the purity of the sacrifice. The reference to the "dung of your festival sacrifices" is a metaphorical image that charges the priests with not preparing the festival sacrifices properly. The concluding statement of the verse reads literally, "and he shall bear you unto it" (contra NRSV), and must be understood as the prophet's statement that YHWH will carry the priests to the dung for disposal just as the priests are to carry away the dung for disposal before the animal is presented at the altar.

Verses 4-7 then turn to the priest's responsibility to observe the terms of their covenant or the covenant of Levi. Verse 4 begins with YHWH's statement to the priests that they should know that YHWH has enjoined them with this commandment. The responsibilities of the Levites are not described specifically with the term "covenant," but the role and the responsibilities are made very clear in Numbers 3–4 (see also Numbers 8; Exod 32:25-29 [cf. Numbers 14]; Numbers 15–20). The concluding speech formula identifies these statements as YHWH's.

Verses 5-7 then define the covenant of Levi as an exchange in which YHWH grants life and peace to the people in return for respect or reverence and awe for YHWH's name on the part of the people. The priests, of course, are responsible for conveying that sense of YHWH's holiness through proper instruction and ritual practice. The teaching role of the Levites is conveyed in verse 6 which states that "true Torah (instruction) was in his mouth, and no wrong was found on his lips. He walked with me in integrity and uprightness, and he turned many from iniquity." The English term "integrity" is employed for *šālôm*, literally "peace" or "wholeness," and "uprightness" is employed for *mîšôr*, "straightness, level" (cf. Pss 45:7; 67:5 [NRSV: 67:4]; Isa 11:4). Again, the statement stresses the responsibilities of the priests with regard to the proper instruction of the people. Verse 7 employs a causative statement to emphasize this role, i.e., the people are to observe knowledge on the lips of the priest and they are to seek Torah from his mouth. The concluding statement of verse 7b well conveys this representative and intermediary function of the priests between the people and YHWH, i.e., the priest is "the messenger of YHWH of Hosts." The term "messenger" is of course the Hebrew *mal'ak*, "messenger, angel," which stands as the basis of the name Malachi. As representative of YHWH, the priest functions much like an angel in carrying out the ritual of the Temple as the holy center of creation. The ritual of the Temple and the role of the priests were considered to be analogous to the ritual of YHWH's heavenly court and the role of the angels in maintaining the stability of that court.[30]

Verses 8-9 then turn to YHWH's charges that the priests have not carried out their properly assigned role and the consequences that will result from that failure. Verse 8 begins with an emphatic "and you" (*wĕgam ʾattâ*) that conveys a series of basic charges by YHWH to the priests of the violation of that covenant, "and you have turned aside from the way; you have caused many to stumble by your instruction; you have corrupted the covenant of Levi." Again, the presence of the speech formula at the end of verse 8 identifies this as a statement by YHWH. Verse 9 employs an element of irony or reversal when YHWH states that the priests will be despised and abased before all the people. The use of the term "despised" (*nibzîm*) reiterates the language in verses 6 and 7, i.e., "O priests who despise (*bôzê*) my Name"; "how have we despised (*bāzînû*) your Name"; "it is despised (*nibzeh*). Just as the priests have despised YHWH, so YHWH despises them. The causative statement in verse 9b reiterates the basic charges of verse 2, i.e., the priests are not observing YHWH's will. The reference to their "showing partiality" suggests that they are not consistent in their practice and teaching of Torah.

The Prophet's Third Speech:
Argument that the People must Sanctify themselves
with Proper Marriage Practice: 2:10-16

The prophet's third speech appears in Mal 2:10-16 in which he charges the men of the community with violating the covenant of their ancestors by marrying foreign women. He argues that such practice profanes the name or sanctity of G–d because it constitutes misuse of "holy seed" and results in the betrayal of the women involved in such

---

[30] See Jon D. Levenson, "The Jerusalem Temple in Devotional and Visionary Experience," *Jewish Spirituality: From the Bible Through the Middle Ages*, ed. Arthur Green (New York: Crossroad, 1988) 32–61; Moshe Weinfeld, "Zion and Jerusalem as Religious and Political Capital: Ideology and Utopia," *The Poet and the Historian: Essays in Literary and Historical Biblical Criticism*, ed. Richard E. Friedman (HSM 26; Chico: Scholars Press, 1983) 75–115.

marriages who must be divorced. Thus, the issue demonstrates the interrelationship of cultic and moral concerns. It is noteworthy that the practice of marrying foreign women was a major issue in the time of Nehemiah and Ezra (see Ezra 9–10; Neh 13:1-3, 23-30) as was the previously-addressed issue of presenting proper offerings at the Jerusalem Temple (Ezra 8; Nehemiah 10; 12:44-47; 13:4-22, 31). Marriage to foreign women was a major issue at this time because of the threat of assimilation that such a practice poses to the identity of the Jewish people. Intermarriage with the seven Canaanite nations is prohibited in Exod 34:11-16 and Deut 7:1-6 because such marriages tend to create a mixed religious environment in which the worship of foreign gods is introduced into the community. Abraham's relationship with Hagar (Genesis 16; 21) and Sarah's or Rebekah's potential relationships with the Pharaoh and the Philistine Abimelech are seen as a potential threat to the covenant (see Genesis 12; 20; 26), and care is taken to make sure that both Isaac and Jacob married women from Abraham's family in Haran rather than Canaanite women as Esau did (Genesis 24; 26:34-35; 28:1-9). Judah's identity as an Israelite line is protected by Tamar, who disguises herself as a prostitute to have relations with her father-in-law following the deaths of Judah's sons who married Canaanite women or otherwise failed to have relations with her (Genesis 38). Samson is betrayed by Philistine women (Judges 13–16), and Solomon's marriages to foreign women are identified as the basic cause of the division of the kingdom following his death because his foreign wives are said to have turned his heart away from Yhwh (see 1 Kings 11, esp. vv. 1-13). Indeed, Neh 13:24 notes that the children of such mixed marriages were unable to speak the language of Judah, and Neh 13:26-27 cites the example of Solomon as part of an argument against such practice.

The reasons for such intermarriages within the early-Persian period Jewish community must also be examined, as it is hardly likely that they were taking place simply for sexual gratification. The conflicts concerning the restoration of Jerusalem and the Temple that broke out between various Samarian authorities and the early groups of Jews who returned with Zerubbabel and Joshua ben Jehozadak must be considered. Ezra 4–6 relates the successful defense against efforts by the Samarian officers, Rehum and Shimshai, as well as by Tattenai, the governor of the Persian province "Across the River," to halt the building of the Temple. Nehemiah 2–6 likewise relates the successful defense against the efforts of Sanballat the Horonite and Tobiah the Ammonite to mobilize the pagan people of the land and the Persian government to halt the restoration of Jerusalem. The latter instance is especially noteworthy because Neh 13:28-29 notes that Jehoiada, son of the high priest Eliashib, was the son-in-law of Sanballat.

Why would Jewish men marry foreign women during this period? It should be noted that 2 Kings 17 claims that the territory of northern Israel was depopulated by the Assyrians and resettled with people from foreign nations who practiced syncretistic forms of Israelite religion. Although such a claim may well be polemical, Jews who returned to the land of Israel from Babylonian exile in the early Persian period may well have married into the local population which would see itself as Israelite. Indeed, archaeological evidence, such as the discovery of numerous mother-goddess figurines, indicates that the Israelite and Judean populations normally engaged in a great deal of practice, both prior to the exile and afterwards, that would have been considered syncretistic by the standards of the Jerusalem priesthood.[31] Furthermore, Israelite law took account of the presence of foreigners within the community by allowing such "resident aliens" to live in Israel as long as they observed the laws of YHWH (see Exod 12:19; 20:10; 23:12; Lev 16:29; 17:8; 25:47; Num 9:14; 15:14; Deut 1:16; 16:11; 26:11). In later times, such persons were considered converts to Judaism. Nevertheless, the wide variety of religious practice evident among the people in various periods would have prompted charges of apostasy, especially during the period when Jerusalem and the Temple were being reestablished and attempts to define consistent and normative cultic practice were undertaken. The issue may be due in part to differing notions of proper Jewish practice and identity within the early-Persian period Jewish community.[32]

Second, it must be recognized that a major portion of the population of Israel had been removed from the land by the Babylonian invasions, and that the early-Persian period was a time when Jews began to return. Although there may well have been an Israelite/Jewish population in the land during the period of the Babylonian exile, there still would have been a significant drop in the population that would have served as an impetus for other groups to move in and begin taking portions of the land for themselves.[33] The identity of Sanballat the

[31] See Ephraim Stern, *Material Culture of the Land of the Bible in the Persian Period, 538–332 B.C.* (Warminster: Aris and Phillips, 1982).

[32] See Morton Smith, *Palestinian Parties and Politics that Shaped the Old Testament* (New York: Columbia University Press, 1971), who argues that a "YHWH alone" party emerged within the Persian period Jewish community and ultimately suppressed other Jewish groups with different understandings of the character of YHWH and Judaism. See also, Shemaryahu Talmon, "The Emergence of Jewish Sectarianism in the Early Second Temple Period," *Ancient Israelite Religion: Essays in Honor of Frank Moore Cross*, ed. P. D. Miller et al. (Philadelphia: Fortress, 1987) 587– 616.

[33] See Hans Barstad, *The Myth of the Empty Land* (Oslo: Scandinavian University Press, 1996), who correctly argues that an Israelite population continued to exist in

Horonite, Tobiah the Ammonite, and Geshem the Arab are particularly important because each of these groups represents population elements of the Trans-Jordan, i.e., Horites were pre-Edomite inhabitants of the Trans-Jordan (Gen 14:6; 36:20-30; Deut 2:12, 22), Ammonites were the people of ancient Ammon in the Trans-Jordan, and the Arabs represented groups who were moving into Edom during this period. Indeed, Edom apparently was displaced from its land by various Arab groups, most notably the Nabateans, during the 6th–2nd centuries B.C.E., and ultimately resettled in the southern portions of Judah.[34] The identity of these figures is especially important as Mal 1:2-5 begins by noting YHWH's "hatred" of Esau, the ancestor of Edom, and the destruction of that nation. Similar encroachments were made from the Philistine regions, where many northern Israelites had been resettled by the Assyrians.[35] Clearly, the possession of land and the identity of the people who possessed it were major issues in the land of Israel during the early Persian period, particularly as the Edomites were displaced and began to move into Judean territory.

Third, many interpreters take this passage to be a prohibition of divorces because YHWH states in verse 16, "'for (I) hate divorce,' says YHWH of Hosts."[36] And yet it is clear that ancient Israelite law envisions the possibility of divorce in Deut 24:1-4 when it discusses the issue of remarriage once a divorce has taken place. Furthermore, Deut 22:29 prohibits a man from divorcing a woman whom he was compelled to marry by having intercourse with her, and Deut 22:19 prohibits a man from divorcing a wife whom he falsely accused of not being a virgin at the time of the marriage. Both laws presuppose the possibility and the legality of divorce. One might also note that Abraham is able to "send away" or "divorce" his concubine Hagar at Sarah's insistence; the issue is not simply one of intermarriage. Insofar as Malachi calls for observance of proper Torah throughout the book, it is difficult to understand how it could prohibit divorces. Indeed, Mal 2:15 states that YHWH "hates" divorce; it does not say that YHWH prohibits it.

---

the land during the period of the exile, although he overstates the continuity in social organization.

[34] See Bartlett, "Edom," *ABD* II:287-95.

[35] Seymor Gitin, "Tel Miqne-Ekron: A Type Site for the Inner Coastal Plain in the Iron Age II Period," *Recent Excavations in Israel: Studies in Iron Age Archaeology*, ed. S. Gitin and W. Dever, AASOR, vol. 49 (Winona Lake: Eisenbrauns, 1989) 23–58, who argues that the Assyrians resettled northern Israelites in Philistia to support a massive olive oil industry.

[36] For a thorough discussion of Malachi and divorce, see Gordon Paul Hugenberger, *Marriage as a Covenant: A Study of Biblical Law and Ethics Governing Marriage, Developed from the Perspective of Malachi*, VTSup, vol. 52 (Leiden: Brill, 1994).

Interestingly, many interpreters presuppose a situation in which Jewish men are betraying the wives of their youth (Mal 2:14-15) in order to marry "the daughter(s) of a foreign god" (Mal 2:11).[37] Why would such divorces take place? Indeed, the polygamous norm of ancient Judean society would render such divorces unnecessary. If a man was already married to a Jewish wife, there would be no need to divorce her in order to marry another woman, Jewish or not. Likewise, the books of Ezra and Nehemiah do not presuppose that Jewish men divorced their Jewish wives in order to marry foreign women; rather, Ezra and Nehemiah portray a situation in which Jewish men are called upon to divorce their foreign wives. There is no hint that Jewish women were divorced by their husbands in this period so that they might marry foreign women. Even Abraham did not have to divorce Sarah in order to take Hagar as a concubine; Sarah was the one who asked him to take Hagar. Of course there was tension in the relationship, and Abraham sent Hagar away only at Sarah's insistence when Hagar's son Ishmael was perceived to be a threat to Isaac's status.

The pattern of argumentation points to the issue of marriage to foreign women as the primary issue under discussion, and divorce enters the picture only as the necessary consequence of such a union. In keeping with the disputational form of Malachi's speeches, the prophet begins in verse 10 by quoting three rhetorical questions that represent the views of those who would contend that marriage to foreign women is acceptable. The first question, "Have we not all one father?" points to the basic equality of all human beings as descendants of Adam (and Eve) and is therefore designed to disarm any argument that human beings must somehow be distinguished. Even when considered in the context of Malachi's concern with Esau and Edomites, it must be noted that Esau and Jacob were both sons of the same father, Isaac, and even Isaac and Ishmael were both sons of the same father, Abraham. And yet Jacob and Isaac bore the covenant of their fathers, whereas Esau and Ishmael did not. The second question, "Has not one G–d created us?" functions in a similar manner by pointing back to the creation of all human beings initially in Adam (and Eve), and thereby pointing to their essential equality. The third question, "Why then are we faithless to one another, profaning the covenant of our ancestors?" then builds naturally upon the previous two by getting to the heart of the matter, i.e., if we are all equal, how then do we betray each other and our covenant with G–d? The connection is especially clear in that the Hebrew term *ʾăbōtênû*, here translated by NRSV as "our ancestors," means literally "our fathers."

[37] E.g., Hill, *Malachi* 222–3, 226–7.

The prophet's rebuttal to this assertion then appears in verses 11-16. It begins with two countertheses that are stated in verses 11-12 and 13. The first is the prophet's assertion that Judah has acted treacherously by committing an abomination in Israel and Jerusalem. The Hebrew term *tôʿēbâ*, "abomination," refers generally to ritual and ethical improprieties that render a person unfit to enter the Temple and present offerings to YHWH (cf. Psalms 15; 24, which state the qualities of one who would stand before YHWH in the Temple). The term may refer to improper or unclean sacrifices (e.g., Exod 8:22 [NRSV: 8:26]), unclean food (Deut 14:3), worship of idols (Isa 41:24), offering children (Deut 12:31), objectionable speech (Prov 8:7), the prayer of the wicked (Prov 28:9), unchastity (Lev 18:22), etc. In the present case, the context makes it clear that marriage to a foreign woman is an abomination because it means marriage to a woman who is identified with a foreign god. The NRSV translates verse 11b, "for Judah has profaned the sanctuary of YHWH, which he loves, and has married the daughter of a foreign god." The Hebrew term *qōdeš*, here translated as "sanctuary," refers more generally to "holiness," in this case, the holiness of YHWH. The statement, "which he loves," more likely qualifies Judah rather than YHWH as indicated by the statement that he has married the daughter of a foreign god. It would therefore state that Judah profanes YHWH's holiness, "when he loves and marries the daughter of a foreign god." Verse 12 then states the penalty for such practice, i.e., that the man should be cut off (from the people), i.e., banished from the community, in keeping with the penalties for various of the incest laws in Leviticus 20, such as failing to execute those who give their children to Moloch (verses 4-5), uncovering the nakedness of a sister (verse 17), or lying with a menstrual woman (verse 18). The statement concerning the man's actions that warrant such punishment is particularly difficult. The NRSV translates, "anyone who does this—any to witness or answer, or to bring an offering to YHWH." This translation presupposes that the man is no longer qualified to testify in a legal matter (cf. Exod 23:1-3; Deut 19:15-21) or to bring an offering to the altar, privileges of adult (male) membership in the community. But this translation presupposes an emendation of the Hebrew expression *ʿēr wĕʿōneh* as *ʿēd wĕʿōneh*, which is based on very questionable textual evidence. It is more likely that the Hebrew term *ʿēr* refers to Judah's first son, born to him by his marriage to a Canaanite woman named Shua (see Gen 38:1-3) and that *ʿōneh* refers to his second son by Shua, Onen (*ʿônān*). When Judah arranged for Er to marry Tamar, Er died because he was considered wicked. The root *ʿrr* to which the name Er is related means "to strip oneself, be destitute, childless" (cf. Gen 15:2; Jer 22:30; Lev 20:20, 21). When Tamar was given to Onan, he spilled his seed on the ground rather than have relations with her, and died as a result of YHWH's displeasure with this act. Although the root *ʿnh* generally means "to answer, respond," one meaning of the root *ʿnh* appears to have sexual connotations as indicated by the noun *ʿōnâ*, "conjugal rights" (Exod 21:10; cf. Hos 10:10). The root can also refer to humiliation, affliction, or rape (e.g., Gen 34:2; Deut 21:14; 22:24, 29; Judg 19:24; 20:5; 2 Sam 13:12, 14; Ezek 22:10, 11; Lam 5:11). Thus, the translation of the statement is not entirely clear, but it seems to refer to a man who is cut off for such acts as one who is "childless and destitute/humiliated from the tents of Jacob." That such a man should bring an offering to YHWH is inappropriate, as elsewhere, those whose reproductive organs are damaged, rendering them unable to father children, are barred from the assembly of YHWH (Deut 23:1). Likewise, those born of improper unions (Deut 23:2) and Ammonites and Moabites (Deut 23:3-6) are banned from the assembly as well. In the present case, one who marries a foreign woman is considered as one who will not have children or who in effect becomes a foreigner himself.

The prophet then turns to the second consequence of marriage with a foreign woman in verse 13, i.e., it results in covering the altar with tears, weeping, and groaning, as the man's offerings at the altar are no longer acceptable. This, of course, builds upon the previous principle that such a man is no longer able to see to the continuity of the community by fathering children who will in turn approach the altar. Again, he is cut off from the community.

Verses 14-16 then present the prophet's elaboration on the principles that are expressed in verses 11-13. He begins by quoting the question that would naturally be posed by those whose marriage practices he has attacked, i.e., "and you say, 'why?'" The answer then comes in the prophet's statement that such action betrays "the wife of your youth" who is "your companion" and "the wife of your covenant." Many interpreters take this as a reference to the Jewish wife of the man whom he betrays by divorcing her so that he might marry a Gentile woman, but there is no reference to the woman's Jewish identity in this verse, and, as noted above, divorce is not necessary for such purposes in a polygamous society. Instead, the woman who is betrayed is the Gentile woman whom the man has married. As the wife of a man who is cut off from the community, she too is cut off and has no possibility of bearing children that will ever be acceptable in the Temple or the Judean community at large. The reference to her as "the wife of your covenant" conveys this sense as Ishmael, born to Abraham by the Egyptian woman Hagar, has no part of the covenant with Abraham, but YHWH makes a separate covenant with him out of compassion for his situation (See Genesis 16). Esau, who married Canaanite and Hittite women, including Ishmael's daughter (Gen 26:34-35; 28:1-9), loses his right to the covenant as well (Gen 25:29–34:27).

Verse 15 continues the prophet's explanation of the situation, but it is very problematic. The NRSV translates, "Did not one G–d make her? Both flesh and spirit are his. And what does the one G–d desire? G–dly offspring. So look to yourselves and do not let anyone be faithless to the wife of his youth." This rendition presupposes a reference to YHWH's creation of Adam and Eve in the Garden of Eden, and a reflection on the interrelationship between flesh and spirit in the human being. This is clearly not the intent of the Hebrew, which reads literally, "and not one has he done, and he has a remnant of spirit. And what does the one seek? The seed of G–d/divine seed, and you should be careful with your spirit." The initial reference to "not one" can hardly refer to G–d; rather it appears to refer to the fact that the men engaged in such marriage practices have not married only one woman, but more than one, which compounds the situation of betrayal of the wife just described, i.e., "and not one has he done (thus)." The reference to "the remnant of spirit" indicates an overabundance of spirit or a sexual appetite that calls for more than one woman. The question, "what does the one seek?" refers to the woman who seeks divine offspring or legitimate children from her marriage to the man, but this is impossible as such marriages are prescribed in YHWH's Torah (Exod 34:10-16; Deut 7:1-6). In short, the prophet indicates that the woman enters the marriage with expectations of legitimate children and status in the community, but she is betrayed by the man who cannot give this to her. Consequently, he enjoins the men to "be careful with your spirit," so that they will not betray their wives.

Verse 16 begins with a causative *kî*, so that it constitutes an explanatory statement to verses 14-15. The prophet presents YHWH's statement, "for (I) hate sending away/divorce." Although divorce is permitted as indicated above, it obviously creates great grief, pain, and disappointment for the parties involved as a relationship that is expected to be permanent is severed. The speech formula in verse 16aα certifies this as a statement by YHWH. A second statement in verse 16aβ, likewise identified as a statement by YHWH, relates YHWH's distaste for "the violence" that covers one's garment as a result of divorce. This apparently functions as a metaphorical expression that is designed to convey the pain, grief, and disillusionment that is inherent in divorce. The verses conclude with YHWH's injunction once again, "and you shall be careful in your spirit so that you do not betray" (cf. NRSV, "so take heed to yourselves and do not be faithless") as a final warning against a practice of intermarriage that must necessarily result in divorce. The grief inherent in such an action is conveyed by references to the fasting, weeping, and mourning of Ezra and the people at large over the prospect of sending away the foreign wives and children (Ezra 9–10).

The Prophet's Fourth Speech:
Argument that YHWH's Messenger will
Come to Establish Justice: 2:17–3:7

The prophet's fourth speech appears in Mal 2:17–3:7 in which he argues that YHWH's messenger will come to establish justice as YHWH returns to the Temple to judge the wicked. The passage begins in verse 17aα with the prophet's assertion to the people that they have wearied YHWH or tried YHWH's patience. He follows immediately in verse 17aβ with a quotation of a question that might be posed by his audience, "and you have said, 'how have we wearied him?'" The prophet's answer then appears in verse 17b with his presentation of statements purportedly made by his audience. The first is an assertion that all who do evil are considered to be good in the eyes of YHWH, and that YHWH favors those who do evil. This of course reverses the normal expectations of moral order and suggests a morally perverted worldview on the part of the audience. The second is a question, "where is the G–d of justice?" that suggests that indeed there is no G–d of justice nor is there any moral order in the world. We have no idea whether or not Malachi's audience ever actually made these statements, but his presentation enables him to characterize his audience as a morally challenged people that rejects the notion of a just G–d. This provides the basis for his following announcement concerning the coming messenger of YHWH.

The prophet's announcement concerning YHWH's messenger appears in 3:1-7. The announcement appears in two parts in verses 1-4 and 5-7, each of which begins with the prophet's presentation of a statement by YHWH followed by his own comments.

The first appears in verses 1-4, and begins with the presentation of YHWH's words in verse 1. YHWH states, "behold, I am sending my messenger, and he shall prepare a way before me, and suddenly, the lord whom you seek will come to his palace, and the messenger of the covenant whom you desire, behold, he comes." The concluding speech formula identifies this as a speech by YHWH. The Hebrew term *malʾākî*, "my messenger," apparently provides the basis for the identification of the prophet in the superscription of the book. It is not a proper name per se, and the prophet's reference to YHWH's messenger as a figure who will come probably indicates that the messenger is not even to be identified with the prophet. As noted above, the term *malʾāk* generally

refers to some emissary or representative of YHWH, such as an angel
(Gen 19:1, 15), prophet (Isa 42:19; 2 Chr 36:15, 16; Hag 1:13), or possibly
a priest (Qoh 5:5). YHWH's messengers or angels appear especially in
the context of theophany where they represent YHWH or otherwise prepare for YHWH's presence. Examples include the angel who appears to
Hagar in the wilderness (Gen 21:17), to Moses in the burning bush
(Exod 3:2), or to Israel at Bochim (Judg 2:1-5). YHWH's angel, sometimes
called "my angel/messenger" (*malʾākî;* Exod 23:23; 32:34), is particularly noted for its role in leading the people of Israel from Egyptian
bondage, through the wilderness, and into the promised land (see
Exod 14:19; Num 20:16; cf. Josh 5:13-15). The angel is positioned together with the pillar of cloud and fire that stands between Israel and
the Egyptians before the sea in Exod 14:19-20. The pillar of cloud and
fire is also identified as a symbol for YHWH's leading the people in Exod
13:17-22. Insofar as the pillar of cloud and fire employs the imagery of
the lighted altar from the Temple to symbolize YHWH's theophanic
presence, it would appear that the messenger in Mal 3:1 also is to be
identified with YHWH's theophany in the Temple as symbolized by the
altar, lit with the fires that consume the sacrificial offerings of Israel.
When the altar is in operation, the doors to the Holy of Holies of the
Temple are open, and YHWH's presence is manifested in the Temple (1
Kings 8; 2 Chr 5:2–7:11), i.e., the lighting of the altar takes place before
the open holy of holies where the ark, symbolizing YHWH's presence,
resides. YHWH's statements in verse 3 concerning the messenger who
prepares for the entry of the lord into the Temple presuppose the image
of the altar in operation and the manifestation of YHWH's presence in
the Temple. The reference to the "messenger of the covenant" likewise
presupposes this role as the functioning Temple symbolizes the covenant relationship that binds YHWH and Israel together. As noted in the
discussion of Mal 3:23 [NRSV: 4:5] below, the messenger is best identified as the prophet Elijah.

The prophet then develops this portrayal of the messenger's and
YHWH's appearance in the Temple in verses 2-4 by employing the imagery of smelting metals. This of course lends itself easily to the symbolism of the lit altar consuming the sacrificial offerings of the people.
He begins in verse 2a with two rhetorical questions that convey the holiness and unapproachable nature of YHWH, i.e., "who can endure the
day of his coming and who can stand when he appears?" The following causative statement then establishes the metaphorical portrayal of
YHWH's messenger as the fire of a refiner and the soap used for washing. Both images convey the purification that is necessary to enable the
presence of human beings in the Temple before YHWH. Such purification is symbolized by the priests who are required to immerse them-

selves in water, don white linen garments, and be morally fit before appearing at the altar (Exodus 29; Leviticus 8; 21). The imagery of refining and purifying gold and silver in verse 3 aids in establishing the precious nature of such purification. The concluding statements of verses 3b-4 indicates that this is necessary for one to make a proper offering to YHWH as it was done in the past.

The second portion of the prophet's presentation of YHWH's statements appears in verses 5-6. Verse 5 states YHWH's intention to serve as a judge and swift witness against all those who are considered to be morally unfit among the people. The enumeration and identification of such persons includes sorcerers, adulterers, those swearing false oaths, those who withhold the wages of a worker, the widow, the orphan, those who turn away a resident alien, and those who do not fear YHWH. The concluding speech formula identifies YHWH as the speaker. This brief catalogue includes a rather full range of cultic and moral wrongdoing that render one unfit for presenting sacrifice at the altar. The reference to sorcerers of course indicates one who consults with the spirits of the dead or otherwise engages other gods, and sometimes relates to improper sexual relations (see 2 Kgs 9:22; Isa 47:9, 12). Female sorcerers are condemned to death in Exod 22:17. Adultery is likewise forbidden as a capital offense (Exod 20:14; Deut 5:17; Lev 20:10), and frequently is associated with apostasy (Isa 57:3; Jer 3:8, 9; Ezek 16:38; Hos 4:2). Swearing a false oath entails an oath that is sworn in the name of YHWH and failing to fulfill it, thereby profaning YHWH's name (Lev 19:12; Exod 20:16; Deut 5:20). It is frequently employed in relation to legal testimony (Exod 23:1-3; Num 35:30; Deut 19:15-19), so that false testimony results in the miscarriage of justice. Withholding wages is forbidden by Israelite law as an affront against the holiness of the community (Lev 19:13; Deut 24:14-15). The proper treatment of widows, orphans, and resident aliens stands at the basis of Israelite legal thinking as the nation is frequently reminded of its former alien status in Egypt (Exod 22:20-23; 23:6-18; Deut 24:17-22). The treatment of widows and orphans is frequently cited as the primary measure of a just society in the ancient near eastern world.[38] YHWH's concluding statement in verse 5, "and they do not fear me," summarizes the basic stance of those enumerated here, i.e., those who fear or respect YHWH do not engage in such acts.

The presentation of YHWH's speech concludes in verses 6-7a with a causative statement that attempts to differentiate YHWH's basic character with that of the people. It begins with YHWH's statement that YHWH

---

[38] F. C. Fensham, "Widow, Orphan, and the Poor in Ancient Near Eastern Legal and Wisdom Literature," *JNES* 21 (1962) 129–39.

has not changed and that the sons of Jacob, i.e., the people of Israel, have not perished, which testifies to Yʜᴡʜ's fidelity to the relationship with Israel. This is in contrast with the charge that the people have failed to observe Yʜᴡʜ's statutes from the time of the ancestors, which of course charges that the people have not maintained their responsibilities to the relationship. Nevertheless, Yʜᴡʜ holds open the possibility of a restoration of the relationship. If the people return to Yʜᴡʜ, Yʜᴡʜ will return to the people. The speech formula identifies this as a statement by Yʜᴡʜ. The prophet's concluding statement, "and you said, 'how shall we return?'" is enigmatic in that it could suggest the prophet's belief that the people will not accept the offer because they question the charge that they have acted immorally or it could suggest the prophet's belief in the possibility that the people will accept this offer because they now ask what they must do to return to Yʜᴡʜ. In either case, the question prepares for the next argument, either to refute the objection of the people or to demonstrate to them what they must do.

The Prophet's Fifth Speech: Argument that Proper Tithes will Result in Blessing from Yʜᴡʜ: 3:8-12

The prophet's fifth speech appears in Mal 3:8-12, in which the prophet charges the nation with withholding its tithes and offerings from Yʜᴡʜ. The purpose of the prophet's contention is not to condemn the nation per se, but to prompt it to present proper tithes and offerings to Yʜᴡʜ and to receive Yʜᴡʜ's blessings for the produce of the land in return.

The prophet begins his argument by presenting Yʜᴡʜ's rhetorical question, "Do humans rob G–d?" followed immediately by the assertion, "for you are robbing me." The initial question employs the rare verb *qbʿ*, "to rob," which appears elsewhere only in Prov 22:23 as a parallel to *gzl*, "to plunder." Some follow the translation of the ʟxx, which renders the verb as a transposition of the verb *ʿqb*, "to cheat, circumvent, overreach," which forms the basis of the name Jacob.[39] Such a contention suggests that the people's actions in relation to Yʜᴡʜ are somehow related to their identification as Jacob in Mal 1:2, but there is no indication that this motif plays a role in the book beyond the initial reference to Jacob. The use of the generic terms *ʾādām*, "human," *ʾlhym*,

---

[39] See the discussion in Hill, *Malachi* 303–4.

"G–d," recalls the creation accounts of Genesis 1–3 in which G–d creates "Adam," and thereby establishes human dependence upon G–d, particularly after Adam and Eve are expelled from the garden for eating forbidden fruit. Indeed, such an act constituted robbery of that forbidden by G–d to humans, and the prophet recalls that past tradition to assert human robbery of G–d once again. The purpose of the question and its corresponding assertion is therefore to instill a sense of guilt or wrongdoing in the audience and thereby to lay a basis for the later appeal to provide proper tithes and offerings at the Temple.

By presenting the people's rhetorical question, "how have we robbed you?" verse 8b provides the opportunity for the prophet to state through YHWH the main topic of his concern, i.e., the tithes and the offerings. The tithe, *ma'ăśēr*, designates the one-tenth of an Israelite's/Judean's income in the flocks, herds, harvest, etc., that is due as an offering or tax to support the Levites (see Gen 14:20; Num 18:21-32; Lev 27:30-33; Deut 14:22-29).[40] The offering, *tĕrûmâ*, designates the offerings that are made for specific services or from the first fruits of flock, herd, and harvest to support the priests (Num 5:9-10; 18:8-20; Ezek 44:28-31).[41] The term is also employed to designate the land or other items allotted to the Temple and thus to the priests (Ezek 45:1-5; Exod 25:2, 3; 35:5, 21, 24; 30:14-15). In short, the prophet is concerned with providing proper support for the Temple and its staff of priests and Levites.

Verses 9-12 then elaborate upon the initial premise established in verse 8 by pointing to the benefits to be had in return for providing proper tithes. Verse 9 begins the prophet's argument by asserting that the people are under "curse," *mĕʾērâ*. The same term was employed in Mal 2:2 as part of the prophet's effort to convince the priests to honor YHWH properly. It is drawn from the blessings and curses of Deuteronomy (see Deut 28:20), where it functions as a means to persuade the people to observe YHWH's commands by presenting the consequences for non-observance and the benefits of observance. The curse is a withered land, enemies, etc., and the benefit is fecundity in the land, prosperity, and security. The statement employs an element of irony. Although the people are already under the curse, and thus do not enjoy the benefit of fecundity in the land, they nevertheless continue to rob G–d, and thereby ensure the continuance of the curse. The final two words of verse 9 indicate that the entire nation is addressed.

Verse 10 then presents YHWH's proposal that the people bring the tithe to the Temple so that they might test YHWH to see what the result

[40] See esp., "Tithe," *Encyclopaedia Judaica* 15:1156-62.
[41] See esp. "Terumot and Ma'aserot," *Encyclopaedia Judaica* 15:1025-8.

will be. Some have questioned the term *ṭerep*, "food," because it is derived from the same root as *ṭĕrēpâ*, "unclean meat/food," that is not fit either for human consumption or presentation in the Temple.[42] Both terms are derived from the root *ṭrp*, "to be torn." In the case of *ṭĕrēpâ* it refers to meat torn by a wild animal and left to die, and it is therefore unfit for human use. Indeed *ṭerep* sometimes refers to prey (Amos 3:4; Isa 5:29) but it also refers to freshly cut meat that is fit for consumption or presentation (see Ps 111:5; Prov 31:15). The speech formula at the end of verse 10a certifies this as a statement by Yhwh. The oath formula *ʾim-lōʾ*, "if," at the beginning of verse 10b opens Yhwh's assertion that Yhwh will indeed open the windows of heavens to provide rain as the blessing due to the people in return to their reverence for Yhwh. Verse 11 continues with Yhwh's promise to rebuke the "locust," literally "the devourer" (cf. Joel 2:5, which describes locusts as a devouring fire, and Joel 2:25).[43] The identification of the locust as "the devourer" is clear from the following statement concerning Yhwh's refusal to allow the "devourer" to destroy the fruit of the land or to make vines barren. Again, the speech formula at the end of the verse certifies this as a statement by Yhwh. Finally, verse 12 points to the motif of the nations' recognition of the nation and of Yhwh for the bounty, prosperity, and happiness that will be evident in the land. Of course, this is the concluding point in an argument by the prophet to prompt the people to bring proper tithes and offerings to the Temple. Again, the concluding speech formula identifies Yhwh as the speaker.

The Prophet's Sixth Speech:
Exhortation to Observe Yhwh's Torah: 3:13-24 [NRSV: 3:13–4:6]

The prophet's sixth and final speech appears in Mal 3:13-24 [NRSV: 3:13–4:6] in which he asserts that Yhwh is indeed just, and will act to punish the wicked and reward the righteous. Although the speech begins with the assertion of a principle for argumentation, i.e., the doubts about Yhwh's efficacy and justice in verses 13-15, the balance of the passage does not contain an explicit refutation of that position. Rather, it reports that Yhwh heard those who fear Yhwh's name speak among themselves, presumably to express their resolve to follow Yhwh, and that Yhwh recorded them in a book of remembrance so that they might

[42] See the discussion of this term in Beth Glazier-McDonald, *Malachi: The Divine Messenger,* SBLDS, vol. 98 (Atlanta: Scholars Press, 1987) 194–5.

[43] Hill, *Malachi* 317.

be spared when the day of judgment against the wicked was to be realized. The following speech by YHWH in verses 17-21 [NRSV: 3:17–4:3]
then expresses YHWH's intention to act on the coming Day of YHWH to
punish the wicked and spare the righteous. The concluding verses 22-
24 [NRSV: 4:4-6] call upon the audience to remember the Torah of Moses
that YHWH commanded and to anticipate the coming of Elijah the
prophet who will prepare for the coming Day of YHWH. Such assertions
implicitly refute the view of YHWH's inefficacy expressed in verses 13-
15, but more importantly, they are designed to motivate the audience to
provide support for the Temple and thereby to be counted among the
righteous who will receive YHWH's blessings.

The speech begins in verses 13-15 with the prophet's presentation of
YHWH's characterization of the people as lacking faith in YHWH's justice
or capacity to act. YHWH addresses the people in verse 13a with the
statement, "your words have been strong against me." The following
speech formula identifies YHWH as the speaker. Although the specific
meaning of this statement becomes clear only as YHWH's discourse continues, it is clear that YHWH characterizes the audience as speaking
against YHWH. Two successive quotes of the people's words then lay
out YHWH's characterization of the people's views. In verse 13b, YHWH
states that the people have asked, "How have we spoken against you?"
This question provides little more than the rhetorical platform by
which the second quote in verses 14-15 specifies the charge made in
verse 13a. The series of assertions made by the people indicate that the
audience is a group of people who would normally be considered
righteous, but who have come to doubt YHWH's justice and power because wickedness is allowed to run unchecked within the community.
Apparently, it is this group that the prophet seeks to motivate to provide support for YHWH and thus to constitute the basis of the restored
Jewish community.

The first series of statements and assertions in verse 14 indicate that
it is futile to depend upon YHWH. Indeed, the first statement, "It is vain
to serve G–d," says as much. The Hebrew word *šāwʾ*, "vain," appears in
one of the Ten Commandments, "you shall not take the name of YHWH
your G–d in vain" (Exod 20:7; Deut 5:11), where it refers to invoking
the name of G–d to make a false accusation or testimony in a legal situation. Such misuse of the name of G–d necessarily entails a miscarriage
of justice that cannot be tolerated in the Israelite/Judean nation. The
use of this term in the present context points to the same situation, i.e.,
there is no justice in the land, and the people have therefore come to the
conclusion that G–d is empty. The second question, "what is the profit
that we have kept his charge and that we have walked in darkness/
mourning before YHWH of Hosts?" correctly follows from the first state-

ment by asserting that in fact there is no profit in adhering to YHWH. The Hebrew term *beṣ'a*, "profit," generally refers to "unjust gain" (Exod 18:21; Mic 4:13), and the asking of the question suggests that the people now live in a world in which "unjust gain" has become the expected norm. The reference to observance of YHWH's "charge," *mišmeret*, employs a term that generally refers to priestly service at the Temple (Lev 8:35; Num 1:53; 3:38; Ezek 40:45; 44:15), and indicates that the prophet's primary audience is the priests in the Temple. The reference to the people walking in "darkness" or "mourning" employs the term *qĕdōranît*, which appears only here. Insofar as the root *qdr* refers to darkness, the term is understood as a reference to mourning. More likely, the reference to walking in darkness is intended to contrast with walking in the "light" of YHWH when one observes YHWH's Torah or instruction (e.g., Isa 2:2-5; 42:6; 49:6; 51:4; 60:19, 20; Prov 6:23).

The second series in verse 15 point to the basis why the audience has come to the conclusion that serving YHWH is vain. The introductory *wĕ'attâ*, "and now," highlights the contrast between reality and expectation while introducing a series of statements that should be inconsistent in a morally-ordered world. The first is that the arrogant are counted happy, whereas Psalm 1:1-2 states the very opposite, i.e., that "happy is the man who does not walk in the council of the wicked . . . but whose desire is in the Torah of YHWH and who meditates on his Torah day and night." The second statement, that evil doers prosper, contradicts the basic moral outlook of Judaism throughout both the biblical and post-biblical traditions. The final assertion, that those who test YHWH escape, indicates that those who violate the basic moral order as expressed in YHWH's Torah are able to do so at will as no penalties are forthcoming. Such observations are not unlike those of the modern world in which evil such as the Shoah is allowed to proceed unchecked while those who are purportedly responsible for morality in the world, whether they be governments, religious establishments, banking institutions, or entire nations, stand silent as the murders, plunderings, and denials are carried out.

Verses 16-24 then turn from the argumentative character of the preceding verses to a report of YHWH's response to those who indicated their willingness to abide by YHWH's wishes for proper respect and sanctification. Basically, verse 16 indicates YHWH's response by recording the actions of those who fear YHWH, and verses 17-24 [NRSV: 3:17–4:6] provide substantiation for the claim that YHWH will indeed take action to punish the wicked and to sustain the righteous. Altogether, this section, including the exhortational statements that conclude the pericope in verses 22-24 [NRSV: 4:4-6] demonstrate that Mal 3:13-24 [NRSV: 3:13–4:6] is not simply the sixth argument in the prophet's disputation;

rather it constitutes a concluding exhortation that is designed to elicit the support of the audience for the prophet's program and its adherence to YHWH's expectations as defined throughout the book. It does so by providing confirmation, through YHWH's recording of those who are righteous, that YHWH will indeed act to punish the wicked and to sustain the righteous.

Verse 16 is formulated as third person narrative that begins in verse 16a with a report that those who fear or respect YHWH talked together. It provides no explicit information concerning the topic of their conversation, but the preceding material in verses 13-15 suggests that they were reconsidering their position of doubt concerning YHWH's ability or will to act and that the result would be a renewed effort to lead the community in meeting YHWH's requirements. Verse 16b reports that YHWH heard these conversations, paid attention to them, and recorded them in a "book of remembrance" so that those who fear YHWH and meditate upon YHWH's name would be remembered when the time came for YHWH to take action. YHWH's book of remembrance is mentioned or alluded to elsewhere in Exod 17:14; 32:32-33; Pss 40:7; 56:8). It appears to reflect the practice of the Persian monarchs who recorded important events for future recollection or action (cf. Esth 6:1) or the role of the Temple as a symbolic representation or remembrance of YHWH's actions in the world and expectations of the people. Jewish tradition regards Yom Kippur or the Day of Atonement (cf. Leviticus 16; 23:26-32; Num 29:7-11) as the day when YHWH reviews the actions of all persons during the past year, makes the final decisions concerning their fate for the coming year, and records the decisions in a book so that they might be carried out.[44]

The prophet then presents YHWH's statements concerning plans to act on behalf of the righteous and against the wicked as a result of the recording reported in verse 16. The speech formula in verse 17a identifies verses 17-18 as a speech by YHWH. YHWH begins by stating YHWH's own perspectives and actions on behalf of the righteous. The statement, "they shall be mine," indicates YHWH's pledge to protect the righteous as indicated in the balance of the verse. YHWH refers to the day when YHWH will act and the righteous will be considered a "special possession" or "treasure" (*sĕgullâ*). The term is employed for royal treasures in 1 Chr 29:3 and Qoh 2:8, and designates Israel's status as YHWH's chosen people in Exod 19:5; Deut 7:6; 14:2; and 26:18. YHWH's statement that YHWH will spare those who serve YHWH like a man who spares a son, indicates that a judgment is coming against the wicked from which the righteous will be spared. YHWH addresses the people,

---

[44] See "Day of Atonement," *Encyclopaedia Judaica* 5:1376-87.

presumably those who identify with Yhwh, with a statement of confirmation that indicates that they will witness the different fates of those who serve Yhwh versus those who do not. Such a contention of course reinforces the exhortational character of the passage by calling subtly upon the audience to be sure that they are among those who are aligned with Yhwh and will therefore be spared when the punishment comes.

Verses 19-21 [NRSV: 4:1-3], introduced by a causative *kî*, then reinforce Yhwh's statements in verses 17-18 by describing in some detail the day in which Yhwh will act. Again, the speech formulas in verses 19 and 21 [NRSV: 4:1 and 3] indicate that Yhwh is the speaker. Verse 19 begins by employing theophanic images to describe the day as one of punishment against the wicked. The image is that of a burning oven in which the wicked and arrogant are to be burned like chaff, leaving neither root nor branch. The reference to root and branch is particularly important because roots and branches play important roles in sustaining a plant. Without them, the plant cannot survive. The metaphor therefore conveys complete destruction of the wicked.

Verses 20-21 then turn to Yhwh's actions on behalf of the righteous. The speech employs second person address forms to indicate that the righteous are the audience to which Yhwh's words are addressed. Again, such a direct address form supports the general exhortational character of the passage by calling upon the audience to identify with the righteous. The image of the rising sun builds upon the image of the sun that rises in the east and thus illumines the entrance to the Temple and its interior, thereby signifying the rebirth of creation each day (n.b., Gen 1:3-5 indicates that light is the first element of creation), and Ezek 40:6 indicates that the Temple faces east, which allows the morning sun to illumine the interior of the Temple at sunrise (cf. Psalms 8; 19; Deut 33:2; Judg 5:4; Habakkuk 3, which portray Yhwh with solar imagery). Psalm 19 is especially clear in associating the imagery of the sun or light with Yhwh's Torah, which seems to underlie the references to the righteousness and healing capacities of the sun. The dancing of the audience like calves from a stall of course recounts the morning activities of shepherds who take their cattle out to feed at morning light, and thus draws the connection between the rising of the sun and the sustenance of life in creation. An element of threat is also present, as Yhwh's emergence represents Yhwh's assault against enemies who threaten the order of creation (e.g., Habakkuk 3). Thus verse 21 [NRSV: 4:3] relates the trampling of the wicked, perhaps under the hooves of the cattle, on the day when Yhwh acts.

Verses 22-24 [NRSV: 4:4-6] constitute the final exhortation of Yhwh's concluding speech and indeed of the book as a whole. Again, these verses appear as a first person speech by Yhwh directed to a second person masculine plural audience, i.e., those who choose to follow YHWH as indicated in verses 13-15, 16 above. The initial statement of this section in verse 22 [NRSV: 4:4] is formulated as an imperative to "remember the Torah of Moses, my servant, which I have commanded him at Horeb concerning all Israel, statutes and laws." The exhortational character of the passage is inherent in the command to remember the Torah of Moses, which embodies the appeal to observe proper respect for YHWH as articulated throughout the book. It also indicates once again that YHWH's statements are addressed first to the priests who serve as the representatives of all Israel before YHWH. Horeb represents the alternative name for Mt. Sinai that appears especially in the Deuteronomic traditions (Deut 1:2, 6, 19; 4:10, 15; 1 Kgs 8:9; 19:8; see also 2 Chr 5:10; Ps 106:19; Exod 17:6; 33:6). Verses 23-24 [NRSV: 4:5-6] state YHWH's intentions to send Elijah the prophet prior to the coming Day of YHWH on which the judgment of the wicked will take place. The choice of Elijah as the precursor to the Day of YHWH makes a great deal of sense as Elijah is also identified with Mt. Horeb. Like Moses who experienced a revelation of YHWH at Horeb/Sinai in the context of Israel's apostasy with the golden calf (Exodus 32–33), Elijah fled to Mt. Horeb at the time of Israel's apostasy in the reign of Ahab and Jezebel and experienced a revelation of YHWH in the form of the "still, small voice" (1 Kings 19). Like Moses, whose burial site is unknown, Elijah has no burial site, but ascended to heaven in a fiery chariot (2 Kings 2). Because Elijah does not die in biblical tradition and because he resembles Moses in many respects, he is identified as the prophet who will return to Israel prior to the coming of the Messiah in Jewish tradition.[45] That role appears to be articulated in the present context in which he returns prior to the Day of YHWH when the wicked are judged and the righteous are spared. Thus, Elijah appears to be identified with "my messenger" whom YHWH is sending to prepare the way in Mal 3:1. The fact that Elijah never died would suggest that he is to be conceived as one of YHWH's angels or messengers. The Day of YHWH is well-known in prophetic tradition as a day of judgment against Israel's enemies (e.g., Isaiah 13; 34; Joel; Obadiah; Zechariah 14), against the wicked within Israel (e.g., Amos 5:18-20; Zephaniah 1), and against all the arrogant of the world (e.g., Isa 2:6-21). It is apparently rooted in the traditions of YHWH's theophanic appearance at the festival of Shavuot, which also commemorates the anniversary of the giving of the Torah to Israel. The concluding statement that the hearts of the fathers will return to the sons and those of the sons to the fathers points to the exhortational character of the book once again, in that Malachi's rhetorical goal

---

[45] See esp., "Elijah," *Encyclopaedia Judaica* 6:632-42.

appears not only to be to exhort the priests and people to observe YHWH's Torah but to convince them to do so as a united community in which the strife that has divided its members over proper understanding of YHWH and observance of YHWH's Torah is overcome. The final statement that such reconciliation will avert YHWH's plans to destroy the land entirely serves as a final motivation for such unified action.

FOR FURTHER READING

COMMENTARIES

Chary, Théophane. *Aggée-Zacharie, Malachie.* Sources bibliques; Paris: Gabalda, 1969.

Hill, Andrew E. *Malachi.* Anchor Bible, 25D. New York: Doubleday, 1998.

Petersen, David L. *Zechariah 9–14 and Malachi.* Old Testament Library. Louisville: Westminster John Knox, 1995.

Redditt, Paul L. *Haggai, Zechariah, Malachi.* New Century Bible Commentary. London: Marshall Pickering; Grand Rapids: William Eerdmans, 1995.

Reventlow, Henning Graf. *Die Propheten Haggai, Sacharja und Maleachi.* Das Alte Testament Deutsch, 25, 2. Göttingen: Vandenhoeck & Ruprecht, 1993.

Robinson, Theodore H. with Friedrich Horst. *Die Zwölf Kleinen Propheten.* Handbuch zum Alten Testament, 14. 3rd edition. Tübingen: J. C. B. Mohr (Paul Siebeck), 1964.

Rudolph, Wilhelm. *Haggai–Sacharja 1–8–Sacharja 9–14–Maleachi.* Kommentar zum Alten Testament, XIII/4. Gütersloh: Gerd Mohn, 1976.

Schuller, Eileen M. "The Book of Malachi: Introduction, Commentary, and Reflections," *The New Interpreter's Bible. Volume VII: Introduction to Apocalyptic Literature, Daniel, The Twelve Prophets,* ed. Leander E. Keck et al. Nashville: Abingdon, 1996.

Smith, John Merlin Powis with Hinckley G. Mitchell and Julius A. Bewer. *A Critical and Exegetical Commentary on Haggai, Zechariah, Malachi, and Jonah.* International Critical Commentary. Edinburgh: T. and T. Clark, 1912.

Smith, Ralph L. *Micah–Malachi.* Word Biblical Commentary, 32. Waco: Word: 1984.

Vuilleumier, René with Samuel Amsler and André Lacoque. *Aggée, Zacharie, Malachie.* Commentaire de l'ancien Testament, XIc. 2nd edition. Geneva: Labor et Fides, 1988.

STUDIES

Coggins, R. J. *Haggai, Zechariah, Malachi.* Old Testament Guides. Sheffield: JSOT Press, 1987.
Glazier-McDonald, Beth. *Malachi: The Divine Messenger.* Society of Biblical Literature Dissertation Series, 98. Atlanta: Scholars Press, 1987.
Hanson, Paul. *The Dawn of Apocalyptic: The Historical and Sociological Roots of Jewish Apocalyptic Eschatology.* Philadelphia: Fortress, 1975.
Hugenberger, Gordon Paul. *Marriage as Covenant: A Study of Biblical Law and Ethics Governing Marriage, Developed from the Perspective of Malachi.* Vetus Testamentum Supplements, 52; Leiden: Brill, 1994.
Mason, R. A. *Preaching the Tradition. Homily and Hermeneutics after the Exile.* Cambridge: Cambridge University Press, 1990.
O'Brien, Julia M. "Malachi in Recent Research." *Currents in Research: Biblical Studies* 3 (1995) 81–94.
O'Brien, Julia M. *Priest and Levite in Malachi.* Society of Biblical Literature Dissertation Series, 121. Atlanta: Scholars Press, 1990.
Pfeiffer, Egon. "Die Disputationsworte im Buche Maleachi (Ein Beitrag zur formgeschichtlichen Struktur)." *Evangelische Theologie* 12 (1959) 546–68.
Utzschneider, Helmut. *Künder oder Schreiber? Eine These zum Problem der "Schriftprophetie" auf Grund von Maleachi 1,6-2,9.* Beiträge zur Erforschung des Alten Testaments und des Antiken Judentums, 19. Frankfurt am Main: Peter Lang, 1989.

INDICES

AUTHOR INDEX

SCRIPTURE INDEX 1

Introduction, Hosea, Joel

SCRIPTURE INDEX 2

Amos, Obadiah, Jonah

SCRIPTURE INDEX 3

Micah, Nahum, Habakkuk, Zephaniah

1:8	463	*Lamentations*		16	504
1:9	475	2:7	471	16:10	523
1:23	470	2:22	471	18:3	411
3:1	463	3:8	463	21–22	386
3:11	470	4:21	409	23:20	344
3:21	401	5:1	516	23:32	454, 469
4:2	463			24:24-25	344
5:12	470	*Daniel*			
6:20	463	1:17	423, 460	*2 Chronicles*	
6:23	463	9:24	423, 460	5:14	476
7:2	463	11:18	369	6:1	509
7:24	349	LXX 14:1	454, 461	7:1	476
8:14	401			7:2	476
10:1	361, 473			7:3	476
10:6	463	*Ezra*		7:6	460, 469
10:11	463	3:2	463	8:14	460, 469
11:1	506	3:11	523	11:5-12	356
11:2	400	3:13	523	11:7	356
11:31	472	7:6	463	11:8	344
13:14	463	10:8	386	11:9	356
14:28	402			15:9-15	356
15:11	472			25:23	366
17:7	472	*Nehemiah*		25:27	356
18:18	362	1:3	516	27:3	383
20:3	506	1:9	502	29–32	495
25:1	473	3:3	507	32:30	385
27:5	470	3:26	383	32:32	460
28:4-7	463	3:35	366	33:14	383, 385, 507
28:9	463	8:1	463	33:21–35:26	493–4
28:16	386	8:3	463	34:3	505
29:15	470	8:18	463	34:20	344
29:18	423, 460	9:3	463	34:22	507
30:18	390	11:21	383	35:2	460, 469
31:24	507	12:9	454		
31:26	463	12:39	507		
		12:45	469	**Apocryphal/Deutero-**	
		13:30	460	**Canonical Books**	
Ruth					
1:2	387	*1 Chronicles*		*Bel and the Dragon*	
2:7	500	1:8	445	1:1	454, 461
3:11	524	1:10	390		
4	359	4:4	387		
4:11	387	5:5	344	**Pseudepigraphical**	
		5:29	397	**Works**	
Song of Songs/Canticles		8:34-35	344		
4:16	483	14:11	366	*Life of Habakkuk*	
6:5	412	15:16-24	488	1–9	454, 461

SCRIPTURE INDEX 4

Haggai, Zechariah, Malachi